UNIFORM COMMERCIAL CODE ANALYSIS OF REVISED ARTICLE 9

With Full Text and Official Comments of 1998 Revised Article 9

Analysis by
JULIAN B. McDONNELL

John A. Sibley Professor of Law
University of Georgia

1999

MATTHEW BENDER

QUESTIONS ABOUT THIS PUBLICATION?

For questions about the **Editorial Content** appearing in these volumes or reprint permission, please call:

Michael A. Bruno, J.D. at .... (800) 252-9257 (Ext. 2518)
Michael A. Starvaggi, J.D. at .... (800) 252-9257 (Ext. 2302)
Outside the United States and Canada please call .... (212) 448-2000

For assistance with replacement pages, shipments, billing or other customer service matters, please call:

Customer Services Department at .... (800) 833-9844
Outside the United States and Canada, please call .... (518) 487-3000
Fax number .... (518) 487-3584

For information on other Matthew Bender publications, please call
Your account manager or .... (800) 223-1940
Outside the United States and Canada, please call .... (518) 487-3000

Library of Congress Card Catalog Number: 99-20266
ISBN 0-8205-3869-8

MATTHEW◆BENDER

MATTHEW BENDER & COMPANY, INCORPORATED
Editorial Offices
2 Park Avenue, New York, NY 10016-5675 (212) 448-2000
201 Mission St., San Francisco, CA 94105-1831 (415) 908-3200

Publisher's Editorial Staff

Statement on Fair Use

Matthew Bender recognizes the balance that must be achieved between the operation of the fair use doctrine, whose basis is to avoid the rigid application of the copyright statute, and the protection of the creative rights and economic interests of authors, publishers and other copyright holders.

We are also aware of the countervailing forces that exist between the ever greater technological advances for making both print and electronic copies and the reduction in the value of copyrighted works that must result from a consistent and pervasive reliance on these new copying technologies. It is Matthew Bender's position that if the "progress of science and useful arts" is promoted by granting copyright protection to authors, such progress may well be impeded if copyright protection is diminished in the name of fair use. (See *Nimmer on Copyright* §13.05[E][1].) This holds true whether the parameters of the fair use doctrine are considered in either the print or the electronic environment as it is the integrity of the copyright that is at issue, not the media under which the protected work may become available. Therefore, the fair use guidelines we propose apply equally to our print and electronic information, and apply, within §§107 and 108 of the Copyright Act, regardless of the professional status of the user.

Our draft guidelines would allow for the copying of limited materials, which would include synopses and tables of contents, primary source and government materials that may have a minimal amount of editorial enhancements, individual forms to aid in the drafting of applications and pleadings, and miscellaneous pages from any of our newsletters, treatises and practice guides. This copying would be permitted provided it is performed for internal use and solely for the purpose of facilitating individual research or for creating documents produced in the course of the user's professional practice, and the original from which the copy is made has been purchased or licensed as part of the user's existing in-house collection.

Matthew Bender fully supports educational awareness programs designed to increase the public's recognition of its fair use rights. We also support the operation of collective licensing organizations with regard to our print and electronic information.

UNIFORM COMMERCIAL CODE
ANALYSIS OF REVISED ARTICLE 9
With Full Text and Official Comments of 1998
Revised Article 9

Analysis by
Julian B. McDonnell
John A. Sibley Professor of Law
University of Georgia

Introduction

1. Why Rewrite Article 9?

Revised Article 9 of the Uniform Commercial Code, approved by the sponsoring organizations in 1998, is a comprehensive restatement of the law of personal property security transactions. Unlike the selective amendments to Article 9 approved by the sponsors in 1972, the Revised Article 9 of 1998 is a reorganized, renumbered and rewritten Article. Not counting transition provisions or conforming amendments proposed for other articles, the revised article contains 126 sections. Of this total, 36 sections are entirely new, having no counterpart in the pre-1998 U.C.C., and 71 other sections contain new language not found in the parallel provisions of the old Article 9. In terms of how the law is expressed, it would be more accurate to label the 1998 Article 9 as "new" rather than "revised."

Why did the National Conference of Commissioners on Uniform State Laws and the American Law Institute decide to rewrite Article 9? Certainly not to reject the central policy thrust of the old article. Instead, one major goal of the revision is to make it easier to create and perfect Article

9 security interests over a greater range of assets. A second and related reason is to adapt Article 9 to electronic commerce. The objective is to induce more and cheaper financing for the small and middle-size firms and the consumers who depend on secured financing. Thus, Revised Article 9 features electronic security agreements; electronic filing; electronic notifications; automatic security interests in "supporting obligations," in collateral securing collateral which is a monetary obligation, and in an expanded category of proceeds; security interests in bank accounts as original collateral as well as in commercial tort claims; filing as to corporate debtors in the state of incorporation, rather than where the collateral is located; financing statements containing super-generic collateral descriptions (*e.g.* "all assets") which are authorized rather than signed by the debtor; security interests perfected by "control," rather than filing or change in possession; automatic perfection of sales of promissory notes and payment intangibles; priority over lien creditors based on filing alone, rather than perfection of the security interest; power in the first-filed creditor to "sell" its priority by filing an amendment statement naming a substitute secured creditor; and other goodies designed to make life easier for secured creditors. The revision is, in the words of the late Barry Zaretsky, "a love feast for secured creditors," paid for with a few new delimited protections for consumer debtors and a few adjustments needed to sell security interests in deposit accounts. But all of these changes did not demand a total rewrite.

A third motive for the revision is to state the law of secured transactions with greater clarity, detail, and precision in the hope of achieving greater transactional certainty. The Revised Article 9 is a product of professional specialization. The original Article 9 was drafted by gifted generalists who provided a new charter defining a new area of law and giving rise to a new area of practice. The Revised Article 9 was drafted by gifted specialists. The Article 9 Drafting Committee resolved to make its mark by resolving the technical problems which courts, practitioners and scholars have uncovered in dealing with increasingly sophisticated transactions over the last forty-five years. For example, when national and international deals are the norm, it seems much more important to be very precise about choice of law rules. The quest for enhanced certainty in planning and executing transactions led to the comprehensive rewrite of Article 9. In sum, Revised Article 9 embodies a specialists' version of the personal property security law needed to fuel the future of finance capitalism.

Since the time of *Twyne's Case* (1602), the whole idea of security interests in personal property has been controversial. Today the supporters of secured credit see it as the linchpin of prosperity. But at the same time vigorous attacks question the efficiency and fairness of the whole system. This new "fast-lane" Article 9, which so unreservedly embraces secured credit, may well intensify the debate. Will Revised Article 9 allow creditors adhesively to extract electronic consents to security interests and financing statements from consumers and small businesses? Will the more-comprehensive floating liens permitted by Revised Article 9 give secured creditors a veto over corporate reorganizations by eliminating any "free assets" to support reorganization attempts? Will Revised Article 9 encourage preemptive filings against all assets of a firm even though no financing is contemplated in the foreseeable future? Will Revised Article 9 undermine the long-standing policy of public notice by expanding the list of interests which are automatically perfected or can be perfected by control? These are the concerns which the future will dispel or confirm—assuming, as most predict, that Revised Article 9 is adopted by the states.

2. Role of the book.

In this book the text and official comments of the Revised Article 9 are supplemented by text analysis designed to probe the implications of the changes made by the Revised Article 9. Such text analysis is designated by a shaded background. Examples are provided to illustrate the actual operation of new rules and the interaction of provisions. *It is important to recognize that the shaded text analysis is analysis which I have written; it is not material in any way approved by the sponsors, the reporters or the Article 9 Drafting Committee.* For more extensive comparison of the old and revised articles, references are provided to P. Coogan, W. Hogan, D. Vagts and J. McDonnell, *Secured Transactions Under the Commercial Code* (Matthew Bender

1999)(herein "*Secured Transactions*"). The Revised Article 9 carries a delayed effective date of July 1, 2001. But many of its provisions will have immediate impact because they will be deemed to be clarifications, rather than substantive changes, in existing law.

Julian B. McDonnell
Athens, Georgia
March, 1999

UNIFORM COMMERCIAL CODE

NATIONAL CONFERENCE OF COMMISSIONERS ON UNIFORM STATE LAWS

REVISED ARTICLE 9. SECURED TRANSACTIONS
(With Conforming Amendments to Articles 1, 2, 2a, 4, 5, 6, 7, and 8)

APPROVED AND RECOMMENDED FOR ENACTMENT IN ALL THE
STATES
at its
ANNUAL CONFERENCE
MEETING IN ITS ONE-HUNDRED-AND-SEVENTH YEAR
CLEVELAND, OHIO
JULY 24-31, 1998

With Comments

DRAFTING COMMITTEE TO REVISE UNIFORM COMMERCIAL CODE

ARTICLE 9 – SECURED TRANSACTIONS

WILLIAM M. BURKE, 20th Floor, Standard Chartered Bank Building, 4 Des Voeux Road, Hong Kong, China, *Chair*

MARION W. BENFIELD, JR., University of Texas, School of Law, 10 Overlook Circle, New Braunfels, TX 78132

NEIL B. COHEN, Brooklyn Law School, Room 904A, 250 Joralemon Street, Brooklyn, NY 11201, *The American Law Institute Representative* DALE G. HIGER, Suite 1900, 101 S. Capitol Boulevard, Boise, ID 83702-5958

WILLIAM C. HILLMAN, U.S. Bankruptcy Court, Room 1101, 10 Causeway Street, Boston, MA 02222

MICHAEL HOUGHTON, P.O. Box 1347, 18th Floor, 1201 N. Market Street, Wilmington, DE 19899 RANDAL C. PICKER, University of Chicago Law School, 1111 E. 60th Street, Chicago, IL 60637

DONALD J. RAPSON, Room 3338, 650 CIT Drive, Livingston, NJ 07039-0491, *The American Law Institute Representative*

HARRY C. SIGMAN, P.O. Box 67E08, Los Angeles, CA 90067, *The American Law Institute Representative*

BRADLEY Y. SMITH, 20th Floor, 450 Lexington Avenue, New York, NY 10017, *The American Law Institute Representative*

EDWIN E. SMITH, 15th Floor, 150 Federal Street, Boston, MA 02110

SANDRA S. STERN, 509 Madison Avenue, Suite 612, New York, NY 10022

STEVEN L. HARRIS, Chicago-Kent College of Law, 565 W. Adams Street, Chicago, IL 60661-3691, *Co-Reporter*

CHARLES W. MOONEY, JR., University of Pennsylvania, School of Law, 3400 Chestnut Street, Philadelphia, PA 19104, *Co-Reporter*

EX OFFICIO

GENE N. LEBRUN, P.O. Box 8250, 9th Floor, 909 St. Joseph Street, Rapid City, SD 57709, *President*

HENRY M. KITTLESON, P.O. Box 32092, 92 Lake Wire Drive, Lakeland, FL 33802-2092, *Division Chair*

AMERICAN BAR ASSOCIATION ADVISORS

ROBERT BAUER, 1300 N. 17th Street, #1800, Arlington, VA 22209, *Intellectual Property Law Section Advisor*

RICHARD E. CHERIN, 1 Riverfront Plaza, Newark, NJ 07102, *Business Law Section Advisor*

RICHARD R. GOLDBERG, 51st Floor, 1735 Market Street, Philadelphia, PA 19103, *Real Property, Probate & Trust Law Section Advisor*

LAWRENCE A. MANZANARES, City & County Building, 1437 Bannock Street, Courtroom 303W, Denver, CO 80202, *Judicial Administration Division, National Conference of Special Court Judges Advisor*

STEVEN O. WEISE, 40th Floor, 601 S. Figueroa Street, Los Angeles, CA 90017, *Advisor*

EXECUTIVE DIRECTOR

FRED H. MILLER, University of Oklahoma, College of Law, 300 Timberdell Road, Norman, OK 73019, *Executive Director*

WILLIAM J. PIERCE, 1505 Roxbury Road, Ann Arbor, MI 48104, *Executive Director Emeritus*

Copies of this Act may be obtained from:
NATIONAL CONFERENCE OF COMMISSIONERS
ON UNIFORM STATE LAWS
211 E. Ontario Street, Suite 1300
Chicago, Illinois 60611
312/915-0195

REVISION OF UNIFORM COMMERCIAL CODE
ARTICLE 9 — SECURED TRANSACTIONS

Table Of Disposition Of Sections In Former Article 9 And Other Code Sections

Table Indicating Sources Or Derivations Of New Article 9 Sections And Conforming Amendments

PART 1 – GENERAL PROVISIONS

[SUBPART 1. SHORT TITLE, DEFINITIONS, AND GENERAL CONCEPTS]

[SUBPART 2. APPLICABILITY OF ARTICLE]

PART 2 – EFFECTIVENESS OF SECURITY AGREEMENT; ATTACHMENT OF SECURITY INTEREST; RIGHTS OF PARTIES TO SECURITY AGREEMENT

[SUBPART 1. EFFECTIVENESS AND ATTACHMENT]

[SUBPART 2. RIGHTS AND DUTIES]

PART 3 – PERFECTION AND PRIORITY

[SUBPART 1. LAW GOVERNING PERFECTION AND PRIORITY]

[SUBPART 2. PERFECTION]

[SUBPART 2. DUTIES AND OPERATION OF FILING OFFICE]

PART 6 – DEFAULT

[SUBPART 1. DEFAULT AND ENFORCEMENT OF SECURITY INTEREST]

[SUBPART 2. NONCOMPLIANCE WITH ARTICLE]

PART 7 – TRANSITION

APPENDIX II MODEL PROVISIONS FOR PRODUCTION-MONEY PRIORITY

TABLE OF DISPOSITION OF SECTIONS IN FORMER ARTICLE 9 AND OTHER CODE SECTIONS

OLD ARTICLE 9	NEW ARTICLE 9
9-101	9-101
9-102	9-109
9-103(1)(a), (b); (c) omitted	9-301
9-103(1)(d)	9-316
9-103(2)(a), (b); (c) omitted	9-303, 9-316
9-103(2)(d)	9-337
9-103(3)(a), (b); (c) omitted	9-301
9-103(3)(d)	9-307
9-103(3)(e)	9-316
9-103(4)	9-301
9-103(5)	9-301
9-103(6)	9-304, 9-305, 9-306
9-104	9-109
9-105	9-102
9-106	9-102
9-107	9-103
9-108	Omitted as no longer needed
9-109	9-102
9-110	9-108
9-111	Deleted as unnecessary
9-112	Omitted - see 9-102(a)(28)
9-113	9-110
9-114	Omitted - see 9-103 and 9-324

OLD ARTICLE 9	NEW ARTICLE 9
9-115(1)	9-102, 9-106
9-115(2)	9-203, 9-308
9-115(3)	9-108
9-115(4)	9-309, 9-312, 9-314
9-115(5)	9-327, 9-328, 9-329
9-115(6)	9-203, 9-313
9-115(e)	9-106
9-116	9-206, 9-309
9-201	9-201
9-202	9-202
9-203(1) - (3)	9-203
9-203(4)	9-201
9-204	9-204
9-205	9-205
9-206	9-403
9-207	9-207
9-208	9-210
9-301(1) - (2)	9-317
9-301(3)	9-102
9-301(4)	9-323
9-302(1)	9-309, 9-310
9-302(2)	9-310
9-302(3), (4)	9-311
9-303	9-308
9-304	9-312
9-305	9-306, 9-313

OLD ARTICLE 9	NEW ARTICLE 9
9-306	9-315
9-307(1) - (2)	9-320
9-307(3)	9-323
9-308	9-330
9-309	9-331
9-310	9-333
9-311	9-401
9-312(1)	9-322
9-312(2) omitted	See Appendix II
9-312(3), (4)	9-324
9-312(5), (6)	9-322
9-312(7)	9-323
9-313(1) - (7)	9-334
9-313(8)	9-604
9-314	9-335
9-315	9-336
9-316	9-339
9-317	9-402
9-318(1)	9-404
9-318(2)	9-405
9-318(3), (4)	9-406
9-401	9-501
9-402(1)	9-504, 9-502
9-402(2)	Omitted as unnecessary
9-402(3)	9-521
9-402(4)	9-512

OLD ARTICLE 9	NEW ARTICLE 9
9-402(5), (6)	9-502
9-402(7)	9-503(a)(4), 9-507
9-402(8)	9-506
9-403(1)	9-516(a)
9-403(2)	9-515
9-403(3)	9-515, 9-522
9-403(4)	9-519
9-403(5)	9-525
9-403(6)	9-515
9-403(7)	9-519
9-404	9-513
9-405	9-514, 9-519
9-406	9-512
9-407	9-523
9-408	9-505
9-501(1), (2)	9-601
9-501(3)	9-602, 9-603
9-501(4)	9-604
9-501 (5)	9-601
9-502	9-607, 9-608
9-503	9-609
9-504(1)	9-610, 9-615
9-504(2)	9-615
9-504(3)	9-610, 9-611, 9-624
9-504(4)	9-617
9-504(5)	9-618

OLD ARTICLE 9	NEW ARTICLE 9
9-505	9-620, 9-621, 9-624
9-506	9-623, 9-624
9-507	9-625, 9-627

OTHER CODE SECTIONS	NEW ARTICLE 9
2-326(3)	9-102
2A-303(3)	9-407
2A-307(2)(b) and (c)	9-317
2A-307(3)	9-321
2A-307(4)	9-323

TABLE INDICATING SOURCES OR DERIVATIONS OF NEW ARTICLE 9 SECTIONS AND CONFORMING AMENDMENTS

NEW ARTICLE 9 SECTIONS (NOTE MANY SECTIONS CONTAIN SOME NEW COVERAGE)	PRIMARY OLD ARTICLE 9 AND OTHER CODE SECTIONS
9-101	9-101
9-102	9-105, 9-106, 9-109, 9-301(3), 9-306 (1), 9-115, 2-326(3)
9-103	9-107
9-104 (New)	Derived from 8-106
9-105 (New)	Derived from 8-106
9-106	8-106 and 9-115(e)
9-107 (New)	Derived from 8-106
9-108	9-110, 9-115(3)
9-109	9-102, 9-104
9-110	9-113
9-201	9-201, 9-203(4)
9-202	9-202
9-203	9-203, 9-115(2), (6)
9-204	9-204
9-205	9-205
9-206	9-116
9-207	9-207
9-208 (New)	
9-209 (New)	

NEW ARTICLE 9 SECTIONS (NOTE MANY SECTIONS CONTAIN SOME NEW COVERAGE)	PRIMARY OLD ARTICLE 9 AND OTHER CODE SECTIONS
9-210	9-208
9-301	9-103(1)(a), (b), 9-103(3)(a), (b),9-103(4) 9-103(5) substantially modified
9-302 (New)	
9-303	9-103(2)(a), (b), substantially revised
9-304 (New)	Derived from 8-110(e) and former 9-103(6)
9-305	9-103(6)
9-306 (New)	Derived in part from 8-110(e) and 9-305 and former 9-103(6)
9-307	9-103(3)(d), as substantially revised
9-308	9-303, 9-115(2)
9-309	9-302(1), 9-115(4)(c), (d), 9-116
9-310	9-302(1), (2)
9-311	9-302(3), (4)
9-312	9-115(4) and 9-304, with additions and some changes
9-313	9-305, 9-115(6)
9-314 (New in part)	9-115(4) and derived from 8-106
9-315	9-306
9-316	9-103(1)(d), (2)(b), (3)(e), as modified

NEW ARTICLE 9 SECTIONS (NOTE MANY SECTIONS CONTAIN SOME NEW COVERAGE)	PRIMARY OLD ARTICLE 9 AND OTHER CODE SECTIONS
9-317	9-301, 2A-307(2)
9-318 (New)	
9-319 (New)	
9-320	9-307
9-321	2A-103(1)(o), 2A-307(3)
9-322	9-312(5), (6)
9-323	9-312(7), 9-301(4), 9-307(3), 2A-307(4)
9-324	9-312(3), (4)
9-325 (New)	But see 9-402(7)
9-326 (New)	But see 9-402(7)
9-327	Derived from 9-115(5)
9-328	9-115(5)
9-329 (New)	Loosely modeled after former 9-115(5). See also 5-114 and 5-118
9-330	9-308
9-331	9-309
9-332 (New)	But see Comment 2(c) to 9-306
9-333	9-310
9-334	9-313
9-335 (New)	Section replaces former 9-314
9-336 (New)	Section replaces former 9-315

NEW ARTICLE 9 SECTIONS (NOTE MANY SECTIONS CONTAIN SOME NEW COVERAGE)	PRIMARY OLD ARTICLE 9 AND OTHER CODE SECTIONS
9-337	Derived from 9-103(2)(d)
9-338 (New)	
9-339	9-316
9-340 (New)	
9-341 (New)	
9-342 (New)	Derived from 8-106(g)
9-401	9-311
9-402	9-317
9-403	9-206
9-404	9-318(1)
9-405	9-318(2)
9-406	9-318(3), (4)
9-407	2A-303
9-408 (New)	
9-409 (New)	See also 5-114
9-501	Derived from former 9-401
9-502	9-402(1), (5), (6)
9-503 (New)	Subsection (a)(4),(b) and (c) derive from former 9-402(7); otherwise, new
9-504	9-402(1)
9-505	9-408
9-506	9-402(8)
9-507	9-402(7)

NEW ARTICLE 9 SECTIONS (NOTE MANY SECTIONS CONTAIN SOME NEW COVERAGE)	PRIMARY OLD ARTICLE 9 AND OTHER CODE SECTIONS
9-508 (New)	But see 9-402(7)
9-509 (New)	
9-510 (New)	
9-511 (New)	
9-512	9-402(4)
9-513	9-404
9-514	9-405
9-515	9-403(2), (3), (6)
9-516 (Basically New)	Subsection (a) is former 9-403(1); the remainder is new
9-517 (New)	
9-518 (New)	
9-519	9-403(4), (7); 9-405(2)
9-520 (New)	
9-521 (New)	
9-522	9-403(3), revised substantially
9-523	9-407; subsections (d) and (e) are new
9-524 (New)	Derived from 4-109
9-525	Various sections of former Part 4
9-526 (New)	Subsection (b) derives in part from the Uniform Consumer Credit Code (1974)

NEW ARTICLE 9 SECTIONS (NOTE MANY SECTIONS CONTAIN SOME NEW COVERAGE)	PRIMARY OLD ARTICLE 9 AND OTHER CODE SECTIONS
9-527 (New)	Derived in part from the Uniform Consumer Credit Code (1974)
9-601	9-501(1), (2), (5)
9-602	9-501(3)
9-603	9-501(3)
9-604	9-501(4), 9-313(8)
9-605 (New)	
9-606 (New)	
9-607	9-502, subsections (b), (d), and (e) are new
9-608	Subsection (a) is new. Subsection (b) derives from former 9-502(2)
9-609	9-503
9-610	9-504(1), (3)
9-611	9-504(3)
9-612 (New)	
9-613 (New)	
9-614 (New)	
9-615	9-504(1), (2)
9-616 (New)	
9-617	9-504(4)
9-618	9-504(5)
9-619 (New)	

NEW ARTICLE 9 SECTIONS (NOTE MANY SECTIONS CONTAIN SOME NEW COVERAGE)	PRIMARY OLD ARTICLE 9 AND OTHER CODE SECTIONS
9-620	9-505
9-621	9-505
9-622 (New)	
9-623	9-506
9-624	9-504(3), 9-505, 9-506
9-625	9-507
9-626 (New)	
9-627	9-507(2)
9-628 (New)	
9-701	No comparable provision in Article 9 (See Article 10)
9-702	No comparable provision in Article 9 (See Article 10)
9-703	No comparable provision in Article 9 (See Article 10)
9-704	No comparable provision in Article 9 (See Article 10)
9-705	No comparable provision in Article 9 (See Article 10)
9-706	No comparable provision in Article 9 (See Article 10)
9-707	No comparable provision in Article 9 (See Article 10)

CONFORMING AMENDMENTS TO OTHER CODE SECTIONS AND COMMENTS

1-105(2)
1-201(9), (32), (37)
2-103(3)
2-210; New subsection (3) added
2-312; Comment
2-326(3)
2-502 (1) and (2)
2-716(3)
2A-103(3)
2A-303
2A-307
2A-309
4-210
5-118 (New)
Article 6 (unless repealed)
7-503
8-102 Comment
8-103 (f)
8-106 and Comment
8-110
8-301 (3)
8-302 (a)
8-502 Comment
8-510

REVISION OF UNIFORM COMMERCIAL CODE
ARTICLE 9—SECURED TRANSACTIONS

ANALYSIS

The title to the new Article 9 is shortened. Given the expansion in the scope of the new article, it is no longer possible to attempt to capture the full reach of the article in a title. The basic scope provision of the old Article 9 (old § 9-102) provided that Article 9 applied to any transaction intended to create a security interest in personal property or fixtures and to any sale of accounts or chattel paper. The new Article 9 retains this coverage. But under the new basic scope provision (new § 9-109) at least *some* of the rules of Article 9 also apply to agricultural liens and consignments, and to sales of payment intangibles and promissory notes. One of the central policy objectives of the revisers was to expand the Article 9 universe. *See Secured Transactions* §§ 1A.03 and 3.02.

PART 1 GENERAL PROVISIONS

[SUBPART 1. SHORT TITLE, DEFINITIONS, AND GENERAL CONCEPTS]

§ 9-101. SHORT TITLE. This article may be cited as Uniform Commercial Code-Secured Transactions.

Official Comment

1. **Source.** This Article supersedes former Uniform Commercial Code (UCC) Article 9. As did its predecessor, it provides a comprehensive scheme for the regulation of security interests in personal property and fixtures. For the most part this Article follows the general approach and retains much of the terminology of former Article 9. In addition to describing many aspects of the operation and interpretation of this Article, these Comments explain the material changes that this Article makes to former Article 9. Former Article 9 superseded the wide variety of pre-UCC security devices. Unlike the Comments to former Article 9, however, these Comments dwell very little on the pre-UCC state of the law. For that reason, the Comments to former Article 9 will remain of substantial historical value and interest. They also will remain useful in understanding the background and general conceptual approach of this Article.

Citations to "Bankruptcy Code Section" in these Comments are to Title 11 of the United States Code as in effect on December 31, 1998.

2. **Background and History.** In 1990, the Permanent Editorial Board for the UCC with the support of its sponsors, The American Law Institute and the National Conference of Commissioners on Uniform State Laws, established a committee to study Article 9 of the UCC. The study committee issued its report as of December 1, 1992, recommending the creation of a drafting committee for the revision of Article 9 and also recommending numerous specific changes to Article 9. Organized in 1993, a drafting committee met fifteen times from 1993 to 1998. This Article was approved by its sponsors in 1998.

3. **Reorganization and Renumbering; Captions; Style.** This Article reflects a substantial reorganization of former Article 9 and renumbering of most sections. New Part 4 deals with several aspects of third-party rights and duties that are unrelated to perfection and priority. Some of these were covered by Part 3 of former Article 9. Part 5 deals with filing (covered by former Part 4) and Part 6 deals with default and enforcement (covered by former Part 5). Appendix I contains conforming revisions to other articles of the UCC, and Appendix II contains model provisions for production-money priority.

This Article also includes headings for the subsections as an aid to readers. Unlike section captions, which are part of the UCC, see Section 1-109, subsection headings are not a part of the official text itself and have not been approved by the sponsors. Each jurisdiction in which this Article is introduced may consider whether to adopt the headings as a part of the statute and whether to adopt a provision clarifying the effect, if any, to be given to the headings. This Article also has been conformed to current style conventions.

4. **Summary of Revisions.** Following is a brief summary of some of the more significant revisions of Article 9 that are included in this Article.

a. **Scope of Article 9.** This Article expands the scope of Article 9 in several respects.

Deposit accounts. Section 9-109 includes within this Article's scope deposit accounts as original collateral, except in consumer transactions. Former Article 9 dealt with deposit accounts only as proceeds of other collateral.

Sales of payment intangibles and promissory notes. Section 9-109 also includes within the scope of this Article most sales of "payment intangibles" (defined in Section 9-102 as general intangibles under which an account debtor's principal obligation is monetary) and "promissory notes" (also defined in Section 9-102). Former Article 9 included sales of accounts and chattel paper, but not sales of payment intangibles or promissory notes. In its inclusion of sales of payment intangibles and promissory notes, this Article continues the drafting convention found in former Article 9; it provides that the sale of accounts, chattel paper, payment intangibles, or promissory notes creates a "security interest." The definition of "account" in Section 9-102 also has been expanded to include various rights to payment that were general intangibles under former Article 9.

Health-care-insurance receivables. Section 9-109 narrows Article 9's exclusion of transfers of interests in insurance policies by carving out of the exclusion "health-care-insurance receivables" (defined in Section 9-102). A health-care-insurance receivable is included within the definition of "account" in Section 9-102.

Nonpossessory statutory agricultural liens. Section 9-109 also brings nonpossessory statutory agricultural liens within the scope of Article 9.

Consignments. Section 9-109 provides that "true" consignments-bailments for the purpose of sale by the bailee-are security interests covered by Article 9, with certain exceptions. See Section 9-102 (defining "consignment"). Currently, many consignments are subject to Article 9's filing requirements by operation of former Section 2-326.

Supporting obligations and property securing rights to payment. This Article also addresses explicitly (i) obligations, such as guaranties and letters of credit, that support payment or performance of collateral such as accounts, chattel paper, and payment intangibles, and (ii) any property (including real property) that secures a right to payment or performance that is subject to an Article 9 security interest. See Sections 9-203, 9-308.

Commercial tort claims. Section 9-109 expands the scope of Article 9 to include the assignment of commercial tort claims by narrowing the exclusion of tort claims generally. However, this Article continues to exclude tort claims for bodily injury and other non-business tort claims of a natural person. See Section 9-102 (defining "commercial tort claim").

Transfers by States and governmental units of States. Section 9-109 narrows the exclusion of transfers by States and their governmental units. It excludes only transfers covered by another statute (other than a statute generally applicable to security interests) to the extent the statute governs the creation, perfection, priority, or enforcement of security interests.

Nonassignable general intangibles, promissory notes, health-care-insurance receivables, and letter-of-credit rights. This Article enables a security interest to attach to letter-of-credit rights, health-care-insurance receivables, promissory notes, and general intangibles, including contracts, permits, licenses, and franchises, notwithstanding a contractual or statutory prohibition against or limitation on assignment. This Article explicitly protects third parties against any adverse effect of the creation or attempted enforcement of the security interest. See Sections 9-408, 9-409.

Subject to Sections 9-408 and 9-409 and two other exceptions (Sections 9-406, concerning accounts, chattel paper, and payment intangibles, and 9-407, concerning interests in leased goods), Section 9-401 establishes a baseline rule that the inclusion of transactions and collateral within the scope of Article 9 has no effect on non-Article 9 law dealing with the alienability or inalienability of property. For example, if a commercial tort claim is nonassignable under other applicable law, the fact that a security interest in the claim is within the scope of Article 9 does not override the other applicable law's effective prohibition of assignment.

b. **Duties of Secured Party.** This Article provides for expanded duties of secured parties.

Release of control. Section 9-208 imposes upon a secured party having control of a deposit account, investment property, or a letter-of-credit right the duty to release control when there is no secured obligation and no commitment to give value. Section 9-209 contains analogous provisions when an account debtor has been notified to pay a secured party.

Information. Section 9-210 expands a secured party's duties to provide the debtor with information concerning collateral and the obligations that it secures.

Default and enforcement. Part 6 also includes some additional duties of secured parties in connection with default and enforcement. See, e.g., Section 9-616 (duty to explain calculation of deficiency or surplus in a consumer-goods transaction).

c. **Choice of Law.** The choice-of-law rules for the law governing perfection, the effect of perfection or nonperfection, and priority are found in Part 3, Subpart 1 (Sections 9-301 through 9-307). See also Section 9-316.

Where to file: Location of debtor. This Article changes the choice-of-law rule governing perfection (i.e., where to file) for most collateral to the law of the jurisdiction where the debtor is located. See Section 9-301. Under former Article 9, the jurisdiction of the debtor's location governed only perfection and priority of a security interest in accounts, general intangibles, mobile goods, and, for purposes of perfection by filing, chattel paper and investment property.

Determining debtor's location. As a baseline rule, Section 9-307 follows former Section 9-103, under which the location of the debtor is the debtor's place of business (or chief executive office, if the debtor has more than one place of business). Section 9-307 contains three major exceptions. First, a "registered organization," such as a corporation or limited liability company, is located in the State under whose law the debtor is organized, e.g., a corporate debtor's State of incorporation. Second, an individual debtor is located at his or her principal residence. Third, there are special rules for determining the location of the United States and registered organizations organized under the law of the United States.

Location of non-U.S. debtors. If, applying the foregoing rules, a debtor is located in a jurisdiction whose law does not require public notice as a condition of perfection of a nonpossessory security interest, the entity is deemed located in the District of Columbia. See Section 9-307. Thus, to the extent that this Article applies to non-U.S. debtors, perfection could be accomplished in many cases by a domestic filing.

Priority. For tangible collateral such as goods and instruments, Section 9-301 provides that the law applicable to priority and the effect of perfection or nonperfection will remain the law of the jurisdiction where the collateral is located, as under former Section 9-103 (but without the confusing "last event" test). For intangible collateral, such as accounts, the applicable law for priority will be that of the jurisdiction in which the debtor is located.

Possessory security interests; agricultural liens. Perfection, the effect of perfection or nonperfection, and priority of a possessory security interest or an agricultural lien are governed by the law of the jurisdiction where the collateral subject to the security interest or lien is located. See Sections 9-301, 9-302.

Goods covered by certificates of title; deposit accounts; letter-of-credit rights; investment property. This Article includes several refinements to the treatment of choice-of-law matters for goods covered by certificates of title. See Section 9-303. It also provides special choice-of-law rules, similar to those for investment property under current Articles 8 and 9, for deposit accounts (Section 9-304), investment property (Section 9-305), and letter-of-credit rights (Section 9-306).

Change in applicable law. Section 9-316 addresses perfection following a change in applicable law.

d. **Perfection.** The rules governing perfection of security interests and agricultural liens are found in Part 3, Subpart 2 (Sections 9-308 through 9-316).

Deposit accounts; letter-of-credit rights. With certain exceptions, this Article provides that a security interest in a deposit account or a letter-of-credit right may be perfected *only* by the secured party's acquiring "control" of the deposit account or letter-of-credit right. See Sections 9-312, 9-314. Under Section 9-104, a secured party has "control" of a deposit account when, with the consent of the debtor, the secured party obtains the depositary bank's agreement to act on the secured party's instructions (including when the secured party becomes the account holder) or when the secured party is itself the depositary bank. The control requirements are patterned on Section 8-106, which specifies the requirements for control of investment property. Under Section 9-107, "control" of a letter-of-credit right occurs when the issuer or nominated person consents to an assignment of proceeds under Section 5-114.

Electronic chattel paper. Section 9-102 includes a new defined term: "electronic chattel paper." Electronic chattel paper is a record or records consisting of information stored in an electronic medium (i.e., it is not written). Perfection of a security interest in electronic chattel paper may be by control or filing. See Sections 9-105 (*sui generis* definition of control of electronic chattel paper), 9-312 (perfection by filing), 9-314 (perfection by control).

Investment property. The perfection requirements for "investment property" (defined in Section 9-102), including perfection by control under Section 9-106, remain substantially unchanged. However, a new provision in Section 9-314 is designed to ensure that a secured party retains control in "repledge" transactions that are typical in the securities markets.

Instruments, agricultural liens, and commercial tort claims. This Article expands the types of collateral in which a security interest may be perfected by filing to include instruments. See Section 9-312. Agricultural liens and security interests in commercial tort claims also are perfected by filing, under this Article. See Sections 9-308, 9-310.

Sales of payment intangibles and promissory notes. Although former Article 9 covered the outright sale of accounts and chattel paper, sales of most other types of receivables also are financing transactions to which Article 9 should apply. Accordingly, Section 9-102 expands the definition of "account" to include many types of receivables (including "health-care-insurance receivables," defined in Section 9-102) that former Article 9 classified as "general intangibles." It thereby subjects to Article 9's filing system sales of more types of receivables than did former Article 9. Certain sales of payment intangibles-primarily bank loan participation transactions-should not be subject to the Article 9 filing rules. These transactions fall in a residual category of collateral, "payment intangibles" (general intangibles under which the account debtor's principal obligation is monetary), the sale of which is exempt from the filing requirements of Article 9. See Sections 9-102, 9-109, 9-309 (perfection upon attachment). The perfection rules for sales of promissory notes are the same as those for sales of payment intangibles.

Possessory security interests. Several provisions of this Article address aspects of security interests involving a secured party or a third party who is in possession of the collateral. In particular, Section 9-313 resolves a number of uncertainties under former Section 9-305. It provides that a security interest in collateral in the possession of a third party is perfected when the third party acknowledges in an authenticated record that it holds for the secured party's benefit. Section 9-313 also provides that a third party need not so acknowledge and that its acknowledgment does not impose any duties on it, unless it otherwise agrees. A special rule in Section 9-313 provides that if a secured party already is in possession of collateral, its security interest remains perfected by possession if it delivers the collateral to a third party and the collateral is accompanied by instructions to hold it for the secured party or to redeliver it to the secured party. Section 9-313 also clarifies the limited circumstances under which a security interest in goods covered by a certificate of title may be perfected by the secured party's taking possession.

Automatic perfection. Section 9-309 lists various types of security interests as to which no public-notice step is required for perfection (e.g., purchase-money security interests in consumer goods other than automobiles). This automatic perfection also extends to a transfer of a health-care-insurance receivable *to* a health-care provider. Those transfers normally will be made by natural persons who receive health-care services; there is little value in requiring filing for perfection in that context. Automatic perfection also applies to security interests created by sales of payment intangibles and promissory notes. Section 9-308 provides that a perfected security interest in collateral supported by a "supporting obligation" (such as an account supported by a guaranty) also is a perfected security interest in the supporting obligation, and that a perfected security interest in an obligation secured by a security interest or lien on property (e.g., a real-property mortgage) also is a perfected security interest in the security interest or lien.

e. **Priority; Special Rules for Banks and Deposit Accounts.** The rules governing priority of security interests and agricultural liens are found in Part 3, Subpart 3 (Sections 9-317 through 9-342). This Article includes several new priority rules and some special rules relating to banks and deposit accounts (Sections 9-340 through 9-342).

Purchase-money security interests: General; consumer-goods transactions; inventory. Section 9-103 substantially rewrites the definition of purchase-money security interest (PMSI) (although the term is not formally "defined"). The substantive changes, however, apply only to non-consumer-goods transactions. (Consumer transactions and consumer-goods transactions are discussed below in Comment 4.j.) For non-consumer-goods transactions,

Section 9-103 makes clear that a security interest in collateral may be (to some extent) both a PMSI as well as a non-PMSI, in accord with the "dual status" rule applied by some courts under former Article 9 (thereby rejecting the "transformation" rule). The definition provides an even broader conception of a PMSI in inventory, yielding a result that accords with private agreements entered into in response to the uncertainty under former Article 9. It also treats consignments as purchase-money security interests in inventory. Section 9-324 revises the PMSI priority rules, but for the most part without material change in substance. Section 9-324 also clarifies the priority rules for competing PMSIs in the same collateral.

Purchase-money security interests in livestock; agricultural liens. Section 9-324 provides a special PMSI priority, similar to the inventory PMSI priority rule, for livestock. Section 9-322 (which contains the baseline first-to-file-or-perfect priority rule) also recognizes special non-Article 9 priority rules for agricultural liens, which can override the baseline first-in-time rule.

Purchase-money security interests in software. Section 9-324 contains a new priority rule for a software purchase-money security interest. (Section 9-102 includes a definition of "software.") Under Section 9-103, a software PMSI includes a PMSI in software that is used in goods that are also subject to a PMSI. (Note also that the definition of "chattel paper" has been expanded to include records that evidence a monetary obligation and a security interest in specific goods and software used in the goods.)

Investment property. The priority rules for investment property are substantially similar to the priority rules found in former Section 9-115, which was added in conjunction with the 1994 revisions to UCC Article 8. Under Section 9-328, if a secured party has control of investment property (Sections 8-106, 9-106), its security interest is senior to a security interest perfected in another manner (e.g., by filing). Also under Section 9-328, security interests perfected by control generally rank according to the time that control is obtained or, in the case of a security entitlement or a commodity contract carried in a commodity account, the time when the control arrangement is entered into. This is a change from former Section 9-115, under which the security interests ranked equally. However, as between a securities intermediary's security interest in a security entitlement that it maintains for the debtor and a security interest held by another secured party, the securities intermediary's security interest is senior.

Deposit accounts. This Article's priority rules applicable to deposit accounts are found in Section 9-327. They are patterned on and are similar to those for investment property in former Section 9-115 and Section 9-328 of this Article. Under Section 9-327, if a secured party has control of a deposit account, its security interest is senior to a security interest perfected in another manner (i.e., as cash proceeds). Also under Section 9-327, security interests perfected by control rank according to the time that control is obtained, but as between a depositary bank's security interest and one held by another secured party, the depositary bank's security interest is senior. A corresponding rule in Section 9-340 makes a depositary bank's right of set-off generally senior to a security interest held by another secured party. However, if the other secured party becomes the depositary bank's customer with respect to the deposit account, then its security interest is senior to the depositary bank's security interest and right of set-off. Sections 9-327, 9-340.

Letter-of-credit rights. The priority rules for security interests in letter-of-credit rights are found in Section 9-329. They are somewhat analogous to those for deposit accounts. A security interest perfected by control has priority over one perfected in another manner (i.e., as a supporting obligation for the collateral in which a security interest is perfected). Security interests in a letter-of-credit right perfected by control rank according to the time that control is obtained. However, the rights of a transferee beneficiary or a nominated person are independent and superior to the extent provided in Section 5-114. See Section 9-109(c)(4).

Chattel paper and instruments. Section 9-330 is the successor to former Section 9-308. As under former Section 9-308, differing priority rules apply to purchasers of chattel paper who give new value and take possession (or, in the case of electronic chattel paper, obtain control) of the collateral depending on whether a conflicting security interest in the collateral is claimed merely as proceeds. The principal change relates to the role of knowledge and the effect of an indication of a previous assignment of the collateral. Section 9-330 also affords priority to purchasers of instruments who take possession in good faith and without knowledge that the purchase violates the rights of the competing secured party. In addition, to qualify for priority, purchasers of chattel paper, but not of instruments, must purchase in the ordinary course of business.

Proceeds. Section 9-322 contains new priority rules that clarify when a special priority of a security interest in collateral continues or does not continue with respect to proceeds of the collateral. Other refinements to the priority rules for proceeds are included in Sections 9-324 (purchase-money security interest priority) and 9-330 (priority of certain purchasers of chattel paper and instruments).

Miscellaneous priority provisions. This Article also includes (i) clarifications of selected good-faith-purchase and similar issues (Sections 9-317, 9-331); (ii) new priority rules to deal with the "double debtor" problem arising when a debtor creates a security interest in collateral acquired by the debtor subject to a security interest created by another person (Section 9-325); (iii) new priority rules to deal with the problems created when a change in corporate structure or the like results in a new entity that has become bound by the original debtor's after-acquired property agreement (Section 9-326); (iv) a provision enabling most transferees of funds from a deposit account or money to take free of a security interest (Section 9-332); (v) substantially rewritten and refined priority rules dealing with accessions and commingled goods (Sections 9-335, 9-336); (vi) revised priority rules for security interests in goods covered by a certificate of title (Section 9-337); and (vii) provisions designed to ensure that security interests in deposit accounts will not extend to most transferees of funds on deposit or payees from deposit accounts and will not otherwise "clog" the payments system (Sections 9-341, 9-342).

Model provisions relating to production-money security interests. Appendix II to this Article contains model definitions and priority rules relating to "production-money security interests" held by secured parties who give new value used in the production of crops. Because no consensus emerged on the wisdom of these provisions during the drafting process, the sponsors make no recommendation on whether these model provisions should be enacted.

f. **Proceeds.** Section 9-102 contains an expanded definition of "proceeds" of collateral which includes additional rights and property that arise out of collateral, such as distributions on account of collateral and claims arising out of the loss or nonconformity of, defects in, or damage to collateral. The term also includes collections on account of "supporting obligations," such as guarantees.

g. **Part 4: Additional Provisions Relating to Third-Party Rights.** New Part 4 contains several provisions relating to the relationships between certain third parties and the parties to secured transactions. It contains new Sections 9-401 (replacing former Section 9-311) (alienability of debtor's rights), 9-402 (replacing former Section 9-317) (secured party not obligated on debtor's contracts), 9-403 (replacing former Section 9-206) (agreement not to assert defenses against assignee), 9-404, 9-405, and 9-406 (replacing former Section 9-318) (rights acquired by assignee, modification of assigned contract, discharge of account debtor, restrictions on assignment of account, chattel paper, promissory note, or payment intangible ineffective), 9-407 (replacing some provisions of former Section 2A-303) (restrictions on creation or enforcement of security interest in leasehold interest or lessor's residual interest ineffective). It also contains new Sections 9-408 (restrictions on assignment of promissory notes, health-care-insurance receivables ineffective, and certain general intangibles ineffective) and 9-409 (restrictions on assignment of letter-of-credit rights ineffective), which are discussed above.

h. **Filing.** Part 5 (formerly Part 4) of Article 9 has been substantially rewritten to simplify the statutory text and to deal with numerous problems of interpretation and implementation that have arisen over the years.

Medium-neutrality. This Article is "medium-neutral"; that is, it makes clear that parties may file and otherwise communicate with a filing office by means of records communicated and stored in media other than on paper.

Identity of person who files a record; authorization. Part 5 is largely indifferent as to the person who effects a filing. Instead, it addresses whose authorization is necessary for a person to file a record with a filing office. The filing scheme does not contemplate that the identity of a "filer" will be a part of the searchable records. This approach is consistent with, and a necessary aspect of, eliminating signatures or other evidence of authorization from the system (except to the extent that filing offices may choose to employ authentication procedures in connection with electronic communications). As long as the appropriate person authorizes the filing, or, in the case of a termination statement, the debtor is entitled to the termination, it is largely insignificant whether the secured party or another person files any given record.

Section 9-509 collects in one place most of the rules that determine when a record may be filed. In general, the debtor's authorization is required for the filing of an initial financing statement or an amendment that adds collateral. With one further exception, a secured party of record's authorization is required for the filing of other amendments. The exception arises if a secured party has failed to provide a termination statement that is required because there is no outstanding secured obligation or commitment to give value. In that situation, a debtor is authorized to file a termination statement indicating that it has been filed by the debtor.

Financing statement formal requisites. The formal requisites for a financing statement are set out in Section 9-502. A financing statement must provide the name of the debtor and the secured party and an indication of the collateral that it covers. Sections 9-503 and 9-506 address the sufficiency of a name provided on a financing statement and clarify when a debtor's name is correct and when an incorrect name is insufficient. Section 9-504 addresses the indication of collateral covered. Under Section 9-504, a super-generic description (e.g., "all assets" or "all personal property") in a financing statement is a sufficient indication of the collateral. (Note, however, that a super-generic description is inadequate for purposes of a security agreement. See Sections 9-108, 9-203.) To facilitate electronic filing, this Article does not require that the debtor's signature or other authorization appear on a financing statement. Instead, it prohibits the filing of unauthorized financing statements and imposes liability upon those who violate the prohibition. See Sections 9-509, 9-626.

Filing-office operations. Part 5 contains several provisions governing filing operations. First, it prohibits the filing office from rejecting an initial financing statement or other record for a reason other than one of the few that are specified. See Sections 9-520, 9-516. Second, the filing office is obliged to link all subsequent records (e.g., assignments, continuation statements, etc.) to the initial financing statement to which they relate. See Section 9-519. Third, the filing office may delete a financing statement and related records from the files no earlier than one year after lapse (lapse normally is five years after the filing date), and then only if a continuation statement has not been filed. See Sections 9-515, 9-519, 9-522. Thus, a financing statement and related records would be discovered by a search of the files even after the filing of a termination statement. This approach helps eliminate filing-office discretion and also eases problems associated with multiple secured parties and multiple partial assignments. Fourth, Part 5 mandates performance standards for filing offices. See Sections 9-519, 9-520, 9-523. Fifth, it provides for the promulgation of filing-office rules to deal with details best left out of the statute and requires the filing office to submit periodic reports. See Sections 9-526, 9-527.

Correction of records: Defaulting or missing secured parties and fraudulent filings. In some areas of the country, serious problems have arisen from fraudulent financing statements that are filed against public officials and other persons. This Article addresses the fraud problem by providing the opportunity for a debtor to file a termination statement when a secured party wrongfully refuses or fails to provide a termination statement. See Section 9-509. This opportunity also addresses the problem of secured parties that simply disappear through mergers or liquidations. In addition, Section 9-518 affords a statutory method by which a debtor who believes that a filed record is inaccurate or was wrongfully filed may indicate that fact in the files by filing a correction statement, albeit without affecting the efficacy, if any, of the challenged record.

Extended period of effectiveness for certain financing statements. Section 9-515 contains an exception to the usual rule that financing statements are effective for five years unless a continuation statement is filed to continue the effectiveness for another five years. Under that section, an initial financing statement filed in connection with a "public-finance transaction" or a "manufactured-home transaction" (terms defined in Section 9-102) is effective for 30 years.

National form of financing statement and related forms. Section 9-521 provides for uniform, national written forms of financing statements and related written records that must be accepted by a filing office that accepts written records.

  i. **Default and Enforcement.** Part 6 of Article 9 extensively revises former Part 5. Provisions relating to enforcement of consumer-goods transactions and consumer transactions are discussed in Comment 4.j.

Debtor, secondary obligor; waiver. Section 9-602 clarifies the identity of persons who have rights and persons to whom a secured party owes specified duties under Part 6. Under that section, the rights and duties are enjoyed by and run to the "debtor," defined in Section 9-102 to mean any person with a non-lien property interest in collateral, and to any "obligor." However, with one exception (Section 9-616, as it relates to a consumer obligor), the rights and duties concerned affect non-debtor obligors only if they are "secondary obligors." "Secondary obligor" is defined in Section 9-102 to include one who is secondarily obligated on the secured obligation, e.g., a guarantor, or one who has a right of recourse against the debtor or another obligor with respect to an obligation secured by collateral. However, under Section 9-628, the secured party is relieved from any duty or liability to any person unless the secured party knows that the person is a debtor or obligor. Resolving an issue on which courts disagreed under former Article 9, this Article generally prohibits waiver by a secondary obligor of its rights and a secured party's duties under Part 6. See Section 9-602. However, Section 9-624 permits a secondary obligor or debtor to waive the right to notification of disposition of collateral and, in a non-consumer transaction, the right to redeem collateral, if the secondary obligor or debtor agrees to do so after default.

Rights of collection and enforcement of collateral. Section 9-607 explains in greater detail than former 9-502 the rights of a secured party who seeks to collect or enforce collateral, including accounts, chattel paper, and payment intangibles. It also sets forth the enforcement rights of a depositary bank holding a security interest in a deposit account maintained with the depositary bank. Section 9-607 relates solely to the rights of a secured party *vis-a-vis* a debtor with respect to collections and enforcement. It does not affect the rights or duties of third parties, such as account debtors on collateral, which are addressed elsewhere (e.g., Section 9-406). Section 9-608 clarifies the manner in which proceeds of collection or enforcement are to be applied.

Disposition of collateral: Warranties of title. Section 9-610 imposes on a secured party who disposes of collateral the warranties of title, quiet possession, and the like that are otherwise applicable under other law. It also provides rules for the exclusion or modification of those warranties.

Disposition of collateral: Notification, application of proceeds, surplus and deficiency, other effects. Section 9-611 requires a secured party to give notification of a disposition of collateral to other secured parties and lienholders who have filed financing statements against the debtor covering the collateral. (That duty was eliminated by the 1972 revisions to Article 9.) However, that section relieves the secured party from that duty when the secured party undertakes a search of the records and a report of the results is unreasonably delayed. Section 9-613, which applies only to non-consumer transactions, specifies the contents of a sufficient notification of disposition and provides that a notification sent 10 days or more before the earliest time for disposition is sent within a reasonable time. Section 9-615 addresses the application of proceeds of disposition, the entitlement of a debtor to any surplus, and the liability of an obligor for any deficiency. Section 9-619 clarifies the effects of a disposition by a secured party, including the rights of transferees of the collateral.

Rights and duties of secondary obligor. Section 9-618 provides that a secondary obligor obtains the rights and assumes the duties of a secured party if the secondary obligor receives an assignment of a secured obligation, agrees to assume the secured party's rights and duties upon a transfer to it of collateral, or becomes subrogated to the rights of the secured party with respect to the collateral. The assumption, transfer, or subrogation is not a disposition of collateral under Section 9-610, but it does relieves the former secured party of further duties. Former Section 9-504(5) did not address whether a secured party was relieved of its duties in this situation.

Transfer of record or legal title. Section 9-619 contains a new provision making clear that a transfer of record or legal title to a secured party is not of itself a disposition under Part 6. This rule applies regardless of the circumstances under which the transfer of title occurs.

Strict foreclosure. Section 9-620, unlike former Section 9-505, permits a secured party to accept collateral in partial satisfaction, as well as full satisfaction, of the obligations secured. This right of strict foreclosure extends to intangible as well as tangible property. Section 9-622 clarifies the effects of an acceptance of collateral on the rights of junior claimants. It rejects the approach taken by some courts-deeming a secured party to have constructively retained collateral in satisfaction of the secured obligations-in the case of a secured party's unreasonable delay in the disposition of collateral. Instead, unreasonable delay is relevant when determining whether a disposition under Section 9-610 is commercially reasonable.

Effect of noncompliance: "Rebuttable presumption" test. Section 9-626 adopts the "rebuttable presumption" test for the failure of a secured party to proceed in accordance with certain provisions of Part 6. (As discussed in Comment 4.j., the test does not necessarily apply to consumer transactions.) Under this approach, the deficiency claim of a noncomplying secured party is calculated by crediting the obligor with the greater of the actual net proceeds of a disposition and the amount of net proceeds that would have been realized if the disposition had been conducted in accordance with Part 6 (e.g., in a commercially reasonable manner). For non-consumer transactions, Section 9-626 rejects the "absolute bar" test that some courts have imposed; that approach bars a noncomplying secured party from recovering any deficiency, regardless of the loss (if any) the debtor suffered as a consequence of the noncompliance.

"Low-price" dispositions: Calculation of deficiency and surplus. Section 9-615(f) addresses the problem of procedurally regular dispositions that fetch a low price. Subsection (f) provides a special method for calculating a deficiency if the proceeds of a disposition of collateral to a secured party, a person related to the secured party, or a secondary obligor are "significantly below the range of proceeds that a complying disposition to a person other than the secured party, a person related to the secured party, or a secondary obligor would have brought." ("Person related to" is defined in Section 9-102.) In these situations there is reason to suspect that there may be inadequate incentives to obtain a better price. Consequently, instead of calculating a deficiency (or surplus) based on the actual net proceeds, the deficiency (or surplus) would be calculated based on the proceeds that would have been received in a disposition to person other than the secured party, a person related to the secured party, or a secondary obligor.

j. **Consumer Goods, Consumer-Goods Transactions, and Consumer Transactions.** This Article (including the accompanying conforming revisions (see Appendix I)) includes several special rules for "consumer goods," "consumer transactions," and "consumer-goods transactions." Each term is defined in Section 9-102.

(i) Revised Sections 2-502 and 2-716 provide a buyer of consumer goods with enhanced rights to possession of the goods, thereby accelerating the opportunity to achieve "buyer in ordinary course of business" status under Section 1-201.

(ii) Section 9-103(e) (allocation of payments for determining extent of purchase-money status), (f) (purchase-money status not affected by cross-collateralization, refinancing, restructuring, or the like), and (g) (secured party has burden of establishing extent of purchase-money status) do not apply to consumer-goods transactions. Sections 9-103 also provides that the limitation of those provisions to transactions other than consumer-goods transactions leaves to the courts the proper rules for consumer-goods transactions and prohibits the courts from drawing inferences from that limitation.

(iii) Section 9-108 provides that in a consumer transaction a description of consumer goods, a security entitlement, securities account, or commodity account "only by [UCC-defined] type of collateral" is not a sufficient collateral description in a security agreement.

(iv) Sections 9-403 and 9-404 make effective the Federal Trade Commission's anti-holder-in-due-course rule (when applicable), 16 C.F.R. Part 433, even in the absence of the required legend.

(v) The 10-day safe-harbor for notification of a disposition provided by Section 9-612 does not apply in a consumer transaction.

(vi) Section 9-613 (contents and form of notice of disposition) does not apply to a consumer-goods transaction.

(vii) Section 9-614 contains special requirements for the contents of a notification of disposition and a safe-harbor, "plain English" form of notification, for consumer-goods transactions.

(viii) Section 9-616 requires a secured party in a consumer-goods transaction to provide a debtor with a notification of how it calculated a deficiency at the time it first undertakes to collect a deficiency.

(ix) Section 9-620 prohibits partial strict foreclosure with respect to consumer goods collateral and, unless the debtor agrees to waive the requirement in an authenticated record after default, in certain cases requires the secured party to dispose of consumer goods collateral which has been repossessed.

(x) Section 9-626 ("rebuttable presumption" rule) does not apply to a consumer transaction. Section 9-626 also provides that its limitation to transactions other than consumer transactions leaves to the courts the proper rules for consumer transactions and prohibits the courts from drawing inferences from that limitation.

k. **Good Faith.** Section 9-102 contains a new definition of "good faith" that includes not only "honesty in fact" but also "the observance of reasonable commercial standards of fair dealing." The definition is similar to the ones adopted in connection with other, recently completed revisions of the UCC.

l. **Transition Provisions.** Part 7 (Sections 9-701 through 9-707) contains transition provisions. Transition from former Article 9 to this Article will be particularly challenging in view of its expanded scope, its modification of choice-of-law rules for perfection and priority, and its expansion of the methods of perfection.

m. **Conforming and Related Amendments to Other UCC Articles.** Appendix I contains several proposed revisions to the provisions and Comments of other UCC articles. For the most part the revisions are explained in the Comments to the proposed revisions. Cross-references in other UCC articles to sections of Article 9 also have been revised.

Article 1. Revised Section 1-201 contains revisions to the definitions of "buyer in ordinary course of business," "purchaser," and "security interest."

Articles 2 and 2A. Sections 2-210, 2-326, 2-502, 2-716, 2A-303, and 2A-307 have been revised to address the intersection between Articles 2 and 2A and Article 9.

Article 5. New Section 5-118 is patterned on Section 4-210. It provides for a security interest in documents presented under a letter of credit in favor of the issuer and a nominated person on the letter of credit.

Article 8. Revisions to Section 8-106, which deals with "control" of securities and security entitlements, conform it to Section 8-302, which deals with "delivery." Revisions to Section 8-110, which deals with a "securities intermediary's jurisdiction," conform it to the revised treatment of a "commodity intermediary's jurisdiction" in Section 9-305. Sections 8-301 and 8-302 have been revised for clarification. Section 8-510 has been revised to conform it to the revised priority rules of Section 9-328. Several Comments in Article 8 also have been revised.

§ 9-102. DEFINITIONS AND INDEX OF DEFINITIONS.

(a) **[Article 9 definitions.]** In this article:

(1) "Accession" means goods that are physically united with other goods in such a manner that the identity of the original goods is not lost.

ANALYSIS

This definition of accessions extends beyond common law accessions which were required to be an integral part of the principal asset to which they were attached to also embrace accessories which are simply united to the larger goods. Old § 9-314 was similarly designed, but the case law as to what is and is not an accession under that section is not consistent. *See Secured Transactions*, Chapter 17 particularly §§ 17.01[3] and 17.02. Under Revised Article 9 the functional importance of the accessions category is reduced. New § 9-335 makes normal priority principles applicable to accessions except that an accessions interest is subordinate to an interest in the whole perfected by compliance with a certificate of title statute.

(2) "Account", except as used in "account for", means a right to payment of a monetary obligation, whether or not earned by performance, (i) for property that has been or is to be sold, leased, licensed, assigned, or otherwise disposed of, (ii) for services rendered or to be rendered, (iii) for a policy of insurance issued or to be issued, (iv) for a secondary obligation incurred or to be incurred, (v) for energy provided or to be provided, (vi) for the use or hire of a vessel under a charter or other contract, (vii) arising out of the use of a credit or charge card or information contained on or for use with the card, or (viii) as winnings in a lottery or other game of chance operated or sponsored by a State, governmental unit of a State, or person licensed or authorized to operate the game by a State or governmental unit of a State. The term includes health-care-insurance receivables. The term does not include (i) rights to payment evidenced by chattel paper or an instrument, (ii) commercial tort claims, (iii) deposit accounts, (iv) investment property, (v) letter-of-credit rights or letters of credit, or (vi) rights to payment for money or funds advanced or sold, other than rights arising out of the use of a credit or charge card or information contained on or for use with the card.

ANALYSIS

This definition greatly expands the "accounts" category. Under old § 9-106 "accounts" were limited to the right to payment for goods sold or leased or for services rendered. This expansion of accounts very much reduces the range of assets which will qualify as general intangibles or fall into the new sub-category of payment intangibles. A right to payment under a real estate sales contract (which is not an instrument) would now qualify as an account as would a right to payment under a license allowing a book to be published. *See Secured Transactions* § 1A.03[3].

(3) "Account debtor" means a person obligated on an account, chattel paper, or general intangible. The term does not include persons obligated to pay a negotiable instrument, even if the instrument constitutes part of chattel paper.

ANALYSIS

An account debtor is not limited to someone that owes payment of a monetary obligation. A licensor of software may qualify because the license itself, as opposed to the right to payment under it, is a general intangible. However, an obligor on a non-negotiable instrument cannot be an "account debtor" and the rules of the Part 4 of the new article which apply solely to account debtors do not apply to such an obligor. *See Secured Transactions* § 1A.03[3].

(4) "Accounting", except as used in "accounting for", means a record:

(A) authenticated by a secured party;

(B) indicating the aggregate unpaid secured obligations as of a date not more than 35 days earlier or 35 days later than the date of the record; and

(C) identifying the components of the obligations in reasonable detail.

(5) "Agricultural lien" means an interest, other than a security interest, in farm products:

(A)   which secures payment or performance of an obligation for:

(i)   goods or services furnished in connection with a debtor's farming operation; or

(ii)   rent on real property leased by a debtor in connection with its farming operation;

(B)   which is created by statute in favor of a person that:

(i)   in the ordinary course of its business furnished goods or services to a debtor in connection with a debtor's farming operation; or

(ii)   leased real property to a debtor in connection with the debtor's farming operation; and

(C)   whose effectiveness does not depend on the person's possession of the personal property.

(6)   "As-extracted collateral" means:

(A)   oil, gas, or other minerals that are subject to a security interest that:

(i)   is created by a debtor having an interest in the minerals before extraction; and

(ii)   attaches to the minerals as extracted; or

(B)   accounts arising out of the sale at the wellhead or minehead of oil, gas, or other minerals in which the debtor had an interest before extraction.

(7)   "Authenticate" means:

(A)   to sign; or

(B)   to execute or otherwise adopt a symbol, or encrypt or similarly process a record in whole or in part, with the present intent of the authenticating person to identify the person and adopt or accept a record.

ANALYSIS

The definition of "authenticate" is critical because it defines how far creditors will be able to go with electronic security agreements. Under new § 9-203 it is no longer necessary that a debtor sign a written security agreement, only that a record in written or electronic form be authenticated by the debtor. This definition should allow telemarketers and those selling by computer to devise rituals which will allow for electronic authentication. For example, if a debtor is asked to speak her name at the end of a recorded phone conversation to identify herself and to accept the recorded conversation as a record then the recording would apparently serve as a security agreement if in the conversation the debtor agrees to the security interest and the collateral is described. Note that Official Comment 9a to this new § 9-102 indicates that information stored other than in the human memory can be a record. The courts will ultimately determine what is required for electronic authentication.

(8)   "Bank" means an organization that is engaged in the business of banking. The term includes savings banks, savings and loan associations, credit unions, and trust companies.

(9)   "Cash proceeds" means proceeds that are money, checks, deposit accounts, or the like.

(10)   "Certificate of title" means a certificate of title with respect to which a statute provides for the security interest in question to be indicated on the certificate as a condition or result of the security interest's obtaining priority over the rights of a lien creditor with respect to the collateral.

(11)   "Chattel paper" means a record or records that evidence both a monetary obligation and a security interest in specific goods, a security interest in specific goods and software used in the goods, or a lease of specific goods. The term does not include charters or other contracts involving the use or hire of a vessel. If a transaction is evidenced both by a security agreement or lease and by an instrument or series of instruments, the group of records taken together constitutes chattel paper.

(12)   "Collateral" means the property subject to a security interest or agricultural lien. The term includes:

(A)   proceeds to which a security interest attaches;

(B)   accounts, chattel paper, payment intangibles, and promissory notes that have been sold; and

(C)   goods that are the subject of a consignment.

(13)   "Commercial tort claim" means a claim arising in tort with respect to which:

(A)   the claimant is an organization; or

(B)   the claimant is an individual and the claim:

    (i)   arose in the course of the claimant's business or profession; and

    (ii)   does not include damages arising out of personal injury to or the death of an individual.

(14)   "Commodity account" means an account maintained by a commodity intermediary in which a commodity contract is carried for a commodity customer.

(15)   "Commodity contract" means a commodity futures contract, an option on a commodity futures contract, a commodity option, or another contract if the contract or option is:

(A)   traded on or subject to the rules of a board of trade that has been designated as a contract market for such a contract pursuant to federal commodities laws; or

(B)   traded on a foreign commodity board of trade, exchange, or market, and is carried on the books of a commodity intermediary for a commodity customer.

(16)   "Commodity customer" means a person for which a commodity intermediary carries a commodity contract on its books.

(17)   "Commodity intermediary" means a person that:

(A)   is registered as a futures commission merchant under federal commodities law; or

(B)   in the ordinary course of its business provides clearance or settlement services for a board of trade that has been designated as a contract market pursuant to federal commodities law.

(18)   "Communicate" means:

(A)   to send a written or other tangible record;

(B)   to transmit a record by any means agreed upon by the persons sending and receiving the record; or

(C)   in the case of transmission of a record to or by a filing office, to transmit a record by any means prescribed by filing-office rule.

(19)   "Consignee" means a merchant to which goods are delivered in a consignment.

(20)   "Consignment" means a transaction, regardless of its form, in which a person delivers goods to a merchant for the purpose of sale and:

(A)   the merchant:

(i)   deals in goods of that kind under a name other than the name of the person making delivery;

(ii)   is not an auctioneer; and

(iii)   is not generally known by its creditors to be substantially engaged in selling the goods of others;

(B)   with respect to each delivery, the aggregate value of the goods is $1,000 or more at the time of delivery;

(C)   the goods are not consumer goods immediately before delivery; and

(D)   the transaction does not create a security interest that secures an obligation.

ANALYSIS

Bailments for purposes other than the sale of the goods (*e.g.* for processing, cleaning, storage) do not qualify as consignments under this definition. Therefore, the case law under old Article 9 holding that bailees for such non-sale purposes lack sufficient "rights" in the bailed goods to create security interests remains viable. *See Secured Transactions* § 2B.06.

(21)   "Consignor" means a person that delivers goods to a consignee in a consignment.

(22)   "Consumer debtor" means a debtor in a consumer transaction.

(23)   "Consumer goods" means goods that are used or bought for use primarily for personal, family, or household purposes.

(24)   "Consumer-goods transaction" means a consumer transaction in which:

(A)   an individual incurs an obligation primarily for personal, family, or household purposes; and

(B)   a security interest in consumer goods secures the obligation.

(25)   "Consumer obligor" means an obligor who is an individual and who incurred the obligation as part of a transaction entered into primarily for personal, family, or household purposes.

(26)   "Consumer transaction" means a transaction in which (i) an individual incurs an obligation primarily for personal, family, or

household purposes, (ii) a security interest secures the obligation, and (iii) the collateral is held or acquired primarily for personal, family, or household purposes. The term includes consumer-goods transactions.

ANALYSIS

Very few provisions of the old Article 9 provide distinctive treatment for consumers. They refer to transactions involving consumer goods. *See* old §§ 9-204(2); 9-505(2); 9-507(1). The Revised Article 9 introduces the new defined terms "consumer transactions," "consumer-goods transaction" and "consumer obligor" to facilitate different treatments of certain consumers and commercial actors. Note that "consumer transaction" requires both a consumer purpose and consumer collateral. "Consumer-goods transaction" is narrower requiring a consumer purpose and consumer goods.

> *Example A*: Joe Smith secures his borrowing from First Bank with a car used primarily for personal and family purposes and a deposit account used primarily to pay consumer obligations. Joe uses the money to finance a vacation. The entire transaction is a consumer transaction. But the transaction is a consumer-goods transaction only as to the car collateral. After default, First Bank must give the special notification of disposition of the car required by new § 9-614 in consumer goods transactions.

> *Example B*: Same as above except Joe uses the loan proceeds to acquire equipment for his laundry business.

> The transaction is neither a consumer transaction nor a consumer goods transaction. After default, First Bank may give the less-detailed notification of deposition required by § 9-613.

With "consumer obligor" the key is the motive for the incurrence of the obligation, not the use of the collateral.

> *Example C*: Joe Smith grants a security interest in his equipment to secure advances incurred to finance a vacation. Joe Smith is a consumer obligor.

(27) "Continuation statement" means an amendment of a financing statement which:

(A)   identifies, by its file number, the initial financing statement to which it relates; and

(B)   indicates that it is a continuation statement for, or that it is filed to continue the effectiveness of, the identified financing statement.

(28)   "Debtor" means:

(A)   a person having an interest, other than a security interest or other lien, in the collateral, whether or not the person is an obligor;

(B)   a seller of accounts, chattel paper, payment intangibles, or promissory notes; or

(C)   a consignee.

ANALYSIS

At first glance the old Article 9 seemed to be a bi-polar drama focusing on a debtor and secured party. Of course, we knew on a moment's reflection that there were other actors too, such as lien creditors, purchasers and guarantors. Moreover, the definition of debtor in old § 9-105(1)(d) wobbled, at times pointing to the person owing performance, at times to the owner of the collateral and even sometimes referring simultaneously to both of these persons.

The basic cast of characters is different under the new Article 9. One must learn to distinguish between a debtor and an obligor and between a primary obligor and a secondary one. The easiest way to grasp the new cast is to oversimplify the technical statutory definitions, concentrating first on the core concepts and then providing illustrations. Following this advice, a debtor is the person who has a property interest (other than a security interest or lien) in the collateral while the obligor is the person who owes payment of the secured obligation. *See* new § 9-102(a)(28). An obligor is the person who owes payment or performance of the obligation. *See* new § 9-102(a)(59). An obligor whose obligation is that of a surety or who has rights of recourse against the debtor, another obligor or the property of either is a secondary obligor. *See* new § 9-102(a)(71). All other obligors are primary obligors. (The text of the new Article 9 does not itself use or define the term "primary obligor" but clearly this is a contrast category involved in the statutory scheme). In many, but not all, transactions, the same person will be both debtor and obligor.

Example A: If Mary Smith makes a secured purchase of a car from Mountain Motors, then Mary Smith is simultaneously a debtor (because she owns the car) and an obligor (because she owes the price).

Example B: If Mary Smith borrows money from First Bank without granting a security interest in any of her assets and Tom Jones, without himself incurring a monetary obligation, grants a security interest in his diamond ring to secure the loan made to Mary, then Mary Smith is simply an obligor and Tom Jones is simply a debtor.

Example C: The transaction described in Example B might more typically be structured by having Tom Jones guaranty Mary Jones' loan obligation and then secure his loan obligation by granting a security interest in the ring. In this event, Mary Smith is still a pure obligor but Tom Jones is now both an obligor and a debtor. Because Jones' obligation arises by way of a suretyship commitment, Jones is a secondary obligor. *See* new § 9-102(a)(71). Mary Smith's obligation is that of a primary obligor, not that of a surety or of someone who has a right of recourse.

This new definitional set clears the way for the revisers to drop the old § 9-112 and to specify in Part 6 of the new Article that the secured party's duties in disposing of collateral after default (*e.g.* the duty to give notification of disposition) run to the debtor and any secondary obligors, but not to pure primary obligors. *See Secured Transactions* § 8.06[7][b]. The revisers also hoped to use this definitional scheme to specify that a secondary obligor could in the initial guaranty agreement waive Article 9 defenses relating to disposition of collateral. However, protests forced the Drafting Committee to back down on this latter initiative. Pre-default waivers of Article 9 default protections are not permitted by either debtors or secondary obligors. *See* new § 9-602 and *Secured Transactions* § 1A.08[1]. Finally, the precise specification of who is a debtor under this new definition defines who must authenticate the security agreement under new § 9-203(b) and whose name must appear as debtor in the financing statement as required by new § 9-502(a).

Example D: Assume that Tom Jones orally authorizes Mary Smith, his wife, to grant a security interest in his diamond ring to First Bank to secure Smith's debt to the bank. In this context under the present Article 9 the decisions are in conflict as to whether Smith's signature on the security agreement qualifies as the debtor's signature. *See Secured Transactions*

§ 2A.03[4]. And there are cases holding that the names of both Mary Smith and Tom Jones must appear as debtor on the financing statement. *See Secured Transactions* § 6C.05[4]. The revision appears to specify that Tom Jones' authentication on the security agreement and his name on the financing statement are alone required and effective.

(29)   "Deposit account" means a demand, time, savings, passbook, or similar account maintained with a bank. The term does not include investment property or accounts evidenced by an instrument.

(30)   "Document" means a document of title or a receipt of the type described in Section 7-201(2).

(31)   "Electronic chattel paper" means chattel paper evidenced by a record or records consisting of information stored in an electronic medium.

(32)   "Encumbrance" means a right, other than an ownership interest, in real property. The term includes mortgages and other liens on real property.

(33)   "Equipment" means goods other than inventory, farm products, or consumer goods.

(34)   "Farm products" means goods, other than standing timber, with respect to which the debtor is engaged in a farming operation and which are:

(A)   crops grown, growing, or to be grown, including:

(i)   crops produced on trees, vines, and bushes; and

(ii)   aquatic goods produced in aquacultural operations;

(B)   livestock, born or unborn, including aquatic goods produced in aquacultural operations;

(C)   supplies used or produced in a farming operation; or

(D)   products of crops or livestock in their unmanufactured states.

(35)   "Farming operation" means raising, cultivating, propagating, fattening, grazing, or any other farming, livestock, or aquacultural operation.

(36)   "File number" means the number assigned to an initial financing statement pursuant to Section 9-519(a).

(37)   "Filing office" means an office designated in Section 9-501 as the place to file a financing statement.

(38)   "Filing-office rule" means a rule adopted pursuant to Section 9-526.

(39)   "Financing statement" means a record or records composed of an initial financing statement and any filed record relating to the initial financing statement.

(40)   "Fixture filing" means the filing of a financing statement covering goods that are or are to become fixtures and satisfying Section 9-502(a) and (b). The term includes the filing of a financing statement covering goods of a transmitting utility which are or are to become fixtures.

(41)   "Fixtures" means goods that have become so related to particular real property that an interest in them arises under real property law.

(42)   "General intangible" means any personal property, including things in action, other than accounts, chattel paper, commercial tort claims, deposit accounts, documents, goods, instruments, investment property, letter-of-credit rights, letters of credit, money, and oil, gas, or other minerals before extraction. The term includes payment intangibles and software.

ANALYSIS

The expansion of the account category correspondingly reduces the range of assets which qualify as general intangibles. *See* new § 9-102(a)(2). While the licensor's right to payment under a software license is an account, the license itself as an interest of the debtor is a general intangible. *See* new § 9-408.

(43)   "Good faith" means honesty in fact and the observance of reasonable commercial standards of fair dealing.

(44)   "Goods" means all things that are movable when a security interest attaches. The term includes (i) fixtures, (ii) standing timber that is to be cut and removed under a conveyance or contract for sale, (iii) the unborn young of animals, (iv) crops grown, growing, or to be grown, even if the crops are produced on trees, vines, or bushes, and (v) manufactured homes. The term also includes a computer program embedded in goods and any supporting information provided in connection with a transaction relating to the

program if (i) the program is associated with the goods in such a manner that it customarily is considered part of the goods, or (ii) by becoming the owner of the goods, a person acquires a right to use the program in connection with the goods. The term does not include a computer program embedded in goods that consist solely of the medium in which the program is embedded. The term also does not include accounts, chattel paper, commercial tort claims, deposit accounts, documents, general intangibles, instruments, investment property, letter-of-credit rights, letters of credit, money, or oil, gas, or other minerals before extraction.

(45)   "Governmental unit" means a subdivision, agency, department, county, parish, municipality, or other unit of the government of the United States, a State, or a foreign country. The term includes an organization having a separate corporate existence if the organization is eligible to issue debt on which interest is exempt from income taxation under the laws of the United States.

(46)   "Health-care-insurance receivable" means an interest in or claim under a policy of insurance which is a right to payment of a monetary obligation for health-care goods or services provided.

(47)   "Instrument" means a negotiable instrument or any other writing that evidences a right to the payment of a monetary obligation, is not itself a security agreement or lease, and is of a type that in ordinary course of business is transferred by delivery with any necessary indorsement or assignment. The term does not include (i) investment property, (ii) letters of credit, or (iii) writings that evidence a right to payment arising out of the use of a credit or charge card or information contained on or for use with the card.

ANALYSIS

Under U.C.C. § 3-103 a negotiable instrument must be in writing. Thus, this definition of the term "instrument" is the only category under the new Article 9 which requires a writing as opposed to a media-neutral record. A right to payment stored or expressed in electronic form is not an Article 9 instrument, but will be either an account, chattel paper, or general intangible.

(48)   "Inventory" means goods, other than farm products, which:

(A)   are leased by a person as lessor;

(B)   are held by a person for sale or lease or to be furnished under a contract of service;

(C)   are furnished by a person under a contract of service; or

(D)   consist of raw materials, work in process, or materials used or consumed in a business.

(49)   "Investment property" means a security, whether certificated or uncertificated, security entitlement, securities account, commodity contract, or commodity account.

(50)   "Jurisdiction of organization", with respect to a registered organization, means the jurisdiction under whose law the organization is organized.

ANALYSIS

"Jurisdiction" is a broader term than "state." Under new § 9-102(a)(76) "state" is limited to a location that flies the U.S. flag. But jurisdiction includes a foreign nation. International waters and space are neither a state nor a jurisdiction.

(51)   "Letter-of-credit right" means a right to payment or performance under a letter of credit, whether or not the beneficiary has demanded or is at the time entitled to demand payment or performance. The term does not include the right of a beneficiary to demand payment or performance under a letter of credit.

(52)   "Lien creditor" means:

(A)   a creditor that has acquired a lien on the property involved by attachment, levy, or the like;

(B)   an assignee for benefit of creditors from the time of assignment;

(C)   a trustee in bankruptcy from the date of the filing of the petition; or

(D)   a receiver in equity from the time of appointment.

(53)   "Manufactured home" means a structure, transportable in one or more sections, which, in the traveling mode, is eight body feet or more in width or 40 body feet or more in length, or, when

erected on site, is 320 or more square feet, and which is built on a permanent chassis and designed to be used as a dwelling with or without a permanent foundation when connected to the required utilities, and includes the plumbing, heating, air-conditioning, and electrical systems contained therein. The term includes any structure that meets all of the requirements of this paragraph except the size requirements and with respect to which the manufacturer voluntarily files a certification required by the United States Secretary of Housing and Urban Development and complies with the standards established under Title 42 of the United States Code.

(54)   "Manufactured-home transaction" means a secured transaction:

(A)   that creates a purchase-money security interest in a manufactured home, other than a manufactured home held as inventory; or

(B)   in which a manufactured home, other than a manufactured home held as inventory, is the primary collateral.

(55)   "Mortgage" means a consensual interest in real property, including fixtures, which secures payment or performance of an obligation.

(56)   "New debtor" means a person that becomes bound as debtor under Section 9-203(d) by a security agreement previously entered into by another person.

(57)   "New value" means (i) money, (ii) money's worth in property, services, or new credit, or (iii) release by a transferee of an interest in property previously transferred to the transferee. The term does not include an obligation substituted for another obligation.

ANALYSIS

A promise of future financing will not ordinarily qualify as money's worth in new credit because the promise will ordinarily be revocable if the promisor learns of rival interests in the collateral. *See* the discussion of new value under the old § 9-309 in *Secured Transactions* § 28.06[5]. However, an irrevocable letter of credit commitment could be considered to be new value.

(58)   "Noncash proceeds" means proceeds other than cash proceeds.

(59)   "Obligor" means a person that, with respect to an obligation secured by a security interest in or an agricultural lien on the collateral, (i) owes payment or other performance of the obligation, (ii) has provided property other than the collateral to secure payment or other performance of the obligation, or (iii) is otherwise accountable in whole or in part for payment or other performance of the obligation. The term does not include issuers or nominated persons under a letter of credit.

(60)   "Original debtor" means a person that, as debtor, entered into a security agreement to which a new debtor has become bound under Section 9-203(d).

(61)   "Payment intangible" means a general intangible under which the account debtor's principal obligation is a monetary obligation.

(62)   "Person related to", with respect to an individual, means:

(A)   the spouse of the individual;

(B)   a brother, brother-in-law, sister, or sister-in-law of the individual;

(C)   an ancestor or lineal descendant of the individual or the individual's spouse; or

(D)   any other relative, by blood or marriage, of the individual or the individual's spouse who shares the same home with the individual.

(63)   "Person related to", with respect to an organization, means:

(A)   a person directly or indirectly controlling, controlled by, or under common control with the organization;

(B)   an officer or director of, or a person performing similar functions with respect to, the organization;

(C)   an officer or director of, or a person performing similar functions with respect to, a person described in subparagraph (A);

(D)   the spouse of an individual described in subparagraph (A), (B), or (C); or

(E)   an individual who is related by blood or marriage to an individual described in subparagraph (A), (B), (C), or (D) and shares the same home with the individual.

(64)   "Proceeds" means the following property:

(A)   whatever is acquired upon the sale, lease, license, exchange, or other disposition of collateral;

(B)   whatever is collected on, or distributed on account of, collateral;

(C)   rights arising out of collateral;

(D)   to the extent of the value of collateral, claims arising out of the loss, nonconformity, or interference with the use of, defects or infringement of rights in, or damage to, the collateral; or

(E)   to the extent of the value of collateral and to the extent payable to the debtor or the secured party, insurance payable by reason of the loss or nonconformity of, defects or infringement of rights in, or damage to, the collateral.

ANALYSIS

Under both the old and Revised Article 9, a secured party automatically gets a security interest in the proceeds of the collateral described in its security agreement. The new Article 9 gives the secured party a larger security interest by expanding the range of assets that will qualify as proceeds. Under old § 9-306(1) proceeds could only be generated by a sale, exchange, collection or other disposition of collateral. Under this new definition a lease or license of collateral will produce proceeds. Moreover, this new definition disconnects proceeds from disposition by including what is collected on or distributed on account of collateral as well as rights arising out of collateral. *See Secured Transactions* § 1A.04[1] and 24.03.

(65)   "Promissory note" means an instrument that evidences a promise to pay a monetary obligation, does not evidence an order to pay, and does not contain an acknowledgment by a bank that the bank has received for deposit a sum of money or funds.

(66)   "Proposal" means a record authenticated by a secured party which includes the terms on which the secured party is willing to accept collateral in full or partial satisfaction of the obligation it secures pursuant to Sections 9-620, 9-621, and 9-622.

(67)   "Public-finance transaction" means a secured transaction in connection with which:

(A)   debt securities are issued;

(B)   all or a portion of the securities issued have an initial stated maturity of at least 20 years; and

(C)   the debtor, obligor, secured party, account debtor or other person obligated on collateral, assignor or assignee of a secured obligation, or assignor or assignee of a security interest is a State or a governmental unit of a State.

(68)   "Pursuant to commitment", with respect to an advance made or other value given by a secured party, means pursuant to the secured party's obligation, whether or not a subsequent event of default or other event not within the secured party's control has relieved or may relieve the secured party from its obligation.

(69)   "Record", except as used in "for record", "of record", "record or legal title", and "record owner", means information that is inscribed on a tangible medium or which is stored in an electronic or other medium and is retrievable in perceivable form.

ANALYSIS

"Record" is the key term used to implement the revisers' policy of media neutrality. Under the Revised Article 9 agreements, notifications and communications may generally be in electronic or written form. The new definition of "communicate" and "send" allow the electronic option. *See* new § 9-102(a)(18) and (74); *see also Secured Transactions* § 1A.06.

(70)   "Registered organization" means an organization organized solely under the law of a single State or the United States and as to which the State or the United States must maintain a public record showing the organization to have been organized.

ANALYSIS

Determining whether a debtor is a registered organization is critical to determining where to file and search under the Revised Article 9. If the debtor is a registered organization, the state of organization controls; for other debtors, the place of business or residence controls. Domestic corporations, limited liability companies and limited partnerships are registered organizations, proprietorships and foreign corporations are not. Official Comment 11 to this new § 9-102 indicates that revisers intend to exclude general partnerships from the category of registered organizations even if they file a statement of partnership authority under Section 303 of the Uniform Partnership Act (1994).

(71) "Secondary obligor" means an obligor to the extent that:

(A) the obligor's obligation is secondary; or

(B) the obligor has a right of recourse with respect to an obligation secured by collateral against the debtor, another obligor, or property of either.

(72) "Secured party" means:

(A) a person in whose favor a security interest is created or provided for under a security agreement, whether or not any obligation to be secured is outstanding;

(B) a person that holds an agricultural lien;

(C) a consignor;

(D) a person to which accounts, chattel paper, payment intangibles, or promissory notes have been sold;

(E) a trustee, indenture trustee, agent, collateral agent, or other representative in whose favor a security interest or agricultural lien is created or provided for; or

(F) a person that holds a security interest arising under Section 2-401, 2-505, 2-711(3), 2A-508(5), 4-210, or 5-118.

(73) "Security agreement" means an agreement that creates or provides for a security interest.

(74) "Send", in connection with a record or notification, means:

(A) to deposit in the mail, deliver for transmission, or transmit by any other usual means of communication, with postage or cost of transmission provided for, addressed to any address reasonable under the circumstances; or

(B) to cause the record or notification to be received within the time that it would have been received if properly sent under subparagraph (A).

(75) "Software" means a computer program and any supporting information provided in connection with a transaction relating to the program. The term does not include a computer program that is included in the definition of goods.

(76) "State" means a State of the United States, the District of Columbia, Puerto Rico, the United States Virgin Islands, or any territory or insular possession subject to the jurisdiction of the United States.

(77) "Supporting obligation" means a letter-of-credit right or secondary obligation that supports the payment or performance of an account, chattel paper, a document, a general intangible, an instrument, or investment property.

(78) "Tangible chattel paper" means chattel paper evidenced by a record or records consisting of information that is inscribed on a tangible medium.

(79) "Termination statement" means an amendment of a financing statement which:

(A) identifies, by its file number, the initial financing statement to which it relates; and

(B) indicates either that it is a termination statement or that the identified financing statement is no longer effective.

(80) "Transmitting utility" means a person primarily engaged in the business of:

(A) operating a railroad, subway, street railway, or trolley bus;

(B) transmitting communications electrically, electromagnetically, or by light;

(C) transmitting goods by pipeline or sewer; or

(D) transmitting or producing and transmitting electricity, steam, gas, or water.

(b) [Definitions in other articles.] The following definitions in other articles apply to this article:

"Applicant" . . . . Section 5-102.
"Beneficiary" . . . . Section 5-102.
"Broker" . . . . Section 8-102.
"Certificated security" . . . . Section 8-102.
"Check" . . . . Section 3-104.
"Clearing corporation" . . . . Section 8-102.
"Contract for sale" . . . . Section 2-106.
"Customer" . . . . Section 4-104.
"Entitlement holder" . . . . Section 8-102.
"Financial asset" . . . . Section 8-102.
"Holder in due course" . . . . Section 3-302.
"Issuer" (with respect to a letter of credit or   Section 5-102.
letter-of-credit right) . . . .
"Issuer" (with respect to a security) . . . . Section 8-201.

(c) [Article 1 definitions and principles.] Article 1 contains general definitions and principles of construction and interpretation applicable throughout this article.

Official Comment

1. **Source.** All terms that are defined in Article 9 and used in more than one section are consolidated in this section. Note that the definition of "security interest" is found in Section 1-201, not in this Article, and has been revised. See Appendix I. Many of the definitions in this section are new; many others derive from those in former Section 9-105. The following Comments also indicate other sections of former Article 9 that defined (or explained) terms.

2. **Parties to Secured Transactions.**

a. **"Debtor"; "Obligor"; "Secondary Obligor."** Determining whether a person was a "debtor" under former Section 9-105(1)(d) required a close examination of the context in which the term was used. To reduce the need for this examination, this Article redefines "debtor" and adds new defined terms, "secondary obligor" and "obligor." In the context of Part 6 (default and enforcement), these definitions distinguish among three classes of persons: (i) those persons who may have a stake in the proper enforcement of a security interest by virtue of their non-lien property interest (typically, an ownership interest) in the collateral, (ii) those persons who may have a stake in the proper enforcement of the security interest because of their obligation to pay the secured debt, and (iii) those persons who have an obligation to pay the secured debt but have no stake in the proper enforcement of the security interest. Persons in the first class are debtors. Persons in the second class are secondary obligors if any portion of the obligation is secondary or if the obligor has a right of recourse against the debtor or another obligor with respect to an obligation secured by collateral. One must consult the law of suretyship to determine whether an obligation is secondary. The Restatement (3d), Suretyship and Guaranty § 1 (1996), contains a useful explanation of the concept. Obligors in the third class are neither debtors nor secondary obligors. With one exception (Section 9-616, as it relates to a consumer obligor), the rights and duties in provided by Part 6 affect non-debtor obligors only if they are "secondary obligors."

By including in the definition of "debtor" all persons with a property interest (other than a security interest in or other lien on collateral), the definition includes transferees of collateral, whether or not the secured party knows of the transfer or the transferee's identity. Exculpatory provisions in Part 6 protect the secured party in that circumstance. See Sections 9-605 and 9-628. The definition renders unnecessary former Section 9-112, which governed situations in which collateral was not owned by the debtor. The definition also includes a "consignee," as defined in this section, as well as a seller of accounts, chattel paper, payment intangibles, or promissory notes.

Secured parties and other lienholders are excluded from the definition of "debtor" because the interests of those parties normally derive from and encumber a debtor's interest. However, if in a *separate* secured transaction a secured party grants, *as debtor*, a security interest in its own interest (i.e., its security interest and any obligation that it secures), the secured party is a debtor *in that transaction.* This typically occurs when a secured party with a security interest in specific goods assigns chattel paper.

Consider the following examples:

Example 1: Behnfeldt borrows money and grants a security interest in her Miata to secure the debt. Behnfeldt is a debtor and an obligor.

Example 2: Behnfeldt borrows money and grants a security interest in her Miata to secure the debt. Bruno co-signs a negotiable note as maker. As before, Behnfeldt is the debtor and an obligor. As an accommodation party (see Section 3-419), Bruno is a secondary obligor. Bruno has this status even if the note states that her obligation is a primary obligation and that she waives all suretyship defenses.

Example 3: Behnfeldt borrows money on an unsecured basis. Bruno co-signs the note and grants a security interest in her Honda to secure her obligation. Inasmuch as Behnfeldt does not have a property interest in the Honda, Behnfeldt is not a debtor. Having granted the security interest, Bruno is the debtor. Because Behnfeldt is a principal obligor, she is not a secondary obligor. Whatever the outcome of enforcement of the security interest against the Honda or Bruno's secondary obligation, Bruno will look to Behnfeldt for her losses. The enforcement will not affect Behnfeldt's aggregate obligations.

When the principal obligor (borrower) and the secondary obligor (surety) each has granted a security interest in different collateral, the status of each is determined by the collateral involved.

Example 4: Behnfeldt borrows money and grants a security interest in her Miata to secure the debt. Bruno co-signs the note and grants a security interest in her Honda to secure her obligation. When the secured party enforces the security interest in Behnfeldt's Miata, Behnfeldt is the debtor, and Bruno is a secondary obligor. When the secured party enforces the security interest in the Honda, Bruno is the "debtor." As in Example 3, Behnfeldt is an obligor, but not a secondary obligor.

b. **"Secured Party."** The secured party is the person in whose favor the security interest has been created, as determined by reference to the security agreement. This definition controls, among other things, which person has the duties and potential liability that Part 6 imposes upon a secured party. The definition of "secured party" also includes a "consignee," a person to which accounts, chattel paper, payment intangibles, or promissory notes have been sold, and the holder of an agricultural lien.

The definition of "secured party" clarifies the status of various types of representatives. Consider, for example, a multi-bank facility under which Bank A, Bank B, and Bank C are lenders and Bank A serves as the collateral agent. If the security interest is granted to the banks, then they are the secured parties. If the security interest is granted to Bank A as collateral agent, then Bank A is the secured party.

c. **Other Parties.** A "consumer obligor" is defined as the obligor in a consumer transaction. Definitions of "new debtor" and "original debtor" are used in the special rules found in Sections 9-326 and 9-508.

3. **Definitions Relating to Creation of a Security Interest.**

a. **"Collateral."** As under former Section 9-105, "collateral" is the property subject to a security interest and includes accounts and chattel paper that have been sold. It has been expanded in this Article. The term now explicitly includes proceeds subject to a security interest. It also reflects the broadened scope of the Article. It includes property subject to an agricultural lien as well as payment intangibles and promissory notes that have been sold.

b. **"Security Agreement."** The definition of "security agreement" is substantially the same as under former Section 9-105-an agreement that creates or provides for a security interest. However, the term frequently was used colloquially in former Article 9 to refer to the document or writing that contained a debtor's security agreement. This Article eliminates that usage, reserving the term for the more precise meaning specified in the definition.

Whether an agreement creates a security interest depends not on whether the parties intend that the law *characterize* the transaction as a security interest but rather on whether the transaction falls within the definition of "security interest" in Section 1-201. Thus, an agreement that the parties characterize as a "lease" of goods may be a "security agreement," notwithstanding the parties' stated intention that the law treat the transaction as a lease and not as a secured transaction.

4. **Goods-Related Definitions.**

a. **"Goods"; "Consumer Goods"; "Equipment"; "Farm Products"; "Farming Operation"; "Inventory."** The definition of "goods" is substantially the same as the definition in former Section 9-105. This Article also retains the four mutually-exclusive "types" of collateral that consist of goods: "consumer goods," "equipment," "farm products," and "inventory." The revisions are primarily for clarification.

The classes of goods are mutually exclusive. For example, the same property cannot simultaneously be both equipment and inventory. In borderline cases-a physician's car or a farmer's truck that might be either consumer goods or equipment-the principal use to which the property is put is determinative. Goods can fall into different classes at different times. For example, a radio may be inventory in the hands of a dealer and consumer goods in the hands of a consumer. As under former Article 9, goods are "equipment" if they do not fall into another category.

The definition of "consumer goods" follows former Section 9-109. The classification turns on whether the debtor uses or bought the goods for use "primarily for personal, family, or household purposes."

Goods are inventory if they are leased by a lessor or held by a person for sale or lease. The revised definition of "inventory" makes clear that the term includes goods leased by the debtor to others as well as goods held for lease. (The same result should have obtained under the former definition.) Goods to be furnished or furnished under a service contract, raw materials, and work in process also are inventory. Implicit in the definition is the criterion that the sales or leases are or will be in the ordinary course of business. For example, machinery used in manufacturing is equipment, not inventory, even though it is the policy of the debtor to sell machinery when it becomes obsolete or worn. Inventory also includes goods that are consumed in a business (e.g., fuel used in operations). In general, goods used in a business are equipment if they are fixed assets or have, as identifiable units, a relatively long period of use, but are inventory, even though not held for sale or lease, if they are used up or consumed in a short period of time in producing a product or providing a service.

Goods are "farm products" if the debtor is engaged in farming operations with respect to the goods. Animals in a herd of livestock are covered whether the debtor acquires them by purchase or as a result of natural increase. Products of crops or livestock remain farm products as long as they have not been subjected to a manufacturing process. The terms "crops" and "livestock" are not defined. The new definition of "farming operations" is for clarification only.

Crops, livestock, and their products cease to be "farm products" when the debtor ceases to be engaged in farming operations with respect to them. If, for example, they come into the possession of a marketing agency for sale or distribution or of a manufacturer or processor as raw materials, they become inventory. Products of crops or livestock, even though they remain in the possession of a person engaged in farming operations, lose their status as farm products if they are subjected to a manufacturing process. What is and what is not a manufacturing operation is not specified in this Article. At one end of the spectrum, some processes are so closely connected with farming-such as pasteurizing milk or boiling sap to produce maple syrup or sugar-that they would not constitute manufacturing. On the other hand an extensive canning operation would be manufacturing. Once farm products have been subjected to a manufacturing operation, they normally become inventory.

The revised definition of "farm products" clarifies the distinction between crops and standing timber and makes clear that aquatic goods produced in aquacultural operations may be either crops or livestock. Although aquatic goods that are vegetable in nature often would be crops and those that are animal would be livestock, this Article leaves the courts free to classify the goods on a case-by-case basis. See Section 9-324, Comment 11.

b. **"Accession"; "Manufactured Home"; "Manufactured-Home Transaction."** Other specialized definitions of goods include "accession" (see the special priority and enforcement rules in Section 9-335), and "manufactured home" (see Section 9-515, permitting a financing statement in a "manufactured-home transaction" to be effective for 30 years). The definition of "manufactured home" borrows from the federal Manufactured Housing Act, 42 U.S.C. §§ 5401 *et seq.*, and is intended to have the same meaning.

c. **"As-Extracted Collateral."** Under this Article, oil, gas, and other minerals that have not been extracted from the ground are treated as real property, to which this Article does not apply. Upon extraction, minerals become personal property (goods) and eligible to be collateral under this Article. See the definition of "goods," which excludes "oil, gas, and other minerals before extraction." To take account of financing practices reflecting the shift from real to personal property, this Article contains special rules for perfecting security interests in minerals which attach upon extraction and in accounts resulting from the sale of minerals at the wellhead or minehead. See, e.g., Sections 9-301(6) (law governing perfection and priority); 9-501 (place of filing), 9-502 (contents of financing statement), 9-519 (indexing of records). The new term, "as-extracted collateral," refers to the minerals and related accounts to which the special rules apply. The term "at the wellhead" encompasses arrangements based on a sale of the produce at the moment that it issues from the ground and is measured, without technical distinctions as to whether title passes at the "Christmas tree" of a well, the far side of a gathering tank, or at some other point. The term "at . . . the minehead" is comparable.

The following examples explain the operation of these provisions.

Example 5: Debtor owns an interest in oil that is to be extracted. To secure Debtor's obligations to Lender, Debtor enters into an authenticated agreement granting Lender an interest in the oil. Although Lender may acquire an interest in the oil under real-property law, Lender does not acquire a security interest under this Article until the oil becomes personal property, i.e., until is extracted and becomes "goods" to which this Article applies. Because Debtor had an interest in the oil before extraction and Lender's security interest attached to the oil as extracted, the oil is "as-extracted collateral."

Example 6: Debtor owns an interest in oil that is to be extracted and contracts to sell the oil to Buyer at the wellhead. In an authenticated agreement, Debtor agrees to sell to Lender the right to payment from Buyer. This right to payment is an account that constitutes "as-extracted collateral." If Lender then resells the account to Financer, Financer acquires a security interest. However, inasmuch as the debtor-seller in that transaction, Lender, had no interest in the oil before extraction, Financer's collateral (the account it owns) is not "as-extracted collateral."

Example 7: Under the facts of Example 6, before extraction, Buyer grants a security interest in the oil to Bank. Although Bank's security interest attaches when the oil is extracted, Bank's security interest is not in "as-extracted collateral," inasmuch as its debtor, Buyer, did not have an interest in the oil before extraction.

5. Receivables-related Definitions.

a. **"Account"; "Health-Care-Insurance Receivable"; "As-Extracted Collateral."** The definition of "account" has been expanded and reformulated. It is no longer limited to rights to payment relating to goods or services. Many categories of rights to payment that were classified as general intangibles under former Article 9 are accounts under this Article. Thus, if they are sold, a financing statement must be filed to perfect the buyer's interest in them. Among the types of property that are expressly excluded from the definition is "a right to payment for money or funds advanced or sold." As defined in Section 1-201, "money" is limited essentially to currency. As used in the exclusion from the definition of "account," however, "funds" is a broader concept (although the term is not defined). For example, when a bank-lender credits a borrower's deposit account for the amount of a loan, the bank's advance of funds is not a transaction giving rise to an account.

The definition of "health-care-insurance receivable" is new. It is a subset of the definition of "account." However, the rules generally applicable to account debtors on accounts do not apply to insurers obligated on health-care-insurance receivables. See Sections 9-404(e), 9-405(d), 9-406(i).

Note that certain accounts also are "as-extracted collateral." See Comment 4.c., Examples 6 and 7.

b. **"Chattel Paper"; "Electronic Chattel Paper"; "Tangible Chattel Paper."** "Chattel paper" consists of a monetary obligation together with a security interest in or a lease of specific goods if the obligation and security interest or lease are evidenced by "a record or records." The definition has been expanded from that found in former Article 9 to include records that evidence a monetary obligation and a security interest in specific goods and software used in the goods. Charters of vessels are expressly excluded from the definition of chattel paper; they are accounts. The term "charter" as used in this section includes bareboat charters, time charters, successive voyage charters, contracts of affreightment, contracts of carriage, and all other arrangements for the use of vessels. Under former Section 9-105, only if the evidence of an obligation consisted of "a writing or writings" could an obligation qualify as chattel paper. In this Article, traditional, written chattel paper is included in the definition of "tangible chattel paper." "Electronic chattel paper" is chattel paper that is stored in an electronic medium instead of in tangible form. The concept of an electronic medium should be construed liberally to include electrical, digital, magnetic, optical, electromagnetic, or any other current or similar emerging technologies.

The definition of electronic chattel paper does not dictate that it be created in any particular fashion. For example, a record consisting of a tangible writing may be converted to electronic form (e.g., by creating electronic images of a signed writing). Or, records may be initially created and executed in electronic form (e.g., a lessee might authenticate an electronic record of a lease that is then stored in electronic form). In either case the resulting records are electronic chattel paper.

c. **"Instrument"; "Promissory Note."** The definition of "instrument" includes a negotiable instrument. As under former Section 9-105, it also includes any other right to payment of a monetary obligation that is evidenced by a writing of a type that in ordinary course of business is transferred by delivery (and, if necessary, an indorsement or assignment). Except in the case of chattel paper, the fact that an instrument is secured by a security interest or encumbrance on property does not change the character of the instrument as such or convert the combination of the instrument and collateral into a separate classification of personal property. The definition makes clear that rights to payment arising out of credit-card transactions are not instruments. The definition of "promissory note" is new, necessitated by the inclusion of sales of promissory notes within the scope of Article 9. It explicitly excludes obligations arising out of "orders" to pay (e.g., checks) as opposed to "promises" to pay. See Section 3-104.

d. **"General Intangible"; "Payment Intangible."** "General intangible" is the residual category of personal property, including things in action, that is not included in the other defined types of collateral. Examples are various categories of intellectual property and the right to payment of a loan of funds that is not evidenced by chattel paper or an instrument. The definition has been revised to exclude commercial tort claims, deposit accounts, and letter-of-credit rights. Each of the three is a separate type of collateral. One important consequence of this exclusion is that tortfeasors (commercial tort claims), banks (deposit accounts), and persons obligated on letters of credit (letter-of-credit rights) are not "account debtors" having the rights and obligations set forth in Sections 9-404, 9-405, and 9-406. In particular, tortfeasors, banks, and persons obligated on letters of credit are not obligated to pay an assignee (secured party) upon receipt of the notification described in Section 9-404(a). See Comment 5.h. Another important consequence relates to the adequacy of the description in the security agreement. See Section 9-108.

"Payment intangible" is a subset of the definition of "general intangible." The sale of a payment intangible is subject to this Article. See Section 9-109(a)(3). Virtually any intangible right could give rise to a right to payment of money once one hypothesizes, for example, that the account debtor is in breach of its obligation. The term "payment intangible," however, embraces only those general intangibles "under which the account debtor's *principal* obligation is a monetary obligation." (Emphasis added.)

In classifying intangible collateral, a court should begin by identifying the particular rights that have been assigned. The account debtor (promisor) under a particular contract may owe several types of monetary obligations as well as other, nonmonetary obligations. If the promisee's right to payment of money is assigned separately, the right is an account or payment intangible, depending on how the account debtor's obligation arose. When all the promisee's rights are assigned together, an account, a payment intangible, and a general intangible all may be involved, depending on the nature of the rights.

A right to the payment of money is frequently buttressed by ancillary covenants, such as covenants in a purchase agreement, note, or mortgage requiring insurance on the collateral or forbidding removal of the collateral, or covenants to preserve the creditworthiness of the promisor, such as covenants restricting dividends and the like. This Article does not treat these ancillary rights separately from the rights to payment to which they relate. For example, attachment and perfection of an assignment of a right to payment of a monetary obligation, whether it be an account or payment intangible, also carries these ancillary rights.

Every "payment intangible" is also a "general intangible." Likewise, "software" is a "general intangible" for purposes of this Article. See Comment 25. Accordingly, except as otherwise provided, statutory provisions applicable to general intangibles apply to payment intangibles and software.

e. **"Letter-of-Credit Right."** The term "letter-of-credit right" embraces the rights to payment and performance under a letter of credit (defined in

Section 5-102). However, it does not include a beneficiary's right to demand payment or performance. Transfer of those rights to a transferee beneficiary is governed by Article 5. See Sections 9-107, Comment 4, and 9-329, Comments 3 and 4.

f. **"Supporting Obligation."** This new term covers the most common types of credit enhancements-suretyship obligations (including guarantees) and letter-of-credit rights that support one of the types of collateral specified in the definition. As explained in Comment 2.a., suretyship law determines whether an obligation is "secondary" for purposes of this definition. Section 9-109 generally excludes from this Article transfers of interests in insurance policies. However, the regulation of a secondary obligation as an insurance product does not necessarily mean that it is a "policy of insurance" for purposes of the exclusion in Section 9-109. Thus, this Article may cover a secondary obligation (as a supporting obligations), even if the obligation is issued by a regulated insurance company and the obligation is subject to regulation as an "insurance" product.

This Article contains rules explicitly governing attachment, perfection, and priority of security interests in supporting obligations. See Sections 9-203, 9-308, 9-310, and 9-322. These provisions reflect the principle that a supporting obligation is an incident of the collateral it supports.

Collections of or other distributions under a supporting obligation are "proceeds" of the supported collateral as well as "proceeds" of the supporting obligation itself. See Section 9-102 (defining "proceeds") and Comment 13.b. As such, the collections and distributions are subject to the priority rules applicable to proceeds generally. See Section 9-322. However, under the special rule governing security interests in a letter-of-credit right, a secured party's failure to obtain control (Section 9-107) of a letter-of-credit right supporting collateral may leave its security interest exposed to a priming interest of a party who does take control. See Section 9-329 (security interest in a letter-of-credit right perfected by control has priority over a conflicting security interest).

g. **"Commercial Tort Claim."** This term is new. A tort claim may serve as original collateral under this Article only if it is a "commercial tort claim." See Section 9-109(d). Although security interests in commercial tort claims are within its scope, this Article does not override other applicable law restricting the assignability of a tort claim. See Section 9-401. A security interest in a tort claim also may exist under this Article if the claim is proceeds of other collateral.

h. **"Account Debtor."** An "account debtor" is a person obligated on an account, chattel paper, or general intangible. The account debtor's obligation often is a monetary obligation; however, this is not always the case. For example, if a franchisee uses its rights under a franchise agreement (a general intangible) as collateral, then the franchisor is an "account debtor." As a general matter, Article 3, and not Article 9, governs obligations on negotiable instruments. Accordingly, the definition of "account debtor" excludes obligors on negotiable instruments constituting part of chattel paper. The principal effect of this change from the definition in former Article 9 is that the rules in Sections 9-403, 9-404, 9-405, and 9-406, dealing with the rights of an assignee and duties of an account debtor, do not apply to an assignment of chattel paper in which the obligation to pay is evidenced by a negotiable instrument. (Section 9-406(d), however, does apply to promissory notes, including negotiable promissory notes.) Rather, the assignee's rights are governed by Article 3. Similarly, the duties of an obligor on a nonnegotiable instrument are governed by non-Article 9 law unless the nonnegotiable instrument is a part of chattel paper, in which case the obligor is an account debtor.

i. **Receivables Under Government Entitlement Programs**. This Article does not contain a defined term that encompasses specifically rights to payment or performance under the many and varied government entitlement programs. Depending on the nature of a right under a program, it could be an account, a payment intangible, a general intangible other than a payment intangible, or another type of collateral. The right also might be proceeds of collateral (e.g., crops).

6. **Investment-Property-Related Definitions: "Commodity Account"; "Commodity Contract"; "Commodity Customer"; "Commodity Intermediary"; "Investment Property."** These definitions are substantially the same as the corresponding definitions in former Section 9-115. "Investment property" includes securities, both certificated and uncertificated, securities accounts, security entitlements, commodity accounts, and commodity contracts. The term investment property includes a "securities account" in order to facilitate transactions in which a debtor wishes to create a security interest in all of the investment positions held through a particular account rather than in particular positions carried in the account. Former Section 9-115 was added in conjunction with Revised Article 8 and contained a variety of rules applicable to security interests in investment property. These rules have been relocated to the appropriate sections of Article 9. See, e.g., Sections 9-203 (attachment), 9-314 (perfection by control), 9-328 (priority).

The terms "security," "security entitlement," and related terms are defined in Section 8-102, and the term "securities account" is defined in Section 8-501. The terms "commodity account," "commodity contract," "commodity customer," and "commodity intermediary" are defined in this section. Commodity contracts are not "securities" or "financial assets" under Article 8. See Section 8-103(f). Thus, the relationship between commodity intermediaries and commodity customers is not governed by the indirect-holding-system rules of Part 5 of Article 8. For securities, Article 9 contains rules on security interests, and Article 8 contains rules on the rights of transferees, including secured parties, on such matters as the rights of a transferee if the transfer was itself wrongful and gives rise to an adverse claim. For commodity contracts, Article 9 establishes rules on security interests, but questions of the sort dealt with in Article 8 for securities are left to other law.

The indirect-holding-system rules of Article 8 are sufficiently flexible to be applied to new developments in the securities and financial markets, where that is appropriate. Accordingly, the definition of "commodity contract" is narrowly drafted to ensure that it does not operate as an obstacle to the application of the Article 8 indirect-holding-system rules to new products. The term "commodity contract" covers those contracts that are traded on or subject to the rules of a designated contract market and foreign commodity contracts that are carried on the books of American commodity intermediaries. The effect of this definition is that the category of commodity contracts that are excluded from Article 8 but governed by Article 9 is essentially the same as the category of contracts that fall within the exclusive regulatory jurisdiction of the federal Commodity Futures Trading Commission.

Commodity contracts are different from securities or other financial assets. A person who enters into a commodity futures contract is not buying an asset having a certain value and holding it in anticipation of increase in value. Rather the person is entering into a contract to buy or sell a commodity at set price for delivery at a future time. That contract may become advantageous or disadvantageous as the price of the commodity fluctuates during the term of the contract. The rules of the commodity exchanges require that the contracts be marked to market on a daily basis; that is, the customer pays or receives any increment attributable to that day's price change. Because commodity customers may incur obligations on their contracts, they are required to provide collateral at the outset, known as "original margin," and may be required to provide additional amounts, known as "variation margin," during the term of the contract.

The most likely setting in which a person would want to take a security interest in a commodity contract is where a lender who is advancing funds to finance an inventory of a physical commodity requires the borrower to enter into a commodity contract as a hedge against the risk of decline in the value of the commodity. The lender will want to take a security interest in both the commodity itself and the hedging commodity contract. Typically, such arrangements are structured as security interests in the entire commodity account in which the borrower carries the hedging contracts, rather than in individual contracts.

One important effect of including commodity contracts and commodity accounts in Article 9 is to provide a clearer legal structure for the analysis of the rights of commodity clearing organizations against their participants and futures commission merchants against their customers. The rules and agreements of commodity clearing organizations generally provide that the clearing organization has the right to liquidate any participant's positions in order to satisfy obligations of the participant to the clearing corporation. Similarly, agreements between futures commission merchants and their customers generally provide that the futures commission merchant has the right to liquidate a customer's positions in order to satisfy obligations of the customer to the futures commission merchant.

The main property that a commodity intermediary holds as collateral for the obligations that the commodity customer may incur under its commodity contracts is not other commodity contracts carried by the customer but the other property that the customer has posted as margin. Typically, this property will be securities. The commodity intermediary's security interest in such securities is governed by the rules of this Article on security interests in securities, not the rules on security interests in commodity contracts or commodity accounts.

Although there are significant analytic and regulatory differences between commodities and securities, the development of commodity contracts on financial products in the past few decades has resulted in a system in which the commodity markets and securities markets are closely linked. The rules on security interests in commodity contracts and commodity accounts provide a structure that may be essential in times of stress in the financial markets. Suppose, for example that a firm has a position in a securities market that is hedged by a position in a commodity market, so that payments that the firm is obligated to make with respect to the securities position will be covered by the receipt of funds from the commodity position. Depending upon the settlement cycles of the different markets, it is possible that the firm could find itself in a position where it is obligated to make the payment with respect to the securities position before it receives the matching funds from the commodity position. If cross-margining arrangements have not been developed between the two markets, the firm may need to borrow funds temporarily to make the earlier payment. The rules on security interests in investment property would facilitate the use of positions in one market as collateral for loans needed to cover obligations in the other market.

7. Consumer-Related Definitions: "Consumer Debtor"; "Consumer Goods"; "Consumer-goods transaction"; "Consumer Obligor"; "Consumer Transaction." The definition of "consumer goods" (discussed above) is substantially the same as the definition in former Section 9-109. The definitions of "consumer debtor," "consumer obligor," "consumer-goods transaction," and "consumer transaction" have been added in connection with various new (and old) consumer-related provisions and to designate certain provisions that are inapplicable in consumer transactions.

"Consumer-goods transaction" is a subset of "consumer transaction." Under each definition, both the obligation secured and the collateral must have a personal, family, or household purpose. However, "mixed" business and personal transactions also may be characterized as a consumer-goods transaction or consumer transaction. Subparagraph (A) of the definition of consumer-goods transactions and clause (i) of the definition of consumer transaction are primary purposes tests. Under these tests, it is necessary to determine the primary purpose of the obligation or obligations secured.

Subparagraph (B) and clause (iii) of these definitions are satisfied if any of the collateral is consumer goods, in the case of a consumer-goods transaction, or "is held or acquired primarily for personal, family, or household purposes," in the case of a consumer transaction. The fact that some of the obligations secured or some of the collateral for the obligation does not satisfy the tests (e.g., some of the collateral is acquired for a business purpose) does not prevent a transaction from being a "consumer transaction" or "consumer-goods transaction."

8. **Filing-Related Definitions: "Continuation Statement"; "File Number";"Filing Office"; "Filing-office Rule"; "Financing Statement"; "Fixture Filing"; "Manufactured-Home Transaction"; "New Debtor";"Original Debtor"; "Public-Finance Transaction"; "Termination Statement"; "Transmitting Utility."** These definitions are used exclusively or primarily in the filing-related provisions in Part 5. Most are self-explanatory and are discussed in the Comments to Part 5. A financing statement filed in a manufactured-home transaction or a public-finance transaction may remain effective for 30 years instead of the 5 years applicable to other financing statements. See Section 9-515(b). The definitions relating to medium neutrality also are significant for the filing provisions. See Comment 9.

The definition of "transmitting utility" has been revised to embrace the business of transmitting communications generally to take account of new and future types of communications technology. The term designates a special class of debtors for whom separate filing rules are provided in Part 5, thereby obviating the many local fixture filings that would be necessary under the rules of Section 9-501 for a far-flung public-utility debtor. A transmitting utility will not necessarily be regulated by or operating as such in a jurisdiction where fixtures are located. For example, a utility might own transmission lines in a jurisdiction, although the utility generates no power and has no customers in the jurisdiction.

9. **Definitions Relating to Medium Neutrality.**

a. **"Record."** In many, but not all, instances, the term "record" replaces the term "writing" and "written." A "record" includes information that is in intangible form (e.g., electronically stored) as well as tangible form (e.g., written on paper). Given the rapid development and commercial adoption of modern communication and storage technologies, requirements that documents or communications be "written," "in writing," or otherwise in tangible form do not necessarily reflect or aid commercial practices.

A "record" need not be permanent or indestructible, but the term does not include any oral or other communication that is not stored or preserved by any means. The information must be stored on paper or in some other medium. Information that has not been retained other than through human memory does not qualify as a record. Examples of current technologies commercially used to communicate or store information include, but are not limited to, magnetic media, optical discs, digital voice messaging systems, electronic mail, audio tapes, and photographic media, as well as paper. "Record" is an inclusive term that includes all of these methods of storing or communicating information. Any "writing" is a record. A record may be authenticated. See Comment 9.b. A record may be created without the knowledge or intent of a particular person.

Like the terms "written" or "in writing," the term "record" does not establish the purposes, permitted uses, or legal effect that a record may have under any particular provision of law. Whatever is filed in the Article 9 filing system, including financing statements, continuation statements, and termination statements, whether transmitted in tangible or intangible form, would fall within the definition. However, in some instances, statutes or filing-office rules may require that a paper record be filed. In such cases, even if this Article permits the filing of an electronic record, compliance with those statutes or rules is necessary. Similarly, a filer must comply with a statute or rule that requires a particular type of encoding or formatting for an electronic record.

This Article sometimes uses the terms "for record," "of record," "record or legal title," and "record owner." Some of these are terms traditionally used in real-property law. The definition of "record" in this Article now explicitly excepts these usages from the defined term. Also, this Article refers to a record that is filed or recorded in real-property recording systems to record a mortgage as a "record of a mortgage." This usage recognizes that the defined term "mortgage" means an interest in real property; it does not mean the record that evidences, or is filed or recorded with respect to, the mortgage.

b. **"Authenticate"; "Communicate"; "Send."** The terms "authenticate" and "authenticated" generally replace "sign" and "signed." "Authenticated" replaces and broadens the definition of "signed," in Section 1-201, to encompass authentication of all records, not just writings. (References to authentication of, e.g., an agreement, demand, or notification mean, of course, authentication of a record containing an agreement, demand, or notification.) The terms "communicate" and "send" also contemplate the possibility of communication by nonwritten media. These definitions include the act of transmitting both tangible and intangible records. The definition of "send" replaces, for purposes of this Article, the corresponding term in Section 1-201. The reference to "usual means of communication" in that definition contemplates an inquiry into the appropriateness of the method of transmission used in the particular circumstances involved.

10. **Scope-Related Definitions.**

a. **Expanded Scope of Article: "Agricultural Lien"; "Consignment"; "Payment Intangible"; "Promissory Note."** These new definitions reflect the expanded scope of Article 9, as provided in Section 9-109(a).

b. **Reduced Scope of Exclusions: "Governmental Unit"; "Health-Care-Insurance Receivable"; "Commercial Tort Claims."** These new definitions reflect the reduced scope of the exclusions, provided in Section 9-109(c) and (d), of transfers by governmental debtors and assignments of interests in insurance policies and commercial tort claims.

11. **Choice-of-Law-Related Definitions: "Certificate of Title"; "Governmental Unit"; "Jurisdiction of Organization"; "Registered Organization"; "State."** These new definitions reflect the changes in the law governing perfection and priority of security interests and agricultural liens provided in Part 3, Subpart 1.

Not every organization that may provide information about itself in the public records is a "registered organization." For example, a general partnership is not a "registered organization," even if it files a statement of partnership authority under Section 303 of the Uniform Partnership Act (1994) or an assumed name ("dba") certificate. This is because the State under whose law the partnership is organized is not required to maintain a public record showing that the partnership has been organized. In contrast, corporations, limited liability companies, and limited partnerships are "registered organizations."

12. **Deposit-Account-Related Definitions: "Deposit Account"; "Bank."** The revised definition of "deposit account" incorporates the definition of "bank," which is new. The definition derives from the definitions of "bank" in Sections 4-105(1) and 4A-105(a)(2), which focus on whether the organization is "engaged in the business of banking."

Deposit accounts evidenced by Article 9 "instruments" are excluded from the term "deposit account." In contrast, former Section 9-105 excluded from the former definition "an account evidenced by a certificate of deposit." The revised definition clarifies the proper treatment of nonnegotiable or uncertificated certificates of deposit. Under the definition, an uncertificated certificate of deposit would be a deposit account (assuming there is no writing evidencing the bank's obligation to pay) whereas a nonnegotiable certificate of deposit would be a deposit account only if it is not an "instrument" as defined in this section (a question that turns on whether the nonnegotiable certificate of deposit is "of a type that in ordinary course of business is transferred by delivery with any necessary indorsement or assignment.")

A deposit account evidenced by an instrument is subject to the rules applicable to instruments generally. As a consequence, a security interest in such an instrument cannot be perfected by "control" (see Section 9-104), and the special priority rules applicable to deposit accounts (see Sections 9-327 and 9-340) do not apply.

The term "deposit account" does not include "investment property," such as securities and security entitlements. Thus, the term also does not include shares in a money-market mutual fund, even if the shares are redeemable by check.

13. **Proceeds-Related Definitions: "Cash Proceeds"; "Noncash Proceeds"; "Proceeds."** The revised definition of "proceeds" expands the

definition beyond that contained in former Section 9-306 and resolves ambiguities in the former section.

a. **Distributions on Account of Collateral.** The phrase "whatever is collected on, or distributed on account of, collateral," in subparagraph (B), is broad enough to cover cash or stock dividends distributed on account of securities or other investment property that is original collateral. Compare former Section 9-306 ("Any payments or distributions made with respect to investment property collateral are proceeds."). This section rejects the holding of *Hastie v. FDIC*, 2 F.3d 1042 (10th Cir. 1993) (postpetition cash dividends on stock subject to a prepetition pledge are not "proceeds" under Bankruptcy Code Section 552(b)), to the extent the holding relies on the Article 9 definition of "proceeds."

b. **Distributions on Account of Supporting Obligations.** Under subparagraph (B), collections on and distributions on account of collateral consisting of various credit-support arrangements ("supporting obligations," as defined in Section 9-102) also are proceeds. Consequently, they are afforded treatment identical to proceeds collected from or distributed by the obligor on the underlying (supported) right to payment or other collateral. Proceeds of supporting obligations also are proceeds of the underlying rights to payment or other collateral.

c. **Proceeds of Proceeds.** The definition of "proceeds" no longer provides that proceeds of proceeds are themselves proceeds. That idea is expressed in the revised definition of "collateral" in Section 9-102. No change in meaning is intended.

d. **Proceeds Received by Person Who Did Not Create Security Interest.** When collateral is sold subject to a security interest and the buyer then resells the collateral, a question arose under former Article 9 concerning whether the "debtor" had "received" what the buyer received on resale and, therefore, whether those receipts were "proceeds" under former Section 9-306(2). This Article contains no requirement that property be "received" by the debtor for the property to qualify as proceeds. It is necessary only that the property be traceable, directly or indirectly, to the original collateral.

e. **Cash Proceeds and Noncash Proceeds.** The definition of "cash proceeds" is substantially the same as the corresponding definition in former Section 9-306. The phrase "and the like" covers property that is functionally equivalent to "money, checks, or deposit accounts," such as some money-market accounts that are securities or part of securities entitlements. Proceeds other than cash proceeds are noncash proceeds.

14. **Consignment-Related Definitions: "Consignee"; "Consignment"; "Consignor."** The definition of "consignment" excludes, in subparagraphs (B) and (C), transactions for which filing would be inappropriate or of insufficient benefit to justify the costs. A consignment excluded from the application of this Article by one of those subparagraphs may still be a true consignment; however, it is governed by non-Article 9 law. The definition

also excludes, in subparagraph (D), what have been called "consignments intended for security." These "consignments" are not bailments but secured transactions. Accordingly, all of Article 9 applies to them. See Sections 1-201(37), 9-109(a)(1). The "consignor" is the person who delivers goods to the "consignee" in a consignment.

The definition of "consignment" requires that the goods be delivered "to a merchant for the purpose of sale." If the goods are delivered for another purpose as well, such as milling or processing, the transaction is a consignment nonetheless because a purpose of the delivery is "sale." On the other hand, if a merchant-processor-bailee will not be selling the goods itself but will be delivering to buyers to which the owner-bailor agreed to sell the goods, the transaction would not be a consignment.

15. **"Accounting."** This definition describes the record and information that a debtor is entitled to request under Section 9-210.

16. **"Document."** The definition of "document" is unchanged in substance from the corresponding definitions in former Section 9-105. See Section 1-201(15) and Comment 15.

17. **"Encumbrance"; "Mortgage."** The definitions of "encumbrance" and "mortgage" are unchanged in substance from the corresponding definitions in former Section 9-105. They are used primarily in the special real-property-related priority and other provisions relating to crops, fixtures, and accessions.

18. **"Fixtures."** This definition is unchanged in substance from the corresponding definition in former Section 9-313. See Section 9-334 (priority of security interests in fixtures and crops).

19. **"Good Faith."** This Article expands the definition of "good faith" to include "the observance of reasonable commercial standards of fair dealing." The definition in this section applies when the term is used in this Article, and the same concept applies in the context of this Article for purposes of the obligation of good faith imposed by Section 1-203. See subsection (c).

20. **"Lien Creditor"** This definition is unchanged in substance from the corresponding definition in former Section 9-301.

21. **"New Value."** This Article deletes former Section 9-108. Its broad formulation of new value, which embraced the taking of after-acquired collateral for a pre-existing claim, was unnecessary, counterintuitive, and ineffective for its original purpose of sheltering after-acquired collateral from attack as a voidable preference in bankruptcy. The new definition derives from Bankruptcy Code Section 547(a). The term is used with respect to temporary perfection of security interests in instruments, certificated securities, or negotiable documents under Section 9-312(e) and with respect to chattel paper priority in Section 9-330.

22. **"Person Related To."** Section 9-615 provides a special method for calculating a deficiency or surplus when "the secured party, a person related to the secured party, or a secondary obligor" acquires the collateral at a

foreclosure disposition. Separate definitions of the term are provided with respect to an individual secured party and with respect to a secured party that is an organization. The definitions are patterned on the corresponding definition in Section 1.301(32) of the Uniform Consumer Credit Code (1974).

23. **"Proposal."** This definition describes a record that is sufficient to propose to retain collateral in full or partial satisfaction of a secured obligation. See Sections 9-620, 9-621, 9-622.

24. **"Pursuant to Commitment."** This definition is unchanged in substance from the corresponding definition in former Section 9-105. It is used in connection with special priority rules applicable to future advances. See Section 9-323.

25. **"Software."** The definition of "software" is used in connection with the priority rules applicable to purchase-money security interests. See Sections 9-103, 9-324. Software, like a payment intangible, is a type of general intangible for purposes of this Article.

26. **Terminology: "Assignment" and "Transfer."** In numerous provisions, this Article refers to the "assignment" or the "transfer" of property interests. These terms and their derivatives are not defined. This Article generally follows common usage by using the terms "assignment" and "assign" to refer to transfers of rights to payment, claims, and liens and other security interests. It generally uses the term "transfer" to refer to other transfers of interests in property. Except when used in connection with a letter-of-credit transaction (see Section 9-107, Comment 4), no significance should be placed on the use of one term or the other. Depending on the context, each term may refer to the assignment or transfer of an outright ownership interest or to the assignment or transfer of a limited interest, such as a security interest.

§ 9-103. PURCHASE-MONEY SECURITY INTEREST; APPLICATION OF PAYMENTS; BURDEN OF ESTABLISHING.

(a)　**[Definitions.]** In this section:

(1)　"purchase-money collateral" means goods or software that secures a purchase-money obligation incurred with respect to that collateral; and

(2)　"purchase-money obligation" means an obligation of an obligor incurred as all or part of the price of the collateral or for value given to enable the debtor to acquire rights in or the use of the collateral if the value is in fact so used.

(b)　**[Purchase-money security interest in goods.]** A security interest in goods is a purchase-money security interest:

(1) to the extent that the goods are purchase-money collateral with respect to that security interest;

(2) if the security interest is in inventory that is or was purchase-money collateral, also to the extent that the security interest secures a purchase-money obligation incurred with respect to other inventory in which the secured party holds or held a purchase-money security interest; and

(3) also to the extent that the security interest secures a purchase-money obligation incurred with respect to software in which the secured party holds or held a purchase-money security interest.

(c) [Purchase-money security interest in software.] A security interest in software is a purchase-money security interest to the extent that the security interest also secures a purchase-money obligation incurred with respect to goods in which the secured party holds or held a purchase-money security interest if:

(1) the debtor acquired its interest in the software in an integrated transaction in which it acquired an interest in the goods; and

(2) the debtor acquired its interest in the software for the principal purpose of using the software in the goods.

(d) [Consignor's inventory purchase-money security interest.] The security interest of a consignor in goods that are the subject of a consignment is a purchase-money security interest in inventory.

(e) [Application of payment in non-consumer-goods transaction.] In a transaction other than a consumer-goods transaction, if the extent to which a security interest is a purchase-money security interest depends on the application of a payment to a particular obligation, the payment must be applied:

(1) in accordance with any reasonable method of application to which the parties agree;

(2) in the absence of the parties' agreement to a reasonable method, in accordance with any intention of the obligor manifested at or before the time of payment; or

(3) in the absence of an agreement to a reasonable method and a timely manifestation of the obligor's intention, in the following order:

(A) to obligations that are not secured; and

(B) if more than one obligation is secured, to obligations secured by purchase-money security interests in the order in which those obligations were incurred.

(f) [No loss of status of purchase-money security interest in non-consumer-goods transaction.] In a transaction other than a consumer-goods transaction, a purchase-money security interest does not lose its status as such, even if:

(1)   the purchase-money collateral also secures an obligation that is not a purchase-money obligation;

(2)   collateral that is not purchase-money collateral also secures the purchase-money obligation; or

(3)   the purchase-money obligation has been renewed, refinanced, consolidated, or restructured.

(g) [Burden of proof in non-consumer-goods transaction.] In a transaction other than a consumer-goods transaction, a secured party claiming a purchase-money security interest has the burden of establishing the extent to which the security interest is a purchase-money security interest.

(h) [Non-consumer-goods transactions; no inference.] The limitation of the rules in subsections (e), (f), and (g) to transactions other than consumer-goods transactions is intended to leave to the court the determination of the proper rules in consumer-goods transactions. The court may not infer from that limitation the nature of the proper rule in consumer-goods transactions and may continue to apply established approaches.

ANALYSIS

This section will allow financers of inventory and equipment to use "all obligations" and after-acquired property clauses without totally forfeiting purchase-money priority. Under the "dual status" rule (which this provision adopts for transactions other than consumer goods transactions) cross-collateralization or refinancing extending the security interest beyond the price of an item or adding other collateral to secure the price does not completely destroy purchase-money status. Decisions such as *Southtrust Bank v. Borg-Warner Acceptance Corp.*, 760 F.2d 1240 (11th Cir. 1985) are overruled. Instead, the interest in a particular item of equipment will remain a purchase-money security interest to the extent the financer can show that the item continues to secure all or part of its price. An interest in an item of inventory will remain a purchase-money interest to the extent that the financer can show that the item continues to secure all or part of its price or the price of other inventory in which the financer holds or has held a purchase-money interest. If a financer finances all of the inventory of the debtor and is cross-collateralized, it should have a purchase-money interest in all of the unpaid-for inventory to secure the total unpaid price of all inventory items. A contractual formula stipulating how payments are to be credited will control calculation of the unpaid price so long as it is reasonable. The fact that an appropriate evidentiary showing may preserve a partial purchase-money priority may not be enough for the financers of new goods. They may still deem it prudent to require subordination by earlier-filed creditors.

This section does limit purchase-money interests to interests in goods and software acquired in an integrated transaction with the goods in which it is to be used. In contrast to old §§ 9-107 and 9-312(4) which allowed a purchase-money interest in collateral in general, the new Article 9 will not (apart from the software exception) permit a purchase-money interest in non-goods collateral such as accounts, general intangibles, instruments or chattel paper. *See Secured Transactions* § 7B.12. Even if the creditor lends the money to enable the debtor to purchase those assets as opposed to generating them in its business operations, the creditor will not be able to jump ahead of an earlier-filed creditor. This change will buttress the position of a first-filed floating lienor.

> ***Example A***: Assume that Debtor A first grants a security interest in all of its inventory, equipment, chattel paper, general intangibles and accounts (including after-acquired assets) to Bank One and that Bank One perfects by filing first as to those classes of collateral. Then Debtor A acquires all of the assets of Enterprise Z with financing provided by Bank Two. If it follows the rules of new § 9-324, Bank Two will qualify for a purchase-money priority over Bank One as to the inventory and equipment. But Bank Two has no chance for a purchase money priority over Bank One as to the chattel paper, general intangibles and accounts acquired by Debtor A in this acquisition.

This change gives the first-filed floating lienor more leverage to prevent new acquisitions by the debtor. The acquisition is likely to occur only if Bank One provides the financing or agrees to subordinate to Bank Two.

Official Comment

1. **Source.** Former Section 9-107.

2. **Scope of This Section.** Under Section 9-309(1), a purchase-money security interest in consumer goods is perfected when it attaches. Sections 9-317 and 9-324 provide special priority rules for purchase-money security interests in a variety of contexts. This section explains when a security interest enjoys purchase-money status.

3. **"Purchase-Money Collateral"; "Purchase-Money Obligation"; "Purchase-Money Security Interest."** Subsection (a) defines "purchase-money collateral" and "purchase-money obligation." These terms are essential to the description of what constitutes a purchase-money security interest under subsection (b). As used in subsection (a)(2), the definition of "purchase-money obligation," the "price" of collateral or the "value given to enable" includes obligations for expenses incurred in connection with acquiring rights in the collateral, sales taxes, duties, finance charges, interest, freight charges, costs of storage in transit, demurrage, administrative charges, expenses of collection and enforcement, attorney's fees, and other similar obligations.

The concept of "purchase-money security interest" requires a close nexus between the acquisition of collateral and the secured obligation. Thus, a security interest does not qualify as a purchase-money security interest if a debtor acquires property on unsecured credit and subsequently creates the security interest to secure the purchase price.

4. **Cross-Collateralization of Purchase-Money Security Interests in Inventory.** Subsection (b)(2) deals with the problem of cross-collateralized purchase-money security interests in inventory. Consider a simple example:

Example: Seller (S) sells an item of inventory (Item-1) to Debtor (D), retaining a security interest in Item-1 to secure Item-1's price and all other obligations, existing and future, of D to S. S then sells another item of inventory to D (Item-2), again retaining a security interest in Item-2 to secure Item-2's price as well as all other obligations of D to S. D then pays to S Item-1's price. D then sells Item-2 to a buyer in ordinary course of business, who takes Item-2 free of S's security interest.

Under subsection (b)(2), S's security interest in *Item-1* securing *Item-2's unpaid price* would be a purchase-money security interest. This is so because S has a purchase-money security interest in Item-1, Item-1 secures the price of (a "purchase-money obligation incurred with respect to") Item-2 ("other inventory"), and Item-2 itself was subject to a purchase-money security interest. Note that, to the extent Item-1 secures the price of Item-2, S's security interest in Item-1 would not be a purchase-money security interest under subsection (b)(1). The security interest in Item-1 is a purchase-money security interest under subsection (b)(1) only to the extent that Item-1 is "purchase-money collateral," i.e., only to the extent that Item-1 "secures a purchase-money obligation incurred with respect to that collateral" (i.e., Item-1). See subsection (a)(1).

5. **Purchase-Money Security Interests in Goods and Software.** Subsections (b) and (c) limit purchase-money security interests to security interests

in goods, including fixtures, and software. Otherwise, no change in meaning from former Section 9-107 is intended. The second sentence of former Section 9-115(5)(f) made the purchase-money priority rule (former Section 9-312(4)) inapplicable to investment property. This section's limitation makes that provision unnecessary.

Subsection (c) describes the limited circumstances under which a security interest in goods may be accompanied by a purchase-money security interest in software. The software must be acquired by the debtor in a transaction integrated with the transaction in which the debtor acquired the goods, and the debtor must acquire the software for the principal purpose of using the software in the goods. "Software" is defined in Section 9-102.

6. **Consignments.** Under former Section 9-114, the priority of the consignor's interest is similar to that of a purchase-money security interest. Subsection (d) achieves this result more directly, by defining the interest of a "consignor," defined in Section 9-102, to be a purchase-money security interest in inventory for purposes of this Article. This drafting convention obviates any need to set forth special priority rules applicable to the interest of a consignor. Rather, the priority of the consignor's interest as against the rights of lien creditors of the consignee, competing secured parties, and purchasers of the goods from the consignee can be determined by reference to the priority rules generally applicable to inventory, such as Sections 9-317, 9-320, 9-322, and 9-324. For other purposes, including the rights and duties of the consignor and consignee as between themselves, the consignor would remain the owner of goods under a bailment arrangement with the consignee. See Section 9-319.

7. **Provisions Applicable Only to Non-Consumer-Goods Transactions.**

a. **"Dual-Status" Rule.** For transactions other than consumer-goods transactions, this Article approves what some cases have called the "dual-status" rule, under which a security interest may be a purchase-money security interest to some extent and a non-purchase-money security interest to some extent. (Concerning consumer-goods transactions, see subsection (h) and Comment 8.) Some courts have found this rule to be explicit or implicit in the words "to the extent," found in former Section 9-107 and continued in subsections (b)(1) and (b)(2). The rule is made explicit in subsection (e). For non-consumer-goods transactions, this Article rejects the "transformation" rule adopted by some cases, under which any cross-collateralization, refinancing, or the like destroys the purchase-money status entirely.

Consider, for example, what happens when a $10,000 loan secured by a purchase-money security interest is refinanced by the original lender, and, as part of the transaction, the debtor borrows an additional $2,000 secured by the collateral. Subsection (f) resolves any doubt that the security interest remains a purchase-money security interest. Under subsection (b), however, it enjoys purchase-money status only to the extent of $10,000.

b. **Allocation of Payments.** Continuing with the example, if the debtor makes a $1,000 payment on the $12,000 obligation, then one must determine the extent to which the security interest remains a purchase-money security interest-$9,000 or $10,000. Subsection (e)(1) expresses the overriding principle, applicable in cases other than consumer-goods transactions, for determining the extent to which a security interest is a purchase-money security interest under these circumstances: freedom of contract, as limited by principle of reasonableness. An unconscionable method of application, for example, is not a reasonable one and so would not be given effect under subsection (e)(1). In the absence of agreement, subsection (e)(2) permits the obligor to determine how payments should be allocated. If the obligor fails to manifest its intention, obligations that are not secured will be paid first. (As used in this Article, the concept of "obligations that are not secured" means obligations for which the debtor has not created a security interest. This concept is different from and should not be confused with the concept of an "unsecured claim" as it appears in Bankruptcy Code Section 506(a).) The obligor may prefer this approach, because unsecured debt is likely to carry a higher interest rate than secured debt. A creditor who would prefer to be secured rather than unsecured also would prefer this approach.

After the unsecured debt is paid, payments are to be applied first toward the obligations secured by purchase-money security interests. In the event that there is more than one such obligation, payments first received are to be applied to obligations first incurred. See subsection (e)(3). Once these obligations are paid, there are no purchase-money security interests and no additional allocation rules are needed.

Subsection (f) buttresses the dual-status rule by making it clear that (in a transaction other than a consumer-goods transaction) cross-collateralization and renewals, refinancings, and restructurings do not cause a purchase-money security interest to lose its status as such. The statutory terms "renewed," "refinanced," and "restructured" are not defined. Whether the terms encompass a particular transaction depends upon whether, under the particular facts, the purchase-money character of the security interest fairly can be said to survive. Each term contemplates that an identifiable portion of the purchase-money obligation could be traced to the new obligation resulting from a renewal, refinancing, or restructuring.

c. **Burden of Proof.** As is the case when the extent of a security interest is in issue, under subsection (g) the secured party claiming a purchase-money security interest in a transaction other than a consumer-goods transaction has the burden of establishing whether the security interest retains its purchase-money status. This is so whether the determination is to be made following a renewal, refinancing, or restructuring or otherwise.

8. **Consumer-Goods Transactions; Characterization Under Other Law.** Under subsection (h), the limitation of subsections (e), (f), and (g) to transactions other than a consumer-goods transactions leaves to the court the

determination of the proper rules in consumer-goods transactions. Subsection (h) also instructs the court not to draw any inference from this limitation as to the proper rules for consumer-goods transactions and leaves the court free to continue to apply established approaches to those transactions.

This section addresses only whether a security interest is a "purchase-money security interest" under this Article, primarily for purposes of perfection and priority. See, e.g., Sections 9-317, 9-324. In particular, its adoption of the dual-status rule, allocation of payments rules, and burden of proof standards for non-consumer-goods transactions is not intended to affect or influence characterizations under other statutes. Whether a security interest is a "purchase-money security interest" under other law is determined by that law. For example, decisions under Bankruptcy Code Section 522(f) have applied both the dual-status and the transformation rules. The Bankruptcy Code does not expressly adopt the state law definition of "purchase-money security interest." Where federal law does not defer to this Article, this Article does not, and could not, determine a question of federal law.

§ 9-104. CONTROL OF DEPOSIT ACCOUNT.

(a) [**Requirements for control.**] A secured party has control of a deposit account if:

(1) the secured party is the bank with which the deposit account is maintained;

(2) the debtor, secured party, and bank have agreed in an authenticated record that the bank will comply with instructions originated by the secured party directing disposition of the funds in the account without further consent by the debtor; or

(3) the secured party becomes the bank's customer with respect to the deposit account.

(b) [**Debtor's right to direct disposition.**] A secured party that has satisfied subsection (a) has control, even if the debtor retains the right to direct the disposition of funds from the deposit account.

ANALYSIS

The Revised Article 9 will for the first time apply to security interests in deposit accounts taken as original collateral. Under new §§ 9-312(b)(1) and 9-314(a) a security interest in a deposit account can only be perfected by control. In contrast to filing or taking possession, control as a method of perfection is not calculated to give public notice of the security interest. *See Secured Transactions* § 6D.02[7]. Under any of the three paths to control in new § 9-104, there is no requirement that the debtor be denied access to the funds. In contrast, the law of some states today demands that the creditor take a common law pledge or assignment of the bank account. *See Secured Transactions* §§ 3.14[4] and 24A.02. Debtor access to the funds can be deemed to be inconsistent with such a pledge or assignment. It is even possible that leaving the debtor with access to the funds will make the arrangement fraudulent under *Benedict v. Ratner*, 268 U.S. 353 (1925). Old § 9-205 does not overrule *Benedict* as to deposit accounts because interests in deposit accounts as original collateral are excluded from Article 9 by old § 9-104(l). The new Article 9 accomplishes that repeal by bringing commercial deposit accounts transactions within Article 9. *See* new §§ 9-109 and 9-205.

Under the Revised Article 9 a bank secured lender can be expected to insist on security interests in deposit accounts maintained with it. The bank lender will automatically have control of such deposit accounts under new § 9-104(a)(1) and will normally have priority over other secured creditors under new § 9-327(3). The debtor may still enjoy access to the account, but the bank will have a perfected interest in the account even though no public disclosure of the interest is required. Presumably, third parties will assume that the debtor's bank accounts are or may be subject to a security interest.

Official Comment

1. **Source.** New; derived from Section 8-106.

2. **Why "Control" Matters.** This section explains the concept of "control" of a deposit account. "Control" under this section may serve two functions. First, "control . . . pursuant to the debtor's agreement" may substitute for an authenticated security agreement as an element of attachment. See Section 9-203(b)(3)(D). Second, when a deposit account is taken as original collateral, the only method of perfection is obtaining control under this section. See Section 9-312(b)(1).

3. **Requirements for "Control."** This section derives from Section 8-106 of Revised Article 8, which defines "control" of securities and certain other investment property. Under subsection (a)(1), the bank with which the deposit account is maintained has control. The effect of this provision is to afford the bank automatic perfection. No other form of public notice is necessary; all actual and potential creditors of the debtor are always on notice that the bank with which the debtor's deposit account is maintained may assert a claim against the deposit account.

Under subsection (a)(2), a secured party may obtain control by obtaining the bank's authenticated agreement that it will comply with the secured party's instructions without further consent by the debtor. The analogous provision in Section 8-106 does not require that the agreement be authenticated. An agreement to comply with the secured party's instructions suffices for "control" of a deposit account under this section even if the bank's agreement is subject to specified conditions, e.g., that the secured party's instructions are accompanied by a certification that the debtor is in default. (Of course, if the condition is the *debtor's* further consent, the statute explicitly provides that the agreement would *not* confer control.) See revised Section 8-106, Comment 7.

Under subsection (a)(3), a secured party may obtain control by becoming the bank's "customer," as defined in Section 4-104. As the customer, the secured party would enjoy the right (but not necessarily the exclusive right) to withdraw funds from, or close, the deposit account. See Sections 4-401(a), 4-403(a).

Although the arrangements giving rise to control may themselves prevent, or may enable the secured party at its discretion to prevent, the debtor from reaching the funds on deposit, subsection (b) makes clear that the debtor's ability to reach the funds is not inconsistent with "control."

Perfection by control is not available for bank accounts evidenced by an instrument (e.g., certain certificates of deposit), which by definition are "instruments" and not "deposit accounts." See Section 9-102 (defining "deposit account" and "instrument").

§ 9-105. CONTROL OF ELECTRONIC CHATTEL PAPER. A secured party has control of electronic chattel paper if the record or records comprising the chattel paper are created, stored, and assigned in such a manner that:

(1) a single authoritative copy of the record or records exists which is unique, identifiable and, except as otherwise provided in paragraphs (4), (5), and (6), unalterable;

(2) the authoritative copy identifies the secured party as the assignee of the record or records;

(3) the authoritative copy is communicated to and maintained by the secured party or its designated custodian;

(4) copies or revisions that add or change an identified assignee of the authoritative copy can be made only with the participation of the secured party;

(5) each copy of the authoritative copy and any copy of a copy is readily identifiable as a copy that is not the authoritative copy; and

(6) any revision of the authoritative copy is readily identifiable as an authorized or unauthorized revision.

ANALYSIS

A security interest in electronic chattel paper may be perfected by filing or control. New §§ 9-312(a); 9-314(a). But control is essential to the special priority given to a purchaser for new value under new § 9-330.

Official Comment

1. **Source.** New.

2. **"Control" of Electronic Chattel Paper.** This Article covers security interests in "electronic chattel paper," a new term defined in Section 9-102. This section governs how "control" of electronic chattel paper may be obtained. A secured party's control of electronic chattel paper (i) may substitute for an authenticated security agreement for purposes of attachment under Section 9-203, (ii) is a method of perfection under Section 9-314, and (iii) is a condition for obtaining special, non-temporal priority under Section 9-330. Because electronic chattel paper cannot be transferred, assigned, or possessed in the same manner as tangible chattel paper, a special definition of control is necessary. In descriptive terms, this section provides that control of electronic chattel paper is the functional equivalent of possession of "tangible chattel paper" (a term also defined in Section 9-102).

3. **"Authoritative Copy" of Electronic Chattel Paper.** One requirement for establishing control is that a particular copy be an "authoritative copy." "Although other copies may exist, they must be distinguished from the authoritative copy. This may be achieved, for example, through the methods of authentication that are used or by business practices involving the marking of any additional copies. When tangible chattel paper is converted to electronic chattel paper, in order to establish that a copy of the electronic chattel paper is the authoritative copy it may be necessary to show that the tangible chattel paper no longer exists or has been permanently marked to indicate that it is not the authoritative copy.

4. **Development of Control Systems.** This Article leaves to the marketplace the development of systems and procedures, through a combination of suitable technologies and business practices, for dealing with control of electronic chattel paper in a commercial context. However, achieving control under this section requires more than the agreement of interested persons that the elements of control are satisfied. For example, paragraph (4) contemplates that control requires that it be a physical impossibility (or sufficiently unlikely

or implausible so as to approach practical impossibility) to add or change an identified assignee without the participation of the secured party (or its authorized representative). It would not be enough for the assignor merely to agree that it will not change the identified assignee without the assignee-secured party's consent. However, the standards applied to determine whether a party is in control of electronic chattel paper should not be more stringent than the standards now applied to determine whether a party is in possession of tangible chattel paper. Control of electronic chattel paper contemplates systems or procedures such that the secured party must take some action (either directly or through its designated custodian) to effect a change or addition to the authoritative copy. But just as a secured party does not lose possession of tangible chattel paper merely by virtue of the possibility that a person acting on its behalf *could* wrongfully redeliver the chattel paper to the debtor, so control of electronic chattel paper would not be defeated by the possibility that the secured party's interest *could* be subverted by the wrongful conduct of a person (such as a custodian) acting on its behalf.

Systems that evolve for control of electronic chattel paper may or may not involve a third party custodian of the relevant records. However, this section and the concept of control of electronic chattel paper are not based on the same concepts as are control of deposit accounts (Section 9-104), security entitlements, a type of investment property (Section 9-106), and letter-of-credit rights (Section 9-107). The rules for control of that collateral are based on existing market practices and legal and regulatory regimes for institutions such as banks and securities intermediaries. Analogous practices for electronic chattel paper are developing nonetheless. The flexible approach adopted by this section, moreover, should not impede the development of these practices and, eventually, legal and regulatory regimes, which may become analogous to those for, e.g., investment property.

§ 9-106. CONTROL OF INVESTMENT PROPERTY.

(a) [Control under Section 8-106.] A person has control of a certificated security, uncertificated security, or security entitlement as provided in Section 8-106.

(b) [Control of commodity contract.] A secured party has control of a commodity contract if:

(1) the secured party is the commodity intermediary with which the commodity contract is carried; or

(2) the commodity customer, secured party, and commodity intermediary have agreed that the commodity intermediary will apply any value distributed on account of the commodity contract as directed by the secured party without further consent by the commodity customer.

(c) [Effect of control of securities account or commodity account.] A secured party having control of all security entitlements or commodity contracts carried in a securities account or commodity account has control over the securities account or commodity account.

ANALYSIS

"Control" as the magic path to perfection and priority of security interests in investment property was introduced with the 1994 revision of Article 8, and is already the law in almost all of the states. Under Section 8-106 the precise way of obtaining control varies depending on whether the collateral is a certificated security in bearer form, a certificated security in registered form, and uncertificated security or a securities entitlement. *See Secured Transactions* §§ 6D.02 and 23.12. In the case of a securities entitlement, control as defined in Section 8-106 does not require that the debtor be denied the power to issue entitlement orders as to the entitlement. Control in this context is not the functional equivalent of common law possession. Control is not calculated to give public notice of the creditor's interest.

Official Comment

1. **Source.** Former Section 9-115(e).

2. **"Control" Under Article 8.** For an explanation of "control" of securities and certain other investment property, see Section 8-106, Comments 4 and 7.

3. **"Control" of Commodity Contracts.** This section, as did former Section 9-115(1)(e), contains provisions relating to control of commodity contracts which are analogous to those in Section 8-106 for other types of investment property.

4. **Securities Accounts and Commodity Accounts.** For drafting convenience, control with respect to a securities account or commodity account is defined in terms of obtaining control over the security entitlements or commodity contracts. Of course, an agreement that provides that (without further consent of the debtor) the securities intermediary or commodity intermediary will honor instructions from the secured party concerning a securities account or commodity account described as such is sufficient. Such an agreement necessarily implies that the intermediary will honor instructions concerning all security entitlements or commodity contracts carried in the account and thus affords the secured party control of all the security entitlements or commodity contracts.

§ 9-107. CONTROL OF LETTER-OF-CREDIT RIGHT. A secured party has control of a letter-of-credit right to the extent of any right to payment or performance by the issuer or any nominated person if the issuer or nominated person has consented to an assignment of proceeds of the letter of credit under Section 5-114(c) or otherwise applicable law or practice.

ANALYSIS

A creditor has two ways of perfecting a security interest in a letter-of-credit right under the new Article 9. One way is by establishing control of the right, which under this new § 9-107 requires that the creditor obtain the consent of the issuer or nominated person to an assignment of the proceeds of the credit. The second path is by perfecting an interest in the account, chattel paper, document, general intangible, instrument or investment property which is supported by the credit. New §§ 9-203, 9-308(d). Perfection by control trumps perfection of the right as a supporting obligation. New § 9-329(1).

Official Comment

1. **Source.** New.

2. **"Control" of Letter-of-Credit Right.** Whether a secured party has control of a letter-of-credit right may determine the secured party's priority as against competing secured parties. See Section 9-329. This section provides that a secured party acquires control of a letter-of-credit right by receiving an assignment if the secured party obtains the consent of the issuer or any nominated person, such as a confirmer or negotiating bank, under Section 5-114 or other applicable law or practice. Because both issuers and nominated persons may give or be obligated to give value under a letter of credit, this section contemplates that a secured party obtains control of a letter-of-credit right with respect to the issuer or a particular nominated person only to the extent that the issuer or that nominated person consents to the assignment. For example, if a secured party obtains control to the extent of an issuer's obligation but fails to obtain the consent of a nominated person, the secured party does not have control to the extent that the nominated person gives value. In many cases the person or persons who will give value under a letter of credit will be clear from its terms. In other cases, prudence may suggest obtaining consent from more than one person. The details of the consenting issuer's or nominated person's duties to pay or otherwise render performance to the secured party are left to the agreement of the parties.

3. **"Proceeds of a Letter of Credit."** Section 5-114 follows traditional banking terminology by referring to a letter of credit beneficiary's assignment of its right to receive payment thereunder as an assignment of the "proceeds of a letter of credit." However, as the seller of goods can assign its right to receive payment (an "account") before it has been earned by delivering the goods to the buyer, so the beneficiary of a letter of credit can assign its contingent right to payment before the letter of credit has been honored. See Section 5-114(b). If the assignment creates a security interest, the security interest can be perfected at the time it is created. An assignment of, including the creation of a security interest in, a letter-of-credit right is an assignment of a present interest.

4. **"Transfer" vs. "Assignment."** Letter-of-credit law and practice distinguish the "transfer" of a letter of credit from an "assignment." Under a transfer, the transferee itself becomes the beneficiary and acquires the right to draw. Whether a new, substitute credit is issued or the issuer advises the transferee of its status as such, the transfer constitutes a novation under which the transferee is the new, substituted beneficiary (but only to the extent of the transfer, in the case of a partial transfer).

Section 5-114(e) provides that the rights of a transferee beneficiary or nominated person are independent of the beneficiary's assignment of the proceeds of a letter of credit and are superior to the assignee's right to the proceeds. For this reason, transfer does not appear in this Article as a means of control or perfection. Section 9-109(c)(4) recognizes the independent and superior rights of a transferee beneficiary under Section 5-114(e); this Article does not apply to the rights of a transferee beneficiary or nominated person to the extent that those rights are independent and superior under Section 5-114.

5. **Supporting Obligation: Automatic Attachment and Perfection.** A letter-of-credit right is a type of "supporting obligation," as defined in Section 9-102. Under Sections 9-203 and 9-308, a security interest in a letter-of-credit right automatically attaches and is automatically perfected if the security interest in the supported obligation is a perfected security interest. However, unless the secured party has control of the letter-of-credit right or itself becomes a transferee beneficiary, it cannot obtain any rights against the issuer or a nominated person under Article 5. Consequently, as a practical matter, the secured party's rights would be limited to its ability to locate and identify proceeds distributed by the issuer or nominated person under the letter of credit.

§ 9-108. SUFFICIENCY OF DESCRIPTION.

(a) [Sufficiency of description.] Except as otherwise provided in subsections (c), (d), and (e), a description of personal or real property is sufficient, whether or not it is specific, if it reasonably identifies what is described.

(b)   [Examples of reasonable identification.] Except as otherwise provided in subsection (d), a description of collateral reasonably identifies the collateral if it identifies the collateral by:

(1)   specific listing;

(2)   category;

(3)   except as otherwise provided in subsection (e), a type of collateral defined in [the Uniform Commercial Code];

(4)   quantity;

(5)   computational or allocational formula or procedure; or

(6)   except as otherwise provided in subsection (c), any other method, if the identity of the collateral is objectively determinable.

(c)   [Supergeneric description not sufficient.] A description of collateral as "all the debtor's assets" or "all the debtor's personal property" or using words of similar import does not reasonably identify the collateral.

(d)   [Investment property.] Except as otherwise provided in subsection (e), a description of a security entitlement, securities account, or commodity account is sufficient if it describes:

(1)   the collateral by those terms or as investment property; or

(2)   the underlying financial asset or commodity contract.

(e)   [When description by type insufficient.] A description only by type of collateral defined in [the Uniform Commercial Code] is an insufficient description of:

(1)   a commercial tort claim; or

(2)   in a consumer transaction, consumer goods, a security entitlement, a securities account, or a commodity account.

ANALYSIS

The listing of the varied ways in which collateral may be identified is borrowed from old § 9-115, added in the Code in 1994 to illustrate ways of identifying the strikingly diverse range of assets that qualify as investment property. The underlying policy theme is the need to allow the drafter flexibility in preparing descriptions. In addition, this provision implicitly blesses the admission of parol evidence of objective circumstances to apply a description to particular assets. Approval of description by type of collateral (*e.g.*, all inventory, all equipment) necessarily implies the admission of parol to determine the use for which particular assets are held by the debtor. The residual test of new § 9-108(b)(6) approving any formulation if it allows the identity of the collateral to be objectively determined confirms this same policy of receptivity to parol clarification. Objective determination contrasts with subjective selection by a debtor or creditor. *See Secured Transactions* § 2A.05[8] for the case law on parol evidence. The definition of "agreement" in U.C.C. § 1-201(3) also supports use of parol evidence in applying the description of security agreements.

Official Comment

1. **Source.** Former Sections 9-110, 9-115(3).

2. **General Rules.** Subsection (a) retains substantially the same formulation as former Section 9-110. Subsection (b) expands upon subsection (a) by indicating a variety of ways in which a description might reasonably identify collateral. Whereas a provision similar to subsection (b) was applicable only to investment property under former Section 9-115(3), subsection (b) applies to all types of collateral, subject to the limitation in subsection (d). Subsection (b) is subject to subsection (c), which follows prevailing case law and adopts the view that an "all assets" or "all personal property" description for purposes of a *security agreement* is *not* sufficient. Note, however, that under Section 9-504, a *financing statement* sufficiently indicates the collateral if it "covers all assets or all personal property."

The purpose of requiring a description of collateral in a security agreement under Section 9-203 is evidentiary. The test of sufficiency of a description under this section, as under former Section 9-110, is that the description do the job assigned to it: make possible the identification of the collateral described. This section rejects any requirement that a description is insufficient unless it is exact and detailed (the so-called "serial number" test).

3. **After-Acquired Collateral.** Much litigation has arisen over whether a description in a security agreement is sufficient to include after-acquired collateral if the agreement does not explicitly so provide. This question is one of contract interpretation and is not susceptible to a statutory rule (other than a rule to the effect that it is a question of contract interpretation). Accordingly, this section contains no reference to descriptions of after-acquired collateral.

4. **Investment Property.** Under subsection (d), the use of the wrong Article 8 terminology does not render a description invalid (e.g., a security agreement

intended to cover a debtor's "security entitlements" is sufficient if it refers to the debtor's "securities"). Note also that given the broad definition of "securities account" in Section 8-501, a security interest in a securities account also includes all other rights of the debtor against the securities intermediary arising out of the securities account. For example, a security interest in a securities account would include credit balances due to the debtor from the securities intermediary, whether or not they are proceeds of a security entitlement. Moreover, describing collateral as a securities account is a simple way of describing all of the security entitlements carried in the account.

5. **Consumer Investment Property; Commercial Tort Claims.** Subsection (e) requires greater specificity of description in order to prevent debtors from inadvertently encumbering certain property. Subsection (e) requires that a description by defined "type" of collateral alone of a commercial tort claim or, in a consumer transaction, of a security entitlement, securities account, or commodity account, is not sufficient. For example, "all existing and after-acquired investment property" or "all existing and after-acquired security entitlements," without more, would be insufficient in a consumer transaction to describe a security entitlement, securities account, or commodity account. The reference to "*only* by type" in subsection (e) means that a description is sufficient if it satisfies subsection (a) and contains a descriptive component beyond the "type" alone. Moreover, if the collateral consists of a securities account or commodity account, a description of the account is sufficient to cover all existing and future security entitlements or commodity contracts carried in the account. See Section 9-203(h), (i).

Under Section 9-204, an after-acquired collateral clause in a security agreement will not reach future commercial tort claims. It follows that when an effective security agreement covering a commercial tort claim is entered into the claim already will exist. Subsection (e) does not require a description to be specific. For example, a description such as "all tort claims arising out of the explosion of debtor's factory" would suffice, even if the exact amount of the claim, the theory on which it may be based, and the identity of the tortfeasor(s) are not described. (Indeed, those facts may not be known at the time.)

[SUBPART 2.   APPLICABILITY OF ARTICLE]

§ 9-109.   SCOPE.

(a)   [General scope of article.] Except as otherwise provided in subsections (c) and (d), this article applies to:

(1)   a transaction, regardless of its form, that creates a security interest in personal property or fixtures by contract;

ANALYSIS

Under old § 9-102(1)(a) the primary test for application of Article 9 is whether the parties intend to create a security interest. The wording of new § 9-109(a)(1) suggests a switch from an *intent* test to an *effects* test. The decisive issue will become whether the transaction has the effect of producing a security interest. However, Official Comment 2 to this section says that no change in meaning is intended. *See Secured Transactions* § 3.02.

(2) an agricultural lien;

(3) a sale of accounts, chattel paper, payment intangibles, or promissory notes;

(4) a consignment;

(5) a security interest arising under Section 2-401, 2-505, 2-711(3), or 2A-508(5), as provided in Section 9-110; and

(6) a security interest arising under Section 4-210 or 5-118.

ANALYSIS

The declaration that Article 9 "applies" does not mean that all of the rules of Article 9 apply. For example, agricultural liens are generally subject to the rules addressing perfection, priority and default, but not to the rules concerning security agreements or attachment of security interests. *See Secured Transactions* § 1A.03[1]. True consignments of the type falling within new § 9-102(a)(20) are definitely subject to the rules on perfection and priority and are seemingly subject to the rules addressing attachment, but are hardly subject to the default rules at all. *See Secured Transactions* § 1A.03[2]. A buyer of payment intangibles and promissory notes enjoys a similar exemption from the default rules. *See Secured Transactions* § 1A.03[3]. A principal reason for applying Article 9 to agricultural liens and true consignments is to require the lienholder or consignor to give public notice of its interest by filing a financing statement. But sales of payment intangibles and promissory notes are automatically perfected. *See* new § 9-309(3) & (4). The revisers were not interested in giving public notice of those sales, but in assuring that a sale could not be undone by a trustee in bankruptcy. It is better to ask whether a particular rule of the new Article 9 governs an aspect of a transaction rather than whether the new Article as a whole applies to a relationship.

For analysis of the priority implications of bringing sales of promissory notes and payment intangibles within Article 9 see the text analysis to new § 9-309.

(b) [Security interest in secured obligation.] The application of this article to a security interest in a secured obligation is not affected by the fact that the obligation is itself secured by a transaction or interest to which this article does not apply.

(c) [Extent to which article does not apply.] This article does not apply to the extent that:

(1)   a statute, regulation, or treaty of the United States preempts this article;

(2)   another statute of this State expressly governs the creation, perfection, priority, or enforcement of a security interest created by this State or a governmental unit of this State;

(3)   a statute of another State, a foreign country, or a governmental unit of another State or a foreign country, other than a statute generally applicable to security interests, expressly governs creation, perfection, priority, or enforcement of a security interest created by the State, country, or governmental unit; or

(4)   the rights of a transferee beneficiary or nominated person under a letter of credit are independent and superior under Section 5-114.

(d) [Inapplicability of article.] This article does not apply to:

(1)   a landlord's lien, other than an agricultural lien;

(2)   a lien, other than an agricultural lien, given by statute or other rule of law for services or materials, but Section 9-333 applies with respect to priority of the lien;

(3)   an assignment of a claim for wages, salary, or other compensation of an employee;

(4)   a sale of accounts, chattel paper, payment intangibles, or promissory notes as part of a sale of the business out of which they arose;

(5)   an assignment of accounts, chattel paper, payment intangibles, or promissory notes which is for the purpose of collection only;

(6)   an assignment of a right to payment under a contract to an assignee that is also obligated to perform under the contract;

(7)   an assignment of a single account, payment intangible, or promissory note to an assignee in full or partial satisfaction of a preexisting indebtedness;

(8)   a transfer of an interest in or an assignment of a claim under a policy of insurance, other than an assignment by or to a health-care provider of a health-care-insurance receivable and any subsequent assignment of the right to payment, but Sections 9-315 and 9-322 apply with respect to proceeds and priorities in proceeds;

(9)   an assignment of a right represented by a judgment, other than a judgment taken on a right to payment that was collateral;

(10)   a right of recoupment or set-off, but:

(A)   Section 9-340 applies with respect to the effectiveness of rights of recoupment or set-off against deposit accounts; and

(B)   Section 9-404 applies with respect to defenses or claims of an account debtor;

(11)   the creation or transfer of an interest in or lien on real property, including a lease or rents thereunder, except to the extent that provision is made for:

(A)   liens on real property in Sections 9-203 and 9-308;

(B)   fixtures in Section 9-334;

(C)   fixture filings in Sections 9-501, 9-502, 9-512, 9-516, and 9-519; and

(D)   security agreements covering personal and real property in Section 9-604;

(12)   an assignment of a claim arising in tort, other than a commercial tort claim, but Sections 9-315 and 9-322 apply with respect to proceeds and priorities in proceeds; or

(13)   an assignment of a deposit account in a consumer transaction, but Sections 9-315 and 9-322 apply with respect to proceeds and priorities in proceeds.

ANALYSIS

The most important expansion in floating lien financing under the Revised Article 9 will spring from the new treatment of interests in deposit accounts. Under old § 9-104(1) a creditor could only have an Article 9 interest in a deposit account as proceeds of some other form of collateral (*e.g.* inventory, accounts). New § 9-109(13) continues that limitation only for consumer transactions. The business debtor's most liquid asset can now be part of the Article 9 collateral package. The business financer will now routinely be asking for an Article 9 interest in the bank accounts of the debtor firm. The firm seeking financing will seldom have the leverage to resist that request. The financer will no longer have to trace bank balances back to other forms of collateral or to struggle with the restrictions placed on a proceeds claim to commingled deposit accounts in bankruptcy. Old § 9-306(4)(d) is repealed by the new Article 9. The financer will only need to establish control over the bank deposits to have assured a perfected interest in them. In this scheme bank financers are preferred. A bank financer automatically has control over deposit accounts maintained with it (new § 9-104(a)(1)) and has a perfected proceeds interest in those funds if they are moved to an account in a different bank (new § 9-315(d)(2)). *See Secured Transactions* §§ 1A.03[4][b], 6D.02[7].

Official Comment

1. **Source.** Former Sections 9-102, 9-104.

2. **Basic Scope Provision.** Subsection (a)(1) derives from former Section 9-102(1) and (2). These subsections have been combined and shortened. No change in meaning is intended. Under subsection (a)(1), all consensual security interests in personal property and fixtures are covered by this Article, except for transactions excluded by subsections (c) and (d). As to which transactions give rise to a "security interest," the definition of that term in Section 1-201 must be consulted. When a security interest is created, this Article applies regardless of the form of the transaction or the name that parties have given to it.

3. **Agricultural Liens.** Subsection (a)(2) is new. It expands the scope of this Article to cover agricultural liens, as defined in Section 9-102.

4. **Sales of Accounts, Chattel Paper, Payment Intangibles, Promissory Notes, and Other Receivables.** Under subsection (a)(3), as under former Section 9-102, this Article applies to sales of accounts and chattel paper. This approach generally has been successful in avoiding difficult problems of distinguishing between transactions in which a receivable secures an obligation and those in which the receivable has been sold outright. In many commercial financing transactions the distinction is blurred.

Subsection (a)(3) expands the scope of this Article by including the sale of a "payment intangible" (defined in Section 9-102 as "a general intangible under which the account debtor's principal obligation is a monetary obligation") and a "promissory note" (also defined in Section 9-102). To a considerable extent, this Article affords these transactions treatment identical to that given sales of accounts and chattel paper. In some respects, however, sales of payment intangibles and promissory notes are treated differently from sales of other receivables. See, e.g., Sections 9-309 (automatic perfection upon attachment), 9-408 (effect of restrictions on assignment). By virtue of the expanded definition of "account" (defined in Section 9-102), this Article now covers sales of (and other security interests in) "health-care-insurance receivables" (also defined in Section 9-102). Although this Article occasionally distinguishes between outright sales of receivables and sales that secure an obligation, neither this Article nor the definition of "security interest" (Section 1-201(37)) delineates how a particular transaction is to be classified. That issue is left to the courts.

5. **Transfer of Ownership in Sales of Receivables.** A "sale" of an account, chattel paper, a promissory note, or a payment intangible includes a sale of a right in the receivable, such as a sale of a participation interest. The term also includes the sale of an enforcement right. For example, a "[p]erson entitled to enforce" a negotiable promissory note (Section 3-301) may sell its ownership rights in the instrument. See Section 3-203, Comment 1 ("Ownership rights in instruments may be determined by principles of the law of property, independent of Article 3, which do not depend upon whether the instrument was transferred under Section 3-203."). Also, the right under Section 3-309 to enforce a lost, destroyed, or stolen negotiable promissory note may be sold to a purchaser who could enforce that right by causing the seller to provide the proof required under that section. This Article rejects decisions reaching a contrary result, e.g., *Dennis Joslin Co. v. Robinson Broadcasting*, 977 F. Supp. 491 (D.D.C. 1997).

Nothing in this section or any other provision of Article 9 prevents the transfer of full and complete ownership of an account, chattel paper, an instrument, or a payment intangible in a transaction of sale. However, as mentioned in Comment 4, neither this Article nor the definition of "security interest" in Section 1-201 provides rules for distinguishing sales transactions from those that create a security interest securing an obligation. This Article applies to both types of transactions. The principal effect of this coverage is to apply this Article's perfection and priority rules to these sales transactions. Use of terminology such as "security interest," "debtor," and "collateral" is merely a drafting convention adopted to reach this end, and its use has no relevance to distinguishing sales from other transactions. See PEB Commentary No. 14.

Following a debtor's outright sale and transfer of ownership of a receivable, the debtor-seller retains no legal or equitable rights in the receivable that has been sold. See Section 9-318(a). This is so whether or not the buyer's security interest is perfected. (A security interest arising from the sale of a promissory note or payment intangible is perfected upon attachment without further action. See Section 9-309.) However, if the buyer's interest in accounts or chattel paper is unperfected, a subsequent lien creditor, perfected secured party, or qualified buyer can reach the sold receivable and achieve priority over (or take free of) the buyer's unperfected security interest under Section 9-317. This is so not because the seller of a receivable retains rights in the property sold; it does not. Nor is this so because the seller of a receivable is a "debtor" and the buyer of a receivable is a "secured party" under this Article (they are). It is so for the simple reason that Sections 9-318(b), 9-317, and 9-322 make it so, as did former Sections 9-301 and 9-312. Because the buyer's security interest is unperfected, for purposes of determining the rights of creditors of and purchasers for value from the debtor-seller, under Section 9-318(b) the debtor-seller is deemed to have the rights and title it sold. Section 9-317 subjects the buyer's unperfected interest in accounts and chattel paper to that of the debtor-seller's lien creditor and other persons who qualify under that section.

6. **Consignments.** Subsection (a)(4) is new. This Article applies to every "consignment." The term, defined in Section 9-102, includes many but not all "true" consignments (i.e., bailments for the purpose of sale). If a transaction is a "sale or return," as defined in revised Section 2-326, it is not a "consignment." In a "sale or return" transaction, the buyer becomes the owner of the goods, and the seller may obtain an enforceable security interest in the goods only by satisfying the requirements of Section 9-203.

Under common law, creditors of a bailee were unable to reach the interest of the bailor (in the case of a consignment, the consignor-owner). Like former Section 2-326 and former Article 9, this Article changes the common-law result; however, it does so in a different manner. For purposes of determining the rights and interests of third-party creditors of, and purchasers of the goods from, the consignee, but not for other purposes, such as remedies of the consignor, the consignee is deemed to acquire under this Article whatever rights and title the consignor had or had power to transfer. See Section 9-319. The interest of a consignor is defined to be a security interest under revised Section 1-201(37), more specifically, a purchase-money security interest in the consignee's inventory. See Section 9-103(d). Thus, the rules pertaining to lien creditors, buyers, and attachment, perfection, and priority of competing security interests apply to consigned goods. The relationship between the consignor and consignee is left to other law. Consignors also have no duties under Part 6. See Section 9-601(g).

Sometimes parties characterize transactions that secure an obligation (other than the bailee's obligation to returned bailed goods) as "consignments." These transactions are not "consignments" as contemplated by Section 9-109(a)(4). See Section 9-102. This Article applies also to these transactions, by virtue of Section 9-109(a)(1). They create a security interest within the meaning of the first sentence of Section 1-201(37).

This Article does not apply to bailments for sale that fall outside the definition of "consignment" in Section 9-102 and that do not create a security interest that secures an obligation.

7. **Security Interest in Obligation Secured by Non-Article 9 Transaction.** Subsection (b) is unchanged in substance from former Section 9-102(3). The following example provides an illustration.

Example 1: O borrows $10,000 from M and secures its repayment obligation, evidenced by a promissory note, by granting to M a mortgage on O's land. This Article does not apply to the creation of the real-property mortgage. However, if M sells the promissory note to X or gives a security interest in the note to secure M's own obligation to X, this Article applies to the security interest thereby created in favor of X. The security interest in the promissory note is covered by this Article even though the note is secured by a real-property mortgage. Also, X's security interest in the note gives X an attached security interest in the mortgage lien that secures the note and, if the security interest in the note is perfected, the security interest in the mortgage lien likewise is perfected. See Sections 9-203, 9-308.

It also follows from subsection (b) that an attempt to obtain or perfect a security interest in a secured obligation by complying with non-Article 9 law, as by an assignment of record of a real-property mortgage, would be ineffective. Finally, it is implicit from subsection (b) that one cannot obtain a security interest in a lien, such as a mortgage on real property, that is not also coupled with an equally effective security interest in the secured obligation. This Article rejects cases such as *In re Maryville Savings & Loan Corp.*, 743 F.2d 413 (6th Cir. 1984), clarified on reconsideration, 760 F.2d 119 (1985).

8. **Federal Preemption.** Former Section 9-104(a) excluded from Article 9 "a security interest subject to any statute of the United States, to the extent that such statute governs the rights of parties to and third parties affected by transactions in particular types of property." Some (erroneously) read the former section to suggest that Article 9 sometimes deferred to federal law even when federal law did not preempt Article 9. Subsection (c)(1) recognizes explicitly that this Article defers to federal law only when and to the extent that it must-i.e., when federal law preempts it.

9. **Governmental Debtors.** Former Section 9-104(e) excluded transfers by governmental debtors. It has been revised and replaced by the exclusions in new paragraphs (2) and (3) of subsection (c). These paragraphs reflect the view that Article 9 should apply to security interests created by a State, foreign country, or a "governmental unit" (defined in Section 9-102) of either except to the extent that another statute governs the issue in question. Under paragraph (2), this Article defers to all statutes of the forum State. (A forum cannot determine whether it should consult the choice-of-law rules in the forum's UCC unless it first determines that its UCC applies to the transaction before it.) Paragraph (3) defers to statutes of another State or a foreign country only to the extent that those statutes contain rules applicable specifically to security interests created by the governmental unit in question.

Example 2: A New Jersey state commission creates a security interest in favor of a New York bank. The validity of the security interest is litigated in New York. The relevant security agreement provides that it is governed by New York law. To the extent that a New Jersey statute contains rules peculiar to creation of security interests by governmental units generally, to creation of security interests by state commissions, or to creation of security interests by this particular state commission, then that law will govern. On the other hand, to the extent that New Jersey law provides that security interests created by governmental units, state commissions, or this state commission are governed by the law generally applicable to secured transactions (i.e., New Jersey's Article 9), then New York's Article 9 will govern.

Example 3: An airline that is an instrumentality of a foreign country creates a security interest in favor of a New York bank. The analysis used in the previous example would apply here. That is, if the matter is litigated in New York, New York law would govern except to the extent that the foreign country enacted a statute applicable to security interests created by governmental units generally or by the airline specifically.

The fact that New York law applies does not necessarily mean that perfection is accomplished by filing in New York. Rather, it means that the court should apply New York's Article 9, including its choice-of-law provisions. Under New York's Section 9-301, perfection is governed by the law of the jurisdiction in which the debtor is located. Section 9-307 determines the debtor's location for choice-of-law purposes.

If a transaction does not bear an appropriate relation to the forum State, then that State's Article 9 will not apply, regardless of whether the transaction would be excluded by paragraph (3).

Example 4: A Belgian governmental unit grants a security interest in its equipment to a Swiss secured party. The equipment is located in Belgium. A dispute arises and, for some reason, an action is brought in a New Mexico state court. Inasmuch as the transaction bears no "appropriate relation" to New Mexico, New Mexico's UCC, including its Article 9, is inapplicable. See Section 1-105(1). New Mexico's Section 9-109(c) on excluded transactions should not come into play. Even if the parties agreed that New Mexico law would govern, the parties' agreement would not be effective because the transaction does not bear a "reasonable relation" to New Mexico. See Section 1-105(1).

Conversely, Article 9 will come into play only if the litigation arises in a UCC jurisdiction or if a foreign choice-of-law rule leads a foreign court to apply the law of a UCC jurisdiction. For example, if issues concerning a security interest granted by a foreign airline to a New York bank are litigated overseas, the court may be bound to apply the law of the debtor's jurisdiction and not New York's Article 9.

10. **Certain Statutory and Common-Law Liens; Interests in Real Property.** With few exceptions (nonconsensual agricultural liens being one), this Article applies only to consensual security interests in personal property. Following former Section 9-104(b) and (j), paragraphs (1) and (11) of

subsection (d) exclude landlord's liens and leases and most other interests in or liens on real property. These exclusions generally reiterate the limitations on coverage (i.e., "by contract," "in personal property and fixtures") made explicit in subsection (a)(1). Similarly, most jurisdictions provide special liens to suppliers of many types of services and materials, either by statute or by common law. With the exception of agricultural liens, it is not necessary for this Article to provide general codification of this lien structure, which is determined in large part by local conditions and which is far removed from ordinary commercial financing. As under former Section 9-104(c), subsection (d)(2) excludes these suppliers' liens (other than agricultural liens) from this Article. However, Section 9-333 provides a rule for determining priorities between certain possessory suppliers' liens and security interests covered by this Article.

11. **Wage and Similar Claims.** As under former Section 9-104(d), subsection (d)(3) excludes assignments of claims for wages and the like from this Article. These assignments present important social issues that other law addresses. The Federal Trade Commission has ruled that, with some exceptions, the taking of an assignment of wages or other earnings is an unfair act or practice under the Federal Trade Commission Act. See 16 C.F.R. Part 444. State statutes also may regulate such assignments.

12. **Certain Sales and Assignments of Receivables; Judgments.** In general this Article covers security interests in (including sales of) accounts, chattel paper, payment intangibles, and promissory notes. Paragraphs (4), (5), (6), and (7) of subsection (d) exclude from the Article certain sales and assignments of receivables that, by their nature, do not concern commercial financing transactions. These paragraphs add to the exclusions in former Section 9-104(f) analogous sales and assignments of payment intangibles and promissory notes. For similar reasons, subsection (d)(9) retains the exclusion of assignments of judgments under former Section 9-104(h) (other than judgments taken on a right to payment that itself was collateral under this Article).

13. **Insurance.** Subsection (d)(8) narrows somewhat the broad exclusion of interests in insurance policies under former Section 9-104(g). This Article now covers assignments by or to a health-care provider of "health-care-insurance receivables" (defined in Section 9-102).

14. **Set-Off.** Subsection (d)(10) adds two exceptions to the general exclusion of set-off rights from Article 9 under former Section 9-104(i). The first takes account of new Section 9-340, which regulates the effectiveness of a set-off against a deposit account that stands as collateral. The second recognizes Section 9-404, which affords the obligor on an account, chattel paper, or general intangible the right to raise claims and defenses against an assignee (secured party).

15. **Tort Claims.** Subsection (d)(12) narrows somewhat the broad exclusion of transfers of tort claims under former Section 9-104(k). This Article

now applies to assignments of "commercial tort claims" (defined in Section 9-102) as well as to security interests in tort claims that constitute proceeds of other collateral (e.g., a right to payment for negligent destruction of the debtor's inventory). Note that once a claim arising in tort has been settled and reduced to a contractual obligation to pay (as in, but not limited to, a structured settlement) the right to payment becomes a payment intangible and ceases to be a claim arising in tort.

This Article contains two special rules governing creation of a security interest in tort claims. First, a description of collateral in a security agreement as "all tort claims" is insufficient to meet the requirement for attachment. See Section 9-108(e). Second, no security interest attaches under an after-acquired property clause to a tort claim. See Section 9-204(b). In addition, this Article does not determine whom the tortfeasor must pay to discharge its obligation. Inasmuch as a tortfeasor is not an "account debtor," the rules governing waiver of defenses and discharge of an obligation by an obligor (Sections 9-403, 9-404, 9-405, and 9-406) are inapplicable to tort-claim collateral.

16. **Deposit Accounts.** Except in consumer transactions, deposit accounts may be taken as original collateral under this Article. Under former Section 9-104(*l*), deposit accounts were excluded as original collateral, leaving security interests in deposit accounts to be governed by the common law. The common law is nonuniform, often difficult to discover and comprehend, and frequently costly to implement. As a consequence, debtors who wished to use deposit accounts as collateral sometimes were precluded from doing so as a practical matter. By excluding deposit accounts from the Article's scope as original collateral in consumer transactions, subsection (d)(13) leaves those transactions to law other than this Article. However, in both consumer and non-consumer transactions, sections 9-315 and 9-322 apply to deposit accounts as proceeds and with respect to priorities in proceeds.

This Article contains several safeguards to protect debtors against inadvertently encumbering deposit accounts and to reduce the likelihood that a secured party will realize a windfall from a debtor's deposit accounts. For example, because "deposit account" is a separate type of collateral, a security agreement covering general intangibles will not adequately describe deposit accounts. Rather, a security agreement must reasonably identify the deposit accounts that are the subject of a security interest, e.g., by using the term "deposit accounts." See Section 9-108. To perfect a security interest in a deposit account as original collateral, a secured party (other than the bank with which the deposit account is maintained) must obtain "control" of the account either by obtaining the bank's authenticated agreement or by becoming the bank's customer with respect to the deposit account. See Sections 9-312(b)(1), 9-104. Either of these steps requires the debtor's consent.

This Article also contains new rules that determine which State's law governs perfection and priority of a security interest in a deposit account

(Section 9-304), priority of conflicting security interests in and set-off rights against a deposit account (Sections 9-327, 9-340), the rights of transferees of funds from an encumbered deposit account (Section 9-332), the obligations of the bank (Section 9-341), enforcement of security interests in a deposit account (Section 9-607(c)), and the duty of a secured party to terminate control of a deposit account (Section 9-208(b)).

§ 9-110. SECURITY INTERESTS ARISING UNDER ARTICLE 2 OR 2A. A security interest arising under Section 2-401, 2-505, 2-711(3), or 2A-508(5) is subject to this article. However, until the debtor obtains possession of the goods:

(1)   the security interest is enforceable, even if Section 9-203(b)(3) has not been satisfied;

(2)   filing is not required to perfect the security interest;

(3)   the rights of the secured party after default by the debtor are governed by Article 2 or 2A; and

(4)   the security interest has priority over a conflicting security interest created by the debtor.

ANALYSIS

This section comes into play when there are priority contests between unpaid suppliers of the debtor and the debtor's secured creditor. The new priority rule of subsection (4) seems to be generally consistent with the results reached in the cases by manipulating the "rights" concept to hold that the debtor-buyer does not obtain rights in the goods until it takes possession of them. *See Secured Transactions* § 2B.04. The unpaid seller seeking to withhold or stop delivery should still be able to prevail under the "rights" analysis even though the right to withhold or stop did not make the list of Article 2 security interest protected by this section. See the reference to § 2-403(1) in Official Comment 5 to this section.

Official Comment

1. **Source.** Former Section 9-113.

2. **Background.** Former Section 9-113, from which this section derives, referred generally to security interests "arising solely under the Article on Sales (Article 2) or the Article on Leases (Article 2A)." Views differed as

to the precise scope of that section. In contrast, Section 9-110 specifies the security interests to which it applies.

3. **Security Interests Under Articles 2 and 2A.** Section 2-505 explains how a seller of goods may reserve a security interest in them. Section 2-401 indicates that a reservation of title by the seller of goods, despite delivery to the buyer, is limited to reservation of a security interest. As did former Article 9, this Article governs a security interest arising solely under one of those sections; however, until the buyer obtains possession of the goods, the security interest is enforceable even in the absence of a security agreement, filing is not necessary to perfect the security interest, and the seller-secured party's rights on the buyer's default are governed by Article 2.

Sections 2-711(3) and 2A-508(5) create a security interest in favor of a buyer or lessee in possession of goods that were rightfully rejected or as to which acceptance was justifiably revoked. As did former Article 9, this Article governs a security interest arising solely under one of those sections; however, until the seller or lessor obtains possession of the goods, the security interest is enforceable even in the absence of a security agreement, filing is not necessary to perfect the security interest, and the secured party's (buyer's or lessee's) rights on the debtor's (seller's or lessor's) default are governed by Article 2 or 2A, as the case may be.

4. **Priority.** This section adds to former Section 9-113 a priority rule. Until the debtor obtains possession of the goods, a security interest arising under one of the specified sections of Article 2 or 2A has priority over conflicting security interests created by the debtor. Thus, a security interest arising under Section 2-401 or 2-505 has priority over a conflicting security interest in the buyer's after-acquired goods, even if the goods in question are inventory. Arguably, the same result would obtain under Section 9-322, but even if it would not, a purchase-money-like priority is appropriate. Similarly, a security interest under Section 2-711(3) or 2A-508(5) has priority over security interests claimed by the seller's or lessor's secured lender. This result is appropriate, inasmuch as the payments giving rise to the debt secured by the Article 2 or 2A security interest are likely to be included among the lender's proceeds.

Example: Seller owns equipment subject to a security interest created by Seller in favor of Lender. Buyer pays for the equipment, accepts the goods, and then justifiably revokes acceptance. As long as Seller does not recover possession of the equipment, Buyer's security interest under Section 2-711(3) is senior to that of Lender.

In the event that a security interest referred to in this section conflicts with a security interest that is created by a person other than the debtor, Section 9-325 applies. Thus, if Lender's security interest in the example was created not by Seller but by the person from whom Seller acquired the goods, Section 9-325 would govern.

5. **Relationship to Other Rights and Remedies Under Articles 2 and 2A.** This Article does not specifically address the conflict between (i) a security interest created by a buyer or lessee and (ii) the seller's or lessor's right to withhold delivery under Section 2-702(1), 2-703(a), or 2A-525, the seller's or lessor's right to stop delivery under Section 2-705 or 2A-526, or the seller's right to reclaim under Section 2-507(2) or 2-702(2). These conflicts are governed by the first sentence of Section 2-403(1), under which the buyer's secured party obtains no greater rights in the goods than the buyer had or had power to convey, or Section 2A-307(1), under which creditors of the lessee take subject to the lease contract.

PART 2 EFFECTIVENESS OF SECURITY AGREEMENT; ATTACHMENT OF SECURITY INTEREST; RIGHTS OF PARTIES TO SECURITY AGREEMENT

[SUBPART 1. EFFECTIVENESS AND ATTACHMENT]

§ 9-201. GENERAL EFFECTIVENESS OF SECURITY AGREEMENT.

   (a) [General effectiveness.] Except as otherwise provided in [the Uniform Commercial Code], a security agreement is effective according to its terms between the parties, against purchasers of the collateral, and against creditors.

   (b) [Applicable consumer laws and other law.] A transaction subject to this article is subject to any applicable rule of law which establishes a different rule for consumers and [insert reference to (i) any other statute or regulation that regulates the rates, charges, agreements, and practices for loans, credit sales, or other extensions of credit and (ii) any consumer-protection statute or regulation].

   (c) [Other applicable law controls.] In case of conflict between this article and a rule of law, statute, or regulation described in subsection (b), the rule of law, statute, or regulation controls. Failure to comply with a statute or regulation described in subsection (b) has only the effect the statute or regulation specifies.

   (d) [Further deference to other applicable law.] This article does not:

   (1) validate any rate, charge, agreement, or practice that violates a rule of law, statute, or regulation described in subsection (b); or

   (2) extend the application of the rule of law, statute, or regulation to a transaction not otherwise subject to it.

Official Comment

   1. **Source.** Former Sections 9-201, 9-203(4).

   2. **Effectiveness of Security Agreement.** Subsection (a) provides that a security agreement is generally effective. With certain exceptions, a security agreement is effective between the debtor and secured party and is likewise effective against third parties. Note that "security agreement" is used here

(and elsewhere in this Article) as it is defined in Section 9-102: "an agreement that creates or provides for a security interest." It follows that subsection (a) does not provide that every term or provision contained in a record that contains a security agreement or that is so labeled is effective. Properly read, former Section 9-201 was to the same effect. Exceptions to the general rule of subsection (a) arise where there is an overriding provision in this Article or any other Article of the UCC. For example, Section 9-317 subordinates unperfected security interests to lien creditors and certain buyers, and several provisions in Part 3 subordinate some security interests to other security interests and interests of purchasers.

3. **Law, Statutes, and Regulations Applicable to Certain Transactions.** Subsection (b) makes clear that certain transactions, although subject to this Article, also are subject to other applicable laws relating to consumers or specified in that subsection. Subsection (c) provides that the other law is controlling in the event of a conflict, and that a violation of other law does not *ipso facto* constitute a violation of this Article. Subsection (d) provides that this Article does not validate violations under or extend the application of the other applicable laws.

§ 9-202.   TITLE TO COLLATERAL IMMATERIAL. Except as otherwise provided with respect to consignments or sales of accounts, chattel paper, payment intangibles, or promissory notes, the provisions of this article with regard to rights and obligations apply whether title to collateral is in the secured party or the debtor.

Official Comment

1. **Source.** Former Section 9-202.

2. **Title Immaterial.** The rights and duties of parties to a secured transaction and affected third parties are provided in this Article without reference to the location of "title" to the collateral. For example, the characteristics of a security interest that secures the purchase price of goods are the same whether the secured party appears to have retained title or the debtor appears to have obtained title and then conveyed title or a lien to the secured party.

3. **When Title Matters.**

a. **Under This Article.** This section explicitly acknowledges two circumstances in which the effect of certain Article 9 provisions turns on ownership (title). First, in some respects sales of accounts, chattel paper, payment intangibles, and promissory notes receive special treatment. See, e.g., Sections 9-207(a), 9-210(b), 9-615(e). Buyers of receivables under former Article 9 were treated specially, as well. See, e.g., former Section 9-502(2). Second, the remedies of a consignor under a true consignment and, for the most part, the remedies of a buyer of accounts, chattel paper, payment intangibles, or promissory notes are determined by other law and not by Part 6. See Section 9-601(g).

b. **Under Other Law.** This Article does not determine which line of interpretation (e.g., title theory or lien theory, retained title or conveyed title) should be followed in cases in which the applicability of another rule of law depends upon who has title. If, for example, a revenue law imposes a tax on the "legal" owner of goods or if a corporation law makes a vote of the stockholders prerequisite to a corporation "giving" a security interest but not if it acquires property "subject" to a security interest, this Article does not attempt to define whether the secured party is a "legal" owner or whether the transaction "gives" a security interest for the purpose of such laws. Other rules of law or the agreement of the parties determines the location and source of title for those purposes.

§ 9-203. ATTACHMENT AND ENFORCEABILITY OF SECURITY INTEREST; PROCEEDS; SUPPORTING OBLIGATIONS; FORMAL REQUISITES.

(a) [Attachment.] A security interest attaches to collateral when it becomes enforceable against the debtor with respect to the collateral, unless an agreement expressly postpones the time of attachment.

(b) [Enforceability.] Except as otherwise provided in subsections (c) through (i), a security interest is enforceable against the debtor and third parties with respect to the collateral only if:

(1) value has been given;

(2) the debtor has rights in the collateral or the power to transfer rights in the collateral to a secured party; and

ANALYSIS

The words "power to transfer rights in the collateral" are new in the Revision. The case law under the old Article 9 treats the debtor as having rights in the collateral even though its rights are based on estoppel, the doctrine of good faith purchase or some other principle of negotiability. The revisers insist that it is more precise to say that in these circumstances the debtor has the power to transfer rights. Presumably, this change was not intended to have substantive impact. But under the new language some courts may find it easier in close cases to say that the debtor has the power to transfer rights. *See Secured Transactions* Ch. 2B.

(3)   one of the following conditions is met:

(A)   the debtor has authenticated a security agreement that provides a description of the collateral and, if the security interest covers timber to be cut, a description of the land concerned;

(B)   the collateral is not a certificated security and is in the possession of the secured party under Section 9-313 pursuant to the debtor's security agreement;

(C)   the collateral is a certificated security in registered form and the security certificate has been delivered to the secured party under Section 8-301 pursuant to the debtor's security agreement; or

(D)   the collateral is deposit accounts, electronic chattel paper, investment property, or letter-of-credit rights, and the secured party has control under Section 9-104, 9-105, 9-106, or 9-107 pursuant to the debtor's security agreement.

(c)   [Other UCC provisions.] Subsection (b) is subject to Section 4-210 on the security interest of a collecting bank, Section 5-118 on the security interest of a letter-of-credit issuer or nominated person, Section 9-110 on a security interest arising under Article 2 or 2A, and Section 9-206 on security interests in investment property.

(d)   [When person becomes bound by another person's security agreement.] A person becomes bound as debtor by a security agreement entered into by another person if, by operation of law other than this article or by contract:

(1)   the security agreement becomes effective to create a security interest in the person's property; or

(2)   the person becomes generally obligated for the obligations of the other person, including the obligation secured under the security agreement, and acquires or succeeds to all or substantially all of the assets of the other person.

ANALYSIS

One of the most troublesome "new entity" situations is the incorporation (without notice to the secured creditor) of a debtor that originally operated as a sole proprietor. *See Secured Transactions* § 22.03. The corporation will typically succeed to the business assets and liabilities of the proprietor, but not to the personal assets and liabilities. Thus, it seems doubtful that the corporation will be bound to a security agreement executed by the proprietor under new § 9-203(d)(2). Note that none of the examples in the official comments to new § 9-326 address this type of case.

(e)   [Effect of new debtor becoming bound.] If a new debtor becomes bound as debtor by a security agreement entered into by another person:

(1)   the agreement satisfies subsection (b)(3) with respect to existing or after-acquired property of the new debtor to the extent the property is described in the agreement; and

(2)   another agreement is not necessary to make a security interest in the property enforceable.

(f)   [Proceeds and supporting obligations.] The attachment of a security interest in collateral gives the secured party the rights to proceeds provided by Section 9-315 and is also attachment of a security interest in a supporting obligation for the collateral.

(g)   [Lien securing right to payment.] The attachment of a security interest in a right to payment or performance secured by a security interest or other lien on personal or real property is also attachment of a security interest in the security interest, mortgage, or other lien.

(h) [Security entitlement carried in securities account.] The attachment of a security interest in a securities account is also attachment of a security interest in the security entitlements carried in the securities account.

(i) [Commodity contracts carried in commodity account.] The attachment of a security interest in a commodity account is also attachment of a security interest in the commodity contracts carried in the commodity account.

ANALYSIS

All statutes of frauds are subject to erosion in our times. In the original Article 9, § 9-203 stated a classic statute of frauds for non-possessory security interests: the security interest would not attach in the absence of a written security agreement signed by the debtor describing the collateral. Each new revision of § 9-203 recognizes new exceptions (some of them hidden in the original statutory scheme) or otherwise relaxes the traditional requirements. This new § 9-203 continues that trend.

It is no longer essential that the agreement be expressed in a writing signed by the debtor. Instead, it only needs to be preserved in a record authenticated by the debtor. Thus, it may be in a writing *or* stored in an electronic or other medium that is "retrievable in perceivable form." *See* new § 9-102(a)(7) & (69) and *Secured Transactions* § 1A.06[1]. If the secured party has "control" over a deposit account, electronic chattel paper, investment property or a letter-of-credit right, the security agreement may be oral. This control exception is more significant than it first seems because control does not require that the debtor be denied access to a deposit account or a securities entitlement and cannot realistically be considered the equivalent of common law possession with respect to these assets. A bank automatically has control over a deposit account maintained with it; a securities firm automatically has control over a securities entitlement with respect to a securities account maintained with it. New §§ 9-104(a); U.C.C. § 8-106(e). *See Secured Transactions* §§ 6D.02[7] and 23.12.

> *Example A*: Debtor Co. orally agrees that Valley Bank will have a security interest in all of the deposit accounts which Debtor Co. maintains with Valley Bank. Valley Bank is in control of those deposit accounts under new § 9-104(a)(1) even though Debtor Co. retains an unrestricted right to draw

on the deposited funds. The security interest of Valley Bank attaches under new § 9-203(b)(3)(D), is perfected under new § 9-314(a), and has priority over conflicting security interests in the deposit account under new § 9-327(3) except where the holder of the rival interest has become the bank's customer with respect to the deposit accounts. *Question*: How likely is it that the bank officer and the President of Debtor Co. will have different memories with respect to whether Debtor Co. orally agreed to such a security interest?

Example B: Investor orally agrees that Broker will have a security interest in the securities entitlement which Investor has *vis a vis* Broker with respect to Coca Cola securities held by Broker for Investor. Broker has control of the entitlement. § 8-106(e). The security interest attaches under new § 9-203(b)(3)(D), is perfected under new § 9-314(a), and has priority over conflicting security interests in the entitlement under § 9-328(3). (This result would also follow under Article 9 as amended in 1994 incident to the revision of Article 8). *Question*: How likely is it that the Investor and the official of the Broker handling the account will have different memories with respect to whether Investor orally agreed to such a security interest?

New § 9-203(d) also continues the erosion of this statute of frauds by binding the assets of entities that were not parties to the security agreement.

Example C: Ocean Inc. grants a security interest in all of its inventory presently owned or thereafter acquired to First Finance to secure advances made by First Finance. Beach Corp. agrees to acquire all of the assets of Ocean Inc. and to pay all of the obligations of Ocean Inc. including the debt owed to First Finance. New §§ 9-203(d)(2) and (e) give First Finance a security interest in the inventory of Beach Corp. then owned or thereafter acquired.

In addition, the new Article 9 erodes the statute of frauds policy by expressly expanding the categories of derivative interests in which the secured party has an interest even though the assets involved are not themselves included in the description of the collateral contained in the security agreement. As under old § 9-203(3), new § 9-203(f) provides that the security interest automatically attaches to the proceeds of described collateral. But the recognition of the derivative proceeds interest has greater significance under the new Article 9 because § 9-102(a)(64) greatly expands the range of assets that will fall in the proceeds bucket. *See Secured Transactions* §§ 1A.04[1] and 24.03.

> **Example D**: Patrick Co. grants a security interest in its equipment to the Bank of Banks. Patrick Co. then leases some of the equipment to Christopher Inc. Under the old § 9-306(1) the cases have held that the rental payments made under the leases are not proceeds of the equipment. *See Secured Transactions* § 24.03[2][a]. New § 9-102(a)(64)(A) declares the rental payments to be proceeds. The Bank of Banks has a security interest in the rental payments even though neither the leases nor the rentals were included in the description of the collateral.

Similarly, new § 9-203(f) for the first time expressly recognizes that the secured party has a derivative interest in supporting obligations.

> **Example E**: Patrick Co. grants a security interest in its accounts to the Bank of Banks. Patrick Co. sells goods on open account to Exporter with Exporter causing Big City Bank to open a letter of credit in favor of Patrick Co. to assure payment of the goods. The Bank of Banks has a security interest in the letter-of-credit rights of Patrick Co. because that right is a supporting obligation with respect to an account of Patrick Co. Under new § 9-102(a)(77) this result follows even though the security agreement of Patrick Co. and the Bank of Banks was silent as to letters of credit. The reporters for the new Article 9 believe this result to be "implicit" in the present law, but the case law on the issue is thin. *See Secured Transactions* § 1A.04[2]. The derivative interests of the Bank of Banks would be inferior to a security interest in the letter-of-credit right perfected through control, *i.e.* through an assignment of the right of Patrick Co. consented to by Big City Bank. New §§ 9-107 and 9-329(1).

The new Article 9 also adds to the list of security interests which arise automatically based on the circumstances of the transaction even though the debtor has not expressly agreed to the interest. The security interest of a collecting bank in a deposited check where that depositary bank has allowed a withdrawal of deposit credit given for the item is an example of such an "automatic" interest. New § 9-206, carrying forward a 1994 addition to the Code, recognizes such an interest in favor of the unpaid securities intermediary selling a securities entitlement or unpaid seller of some of the other financial assets. *See Secured Transactions* § 23.13[2]. Proposed new § 5-118 will recognize an automatic interest in documents accompanying letters of credit on behalf of an issuer or nominated person that honors or gives value for a draw under the credit.

The classic statute of frauds of the original Article 9 (a written agreement signed by the debtor describing the collateral) served evidentiary and cautionary policies that have seemed less compelling to each new revision group than the need ease the establishment of the secured creditor's interest. Each requirement of form imposed for an effective security agreement is a potential trap that the secured creditor may fail to satisfy. Erosion of the statute of frauds diminishes the risk that the secured creditor will stub its toe. In the case of electronic agreements, this erosion allows the creditor to transact, store and retrieve the agreement in what is often the least expensive form.

Official Comment

1. **Source.** Former Sections 9-203, 9-115(2), (6).

2. **Creation, Attachment, and Enforceability.** Subsection (a) states the general rule that a security interest attaches to collateral only when it becomes enforceable against the debtor. Subsection (b) specifies the circumstances under which a security interest becomes enforceable. Subsection (b) states three basic prerequisites to the existence of a security interest: value (paragraph (1)), rights or power to transfer rights in collateral (paragraph (2)), and agreement plus satisfaction of an evidentiary requirement (paragraph (3)). When all of these elements exist, a security interest becomes enforceable between the parties and attaches under subsection (a). Subsection (c) identifies certain exceptions to the general rule of subsection (b).

3. **Security Agreement; Authentication.** Under subsection (b)(3), enforceability requires the debtor's security agreement and compliance with an evidentiary requirement in the nature of a Statute of Frauds. Paragraph (3)(A) represents the most basic of the evidentiary alternatives, under which the debtor must authenticate a security agreement that provides a description of the collateral. Under Section 9-102, a "security agreement" is "an agreement that creates or provides for a security interest." Neither that definition nor the requirement of paragraph (3)(A) rejects the deeply rooted doctrine that a bill of sale, although absolute in form, may be shown in fact to have been given as security. Under this Article, as under prior law, a debtor may show by parol evidence that a transfer purporting to be absolute was in fact for security. Similarly, a self-styled "lease" may serve as a security agreement if the agreement creates a security interest. See Section 1-201(37) (distinguishing security interest from lease).

4. **Possession, Delivery, or Control Pursuant to Security Agreement.** The other alternatives in subsection (b)(3) dispense with the requirement of an authenticated security agreement and provide alternative evidentiary tests.

Under paragraph (3)(B), the secured party's possession substitutes for the debtor's authentication under paragraph (3)(A) if the secured party's possession is "pursuant to the debtor's security agreement." That phrase refers to the debtor's agreement to the secured party's possession for the purpose of creating a security interest. The phrase should not be confused with the phrase "debtor has authenticated a security agreement," used in paragraph (3)(A), which contemplates the debtor's authentication of a record. In the unlikely event that possession is obtained without the debtor's agreement, possession would not suffice as a substitute for an authenticated security agreement. However, once the security interest has become enforceable and has attached, it is not impaired by the fact that the secured party's possession is maintained without the agreement of a subsequent debtor (e.g., a transferee). Possession as contemplated by Section 9-313 is possession for purposes of subsection (b)(3)(B), even though it may not constitute possession "pursuant to the debtor's agreement" and consequently might not serve as a substitute for an authenticated security agreement under subsection (b)(3)(A). Subsection (b)(3)(C) provides that delivery of a certificated security to the secured party under Section 8-301 pursuant to the debtor's security agreement is sufficient as a substitute for an authenticated security agreement. Similarly, under subsection (b)(3)(D), control of investment property, a deposit account, electronic chattel paper, or a letter-of-credit right satisfies the evidentiary test if control is pursuant to the debtor's security agreement.

5. **Collateral Covered by Other Statute or Treaty.** One evidentiary purpose of the formal requisites stated in subsection (b) is to minimize the possibility of future disputes as to the terms of a security agreement (e.g., as to the property that stands as collateral for the obligation secured). One should distinguish the evidentiary functions of the formal requisites of attachment and enforceability (such as the requirement that a security agreement contain a description of the collateral) from the more limited goals of "notice filing" for financing statements under Part 5, explained in Section 9-502, Comment 2. When perfection is achieved by compliance with the requirements of a statute or treaty described in Section 9-311(a), such as a federal recording act or a certificate-of-title statute, the manner of describing the collateral in a registry imposed by the statute or treaty may or may not be adequate for purposes of this section and Section 9-108. However, the description contained in the security agreement, not the description in a public registry or on a certificate of title, controls for purposes of this section.

6. **Debtor's Rights; Debtor's Power to Transfer Rights.** Subsection (b)(2) conditions attachment on the debtor's having "rights in the collateral or the power to transfer rights in the collateral to a secured party." A debtor's limited rights in collateral, short of full ownership, are sufficient for a security interest to attach. However, in accordance with basic personal property conveyancing principles, the baseline rule is that a security interest attaches only to whatever rights a debtor may have, broad or limited as those rights may be.

Certain exceptions to the baseline rule enable a debtor to transfer, and a security interest to attach to, greater rights than the debtor has. See Part 3, Subpart 3 (priority rules). The phrase, "or the power to transfer rights in the collateral to a secured party," accommodates those exceptions. In some cases, a debtor may have power to transfer another person's rights only to a class of transferees that excludes secured parties. See, e.g., Section 2-403(2) (giving certain merchants power to transfer an entruster's rights to a buyer in ordinary course of business). Under those circumstances, the debtor would not have the power to create a security interest in the other person's rights, and the condition in subsection (b)(2) would not be satisfied.

7. **New Debtors.** Subsection (e) makes clear that the enforceability requirements of subsection (b)(3) are met when a new debtor becomes bound under an original debtor's security agreement. If a new debtor becomes bound as debtor by a security agreement entered into by another person, the security agreement satisfies the requirement of subsection (b)(3) as to the existing and after-acquired property of the new debtor to the extent the property is described in the agreement.

Subsection (d) explains when a new debtor becomes bound. Persons who become bound under paragraph (2) are limited to those who both become primarily liable for the original debtor's obligations and succeed to (or acquire) its assets. Thus, the paragraph excludes sureties and other secondary obligors as well as persons who become obligated through veil piercing and other non-successorship doctrines. In many cases, paragraph (2) will exclude successors to the assets and liabilities of a division of a debtor. See also Section 9-508, Comment 3.

8. **Supporting Obligations.** Under subsection (f), a security interest in a "supporting obligation" (defined in Section 9-102) automatically follows from a security interest in the underlying, supported collateral. This result was implicit under former Article 9. Implicit in subsection (f) is the principle that the secured party's interest in a supporting obligation extends to the supporting obligation only to the extent that it supports the collateral in which the secured party has a security interest. Complex issues may arise, however, if a supporting obligation supports many separate obligations of a particular account debtor and if the supported obligations are separately assigned as security to several secured parties. The problems may be exacerbated if a supporting obligation is limited to an aggregate amount that is less than the aggregate amount of the obligations it supports. This Article does not contain provisions dealing with competing claims to a limited supporting obligation. As under former Article 9, the law of suretyship and the agreements of the parties will control.

9. **Collateral Follows Right to Payment or Performance.** Subsection (g) codifies the common-law rule that a transfer of an obligation secured by a security interest or other lien on personal or real property also transfers the security interest or lien. See Restatement (3d), Property (Mortgages) § 5.4(a) (1997). See also Section 9-308(e) (analogous rule for perfection).

10. **Investment Property.** Subsections (h) and (i) make clear that attachment of a security interest in a securities account or commodity account is also attachment in security entitlements or commodity contracts carried in the accounts.

§ 9-204. AFTER-ACQUIRED PROPERTY; FUTURE ADVANCES.

(a)   [After-acquired collateral.] Except as otherwise provided in subsection (b), a security agreement may create or provide for a security interest in after-acquired collateral.

(b)   [When after-acquired property clause not effective.] A security interest does not attach under a term constituting an after-acquired property clause to:

(1)   consumer goods, other than an accession when given as additional security, unless the debtor acquires rights in them within 10 days after the secured party gives value; or

(2)   a commercial tort claim.

(c)   [Future advances and other value.] A security agreement may provide that collateral secures, or that accounts, chattel paper, payment intangibles, or promissory notes are sold in connection with, future advances or other value, whether or not the advances or value are given pursuant to commitment.

Official Comment

1. **Source.** Former Section 9-204.

2. **After-Acquired Property; Continuing General Lien.** Subsection (a) makes clear that a security interest arising by virtue of an after-acquired property clause is no less valid than a security interest in collateral in which the debtor has rights at the time value is given. A security interest in after-acquired property is not merely an "equitable" interest; no further action by the secured party-such as a supplemental agreement covering the new collateral-is required. This section adopts the principle of a "continuing general lien" or "floating lien." It validates a security interest in the debtor's existing and (upon acquisition) future assets, even though the debtor has liberty to use or dispose of collateral without being required to account for proceeds or substitute new collateral. See Section 9-205. Subsection (a), together with subsection (c), also validates "cross-collateral" clauses under which collateral acquired at any time secures advances whenever made.

3. **After-Acquired Consumer Goods.** Subsection (b)(1) makes ineffective an after-acquired property clause covering consumer goods (defined in Section 9-109), except as accessions (see Section 9-335), acquired more than

ten days after the secured party gives value. Subsection (b)(1) is unchanged in substance from the corresponding provision in former Section 9-204(2).

4. **Commercial Tort Claims.** Subsection (b)(2) provides that an after-acquired property clause in a security agreement does not reach future commercial tort claims. In order for a security interest in a tort claim to attach, the claim must be in existence when the security agreement is authenticated. In addition, the security agreement must describe the tort claim with greater specificity than simply "all tort claims." See Section 9-108(e).

5. **Future Advances; Obligations Secured.** Under subsection (c) collateral may secure future as well as past or present advances if the security agreement so provides. This is in line with the policy of this Article toward security interests in after-acquired property under subsection (a). Indeed, the parties are free to agree that a security interest secures any obligation whatsoever. Determining the obligations secured by collateral is solely a matter of construing the parties' agreement under applicable law. This Article rejects the holdings of cases decided under former Article 9 that applied other tests, such as whether a future advance or other subsequently incurred obligation was of the same or a similar type or class as earlier advances and obligations secured by the collateral.

ANALYSIS

The language of new § 9-204(c) does not itself reject the relatedness doctrine. It could therefore be argued that this commentary is not supported by the text of the legislation. It illustrates a trend of stating the law in the commentary, rather than in the statutory text. For discussion of relatedness under old Article 9 see *Secured Transactions* § 7C.02[6].

6. **Sales of Receivables.** Subsections (a) and (c) expressly validate after-acquired property and future advance clauses not only when the transaction is for security purposes but also when the transaction is the sale of accounts, chattel paper, payment intangibles, or promissory notes.. This result was implicit under former Article 9.

7. **Financing Statements.** The effect of after-acquired property and future advance clauses as components of a security agreement should not be confused with the requirements applicable to financing statements under this Article's system of perfection by notice filing. The references to after-acquired property clauses and future advance clauses in this section are limited to security agreements. There is no need to refer to after-acquired property or future advances or other obligations secured in a financing statement. See Section 9-502, Comment 2.

§ 9-205. USE OR DISPOSITION OF COLLATERAL PERMISSIBLE.

(a) [When security interest not invalid or fraudulent.] A security interest is not invalid or fraudulent against creditors solely because:

(1) the debtor has the right or ability to:

(A) use, commingle, or dispose of all or part of the collateral, including returned or repossessed goods;

(B) collect, compromise, enforce, or otherwise deal with collateral;

(C) accept the return of collateral or make repossessions; or

(D) use, commingle, or dispose of proceeds; or

(2) the secured party fails to require the debtor to account for proceeds or replace collateral.

ANALYSIS

Why did the Drafting Committee qualify this repeal of the rule in *Benedict v. Ratner*, 268 U.S. 353 (1925) by introducing the word "solely" into new § 9-205(a)? It does not appear in the old § 9-205. Could this open the door to an attack on a security arrangement as a device intended to hinder, defraud or delay creditors or as being constructively fraudulent based *in part* on the debtor's total control over the collateral and its proceeds? Nothing in the official commentary, other work or drafting philosophy of the revisers suggests that this is so. Indeed, encouraging such a challenge would seem to be directly contrary to what the revisers were otherwise attempting to accomplish in the Revised Article 9.

(b) [Requirements of possession not relaxed.] This section does not relax the requirements of possession if attachment, perfection, or enforcement of a security interest depends upon possession of the collateral by the secured party.

Official Comment

1. **Source.** Former Section 9-205.

2. **Validity of Unrestricted "Floating Lien."** This Article expressly validates the "floating lien" on shifting collateral. See Sections 9-201, 9-204

and Comment 2. This section provides that a security interest is not invalid or fraudulent by reason of the debtor's liberty to dispose of the collateral without being required to account to the secured party for proceeds or substitute new collateral. As did former Section 9-205, this section repeals the rule of *Benedict v. Ratner*, 268 U.S. 353 (1925), and other cases which held such arrangements void as a matter of law because the debtor was given unfettered dominion or control over collateral. The *Benedict* rule did not effectively discourage or eliminate security transactions in inventory and receivables. Instead, it forced financing arrangements to be self-liquidating. Although this section repeals *Benedict*, the filing and other perfection requirements (see Part 3, Subpart 2, and Part 5) provide for public notice that overcomes any potential misleading effects of a debtor's use and control of collateral. Moreover, nothing in this section prevents the debtor and secured party from agreeing to procedures by which the secured party polices or monitors collateral or to restrictions on the debtor's dominion. However, this Article leaves these matters to agreement based on business considerations, not on legal requirements.

3. **Possessory Security Interests.** Subsection (b) makes clear that this section does not relax the requirements for perfection by possession under Section 9-315. If a secured party allows the debtor access to and control over collateral its security interest may be or become unperfected.

4. **Permissible Freedom for Debtor to Enforce Collateral.** Former Section 9-205 referred to a debtor's "liberty. . . to collect or compromise accounts or chattel paper." This section recognizes the broader rights of a debtor to "enforce," as well as to "collect" and "compromise" collateral. This section's reference to collecting, compromising, and enforcing "collateral" instead of "accounts or chattel paper" contemplates the many other types of collateral that a debtor may wish to "collect, compromise, or enforce": e.g., deposit accounts, documents, general intangibles, instruments, investment property, and letter-of-credit rights.

§ 9-206. SECURITY INTEREST ARISING IN PURCHASE OR DELIVERY OF FINANCIAL ASSET.

(a) **[Security interest when person buys through securities intermediary.]** A security interest in favor of a securities intermediary attaches to a person's security entitlement if:

(1) the person buys a financial asset through the securities intermediary in a transaction in which the person is obligated to pay the purchase price to the securities intermediary at the time of the purchase; and

(2) the securities intermediary credits the financial asset to the buyer's securities account before the buyer pays the securities intermediary.

(b) [Security interest secures obligation to pay for finan-cial asset.] The security interest described in subsection (a) se-cures the person's obligation to pay for the financial asset.

(c) [Security interest in payment against delivery trans-action.] A security interest in favor of a person that delivers a certificated security or other financial asset represented by a writing attaches to the security or other financial asset if:

(1)   the security or other financial asset:

(A)   in the ordinary course of business is transferred by delivery with any necessary indorsement or assignment; and

(B)   is delivered under an agreement between persons in the business of dealing with such securities or financial assets; and

(2)   the agreement calls for delivery against payment.

(d) [Security interest secures obligation to pay for deliv-ery.] The security interest described in subsection (c) secures the obligation to make payment for the delivery.

ANALYSIS

An unpaid supplier of goods to a commercial enterprise is not automatically given a security interest in the goods supplied. The supplier must expressly retain a security interest if only by reserving title which operates to create a security interest after delivery. *See* §§ 1-201(37) and 2-401(1) and *Secured Transactions* § 7D.05. But brokers and other securities firms are automatically given a security interest when they perform without obtaining payment. There are no cases decided under the present Article 9 recognizing such a broker's lien. *See Secured Transactions* § 23.13[2].

Official Comment

1. **Source.** Former 9-116.

2. **Codification of "Broker's Lien."** Depending upon a securities interme-diary's arrangements with its entitlement holders, the securities intermediary may treat the entitlement holder as entitled to financial assets before the entitlement holder has actually made payment for them. For example, many brokers permit retail customers to pay for financial assets by check. The

broker may not receive final payment of the check until several days after the broker has credited the customer's securities account for the financial assets. Thus, the customer will have acquired a security entitlement prior to payment. Subsection (a) provides that, in such circumstances, the securities intermediary has a security interest in the entitlement holder's security entitlement. Under subsection (b) the security interest secures the customer's obligation to pay for the financial asset in question. Subsections (a) and (b) codify and adapt to the indirect holding system the so-called "broker's lien," which has long been recognized. See Restatement, Security § 12.

3. **Financial Assets Delivered Against Payment.** Subsection (c) creates a security interest in favor of persons who deliver certificated securities or other financial assets in physical form, such as money market instruments, if the agreed payment is not received. In some arrangements for settlement of transactions in physical financial assets, the seller's securities custodian will deliver physical certificates to the buyer's securities custodian and receive a time-stamped delivery receipt. The buyer's securities custodian will examine the certificate to ensure that it is in good order, and that the delivery matches a trade in which the buyer has instructed the seller to deliver to that custodian. If all is in order, the receiving custodian will settle with the delivering custodian through whatever funds settlement system has been agreed upon or is used by custom and usage in that market. The understanding of the trade, however, is that the delivery is conditioned upon payment, so that if payment is not made for any reason, the security will be returned to the deliverer. Subsection (c) clarifies the rights of persons making deliveries in such circumstances. It provides the person making delivery with a security interest in the securities or other financial assets; under subsection (d), the security interest secures the seller's right to receive payment for the delivery. Section 8-301 specifies when delivery of a certificated security occurs; that section should be applied as well to other financial assets as well for purposes of this section.

4. **Automatic Attachment and Perfection.** Subsections (a) and (c) refer to attachment of a security interest. Attachment under this section has the same incidents (enforceability, right to proceeds, etc.) as attachment under Section 9-203. This section overrides the general attachment rules in Section 9-203. See Section 9-203(c). A securities intermediary's security interest under subsection (a) is perfected by control without further action. See Section 8-106 (control); 9-314 (perfection). Security interests arising under subsection (c) are automatically perfected. See Section 9-309(9).

[SUBPART 2. RIGHTS AND DUTIES]

§ 9-207. RIGHTS AND DUTIES OF SECURED PARTY HAVING POSSESSION OR CONTROL OF COLLATERAL.

(a) **[Duty of care when secured party in possession.]** Except as otherwise provided in subsection (d), a secured party shall use reasonable care in the custody and preservation of collateral in the secured party's possession. In the case of chattel paper or an instrument, reasonable care includes taking necessary steps to preserve rights against prior parties unless otherwise agreed.

(b) **[Expenses, risks, duties, and rights when secured party in possession.]** Except as otherwise provided in subsection (d), if a secured party has possession of collateral:

(1) reasonable expenses, including the cost of insurance and payment of taxes or other charges, incurred in the custody, preservation, use, or operation of the collateral are chargeable to the debtor and are secured by the collateral;

(2) the risk of accidental loss or damage is on the debtor to the extent of a deficiency in any effective insurance coverage;

(3) the secured party shall keep the collateral identifiable, but fungible collateral may be commingled; and

(4) the secured party may use or operate the collateral:

(A) for the purpose of preserving the collateral or its value;

(B) as permitted by an order of a court having competent jurisdiction; or

(C) except in the case of consumer goods, in the manner and to the extent agreed by the debtor.

(c) **[Duties and rights when secured party in possession or control.]** Except as otherwise provided in subsection (d), a secured party having possession of collateral or control of collateral under Section 9-104, 9-105, 9-106, or 9-107:

(1) may hold as additional security any proceeds, except money or funds, received from the collateral;

(2) shall apply money or funds received from the collateral to reduce the secured obligation, unless remitted to the debtor; and

(3)   may create a security interest in the collateral.

ANALYSIS

A bank with a security interest in and control over a deposit account maintained with it may itself create a security interest in the account. Note that the only duty imposed on a creditor in control is to apply money or funds received from the collateral to the secured obligation or remit those collections to the debtor. The absence of duties for the creditor in control is another indication that possession and control are not functionally equivalent.

(d)   [Buyer of certain rights to payment.] If the secured party is a buyer of accounts, chattel paper, payment intangibles, or promissory notes or a consignor:

(1)   subsection (a) does not apply unless the secured party is entitled under an agreement:

(A)   to charge back uncollected collateral; or

(B)   otherwise to full or limited recourse against the debtor or a secondary obligor based on the nonpayment or other default of an account debtor or other obligor on the collateral; and

(2)   subsections (b) and (c) do not apply.

Official Comment

1. **Source.** Former Section 9-207.

2. **Duty of Care for Collateral in Secured Party's Possession.** Like former section 9-207, subsection (a) imposes a duty of care, similar to that imposed on a pledgee at common law, on a secured party in possession of collateral. See Restatement, Security §§ 17, 18. In many cases a secured party in possession of collateral may satisfy this duty by notifying the debtor of action that should be taken and allowing the debtor to take the action itself. If the secured party itself takes action, its reasonable expenses may be added to the secured obligation. The revised definitions of "collateral," "debtor," and "secured party" in Section 9-102 make this section applicable to collateral subject to an agricultural lien if the collateral is in the lienholder's possession. Under Section 1-102 the duty to exercise reasonable care may not be disclaimed by agreement, although under that section the parties remain free

to determine by agreement standards that are not manifestly unreasonable as to what constitutes reasonable care. Unless otherwise agreed, for a secured party in possession of chattel paper or an instrument, reasonable care includes the preservation of rights against prior parties. The secured party's right to have instruments or documents indorsed or transferred to it or its order is dealt with in the relevant sections of Articles 3, 7, and 8. See Sections 3-201, 7-506, 8-304(d).

3. **Specific Rules When Secured Party in Possession or Control of Collateral.** Subsection (b) and (c) provide rules following common-law precedents which apply unless the parties otherwise agree. The rules in subsection (b) apply to typical issues that may arise while a secured party is in possession of collateral, including expenses, insurance, and taxes, risk of loss or damage, identifiable and fungible collateral, and use or operation of collateral. Subsection (c) contains rules that apply in certain circumstances that may arise when a secured party is in either possession or control of collateral. These circumstances include the secured party's receiving proceeds from the collateral and the secured party's creation of a security interest in the collateral.

4. **Applicability Following Default.** This section applies when the secured party has possession of collateral either before or after default. See Sections 9-601(b), 9-609. Subsection (b)(4)(C) limits agreements concerning the use or operation of collateral to collateral other than consumer goods. Under Section 9-602(1), a debtor cannot waive or vary that limitation.

5. **"Repledges" and Right of Redemption.** Subsection (c)(3) eliminates the qualification in former Section 9-207 to the effect that the terms of a "repledge" may not "impair" a debtor's "right to redeem" collateral. The change is primarily for clarification. There is no basis on which to draw from subsection (c)(3) any inference concerning the debtor's right to redeem the collateral. The debtor enjoys that right under Section 9-621; this section need not address it. For example, if the collateral is a negotiable note that the secured party (SP-1) repledges to SP-2, nothing in this section suggests that the debtor (D) does not retain the right to redeem the note upon payment to SP-1 of all obligations secured by the note. But, as explained below, the debtor's unimpaired right to redeem as against the debtor's original secured party nevertheless may not be enforceable as against the new secured party.

In resolving questions that arise from the creation of a security interest by SP-1, one must take care to distinguish D's rights against SP-1 from D's rights against SP-2. Once D discharges the secured obligation, D becomes entitled to the note; SP-1 has no legal basis upon which to withhold it. If, as a practical matter, SP-1 is unable to return the note because SP-2 holds it as collateral for SP-1's unpaid debt, then SP-1 is liable to D under the law of conversion.

Whether SP-2 would be liable to D depends on the relative priority of SP-2's security interest and D's interest. By permitting SP-1 to create a security interest in the collateral (repledge), subsection (c)(3) provides a statutory power for SP-1 to give SP-2 a security interest (subject, of course, to any agreement by SP-1 not to give a security interest). In the vast majority of cases where repledge rights are significant, the security interest of the second secured party, SP-2 in the example, will be senior to the debtor's interest. By virtue of the debtor's consent or applicable legal rules, SP-2 typically would cut off D's rights in investment property or be immune from D's claims. See Sections 9-331, 3-306 (holder in due course), 8-303 (protected purchaser), 8-502 (acquisition of a security entitlement), 8-503(e) (action by entitlement holder). Moreover, the expectations and business practices in some markets, such as the securities markets, are such that D's consent to SP-2's taking free of D's rights inheres in D's creation of SP-1's security interest which gives rise to SP-1's power under this section. In these situations, D would have no right to recover the collateral or recover damages from SP-2. Nevertheless, D would have a damage claim against SP-1 if SP-1 had given a security interest to SP-2 in breach of its agreement with D. Moreover, if SP-2's security interest secures an amount that is less than the amount secured by SP-1's security interest (granted by D), then D's exercise of its right to redeem would provide value sufficient to discharge SP-1's obligations to SP-2.

For the most part this section does not change the law under former Section 9-207, although eliminating the reference to the debtor's right of redemption may alter the secured party's right to repledge in one respect. Former Section 9-207 could have been read to limit the secured party's statutory right to repledge collateral to repledge transactions in which the collateral did not secure a greater obligation than that of the original debtor. Inasmuch as this is a matter normally dealt with by agreement between the debtor and secured party, any change would appear to have little practical effect.

6. **"Repledges" of Investment Property.** The following example will aid the discussion of "repledges" of investment property.

Example. Debtor grants Alpha Bank a security interest in a security entitlement that includes 1000 shares of XYZ Co. stock that Debtor holds through an account with Able & Co. Alpha does not have an account with Able. Alpha uses Beta Bank as its securities custodian. Debtor instructs Able to transfer the shares to Beta, for the account of Alpha, and Able does so. Beta then credits Alpha's account. Alpha has control of the security entitlement for the 1000 shares under Section 8-106(d). (These are the facts of Example 2, Section 8-106, Comment 4.) Although, as between Debtor and Alpha, Debtor may have become the beneficial owner of the new securities entitlement with Beta, Beta has agreed to act on Alpha's entitlement orders because, as between Beta and Alpha, Alpha has become the entitlement holder.

Next, Alpha grants Gamma Bank a security interest in the security entitlement with Beta that includes the 1000 shares of XYZ Co. stock. In order to afford Gamma control of the entitlement, Alpha instructs Beta to transfer the stock to Gamma's custodian, Delta Bank, which credits Gamma's account for 1000 shares. At this point Gamma holds its securities entitlement for its benefit as well as that of its debtor, Alpha. Alpha's derivative rights also are for the benefit of Debtor.

In many, probably most, situations and at any particular point in time, it will be impossible for Debtor or Alpha to "trace" Alpha's "repledge" to any particular securities entitlement or financial asset of Gamma or anyone else. Debtor would retain, of course, a right to redeem the collateral from Alpha upon satisfaction of the secured obligation. However, in the absence of a traceable interest, Debtor would retain only a personal claim against Alpha in the event Alpha failed to restore the security entitlement to Debtor. Moreover, even in the unlikely event that Debtor could trace a property interest, in the context of the financial markets, normally the operation of this section, Debtor's explicit agreement to permit Alpha to create a senior security interest, or legal rules permitting Gamma to cut off Debtor's rights or become immune from Debtor's claims would effectively subordinate Debtor's interest to the holder of a security interest created by Alpha. And, under the shelter principle, all subsequent transferees would obtain interests to which Debtor's interest also would be subordinate.

7. **Buyers of Chattel Paper and Other Receivables; Consignors.** This section has been revised to reflect the fact that a seller of accounts, chattel paper, payment intangibles, or promissory notes retains no interest in the collateral and so is not disadvantaged by the secured party's noncompliance with the requirements of this section. Accordingly, subsection (d) provides that subsection (a) applies only to security interests that secure an obligation and to sales of receivables in which the buyer has recourse against the debtor. (Of course, a buyer of accounts or payment intangibles could not have "possession" of original collateral, but might have possession of proceeds, such as promissory notes or checks.) The meaning of "recourse" in this respect is limited to recourse arising out of the account debtor's failure to pay or other default.

Subsection (d) makes subsections (b) and (c) inapplicable to buyers of accounts, chattel paper, payment intangibles, or promissory notes and consignors. Of course, there is no reason to believe that a buyer of receivables or a consignor could not, for example, create a security interest or otherwise transfer an interest in the collateral, regardless of who has possession of the collateral. However, this section leaves the rights of those owners to law other than Article 9.

§ 9-208. ADDITIONAL DUTIES OF SECURED PARTY HAVING CONTROL OF COLLATERAL.

(a) [Applicability of section.] This section applies to cases in which there is no outstanding secured obligation and the secured party is not committed to make advances, incur obligations, or otherwise give value.

(b) [Duties of secured party after receiving demand from debtor.] Within 10 days after receiving an authenticated demand by the debtor:

(1) a secured party having control of a deposit account under Section 9-104(a)(2) shall send to the bank with which the deposit account is maintained an authenticated statement that releases the bank from any further obligation to comply with instructions originated by the secured party;

(2) a secured party having control of a deposit account under Section 9-104(a)(3) shall:

(A) pay the debtor the balance on deposit in the deposit account; or

(B) transfer the balance on deposit into a deposit account in the debtor's name;

(3) a secured party, other than a buyer, having control of electronic chattel paper under Section 9-105 shall:

(A) communicate the authoritative copy of the electronic chattel paper to the debtor or its designated custodian;

(B) if the debtor designates a custodian that is the designated custodian with which the authoritative copy of the electronic chattel paper is maintained for the secured party, communicate to the custodian an authenticated record releasing the designated custodian from any further obligation to comply with instructions originated by the secured party and instructing the custodian to comply with instructions originated by the debtor; and

(C) take appropriate action to enable the debtor or its designated custodian to make copies of or revisions to the authoritative copy which add or change an identified assignee of the authoritative copy without the consent of the secured party;

(4) a secured party having control of investment property under Section 8-106(d)(2) or 9-106(b) shall send to the securities

intermediary or commodity intermediary with which the security entitlement or commodity contract is maintained an authenticated record that releases the securities intermediary or commodity intermediary from any further obligation to comply with entitlement orders or directions originated by the secured party; and

(5) a secured party having control of a letter-of-credit right under Section 9-107 shall send to each person having an unfulfilled obligation to pay or deliver proceeds of the letter of credit to the secured party an authenticated release from any further obligation to pay or deliver proceeds of the letter of credit to the secured party.

Official Comment

1. **Source.** New.

2. **Scope and Purpose.** This section imposes duties on a secured party who has control of a deposit account, electronic chattel paper, investment property, or a letter-of-credit right. The duty to terminate the secured party's control is analogous to the duty to file a termination statement, imposed by Section 9-513. Under subsection (a), it applies only when there is no outstanding secured obligation and the secured party is not committed to give value. The requirements of this section can be varied by agreement under Section 1-102(3). For example, a debtor could by contract agree that the secured party may release its control of investment property under subsection (a)(1) more than three days following demand. Also, duties under this section should not be read to conflict with the terms of the collateral itself. For example, if the collateral is a time deposit account, subsection (b)(3) should not require a secured party with control to make an early withdrawal of the funds (assuming that were possible) in order to pay them over to the debtor or put them in an account in the debtor's name.

3. **Remedy for Failure to Relinquish Control.** If a secured party fails to comply with the requirements of subsection (b), the debtor has the remedy set forth in Section 9-625(e). This remedy is identical to that applicable to failure to provide or file a termination statement under Section 9-513.

4. **Duty to Relinquish Possession.** Although Section 9-207 addresses directly the duties of a secured party in possession of collateral, that section does not require the secured party to relinquish possession when the secured party ceases to hold a security interest. Under common law, absent agreement to the contrary, the failure to relinquish possession of collateral upon satisfaction of the secured obligation would constitute a conversion. Inasmuch as problems apparently have not surfaced in the absence of statutory duties under former Article 9 and the common-law duty appears to have been sufficient, this Article does not impose a statutory duty to relinquish possession.

§ 9-209. DUTIES OF SECURED PARTY IF ACCOUNT DEBTOR HAS BEEN NOTIFIED OF ASSIGNMENT.

(a) **[Applicability of section.]** Except as otherwise provided in subsection (c), this section applies if:

(1) there is no outstanding secured obligation; and

(2) the secured party is not committed to make advances, incur obligations, or otherwise give value.

(b) **[Duties of secured party after receiving demand from debtor.]** Within 10 days after receiving an authenticated demand by the debtor, a secured party shall send to an account debtor that has received notification of an assignment to the secured party as assignee under Section 9-406(a) an authenticated record that releases the account debtor from any further obligation to the secured party.

(c) **[Inapplicability to sales.]** This section does not apply to an assignment constituting the sale of an account, chattel paper, or payment intangible.

Official Comment

1. **Source.** New.

2. **Scope and Purpose.** Like Sections 9-208 and 9-513, which require a secured party to relinquish control of collateral and to file or provide a termination statement for a financing statement, this section requires a secured party to free up collateral when there no longer is any outstanding secured obligation or any commitment to give value in the future. This section addresses the case in which account debtors have been notified to pay a secured party to whom the receivables have been assigned. It requires the secured party (assignee) to inform the account debtors that they no longer are obligated to make payment to the secured party. See subsection (b). It does not apply to account debtors whose obligations on an account, chattel paper, or payment intangible have been sold. See subsection (c).

§ 9-210. REQUEST FOR ACCOUNTING; REQUEST REGARDING LIST OF COLLATERAL OR STATEMENT OF ACCOUNT.

(a) **[Definitions.]** In this section:

(1) "Request" means a record of a type described in paragraph (2), (3), or (4).

(2) "Request for an accounting" means a record authenticated by a debtor requesting that the recipient provide an accounting of the unpaid obligations secured by collateral and reasonably identifying the transaction or relationship that is the subject of the request.

(3) "Request regarding a list of collateral" means a record authenticated by a debtor requesting that the recipient approve or correct a list of what the debtor believes to be the collateral securing an obligation and reasonably identifying the transaction or relationship that is the subject of the request.

(4) "Request regarding a statement of account" means a record authenticated by a debtor requesting that the recipient approve or correct a statement indicating what the debtor believes to be the aggregate amount of unpaid obligations secured by collateral as of a specified date and reasonably identifying the transaction or relationship that is the subject of the request.

(b) [Duty to respond to requests.] Subject to subsections (c), (d), (e), and (f), a secured party, other than a buyer of accounts, chattel paper, payment intangibles, or promissory notes or a consignor, shall comply with a request within 14 days after receipt:

(1) in the case of a request for an accounting, by authenticating and sending to the debtor an accounting; and

(2) in the case of a request regarding a list of collateral or a request regarding a statement of account, by authenticating and sending to the debtor an approval or correction.

(c) [Request regarding list of collateral; statement concerning type of collateral.] A secured party that claims a security interest in all of a particular type of collateral owned by the debtor may comply with a request regarding a list of collateral by sending to the debtor an authenticated record including a statement to that effect within 14 days after receipt.

(d) [Request regarding list of collateral; no interest claimed.] A person that receives a request regarding a list of collateral, claims no interest in the collateral when it receives the request, and claimed an interest in the collateral at an earlier time shall comply with the request within 14 days after receipt by sending to the debtor an authenticated record:

(1) disclaiming any interest in the collateral; and

(2) if known to the recipient, providing the name and mailing address of any assignee of or successor to the recipient's security interest in the collateral.

(e) [Request for accounting or regarding statement of account; no interest in obligation claimed.] A person that receives a request for an accounting or a request regarding a statement of account, claims no interest in the obligations when it receives the request, and claimed an interest in the obligations at an earlier time shall comply with the request within 14 days after receipt by sending to the debtor an authenticated record:

(1)   disclaiming any interest in the obligations; and

(2)   if known to the recipient, providing the name and mailing address of any assignee of or successor to the recipient's interest in the obligations.

(f) [Charges for responses.] A debtor is entitled without charge to one response to a request under this section during any six-month period. The secured party may require payment of a charge not exceeding $25 for each additional response.

Official Comment

1. **Source.** Former Section 9-208.

2. **Scope and Purpose.** This section provides a procedure whereby a debtor may obtain from a secured party information about the secured obligation and the collateral in which the secured party may claim a security interest. It clarifies and resolves some of the issues that arose under former Section 9-208 and makes information concerning the secured indebtedness readily available to debtors, both before and after default. It applies to agricultural lien transactions (see the definitions of "debtor," secured party," and "collateral" in Section 9-102), but generally not to sales of receivables. See subsection (b).

3. **Requests by Debtors Only.** A financing statement filed under Part 5 may disclose only that a secured party may have a security interest in specified types of collateral. In most cases the financing statement will contain no indication of the obligation (if any) secured, whether any security interest actually exists, or the particular property subject to a security interest. Because creditors of and prospective purchasers from a debtor may have legitimate needs for more detailed information, it is necessary to provide a procedure under which the secured party will be required to provide information. On the other hand, the secured party should not be under a duty to disclose any details of the debtor's financial affairs to any casual inquirer or competitor who may inquire. For this reason, this section gives the right to request information to the debtor only. The debtor may submit a request in connection with negotiations with subsequent creditors and purchasers, as well as for the purpose of determining the status of its credit relationship or demonstrating which of its assets are free of a security interest.

4. **Permitted Types of Requests for Information.** Subsection (a) contemplates that a debtor may request three types of information by submitting three types of "requests" to the secured party. First, the debtor may request the secured party to prepare and send an "accounting" (defined in Section 9-102). Second, the debtor may submit to the secured party a list of collateral for the secured party's approval or correction. Third, the debtor may submit to the secured party for its approval or correction a statement of the aggregate amount of unpaid secured obligations. Inasmuch as a secured party may have numerous transactions and relationships with a debtor, each request must identify the relevant transactions or relationships. Subsections (b) and (c) require the secured party to respond to a request within 14 days following receipt of the request.

5. **Recipients Claiming No Interest in the Transaction.** A debtor may be unaware that a creditor with whom it has dealt has assigned its security interest or the secured obligation. Subsections (d) and (e) impose upon recipients of requests under this section the duty to inform the debtor that they claim no interest in the collateral or secured obligation, respectively, and to inform the debtor of the name and mailing address of any known assignee or successor. As under subsections (b) and (c), a response to a request under subsection (d) or (e) is due 14 days following receipt.

6. **Waiver; Remedy for Failure to Comply.** The debtor's rights under this section may not be waived or varied. See Section 9-602(2). Section 9-625(e) sets forth the remedy for noncompliance with the requirements of this section.

7. **Limitation on Free Responses to Requests.** Under subsection (f), during a six-month period a debtor is entitled to receive from the secured party one free response to a request. The debtor is not entitled to a free response to *each* type of request (i.e., three free responses) during a six-month period.

PART 3   PERFECTION AND PRIORITY

[SUBPART 1.   LAW GOVERNING PERFECTION AND PRIORITY]

§ 9-301.   LAW GOVERNING PERFECTION AND PRIORITY OF SECURITY INTERESTS. Except as otherwise provided in Sections 9-303 through 9-306, the following rules determine the law governing perfection, the effect of perfection or nonperfection, and the priority of a security interest in collateral:

(1)   Except as otherwise provided in this section, while a debtor is located in a jurisdiction, the local law of that jurisdiction governs perfection, the effect of perfection or nonperfection, and the priority of a security interest in collateral.

(2)   While collateral is located in a jurisdiction, the local law of that jurisdiction governs perfection, the effect of perfection or nonperfection, and the priority of a possessory security interest in that collateral.

(3)   Except as otherwise provided in paragraph (4), while negotiable documents, goods, instruments, money, or tangible chattel paper is located in a jurisdiction, the local law of that jurisdiction governs:

(A)   perfection of a security interest in the goods by filing a fixture filing;

(B)   perfection of a security interest in timber to be cut; and

(C)   the effect of perfection or nonperfection and the priority of a nonpossessory security interest in the collateral.

(4)   The local law of the jurisdiction in which the wellhead or minehead is located governs perfection, the effect of perfection or nonperfection, and the priority of a security interest in as-extracted collateral.

ANALYSIS

Choice of law rules are moved from old § 9-103 to this new subpart 1 of Part 3 of the Revised Article 9. This relocation specifies the priority issues controlled by these rules. If the priority provision is located in part 3 (*e.g.* new § 9-320 stating the priority of a buyer in ordinary course, new § 9-324 stating the purchase-money priorities), then these choice of law rules control. In contrast, if the issue involves a provision of Part 4 of Revised Article, these Part 3 choice of law rules are not controlling by their terms.

As to tangible collateral, the general rule of the revision is that the law of the jurisdiction of the collateral's location controls priority questions. New § 9-301(3). But at the same time, the general rule as to all forms of collateral is that perfection of non-possessory security interests is controlled by the debtor's location. This bifurcation of controlling choice of law can be illustrated as follows:

> *Example A*: First Bank takes a security interest in the inventory of Appliance Store Inc., a Delaware Corporation. All of the inventory is located in Texas where Appliance Store Inc. has its sole place of business. In Texas, Gommer buys two refrigerators from Appliance Store Inc. Whether the security interest of First Bank is properly perfected will be governed by the law of Delaware, where the debtor is deemed to be located. New § 9-307(e). Under new § 9-501 First Bank will need to file in Delaware to perfect its interest in the inventory located in Texas. Third parties will need to search in Delaware to detect interests in the debtor's inventory. But the question of whether Gommer qualifies as a buyer in ordinary course and takes free of First Bank's security interest in the refrigerators will be controlled by the law of Texas. *See Secured Transactions* § 1A.07.

Official Comment

1. **Source.** Former Sections 9-103(1)(a), (b), 9-103(3)(a), (b), 9-103(5), substantially modified.

2. **Scope of This Subpart.** Part 3, Subpart 1 (Sections 9-301 through 9-307) contains choice-of-law rules similar to those of former Section 9-103. Former

Section 9-103 generally addresses which State's law governs "perfection and the effect of perfection or non-perfection of" security interests. See, e.g., former Section 9-103(1)(b). This Article follows the broader and more precise formulation in former Section 9-103(6)(b), which was revised in connection with the promulgation of Revised Article 8 in 1994: "perfection, the effect of perfection or non-perfection, and the priority of" security interests. Priority, in this context, subsumes all of the rules in Part 3, including "cut off" or "take free" rules such as Sections 9-317(b), (c), and (d), 9-320(a), (b), and (d), and 9-332. This subpart does not address choice of law for other purposes. For example, the law applicable to issues such as attachment, validity, characterization (e.g., true lease or security interest), and enforcement is governed by the rules in Section 1-105; that governing law typically is specified in the same agreement that contains the security agreement. And, another jurisdiction's law may govern other third-party matters addressed in this Article. See Section 9-401, Comment 3.

3. **Scope of Referral.** In designating the jurisdiction whose law governs, this Article directs the court to apply only the substantive ("local") law of a particular jurisdiction and not its choice-of-law rules.

Example 1: Litigation over the priority of a security interest in accounts arises in State X. State X has adopted the official text of this Article, which provides that priority is determined by the local law of the jurisdiction in which the debtor is located. See Section 9-301(1). The debtor is located in State Y. Even if State Y has retained former Article 9 or enacted a nonuniform choice-of-law rule (e.g., one that provides that perfection is governed by the law of State Z), a State X court should look only to the substantive law of State Y and disregard State Y's choice-of-law rule. State Y's substantive law (e.g., its Section 9-501) provides that financing statements should be filed in a filing office in State Y. Note, however, that if the identical perfection issue were to be litigated in State Y, the court would look to State Y's former Section 9-103 or nonuniform 9-301 and conclude that a filing in State Y is ineffective.

Example 2: In the preceding Example, assume that State X has adopted the official text of this Article, and State Y has adopted a nonuniform Section 9-301(1) under which perfection is governed by the whole law of State X, including its choice-of-law rules. If litigation occurs in State X, the court should look to the substantive law of State Y, which provides that financing statements are to be filed in a filing office in State Y. If litigation occurs in State Y, the court should look to the law of State X, whose choice-of-law rule requires that the court apply the substantive law of State Y. Thus, regardless of the jurisdiction in which the litigation arises, the financing statement should be filed in State Y.

4. **Law Governing Perfection: General Rule.** Paragraph (1) contains the general rule: the law governing perfection of security interests in both tangible and intangible collateral, whether perfected by filing or automatically, is the law of the jurisdiction of the debtor's location, as determined under Section 9-307.

Paragraph (1) substantially simplifies the choice-of-law rules. Former Section 9-103 contained different choice-of-law rules for different types of collateral. Under Section 9-301(1), the law of a single jurisdiction governs perfection with respect to most types of collateral, both tangible and intangible. Paragraph (1) eliminates the need for former Section 9-103(1)(c), which concerned purchase-money security interests in tangible collateral that is intended to move from one jurisdiction to the other. It is likely to reduce the frequency of cases in which the governing law changes after a financing statement is properly filed. (Presumably, debtors change their own location less frequently than they change the location of their collateral.) The approach taken in paragraph (1) also eliminates some difficult priority issues and the need to distinguish between "mobile" and "ordinary" goods, and it reduces the number of filing offices in which secured parties must file or search when collateral is located in several jurisdictions.

5. **Law Governing Perfection: Exceptions.** The general rule is subject to several exceptions. It does not apply to goods covered by a certificate of title (see Section 9-303), deposit accounts (see Section 9-304), investment property (see Section 9-305), or letter-of-credit rights (see Section 9-306). Nor does it apply to possessory security interests, i.e., security interests that the secured party has perfected by taking possession of the collateral (see paragraph (2)), security interests perfected by filing a fixture filing (see paragraph (4)), security interests in timber to be cut (paragraph (5)), or security interests in as-extracted collateral (see paragraph (6)).

a. **Possessory Security Interests.** Paragraph (2) applies to possessory security interests and provides that perfection is governed by the local law of the jurisdiction in which the collateral is located. This is the rule of former Section 9-103(1)(b), except paragraph (2) eliminates the troublesome "last event" test of former law.

The distinction between nonpossessory and possessory security interests creates the potential for the same jurisdiction to apply two different choice-of-law rules to determine perfection in the same collateral. For example, were a secured party in possession of an instrument or document to relinquish possession in reliance on temporary perfection, the applicable law immediately would change from that of the location of the collateral to that of the location of the debtor. The applicability of two different choice-of-law rules for perfection is unlikely to lead to any material practical problems. The perfection rules of one Article 9 jurisdiction are likely to be identical to those of another. Moreover, under paragraph (3), the relative priority of competing security interests in tangible collateral is resolved by reference to the law of the jurisdiction in which the collateral is located, regardless of how the security interests are perfected.

b. **Fixtures.** Application of the general rule in paragraph (1) to perfection of a security interest in fixtures would yield strange results. For example, perfection of a security interest in fixtures located in Arizona and owned by a Delaware corporation would be governed by the law of Delaware. Although Delaware law would send one to a filing office in Arizona for the place to file a financing statement as a fixture filing, see Section 9-501, Delaware law would not take account of local, nonuniform, real-property filing and recording requirements that Arizona law might impose. For this reason, paragraph (3)(A) contains a special rule for security interests perfected by a fixture filing; the law of the jurisdiction in which the fixtures are located governs perfection, including the formal requisites of a fixture filing. Under paragraph (3)(C), the same law governs priority. Fixtures are "goods" as defined in Section 9-102.

c. **Timber to Be Cut.** Application of the general rule in paragraph (1) to perfection of a security interest in timber to be cut would yield undesirable results analogous to those described with respect to fixtures. Paragraph (3)(B) adopts a similar solution: perfection is governed by the law of the jurisdiction in which the timber is located. As with fixtures, under paragraph (3)(C), the same law governs priority. Timber to be cut also is "goods" as defined in Section 9-102.

Paragraph (3)(B) applies only to "timber to be cut," not to timber that has been cut. Consequently, once the timber is cut, the general choice-of-law rule in paragraph (1) becomes applicable. To ensure continued perfection, a secured party should file in both the jurisdiction in which the timber to be cut is located and in the state where the debtor is located. The former filing would be with the office in which a real property mortgage would be filed, and the latter would be a central filing. See Section 9-501.

d. **As-Extracted Collateral.** Paragraph (4) adopts the rule of former Section 9-103(5) with respect to certain security interests in minerals and related accounts. Like security interests in fixtures perfected by filing a fixture filing, security interests in minerals that are as-extracted collateral are perfected by filing in the office designated for the filing or recording of a mortgage on the real property. For the same reasons, the law governing perfection and priority is the law of the jurisdiction in which the wellhead or minehead is located.

6. **Change in Law Governing Perfection.** When the debtor changes its location to another jurisdiction, the jurisdiction whose law governs perfection under paragraph (1) changes, as well. Similarly, the law governing perfection of a possessory security interest in collateral under paragraph (2) changes when the collateral is removed to another jurisdiction. Nevertheless, these changes will not result in an immediate loss of perfection. See Section 9-316(a), (b).

7. **Law Governing Effect of Perfection and Priority: Goods, Documents, Instruments, Money, Negotiable Documents, and Tangible Chattel Paper.** Under former Section 9-103, the law of a single jurisdiction governed both questions of perfection and those of priority. This Article generally adopts that approach. See paragraph (1). But the approach may create problems if the debtor and collateral are located in different jurisdictions. For example, assume a security interest in equipment located in Pennsylvania is perfected by filing in Illinois, where the debtor is located. If the law of the jurisdiction in which the debtor is located were to govern priority, then the priority of an execution lien on goods located in Pennsylvania would be governed by rules enacted by the Illinois legislature.

To address this problem, paragraph (3)(C) divorces questions of perfection from questions of "the effect of perfection or nonperfection and the priority of a security interest." Under paragraph (3)(C), the rights of competing claimants to tangible collateral are resolved by reference to the law of the jurisdiction in which the collateral is located. A similar bifurcation applied to security interests in investment property under former Section 9-103(6). See Section 9-305.

Paragraph (3)(C) applies the law of the situs to determine priority only with respect to goods (including fixtures), instruments, money, negotiable documents, and tangible chattel paper. Compare former Section 9-103(1), which applied the law of the location of the collateral to documents, instruments, and "ordinary" (as opposed to "mobile") goods. This Article does not distinguish among types of goods. The ordinary/mobile goods distinction appears to address concerns about where to file and search, rather than concerns about priority. There is no reason to preserve this distinction under the bifurcated approach.

Particularly serious confusion may arise when the choice-of-law rules of a given jurisdiction result in each of two competing security interests in the same collateral being governed by a different priority rule. The potential for this confusion existed under former Section 9-103(4) with respect to chattel paper: Perfection by possession was governed by the law of the location of the paper, whereas perfection by filing was governed by the law of the location of the debtor. Consider the mess that would have been created if the language or interpretation of former Section 9-308 were to differ in the two relevant States, or if one of the relevant jurisdictions (e.g., a foreign country) had not adopted Article 9. The potential for confusion could have been exacerbated when a secured party perfected both by taking possession in the State where the collateral is located (State A) and by filing in the State where the debtor is located (State B)-a common practice for some chattel paper financers. By providing that the law of the jurisdiction in which the collateral is located governs priority, paragraph (3) substantially diminishes this problem.

8. **Non-U.S. Debtors.** This Article applies the same choice-of-law rules to all debtors, foreign and domestic. For example, it adopts the bifurcated approach for determining the law applicable to security interests in goods and other tangible collateral. See Comment 5.a., above. The Article contains a new rule specifying the location of non-U.S. debtors for purposes of this Part. The rule appears in Section 9-307 and is explained in the Reporters' Comments following that section. Former Section 9-103(3)(c), which contained a special choice-of-law rule governing security interests created by debtors located in a non-U.S. jurisdiction, proved unsatisfactory and was deleted.

§ 9-302. LAW GOVERNING PERFECTION AND PRIORITY OF AGRICULTURAL LIENS. While farm products are located in a jurisdiction, the local law of that jurisdiction governs perfection, the effect of perfection or nonperfection, and the priority of an agricultural lien on the farm products.

ANALYSIS

Specifying a different jurisdiction as controlling the perfection of agricultural liens could create the need for two searches as to farm products: one in the state of the debtor's location for security interests and one in the state where the products are growing as to agricultural liens.

Example A: Farmer Santos resides in South Dakota but farms land in both South Dakota and North Dakota. A third party searching with respect to interests in crops growing in North Dakota must search in South Dakota for filings of security interests since the individual debtor is deemed to be located at his residence even if his place of business is in another jurisdiction. New § 9-307(b)(1). But the third party must also search in North Dakota where the crops are growing for agricultural liens.

Official Comment

1. **Source.** New.

2. **Agricultural Liens.** This section provides choice-of-law rules for agricultural liens on farm products. Perfection, the effect of perfection or nonperfection, and priority all are governed by the law of the jurisdiction in which the farm products are located. Other choice-of-law rules, including Section 1-105, determine which jurisdiction's law governs other matters, such as the secured party's rights on default. See Section 9-301, Comment 2. Inasmuch as no agricultural lien on proceeds arises under this Article, this section does not expressly apply to proceeds of agricultural liens. However, if another statute creates an agricultural lien on proceeds, it may be appropriate for courts to apply the choice-of-law rule in this section to determine priority in the proceeds.

§ 9-303. LAW GOVERNING PERFECTION AND PRIORITY OF SECURITY INTERESTS IN GOODS COVERED BY A CERTIFICATE OF TITLE.

(a) [Applicability of section.] This section applies to goods covered by a certificate of title, even if there is no other relationship between the jurisdiction under whose certificate of title the goods are covered and the goods or the debtor.

(b) [When goods covered by certificate of title.] Goods become covered by a certificate of title when a valid application for the certificate of title and the applicable fee are delivered to the appropriate authority. Goods cease to be covered by a certificate of title at the earlier of the time the certificate of title ceases to be effective under the law of the issuing jurisdiction or the time the goods become covered subsequently by a certificate of title issued by another jurisdiction.

(c) [Applicable law.] The local law of the jurisdiction under whose certificate of title the goods are covered governs perfection, the effect of perfection or nonperfection, and the priority of a security interest in goods covered by a certificate of title from the time the goods become covered by the certificate of title until the goods cease to be covered by the certificate of title.

ANALYSIS

Certificated interests are an exception to the general rules that law of the debtor's jurisdiction controls as to perfection and that the law of the location of collateral controls as to priority. Instead, the law of the first jurisdiction to issue a certificate of title initially controls even if that jurisdiction has no other relation to the goods or the debtor. The law of that first state no longer controls as to perfection of new interests or as to priority issues governed by Part 3 of Revised Article 9 when the goods become covered by the law of a second jurisdiction, but the perfection of an interest perfected under the law of the first state does not automatically lapse because of the change in controlling law. The impact of a change in the controlling law on the perfection of interests perfected under the law of the initial certificate state is controlled by new § 9-316(d) & (e). *See* the Text Analysis to that provision.

> *Example A*: Bubba Martin, who resides in State X is an independent trucker engaged in transporting goods throughout the U.S. In 2002 a truck owned by Bubba is certificated in State Y with First Bank noting its interest on the certificate as required by the law of State Y. The interest of First Bank is perfected even though State Y has no other connection with the transaction.

> *Example B*: Same as above but in January 2003 Bubba Martin moves to State Z and the truck is certificated in State Z. Second Bank takes the action necessary to perfect its interest in the truck under the law of State Z. Second Bank's interest is perfected because after the truck is covered by the certificate of the second state the law of that state thereafter governs the perfection of interests in the truck.

> *Example C*: After Bubba Martin moves to State Z he does not grant any new security interest in the truck but the truck is repaired by Service Co. Whether Service Co. has priority over First Bank under new § 9-333 is governed by the law of State Z because after the issuance of the certificate in that state the priority issues of Part 3 of Revised Article 9 are controlled by the law of State Z.

The significance of allowing Part 3 priority issues to be governed by the law of the second certificate state is not as great as might seem assuming all of the states have enacted the Revised Article 9. In that event, the statutory law of all of the states as to these priority issues will be the same to the extent that the law is stated in Revised Article 9. For example, both states will have the same text of new § 9-333. But both states may not have the same statutes or case law as to other statutory liens which are not possessory liens for services or materials or agricultural liens.

Official Comment

1. **Source.** Former Section 9-103(2)(a), (b), substantially revised.

2. **Scope of This Section.** This section applies to "goods covered by a certificate of title." The new definition of "certificate of title" in Section 9-102 makes clear that this section applies not only to certificate-of-title statutes under which perfection occurs upon notation of the security interest on the certificate but also to those that contemplate notation but provide that perfection is achieved by another method, e.g., delivery of designated documents to an official. Subsection (a), which is new, makes clear that this section applies to certificates of a jurisdiction having no other contacts with the goods or the debtor. This result comports with most of the reported cases on the subject and with contemporary business practices in the trucking industry.

3. **Law Governing Perfection and Priority.** Subsection (c) is the basic choice-of-law rule for goods covered by a certificate of title. Perfection and priority of a security interest are governed by the law of the jurisdiction under whose certificate of title the goods are covered from the time the goods become covered by the certificate of title until the goods cease to be covered by the certificate of title.

Normally, under the law of the relevant jurisdiction, the perfection step would consist of compliance with that jurisdiction's certificate-of-title statute and a resulting notation of the security interest on the certificate of title. See Section 9-311(b). In the typical case of an automobile or over-the-road truck, a person who wishes to take a security interest in the vehicle can ascertain whether it is subject to any security interests by looking at the certificate of title. But certificates of title cover certain types of goods in some States but not in others. A secured party who does not realize this may extend credit and attempt to perfect by filing in the jurisdiction in which the debtor is located. If the goods had been titled in another jurisdiction, the lender would be unperfected.

Subsection (b) explains when goods become covered by a certificate of title and when they cease to be covered. Goods may become covered by a certificate of title, even though no certificate of title has issued. Former

Section 9-103(2)(b) provided that the law of the jurisdiction issuing the certificate ceases to apply upon "surrender" of the certificate. This Article eliminates the concept of "surrender." However, if the certificate is surrendered in conjunction with an appropriate application for a certificate to be issued by another jurisdiction, the law of the original jurisdiction ceases to apply because the goods became covered subsequently by a certificate of title from another jurisdiction. Alternatively, the law of the original jurisdiction ceases to apply when the certificate "ceases to be effective" under the law of that jurisdiction. Given the diversity in certificate-of-title statutes, the term "effective" is not defined.

4. **Continued Perfection.** The fact that the law of one State ceases to apply under subsection (b) does not mean that a security interest perfected under that law becomes unperfected automatically. In most cases, the security interest will remain perfected. See Section 9-316(d), (e). Moreover, a perfected security interest may be subject to defeat by certain buyers and secured parties. See Section 9-337.

5. **Inventory.** Compliance with a certificate-of-title statute generally is *not* the method of perfecting security interests in inventory. Section 9-311(d) provides that a security interest created in inventory held by a person in the business of selling or leasing goods of that kind is subject to the normal filing rules; compliance with a certificate-of-title statute is not necessary or effective to perfect the security interest. Most certificate-of-title statutes are in accord.

The following example explains the subtle relationship between this rule and the choice-of-law rules in Section 9-303 and former Section 9-103(2):

Example: Goods are located in State A and covered by a certificate of title issued under the law of State A. The State A certificate of title is "clean"; it does not reflect a security interest. Owner takes the goods to State B and sells (trades in) the goods to Dealer, who is located (within the meaning of Section 9-307) in State B. As is customary, Dealer retains the duly assigned State A certificate of title pending resale of the goods. Dealer's inventory financer, SP, obtains a security interest in the goods under its after-acquired property clause.

Under Section 9-311(d) of both State A and State B, Dealer's inventory financer, SP, must perfect by filing instead of complying with a certificate-of-title statute. If Section 9-303 were read to provide that the law applicable to perfection of SP's security interest is that of State A, because the goods are covered by a State A certificate, then SP would be required to file in State A under State A's Section 9-501. That result would be anomalous, to say the least, since the principle underlying Section 9-311(d) is that the inventory should be treated as ordinary goods.

Section 9-303 (and former Section 9-103(2)) should be read as providing that the law of State B, not State A, applies. A court looking to the forum's Section 9-303(a) would find that Section 9-303 applies only if two conditions are met: (i) the goods are covered by the certificate as explained in Section

9-303(b), i.e., application had been made for a State (here, State A) to issue a certificate of title covering the goods and (ii) the certificate is a "certificate of title" as defined in Section 9-102, i.e., "a statute provides for the security interest in question to be indicated on the certificate as a condition or result of the security interest's obtaining priority over the rights of a lien creditor." Stated otherwise, Section 9-303 applies only when compliance with a certificate-of-title statute, and not filing, is the appropriate method of perfection. Under the law of State A, *for purposes of perfecting SP's security interest in the dealer's inventory*, the proper method of perfection is filing-not compliance with State A's certificate-of-title statute. For that reason, the goods are not covered by a "certificate of title," and the second condition is not met. Thus, Section 9-303 does not apply to the goods. Instead, Section 9-301 applies, and the applicable law is that of State B, where the debtor (dealer) is located.

6. **External Constraints on This Section.** The need to coordinate Article 9 with a variety of nonuniform certificate-of-title statutes, the need to provide rules to take account of situations in which multiple certificates of title are outstanding with respect to particular goods, and the need to govern the transition from perfection by filing in one jurisdiction to perfection by notation in another all create pressure for a detailed and complex set of rules. In an effort to minimize complexity, this Article does not attempt to coordinate Article 9 with the entire array of certificate-of-title statutes. In particular, Sections 9-303, 9-311, and 9-316(d) and (e) assume that the certificate-of-title statutes to which they apply do not have relation-back provisions (i.e., provisions under which perfection is deemed to occur at a time earlier than when the perfection steps actually are taken). A Legislative Note to Section 9-311 recommends the elimination of relation-back provisions in certificate-of-title statutes affecting perfection of security interests.

Ideally, at any given time, only one certificate of title is outstanding with respect to particular goods. In fact, however, sometimes more than one jurisdiction issues more than one certificate of title with respect to the same goods. This situation results from defects in certificate-of-title laws and the interstate coordination of those laws, not from deficiencies in this Article. As long as the possibility of multiple certificates of title remains, the potential for innocent parties to suffer losses will continue. At best, this Article can identify clearly which innocent parties will bear the losses in familiar fact patterns.

§ 9-304. LAW GOVERNING PERFECTION AND PRIORITY OF SECURITY INTERESTS IN DEPOSIT ACCOUNTS.

(a)   [Law of bank's jurisdiction governs.] The local law of a bank's jurisdiction governs perfection, the effect of perfection or nonperfection, and the priority of a security interest in a deposit account maintained with that bank.

(b) [Bank's jurisdiction.] The following rules determine a bank's jurisdiction for purposes of this part:

(1)   If an agreement between the bank and the debtor governing the deposit account expressly provides that a particular jurisdiction is the bank's jurisdiction for purposes of this part, this article, or [the Uniform Commercial Code], that jurisdiction is the bank's jurisdiction.

(2)   If paragraph (1) does not apply and an agreement between the bank and its customer governing the deposit account expressly provides that the agreement is governed by the law of a particular jurisdiction, that jurisdiction is the bank's jurisdiction.

(3)   If neither paragraph (1) nor paragraph (2) applies and an agreement between the bank and its customer governing the deposit account expressly provides that the deposit account is maintained at an office in a particular jurisdiction, that jurisdiction is the bank's jurisdiction.

(4)   If none of the preceding paragraphs applies, the bank's jurisdiction is the jurisdiction in which the office identified in an account statement as the office serving the customer's account is located.

(5)   If none of the preceding paragraphs applies, the bank's jurisdiction is the jurisdiction in which the chief executive office of the bank is located.

ANALYSIS

Since security interests in deposit accounts can only be perfected by control under the new article, the interests of third parties cannot be adversely affected by allowing the debtor and the bank to select the law which will be deemed to be the law of the bank's jurisdiction. That selection does not designate a place of filing. California, Hawaii, Illinois, Louisiana and Oregon have non-uniform amendments which already allow for Article 9 interests in deposit accounts under their UCCs. But none of these jurisdictions permit perfection by filing. Their present statutes prefigure "control" by allowing automatic perfection of interests granted to the bank with which the account is maintained and by requiring notice to or the consent of the depositary bank in other cases.

Official Comment

1. **Source.** New; derived from Section 8-110(e) and former Section 9-103(6).

2. **Deposit Accounts.** Under this section, the law of the "bank's jurisdiction" governs perfection and priority of a security interest in deposit accounts. Subsection (b) contains rules for determining the "bank's jurisdiction." The substance of these rules is substantially similar to that of the rules determining the "security intermediary's jurisdiction" under former Section 8-110(e), except that subsection (b)(1) provides more flexibility than the analogous provision in former Section 8-110(e)(1). Subsection (b)(1) permits the parties to choose the law of one jurisdiction to govern perfection and priority of security interests and a different governing law for other purposes. The parties' choice is effective, even if the jurisdiction whose law is chosen bears no relationship to the parties or the transaction. Section 8-110(e)(1) has been conformed to subsection (b)(1) of this section, and Section 9-305(b)(1), concerning a commodity intermediary's jurisdiction, makes a similar departure from former Section 9-103(6)(e)(i).

3. **Change in Law Governing Perfection.** When the bank's jurisdiction changes, the jurisdiction whose law governs perfection under subsection (a) changes, as well. Nevertheless, the change will not result in an immediate loss of perfection. See Section 9-316(f), (g).

§ 9-305. LAW GOVERNING PERFECTION AND PRIORITY OF SECURITY INTERESTS IN INVESTMENT PROPERTY.

(a) [Governing law: general rules.] Except as otherwise provided in subsection (c), the following rules apply:

(1) While a security certificate is located in a jurisdiction, the local law of that jurisdiction governs perfection, the effect of perfection or nonperfection, and the priority of a security interest in the certificated security represented thereby.

(2) The local law of the issuer's jurisdiction as specified in Section 8-110(d) governs perfection, the effect of perfection or nonperfection, and the priority of a security interest in an uncertificated security.

(3) The local law of the securities intermediary's jurisdiction as specified in Section 8-110(e) governs perfection, the effect of perfection or nonperfection, and the priority of a security interest in a security entitlement or securities account.

(4) The local law of the commodity intermediary's jurisdiction governs perfection, the effect of perfection or nonperfection, and

the priority of a security interest in a commodity contract or commodity account.

(b) [Commodity intermediary's jurisdiction.] The following rules determine a commodity intermediary's jurisdiction for purposes of this part:

(1)   If an agreement between the commodity intermediary and commodity customer governing the commodity account expressly provides that a particular jurisdiction is the commodity intermediary's jurisdiction for purposes of this part, this article, or [the Uniform Commercial Code], that jurisdiction is the commodity intermediary's jurisdiction.

(2)   If paragraph (1) does not apply and an agreement between the commodity intermediary and commodity customer governing the commodity account expressly provides that the agreement is governed by the law of a particular jurisdiction, that jurisdiction is the commodity intermediary's jurisdiction.

(3)   If neither paragraph (1) nor paragraph (2) applies and an agreement between the commodity intermediary and commodity customer governing the commodity account expressly provides that the commodity account is maintained at an office in a particular jurisdiction, that jurisdiction is the commodity intermediary's jurisdiction.

(4)   If none of the preceding paragraphs applies, the commodity intermediary's jurisdiction is the jurisdiction in which the office identified in an account statement as the office serving the commodity customer's account is located.

(5)   If none of the preceding paragraphs applies, the commodity intermediary's jurisdiction is the jurisdiction in which the chief executive office of the commodity intermediary is located.

(c) [When perfection governed by law of jurisdiction where debtor located.] The local law of the jurisdiction in which the debtor is located governs:

(1)   perfection of a security interest in investment property by filing;

(2)   automatic perfection of a security interest in investment property created by a broker or securities intermediary; and

(3)   automatic perfection of a security interest in a commodity contract or commodity account created by a commodity intermediary.

Official Comment

1. **Source.** Former Section 9-103(6).

2. **Investment Property: General Rules.** This section specifies choice-of-law rules for perfection and priority of security interests in investment property. Subsection (a)(1) covers security interests in certificated securities. Subsection (a)(2) covers security interests in uncertificated securities. Subsection (a)(3) covers security interests in security entitlements and securities accounts. Subsection (a)(4) covers security interests in commodity contracts and commodity accounts. The approach of each of these paragraphs is essentially the same. They identify the jurisdiction's law that governs questions of perfection and priority by using the same principles that Article 8 uses to determine other questions concerning that form of investment property. Thus, for certificated securities, the law of the jurisdiction in which the certificate is located governs. Cf. Section 8-110(c). For uncertificated securities, the law of the issuer's jurisdiction governs. Cf. Section 8-110(a). For security entitlements and securities accounts, the law of the securities intermediary's jurisdiction governs. Cf. Section 8-110(b). For commodity contracts and commodity accounts, the law of the commodity intermediary's jurisdiction governs. Because commodity contracts and commodity accounts are not governed by Article 8, subsection (b) contains rules that specify the commodity intermediary's jurisdiction. These are analogous to the rules in Section 8-110(e) specifying a securities intermediary's jurisdiction. Subsection (b)(1) affords the parties greater flexibility than did former Section 9-103(6)(3). See also Section 9-304(b) (bank's jurisdiction); Revised Section 8-110(e)(1) (securities intermediary's jurisdiction).

3. **Investment Property: Exceptions.** Subsection (c) establishes an exception to the general rules set out in subsection (a). It provides that perfection of a security interest by filing, automatic perfection of a security interest in investment property created by a debtor who is a broker or securities intermediary (see Section 9-309(10)), and automatic perfection of a security interest in a commodity contract or commodity account of a debtor who is a commodity intermediary (see Section 9-309(11) are governed by the law of the jurisdiction in which the debtor is located, as determined under Section 9-307.

4. **Examples:** The following examples illustrate the rules in this section:

Example 1: A customer residing in New Jersey maintains a securities account with Able & Co. The agreement between the customer and Able specifies that it is governed by Pennsylvania law but expressly provides that the law of California is Able's jurisdiction for purposes of the Uniform Commercial Code. Through the account the customer holds securities of a Massachusetts corporation, which Able holds through a clearing corporation located in New York. The customer obtains a margin loan from Able. Subsection (a)(3) provides that California law-the law of the securities intermediary's jurisdiction-governs perfection and priority of the security interest, even if California has no other relationship to the parties or the transaction.

Example 2: A customer residing in New Jersey maintains a securities account with Able & Co. The agreement between the customer and Able specifies that it is governed by Pennsylvania law. Through the account the customer holds securities of a Massachusetts corporation, which Able holds through a clearing corporation located in New York. The customer obtains a loan from a lender located in Illinois. The lender takes a security interest and perfects by obtaining an agreement among the debtor, itself, and Able, which satisfies the requirement of Section 8-106(d)(2) to give the lender control. Subsection (a)(3) provides that Pennsylvania law-the law of the securities intermediary's jurisdiction-governs perfection and priority of the security interest, even if Pennsylvania has no other relationship to the parties or the transaction.

Example 3: A customer residing in New Jersey maintains a securities account with Able & Co. The agreement between the customer and Able specifies that it is governed by Pennsylvania law. Through the account, the customer holds securities of a Massachusetts corporation, which Able holds through a clearing corporation located in New York. The customer borrows from SP-1, and SP-1 files a financing statement in New Jersey. Later, the customer obtains a loan from SP-2. SP-2 takes a security interest and perfects by obtaining an agreement among the debtor, itself, and Able, which satisfies the requirement of Section 8-106(d)(2) to give the SP-2 control. Subsection (c) provides that perfection of SP-1's security interest by filing is governed by the location of the debtor, so the filing in New Jersey was appropriate. Subsection (a)(3), however, provides that Pennsylvania law-the law of the securities intermediary's jurisdiction-governs all other questions of perfection and priority. Thus, Pennsylvania law governs perfection of SP-2's security interest, and Pennsylvania law also governs the priority of the security interests of SP-1 and SP-2.

5. **Change in Law Governing Perfection.** When the issuer's jurisdiction, the securities intermediary's jurisdiction, or commodity intermediary's jurisdiction changes, the jurisdiction whose law governs perfection under subsection (a) changes, as well. Similarly, the law governing perfection of a possessory security interest in a certificated security changes when the collateral is removed to another jurisdiction, see subsection (a)(1), and the law governing perfection by filing changes when the debtor changes its location. See subsection (c). Nevertheless, these changes will not result in an immediate loss of perfection. See Section 9-316.

§ 9-306. LAW GOVERNING PERFECTION AND PRIORITY OF SECURITY INTERESTS IN LETTER-OF-CREDIT RIGHTS.

(a) [Governing law: issuers or nominated person's jurisdiction.] Subject to subsection (c), the local law of the issuer's jurisdiction or a nominated person's jurisdiction governs perfection, the effect of perfection or nonperfection, and the priority of a security interest in a letter-of-credit right if the issuer's jurisdiction or nominated person's jurisdiction is a State.

(b) [Issuer's or nominated person's jurisdiction.] For purposes of this part, an issuer's jurisdiction or nominated person's jurisdiction is the jurisdiction whose law governs the liability of the issuer or nominated person with respect to the letter-of-credit right as provided in Section 5-116.

(c) [When section not applicable.] This section does not apply to a security interest that is perfected only under Section 9-308(d).

Official Comment

1. **Source.** New; derived in part from Section 8-110(e) and former Section 9-103(6).

2. *Sui Generis* **Treatment.** This section governs the applicable law for perfection and priority of security interests in letter-of-credit rights, other than a security interest perfected only under Section 9-308(d) (i.e., as a supporting obligation). The treatment differs substantially from that provided in Section 9-304 for deposit accounts. The basic rule is that the law of the issuer's or nominated person's (e.g., confirmer's) jurisdiction, derived from the terms of the letter of credit itself, controls perfection and priority, but only if the issuer's or nominated person's jurisdiction is a State, as defined in Section 9-102. If the issuer's or nominated person's jurisdiction is not a State, the baseline rule of Section 9-301 applies-perfection and priority are governed by the law of the debtor's location, determined under Section 9-307. Export transactions typically involve a foreign issuer and a domestic nominated person, such as a confirmer, located in a State. The principal goal of this section is to reduce the likelihood that perfection and priority would be governed by the law of a foreign jurisdiction in a transaction that is essentially domestic from the standpoint of the debtor-beneficiary, its creditors, and a domestic nominated person.

3. **Issuer's or Nominated Person's Jurisdiction.** Subsection (b) defers to the rules established under Section 5-116 for determination of an issuer's or nominated person's jurisdiction.

Example: An Italian bank issues a letter of credit that is confirmed by a New York bank. The beneficiary is a Connecticut corporation. The letter of credit provides that the issuer's liability is governed by Italian law, and the confirmation provides that the confirmer's liability is governed by the law of New York. Under Sections 9-306(b) and 5-116(a), Italy is the issuer's jurisdiction and New York is the confirmer's (nominated person's) jurisdiction. Because the confirmer's jurisdiction is a State, the law of New York governs perfection and priority of a security interest in the beneficiary's letter-of-credit right against the confirmer. See Section 9-306(a). However, because the issuer's jurisdiction is not a State, the law of that jurisdiction does not govern. See Section 9-306(a). Rather, the choice-of-law rule in Section 9-301(1) applies to perfection and priority of a security interest in the beneficiary's letter-of-credit right against the issuer. Under that section, perfection and priority are governed by the law of the jurisdiction in which the debtor (beneficiary) is located. That jurisdiction is Connecticut. See Section 9-307.

4. **Scope of this Section.** This section specifies only the law governing perfection, the effect of perfection or nonperfection, and priority of security interests. Section 5-116 specifies the law governing the liability of, and Article 5 (or other applicable law) deals with the rights and duties of, an issuer or nominated person. Perfection, nonperfection, and priority have no effect on those rights and duties.

5. **Change in Law Governing Perfection.** When the issuer's jurisdiction, or nominated person's jurisdiction changes, the jurisdiction whose law governs perfection under subsection (a) changes, as well. Nevertheless, this change will not result in an immediate loss of perfection. See Section 9-316(f), (g).

§ 9-307. LOCATION OF DEBTOR.

(a) ["Place of business."] In this section, "place of business" means a place where a debtor conducts its affairs.

(b) [Debtor's location: general rules.] Except as otherwise provided in this section, the following rules determine a debtor's location:

(1) An debtor who is an individual is located at the individual's principal residence.

(2) A debtor that is an organization and has only one place of business is located at its place of business.

(3) A debtor that is an organization and has more than one place of business is located at its chief executive office.

ANALYSIS

The principal residence of an individual controls as to both personal and business assets. Subsections (b)(2) and (b)(3) apply only to "any other debtor," not the individual of subsection (b)(1). This structure reverses the rule of old § 9-103(3)(d) which gives priority to a debtor's place of business if he has one. *See Secured Transactions* §§ 5.09[4] and 5.13[2].

> *Example A*: Webster resides in New Jersey but operates a business as a sole proprietor in New York. Under the Revised Article 9, filing as to the business assets of Webster located in New York or generated by the New York business must be made in New Jersey.

Revised Article 9 gives prominence to the debtor's principal residence but does not define the term. There is little or no case law defining "residence" under the old § 9-103(3) because it applies only to accounts, general intangibles, mobile goods, and non-possessory interests in chattel paper and directs that the debtor's residence controls as to these business assets only when a debtor does not have a place of business. A court may look to the cases defining "residence" under versions of old § 9-401 that require a local filing within a state at the place of the debtor's residence. *See Secured Transactions* § 5.13[2].

(c) [Limitation of applicability of subsection (b).] Subsection (b) applies only if a debtor's residence, place of business, or chief executive office, as applicable, is located in a jurisdiction whose law generally requires information concerning the existence of a nonpossessory security interest to be made generally available in a filing, recording, or registration system as a condition or result of the security interest's obtaining priority over the rights of a lien creditor with respect to the collateral. If subsection (b) does not apply, the debtor is located in the District of Columbia.

ANALYSIS

Filings as to foreign corporations are not governed by their state of organization because a foreign corporation is not a registered organization as defined in new § 9-102(a)(70). If the foreign corporation has its place of business or chief executive office in a jurisdiction that generally requires filing, recording or registration of non-possessory security interests, that jurisdiction will control under new § 9-307(b)(2) or (3). Otherwise, the debtor is deemed to be located in the District of Columbia.

> *Example A*: Corporation X is organized in Germany and has its chief executive office in that country. Corporation X opens a manufacturing plant in Idaho. It grants a security interest in equipment in the plant to a California Bank. Assuming that German law does not generally provide for filing, recording or registration of non-possessory security interests as a condition for priority over lien creditors, California Bank must file in the District of Columbia to perfect its interest in the equipment. Third parties searching as to the assets of Corporation X must be alert to the need to search in the District of Columbia.

> *Example B*: Same facts except that German law does generally require filing in order to perfect non-possessory security interests. Then the proper place to file and to search as to the Idaho equipment is in Germany. The location-of-the-debtor perfection rule of new § 9-301 includes locations in a foreign jurisdiction if that jurisdiction has the required public notice system.

See Secured Transactions § 5.13[4].

(d) [Continuation of location: cessation of existence, etc.] A person that ceases to exist, have a residence, or have a place of business continues to be located in the jurisdiction specified by subsections (b) and (c).

(e) [Location of registered organization organized under State law.] A registered organization that is organized under the law of a State is located in that State.

ANALYSIS

One of the most important changes made by the Revised Article 9 is to change the place of filing with respect to the goods of a domestic corporation. The "last event" test of old § 9-103(1)(b) required filing in the state where the goods were located. Under the revision filing is required in the state of organization. *See Secured Transactions* §§ 5.05 and 5.13[1]. This provision may be a political "hard sell" in some state legislatures.

(f) [Location of registered organization organized under federal law; bank branches and agencies.] Except as otherwise provided in subsection (i), a registered organization that is organized under the law of the United States and a branch or agency of a bank that is not organized under the law of the United States or a State are located:

(1)   in the State that the law of the United States designates, if the law designates a State of location;

(2)   in the State that the registered organization, branch, or agency designates, if the law of the United States authorizes the registered organization, branch, or agency to designate its State of location; or

(3)   in the District of Columbia, if neither paragraph (1) nor paragraph (2) applies.

(g) [Continuation of location: change in status of registered organization.] A registered organization continues to be located in the jurisdiction specified by subsection (e) or (f) notwithstanding:

(1)   the suspension, revocation, forfeiture, or lapse of the registered organization's status as such in its jurisdiction of organization; or

(2)   the dissolution, winding up, or cancellation of the existence of the registered organization.

(h)   [Location of United States.] The United States is located in the District of Columbia.

(i)   [Location of foreign bank branch or agency if licensed in only one state.] A branch or agency of a bank that is not organized under the law of the United States or a State is located in the State in which the branch or agency is licensed, if all branches and agencies of the bank are licensed in only one State.

(j)   [Location of foreign air carrier.] A foreign air carrier under the Federal Aviation Act of 1958, as amended, is located at the designated office of the agent upon which service of process may be made on behalf of the carrier.

(k)   [Section applies only to this part.] This section applies only for purposes of this part.

Official Comment

1. **Source.** Former Section 9-103(3)(d), substantially revised.

2. **General Rules.** As a general matter, the location of the debtor determines the jurisdiction whose law governs perfection of a security interest. See Sections 9-301(1), 9-305(c). It also governs priority of a security interest in certain types of intangible collateral, such as accounts, electronic chattel paper, and general intangibles. This section determines the location of the debtor for choice-of-law purposes, but not for other purposes. See subsection (k).

Subsection (b) states the general rules: An individual debtor is deemed to be located at the individual's principal residence with respect to both personal and business assets. Any other debtor is deemed to be located at its place of business if it has only one, or at its chief executive office if it has more than one place of business.

As used in this section, a "place of business" means a place where the debtor conducts its affairs. See subsection (a). Thus, every organization, even eleemosynary institutions and other organizations that do not conduct "for profit" business activities, has a "place of business." Under subsection (d), a person who ceases to exist, have a residence, or have a place of business continues to be located in the jurisdiction determined by subsection (b).

The term "chief executive office" is not defined in this Section or elsewhere in the Uniform Commercial Code. "Chief executive office" means the place from which the debtor manages the main part of its business operations or other affairs. This is the place where persons dealing with the debtor would normally look for credit information, and is the appropriate place for filing. With respect to most multi-state debtors, it will be simple to determine which of the debtor's offices is the "chief executive office." Even when a doubt arises, it would be rare that there could be more than two possibilities. A secured party in such a case may protect itself by perfecting under the law of each possible jurisdiction.

Similarly, the term "principal residence" is not defined. If the security interest in question is a purchase-money security interest in consumer goods which is perfected upon attachment, see Section 9-309(1), the choice of law may make no difference. In other cases, when a doubt arises, prudence may dictate perfecting under the law of each jurisdiction that might be the debtor's "principal residence."

The general rule is subject to several exceptions, each of which is discussed below.

3. **Non-U.S. Debtors.** Under the general rules of this section, a non-U.S. debtor normally would be located in a foreign jurisdiction and, as a consequence, foreign law would govern perfection. When foreign law affords no public notice of security interests, the general rule yields unacceptable results.

Accordingly, subsection (c) provides that the normal rules for determining the location of a debtor (i.e., the rules in subsection (b)) apply only if they yield a location that is "a jurisdiction whose law generally requires information concerning the existence of a nonpossessory security interest to be made generally available in a filing, recording, or registration system as a condition or result of the security interest's obtaining priority over the rights of a lien creditor with respect to the collateral." The phrase "generally requires" is meant to include legal regimes that generally require notice in a filing or recording system as a condition of perfecting nonpossessory security interests, but which permit perfection by another method (e.g., control, automatic perfection, temporary perfection) in limited circumstances. A jurisdiction that has adopted this Article or an earlier version of this Article is such a jurisdiction. If the rules in subsection (b) yield a jurisdiction whose law does not generally require notice in a filing or registration system, the debtor is located in the District of Columbia.

Example 1: Debtor is an English corporation with 7 offices in the United States and its chief executive office in London, England. Debtor creates a security interest in its accounts. Under subsection (b)(3), Debtor would be located in England. However, subsection (c) provides that subsection (b) applies only if English law generally conditions perfection on giving public notice in a filing, recording, or registration system. Otherwise, Debtor is located in the District of Columbia. Under Section 9-301(1), perfection, the effect of perfection, and priority are governed by the law of the jurisdiction of the debtor's location-here, England or the District of Columbia (depending on the content of English law).

Example 2: Debtor is an English corporation with 7 offices in the United States and its chief executive office in London, England. Debtor creates a security interest in equipment located in London. Under subsection (b)(3) Debtor would be located in England. However, subsection (c) provides that subsection (b) applies only if English law generally conditions perfection on giving public notice in a filing, recording, or registration system. Otherwise, Debtor is located in the District of Columbia. Under Section 9-301(1), perfection is governed by the law of the jurisdiction of the debtor's location, whereas, under Section 9-301(3), the law of the jurisdiction in which the collateral is located-here, England-governs priority.

The foregoing discussion assumes that each transaction bears an appropriate relation to the forum State. In the absence of an appropriate relation, the forum State's entire UCC, including the choice-of-law provisions in Article 9 (Sections 9-301 through 9-307), will not apply. See Section 9-109, Comment 9.

4. **Registered Organizations Organized Under Law of a State.** Under subsection (e), a registered organization (e.g., a corporation or limited partnership) organized under the law of a "State" (defined in Section 9-102) is located in its State of organization. Subsection (g) makes clear that events affecting the status of a registered organization, such as the dissolution of a corporation or revocation of its charter, do not affect its location for purposes of subsection (e). However, certain of these events may result in, or be accompanied by, a transfer of collateral from the registered organization to another debtor. This section does not determine whether a transfer occurs, nor does it determine the legal consequences of any transfer.

Determining the registered organization-debtor's location by reference to the jurisdiction of organization could provide some important side benefits for the filing systems. A jurisdiction could structure its filing system so that it would be impossible to make a mistake in a registered organization-debtor's name on a financing statement. For example, a filer would be informed if a filed record designated an incorrect corporate name for the debtor. Linking filing to the jurisdiction of organization also could reduce pressure on the system imposed by transactions in which registered organizations cease to exist-as a consequence of merger or consolidation, for example. The jurisdiction of organization might prohibit such transactions unless steps were taken to ensure that existing filings were refiled against a successor or terminated by the secured party.

5. **Registered Organizations Organized Under Law of United States; Branches and Agencies of Banks Not Organized Under Law of United States.** Subsection (f) specifies the location of a debtor that is a registered organization organized under the law of the United States. It defers to law of the United States, to the extent that that law determines, or authorizes the debtor to determine, the debtor's location. Thus, if the law of the United States designates a particular State as the debtor's location, that State is the debtor's location for purposes of this Article's choice-of-law rules. Similarly, if the law of the United States authorizes the registered organization to designate its State of location, the State that the registered organization designates is the State in which it is located for purposes of this Article's choice-of-law rules. In other cases, the debtor is located in the District of Columbia.

Subsection (f) also determines the location of branches and agencies of banks that are not organized under the law of the United States or a State. However, if all the branches and agencies of the bank are licensed only in one State, then they are located in that State. See subsection (i).

6. **United States.** To the extent that Article 9 governs (see Sections 1-105, 9-109(c)), the United States is located in the District of Columbia for purposes of this Article's choice-of-law rules. See subsection (h).

7. **Foreign Air Carriers.** Subsection (j) follows former Section 9-103(3)(d). To the extent that it is applicable, the Convention on the International Recognition of Rights in Aircraft (Geneva Convention) supersedes state

legislation on this subject, as set forth in Section 9-311(b), but some nations are not parties to that Convention.

[SUBPART 2. PERFECTION]

§ 9-308. WHEN SECURITY INTEREST OR AGRICULTURAL LIEN IS PERFECTED; CONTINUITY OF PERFECTION.

(a) [Perfection of security interest.] Except as otherwise provided in this section and Section 9-309, a security interest is perfected if it has attached and all of the applicable requirements for perfection in Sections 9-310 through 9-316 have been satisfied. A security interest is perfected when it attaches if the applicable requirements are satisfied before the security interest attaches.

(b) [Perfection of agricultural lien.] An agricultural lien is perfected if it has become effective and all of the applicable requirements for perfection in Section 9-310 have been satisfied. An agricultural lien is perfected when it becomes effective if the applicable requirements are satisfied before the agricultural lien becomes effective.

(c) [Continuous perfection; perfection by different methods.] A security interest or agricultural lien is perfected continuously if it is originally perfected by one method under this article and is later perfected by another method under this article, without an intermediate period when it was unperfected.

(d) [Supporting obligation.] Perfection of a security interest in collateral also perfects a security interest in a supporting obligation for the collateral.

(e) [Lien securing right to payment.] Perfection of a security interest in a right to payment or performance also perfects a security interest in a security interest, mortgage, or other lien on personal or real property securing the right.

ANALYSIS

"The note is the principal thing, the mortgage is an accessory." That has always been the traditional teaching of real estate law. This teaching has implications when a mortgagee assigns the note and mortgage.

> **Example A**: Homeowners obtain a mortgage loan from Local Mortgage Co. They execute a promissory note payable to Local Mortgage Co. to evidence the loan and secure the note with a mortgage or similar real estate security document covering their home. Local Mortgage Co. then obtains financing from Big Time Finance Co. assigning the note and mortgage to Big Time to secure the financing.

> **Example B**: Same as above except the source of financing for Local Mortgage Co. is not a large institutional entity. Instead, an individual is convinced to "invest" in the Local Mortgage Co. by lending it money secured by an assignment of the note and mortgage executed by Homeowners.

In these transactions, Local Mortgage Co. plays a double role. It is financing the Homeowners, but simultaneously occupies the role of a debtor borrowing from either Big Time Finance or the local "investor." Comment 4 to old § 9-102 was a source of little confusion as to what was necessary to perfect the interests of Big Time and the local "investor." The comment clearly confirmed the message of old § 9-102(3) (now new § 9-109(b)): Article 9 applies to the note even though it is secured by real estate. But the comment also seemed to suggest that compliance with the law of real estate finance might be necessary to perfect the interest of these assignees in the mortgage. This suggestion was inconsistent with the traditional wisdom that the mortgage is accessory to the note. In fact, the cases under the old Article 9 seemed always to end up with the traditional wisdom: they held that the assignee was perfected as to the mortgage and its proceeds if and only if the assignee was perfected as to the note. *See Secured Transactions* § 16.09. Under the old Article 9 a security interest in the note, an Article 9 instrument, could be perfected by taking possession. Old § 9-304(1). Thus Big Time and local "investor," both of whom had taken assignments to secure, would have a perfected interest in the mortgage if and only if they had taken possession of the note. *See Secured Transactions* § 16.09[2].

New § 9-308(e) reaffirms and generalizes the traditional wisdom. The operative slogan becomes: "The monetary obligation is the principal thing, the security for that obligation is the accessory." The monetary obligation may be in the form of a note or contract, it may be written or intangible. The security may be an interest in real estate or in personal property.

In the context of Examples 1 and 2 above, new § 9-308(e) reaffirms that perfecting an interest in the note also perfects the interest in the mortgage. But under Revised Article 9, Big Time and the local "investor" have two perfection options. When they take a security interest in the note to secure a debt owed to them, they can either file as to Local Mortgage Co. as debtor or take possession of the note. New §§ 9-312(a); 9-313(a). If the assignee for security takes possession or makes a proper Article 9 filing, it should have an interest in the mortgage or its proceeds which cannot be invalidated by a trustee in bankruptcy of the Mortgage Co. under § 544(a) of the Bankruptcy Code. On the other hand, if the note is sold outright, the interest of the transferee in the note is automatically perfected under new § 9-309(4) and the buyer's interest in the mortgage is correspondingly perfected under this new § 9-308(e). These results are the point of the whole exercise.

Revised Article 9 also affirms that it is possible to have a security interest in an Article 9 security interest. When a creditor takes a security interest in a monetary obligation, such an interest automatically attaches to the security interest securing the obligation. New § 9-203(g). If the creditor perfects its interest in the monetary obligation, that perfection automatically extends to the security interest. We are used to this type of derivative perfection under the old Article 9 when chattel paper is assigned. *See Secured Transactions* § 28.03. But the idea is less familiar when the security interest is in a pool of assets rather than a specific good.

> *Example C*: First Finance secures advances to Local Appliance Store with a floating lien security interest in all of the inventory of Local Appliance Store. First Finance then sells or grants a security interest in its right to payment from Local Appliance Store (whether embodied in a note or not) to Second Bank. If the transaction is an outright sale, Second Bank automatically has a perfected interest in the note or payment intangible as an asset of First Finance. New § 9-309(3) & (4). If the transaction with Second Bank is for security, Second Bank will need to file as to First Finance as debtor to perfect its interest in any payment intangible *vis a vis* the creditors of First Finance. New § 9-310. As to any instrument transferred as security, Second Bank has the option of filing or taking possession. New §§ 9-312(a), 9-313(a). New § 9-310(c) does not help Second Bank *vis a vis* the creditors of First Finance; it only establishes that no additional step of perfection is needed as to the creditors of Local Appliance Store. Once Second Bank is perfected as to the monetary obligation, it is automatically perfected as to the security interest which First Finance holds in the inventory of Local Appliance Store. What does it mean to have a

security interest in a security interest? Apparently, Second Bank succeeds to the rights of First Finance just as it would if it purchased chattel paper held by First Finance. If Appliance Store files a bankruptcy action, Second Bank will have a perfected interest in any proceeds of inventory received by Appliance Store before the bankruptcy and any post-petition proceeds traceable to pre-petition inventory items. *See* Bankruptcy Code § 552; *Secured Transactions* § 9.09.

(f)   [Security entitlement carried in securities account.] Perfection of a security interest in a securities account also perfects a security interest in the security entitlements carried in the securities account.

(g)   [Commodity contract carried in commodity account.] Perfection of a security interest in a commodity account also perfects a security interest in the commodity contracts carried in the commodity account.

Legislative Note: Any statute conflicting with subsection (e) must be made expressly subject to that subsection.

ANALYSIS

The following chart summarizes methods of perfecting security interests under Revised Article 9. It does not include temporary perfection under new § 9-312(e) or (f) or perfection as to proceeds under new § 9-315.

Interest	Method	Authority
Accounts		
A. Accounts which are not significant part of outstanding accounts	Automatic	9-309(2)
B. Health-care-insurance receivables assigned to provider of health care goods or services	Automatic	9-309(5)
C. Other Accounts	Filing	9-310(a)
Agricultural Liens	Filing	9-310(a)
Chattel Paper		
A. Tangible	Filing or possession	9-312(a); 9-313(a)
B. Electronic	Filing or control under § 9-105	9-312(a); 9-314(a)
Commercial Tort Claim	Filing	9-310
Consumer Goods		
A. Purchase money interests in assets not subject to certificate acts, federal law or treaties	Automatic	9-309(1)
B. Assets subject to certificate of title laws	Compliance with certificate of title acts; possession in cases covered by §§ 9-313(b) and 9-316(d)	9-311(b)
C. Assets subject to federal law or treaties	Compliance with applicable law or treaty	9-311(b)
D. Other consumer goods interests	Possession or filing	9-310(a); 9-313(a)
Deposit Accounts	Control under § 9-104	9-312(b)

Documents		
A. Negotiable	Filing or possession	9-312(a); 9-313(a)
B. Non-negotiable	See goods in possession of bailee who has issued non-negotiable document	
Equipment	Filing	9-310(a); 9-313(a)
Farm Products	Filing or possession	9-310(a); 9-313(a)
General Intangibles		
A. Sale of payment intangible	Automatic	9-309(3)
B. Payment intangible which is not a significant part of payment intangibles	Automatic	9-309(2)
C. Other transactions in General Intangibles	Filing	9-310(a)
Goods in possession of bailee who has issued non-negotiable document	Issuance of document in name of secured party; bailee's receipt of notification; or filing as to goods	9-312(d)
Instruments	Filing or possession	9-312(a); 9-313(a)
Inventory	Filing or possession	9-310(a); 9-313(a)
Interests (Other)		
A. Interests in investment property created by debtor other than broker or intermediary	Filing or control under § 9-106; delivery of certificated securities under § 8-301	9-312(a); 9-314
B. Interests created by broker or intermediary	Automatic	9-309(10)
Letter-of-credit right	Control under § 9-107 or by perfecting as to supported obligation	9-312(b)(2) 9-308(e)
Money	Possession under § 9-313	9-312(b)(3)

Official Comment

1. **Source.** Former Sections 9-303, 9-115(2).

2. **General Rule.** This Article uses the term "attach" to describe the point at which property becomes subject to a security interest. The requisites for attachment are stated in Section 9-203. When it attaches, a security interest may be either perfected or unperfected. "Perfected" means that the security interest has attached and the secured party has taken all the steps required by this Article as specified in Sections 9-310 through 9-316. A perfected security interest may still be or become subordinate to other interests. See, e.g., Sections 9-320, 9-322. However, in general, after perfection the secured party is protected against creditors and transferees of the debtor and, in particular, against any representative of creditors in insolvency proceedings instituted by or against the debtor. See, e.g., Section 9-317.

Subsection (a) explains that the time of perfection is when the security interest has attached and any necessary steps for perfection, such as taking possession or filing, have been taken. The "except" clause refers to the perfection-upon-attachment rules appearing in Section 9-309. It also reflects that other subsections of this section, e.g., subsection (d), contain automatic-perfection rules. If the steps for perfection have been taken in advance, as when the secured party files a financing statement before giving value or before the debtor acquires rights in the collateral, then the security interest is perfected when it attaches.

3. **Agricultural Liens.** Subsection (b) is new. It describes the elements of perfection of an agricultural lien.

4. **Continuous Perfection.** The following example illustrates the operation of subsection (c):

Example 1: Debtor, an importer, creates a security interest in goods that it imports and the documents of title that cover the goods. The secured party, Bank, takes possession of a negotiable bill of lading covering certain imported goods and thereby perfects its security interest in the bill of lading and the goods. See Sections 9-313(a), 9-312(c)(1). Bank releases the bill of lading to the debtor for the purpose of procuring the goods from the carrier and selling them. Under Section 9-312(f), Bank continues to have a perfected security interest in the document and goods for 20 days. Bank files a financing statement covering the collateral before the expiration of the 20-day period. Its security interest now continues perfected for as long as the filing is good.

If the successive stages of Bank's security interest succeed each other without an intervening gap, the security interest is "perfected continuously," and the date of perfection is when the security interest first became perfected (i.e., when Bank received possession of the bill of lading). If, however, there is a gap between stages-for example, if Bank does not file until after the expiration of the 20-day period specified in Section 9-312(f) and leaves the collateral in the debtor's possession-then, the chain being broken, the perfection is no longer continuous. The date of perfection would now be the date of filing (after expiration of the 20-day period). Bank's security interest would be vulnerable to any interests arising during the gap period which under Section 9-317 take priority over an unperfected security interest.

5. **Supporting Obligations.** Subsection (d) is new. It provides for automatic perfection of a security interest in a supporting obligation for collateral if the security interest in the collateral is perfected. This is unlikely to effect any change in the law prior to adoption of this Article.

Example 2: Buyer is obligated to pay Debtor for goods sold. Buyer's president guarantees the obligation. Debtor creates a security interest in the right to payment (account) in favor of Lender. Under Section 9-203(f), the security interest attaches to Debtor's rights under the guarantee (supporting obligation). Under subsection (d), perfection of the security interest in the account constitutes perfection of the security interest in Debtor's rights under the guarantee.

6. **Rights to Payment Secured by Lien.** Subsection (e) is new. It deals with the situation in which a security interest is created in a right to payment that is secured by a security interest, mortgage, or other lien.

Example 3: Owner gives to Mortgagee a mortgage on Blackacre to secure a loan. Owner's obligation to pay is evidenced by a promissory note. In need of working capital, Mortgagee borrows from Financer and creates a security interest in the note in favor of Financer. Section 9-203(g) adopts the traditional view that the mortgage follows the note; i.e., the transferee of the note acquires the mortgage, as well. This subsection adopts a similar principle: perfection of a security interest in the right to payment constitutes perfection of a security interest in the mortgage securing it.

An important consequence of the rules in Section 9-203(g) and subsection (e) is that, by acquiring a perfected security interest in a mortgage (or other secured) note, the secured party acquires a security interest in the mortgage (or other lien) that is senior to the rights of a person who becomes a lien creditor of the mortgagee (Article 9 debtor). See Section 9-317(a)(2). This result helps prevent the separation of the mortgage (or other lien) from the note.

Under this Article, attachment and perfection of a security interest in a secured right to payment do not of themselves affect the obligation to pay. For example, if the obligation is evidenced by a negotiable note, then Article 3 dictates the person whom the maker must pay to discharge the note and any lien securing it. See Section 3-602. If the right to payment is a payment intangible, then Section 9-406 determines whom the account debtor must pay.

Similarly, this Article does not determine who has the power to release a mortgage of record. That issue is determined by real-property law.

7. **Investment Property.** Subsections (f) and (g) follow former Section 9-115(2).

§ 9-309. SECURITY INTEREST PERFECTED UPON ATTACHMENT. The following security interests are perfected when they attach:

(1) a purchase-money security interest in consumer goods, except as otherwise provided in Section 9-311(b) with respect to consumer goods that are subject to a statute or treaty described in Section 9-311(a);

(2) an assignment of accounts or payment intangibles which does not by itself or in conjunction with other assignments to the same assignee transfer a significant part of the assignor's outstanding accounts or payment intangibles;

(3) a sale of a payment intangible;

(4) a sale of a promissory note;

(5) a security interest created by the assignment of a health-care-insurance receivable to the provider of the health-care goods or services;

(6) a security interest arising under Section 2-401, 2-505, 2-711(3), or 2A-508(5), until the debtor obtains possession of the collateral;

(7) a security interest of a collecting bank arising under Section 4-210;

(8) a security interest of an issuer or nominated person arising under Section 5-118;

(9) a security interest arising in the delivery of a financial asset under Section 9-206(c);

(10) a security interest in investment property created by a broker or securities intermediary;

(11) a security interest in a commodity contract or a commodity account created by a commodity intermediary;

(12) an assignment for the benefit of all creditors of the transferor and subsequent transfers by the assignee thereunder; and

(13) a security interest created by an assignment of a beneficial interest in a decedent's estate.

ANALYSIS

"Automatic perfection" has a nice ring to it. But each of these categories validates a secret interest with respect to which no public notice is required. When combined with the categories of interests that may be perfected through control under § 9-314, there is noticeable drift away from the ancient policy against secret interests in personal property assets. For example, the old Article 9 did not apply to a sale of a note. However, Article 3 demands a transfer of possession in order to either transfer or negotiate a negotiable note. *See* §§ 3-201, 3-203. What if a payee in an authenticated record purports to sell the note but retains possession? Except for new Section 9-331 (preserving the rights of a holder in due course), Article 9 primes Article 3. *See* § 3-102(b). The apparent effect of bringing a sale of a promissory note within Revised Article 9 and then allowing for automatic perfection of the sale is that the interest of the buyer of the negotiable note is good as against the creditors of the seller even though the seller still has possession. There is neither a public notice nor a change in possession to alert third parties that the seller is no longer the owner of the note it still possesses. The seller's trustee in bankruptcy cannot avoid the sale under Section 544(a) of the Bankruptcy Code because state law lien creditors do not have priority over the buyer under Revised Article 9. Secret interests are allowed to facilitate securitization of the notes.

The drama becomes even more interesting once one gets to applying the priority rules of new Article 9 to outright sales of notes and payment intangibles which are deemed to give the buyer perfected security interests.

> *Example A*: Assume that Debtor Co. borrows $500,000 from Valley Finance evidencing its obligation to repay the loan by executing a negotiable promissory note. Valley Finance makes an outright sale of the note to Trust One evidencing the sale in an authenticated record meeting the requirements of new Section 9-203, but retaining possession of the note. Unbeknowst to Trust One and in violation of the terms of the record, Valley Finance then sells and transfers the note to Local Finance Co.

If Local Finance qualifies as a holder in due course under Article 3, it will take free of the interest of Trust One. *See* new § 9-331(a). Even if Local Finance is not a holder in due course (*e.g.* it buys when the note is past due), Local Finance may win under new § 9-330(d) as a purchaser in good faith without knowledge that the sale violates the rights of Trust One. But Local Finance can obtain an interest under Article 9 and qualify as a good faith purchaser only if Valley Finance retained rights in the note despite its outright sale to Trust One. New §§ 1-201(37), 9-203(b)(2). And new § 9-318(a) declares that after the sale of a note the debtor has no legal or equitable interest in the note. It appears that the only way for Local Finance to prevail over Trust One is as a holder in due course. Trust One is not otherwise penalized for leaving possession of the note in the hands of Valley Finance.

> **Example B**: Assume that Debtor Co. borrows $500,000 from Valley Finance evidencing its obligation to repay in an electronic record. Valley Finance holds a payment intangible under new §§ 9-102(a)(2), (42) and (61). Valley Finance then makes an outright sale of this payment intangible to Trust One evidencing the sale in an authenticated record meeting the requirements of new Section 9-203. Then Valley Finance grants a security interest in its right to obtain payment to Local Finance, who is unaware of the sale to Trust One. Local Finance files to perfect its interest.

The interest of Trust One is automatically perfected under new § 9-309(3). Local Finance cannot rely on new § 9-330 or 9-331 because no instrument is involved. Priority would be governed by new § 9-322(a)(1) if one assumes that Valley Finance retained rights in the payment intangible despite the outright sale to Trust Co. But new § 9-318(a) provides that after an outright sale of a payment intangible the seller has no rights. Thus, it would not appear that the interest of Local Finance even attached. And even if new § 9-322(a)(1) applied, Trust One would have priority because it was perfected before Local Finance filed.

The bottom line is that bringing sales of payment intangibles within Article 9 and providing for their automatic perfection may discourage financers from taking security interests in such intangibles because they may lose to a buyer of the intangibles who has not filed.

The 1994 Revision of Article 8 introduced automatic perfection of all security interests in investment property granted by brokers or securities intermediaries. These interests are also secret interests validated to accommodate the practices of the securities industry. *See Secured Transactions* § 23.14[1][a].

Official Comment

1. **Source.** Derived from former Sections 9-302(1), 9-115(4)(c), (d), 9-116.

2. **Automatic Perfection.** This section contains the perfection-upon-attachment rules previously located in former Sections 9-302(1), 9-115(4)(c), (d), and 9-116. Rather than continue to state the rule by indirection, this section explicitly provides for perfection upon attachment.

3. **Purchase-Money Security Interest in Consumer Goods.** Former Section 9-302(1)(d) has been revised and appears here as paragraph (1). No filing or other step is required to perfect a purchase-money security interest in consumer goods, other than goods, such as automobiles, that are subject to a statute or treaty described in Section 9-311(a). However, filing is required to perfect a non-purchase-money security interest in consumer goods and is necessary to prevent a buyer of consumer goods from taking free of a security interest under Section 9-320(b). A fixture filing is required for priority over conflicting interests in fixtures to the extent provided in Section 9-334.

4. **Rights to Payment.** Paragraph (2) expands upon former Section 9-302(1)(e) by affording automatic perfection to certain assignments of payment intangibles as well as accounts. The purpose of paragraph (2) is to save from *ex post facto* invalidation casual or isolated assignments-assignments which no one would think of filing. Any person who regularly takes assignments of any debtor's accounts or payment intangibles should file. In this connection Section 9-109(d)(4) through (7), which excludes certain transfers of accounts, chattel paper, payment intangibles, and promissory notes from this Article, should be consulted.

Paragraphs (3) and (4), which are new, afford automatic perfection to sales of payment intangibles and promissory notes, respectively. They reflect the practice under former Article 9. Under that Article, filing a financing statement did not affect the rights of a buyer of payment intangibles or promissory notes, inasmuch as the former Article did not cover those sales. To the extent that the exception in paragraph (2) covers outright sales of payment intangibles, which automatically are perfected under paragraph (3), the exception is redundant.

5. **Health-Care-Insurance Receivables.** Paragraph (5) extends automatic perfection to assignments of health-care-insurance receivables if the assignment is made to the health-care provider that provided the health-care goods or services. The primary effect is that, when an individual assigns a right to payment under an insurance policy to the person who provided health-care goods or services, the provider has no need to file a financing statement against the individual. The normal filing requirements apply to other assignments of health-care-insurance receivables covered by this Article, e.g., assignments from the health-care provider to a financer.

6. **Investment Property.** Paragraph (9) replaces the last clause of former Section 9-116(2), concerning security interests that arise in the delivery of a financial asset.

Paragraphs (10) and (11) replace former Section 9-115(4)(c) and (d), concerning secured financing of securities and commodity firms and clearing corporations. The former sections indicated that, with respect to certain security interests created by a securities intermediary or commodity intermediary, "[t]he filing of a financing statement . . . has no effect for purposes of perfection or priority with respect to that security interest." No change in meaning is intended by the deletion of the quoted phrase.

Secured financing arrangements for securities firms are currently implemented in various ways. In some circumstances, lenders may require that the transactions be structured as "hard pledges," where the securities are transferred on the books of a clearing corporation from the debtor's account to the lender's account or to a special pledge account for the lender where they cannot be disposed of without the specific consent of the lender. In other circumstances, lenders are content with so-called "agreement to pledge" or "agreement to deliver" arrangements, where the debtor retains the positions in its own account, but reflects on its books that the positions have been hypothecated and promises that the securities will be transferred to the secured party's account on demand.

The perfection and priority rules of this Article are designed to facilitate current secured financing arrangements for securities firms as well as to provide sufficient flexibility to accommodate new arrangements that develop in the future. Hard pledge arrangements are covered by the concept of control. See Sections 9-314, 9-106, 8-106. Non-control secured financing arrangements for securities firms are covered by the automatic perfection rule of paragraph (10). Before the 1994 revision of Articles 8 and 9, agreement to pledge arrangements could be implemented under a provision that a security interest in securities given for new value under a written security agreement was perfected without filing or possession for a period of 21 days. Although the security interests were temporary in legal theory, the financing arrangements could, in practice, be continued indefinitely by rolling over the loans at least every 21 days. Accordingly, a knowledgeable creditor of a securities firm realizes that the firm's securities may be subject to security interests that are not discoverable from any public records. The automatic-perfection rule of paragraph (10) makes it unnecessary to engage in the purely formal practice of rolling over these arrangements every 21 days.

ANALYSIS

This commentary treats as a certainty what was only a possibility under the pre-1994 U.C.C. There is no case law upholding the rollover procedure under old §§ 9-304(4) or 8-321(2). Moreover, perpetual rollover seems to be inconsistent with the underlying policy of temporary perfection. *See Secured Transactions* § 23.14[1][a]. The reporters assume the law to be what the industry wants the law to be.

Official Comment

In some circumstances, a clearing corporation may be the debtor in a secured financing arrangement. For example, a clearing corporation that settles delivery-versus-payment transactions among its participants on a net, same-day basis relies on timely payments from all participants with net obligations due to the system. If a participant that is a net debtor were to default on its payment obligation, the clearing corporation would not receive some of the funds needed to settle with participants that are net creditors to the system. To complete end-of-day settlement after a payment default by a participant, a clearing corporation that settles on a net, same-day basis may need to draw on credit lines and pledge securities of the defaulting participant or other securities pledged by participants in the clearing corporation to secure such drawings. The clearing corporation may be the top-tier securities intermediary for the securities pledged, so that it would not be practical for the lender to obtain control. Even where the clearing corporation holds some types of securities through other intermediaries, however, the clearing corporation is unlikely to be able to complete the arrangements necessary to convey "control" over the securities to be pledged in time to complete settlement in a timely manner. However, the term "securities intermediary" is defined in Section 8-102(a)(14) to include clearing corporations. Thus, the perfection rule of paragraph (10) applies to security interests in investment property granted by clearing corporations.

7. **Beneficial Interests in Trusts.** Under former Section 9-302(1)(c), filing was not required to perfect a security interest created by an assignment of a beneficial interest in a trust. Because beneficial interests in trusts are now used as collateral with greater frequency in commercial transactions, under this Article filing is required to perfect a security interest in a beneficial interest.

8. **Assignments for Benefit of Creditors.** No filing or other action is required to perfect an assignment for the benefit of creditors. These assignments are not financing transactions, and the debtor ordinarily will not be engaging in further credit transactions.

§ 9-310. WHEN FILING REQUIRED TO PERFECT SECURITY INTEREST OR AGRICULTURAL LIEN; SECURITY INTERESTS AND AGRICULTURAL LIENS TO WHICH FILING PROVISIONS DO NOT APPLY.

(a) **[General rule: perfection by filing.]** Except as otherwise provided in subsection (b) and Section 9-312(b), a financing statement must be filed to perfect all security interests and agricultural liens.

(b) **[Exceptions: filing not necessary.]** The filing of a financing statement is not necessary to perfect a security interest:

(1)   that is perfected under Section 9-308(d), (e), (f), or (g);

(2)   that is perfected under Section 9-309 when it attaches;

(3)   in property subject to a statute, regulation, or treaty described in Section 9-311(a);

(4)   in goods in possession of a bailee which is perfected under Section 9-312(d)(1) or (2);

(5)   in certificated securities, documents, goods, or instruments which is perfected without filing or possession under Section 9-312(e), (f), or (g);

(6)   in collateral in the secured party's possession under Section 9-313;

(7)   in a certificated security which is perfected by delivery of the security certificate to the secured party under Section 9-313;

(8)   in deposit accounts, electronic chattel paper, investment property, or letter-of-credit rights which is perfected by control under Section 9-314;

(9)   in proceeds which is perfected under Section 9-315; or

(10)   that is perfected under Section 9-316.

(c) **[Assignment of perfected security interest.]** If a secured party assigns a perfected security interest or agricultural lien, a filing under this article is not required to continue the perfected status of the security interest against creditors of and transferees from the original debtor.

Official Comment

1. **Source.** Former Section 9-302(1), (2).

2. **General Rule.** Subsection (a) establishes a central Article 9 principle: Filing a financing statement is necessary for perfection of security interests and agricultural liens. However, filing is not necessary to perfect a security interest that is perfected by another permissible method, see subsection (b), nor does filing ordinarily perfect a security interest in a deposit account, letter-of-credit right, or money. See Section 9-312(b). Part 5 of the Article deals with the office in which to file, mechanics of filing, and operations of the filing office.

3. **Exemptions from Filing.** Subsection (b) lists the security interests for which filing is not required as a condition of perfection, because they are perfected automatically upon attachment (subsections (b)(2) and (b)(9)) or upon the occurrence of another event (subsections (b)(1), (b)(5), and (b)(9)), because they are perfected under the law of another jurisdiction (subsection (b)(10)), or because they are perfected by another method, such as by the secured party's taking possession or control (subsections (b)(3), (b)(4), (b)(5), (b)(6), (b)(7), and (b)(8)).

4. **Assignments of Perfected Security Interests.** Subsection (c) concerns assignment of a perfected security interest or agricultural lien. It provides that no filing is necessary in connection with an assignment by a secured party to an assignee in order to maintain perfection as against creditors of and transferees from the original debtor.

Example 1: Buyer buys goods from Seller, who retains a security interest in them. After Seller perfects the security interest by filing, Seller assigns the perfected security interest to X. The security interest, in X's hands and without further steps on X's part, continues perfected against *Buyer's* transferees and creditors.

Example 2: Dealer creates a security interest in specific equipment in favor of Lender. After Lender perfects the security interest in the equipment by filing, Lender assigns the chattel paper (which includes the perfected security interest in Dealer's equipment) to X. The security interest in the equipment, in X's hands and without further steps on X's part, continues perfected against *Dealer's* transferees and creditors. However, regardless of whether Lender made the assignment to secure Lender's obligation to X or whether the assignment was an outright sale of the chattel paper, the assignment creates a security interest in the chattel paper in favor of X. Accordingly, X must take whatever steps may be required for perfection in order to be protected against *Lender's* transferees and creditors with respect to the chattel paper.

Subsection (c) applies not only to an assignment of a security interest perfected by filing but also to an assignment of a security interest perfected by a method other than by filing, such as by control or by possession. Although subsection (c) addresses explicitly only the absence of an additional filing requirement, the same result normally will follow in the case of an assignment of a security interest perfected by a method other than by filing.

For example, as long as possession of collateral is maintained by an assignee or by the assignor or another person on behalf of the assignee, no further perfection steps need be taken on account of the assignment to continue perfection as against creditors and transferees of the original debtor. Of course, additional action may be required for perfection of the assignee's interest as against creditors and transferees of the *assignor*.

Similarly, subsection (c) applies to the assignment of a security interest perfected by compliance with a statute, regulation, or treaty under Section 9-311(b), such as a certificate-of-title statute. Unless the statute expressly provides to the contrary, the security interest will remain perfected against creditors of and transferees from the original debtor, even if the assignee takes no action to cause the certificate of title to reflect the assignment or to cause its name to appear on the certificate of title. See PEB Commentary No. 12, which discusses this issue under former Section 9-302(3). Compliance with the statute is "equivalent to filing" under Section 9-311(b).

§ 9-311. PERFECTION OF SECURITY INTERESTS IN PROPERTY SUBJECT TO CERTAIN STATUTES, REGULATIONS, AND TREATIES.

(a) [Security interest subject to other law.] Except as otherwise provided in subsection (d), the filing of a financing statement is not necessary or effective to perfect a security interest in property subject to:

(1) a statute, regulation, or treaty of the United States whose requirements for a security interest's obtaining priority over the rights of a lien creditor with respect to the property preempt Section 9-310(a);

(2) [list any certificate-of-title statute covering automobiles, trailers, mobile homes, boats, farm tractors, or the like, which provides for a security interest to be indicated on the certificate as a condition or result of perfection, and any non-Uniform Commercial Code central filing statute]; or

(3) a certificate-of-title statute of another jurisdiction which provides for a security interest to be indicated on the certificate as a condition or result of the security interest's obtaining priority over the rights of a lien creditor with respect to the property.

(b) [Compliance with other law.] Compliance with the requirements of a statute, regulation, or treaty described in subsection (a) for obtaining priority over the rights of a lien creditor is equivalent to the filing of a financing statement under this article. Except as otherwise provided in subsection (d) and Sections 9-313 and 9-316(d) and (e) for goods covered by a certificate of title, a security interest in property subject to a statute, regulation, or treaty described in subsection (a) may be perfected only by compliance with those requirements, and a security interest so perfected remains perfected notwithstanding a change in the use or transfer of possession of the collateral.

(c) [Duration and renewal of perfection.] Except as otherwise provided in subsection (d) and Section 9-316(d) and (e), duration and renewal of perfection of a security interest perfected by compliance with the requirements prescribed by a statute, regulation, or treaty described in subsection (a) are governed by the statute, regulation, or treaty. In other respects, the security interest is subject to this article.

(d) [Inapplicability to certain inventory.] During any period in which collateral is inventory held for sale or lease by a person or leased by that person as lessor and that person is in the business of selling or leasing goods of that kind, this section does not apply to a security interest in that collateral created by that person as debtor.

Legislative Note: This Article contemplates that perfection of a security interest in goods covered by a certificate of title occurs upon receipt by appropriate State officials of a properly tendered application for a certificate of title on which the security interest is to be indicated, without a relation back to an earlier time. States whose certificate-of-title statutes provide for perfection at a different time or contain a relation-back provision should amend the statutes accordingly.

Official Comment

1. **Source.** Former Section 9-302(3), (4).

2. **Federal Statutes, Regulations, and Treaties.** Subsection (a)(1) exempts from the filing provisions of this Article transactions as to which a system of filing-state or federal-has been established under federal law. Subsection (b) makes clear that when such a system exists, perfection of a relevant security interest can be achieved only through compliance with that system (i.e., filing under this Article is not a permissible alternative).

An example of the type of federal statute referred to in subsection (a)(1) is 49 U.S.C. §§ 44107-11, for civil aircraft of the United States. The Assignment of Claims Act of 1940, as amended, provides for notice to contracting and disbursing officers and to sureties on bonds but does not establish a national filing system and therefore is not within the scope of subsection (a)(1). An assignee of a claim against the United States may benefit from compliance with the Assignment of Claims Act. But regardless of whether the assignee complies with that Act, the assignee must file under this Article in order to perfect its security interest against creditors and transferees of its assignor.

Subsection (a)(1) provides explicitly that the filing requirement of this Article defers only to federal statutes, regulations, or treaties whose requirements for a security interest's obtaining priority over the rights of a lien creditor preempt Section 9-310(a). The provision eschews reference to the term "perfection," inasmuch as Section 9-308 specifies the meaning of that term and a preemptive rule may use other terminology.

3. **State Statutes.** Subsections (a)(2) and (3) exempt from the filing requirements of this Article transactions covered by State certificate-of-title statutes covering motor vehicles and the like. The description of certificate-of-title statutes in subsections (a)(2) and (a)(3) tracks the language of the definition of "certificate of title" in Section 9-102. For a discussion of the operation of state certificate-of-title statutes in interstate contexts, see the Comments to Section 9-303.

Some states have enacted central filing statutes with respect to secured transactions in kinds of property that are of special importance in the local economy. Subsection (a)(2) defers to these statutes with respect to filing for that property.

4. **Inventory Covered by Certificate of Title.** Under subsection (d), perfection of a security interest in the inventory of a dealer is governed by the normal perfection rules, even if the inventory is covered by a certificate of title. Under former Section 9-302(3), a secured party who financed a dealer may have needed to perfect by filing for goods held for sale and by compliance with a certificate-of-title statute for goods held for lease. In some cases, this may have required notation on thousands of certificates. The problem would have been compounded by the fact that dealers, particularly of automobiles, often do not know whether a particular item of inventory will be sold or leased. Under subsection (d), notation is both unnecessary and ineffective.

The filing and other perfection provisions of this Article apply to goods covered by a certificate of title only "during any period in which collateral is inventory held for sale or lease or leased." If the debtor takes goods of this kind out of inventory and uses them, say, as equipment, a filed financing statement would not remain effective to perfect a security interest.

5. **Compliance with Perfection Requirements of Other Statute.** Subsection (b) makes clear that compliance with the perfection requirements (i.e., the requirements for obtaining priority over a lien creditor), but not other requirements, of a statute, regulation, or treaty described in subsection (a) is sufficient for perfection under this Article. Perfection of a security interest under a such a statute, regulation, or treaty has all the consequences of perfection under this Article.

The interplay of this section with certain certificate-of-title statutes may create confusion and uncertainty. For example, statutes under which perfection does not occur until a certificate of title is issued will create a gap between the time that the goods are covered by the certificate under Section 9-303 and the time of perfection. If the gap is long enough, it may result in turning some unobjectionable transactions into avoidable preferences under Bankruptcy Code Section 547. (The preference risk arises if more than ten days (or 20 days, in the case of a purchase-money security interest) passes between the time a security interest attaches (or the debtor receives possession of the collateral, in the case of a purchase-money security interest) and the time it is perfected.) Accordingly, the Legislative Note to this section instructs the legislature to amend the applicable certificate-of-title statute to provide that perfection occurs upon receipt by the appropriate State official of a properly tendered application for a certificate of title on which the security interest is to be indicated.

Under some certificate-of-title statutes, including the Uniform Motor Vehicle Certificate of Title and Anti-Theft Act, perfection generally occurs upon delivery of specified documents to a state official but may, under certain circumstances, relate back to the time of attachment. This relation-back feature can create great difficulties for the application of the rules in Sections 9-303 and 9-311(b). Accordingly, the Legislative Note also recommends to legislatures that they remove any relation-back provisions from certificate-of-title statutes affecting security interests.

6. **Compliance with Perfection Requirements of Other Statute as Equivalent to Filing.** Under Subsection (b), compliance with the perfection requirements (i.e., the requirements for obtaining priority over a lien creditor) of a statute, regulation, or treaty described in subsection (a) "is equivalent to the filing of a financing statement."

The quoted phrase appeared in former Section 9-302(3). Its meaning was unclear, and many questions arose concerning the extent to which and manner in which Article 9 rules referring to "filing" were applicable to perfection by compliance with a certificate-of-title statute. This Article takes a variety of approaches for applying Article 9's filing rules to compliance with other statutes and treaties. First, as discussed above in Comment 5, it leaves the determination of some rules, such as the rule establishing time of perfection (Section 9-516(a)), to the other statutes themselves. Second, this Article explicitly applies some Article 9 filing rules to perfection under other statutes or treaties. See, e.g., Section 9-505. Third, this Article makes other Article 9 rules applicable to security interests perfected by compliance with another statute through the "equivalent to... filing" provision in the first sentence of Section 9-311(b). The third approach is reflected for the most part in occasional Comments explaining how particular rules apply when perfection is accomplished under Section 9-311(b). See, e.g., Section 9-310, Comment 4; Section 9-315, Comment 6; Section 9-317, Comment 8. The absence of a

Comment indicating that a particular filing provision applies to perfection pursuant to Section 9-311(b) does not mean the provision is inapplicable.

7. **Perfection by Possession of Goods Covered by Certificate-of-Title Statute.** A secured party who holds a security interest perfected under the law of State A in goods that subsequently are covered by a State B certificate of title may face a predicament. Ordinarily, the secured party will have four months under State B's Section 9-316(c) and (d) in which to (re)perfect as against a purchaser of the goods by having its security interest noted on a State B certificate. This procedure is likely to require the cooperation of the debtor and any competing secured party whose security interest has been noted on the certificate. Comment 4(e) to former Section 9-103 observed that "that cooperation is not likely to be forthcoming from an owner who wrongfully procured the issuance of a new certificate not showing the out-of-state security interest, or from a local secured party finding himself in a priority contest with the out-of-state secured party." According to that Comment, "[t]he only solution for the out-of-state secured party under present certificate of title statutes seems to be to reperfect by possession, i.e., by repossessing the goods." But the "solution" may not have worked: Former Section 9-302(4) provided that a security interest in property subject to a certificate-of-title statute "can be perfected only by compliance therewith."

Sections 9-316(d) and (e), 9-311(c), and 9-313(b) of this Article resolve the conflict by providing that a security interest that remains perfected solely by virtue of Section 9-316(e) can be (re)perfected by the secured party's taking possession of the collateral. These sections contemplate only that taking possession of goods covered by a certificate of title will work as a method of perfection. None of these sections creates a right to take possession. Section 9-609 and the agreement of the parties define the secured party's right to take possession.

§ 9-312. PERFECTION OF SECURITY INTERESTS IN CHATTEL PAPER, DEPOSIT ACCOUNTS, DOCUMENTS, GOODS COVERED BY DOCUMENTS, INSTRUMENTS, INVESTMENT PROPERTY, LETTER-OF-CREDIT RIGHTS, AND MONEY; PERFECTION BY PERMISSIVE FILING; TEMPORARY PERFECTION WITHOUT FILING OR TRANSFER OF POSSESSION.

(a) [Perfection by filing permitted.] A security interest in chattel paper, negotiable documents, instruments, or investment property may be perfected by filing.

(b) [Control or possession of certain collateral.] Except as otherwise provided in Section 9-315(c) and (d) for proceeds:

(1)   a security interest in a deposit account may be perfected only by control under Section 9-314;

(2)   and except as otherwise provided in Section 9-308(d), a security interest in a letter-of-credit right may be perfected only by control under Section 9-314; and

(3)   a security interest in money may be perfected only by the secured party's taking possession under Section 9-313.

(c) [Goods covered by negotiable document.] While goods are in the possession of a bailee that has issued a negotiable document covering the goods:

(1)   a security interest in the goods may be perfected by perfecting a security interest in the document; and

(2)   a security interest perfected in the document has priority over any security interest that becomes perfected in the goods by another method during that time.

(d) [Goods covered by nonnegotiable document.] While goods are in the possession of a bailee that has issued a nonnegotiable document covering the goods, a security interest in the goods may be perfected by:

(1)   issuance of a document in the name of the secured party;

(2)   the bailee's receipt of notification of the secured party's interest; or

(3)   filing as to the goods.

(e) [Temporary perfection: new value.] A security interest in certificated securities, negotiable documents, or instruments is perfected without filing or the taking of possession for a period of 20 days from the time it attaches to the extent that it arises for new value given under an authenticated security agreement.

(f) [Temporary perfection: goods or documents made available to debtor.] A perfected security interest in a negotiable document or goods in possession of a bailee, other than one that has issued a negotiable document for the goods, remains perfected for 20 days without filing if the secured party makes available to the debtor the goods or documents representing the goods for the purpose of:

(1)   ultimate sale or exchange; or

(2)   loading, unloading, storing, shipping, transshipping, manufacturing, processing, or otherwise dealing with them in a manner preliminary to their sale or exchange.

(g) [Temporary perfection: delivery of security certificate or instrument to debtor.] A perfected security interest in a certificated security or instrument remains perfected for 20 days without filing if the secured party delivers the security certificate or instrument to the debtor for the purpose of:

(1)   ultimate sale or exchange; or

(2)   presentation, collection, enforcement, renewal, or registration of transfer.

(h) [Expiration of temporary perfection.] After the 20-day period specified in subsection (e), (f), or (g) expires, perfection depends upon compliance with this article.

Official Comment

1. **Source.** Former Section 9-304, with additions and some changes.

2. **Instruments.** Under subsection (a), a security interest in instruments may be perfected by filing. This rule represents an important change from former Article 9, under which the secured party's taking possession of an instrument was the only method of achieving long-term perfection. The rule is likely to be particularly useful in transactions involving large number of notes that a debtor uses as collateral but continues to collect from the makers. A security interest perfected by filing is subject to defeat by certain subsequent purchasers (including secured parties). Under Section 9-330(d), purchasers for value who take possession of an instrument without knowledge that the purchase violates the rights of the secured party generally would achieve priority over a security interest in the instrument perfected by filing. In addition, Section 9-331 provides that filing a financing statement does not constitute notice that would preclude a subsequent purchaser from becoming a holder in due course and taking free of all claims under Section 3-306.

3. **Chattel Paper; Negotiable Documents.** Subsection (a) further provides that filing is available as a method of perfection for security interests in chattel paper and negotiable documents. Tangible chattel paper is sometimes delivered to the assignee, and sometimes left in the hands of the assignor for collection. Subsection (a) allows the assignee to perfect its security interest by filing in the latter case. Alternatively, the assignee may perfect by taking possession. See Section 9-313(a). An assignee of electronic chattel paper may perfect by taking control. See Sections 9-314(a), 9-105. The security interest of an assignee who takes possession or control may qualify for priority over a competing security interest perfected by filing. See Section 9-330.

Negotiable documents may be, and usually are, delivered to the secured party. The secured party's taking possession will suffice as a perfection step. See Section 9-313(a). However, as is the case with chattel paper, a security interest in a negotiable document may be perfected by filing.

4. **Investment Property.** A security interest in investment property, including certificated securities, uncertificated securities, security entitlements, and securities accounts, may be perfected by filing. However, security interests created by brokers, securities intermediaries, or commodity intermediaries are automatically perfected; filing is of no effect. See Section 9-309(10), (11). A security interest in all kinds of investment property also may be perfected by control, see Sections 9-314, 9-106, and a security interest in a certificated security also may be perfected by the secured party's taking delivery under Section 8-301. See Section 9-313(a). A security interest perfected only by filing is subordinate to a conflicting security interest perfected by control or delivery. See Section 9-328(1), (5). Thus, although filing is a permissible method of perfection, a secured party who perfects by filing takes the risk that the debtor has granted or will grant a security interest in the same collateral to another party who obtains control. Also, perfection by filing would not give the secured party protection against other types of adverse claims, since the Article 8 adverse claim cut-off rules require control. See Section 8-510.

5. **Deposit Accounts.** Under new subsection (b)(1), the only method of perfecting a security interest in a deposit account as original collateral is by control. Filing is ineffective, except as provided in Section 9-315 with respect to proceeds. As explained in Section 9-104, "control" can arise as a result of an agreement among the secured party, debtor, and bank, whereby the bank agrees to comply with instructions of the secured party with respect to disposition of the funds on deposit, even though the debtor retains the right to direct disposition of the funds. Thus, subsection (b)(1) takes an intermediate position between certain non-UCC law, which conditions the effectiveness of a security interest on the secured party's enjoyment of such dominion and control over the deposit account that the debtor is unable to dispose of the funds, and the approach this Article takes to securities accounts, under which a secured party who is unable to reach the collateral without resort to judicial process may perfect by filing. By conditioning perfection on "control," rather than requiring the secured party to enjoy absolute dominion to the exclusion of the debtor, subsection (b)(1) permits perfection in a wide variety of transactions, including those in which the secured party actually relies on the deposit account in extending credit and maintains some meaningful dominion over it, but does not wish to deprive the debtor of access to the funds altogether.

6. **Letter-of-Credit Rights.** Letter-of-credit rights commonly are "supporting obligations," as defined in Section 9-102. Perfection as to the related account, chattel paper, document, general intangible, instrument, or

investment property will perfect as to the letter-of-credit rights. See Section 9-308(d). Subsection (b)(2) provides that, in other cases, a security interest in a letter-of-credit right may be perfected only by control. "Control," for these purposes, is explained in Section 9-107.

7. **Goods Covered by Document of Title.** Subsection (c) applies to goods in the possession of a bailee who has issued a negotiable document covering the goods. Subsection (d) applies to goods in the possession of a bailee who has issued a nonnegotiable document of title, including a document of title that is "non-negotiable" under Section 7-104. Section 9-313 governs perfection of a security interest in goods in the possession of a bailee who has not issued a document of title.

Subsection (c) clarifies the perfection and priority rules in former Section 9-304(2). Consistently with the provisions of Article 7, subsection (c) takes the position that, as long as a negotiable document covering goods is outstanding, title to the goods is, so to say, locked up in the document. Accordingly, a security interest in goods covered by a negotiable document may be perfected by perfecting a security interest in the document. The security interest also may be perfected by another method, e.g., by filing. The priority rule in subsection (c) governs only priority between (i) a security interest in goods which is perfected by perfecting in the document and (ii) a security interest in the goods which becomes perfected by another method while the goods are covered by the document.

Example 1: While wheat is in a grain elevator and covered by a negotiable warehouse receipt, Debtor creates a security interest in the wheat in favor of SP-1 and SP-2. SP-1 perfects by filing a financing statement covering "wheat." Thereafter, SP-2 perfects by filing a financing statement describing the warehouse receipt. Subsection (c)(1) provides that SP-2's security interest is perfected. Subsection (c)(2) provides that SP-2's security interest is senior to SP-1's.

Example 2: The facts are as in Example 1, but SP-1's security interest attached and was perfected before the goods were delivered to the grain elevator. Subsection (c)(2) does not apply, because SP-1's security interest did not become perfected during the time that the wheat was in the possession of a bailee. Rather, the first-to-file-or-perfect priority rule applies. See Section 9-322.

A secured party may become "a holder to whom a negotiable document of title has been duly negotiated" under Section 7-501. If so, the secured party acquires the rights specified by Article 7. Article 9 does not limit those rights, which may include the right to priority over an earlier-perfected security interest. See Section 9-331(a).

Subsection (d) takes a different approach to the problem of goods covered by a nonnegotiable document. Here, title to the goods is not looked on as being locked up in the document, and the secured party may perfect its security interest directly in the goods by filing as to them. The subsection provides two other methods of perfection: issuance of the document in the secured party's name (as consignee of a straight bill of lading or the person to whom delivery would be made under a non-negotiable warehouse receipt) and receipt of notification of the secured party's interest by the bailee. Perfection under subsection (d) occurs when the bailee receives notification of the secured party's interest in the goods, regardless of who sends the notification. Receipt of notification is effective to perfect, regardless of whether the bailee responds. Unlike former Section 9-304(3), from which it derives, subsection (d) does not apply to goods in the possession of a bailee who has not issued a document of title. Section 9-313(c) covers that case and provides that perfection by possession as to goods not covered by a document requires the bailee's acknowledgment.

8. **Temporary Perfection Without Having First Otherwise Perfected.** Subsection (e) follows former Section 9-304(4) in giving perfected status to security interests in certificated securities, instruments, and negotiable documents for a short period (reduced from 21 to 20 days, which is the time period generally applicable in this Article), although there has been no filing and the collateral is in the debtor's possession. The 20-day temporary perfection runs from the date of attachment. There is no limitation on the purpose for which the debtor is in possession, but the secured party must have given "new value" (defined in Section 9-102) under an authenticated security agreement.

9. **Maintaining Perfection After Surrendering Possession.** There are a variety of legitimate reasons-many of them are described in subsections (f) and (g)-why certain types of collateral must be released temporarily to a debtor. No useful purpose would be served by cluttering the files with records of such exceedingly short term transactions.

Subsection (f) affords the possibility of 20-day perfection in negotiable documents and goods in the possession of a bailee but not covered by a negotiable document. Subsection (g) provides for 20-day perfection in certificated securities and instruments. These subsections derive from former Section 9-305(5). However, the period of temporary perfection has been reduced from 21 to 20 days, which is the time period generally applicable in this Article, and "enforcement" has been added in subsection (g) as one of the special and limited purposes for which a secured party can release an instrument or certificated security to the debtor and still remain perfected. The period of temporary perfection runs from the date a secured party who already has a perfected security interest turns over the collateral to the debtor. There is no new value requirement, but the turnover must be for one or more of the purposes stated in subsection (f) or (g). The 20-day period may be extended by perfecting as to the collateral by another method before the period expires. However, if the security interest is not perfected by another method until after the 20-day period expires, there will be a gap during which the security interest is unperfected.

Temporary perfection extends only to the negotiable document or goods under subsections (f) and only to the certificated security or instrument under subsection (g). It does not extend to proceeds. If the collateral is sold, the security interest will continue in the proceeds for the period specified in Section 9-315.

Subsections (f) and (g) deal only with perfection. Other sections of this Article govern the priority of a security interest in goods after surrender of the document covering them. In the case of a purchase-money security interest in inventory, priority may be conditioned upon giving notification to a prior inventory financer. See Section 9-324.

§ 9-313. WHEN POSSESSION BY OR DELIVERY TO SECURED PARTY PERFECTS SECURITY INTEREST WITHOUT FILING.

(a)   [Perfection by possession or delivery.] Except as otherwise provided in subsection (b), a secured party may perfect a security interest in negotiable documents, goods, instruments, money, or tangible chattel paper by taking possession of the collateral. A secured party may perfect a security interest in certificated securities by taking delivery of the certificated securities under Section 8-301.

(b)   [Goods covered by certificate of title.] With respect to goods covered by a certificate of title issued by this State, a secured party may perfect a security interest in the goods by taking possession of the goods only in the circumstances described in Section 9-316(d).

(c)   [Collateral in possession of person other than debtor.] With respect to collateral other than certificated securities and goods covered by a document, a secured party takes possession of collateral in the possession of a person other than the debtor, the secured party, or a lessee of the collateral from the debtor in the ordinary course of the debtor's business, when:

(1)   the person in possession authenticates a record acknowledging that it holds possession of the collateral for the secured party's benefit; or

(2)   the person takes possession of the collateral after having authenticated a record acknowledging that it will hold possession of collateral for the secured party's benefit.

ANALYSIS

Revised Article 9 returns to the common law requirement of attornment when collateral is in the hands of a third party who has not issued a document of title covering the goods. Attornment requires that the third party consent to holding the collateral for the secured party. Requiring such attornment contrasts with the rule of old § 9-305 which simply required notification to the bailee holding the goods. Comment 2 to old § 9-305 stated "this rule rejects the common law doctrine that it is necessary for the bailee to attorn to the secured party or acknowledge that he now holds on his behalf." When the only way to perfect an interest in the collateral is by the secured party taking possession, an attornment requirement allows a first pledgee to veto the perfection of a secondary security interest by refusing to attorn. Under the original Article 9 the only way to perfect an interest in a promissory note or certificated security was by taking possession. *See Secured Transactions* §§ 6A.05[2] and 23.03. Thus, the original drafters rejected the attornment requirement to assure that a debtor could perfect secondary interests in these important assets. This rejection in effect required the first pledgee to act both for itself and for the second creditor when it received notification of the second creditor's interest. Under the Revised Article 9 interests in notes and certificated securities may be perfected by filing. The second creditor no longer needs the first pledgee to hold the collateral for him so that the second creditor can be deemed to be in possession. This change as to methods of perfection cleared the way for the revisers to return the attornment rule. Under the revision, money is the only asset for which possession is the only path to perfection. New § 9-312(b)(3). The attornment requirement will give the first pledgee of money the power to prevent a perfection of a secondary interest.

Under new § 9-313(g) attornment does not impose duties to act for the secured creditor one is attorning to or to disclose the relationship to third parties unless the person making the attornment agrees to do so or such duties are imposed by other law. If other law does not impose any duties, attornment could be considered to be a meaningless ritual insofar as giving notice to third parties. The revisers do not explain why some obligation to a secured party is not implicit in an acknowledgment that the possessor "holds" the collateral for the benefit of the secured party.

The rule of attornment does not apply when goods are in the hands of a bailee who has issued a non-negotiable document of title such as a non-negotiable bill of lading or warehouse receipt. In that event, notification to the issuer of the document alone is sufficient to perfect an interest in the goods under new § 9-312(d)(2) even though filing is also a method of perfection. Differences in business practices with respect to the shipment and storage of goods as opposed to financing on the security of notes and securities may explain this difference in codal treatment.

(d) [Time of perfection by possession; continuation of perfection.] If perfection of a security interest depends upon possession of the collateral by a secured party, perfection occurs no earlier than the time the secured party takes possession and continues only while the secured party retains possession.

(e) [Time of perfection by delivery; continuation of perfection.] A security interest in a certificated security in registered form is perfected by delivery when delivery of the certificated security occurs under Section 8-301 and remains perfected by delivery until the debtor obtains possession of the security certificate.

(f) [Acknowledgment not required.] A person in possession of collateral is not required to acknowledge that it holds possession for a secured party's benefit.

(g) [Effectiveness of acknowledgment; no duties or confirmation.] If a person acknowledges that it holds possession for the secured party's benefit:

(1) the acknowledgment is effective under subsection (c) or Section 8-301(a), even if the acknowledgment violates the rights of a debtor; and

(2) unless the person otherwise agrees or law other than this article otherwise provides, the person does not owe any duty to the secured party and is not required to confirm the acknowledgment to another person.

(h) [Secured party's delivery to person other than debtor.] A secured party having possession of collateral does not relinquish possession by delivering the collateral to a person other than the debtor or a lessee of the collateral from the debtor in the ordinary course of the debtor's business if the person was instructed before the delivery or is instructed contemporaneously with the delivery:

(1)   to hold possession of the collateral for the secured party's benefit; or

(2)   to redeliver the collateral to the secured party.

(i)   [Effect of delivery under subsection (h); no duties or confirmation.] A secured party does not relinquish possession, even if a delivery under subsection (h) violates the rights of a debtor. A person to which collateral is delivered under subsection (h) does not owe any duty to the secured party and is not required to confirm the delivery to another person unless the person otherwise agrees or law other than this article otherwise provides.

Official Comment

1. **Source.** Former Sections 9-305, 9-115(6).

2. **Perfection by Possession.** As under the common law of pledge, no filing is required by this Article to perfect a security interest if the secured party takes possession of the collateral. See Section 9-310(b)(6).

This section permits a security interest to be perfected by the taking of possession only when the collateral is goods, instruments, negotiable documents, money, or tangible chattel paper. Accounts, commercial tort claims, deposit accounts, investment property, letter-of-credit rights, letters of credit, money, and oil, gas, or other minerals before extraction are excluded. (But see Comment 6, below, regarding certificated securities.) A security interest in accounts and payment intangibles-property not ordinarily represented by any writing whose delivery operates to transfer the right to payment-may under this Article be perfected only by filing. This rule would not be affected by the fact that a security agreement or other record described the assignment of such collateral as a "pledge." Section 9-309(2) exempts from filing certain assignments of accounts or payment intangibles which are out of the ordinary course of financing. These exempted assignments are perfected when they attach. Similarly, under Section 9-309(3), sales of payment intangibles are automatically perfected.

3. **"Possession."** This section does not define "possession." In determining whether a particular person has possession, the principles of agency apply. For example, if the collateral clearly is in possession of an agent of the secured party for the purposes of possessing on behalf of the secured party, and if the agent is not also an agent of the debtor, the secured party has taken actual possession without the need to rely on a third-party acknowledgment. See subsection (c) and Comments 4 and 8. However, if the agent is an agent of both the secured party and the debtor, prudence might suggest that the secured party obtain the agent's acknowledgment in order to ensure perfection by possession. The debtor cannot qualify as an agent for the secured party for purposes of the secured party's taking possession. And, under appropriate circumstances, a court may determine that a third person in possession is so

closely connected to or controlled by the debtor that the debtor has retained effective possession, even though the third person may have agreed to take possession on behalf of the secured party. If so, the third person's taking possession would not constitute the secured party's taking possession and would not be sufficient for perfection. See also Section 9-205(b). In a typical escrow arrangement, where the escrowee holds possession of collateral as agent for both the secured party and the debtor, the debtor's relationship to the escrowee is not such as to constitute retention of possession by the debtor.

4. **Goods in Possession of Third Party: Perfection.** Former Section 9-305 permitted perfection of a security interest by notification to a bailee in possession of collateral. This Article distinguishes between goods in the possession of a bailee who has issued a document of title covering the goods and goods in the possession of a third party who has not issued a document. Section 9-312(c) or (d) applies to the former, depending on whether the document is negotiable. Section 9-313(c) applies to the latter. It provides a method of perfection by possession when the collateral is possessed by a third person who is not the secured party's agent.

Notification of a third person does not suffice to perfect under Section 9-313(c). Rather, perfection does not occur unless the third person authenticates an acknowledgment that it holds possession of the collateral for the secured party's benefit. Compare Section 9-312(d), under which receipt of notification of the security party's interest by a bailee holding goods covered by a nonnegotiable document is sufficient to perfect, even if the bailee does not acknowledge receipt of the notification. A third person may acknowledge that it will hold for the secured party's benefit goods to be received in the future. Under these circumstances, perfection by possession occurs when the third person obtains possession of the goods.

Under subsection (c), acknowledgment of notification by a "lessee . . . in . . . ordinary course of . . . business" (defined in Section 2A-103) does not suffice for possession. The section thus rejects the reasoning of *In re Atlantic Systems, Inc.*, 135 B.R. 463 (Bankr. S.D.N.Y. 1992) (holding that notification to debtor-lessor's lessee sufficed to perfect security interest in leased goods). See Steven O. Weise, *Perfection by Possession: The Need for an Objective Test*, 29 Idaho Law Rev. 705 (1992-93) (arguing that lessee's possession in ordinary course of debtor-lessor's business does not provide adequate public notice of possible security interest in leased goods). Inclusion of a per se rule concerning lessees is not meant to preclude a court, under appropriate circumstances, from determining that a third person is so closely connected to or controlled by the debtor that the debtor has retained effective possession. If so, the third person's acknowledgment would not be sufficient for perfection.

5. **No Relation Back.** Former Section 9-305 provided that a security interest is perfected by possession from the time possession is taken "without a relation back." As the Comment to former Section 9-305 observed, the

relation-back theory, under which the taking of possession was deemed to relate back to the date of the original security agreement, has had little vitality since the 1938 revision of the Federal Bankruptcy Act. The theory is inconsistent with former Article 9 and with this Article. See Section 9-313(d). Accordingly, this Article deletes the quoted phrase as unnecessary. Where a pledge transaction is contemplated, perfection dates only from the time possession is taken, although a security interest may attach, unperfected. The only exceptions to this rule are the short, 20-day periods of perfection provided in Section 9-312(e), (f), and (g), during which a debtor may have possession of specified collateral in which there is a perfected security interest.

6. **Certificated Securities.** The second sentence of subsection (a) reflects the traditional rule for perfection of a security interest in certificated securities. Compare Section 9-115(6) (1994 Official Text); Sections 8-321, 8-313(1)(a) (1978 Official Text); Section 9-305 (1972 Official Text). It has been modified to refer to "delivery" under Section 8-301. Corresponding changes appear in Section 9-203(b).

Subsections (e), (f), and (g), which are new, apply to a person in possession of security certificates or holding security certificates for the secured party's benefit under Section 8-301. For delivery to occur when a person other than a secured party holds possession for the secured party, the person may not be a securities intermediary.

Under subsection (e), a possessory security interest in a certificated security remains perfected until the debtor obtains possession of the security certificate. This rule is analogous to that of Section 9-314(c), which deals with perfection of security interests in investment property by control. See Section 9-314, Comment 3.

7. **Goods Covered by Certificate of Title.** Subsection (b) is necessary to effect changes to the choice-of-law rules governing goods covered by a certificate of title. These changes are described in the Comments to Section 9-311. Subsection (b), like subsection (a), does not create a right to take possession. Rather, it indicates the circumstances under which the secured party's taking possession of goods covered by a certificate of title is effective to perfect a security interest in the goods: the goods become covered by a certificate of title issued by this State at a time when the security interest is perfected by any method under the law of another jurisdiction.

8. **Goods in Possession of Third Party: No Duty to Acknowledge; Consequences of Acknowledgment.** Subsections (f) and (g) are new and address matters as to which former Article 9 was silent. They derive in part from Section 8-106(g). Subsection (f) provides that a person in possession of collateral is not required to acknowledge that it holds for a secured party. Subsection (g)(1) provides that an acknowledgment is effective even if wrongful as to the debtor. Subsection (g)(2) makes clear that an acknowledgment does not give rise to any duties or responsibilities under this Article.

Arrangements involving the possession of goods are hardly standardized. They include bailments for services to be performed on the goods (such as repair or processing), for use (leases), as security (pledges), for carriage, and for storage. This Article leaves to the agreement of the parties and to any other applicable law the imposition of duties and responsibilities upon a person who acknowledges under subsection (c). For example, by acknowledging, a third party does not become obliged to act on the secured party's direction or to remain in possession of the collateral unless it agrees to do so or other law so provides.

9. **Delivery to Third Party by Secured Party.** New subsections (h) and (i) address the practice of mortgage warehouse lenders. These lenders typically send mortgage notes to prospective purchasers under cover of letters advising the prospective purchasers that the lenders hold security interests in the notes. These lenders relied on notification to maintain perfection under former 9-305. Requiring them to obtain authenticated acknowledgments from each prospective purchaser under subsection (c) could be unduly burdensome and disruptive of established practices. Under subsection (h), when a secured party in possession itself delivers the collateral to a third party, instructions to the third party would be sufficient to maintain perfection by possession; an acknowledgment would not be necessary. Under subsection (i), the secured party does not relinquish possession by making a delivery under subsection (h), even if the delivery violates the rights of the debtor. That subsection also makes clear that a person to whom collateral is delivered under subsection (h) does not owe any duty to the secured party and is not required to confirm the delivery to another person unless the person otherwise agrees or law other than this Article provides otherwise.

§ 9-314. PERFECTION BY CONTROL.

(a) [Perfection by control.] A security interest in investment property, deposit accounts, letter-of-credit rights, or electronic chattel paper may be perfected by control of the collateral under Section 9-104, 9-105, 9-106, or 9-107.

ANALYSIS

"Control" is not the functional equivalent of possession with respect to deposit accounts or securities entitlements because control over such assets does not require denying the debtor access to them. The depositary bank and the securities intermediary automatically have control over assets which they hold. *See Secured Transactions* §§ 1A.03[4] and 6D.02[5] & [7]. Therefore, these interests must be added to the secret interests permitted by new § 9-309 in assessing the extent to which the Revised Article departs from the public notice policy.

(b) [Specified collateral: time of perfection by control; continuation of perfection.] A security interest in deposit accounts, electronic chattel paper, or letter-of-credit rights is perfected by control under Section 9-104, 9-105, or 9-107 when the secured party obtains control and remains perfected by control only while the secured party retains control.

(c) [Investment property: time of perfection by control; continuation of perfection.] A security interest in investment property is perfected by control under Section 9-106 from the time the secured party obtains control and remains perfected by control until:

(1)   the secured party does not have control; and

(2)   one of the following occurs:

(A)   if the collateral is a certificated security, the debtor has or acquires possession of the security certificate;

(B)   if the collateral is an uncertificated security, the issuer has registered or registers the debtor as the registered owner; or

(C)   if the collateral is a security entitlement, the debtor is or becomes the entitlement holder.

Official Comment

1. **Source.** Substantially new; derived in part from former Section 9-115(4).

2. **Control.** This section provides for perfection by control with respect to investment property, deposit accounts, letter-of-credit rights, and electronic chattel paper. For explanations of how a secured party takes control of these types of collateral, see Sections 9-104 through 9-107. Subsection (b) explains when a security interest is perfected by control and how long a security interest remains perfected by control. Like Section 9-313(d) and for the same reasons, subsection (b) makes no reference to the doctrine of "relation back." See Section 9-313, Comment 5.

3. **Investment Property.** Subsection (c) provides a special rule for investment property. Once a secured party has control, its security interest remains perfected by control until the secured party ceases to have control and the debtor receives possession of collateral that is a certificated security, becomes the registered owner of collateral that is an uncertificated security, or becomes the entitlement holder of collateral that is a security entitlement.

The result is particularly important in the "repledge" context. See Section 9-207, Comment 5.

In a transaction in which a secured party who has control grants a security interest in investment property or sells outright the investment property, by virtue of the debtor's consent or applicable legal rules, a purchaser from the secured party typically will cut off the debtor's rights in the investment property or be immune from the debtor's claims. See Section 9-207, Comments 5 and 6. If the investment property is a security, the debtor normally would retain no interest in the security following the purchase from the secured party, and a claim of the debtor against the secured party for redemption (Section 9-623) or otherwise with respect to the security would be a purely personal claim. If the investment property transferred by the secured party is a financial asset in which the debtor had a security entitlement credited to a securities account maintained with the secured party as a securities intermediary, the debtor's claim against the secured party could arise as a part of its securities account notwithstanding its personal nature. (This claim would be analogous to a "credit balance" in the securities account, which is a component of the securities account even though it is a personal claim against the intermediary.) In the case in which the debtor may retain an interest in investment property notwithstanding a repledge or sale by the secured party, subsection (c) makes clear that the security interest will remain perfected by control.

§ 9-315. SECURED PARTY'S RIGHTS ON DISPOSITION OF COLLATERAL AND IN PROCEEDS.

(a) [Disposition of collateral: continuation of security interest or agricultural lien; proceeds.] Except as otherwise provided in this article and in Section 2-403(2):

(1) a security interest or agricultural lien continues in collateral notwithstanding sale, lease, license, exchange, or other disposition thereof unless the secured party authorized the disposition free of the security interest or agricultural lien; and

(2) a security interest attaches to any identifiable proceeds of collateral.

(b) [When commingled proceeds identifiable.] Proceeds that are commingled with other property are identifiable proceeds:

(1) if the proceeds are goods, to the extent provided by Section 9-336; and

(2) if the proceeds are not goods, to the extent that the secured party identifies the proceeds by a method of tracing, including

application of equitable principles, that is permitted under law other than this article with respect to commingled property of the type involved.

ANALYSIS

The Revised Article 9 not only expands the definition of "proceeds" (see new § 9-102(a)(64)), it also expands the proceeds interest of the secured creditor by omitting the language of old § 9-306(2) suggesting that proceeds must be "received by the debtor" and by omitting entirely old § 9-306(4)(d) limiting proceeds claims to commingled bank accounts in bankruptcy proceedings. *See Secured Transactions* § 24.05[4][f]. The lowest intermediate balance tracing rule, blessed by new § 9-315(b)(2), may under the revision be used both in and outside of bankruptcy to identify the creditor's claim to commingled deposits. *See Secured Transactions* § 24.05[4][b]. The express preservation of a claim to commingled goods proceeds under new § 9-336 is also new with the revision.

> *Example A*: Bank A has a perfected security interest in the receivables of Hardware Store. Hardware Store uses collections from the receivables to buy a shipment of new inventory items (*e.g.* nails, screws etc.). Later Bank B finances another shipment of the same type of items, perfecting a security interest in the items which it finances. The two shipments are subsequently mixed together so that one can no longer segregate the items purchased from receivables collections. New §§ 9-315(b)(1) and 9-336 continue the proceeds interest of Bank A in the collective mass. Under new § 9-336(2) Bank A's interest in the commingled items is equal to the value of the items financed by receivables divided by the value of all items in the pool.

(c) [Perfection of security interest in proceeds.] A security interest in proceeds is a perfected security interest if the security interest in the original collateral was perfected.

(d) [Continuation of perfection.] A perfected security interest in proceeds becomes unperfected on the 21st day after the security interest attaches to the proceeds unless:

(1)   the following conditions are satisfied:

(A)   a filed financing statement covers the original collateral;

(B) the proceeds are collateral in which a security interest may be perfected by filing in the office in which the financing statement has been filed; and

(C) the proceeds are not acquired with cash proceeds;

(2) the proceeds are identifiable cash proceeds; or

(3) the security interest in the proceeds is perfected other than under subsection (c) when the security interest attaches to the proceeds or within 20 days thereafter.

ANALYSIS

The key change made by this subsection is to allow a proceeds interest in identifiable cash proceeds to be automatically perfected even though there was no filed financing statement covering the original collateral. Cash proceeds of control interests in deposit accounts, securities entitlements, electronic chattel paper, and letter of credit rights will continue to be perfected without need for any additional action by the secured party. *See Secured Transactions* § 24.06[2].

(e) [When perfected security interest in proceeds becomes unperfected.] If a filed financing statement covers the original collateral, a security interest in proceeds which remains perfected under subsection (d)(1) becomes unperfected at the later of:

(1) when the effectiveness of the filed financing statement lapses under Section 9-515 or is terminated under Section 9-513; or

(2) the 21st day after the security interest attaches to the proceeds.

Official Comment

1. **Source.** Former Section 9-306.

2. **Continuation of Security Interest or Agricultural Lien Following Disposition of Collateral.** Subsection (a)(1), which derives from former Section 9-306(2), contains the general rule that a security interest survives disposition of the collateral. In these cases, the secured party may repossess the collateral from the transferee or, in an appropriate case, maintain an action for conversion. The secured party may claim both any proceeds and the original collateral but, of course, may have only one satisfaction.

In many cases, a purchaser or other transferee of collateral will take free of a security interest, and the secured party's only right will be to proceeds. For example, the general rule does not apply, and a security interest does not continue in collateral, if the secured party authorized the disposition, in the agreement that contains the security agreement or otherwise. Subsection (a)(1) adopts the view of PEB Commentary No. 3 and makes explicit that the authorized disposition to which it refers is an authorized disposition "free of" the security interest or agricultural lien. The secured party's right to proceeds under this section or under the express terms of an agreement does not in itself constitute an authorization of disposition. The change in language from former Section 9-306(2) is not intended to address the frequently litigated situation in which the effectiveness of the secured party's consent to a disposition is conditioned upon the secured party's receipt of the proceeds. In that situation, subsection (a) leaves the determination of authorization to the courts, as under former Article 9.

This Article contains several provisions under which a transferee takes free of a security interest or agricultural lien. For example, Section 9-317 states when transferees take free of unperfected security interests; Sections 9-320 and 9-321 on goods, 9-321 on general intangibles, 9-330 on chattel paper and instruments, and 9-331 on negotiable instruments, negotiable documents, and securities state when purchasers of such collateral take free of a security interest, even though perfected and even though the disposition was not authorized. Section 9-332 enables most transferees (including non-purchasers) of funds from a deposit account and most transferees of money to take free of a perfected security interest in the deposit account or money.

Likewise, the general rule that a security interest survives disposition does not apply if the secured party entrusts goods collateral to a merchant who deals in goods of that kind and the merchant sells the collateral to a buyer in ordinary course of business. Section 2-403(2) gives the merchant the power to transfer all the secured party's rights to the buyer, even if the sale is wrongful as against the secured party. Thus, under subsection (a)(1), an entrusting secured party runs the same risk as any other entruster.

3. **Secured Party's Right to Identifiable Proceeds.** Under subsection (a)(2), which derives from former Section 9-306(2), a security interest attaches to any identifiable "proceeds," as defined in Section 9-102. See also Section 9-203(f). Subsection (b) is new. It indicates when proceeds commingled with other property are identifiable proceeds and permits the use of whatever methods of tracing other law permits with respect to the type of property involved. Among the "equitable principles" whose use other law may permit is the "lowest intermediate balance rule." See Restatement (2d), Trusts § 202.

4. **Automatic Perfection in Proceeds: General Rule.** Under subsection (c), a security interest in proceeds is a perfected security interest if the security

interest in the original collateral was perfected. This Article extends the period of automatic perfection in proceeds from ten days to 20 days. Generally, a security interest in proceeds becomes unperfected on the 21st day after the security interest attaches to the proceeds. See subsection (d). The loss of perfected status under subsection (d) is prospective only. Compare, e.g., Section 9-515(c) (deeming security interest unperfected retroactively).

5. **Automatic Perfection in Proceeds: Proceeds Acquired with Cash Proceeds.** Subsection (d)(1) derives from former Section 9-306(3)(a). It carries forward the basic rule that a security interest in proceeds remains perfected beyond the period of automatic perfection if a filed financing statement covers the original collateral (e.g., inventory) and the proceeds are collateral in which a security interest may be perfected by filing in the office where the financing statement has been filed (e.g., equipment). A different rule applies if the proceeds are acquired with cash proceeds, as is the case if the original collateral (inventory) is sold for cash (cash proceeds) that is used to purchase equipment (proceeds). Under these circumstances, the security interest in the equipment proceeds remains perfected only if the description in the filed financing indicates the type of property constituting the proceeds (e.g., "equipment").

This section reaches the same result but takes a different approach. It recognizes that the treatment of proceeds acquired with cash proceeds under former Section 9-306(3)(a) essentially was superfluous. In the example, had the filing covered "equipment" as well as "inventory," the security interest in the proceeds would have been perfected under the usual rules governing after-acquired equipment (see former Sections 9-302, 9-303); paragraph (3)(a) added only an exception to the general rule. Subsection (d)(1)(C) of this section takes a more direct approach. It makes the general rule of continued perfection inapplicable to proceeds acquired with cash proceeds, leaving perfection of a security interest in those proceeds to the generally applicable perfection rules under subsection (d)(3).

Example 1: Lender perfects a security interest in Debtor's inventory by filing a financing statement covering "inventory." Debtor sells the inventory and deposits the buyer's check into a deposit account. Debtor draws a check on the deposit account and uses it to pay for equipment. Under the "lowest intermediate balance rule," which is a permitted method of tracing in the relevant jurisdiction, see Comment 3, the funds used to pay for the equipment were identifiable proceeds of the inventory. Because the proceeds (equipment) were acquired with cash proceeds (deposit account), subsection (d)(1) does not extend perfection beyond the 20-day automatic period.

Example 2: Lender perfects a security interest in Debtor's inventory by filing a financing statement covering "all debtor's property." As in Example 1, Debtor sells the inventory, deposits the buyer's check into a deposit account, draws a check on the deposit account, and uses the check to pay for equipment. Under the "lowest intermediate balance rule," which is a permitted method of tracing in the relevant jurisdiction, see Comment 3, the funds used to pay for the equipment were identifiable proceeds of the inventory. Because the proceeds (equipment) were acquired with cash proceeds (deposit account), subsection (d)(1) does not extend perfection beyond the 20-day automatic period. However, because the financing statement is sufficient to perfect a security interest in debtor's equipment, under subsection (d)(3) the security interest in the equipment proceeds remains perfected beyond the 20-day period.

6. **Automatic Perfection in Proceeds: Lapse or Termination of Financing Statement During 20-Day Period; Perfection Under Other Statute or Treaty.** Subsection (e) provides that a security interest in proceeds perfected under subsection (d)(1) ceases to be perfected when the financing statement covering the original collateral lapses or is terminated. If the lapse or termination occurs before the 21st day after the security interest attaches, however, the security interest in the proceeds remains perfected until the 21st day. Section 9-311(b) provides that compliance with the perfection requirements of a statute or treaty described in Section 9-311(a) "is equivalent to the filing of a financing statement." It follows that collateral subject to a security interest perfected by such compliance under Section 9-311(b) is covered by a "filed financing statement" within the meaning of Section 9-315(d) and (e).

7. **Automatic Perfection in Proceeds: Continuation of Perfection in Cash Proceeds.** Former Section 9-306(3)(b) provided that if a filed financing statement covered original collateral, a security interest in identifiable cash proceeds of the collateral remained perfected beyond the ten-day period of automatic perfection. Former Section 9-306(3)(c) contained a similar rule with respect to identifiable cash proceeds of investment property. Subsection (d)(2) extends the benefits of former Sections 9-306(3)(b) and (3)(c) to identifiable cash proceeds of all types of original collateral in which a security interest is perfected by any method. Under subsection (d)(2), if the security interest in the original collateral was perfected, a security interest in identifiable cash proceeds will remain perfected indefinitely, regardless of whether the security interest in the original collateral remains perfected. In many cases, however, a purchaser or other transferee of the cash proceeds will take free of the perfected security interest. See, e.g., Sections 9-330(d) (purchaser of check), 9-331 (holder in due course of check), 9-332 (transferee of money or funds from a deposit account).

8. **Insolvency Proceedings; Returned and Repossessed Goods.** This Article deletes former Section 9-306(4), which dealt with proceeds in insolvency proceedings. Except as otherwise provided by the Bankruptcy Code, the debtor's entering into bankruptcy does not affect a secured party's right to proceeds.

This Article also deletes former Section 9-306(5), which dealt with returned and repossessed goods. Section 9-330, Comments 9 to 11 explain and clarify the application of priority rules to returned and repossessed goods as proceeds of chattel paper.

9. **Proceeds of Collateral Subject to Agricultural Lien.** This Article does not determine whether a lien extends to proceeds of farm products encumbered by an agricultural lien. If, however, the proceeds are themselves farm products on which an "agricultural lien" (defined in Section 9-102) arises under other law, then the agricultural-lien provisions of this Article apply to the agricultural lien on the proceeds in the same way in which they would apply had the farm products not been proceeds.

§ 9-316.　CONTINUED PERFECTION OF SECURITY INTEREST FOLLOWING CHANGE IN GOVERNING LAW.

(a)　[General rule: effect on perfection of change in governing law.] A security interest perfected pursuant to the law of the jurisdiction designated in Section 9-301(1) or 9-305(c) remains perfected until the earliest of:

(1)　the time perfection would have ceased under the law of that jurisdiction;

(2)　the expiration of four months after a change of the debtor's location to another jurisdiction; or

(3)　the expiration of one year after a transfer of collateral to a person that thereby becomes a debtor and is located in another jurisdiction.

(b)　[Security interest perfected or unperfected under law of new jurisdiction.] If a security interest described in subsection (a) becomes perfected under the law of the other jurisdiction before the earliest time or event described in that subsection, it remains perfected thereafter. If the security interest does not become perfected under the law of the other jurisdiction before the earliest time or event, it becomes unperfected and is deemed never to have been perfected as against a purchaser of the collateral for value.

ANALYSIS

The continuation rules of new § 9-316(a) provide the first state creditor a period of grace as against purchasers for value and, by necessary implication, a period of absolute protection as against lien creditors. *See Secured Transactions* § 5.14. These periods are provided only with respect to security interests that have been initially perfected in the proper jurisdiction under new § 9-301, 9-304, 9-305 or 9-306. New § 9-308 continues a technical definition of perfection which insists that an interest cannot be perfected until it has attached. New § 9-203(b) insists that no security interest can attach until the debtor has "rights in the collateral or the power to transfer rights in the collateral." Does this mean that the continuation rules only continue interests in collateral in which the debtor had rights at the time of the change in the applicable law?

> *Example A*: Assume that First Bank takes a security interest in all of the inventory (including after-acquired inventory) of a partnership which does not qualify as a registered organization. Since the chief executive office of the partnership is in Alabama, First Bank properly files in Alabama. New §§ 9-301(1); 9-307(b)(3). Then the partnership moves its chief executive office to Tennessee.

No doubt First Bank enjoys the protection of new § 9-316(a) as to inventory in which the partnership had rights at the time of the move. As to this inventory First Bank had perfected security interests at the time of the change in controlling law. But what of the inventory acquired by the partnership after the move? If the technical definition of perfection controls, First Bank has no protection as to the post-move inventory. Example 5 in Official Comment 2 to this Section indicates that the revisers intend the technical definition of perfection to control.

(c) [Possessory security interest in collateral moved to new jurisdiction.] A possessory security interest in collateral, other than goods covered by a certificate of title and as-extracted collateral consisting of goods, remains continuously perfected if:

(1)   the collateral is located in one jurisdiction and subject to a security interest perfected under the law of that jurisdiction;

(2)   thereafter the collateral is brought into another jurisdiction; and

(3)   upon entry into the other jurisdiction, the security interest is perfected under the law of the other jurisdiction.

(d) [Goods covered by certificate of title from this state.] Except as otherwise provided in subsection (e), a security interest in goods covered by a certificate of title which is perfected by any method under the law of another jurisdiction when the goods become covered by a certificate of title from this State remains perfected until the security interest would have become unperfected under the law of the other jurisdiction had the goods not become so covered.

ANALYSIS

Initially the perfection of a security interest in a certificated asset will be governed by the law of the first state to cover the asset with a certificate of title. *See* new § 9-303. If an interest is perfected under the law of the first state (*e.g.* by applying for a certificate to have a notation of the interest or by having the interest actually noted on the first state certificate), the subsequent certification of the asset in a second state does not cause the perfection of this interest to lapse immediately. As against a lien creditor, perfection of the interest under the law of the first state continues to have extra-territorial effect so long as the certificate of the first state remains effective under the law of the first state. New § 9-316(d). As against a purchaser for value, the secured creditor has a four month period of grace in which to perfect in the second state. Normally, this perfection would occur by the first state creditor repossessing the goods after default. New § 9-316(e). New § 9-313(b) permits repossession to accomplish this perfection. Perfection with the debtor's cooperation under the certificate of title law of the second state should also assure continuous perfection. *See Secured Transactions* § 5.15.

(e) [When subsection (d) security interests becomes unperfected against purchasers.] A security interest described in subsection (d) becomes unperfected as against a purchaser of the goods for value and is deemed never to have been perfected as against a purchaser of the goods for value if the applicable requirements for perfection under Section 9-311(b) or 9-313 are not satisfied before the earlier of:

(1) the time the security interest would have become unperfected under the law of the other jurisdiction had the goods not become covered by a certificate of title from this State; or

(2) the expiration of four months after the goods had become so covered.

ANALYSIS

Revised Article 9 does not define "purchaser for value." Presumably, the definitions of Article 1 control. *See* U.C.C. §§ 1-201 (32) & (44). The statutory text of new § 9-316(e) does not demand that the purchaser acquire its interest without notice of the earlier interest. But § 1-203 does require the second creditor to act in good faith.

> *Example A*: Bubba Martin, who resides in Mississippi, is an independent trucker engaged in transporting goods throughout the United States. In 2002 a truck owned by Bubba is certificated in Tennessee. Bank A perfects its security interest in the truck under Tennessee law by having its security interest noted on the Tennessee certificate. In January 2003 Bubba Martin moves to Texas and the truck is certificated in Texas. In January 2004 Bubba Martin files a bankruptcy action in Texas. Assuming that the Tennessee certificate remains effective under Tennessee law, the interest of Bank A is still perfected and cannot be avoided by Martin's trustee in bankruptcy under § 544(a) of the Bankruptcy Code.

> *Example B*: Same facts except Martin does not file a bankruptcy action. Instead in January 2004 he grants a security interest to Bank B that makes advances to Martin and perfects by complying with the Texas certificate of title provisions and as to it the interest of Bank A is therefore unperfected.

(f) [Change in jurisdiction of bank, issuer, nominated person, securities intermediary, or commodity intermediary.] A security interest in deposit accounts, letter-of-credit rights, or investment property which is perfected under the law of the bank's jurisdiction, the issuer's jurisdiction, a nominated person's jurisdiction, the securities intermediary's jurisdiction, or the commodity intermediary's jurisdiction, as applicable, remains perfected until the earlier of:

(1)   the time the security interest would have become unperfected under the law of that jurisdiction; or

(2)   the expiration of four months after a change of the applicable jurisdiction to another jurisdiction.

(g) [Subsection (f) security interest perfected or unperfected under law of new jurisdiction.] If a security interest described in subsection (f) becomes perfected under the law of the other jurisdiction before the earlier of the time or the end of the period described in that subsection, it remains perfected thereafter. If the security interest does not become perfected under the law of the other jurisdiction before the earlier of that time or the end of that period, it becomes unperfected and is deemed never to have been perfected as against a purchaser of the collateral for value.

ANALYSIS

None of the subsections of new § 9-316 continue the perfection of interests in fixtures perfected by fixture filing or the perfection of an agricultural lien. These perfections lapse as soon as the fixtures or the farm products move to another jurisdiction.

Official Comment

1. **Source.** Former Section 9-103(1)(d), (2)(b), (3)(e), as modified.

2. **Continued Perfection.** This section deals with continued perfection of security interests that have been perfected under the law of another jurisdiction. The fact that the law of a particular jurisdiction ceases to govern perfection under Sections 9-301 through 9-307 does not necessarily mean that a security interest perfected under that law automatically becomes unperfected. To the contrary: This section generally provides that a security interest perfected under the law of one jurisdiction remains perfected for a fixed period of time (four months or one year, depending on the circumstances), even though the jurisdiction whose law governs perfection changes. However, cessation of perfection under the law of the original jurisdiction cuts short the fixed period. The four-month and one-year periods are long enough for a secured party to discover in most cases that the law of a different jurisdiction governs perfection and to reperfect (typically by filing) under the law of that jurisdiction. If a secured party properly reperfects a security interest before it becomes unperfected under subsection (a), then the security interest remains perfected continuously thereafter. See subsection (b).

Example 1: Debtor is a general partnership whose chief executive office is in Pennsylvania. Lender perfects a security interest in Debtor's equipment by filing in Pennsylvania on May 15, 2002. On April 1, 2005, without Lender's knowledge, Debtor moves its chief executive office to New Jersey. Lender's security interest remains perfected for four months after the move. See subsection (a)(2).

Example 2: Debtor is a general partnership whose chief executive office is in Pennsylvania. Lender perfects a security interest in Debtor's equipment by filing in Pennsylvania on May 15, 2002. On April 1, 2007, without Lender's knowledge, Debtor moves its chief executive office to New Jersey. Lender's security interest remains perfected only through May 14, 2007, when the effectiveness of the filed financing statement lapses. See subsection (a)(1). Although, under these facts, Lender would have only a short period of time to discover that Debtor had relocated and to reperfect under New Jersey law, Lender could have protected itself by filing a continuation statement in Pennsylvania before Debtor relocated. By doing so, Lender would have prevented lapse and allowed itself the full four months to discover Debtor's new location and refile there or, if Debtor is in default, to perfect by taking possession of the equipment.

Example 3: Under the facts of Example 2, Lender files a financing statement in New Jersey before the effectiveness of the Pennsylvania financing statement lapses. Under subsection (b), Lender's security interest is continuously perfected beyond May 14, 2007, for a period determined by New Jersey's Article 9.

Subsection (a)(3) allows a one-year period in which to reperfect. The longer period is necessary, because, even with the exercise of due diligence, the secured party may be unable to discover that the collateral has been transferred to a person located in another jurisdiction.

Example 4: Debtor is a Pennsylvania corporation. Lender perfects a security interest in Debtor's equipment by filing in Pennsylvania. Debtor's shareholders decide to "reincorporate" in Delaware. They form a Delaware corporation (Newcorp) into which they merge Debtor. The merger effectuates a transfer of the collateral from Debtor to Newcorp, which thereby becomes a debtor and is located in another jurisdiction. Under subsection (a)(3), the security interest remains perfected for one year after the merger. If a financing statement is filed in Delaware against Newcorp within the year following the merger, then the security interest remains perfected thereafter for a period determined by Delaware's Article 9.

Note that although Newcorp is a "new debtor" as defined in Section 9-102, the application of subsection (a)(3) is not limited to transferees who are new debtors. Note also that, under Section 9-507, the financing statement naming Debtor remains effective even though Newcorp has become the debtor.

This section addresses security interests that are perfected (i.e., that have attached and as to which any required perfection step has been taken) before the debtor changes its location. It does not apply to security interests that have not attached before the location changes.

Example 5: Debtor is a Pennsylvania corporation. Debtor grants to Lender a security interest in Debtor's existing and after-acquired inventory. Lender perfects by filing in Pennsylvania. Debtor's shareholders decide to "reincorporate" in Delaware. They form a Delaware corporation (Newcorp) into which they merge Debtor. By virtue of the merger, Newcorp becomes bound by Debtor's security agreement. See Section 9-203. After the merger, Newcorp acquires inventory to which Lender's security interest attaches. Because Newcorp is located in Delaware, Delaware law governs perfection of a security interest in Newcorp's inventory. See Sections 9-301, 9-307. Having failed to perfect under Delaware law, Lender holds an unperfected security interest in the inventory acquired by Newcorp after the merger. The same result follows regardless of the name of the Delaware corporation (i.e., even if the Delaware corporation and Debtor have the same name).

3. **Retroactive Unperfection.** Subsection (b) sets forth the consequences of the failure to reperfect before perfection ceases under subsection (a): the security interest becomes unperfected prospectively and, as against purchasers for value, including buyers and secured parties, but not as against donees or lien creditors, retroactively. The rule applies to agricultural liens, as well. See also Section 9-515 (taking the same approach with respect to lapse). Although this approach creates the potential for circular priorities, the alternative-retroactive unperfection against lien creditors-would create substantial and unjustifiable preference risks.

Example 6: Under the facts of Example 4, six months after the merger, Buyer bought from Newcorp some equipment formerly owned by Debtor. At the time of the purchase, Buyer took subject to Lender's perfected security interest, of which Buyer was unaware. See Section 9-315(a)(1). However, subsection (b) provides that if Lender fails to reperfect in Delaware within a year after the merger, its security interest becomes unperfected and is deemed never to have been perfected against Buyer. Having given value and received delivery of the equipment without knowledge of the security interest and before it was perfected, Buyer would take free of the security interest. See Section 9-317(b).

Example 7: Under the facts of Example 4, one month before the merger, Debtor created a security interest in certain equipment in favor of Financer, who perfected by filing in Pennsylvania. At that time, Financer's security interest is subordinate to Lender's. See Section 9-322(a)(1). Financer reperfects by filing in Delaware within a year after the merger, but Lender fails to do so. Under subsection (b), Lender's security interest is deemed never to have been perfected against Financer, a purchaser for value. Consequently, under Section 9-322(a)(2), Financer's security interest is now senior.

Of course, the expiration of the time period specified in subsection (a) does not of itself prevent the secured party from later reperfecting under the law of the new jurisdiction. If the secured party does so, however, there will be a gap in perfection, and the secured party may lose priority as a result. Thus, in Example 7, if Lender perfects by filing in Delaware more than one year under the merger, it will have a new date of filing and perfection for purposes of Section 9-322(a)(1). Financer's security interest, whose perfection dates back to the filing in Pennsylvania under subsection (b), will remain senior.

4. **Possessory Security Interests.** Subsection (c) deals with continued perfection of possessory security interests. It applies not only to security interests perfected solely by the secured party's having taken possession of the collateral. It also applies to security interests perfected by a method that includes as an element of perfection the secured party's having taken possession, such as perfection by taking delivery of a certificated security in registered form, see Section 9-313(a) and perfection by obtaining control over a certificated security. See Section 9-314(a).

5. **Goods Covered by Certificate of Title.** Subsections (d) and (e) address continued perfection of a security interest in goods covered by a certificate of title. The following examples explain the operation of those subsections.

Example 8: Debtor's automobile is covered by a certificate of title issued by Illinois. Lender perfects a security interest in the automobile by complying with Illinois' certificate-of-title statute. Thereafter, Debtor applies for a certificate of title in Indiana. Six months thereafter, Creditor acquires a judicial lien on the automobile. Under Section 9-303(b), Illinois law ceases to govern perfection; rather, once Debtor delivers the application and applicable fee to the appropriate Indiana authority, Indiana law governs. Nevertheless, under Indiana's Section 9-316(d), Lender's security interest remains perfected until it would become unperfected under Illinois law had no certificate of title been issued by Indiana. (For example, Illinois' certificate-of-title statute may provide that the surrender of an Illinois certificate of title in connection with the issuance of a certificate of title by another jurisdiction causes a security interest noted thereon to become unperfected.) If Lender's security interest remains perfected, it is senior to Creditor's judicial lien.

Example 9: Under the facts in Example 8, five months after Debtor applies for an Indiana certificate of title, Debtor sells the automobile to Buyer. Under subsection (e)(2), because Lender did not reperfect within the four months after the goods became covered by the Indiana certificate of title, Lender's security interest is deemed never to have been perfected against Buyer. Under Section 9-317(b), Buyer is likely to take free of the security interest. Lender could have protected itself by perfecting its security interest either under Indiana's certificate-of-title statute, see Section 9-311, or, if it had a right to do so under an agreement or Section 9-610, by taking possession of the automobile. See Section 9-313(b).

The results in Examples 8 and 9 do not depend on the fact that the original perfection was achieved by notation on a certificate of title. Subsection (d) applies regardless of the method by which a security interest is perfected under the law of another jurisdiction when the goods became covered by a certificate of title from this State.

Section 9-337 affords protection to a limited class of persons buying or acquiring a security interest in the goods while a security interest is perfected under the law of another jurisdiction but after this State has issued a clean certificate of title.

6. Deposit Accounts, Letter-of-Credit Rights, and Investment Property. Subsections (f) and (g) address changes in the jurisdiction of a bank, issuer of an uncertificated security, issuer of or nominated person under a letter of credit, securities intermediary, and commodity intermediary. The provisions are analogous to those of subsections (a) and (b).

7. Agricultural Liens. This section does not apply to agricultural liens.

Example 10: Supplier holds an agricultural lien on corn. The lien arises under an Iowa statute. Supplier perfects by filing a financing statement in Iowa, where the corn is located. See Section 9-302. Debtor stores the corn in Missouri. Assume the Iowa agricultural lien survives or an agricultural lien arises under Missouri law (matters that this Article does not govern). Once the corn is located in Missouri, Missouri becomes the jurisdiction whose law governs perfection. See Section 9-302. Thus, the agricultural lien will not be perfected unless Supplier files a financing statement in Missouri.

[SUBPART 3.   PRIORITY]

§ 9-317.   INTERESTS THAT TAKE PRIORITY OVER OR TAKE FREE OF UNPERFECTED SECURITY INTEREST OR AGRICULTURAL LIEN.

(a)   [Conflicting security interests and rights of lien creditors.] An unperfected security interest or agricultural lien is subordinate to the rights of:

(1)   a person entitled to priority under Section 9-322; and

(2)   except as otherwise provided in subsection (e), a person that becomes a lien creditor before the earlier of the time the security interest or agricultural lien is perfected or a financing statement covering the collateral is filed.

ANALYSIS

This section changes the most basic rule of priority—the rule governing contests between secured creditors and lien creditors. Under old § 9-301(1)(b) the secured creditor was subordinate to a lien creditor whose lien arose before the security interest was *perfected.* Under the revision, the lien creditor prevails only if its lien arises before the security interest is *"perfected or a financing statement covering the collateral is filed."* By filing as to assets in which interests can be perfected by filing, a financer, actual or prospective, can assure that lien creditors will not thereafter gain priority over it, subject only to the rules as to future advances now stated in new § 9-323. This change not only places the first advance by a secured creditor on the same level as later advances, it also creates the possibility that more preemptive filings will be made against prospective debtors to assure priority in the event that financing is extended in the future.

> *Example A*: Feb. 2002 – First Finance properly files as to the equipment of Debtor Co. but does not take a security agreement or advance value. Debtor Co. authorizes the filing because it believes that being cooperative will impress First Finance.
>
> June 2004 – Tort Victim secures a $10 million judgment against Debtor Co. and levies on its equipment which is worth $5 million. The levy qualifies Tort Victim as a lien creditor under new § 9-102(a)(52).
>
> November 2004 – First Finance takes a security agreement and simultaneously advances $5 million to Debtor Co.

On these facts, First Finance has the priority claim to the full value of the equipment under new § 9-317 because it was filed before the lien arose. First Finance arguably does not lose this priority under new § 9-323 because its $5 million advance is an original advance, not a future advance, and because new § 9-323(b) only applies to a lien creditor who becomes a lien creditor while the security interest is perfected. First Finance was not perfected until after the lien of Tort Victim was established. *But see* Official Comment 4 suggesting that the revisers may believe that § 9-323(b) applies. Of course, courts may resist such a technical reading that immunizes Debtor Co. from tort claims over the life of a U.C.C. filing. Moreover, if bankruptcy intervenes before First Finance takes and perfects its interest, First Finance would be barred by Bankruptcy Code Section 549 from taking the interest. But in that event, First Finance would never make the $5 million advance. In this analysis any pre-bankruptcy security interest created in the equipment will be immune from avoidance by the trustee under Bankruptcy Code § 544(a) because a lien creditor will be unable to subordinate the interest under new § 9-317(a)(2).

Does the change in this basic rule of priority assist the debtor and a financer in judgment-proofing the debtor? In assessing this risk note that proposed § 9-512 clearly allows a creditor who has filed to sell its priority by filing an amendment statement changing the name of the secured party. A firm recognizing that it may face future tort judgments could authorize a friendly person to file a financing statement covering all of the firm's assets (*see* new § 9-504(2)). If judgments are recorded, the friend could sell its priority to the financer who will place new money in the firm and enjoy priority over all tort victims as to all assets covered by the filing. The tort victims are left to chase the new money as best they can. The potential interaction of the changes made by new §§ 9-317(a)(a), 9-504(2) and 9-512 seems to pose a risk of preemptive filings calculated to shield assets of a firm. *See* the text analysis to new § 9-504.

(b) [Buyers that receive delivery.] Except as otherwise provided in subsection (e), a buyer, other than a secured party, of tangible chattel paper, documents, goods, instruments, or a security certificate takes free of a security interest or agricultural lien if the buyer gives value and receives delivery of the collateral without knowledge of the security interest or agricultural lien and before it is perfected.

(c) [Lessees that receive delivery.] Except as otherwise provided in subsection (e), a lessee of goods takes free of a security interest or agricultural lien if the lessee gives value and receives delivery of the collateral without knowledge of the security interest or agricultural lien and before it is perfected.

(d) [Licensees and buyers of certain collateral.] A licensee of a general intangible or a buyer, other than a secured party, of accounts, electronic chattel paper, general intangibles, or investment property other than a certificated security takes free of a security interest if the licensee or buyer gives value without knowledge of the security interest and before it is perfected.

(e) [Purchase-money security interest.] Except as otherwise provided in Sections 9-320 and 9-321, if a person files a financing statement with respect to a purchase-money security interest before or within 20 days after the debtor receives delivery of the collateral, the security interest takes priority over the rights of a buyer, lessee, or lien creditor which arise between the time the security interest attaches and the time of filing.

Official Comment

1. **Source.** Former Sections 9-301, 2A-307(2).

2. **Scope of This Section.** As did former Section 9-301, this section lists the classes of persons who take priority over, or take free of, an unperfected security interest. Section 9-308 explains when a security interest or agricultural lien is "perfected." A security interest that has attached (see Section 9-203) but as to which a required perfection step has not been taken is "unperfected." Certain provisions have been moved from former Section 9-301. The definition of "lien creditor" now appears in Section 9-102, and the rules governing priority in future advances are found in Section 9-323.

3. **Competing Security Interests.** Section 9-322 states general rules for determining priority among conflicting security interests and refers to other sections that state special rules of priority in a variety of situations. The security interests given priority under Section 9-322 and the other sections to which it refers take priority in general even over a perfected security interest. *A fortiori* they take priority over an unperfected security interest. Paragraph (a)(1) of this section so states.

4. **Filed but Unattached Security Interest vs. Lien Creditor.** Under former Section 9-301(1)(b), a lien creditor's rights had priority over an unperfected security interest. Perfection required attachment (former Section 9-303) and attachment required the giving of value (former Section 9-203). It followed that, if a secured party had filed a financing statement but had not yet given value, an intervening lien creditor whose lien arose after filing but before attachment of the security interest acquired rights that are senior to those of the secured party who later gives value. This result comported with the *nemo dat* concept: When the security interest attached, the collateral was already subject to the judicial lien.

On the other hand, this result treated the first secured advance differently from all other advances. The special rule for future advances in former Section 9-301(4) (substantially reproduced in Section 9-323(b)) afforded priority to a discretionary advance made by a secured party within 45 days after the lien creditor's rights arose as long as the secured party was "perfected" when the lien creditor's lien arose-i.e., as long as the advance was not the first one and an earlier advance had been made.

Subsection (a)(2) revises former Section 9-301(1)(b) and treats the first advance the same as subsequent advances. That is, a judicial lien that arises after a financing statement is filed and before the security interest attaches and becomes perfected is subordinate to all advances secured by the security interest, even the first advance, except as otherwise provided in Section 9-323(b). However, if the security interest becomes unperfected (e.g., because the effectiveness of the filed financing statement lapses) before the judicial lien arises, the security interest is subordinate. If a financing statement is filed but a security interest does not attach, then no priority contest arises. The lien creditor has the only claim to the property.

5. **Security Interest of Consignor or Receivables Buyer vs. Lien Creditor.** Section 1-201(37) defines "security interest" to include the interest of most true consignors of goods and the interest of most buyers of certain receivables (accounts, chattel paper, payment intangibles, and promissory notes). A consignee of goods or a seller of accounts or chattel paper each is deemed to have rights in the collateral which a lien creditor may reach, as long as the competing security interest of the consignor or buyer is unperfected. This is so even though, as between the consignor and the debtor-consignee, the latter has only limited rights, and, as between the buyer and debtor-seller, the latter does not have any rights in the collateral. See Sections 9-318 (seller), 9-319 (consignee). Security interests arising from sales of payment intangibles and promissory notes are automatically perfected. See Section 9-309. Accordingly, a subsequent judicial lien always would be subordinate to the rights of a buyer of those types of receivables.

6. **Purchasers Other Than Secured Parties.** Subsections (b), (c), and (d) afford priority over an unperfected security interest to certain purchasers (other than secured parties) of collateral. They derive from former Sections 9-301(1)(c), 2A-307(2), and 9-301(d). Former Section 9-301(1)(c) and (1)(d) provided that unperfected security interests are "subordinate" to the rights of certain purchasers. But, as former Comment 9 suggested, the practical effect of subordination in this context is that the purchaser takes free of the security interest. To avoid any possible misinterpretation, subsections (b) and (d) of this section use the phrase "takes free."

Subsection (b) governs goods, as well as intangibles of the type whose transfer is effected by physical delivery of the representative piece of paper (tangible chattel paper, documents, instruments, and security certificates). To obtain priority, a buyer must both give value and receive delivery of the collateral without knowledge of the existing security interest and before perfection. Even if the buyer gave value without knowledge and before perfection, the buyer would take subject to the security interest if perfection occurred before physical delivery of the collateral to the buyer. Subsection (c) contains a similar rule with respect to lessees of goods. Note that a lessee of goods in ordinary course of business takes free of all security interests created by the lessor, even if perfected. See Section 9-321.

Normally, there will be no question when a buyer of chattel paper, documents, instruments, or security certificates "receives delivery" of the property. See Section 1-201 (defining "delivery"). However, sometimes a buyer or lessee of goods, such as complex machinery, takes delivery of the goods in stages and completes assembly at its own location. Under those circumstances, the buyer or lessee "receives delivery" within the meaning of subsections (b) and (c) when, after an inspection of the portion of the goods remaining with the seller or lessor, it would be apparent to a potential lender to the seller or lessor that another person might have an interest in the goods.

The rule of subsection (b) obviously is not appropriate where the collateral consists of intangibles and there is no representative piece of paper whose physical delivery is the only or the customary method of transfer. Therefore, with respect to such intangibles (accounts, electronic chattel paper, general intangibles, and investment property other than certificated securities), subsection (d) gives priority to any buyer who gives value without knowledge, and before perfection, of the security interest. A licensee of a general intangible takes free of an unperfected security interest in the general intangible under the same circumstances. Note that a licensee of a general intangible in ordinary course of business takes rights under a nonexclusive license free of security interests created by the licensor, even if perfected. See Section 9-321.

Unless Section 9-109 excludes the transaction from this Article, a buyer of accounts, chattel paper, payment intangibles, or promissory notes is a "secured party" (defined in Section 9-102), and subsections (b) and (d) do not determine priority of the security interest created by the sale. Rather, the priority rules generally applicable to competing security interests apply. See Section 9-322.

7. **Agricultural Liens.** Subsections (a), (b), and (c) subordinate unperfected agricultural liens in the same manner in which they subordinate unperfected security interests.

8. **Purchase-Money Security Interests.** Subsection (e) derives from former Section 9-301(2). It provides that, if a purchase-money security interest is perfected by filing no later than 20 days after the debtor receives delivery of the collateral, the security interest takes priority over the rights of buyers, lessees, or lien creditors which arise between the time the security interest attaches and the time of filing. Subsection (e) differs from former Section 9-301(2) in two significant respects. First, subsection (e) protects a purchase-money security interest against all buyers and lessees, not just against transferees in bulk. Second, subsection (e) conditions this protection on filing within 20, as opposed to ten, days after delivery.

Section 9-311(b) provides that compliance with the perfection requirements of a statute or treaty described in Section 9-311(a) "is equivalent to the filing of a financing statement." It follows that a person who perfects a security interest in goods covered by a certificate of title by complying with the perfection requirements of an applicable certificate-of-title statute "files a financing statement" within the meaning of subsection (e).

§ 9-318. NO INTEREST RETAINED IN RIGHT TO PAYMENT THAT IS SOLD; RIGHTS AND TITLE OF SELLER OF ACCOUNT OR CHATTEL PAPER WITH RESPECT TO CREDITORS AND PURCHASERS.

(a) [Seller retains no interest.] A debtor that has sold an account, chattel paper, payment intangible, or promissory note does not retain a legal or equitable interest in the collateral sold.

(b) [Deemed rights of debtor if buyer's security interest unperfected.] For purposes of determining the rights of creditors of, and purchasers for value of an account or chattel paper from, a debtor that has sold an account or chattel paper, while the buyer's security interest is unperfected, the debtor is deemed to have rights and title to the account or chattel paper identical to those the debtor sold.

ANALYSIS

A seller who has sold an account or chattel paper actually has no rights in the asset sold, but for a limited purpose is deemed to have rights so long as the sale is unperfected. The stipulated rights allow the seller to sell the asset again or to grant security interests in it. The interest of the later buyer or secured creditor is thus allowed to attach under Section 9-203. The law on this question under the old Article 9 is not explicit. *See Secured Transactions* § 2B.07[3]. Note that subsection (b) does not apply to sales of promissory notes or other payment intangibles, which are automatically perfected pursuant to new §§ 9-307(4) & (5). Revised Article 9 pursues a policy of requiring sales of accounts and chattel paper to be publicly disclosed but of allowing sales of payment intangibles and promissory notes to be secret. For discussion of the priority implications as to sales of notes and payment intangibles see the text analysis to new § 9-309.

New § 9-318 also supports a negative inference that once the buyer of the accounts or chattel paper has perfected its interest, the seller no longer has "rights" in the assets for any purpose. This inference in turn supports the position that after the outright sale and perfection the transferred accounts or chattel paper are no longer part of the bankruptcy estate of the seller. Language to the contrary in *Octagon Gas Systems Inc. v. Rimmer*, 995 F.2d 948 (10th Cir. 1993), is therefore implicitly rejected. *See Secured Transactions* § 9.01[2][a]. All of this is designed to facilitate securitization of a firm's accounts, chattel paper, notes and payment intangibles.

Official Comment

1. **Source.** New.

2. **Sellers of Accounts, Chattel Paper, Payment Intangibles, and Promissory Notes.** Section 1-201(37) defines "security interest" to include the interest of a buyer of accounts, chattel paper, payment intangibles, or promissory notes. See also Section 9-109(a) and Comment 5. Subsection (a) makes explicit what was implicit, but perfectly obvious, under former Article 9: The fact that a sale of an account or chattel paper gives rise to a "security interest" does not imply that the seller retains an interest in the property that has been sold. To the contrary, a seller of an account or chattel paper retains no interest whatsoever in the property to the extent that it has been sold. Subsection (a) also applies to sales of payment intangibles and promissory notes, transactions that were not covered by former Article 9. Neither this Article nor the definition of "security interest" in Section 1-201 provides rules for distinguishing sales transactions from those that create a security interest securing an obligation.

3. **Buyers of Accounts and Chattel Paper.** Another aspect of sales of accounts and chattel paper also was implicit, and equally obvious, under former Article 9: If the buyer's security interest is unperfected, then for purposes of determining the rights of certain third parties, the seller (debtor) is deemed to have all rights and title that the seller sold. The seller is deemed to have these rights even though, as between the parties, it has sold all its rights to the buyer. Subsection (b) makes this explicit. As a consequence of subsection (b), if the buyer's security interest is unperfected, the seller can transfer, and the creditors of the seller can reach, the account or chattel paper as if it had not been sold.

Example: Debtor sells accounts or chattel paper to Buyer-1 and retains no interest in them. Buyer-1 does not file a financing statement. Debtor then sells the same receivables to Buyer-2. Buyer-2 files a proper financing statement. Having sold the receivables to Buyer-1, Debtor would not have any rights in the collateral so as to permit Buyer-2's security (ownership) interest to attach. Nevertheless, under this section, for purposes of determining the rights of purchasers for value from Debtor, Debtor is deemed to have the rights that Debtor sold. Accordingly, Buyer-2's security interest attaches, is perfected by the filing, and, under Section 9-322, is senior to Buyer-1's interest.

4. **Effect of Perfection.** If the security interest of a buyer of accounts or chattel paper is perfected the usual result would take effect: transferees from and creditors of the seller could not acquire an interest in the sold accounts or chattel paper. The same result would occur if payment intangibles or promissory notes were sold, inasmuch as the buyer's security interest is automatically perfected under Section 9-309.

§ 9-319. RIGHTS AND TITLE OF CONSIGNEE WITH RESPECT TO CREDITORS AND PURCHASERS.

(a) [Consignee has consignor's rights.] Except as otherwise provided in subsection (b), for purposes of determining the rights of creditors of, and purchasers for value of goods from, a consignee, while the goods are in the possession of the consignee, the consignee is deemed to have rights and title to the goods identical to those the consignor had or had power to transfer.

(b) [Applicability of other law.] For purposes of determining the rights of a creditor of a consignee, law other than this article determines the rights and title of a consignee while goods are in the consignee's possession if, under this part, a perfected security interest held by the consignor would have priority over the rights of the creditor.

ANALYSIS

Under Revised Article 9 true consignments (as defined in new § 9-102(a)(20)) are deemed to give rise to a purchase-money security interest in favor of the consignor. New § 9-103(d). Even though the consignor and consignee do not intend the transaction to be a security arrangement, it is deemed to be one. This new § 9-318 confirms the consequences of the fictional security interest.

> *Example A*: Supplier Co. delivers jewelry to Retailer in a transaction which qualifies as a consignment under § 9-102(a)(20) but does not file a financing statement to perfect its interest. Retailer Co. grants a security interest in the jewelry to First Bank which perfects by filing. Under Revised Article 9 First Bank would have priority over Supplier Co. as the first and only secured party to file if we visualize these

parties as having Article 9 interests. *See* new §§ 9-322(1); 9-324(a). Therefore, new § 9-319(a) applies and Retailer Co. has all of the rights and title of Supplier Co. in the jewelry for purposes of defining the security interest of First Bank. The security interest of First Bank attaches to the full ownership interest of Retailer Co., not just to Retailer's interest as a bailee. First Bank has the priority claim to all proceeds obtained in disposing of the jewelry.

Example B: Same as above except that Supplier Co. files to perfect before First bank files *or* Supplier Co. files and gives notification so as to qualify for purchase-money priority over First Bank under new § 9-324 even though First Bank was first filed. Since Supplier Co. would not have priority over First Bank if we visualize the parties as competing secured creditors, new § 9-319(b) applies. Other law (*i.e.* the law of bailment) defines the extent of Retailer's interest in the goods to which the security interest can attach.

See Secured Transactions § 1A.03[2] for more on the priority visualization process required by new § 9-319.

Official Comment

1. **Source.** New.

2. **Consignments.** This section takes an approach to consignments similar to that taken by Section 9-318 with respect to buyers of accounts and chattel paper. Revised Section 1-201(37) defines "security interest" to include the interest of a consignor of goods under many true consignments. Section 9-319(a) provides that, for purposes of determining the rights of certain third parties, the consignee is deemed to acquire all rights and title that the consignor had, if the consignor's security interest is unperfected. The consignee acquires these rights even though, as between the parties, it purchases a limited interest in the goods (as would be the case in a true consignment, under which the consignee acquires only the interest of a bailee). As a consequence of this section, creditors of the consignee can acquire judicial liens and security interests in the goods.

Insofar as creditors of the consignee are concerned, this Article to a considerable extent reformulates the former law, which appeared in former Sections 2-326 and 9-114, without changing the results. However, neither Article 2 nor former Article 9 specifically addresses the rights of non-ordinary course buyers from the consignee. Former Section 9-114 contained priority rules applicable to security interests in consigned goods. Under this Article, the priority rules for purchase-money security interests in inventory apply to consignments. See Section 9-103(d). Accordingly, a special section containing priority rules for consignments no longer is needed. Section 9-317 determines whether the rights of a judicial lien creditor are senior to the interest of the consignor, Sections 9-322 and 9-324 govern competing security interests in consigned goods, and Sections 9-317, 9-315, and 9-320 determine whether a buyer takes free of the consignor's interest.

The following example explains the operation of this section:

Example 1: SP-1 delivers goods to Debtor in a transaction constituting a "consignment" as defined in Section 9-102. SP-1 does not file a financing statement. Debtor then grants a security interest in the goods to SP-2. SP-2 files a proper financing statement. Assuming Debtor is a mere bailee, as in a "true" consignment, Debtor would not have any rights in the collateral (beyond those of a bailee) so as to permit SP-2's security interest to attach to any greater rights. Nevertheless, under this section, for purposes of determining the rights of Debtor's creditors, Debtor is deemed to acquire SP-1's rights. Accordingly, SP-2's security interest attaches, is perfected by the filing, and, under Section 9-322, is senior to SP-1's interest.

3. **Effect of Perfection.** Subsection (b) contains a special rule with respect to consignments that are perfected. If application of this Article would result in the consignor having priority over a competing creditor, then other law determines the rights and title of the consignee.

Example 2: SP-1 delivers goods to Debtor in a transaction constituting a "consignment" as defined in Section 9-102. SP-1 files a proper financing statement. Debtor then grants a security interest in the goods to SP-2. Under Section 9-322, SP-1's security interest is senior to SP-2's. Subsection (b) indicates that, for purposes of determining SP-2's rights, other law determines the rights and title of the consignee. If, for example, a consignee obtains only the special property of a bailee, then SP-2's security interest would attach only to that special property.

Example 3: SP-1 obtains a security interest in all Debtor's existing and after-acquired inventory. SP-1 perfects its security interest with a proper filing. Then SP-2 delivers goods to Debtor in a transaction constituting a "consignment" as defined in Section 9-102. SP-2 files a proper financing statement but does not send notification to SP-1 under Section 9-324(b). Accordingly, SP-2's security interest is junior to SP-1's under Section 9-322(a). Under Section 9-319(a), Debtor is deemed to have the consignor's rights and title, so that SP-1's security interest attaches to SP-2's ownership interest in the goods. Thereafter, Debtor grants a security interest in the goods to SP-3, and SP-3 perfects by filing. Because SP-2's perfected security interest is senior to SP-3's under Section 9-322(a), Section 9-319(b) applies: Other law determines Debtor's rights and title to the goods insofar as SP-3 is concerned, and SP-3's security interest attaches to those rights.

§ 9-320. BUYER OF GOODS.

(a) [Buyer in ordinary course of business.] Except as otherwise provided in subsection (e), a buyer in ordinary course of business, other than a person buying farm products from a person engaged in farming operations, takes free of a security interest created by the buyer's seller, even if the security interest is perfected and the buyer knows of its existence.

(b) [Buyer of consumer goods.] Except as otherwise provided in subsection (e), a buyer of goods from a person who used or bought the goods for use primarily for personal, family, or household purposes takes free of a security interest, even if perfected, if the buyer buys:

(1) without knowledge of the security interest;

(2) for value;

(3) primarily for the buyer's personal, family, or household purposes; and

(4) before the filing of a financing statement covering the goods.

(c) [Effectiveness of filing for subsection (b).] To the extent that it affects the priority of a security interest over a buyer of goods under subsection (b), the period of effectiveness of a filing made in the jurisdiction in which the seller is located is governed by Section 9-316(a) and (b).

(d) [Buyer in ordinary course of business at wellhead or minehead.] A buyer in ordinary course of business buying oil, gas, or other minerals at the wellhead or minehead or after extraction takes free of an interest arising out of an encumbrance.

(e) [Possessory security interest not affected.] Subsections (a) and (b) do not affect a security interest in goods in the possession of the secured party under Section 9-313.

ANALYSIS

New § 9-320(e) overrides *Tanbro Fabrics Corp. v. Deering Milliken, Inc.*, 29 N.Y.2d 632 350 N.E.2d 590 (1976). Under the Revised Article 9 a buyer in ordinary course will not take free of a security interest in goods in the possession of a secured creditor as possession is defined in new § 9-313. That provision requires that a third party in possession of the goods, which are not covered by a document to attorn to the secured creditor in order for the secured creditor to be deemed to be in possession. *See* the text analysis to new § 9-313. If goods have been shipped or stored under a non-negotiable document of title, notification alone to the transportation or warehouse company will perfect the secured party's interest under new § 9-312(d)(2). But if the transportation or warehouse company does not attorn by acknowledging that it holds for the secured party, will the secured party be deemed to have possession under § 9-313? Arguably, notification under § 9-313(a)(2) should be deemed to be possession under 9-313(a) for goods which are subject to a document.

The larger issue is whether the override of *Tanbro* will slow purchase transactions. Under new § 9-320(e) a buyer that pays for goods in possession of a secured creditor takes subject to the interest of the secured creditor, assuming that the secured creditor has not authorized the sale free of its interest under new § 9-315(a)(1). When a seller is not itself in possession, a buyer needs to be alert to the possibility that the secured creditor will be deemed to be in possession under § 9-311 even though the goods are physically controlled by a supplier of the seller, a transportation company or a warehouse.

Official Comment

1. **Source.** Former Section 9-307.

2. **Scope of This Section.** This section states when buyers of goods take free of a security interest even though perfected. Of course, a buyer who takes free of a perfected security interest takes free of an unperfected one. Section 9-317 should be consulted to determine what purchasers, in addition to the buyers covered in this section, take free of an unperfected security interest. Article 2 states general rules on purchase of goods from a seller with defective or voidable title (Section 2-403).

3. **Buyers in Ordinary Course.** Subsection (a) derives from former Section 9-307(1). The definition of "buyer in ordinary course of business" in Section 1-201 restricts its application to buyers "from a person, other than a pawnbroker, in the business of selling goods of that kind." Thus subsection (a) applies primarily to inventory collateral. The subsection further excludes from its operation buyers of "farm products" (defined in Section 9-102) from a person engaged in farming operations. The buyer in ordinary course of business is defined as one who buys goods "in good faith, without knowledge that the sale violates the rights of another person and in the ordinary course." Subsection (a) provides that such a buyer takes free of a security interest, even though perfected, and even though the buyer knows the security interest

exists. Reading the definition together with the rule of law results in the buyer's taking free if the buyer merely knows that a security interest covers the goods but taking subject if the buyer knows, in addition, that the sale violates a term in an agreement with the secured party.

As did former Section 9-307(1), subsection (a) applies only to security interests created by the seller of the goods to the buyer in ordinary course. However, under certain circumstances a buyer in ordinary course who buys goods that were encumbered with a security interest created by a person other than the seller may take free of the security interest, as Example 2 explains. See also Comment 6, below.

Example 1: Manufacturer, who is in the business of manufacturing appliances, owns manufacturing equipment subject to a perfected security interest in favor of Lender. Manufacturer sells the equipment to Dealer, who is in the business of buying and selling used equipment. Buyer buys the equipment from Dealer. Even if Buyer qualifies as a buyer in the ordinary course of business, Buyer does not take free of Lender's security interest under subsection (a), because Dealer did not create the security interest; Manufacturer did.

Example 2: Manufacturer, who is in the business of manufacturing appliances, owns manufacturing equipment subject to a perfected security interest in favor of Lender. Manufacturer sells the equipment to Dealer, who is in the business of buying and selling used equipment. Lender learns of the sale but does nothing to assert its security interest. Buyer buys the equipment from Dealer. Inasmuch as Lender's acquiescence constitutes an "entrusting" of the goods to Dealer within the meaning of Section 2-403(3) Buyer takes free of Lender's security interest under Section 2-403(2) if Buyer qualifies as a buyer in ordinary course of business.

4. **Buyers of Farm Products.** This section does not enable a buyer of farm products to take free of a security interest created by the seller, even if the buyer is a buyer in ordinary course of business. However, a buyer of farm products may take free of a security interest under Section 1324 of the Food Security Act of 1985, 7 U.S.C. § 1631.

5. **Buyers of Consumer Goods.** Subsection (b), which derives from former Section 9-307(2), deals with buyers of collateral that the debtor-seller holds as "consumer goods" (defined in Section 9-102). Under Section 9-309(1), a purchase-money interest in consumer goods, except goods that are subject to a statute or treaty described in Section 9-311(a) (such as automobiles that are subject to a certificate-of-title statute), is perfected automatically upon attachment. There is no need to file to perfect. Under subsection (b) a buyer of consumer goods takes free of a security interest, even though perfected, if the buyer buys (1) without knowledge of the security interest, (2) for value, (3) primarily for the buyer's own personal, family, or household purposes, and (4) before a financing statement is filed.

As to purchase money security interests which are perfected without filing under Section 9-309(1): A secured party may file a financing statement, although filing is not required for perfection. If the secured party does file, all buyers take subject to the security interest. If the secured party does not file, a buyer who meets the qualifications stated in the preceding paragraph takes free of the security interest.

As to security interests for which a perfection step is required: This category includes all non-purchase-money security interests, and all security interests, whether or not purchase-money, in goods subject to a statute or treaty described in Section 9-311(a), such as automobiles covered by a certificate-of-title statute. As long as the required perfection step has not been taken and the security interest remains unperfected, not only the buyers described in subsection (b) but also the purchasers described in Section 9-317 will take free of the security interest. After a financing statement has been filed or the perfection requirements of the applicable certificate-of-title statute have been complied with (compliance is the equivalent of filing a financing statement; see Section 9-311(b)), all subsequent buyers, under the rule of subsection (b), are subject to the security interest.

The rights of a buyer under subsection (b) turn on whether a financing statement has been filed against consumer goods. Occasionally, a debtor changes his or her location after a filing is made. Subsection (c), which derives from former Section 9-103(1)(d)(iii), deals with the continued effectiveness of the filing under those circumstances. It adopts the rules of Sections 9-316(a) and (b). These rules are explained in the Comments to that section.

6. **Authorized Dispositions.** The limitations that subsections (a) and (b) impose on the persons who may take free of a security interest apply of course only to unauthorized sales by the debtor. If the secured party authorized the sale in an express agreement or otherwise, the buyer takes free under Section 9-315(a) without regard to the limitations of this section. (That section also states the right of a secured party to the proceeds of a sale, authorized or unauthorized.) Moreover, the buyer also takes free if the secured party waived or otherwise is precluded from asserting its security interest against the buyer. See Section 1-103.

7. **Oil, Gas, and Other Minerals.** Under subsection (d), a buyer in ordinary course of business of minerals at the wellhead or minehead or after extraction takes free of a security interest created by the seller. Specifically, it provides that qualified buyers take free not only of Article 9 security interests but also of interests "arising out of an encumbrance." As defined in Section 9-102, the term "encumbrance" means "a right, other than an ownership interest, in real property." Thus, to the extent that a mortgage encumbers minerals not only before but also after extraction, subsection (d) enables a buyer in ordinary course of the minerals to take free of the mortgage. This subsection does not, however, enable these buyers to take free of interests arising out of ownership interests in the real property. This issue is significant only in

a minority of states. Several of them have adopted special statutes and nonuniform amendments to Article 9 to provide special protections to mineral owners, whose interests often are highly fractionalized in the case of oil and gas. See Terry I. Cross, *Oil and Gas Product Liens—Statutory Security Interests for Producers and Royalty Owners Under the Statutes of Kansas, New Mexico, Oklahoma, Texas and Wyoming*, 50 Consumer Fin. L. Q. Rep. 418 (1996). Inasmuch as a complete resolution of the issue would require the addition of complex provisions to this Article, and there are good reasons to believe that a uniform solution would not be feasible, this Article leaves its resolution to other legislation.

8. **Possessory Security Interests.** Subsection (e) is new. It rejects the holding of *Tanbro Fabrics Corp. v. Deering Milliken, Inc.*, 350 N.E.2d 590 (N.Y. 1976) and, together with Section 9-317(b), prevents a buyer of goods collateral from taking free of a security interest if the collateral is in the possession of the secured party. "The secured party" referred in subsection (e) is the holder of the security interest referred to in subsection (a) or (b). Section 9-313 determines whether a secured party is in possession for purposes of this section. Under some circumstances, Section 9-313 provides that a secured party is in possession of collateral even if the collateral is in the physical possession of a third party.

§ 9-321. LICENSEE OF GENERAL INTANGIBLE AND LESSEE OF GOODS IN ORDINARY COURSE OF BUSINESS.

(a) ["Licensee in ordinary course of business."] In this section, "licensee in ordinary course of business" means a person that becomes a licensee of a general intangible in good faith, without knowledge that the license violates the rights of another person in the general intangible, and in the ordinary course from a person in the business of licensing general intangibles of that kind. A person becomes a licensee in the ordinary course if the license to the person comports with the usual or customary practices in the kind of business in which the licensor is engaged or with the licensor's own usual or customary practices.

(b) [Rights of licensee in ordinary course of business.] A licensee in ordinary course of business takes its rights under a nonexclusive license free of a security interest in the general intangible created by the licensor, even if the security interest is perfected and the licensee knows of its existence.

(c) [Rights of lessee in ordinary course of business.] A lessee in ordinary course of business takes its leasehold interest free of a security interest in the goods created by the lessor, even if the security interest is perfected and the lessee knows of its existence.

ANALYSIS

Under Revised Article 9 a lessee in ordinary course may be better off than a buyer in ordinary course in that the lessee seemingly takes free of the security interest even though the secured party is in possession of the goods when the lease is executed. *See* U.C.C. § 2A-103(o).

Official Comment

1. **Source.** Derived from Sections 2A-103(1)(o), 2A-307(3).

2. **Licensee in Ordinary Course.** Like the analogous rules in Section 9-320(a) with respect to buyers in ordinary course and subsection (c) with respect to lessees in ordinary course, the new rule in subsection (b) reflects the expectations of the parties and the marketplace: a licensee under a nonexclusive license takes subject to a security interest unless the secured party authorizes the license free of the security interest or other, controlling law such as that of this section (protecting ordinary-course licensees) dictates a contrary result. See Sections 9-201, 9-315. The definition of "licensee in ordinary course of business" in subsection (a) is modeled upon that of "buyer in ordinary course of business."

3. **Lessee in Ordinary Course.** Subsection (c) contains the rule formerly found in Section 2A-307(3). The rule works in the same way as that of Section 9-320(a).

§ 9-322. PRIORITIES AMONG CONFLICTING SECURITY INTERESTS IN AND AGRICULTURAL LIENS ON SAME COLLATERAL.

(a) [General priority rules.] Except as otherwise provided in this section, priority among conflicting security interests and agricultural liens in the same collateral is determined according to the following rules:

(1) Conflicting perfected security interests and agricultural liens rank according to priority in time of filing or perfection. Priority dates from the earlier of the time a filing covering the collateral is first made or the security interest or agricultural lien is first perfected, if there is no period thereafter when there is neither filing nor perfection.

(2)   A perfected security interest or agricultural lien has priority over a conflicting unperfected security interest or agricultural lien.

(3)   The first security interest or agricultural lien to attach or become effective has priority if conflicting security interests and agricultural liens are unperfected.

(b)   [Time of perfection: proceeds and supporting obligations.] For the purposes subsection (a)(1):

(1)   the time of filing or perfection as to a security interest in collateral is also the time of filing or perfection as to a security interest in proceeds; and

(2)   the time of filing or perfection as to a security interest in collateral supported by a supporting obligation is also the time of filing or perfection as to a security interest in the supporting obligation.

(c)   [Special priority rules: proceeds and supporting obligations.] Except as otherwise provided in subsection (f), a security interest in collateral which qualifies for priority over a conflicting security interest under Section 9-327, 9-328, 9-329, 9-330, or 9-331 also has priority over a conflicting security interest in:

(1)   any supporting obligation for the collateral; and

(2)   proceeds of the collateral if:

(A)   the security interest in proceeds is perfected;

(B)   the proceeds are cash proceeds or of the same type as the collateral; and

(C)   in the case of proceeds that are proceeds of proceeds, all intervening proceeds are cash proceeds, proceeds of the same type as the collateral, or an account relating to the collateral.

(d)   [First-to-file priority rule for certain collateral.] Subject to subsection (e) and except as otherwise provided in subsection (f), if a security interest in chattel paper, deposit accounts, negotiable documents, instruments, investment property, or letter-of-credit rights is perfected by a method other than filing, conflicting perfected security interests in proceeds of the collateral rank according to priority in time of filing.

(e)   [Applicability of subsection (d).] Subsection (d) applies only if the proceeds of the collateral are not cash proceeds, chattel paper, negotiable documents, instruments, investment property, or letter-of-credit rights.

(f) [Limitations on subsections (a) through (e).] Subsections (a) through (e) are subject to:

(1)   subsection (g) and the other provisions of this part;

(2)   Section 4-210 with respect to a security interest of a collecting bank;

(3)   Section 5-118 with respect to a security interest of an issuer or nominated person; and

(4)   Section 9-110 with respect to a security interest arising under Article 2 or 2A.

(g) [Priority under agricultural lien statute.] A perfected agricultural lien on collateral has priority over a conflicting security interest in or agricultural lien on the same collateral if the statute creating the agricultural lien so provides.

ANALYSIS

At times the drafters of Revised Article 9 push the limits of codification. That is certainly the case with the intricate treatment of priority in proceeds provided by this section. Consider the following translation:

1. When there are conflicting perfected security interests or agricultural liens in the same collateral, the general rule of priority is first-to-file or perfect (FTFOP). New § 9-322(a)(1). The assumption is that creditors who take and file security interests routinely search the record before disbursing funds or becoming unconditionally liable to make any disbursements. These creditors make their credit decisions in reliance on having the first priority interest which FTFOP provides.

2. *Principal* exceptions to FTFOP are the purchase-money priorities of new § 9-324 and the priorities predicated on possession or control recognized by new §§ 9-327 through 9-331. To determine the priority of a purchase-money financer in proceeds one must consult § 9-324. The collateral assets which may be subject to the possession or control priorities are chattel paper, deposit accounts, negotiable documents, instruments, investment property and letter of credit rights. The revisers refer to these assets as "non-filing collateral." However, interests in chattel paper, negotiable documents, instruments and investment property can all be perfected by filing. New § 9-312(a). A better moniker for these collateral assets may be collateral subject to possession or control priorities (CSTPOCP). The assumption is that some creditors who take possession or control of these assets routinely do not search the record prior to their credit decision.

3. When a secured party has priority under FTFOP, the priority it enjoys as to original collateral normally flows through to the proceeds of the collateral. New § 9-322(b)(1).

> *Example*: If Creditor A, who is first filed or perfected as to the inventory of a firm, finds itself in a priority contest with Creditor B, the holder of an interest in the same collateral that is not entitled to a purchase-money priority, then it is clear that Creditor A has priority over Creditor B as to the proceeds of the inventory as well as to the inventory items themselves.

4. The priority flow through principle is restricted or displaced when the original collateral is CSTPOCP. The restriction or displacement is deemed necessary to protect creditors relying on FTFOP. Under new § 9-322(d) if the original collateral is CSTPOCP, the perfection is by a method other than filing, and the proceeds generated are not CTSPOCP or cash proceeds, then the priority flow through is entirely displaced. Instead, priority as to proceeds is governed by a first to file rule.

> *Example A*: Creditor B perfects an interest in a deposit account by control. Creditor A first files as to equipment. The deposit account is used to purchase equipment. Creditor A has priority as to the equipment collateral because it is likely that it made its credit decision based on the record showing no filings as to equipment.

5. If a creditor has a priority in CSTPOCP based upon the possession or control priority of new §§ 9-327 through 9-331, then the flow through of the priority to proceeds is limited to proceeds in which the creditor has a perfected interest which are cash proceeds, or proceeds of the same type (under the Article classification scheme) as the CSTPOCP involved as original collateral. Additionally, any claim to proceeds of proceeds in this situation, must involve a proceeds trail that involves only cash proceeds or assets of the same type as the original CSTPOCP. New § 9-322(c).

> *Example B*: Creditor A establishes control over deposit account. Creditor B files as to equipment. Funds from the deposit account are used to acquire equipment. Creditor B has priority because the equipment is neither cash proceeds nor CSTPOCP. Creditor B is protected because it may have relied on the priority of being first filed as to equipment.

> 6. Just to assure that everyone is intellectually alert, all of these rules are subject to "other provisions of this part."

Official Comment

1. **Source.** Former Section 9-312(5), (6).

2. **Scope of This Section.** In a variety of situations, two or more people may claim a security interest in the same collateral. This section states general rules of priority among conflicting security interests. As subsection (f) provides, the general rules in subsections (a) through (e) are subject to the rule in subsection (g) governing perfected agricultural liens and to the other rules in this Part of this Article. Rules that override this section include those applicable to purchase-money security interests (Section 9-324) and those qualifying for special priority in particular types of collateral. See, e.g., Section 9-327 (deposit accounts); Section 9-328 (investment property); Section 9-329 (letter-of-credit rights); Section 9-330 (chattel paper and instruments); Section 9-334 (fixtures). In addition, the general rules of sections (a) through (e) are subject to priority rules governing security interests arising under Articles 2, 2A, 4, and 5.

3. **General Rules.** Subsection (a) contains three general rules. Subsection (a)(1) governs the priority of competing perfected security interests. Subsection (a)(2) governs the priority of competing security interests if one is perfected and the other is not. Subsection (a)(3) governs the priority of competing unperfected security interests. The rules may be regarded an adaptations of the idea, deeply rooted at common law, of a race of diligence among creditors. The first two rules are based on precedence in the time as of which the competing secured parties either filed their financing statements or obtained perfected security interests. Under subsection (a)(1), the first secured party who files or perfects has priority. Under subsection (a)(2), which is new, a perfected security interest has priority over an unperfected one. Under subsection (a)(3), if both security interests are unperfected, the first to attach has priority. Note that Section 9-708(b) may affect the application of subsection (a) to a filing that occurred before the effective date of this Article and which would be ineffective to perfect a security interest under former Article 9 but effective under this Article.

4. **Competing Perfected Security Interests.** When there is more than one perfected security interest, the security interests rank according to priority in time of filing or perfection. "Filing," of course, refers to the filing of an effective financing statement. "Perfection" refers to the acquisition of a perfected security interest, i.e., one that has attached and as to which any required perfection step has been taken. See Section 9-308.

Example 1: On February 1, A files a financing statement covering a certain item of Debtor's equipment. On March 1, B files a financing statement covering the same equipment. On April 1, B makes a loan to Debtor and obtains a security interest in the equipment. On May 1, A makes a loan to Debtor and obtains a security interest in the same collateral. A has priority even though B's loan was made earlier and was perfected when made. It makes no difference whether A knew of B's security interest when A made its advance.

The problem stated in Example 1 is peculiar to a notice-filing system under which filing may occur before the security interest attaches (see Section 9-502). The justification for determining priority by order of filing lies in the necessity of protecting the filing system-that is, of allowing the first secured party who has filed to make subsequent advances without each time having to check for subsequent filings as a condition of protection. Note, however, that this first-to-file protection is not absolute. For example, Section 9-324 affords priority to certain purchase-money security interests, even if a competing secured party was the first to file or perfect.

Example 2: A and B make non-purchase-money advances secured by the same collateral. The collateral is in Debtor's possession, and neither security interest is perfected when the second advance is made. Whichever secured party first perfects its security interest (by taking possession of the collateral or by filing) takes priority. It makes no difference whether that secured party knows of the other security interest at the time it perfects its own.

The rule of subsection (a)(1), affording priority to the first to file or perfect, applies to security interests that are perfected by any method, including temporarily (Section 9-312) or upon attachment (Section 9-309), even though there may be no notice to creditors or subsequent purchasers and notwithstanding any common-law rule to the contrary. The form of the claim to priority, i.e., filing or perfection, may shift from time to time, and the rank will be based on the first filing or perfection as long as there is no intervening period without filing or perfection. See Section 9-308(c).

Example 3: On October 1, A acquires a temporarily perfected (20-day) security interest, unfiled, in a negotiable document in the debtor's possession under Section 9-312(e). On October 5, B files and thereby perfects a security interest that previously had attached to the same document. On October 10, A files. A has priority, even after the 20-day period expires, regardless of whether A knows of B's security interest when A files. A was the first to perfect and maintained continuous perfection or filing since the start of the 20-day period. However, the perfection of A's security interest extends only "to the extent it arises for new value given." To the extent A's security interest secures advances made by A beyond the 20-day period, its security interest would be subordinate to B's, inasmuch as B was the first to file.

In general, the rule in subsection (a)(1) does not distinguish among various advances made by a secured party. The priority of every advance dates from the earlier of filing or perfection. However, in rare instances, the priority of an advance dates from the time the advance is made. See Example 3 and Section 9-323.

5. **Priority in After-Acquired Property.** The application of the priority rules to after-acquired property must be considered separately for each item of collateral. Priority does not depend only on time of perfection but may also be based on priority in filing before perfection.

Example 4: On February 1, A makes advances to Debtor under a security agreement covering "all Debtor's machinery, both existing and after-acquired." A promptly files a financing statement. On April 1, B takes a security interest in all Debtor's machinery, existing and after-acquired, to secure an outstanding loan. The following day, B files a financing statement. On May 1, Debtor acquires a new machine. When Debtor acquires rights in the new machine, both A and B acquire security interests in the machine simultaneously. Both security interests are perfected simultaneously. However, A has priority because A filed before B.

When after-acquired collateral is encumbered by more than one security interest, one of the security interests often is a purchase-money security interest that is entitled to special priority under Section 9-324.

6. **Priority in Proceeds: General Rule.** Subsection (b)(1) follows former Section 9-312(6). It provides that the baseline rules of subsection (a) apply generally to priority conflicts in proceeds except where otherwise provided (e.g., as in subsections (c) through (e)). Under Section 9-203, attachment cannot occur (and therefore, under Section 9-308, perfection cannot occur) as to particular collateral until the collateral itself comes into existence and the debtor has rights in it. Thus, a security interest in proceeds of original collateral does not attach and is not perfected until the proceeds come into existence and the debtor acquires rights in them.

Example 5: On April 1, Debtor authenticates a security agreement granting to A a security interest in all Debtor's existing and after-acquired inventory. The same day, A files a financing statement covering inventory. On May 1, Debtor authenticates a security agreement granting B a security interest in all Debtor's existing and future accounts. On June 1, Debtor sells inventory to a customer on 30-day unsecured credit. When Debtor acquires the account, B's security interest attaches to it and is perfected by B's financing statement. At the very same time, A's security interest attaches to the account as proceeds of the inventory and is automatically perfected. See Section 9-315. Under subsection (b) of this section, for purposes of determining A's priority in the account, the time of filing as to the original collateral (April 1, as to inventory) is also the time of filing as to proceeds (account). Accordingly, A's security interest in the account has priority over B's. Of course, had B filed its financing statement on before A filed (e.g., on March 1), then B would have priority in the accounts.

Section 9-324 governs the extent to which a special purchase-money priority in goods or software carries over into the proceeds of the original collateral.

7. Priority in Proceeds: Special Rules. Subsections (c), (d), and (e), which are new, provide additional priority rules for proceeds of collateral in situations where the temporal (first-in-time) rules of subsection (a)(1) are not appropriate. These new provisions distinguish what these Comments refer to as "non-filing collateral" from what they call "filing collateral." As used in these Comments, non-filing collateral is collateral of a type for which perfection may be achieved by a method other than filing (possession or control, mainly) and for which secured parties who so perfect generally do not expect or need to conduct a filing search. More specifically, non-filing collateral is chattel paper, deposit accounts, negotiable documents, instruments, investment property, and letter-of-credit rights. Other collateral-accounts, commercial tort claims, general intangibles, goods, nonnegotiable documents, and payment intangibles-is filing collateral.

8. Proceeds of Non-Filing Collateral: Non-Temporal Priority. Subsection (c)(2) provides a baseline priority rule for proceeds of non-filing collateral which applies if the secured party has taken the steps required for non-temporal priority over a conflicting security interest in non-filing collateral (e.g., control, in the case of deposit accounts, letter-of-credit rights, and investment property). This rule determines priority in proceeds of non-filing collateral whether or not there exists an actual conflicting security interest in the original non-filing collateral. Under subsection (c)(2), the priority in the original collateral continues in proceeds if the security interest in proceeds is perfected and the proceeds are cash proceeds or non-filing proceeds "of the same type" as the original collateral. As used in subsection (c)(2), "type" means a type of collateral defined in the Uniform Commercial Code and should be read broadly. For example, a security is "of the same type" as a security entitlement (i.e., investment property), and a promissory note is "of the same type" as a draft (i.e., an instrument).

Example 6: SP-1 perfects its security interest in investment property by filing. SP-2 perfects subsequently by taking control of a certificated security. Debtor receives cash proceeds of the security (e.g., dividends deposited into Debtor's deposit account). If the first-to-file-or-perfect rule of subsection (a)(1) were applied, SP-1's security interest in the cash proceeds would be senior, although SP-2's security interest continues perfected under Section 9-315 beyond the 20-day period of automatic perfection. This was the result under former Article 9. Under subsection (c), however, SP-2's security interest is senior.

Note that a different result would obtain in Example 1 (i.e., SP-1's security interest would be senior) if SP-1 were to obtain control of the deposit-account proceeds. This is so because subsection (c) is subject to subsection (f), which in turn provides that the priority rules under subsections (a) through (e) are subject to "the other provisions of this part." One of those "other provisions" is Section 9-327, which affords priority to a security interest perfected by control. See Section 9-327(1).

Example 7: SP-1 perfects its security interest in investment property by filing. SP-2 perfects subsequently by taking control of a certificated security. Debtor receives proceeds of the security consisting of a new certificated security issued as a stock dividend on the original collateral. Although the new security is of the same type as the original collateral (i.e., investment property), once the 20-day period of automatic perfection expires (see Section 9-315(d)), SP-2's security interest is unperfected. (SP-2 has not filed or taken delivery or control, and no temporary-perfection rule applies.) Consequently, once the 20-day period expires, subsection (c) does not confer priority, and, under subsection (a)(2), SP-1's security interest in the security is senior. This was the result under former Article 9.

Example 8: SP-1 perfects its security interest in investment property by filing. SP-2 perfects subsequently by taking control of a certificated security and also by filing against investment property. Debtor receives proceeds of the security consisting of a new certificated security issued as a stock dividend of the collateral. Because the new security is of the same type as the original collateral (i.e., investment property) and (unlike Example 7) SP-2's security interest is perfected by filing, SP-2's security interest is senior under subsection (c). If the new security were redeemed by the issuer upon surrender and yet another security were received by Debtor, SP-2's security interest would continue to enjoy priority under subsection (c). The new security would be proceeds of proceeds.

Example 9: SP-1 perfects its security interest in instruments by filing. SP-2 subsequently perfects its security interest in investment property by taking control of a certificated security and also by filing against investment property. Debtor receives proceeds of the security consisting of a dividend check that it deposits to a deposit account. Because the check and the deposit account are cash proceeds, SP-1's and SP-2's security interests in the cash proceeds are perfected under Section 9-315 beyond the 20-day period of automatic perfection. However, SP-2's security interest is senior under subsection (c).

Example 10: SP-1 perfects its security interest in investment property by filing. SP-2 perfects subsequently by taking control of a certificated security and also by filing against investment property. Debtor receives an instrument as proceeds of the security. (Assume that the instrument is not cash proceeds.) Because the instrument is not of the same type as the original collateral (i.e., investment property), SP-2's security interest, although perfected by filing, does not achieve priority under subsection (c). Under the first-to-file-or-perfect rule of subsection (a)(1), SP-1's security interest in the proceeds is senior.

The proceeds of proceeds are themselves proceeds. See Section 9-102 (defining "proceeds" and "collateral"). Sometimes competing security interests arise in proceeds that are several generations removed from the original collateral. As the following example explains, the applicability of subsection (c) may turn on the nature of the intervening proceeds.

Example 11: SP-1 perfects its security interest in Debtor's deposit account by obtaining control. Thereafter, SP-2 files against inventory, (presumably) searches, finds no indication of a conflicting security interest, and advances against Debtor's existing and after-acquired inventory. Debtor uses funds from the deposit account to purchase inventory, which SP-1 can trace as identifiable proceeds of its security interest in Debtor's deposit account, and which SP-2 claims as original collateral. The inventory is sold and the proceeds deposited into *another* deposit account, as to which SP-1 has not obtained control. Subsection (c) does not govern priority in this other deposit account. This deposit account is cash proceeds and is also the same type of collateral as SP-1's original collateral, as required by subsections (c)(2)(A) and (B). However, SP-1's security interest does not satisfy subsection (c)(2)(C) because the inventory proceeds, which intervened between the original deposit account and the deposit account constituting the proceeds at issue, are not cash proceeds, proceeds of the same type as the collateral (original deposit account), or an account relating to the collateral. Stated otherwise, once proceeds other than cash proceeds, proceeds of the same type as the original collateral, or an account relating to the original collateral intervene in the chain of proceeds, priority under subsection (c) is thereafter unavailable. The special priority rule in subsection (d) also is inapplicable to this case. See Comment 9, Example 13, below. Instead, the general first-to-file-or-perfect rule of subsections (a) and (b) apply. Under that rule, SP-1 has priority unless its security interest in the inventory proceeds became unperfected under Section 9-315(d). Had SP-2 filed against inventory before SP-1 obtained control of the original deposit account, the SP-2 would have had priority even if SP-1's security interest in the inventory proceeds remained perfected.

9. **Proceeds of Non-Filing Collateral: Special Temporal Priority.** Under subsections (d) and (e), if a security interest in non-filing collateral is perfected by a method other than filing (e.g., control or possession), it does not retain its priority over a conflicting security interest in proceeds that are filing collateral. Moreover, it is not entitled to priority in proceeds under the first-to file-or-perfect rule of subsections (a)(1) and (b). Instead, under subsection (d), priority is determined by a new first-to-file rule.

Example 12: SP-1 perfects its security interest in Debtor's deposit account by obtaining control. Thereafter, SP-2 files against equipment, (presumably) searches, finds no indication of a conflicting security interest, and advances against Debtor's equipment. SP-1 then files against Debtor's equipment. Debtor uses funds from the deposit account to purchase equipment, which SP-1 can trace as proceeds of its security interest in Debtor's deposit account. If the first-to-file-or-perfect rule were applied, SP-1's security interest would be senior under subsections (a)(1) and (b), because it was the first to perfect in the original collateral and there was no period during which its security interest was unperfected. Under subsection (d), however, SP-2's security interest would be senior because it filed first. This corresponds with the likely expectations of the parties.

Note that under subsection (e), the first-to-file rule of subsection (d) applies only if the proceeds in question are other than non-filing collateral (i.e., if the proceeds are filing collateral). If the proceeds are non-filing collateral, either the first-to-file-or-perfect rule under subsections (a) and (b) or the non-temporal priority rule in subsection (c) would apply, depending on the facts.

Example 13: SP-1 perfects its security interest in Debtor's deposit account by obtaining control. Thereafter, SP-2 files against inventory, (presumably) searches, finds no indication of a conflicting security interest, and advances against Debtor's existing and after-acquired inventory. Debtor uses funds from the deposit account to purchase inventory, which SP-1 can trace as identifiable proceeds of its security interest in Debtor's deposit account, and which SP-2 claims as original collateral. The inventory is sold and the proceeds deposited into *another* deposit account, as to which SP-1 has not obtained control. As discussed above in Comment 8, Example 11, subsection (c) does not govern priority in this deposit account. Subsection (d) also does not govern, because the proceeds at issue (the deposit account) are cash proceeds. See subsection (e). Rather, the general rules of subsections (a) and (b) govern.

10. **Priority in Supporting Obligations.** Under subsections (b)(2) and (c)(1), a security interest having priority in collateral also has priority in a supporting obligation for that collateral. However, the rules in these subsections are subject to the special rule in Section 9-329 governing the priority of security interests in a letter-of-credit right. See subsection (f). Under Section 9-329, a secured party's failure to obtain control (Section 9-107) of a letter-of-credit right that serves as supporting collateral leaves its security interest exposed to a priming interest of a party who does take control.

11. **Unperfected Security Interests.** Under subsection (a)(3), if conflicting security interests are unperfected, the first to attach has priority. This rule may be of merely theoretical interest, inasmuch as it is hard to imagine a situation where the case would come into litigation without either secured party's having perfected its security interest. If neither security interest had been perfected at the time of the filing of a petition in bankruptcy, ordinarily neither would be good against the trustee in bankruptcy under the Bankruptcy Code.

12. **Agricultural Liens.** Statutes other than this Article may purport to grant priority to an agricultural lien as against a conflicting security interest or agricultural lien. Under subsection (g), if another statute grants priority to an agricultural lien, the agricultural lien has priority only if the same statute creates the agricultural lien and the agricultural lien is perfected. Otherwise, subsection (a) applies the same priority rules to an agricultural lien as to a security interest, regardless of whether the agricultural lien conflicts with another agricultural lien or with a security interest.

Inasmuch as no agricultural lien on proceeds arises under this Article, subsections (b) through (e) do not apply to proceeds of agricultural liens.

However, if an agricultural lien has priority under subsection (g) and the statute creating the agricultural lien gives the secured party a lien on proceeds of the collateral subject to the lien, a court should apply the principle of subsection (g) and award priority in the proceeds to the holder of the perfected agricultural lien.

§ 9-323. FUTURE ADVANCES.

(a) [When priority based on time of advance.] Except as otherwise provided in subsection (c), for purposes of determining the priority of a perfected security interest under Section 9-322(a)(1), perfection of the security interest dates from the time an advance is made to the extent that the security interest secures an advance that:

(1)   is made while the security interest is perfected only:

(A)   under Section 9-309 when it attaches; or

(B)   temporarily under Section 9-312(e), (f), or (g); and

(2)   is not made pursuant to a commitment entered into before or while the security interest is perfected by a method other than under Section 9-309 or 9-312(e), (f), or (g).

ANALYSIS

If a creditor relies solely on automatic or temporary perfection, the creditor's priority as to new advances is as of the time of the advances.

Example A: On March 1 Uptown Loan Co. makes an advance to enable Consumer to purchase a boat to be used for pleasure. The boat is not certificated. Uptown takes a security interest in the boat but does not file. The security agreement contains an "all obligations" clause. On May 1 Downtown Loan Co. makes a loan to Consumer secured by the boat and files to perfect its interest. On July 1 Uptown makes a new advance to Consumer. The new advance is secured by the boat pursuant to the "all obligations" clause of the March 1 secured agreement. However, Uptown's priority over Downtown is limited to the amount outstanding with respect to the March 1 advance. Uptown is secondary to Downtown with respect to the July 1 advance.

As a practical matter, the exposure of a lender such as Uptown in this context may be limited to consumer goods not protected by the

FTC's Credit Practices Rule. 16 C.F.R. §§ 441.1–444.5. If the household goods are protected by the FTC's Rule, then Downtown would violate that rule by taking a non-purchase-money interest in them. *See Secured Transactions* §§ 20.03, 20.04. It is not clear however, that a violation of the Rule would invalidate the interest or priority of Downtown.

> *Example B*: On March 1 Bank makes loan to Debtor taking a security interest in certificated securities to be delivered by Debtor within 20 days. On March 10 Bank makes a new advance which is also secured by the March 1 agreement. On March 19 Debtor delivers the security certificates. The Bank's interest in the securities was initially and temporarily perfected on March 1 pursuant to new § 9-312(e). But the Bank's priority as to the March 10 advance dates from March 10, not the initial temporary perfection date.

(b) [Lien creditor.] Except as otherwise provided in subsection (c), a security interest is subordinate to the rights of a person that becomes a lien creditor while the security interest is perfected only to the extent that it secures advances made more than 45 days after the person becomes a lien creditor unless the advance is made:

(1) without knowledge of the lien; or

(2) pursuant to a commitment entered into without knowledge of the lien.

ANALYSIS

What if the lien of the lien creditor arises after a filing by the secured creditor but before the security interest is perfected? New § 9-323(b) limits the priority of the secured creditor as to future advances when the lien arises "while the security interest is perfected." Thus, it would seem that the creditor's advances when the lien arises before perfection would be governed by the general FTFOP rule of new § 9-322. Under new § 9-317 the secured creditor has priority if it is filed before the lien arises. Why should the creditor be better off when the lien creditor's claim arises before perfection of the security interest? Perhaps new § 9-323(b) was not worded to keep up with the change in priority provided by new § 9-317(a)(2). *See* the text analysis to new § 9-317.

(c) [Buyer of receivables.] Subsections (a) and (b) do not apply to a security interest held by a secured party that is a buyer of accounts, chattel paper, payment intangibles, or promissory notes or a consignor.

(d) [Buyer of goods.] Except as otherwise provided in subsection (e), a buyer of goods other than a buyer in ordinary course of business takes free of a security interest to the extent that it secures advances made after the earlier of:

(1) the time the secured party acquires knowledge of the buyer's purchase; or

(2) 45 days after the purchase.

(e) [Advances made pursuant to commitment: priority of buyer of goods.] Subsection (d) does not apply if the advance is made pursuant to a commitment entered into without knowledge of the buyer's purchase and before the expiration of the 45-day period.

(f) [Lessee of goods.] Except as otherwise provided in subsection (g), a lessee of goods, other than a lessee in ordinary course of business, takes the leasehold interest free of a security interest to the extent that it secures advances made after the earlier of:

(1) the time the secured party acquires knowledge of the lease; or

(2)   45 days after the lease contract becomes enforceable.

(g) [Advances made pursuant to commitment: priority of lessee of goods.] Subsection (f) does not apply if the advance is made pursuant to a commitment entered into without knowledge of the lease and before the expiration of the 45-day period.

Official Comment

1. **Source.** Former Sections 9-312(7), 9-301(4), 9-307(3), 2A-307(4).

2. **Scope of This Section.** A security agreement may provide that collateral secures future advances. See Section 9-204(c). This section collects all of the special rules dealing with the priority of advances made by a secured party after a third party acquires an interest in the collateral. Subsection (a) applies when the third party is a competing secured party. It replaces and clarifies former Section 9-312(7). Subsection (b) deals with lien creditors and replaces former Section 9-301(4). Subsections (d) and (e) deal with buyers and replace former Section 9-307(3). Subsections (f) and (g) deal with lessees and replace former Section 2A-307(4).

3. **Competing Security Interests.** Under a proper reading of the first-to-file-or perfect rule of Section 9-322(a)(1) (and former Section 9-312(5)), it is abundantly clear that the time when an advance is made plays no role in determining priorities among conflicting security interests except when a financing statement was not filed and the advance is the giving of value as the last step for attachment and perfection. Thus, a secured party takes subject to all advances secured by a competing security interest having priority under Section 9-322(a)(1). This result generally obtains regardless of how the competing security interest is perfected and regardless of whether the advances are made "pursuant to commitment" (Section 9-102). Subsection (a) of this section states the only other instance when the time of an advance figures in the priority scheme in Section 9-322: when the security interest is perfected only automatically under Section 9-309 or temporarily under Section 9-312(e), (f), or (g), and the advance is not made pursuant to a commitment entered into while the security interest was perfected by another method. Thus, an advance has priority from the date it is made only in the rare case in which it is made without commitment and while the security interest is perfected only temporarily under Section 9-312.

The new formulation in subsection (a) clarifies the result when the initial advance is paid and a new ("future") advance is made subsequently. Under former Section 9-312(7), the priority of the new advance turned on whether it was "made while a security interest is perfected." This section resolves any ambiguity by omitting the quoted phrase.

Example 1: On February 1, A makes an advance secured by machinery in the debtor's possession and files a financing statement. On March 1, B makes an advance secured by the same machinery and files a financing statement. On April 1, A makes a further advance, under the original security agreement, against the same machinery. A was the first to file and so, under the first-to-file-or-perfect rule of Section 9-322(a)(1), A's security interest has priority over B's, B both as to the February 1 and as to the April 1 advance. It makes no difference whether A knows of B's intervening advance when A makes the second advance. Note that, as long as A was the first to file or perfect, A would have priority with respect to both advances if either A or B had perfected by taking possession of the collateral. Likewise, A would have priority if A's April 1 advance was not made under the original agreement with the debtor, but was under a new agreement.

Example 2: On October 1, A acquires a temporarily perfected (20-day) security interest, unfiled, in a negotiable document in the debtor's possession under Section 9-312(e) or (f). The security interest secures an advance made on that day as well as future advances. On October 5, B files and thereby perfects a security interest that previously had attached to the same document. On October 8, A makes an additional advance. On October 10, A files. Under Section 9-322(a)(1), because A was the first to perfect and maintained continuous perfection or filing since the start of the 20-day period, A has priority, even after the 20-day period expires. See Section 9-322, Comment 4, Example 3. However, under this section, for purposes of Section 9-322(a)(1), to the extent A's security interest secures the October 8 advance, the security interest was perfected on October 8. Inasmuch as B perfected on October 5, B has priority over the October 8 advance.

The rule in subsection (a) is more liberal toward the priority of future advances than the corresponding rules applicable to intervening lien creditors (subsection (b)), buyers (subsections (d) and (e), and lessees (subsections (f) and (g)).

4. **Competing Lien Creditors.** Subsection (b) replaces former Section 9-301(4). It addresses the problem considered by PEB Commentary No. 2 and removes the ambiguity that necessitated the Commentary. Former Section 9-301(4) appeared to state a general rule that a lien creditor has priority over a perfected security interest and is "subject to" the security interest "only" in specified circumstances. Because that section spoke to the making of an "advance," it arguably implied that to the extent a security interest secured non-advances (expenses, interest, etc.), it was junior to the lien creditor's interest. Under Section 9-317(a)(2), a perfected security interest is senior to the rights of a subsequent lien creditor. Subsection (b) of this section eliminates the erroneous implication of former law by providing that a perfected security interest is subordinate only to the extent that the specified circumstances occur.

As under former Section 9-301(4), a secured party's knowledge does not cut short the 45-day period during which future advances can achieve priority over an intervening lien creditor's interest. Rather, because of the impact of the rule in subsection (b) on the question whether the security interest for future advances is "protected" under Section 6323(c)(2) and (d) of the Internal Revenue Code as amended by the Federal Tax Lien Act of 1966, the priority of the security interest for future advances over a lien creditor is made absolute for 45 days regardless of knowledge of the secured party concerning the lien. If, however, the advance is made after the 45 days, the advance will not have priority unless it was made or committed without knowledge of the lien.

5. **Sales of Receivables; Consignments.** Subsections (a) and (b) do not apply to outright sales of accounts, chattel paper, payment intangibles, or promissory notes, nor do they apply to consignments.

6. **Competing Buyers and Lessees.** Under subsections (d) and (e), a buyer will not take subject to a security interest to the extent it secures advances made after the secured party has knowledge that the buyer has purchased the collateral or more than 45 days after the purchase unless the advances were made pursuant to a commitment entered into before the expiration of the 45-day period and without knowledge of the purchase. Subsections (f) and (g) provide an analogous rule for lessees. Of course, a buyer in ordinary course who takes free of the security interest under Section 9-320 and a lessee in ordinary course who takes free under Section 9-321 are not subject to any future advances. Subsections (d) and (e) replace former Section 9-307(3), and subsections (f) and (g) replace former Section 2A-307(4). No change in meaning is intended.

§ 9-324. PRIORITY OF PURCHASE-MONEY SECURITY INTERESTS.

(a)   [General rule: purchase-money priority.] Except as otherwise provided in subsection (g), a perfected purchase-money security interest in goods other than inventory or livestock has priority over a conflicting security interest in the same goods, and, except as otherwise provided in Section 9-327, a perfected security interest in its identifiable proceeds also has priority, if the purchase-money security interest is perfected when the debtor receives possession of the collateral or within 20 days thereafter.

(b)   [Inventory purchase-money priority.] Subject to subsection (c) and except as otherwise provided in subsection (g), a perfected purchase-money security interest in inventory has priority over a conflicting security interest in the same inventory, has priority over a conflicting security interest in chattel paper or an instrument constituting proceeds of the inventory and in proceeds of the chattel paper, if so provided in Section 9-330, and, except as otherwise provided in Section 9-327, also has priority in identifiable cash proceeds of the inventory to the extent the identifiable cash proceeds are received on or before the delivery of the inventory to a buyer, if:

(1)   the purchase-money security interest is perfected when the debtor receives possession of the inventory;

(2)   the purchase-money secured party sends an authenticated notification to the holder of the conflicting security interest;

(3)   the holder of the conflicting security interest receives the notification within five years before the debtor receives possession of the inventory; and

(4)   the notification states that the person sending the notification has or expects to acquire a purchase-money security interest in inventory of the debtor and describes the inventory.

ANALYSIS

Under old § 9-312(3) the priority of the purchase-money financer of inventory "flowed through" a disposition of the inventory by the debtor only to "identifiable cash proceeds received on or before the delivery of the inventory" to a buyer. Under new § 9-324 the priority also reaches proceeds in the form of chattel paper or instruments if the purchase-money financer would be entitled to priority in these assets under new § 9-330. But at the same time the purchase-money creditor's claim to cash proceeds placed in a deposit account is subordinate to a control security interest held by a rival creditor in the deposit account.

> *Example A*: In 2002 Appliance Store grants a floating lien security interest in all of its inventory (including after-acquired inventory) to First Bank. First Bank makes its advances based solely on the inventory which Appliance Store has on hand. First Bank is first-filed. In 2003 Appliance Store grants a purchase-money security interest in a new shipment of inventory to Second Bank. Second Bank takes the steps required by new § 9-324(b) for priority as to the new shipment over First Bank. Appliance Store sells an item of inventory to Consumer X in a secured credit sale. The sales contract between Appliance Store and Consumer X is tangible chattel paper. The chattel paper is not legended to show the interest of First Bank. Second Bank takes possession of the chattel paper. Second Bank is deemed to have given new value for the chattel paper under new § 9-330(e). Assuming that Second Bank acted in good faith and in the ordinary course of its business it has priority over First Bank under new § 9-330(a). The claim of First Bank is a claim to the chattel paper merely as proceeds of the inventory.

Example B: Same as above except that Consumer X, after buying the appliances, makes a payment to Appliance Store by check and that Second Bank takes possession of the check. Second Bank has the priority claim to the check as cash proceeds of the chattel paper.

Example C: The sale to Consumer X was on open account. No security interest or instrument was given to Appliance Store. Second Bank has no priority over First Bank as to the account or payments made on the account.

Example D: Appliance Store sells the inventory item to Consumer X who pays by check before taking delivery. Appliance Store places the check into an account at Third Bank. Appliance Store has previously granted a security interest in this account to Third Bank. Since the deposit account is maintained with Third Bank, Third Bank has control over the deposit account. Third Bank's control interest in the deposited proceeds trumps Second Bank's purchase-money priority under new § 9-327.

Example E: Consumer X first gives tangible chattel paper for the inventory item. Second Bank has the priority claim to the chattel paper under § 9-330. Consumer X makes a payment by check which Appliance Store deposits into its bank account at Third Bank, which is subject to a control security interest of Third Bank. Since the struggle is now over the deposit account, new § 9-324 seems to specify that Third Bank's control interest should still trump Second Bank's purchase-money priority under new § 9-327. Since Third Bank's interest is perfected by control, one could argue that Third Bank should be subordinated to Second Bank that filed under Section 9-322. But the rules on proceeds in that Section are subject to "other provisions of this part."

(c)   [Holders of conflicting inventory security interests to be notified.] Subsections (b)(2) through (4) apply only if the holder of the conflicting security interest had filed a financing statement covering the same types of inventory:

(1)   if the purchase-money security interest is perfected by filing, before the date of the filing; or

(2)   if the purchase-money security interest is temporarily perfected without filing or possession under Section 9-312(f), before the beginning of the 20-day period thereunder.

(d) [Livestock purchase-money priority.] Subject to subsection (e) and except as otherwise provided in subsection (g), a perfected purchase-money security interest in livestock that are farm products has priority over a conflicting security interest in the same livestock, and, except as otherwise provided in Section 9-327, a perfected security interest in their identifiable proceeds and identifiable products in their unmanufactured states also has priority, if:

(1)   the purchase-money security interest is perfected when the debtor receives possession of the livestock;

(2)   the purchase-money secured party sends an authenticated notification to the holder of the conflicting security interest;

(3)   the holder of the conflicting security interest receives the notification within six months before the debtor receives possession of the livestock; and

(4)   the notification states that the person sending the notification has or expects to acquire a purchase-money security interest in livestock of the debtor and describes the livestock.

(e) [Holders of conflicting livestock security interests to be notified.] Subsections (d)(2) through (4) apply only if the holder of the conflicting security interest had filed a financing statement covering the same types of livestock:

(1)   if the purchase-money security interest is perfected by filing, before the date of the filing; or

(2)   if the purchase-money security interest is temporarily perfected without filing or possession under Section 9-312(f), before the beginning of the 20-day period thereunder.

(f) [Software purchase-money priority.] Except as otherwise provided in subsection (g), a perfected purchase-money security interest in software has priority over a conflicting security interest in the same collateral, and, except as otherwise provided in Section 9-327, a perfected security interest in its identifiable proceeds also has priority, to the extent that the purchase-money security interest in the goods in which the software was acquired for use has priority in the goods and proceeds of the goods under this section.

ANALYSIS

Under new § 9-103(c) a purchase-money security interest in software exists only when the debtor acquires the software in an integrated transaction with goods in which the creditor also holds a purchase-money interest and for the principal purpose of using them in the software.

(g) [Conflicting purchase-money security interests.] If more than one security interest qualifies for priority in the same collateral under subsection (a), (b), (d), or (f):

(1)   a security interest securing an obligation incurred as all or part of the price of the collateral has priority over a security interest securing an obligation incurred for value given to enable the debtor to acquire rights in or the use of collateral; and

(2)   in all other cases, Section 9-322(a) applies to the qualifying security interests.

ANALYSIS

Old § 9-312(4) allowed a purchase-money priority in "other collateral." Under Revised Article 9 it is not possible to have a purchase-money interest in non-goods collateral other than software purchased in an integrated transaction with the goods in which it is to be used. *See* new § 9-103 and the text analysis thereto.

Official Comment

1. **Source.** Former Section 9-312(3), (4).

2. **Priority of Purchase-Money Security Interests.** This section contains the priority rules applicable to purchase-money security interests, as defined in Section 9-103. It affords a special, non-temporal priority to those purchase-money security interests that satisfy the statutory conditions. In most cases, priority will be over a security interest asserted under an after-acquired property clause. See Section 9-204 on the extent to which security interests in after-acquired property are validated.

A purchase-money security interest can be created only in goods and software. See Section 9-103. Section 9-324(a), which follows former Section 9-312(4), contains the general rule for purchase-money security interests in goods. It is subject to subsections (b) and (c), which derive from former Section 9-312(3) and apply to purchase-money security interests in inventory, and subsections (d) and (e), which apply to purchase-money security interests in livestock that are farm products. Subsection (f) applies to purchase-money security interests in software. Subsection (g) deals with the relatively unusual case in which a debtor creates two purchase-money security interests in the same collateral and both security interests qualify for special priority under one of the other subsections.

Former Section 9-312(2) contained a rule affording special priority to those who provided secured credit that enabled a debtor to produce crops. This rule proved unworkable and has been eliminated from this Article. Instead, model Section 9-324A contains a revised production-money priority rule. That section is a model, not uniform, provision. The sponsors of the UCC have taken no position as to whether it should be enacted, instead leaving the matter for state legislatures to consider if they are so inclined.

3. **Purchase-Money Priority in Goods Other Than Inventory and Livestock.** Subsection (a) states a general rule applicable to all types of goods except inventory and farm-products livestock: the purchase-money interest takes priority if it is perfected when the debtor receives possession of the collateral or within 20 days thereafter. (As to the 20-day "grace period," compare Section 9-317(e). Former Sections 9-312(4) and 9-301(2) contained a 10-day grace period.) The perfection requirement means that the purchase-money secured party either has filed a financing statement before that time or has a temporarily perfected security interest in goods covered by documents under Section 9-312(e) and (f) which is continued in a perfected status by filing before the expiration of the 20-day period specified in that section. A purchase-money security interest qualifies for priority under subsection (a), even if the purchase-money secured party knows that a conflicting security interest has been created and or that the holder of the conflicting interest has filed a financing statement covering the collateral.

Normally, there will be no question when "the debtor receives possession of the collateral" for purposes of subsection (a). However, sometimes a debtor buys goods and takes possession of them in stages, and then assembly and testing are completed (by the seller or debtor-buyer) at the debtor's location. Under those circumstances, the buyer "takes possession" within the meaning of subsection (a) when, after an inspection of the portion of the goods in the debtor's possession, it would be apparent to a potential lender to the debtor that the debtor has acquired an interest in the goods taken as a whole.

A similar issue concerning the time when "the debtor receives possession" arises when a person acquires possession of goods under a transaction that is not governed by this Article and then later agrees to buy the goods on secured credit. For example, a person may take possession of goods as lessee under a lease contract and then exercise an option to purchase the goods from the lessor on secured credit. Under Section 2A-307(1), creditors of the lessee generally take subject to the lease contract; filing a financing statement against the lessee is unnecessary to protect the lessor's leasehold or residual interest. Once the lease is converted to a security interest, filing a financing statement is necessary to protect the seller's (former lessor's) security interest. Accordingly, the 20-day period in subsection (a) does not commence until a the goods become "collateral" (defined in Section 9-102), i.e., until they are subject to a security interest.

4. **Purchase-Money Security Interests in Inventory.** Subsections (b) and (c) afford a means by which a purchase-money security interest in inventory can achieve priority over an earlier-filed security interest in the same collateral. To achieve priority, the purchase-money security interest must be perfected when the debtor receives possession of the inventory. For a discussion of when "the debtor receives possession," see Comment 3, above. The 20-day grace period of subsection (a) does not apply.

The arrangement between an inventory secured party and its debtor typically requires the secured party to make periodic advances against incoming inventory or periodic releases of old inventory as new inventory is received. A fraudulent debtor may apply to the secured party for advances even though it has already given a purchase-money security interest in the inventory to another secured party. For this reason, subsections (b)(2) through (4) and (c) impose a second condition for the purchase-money security interest's achieving priority: the purchase-money secured party must give notification to the holder of a conflicting security interest who filed against the same item or type of inventory before the purchase-money secured party filed or its security interest became perfected temporarily under Section 9-312(e) or (f). The notification requirement protects the non-purchase-money inventory secured party in such a situation: if the inventory secured party has received notification, it presumably will not make an advance; if it has not received notification (or if the other security interest does not qualify as purchase-money), any advance the inventory secured party may make ordinarily will have priority under Section 9-322. Inasmuch as an arrangement for periodic advances against incoming goods is unusual outside the inventory field, subsection (a) does not contain a notification requirement.

5. **Notification to Conflicting Inventory Secured Party: Timing.** Under subsection (b)(3), the perfected purchase-money security interest achieves priority over a conflicting security interest only if the holder of the conflicting security interest receives a notification within five years before the debtor receives possession of the purchase-money collateral. If the debtor never receives possession, the five-year period never begins, and the purchase-money security interest has priority, even if notification is not given. However, where the purchase-money inventory financing began by the purchase-money secured party's possession of a negotiable document of title, to retain priority the secured party must give the notification required by subsection (b) at or before the usual time, i.e., when the debtor gets possession of the inventory, even though the security interest remains perfected for 20 days under Section 9-312(e) or (f).

Some people have mistakenly read former Section 9-312(3)(b) to require, as a condition of purchase-money priority in inventory, that the purchase-money secured party give the notification before it files a financing statement. Read correctly, the "before" clauses compare (i) the time when the holder of the conflicting security interest filed a financing statement with (ii) the time when the purchase-money security interest becomes perfected by filing or automatically perfected temporarily. Only if (i) occurs before (ii) must notification be given to the holder of the conflicting security interest. Subsection (c) has been rewritten to clarify this point.

6. **Notification to Conflicting Inventory Secured Party: Address.** Inasmuch as the address provided as that of the secured party on a filed financing statement is an "address that is reasonable under the circumstances," the holder of a purchase-money security interest may satisfy the requirement to "send" notification to the holder of a conflicting security interest in inventory by sending a notification to that address, even if the address is or becomes incorrect. See Section 9-102 (definition of "send"). Similarly, because the address is "held out by [the holder of the conflicting security interest] as the place for receipt of such communications [i.e., communications relating to security interests]," the holder is deemed to have "received" a notification delivered to that address. See Section 1-201(26).

7. **Consignments.** Subsections (b) and (c) also determine the priority of a consignor's interest in consigned goods as against a security interest in the goods created by the consignee. Inasmuch as a consignment subject to this Article is defined to be a purchase-money security interest, see Section 9-103(d), no inference concerning the nature of the transaction should be drawn from the fact that a consignor uses the term "security interest" in its notice under subsection (b)(4). Similarly, a notice stating that the consignor has delivered or expects to deliver goods, properly described, "on consignment" meets the requirements of subsection (b)(4), even if it does not contain the term "security interest," and even if the transaction subsequently is determined to be a security interest. Cf. Section 9-505 (use of "consignor" and "consignee" in financing statement).

8. **Priority in Proceeds: General.** When the purchase-money secured party has priority over another secured party, the question arises whether this priority extends to the proceeds of the original collateral. Subsections (a), (d), and (f) give an affirmative answer, but only as to proceeds in which the security interest is perfected (see Section 9-315). Although this qualification did not appear in former Section 9-312(4), it was implicit in that provision.

In the case of inventory collateral under subsection (b), where financing frequently is based on the resulting accounts, chattel paper, or other proceeds, the special priority of the purchase-money secured interest carries over into only certain types of proceeds. As under former Section 9-312(3), the purchase-money priority in inventory under subsection (b) carries over into identifiable cash proceeds (defined in Section 9-102) received on or before the delivery of the inventory to a buyer.

As a general matter, also like former Section 9-312(3), the purchase-money priority in inventory does *not* carry over into proceeds consisting of accounts or chattel paper. Many parties financing inventory are quite content to protect their first-priority security interest in the inventory itself. They realize that when the inventory is sold, someone else will be financing the resulting receivables (accounts or chattel paper), and the priority for inventory will not run forward to the receivables constituting the proceeds. Indeed, the cash supplied by the receivables financer often will be used to pay the inventory financing. In some situations, the party financing the inventory on a purchase-money basis makes contractual arrangements that the proceeds of receivables financing by another be devoted to paying off the inventory security interest.

However, the purchase-money priority in inventory *does* carry over to proceeds consisting of chattel paper and its proceeds (and also to instruments) to the extent provided in Section 9-330. Under Section 9-330(e), the holder of a purchase-money security interest in inventory is deemed to give new value for proceeds consisting of chattel paper. Taken together, Sections 9-324(b) and 9-330(e) enable a purchase-money inventory secured party to obtain priority in chattel paper constituting proceeds of the inventory, even if the secured party does not actually give new value for the chattel paper, provided the purchase-money secured party satisfies the other conditions for achieving priority.

When the proceeds of original collateral (goods or software) consist of a deposit account, Section 9-327 governs priority to the extent it conflicts with the priority rules of this section.

9. **Priority in Accounts Constituting Proceeds of Inventory.** The application of the priority rules in subsection (b) is shown by the following examples:

Example 1: Debtor creates a security interest in its existing and after-acquired inventory in favor of SP-1, who files a financing statement covering inventory. SP-2 subsequently takes a purchase-money security interest in certain inventory and, under subsection (b), achieves priority in this inventory over SP-1. This inventory is then sold, producing accounts. Accounts are not cash proceeds, and so the special purchase-money priority in the inventory does not control the priority in the accounts. Rather, the first-to-file-or-perfect rule of Section 9-322(a)(1) applies. The time of SP-1's filing as to the inventory is also the time of filing as to the accounts under Section 9-322 (b). Assuming that each security interest in the accounts proceeds remains perfected under Section 9-315, SP-1 has priority as to the accounts.

Example 2: In Example 1, if SP-2 had filed directly against accounts, the date of that filing as to accounts would be compared with the date of SP-1's filing as to the inventory. The first filed would prevail under Section 9-322(a)(1).

Example 3: If SP-3 had filed against accounts in Example 1 before either SP-1 or SP-2 filed against inventory, SP-3's filing against accounts would have priority over the filings of SP-1 and SP-2. This result obtains even though the filings against inventory are effective to continue the perfected status of SP-1's and SP-2's security interest in the accounts beyond the 20-day period of automatic perfection. See Section 9-315. SP-1's and SP-2's position as to the inventory does not give them a claim to accounts (as proceeds of the inventory) which is senior to someone who has filed earlier against accounts. If, on the other hand, either SP-1's or SP-2's filing against the inventory preceded SP-3's filing against accounts, SP-1 or SP-2 would outrank SP-3 as to the accounts.

10. **Purchase-Money Security Interests in Livestock.** New subsections (d) and (e) provide a purchase-money priority rule for farm-products livestock. They are patterned on the purchase-money priority rule for inventory found in subsections (b) and (c) and include a requirement that the purchase-money secured party notify earlier-filed parties. Two differences between subsections (b) and (d) are noteworthy. First, unlike the purchase-money inventory lender, the purchase-money livestock lender enjoys priority in *all* proceeds of the collateral. Thus, under subsection (d), the purchase-money secured party takes priority in accounts over an earlier-filed accounts financer. Second, subsection (d) affords priority in certain products of the collateral as well as proceeds.

11. **Purchase-Money Security Interests in Aquatic Farm Products.** Aquatic goods produced in aquacultural operations (e.g., catfish raised on a catfish farm) are farm products. See Section 9-102 (definition of "farm products"). The definition does not indicate whether aquatic goods are "crops," as to which the model production money security interest priority in Section 9-324A applies, or "livestock," as to which the purchase-money priority in subsection (d) of this section applies. This Article leaves courts free to determine the classification of particular aquatic goods on a case-by-case basis, applying whichever priority rule makes more sense in the overall context of the debtor's business.

12. **Purchase-Money Security Interests in Software.** Subsection (f) governs the priority of purchase-money security interests in software. Under Section 9-103(c), a purchase-money security interest arises in software only if the debtor acquires its interest in the software for the principal purpose of using the software in goods subject to a purchase-money security interest. Under subsection (f), a purchase-money security interest in software has the same priority as the purchase-money security interest in the goods in which the software was acquired for use. This priority is determined under subsections (b) and (c) (for inventory) or (a) (for other goods).

13. **Multiple Purchase-Money Security Interests.** New subsection (g) governs priority among multiple purchase-money security interests in the same collateral. It grants priority to purchase-money security interests securing the price of collateral (i.e., created in favor of the seller) over purchase-money security interests that secure enabling loans. Section 7.2(c)

of the Restatement (3d) of the Law of Property (Mortgages) (1997) adopts this rule with respect to real property mortgages. As Comment *d* to that section explains:

> the equities favor the vendor. Not only does the vendor part with specific real estate rather than money, but the vendor would never relinquish it at all except on the understanding that the vendor will be able to use it to satisfy the obligation to pay the price. This is the case even though the vendor may know that the mortgagor is going to finance the transaction in part by borrowing from a third party and giving a mortgage to secure that obligation. In the final analysis, the law is more sympathetic to the vendor's hazard of losing real estate previously owned than to the third party lender's risk of being unable to collect from an interest in real estate that never previously belonged to it.

The first-to-file-or-perfect rule of Section 9-322 applies to multiple purchase-money security interests securing enabling loans.

§ 9-325. PRIORITY OF SECURITY INTERESTS IN TRANSFERRED COLLATERAL.

(a) [Subordination of security interest in transferred collateral.] Except as otherwise provided in subsection (b), a security interest created by a debtor is subordinate to a security interest in the same collateral created by another person if:

(1) the debtor acquired the collateral subject to the security interest created by the other person;

(2) the security interest created by the other person was perfected when the debtor acquired the collateral; and

(3) there is no period thereafter when the security interest is unperfected.

(b) [Limitation of subsection (a) subordination.] Subsection (a) subordinates a security interest only if the security interest:

(1) otherwise would have priority solely under Section 9-322(a) or 9-324; or

(2) arose solely under Section 2-711(3) or 2A-508(5).

ANALYSIS

Creditors financing the inventory of retailers should note this resolution of the dual debtor dilemma in light of the revision's simultaneous override of the *Tanbro* decision. *See* new § 9-320(e). The financer of inventory moving down the chain of distribution that retains possession of the inventory no longer loses its interest under the buyer in ordinary course rule. An interest created by a subsequent transferee will apparently be subordinated by new § 9-325 if the original financer has retained possession and has not authorized sales free of its interest under new § 9-315(a)(1).

> *Example A*: Supplier Co. sells 10 computers to Distributor Co. retaining a security interest in the computers and retaining possession of the computers. The agreement of these parties provides that Distributor Co. will not sell the computers until Supplier Co. is paid in full. In violation of this agreement, Distributor Co. sells the machines to Retailer identifying them by serial numbers. Valley Finance finances the acquisition of the machines by Retailer. Valley Finance is first filed as to the inventory of Retailer. Even if it were not first-filed, it could qualify for a purchase-money priority under new § 9-324(b).

Assuming that the computers never left the possession of Supplier Co., it holds a continuously perfected interest in them. Nothing in the text of new § 9-325 or its commentary says that a debtor must take possession as a pre-condition to its interests being subordinated. Under U.C.C. § 2-401, title can pass based on the agreement of the parties—a transfer of possession is not required. Thus, Supplier Co. appears to be entitled to priority under § 9-325 because Distributor Co. (and Retailer as its transferee) did not take free of Supplier Co.'s interest as a buyer in ordinary course. The financer of the retailer would be well advised to assure that the inventory it is financing is not subject to an upstream possessory security interest. For discussion of the dual debtor dilemma under the old Article 9 see *Secured Transactions* § 7B.03[3].

Official Comment

1. **Source.** New.

2. **"Double Debtor Problem."** This section addresses the "double debtor" problem, which arises when a debtor acquires property that is subject to a security interest created by another debtor.

3. **Taking Subject to Perfected Security Interest.** Consider the following scenario:

Example 1: A owns an item of equipment subject to a perfected security interest in favor of SP-A. A sells the equipment to B, not in the ordinary course of business. B acquires its interest subject to SP-A's security interest. See Sections 9-201, 9-315(a)(1). Under this section, if B creates a security interest in the equipment in favor of SP-B, SP-B's security interest is subordinate to SP-A's security interest, even if SP-B filed against B before SP-A filed against A, and even if SP-B took a purchase-money security interest. Normally, SP-B could have investigated the source of the equipment and discovered SP-A's filing before making an advance against the equipment, whereas SP-A had no reason to search the filings against someone other than its debtor, A.

4. **Taking Subject to Unperfected Security Interest.** This section applies only if the security interest in the transferred collateral was perfected when the transferee acquired the collateral. See subsection (a)(2). If this condition is not met, then the normal priority rules apply.

Example 2: A owns an item of equipment subject to an unperfected security interest in favor of SP-A. A sells the equipment to B, who gives value and takes delivery of the equipment without knowledge of the security interest. B takes free of the security interest. See Section 9-317(b). If B then creates a security interest in favor of SP-B, no priority issue arises; SP-B has the only security interest in the equipment.

Example 3: The facts are as in Example 2, except that B knows of SP-A's security interest and therefore takes the equipment subject to it. If B creates a security interest in the equipment in favor of SP-B, this section does not determine the relative priority of the security interests. Rather, the normal priority rules govern. If SP-B perfects its security interest, then, under Section 9-322(a)(2), SP-A's unperfected security interest will be junior to SP-B's perfected security interest. The award of priority to SP-B is premised on the belief that SP-A's failure to file could have misled SP-B.

5. **Taking Subject to Perfected Security Interest that Becomes Unperfected.** This section applies only if the security interest in the transferred collateral did not become unperfected at any time after the transferee acquired the collateral. See subsection (a)(3). If this condition is not met, then the normal priority rules apply.

Example 4: As in Example 1, A owns an item of equipment subject to a perfected security interest in favor of SP-A. A sells the equipment to B, not in the ordinary course of business. B acquires its interest subject to SP-A's security interest. See Sections 9-201, 9-315(a)(1). B creates a security interest in favor of SP-B, and SP-B perfects its security interest. This section provides that SP-A's security interest is senior to SP-B's. However, if SP-A's financing statement lapses while SP-B's security interest is perfected, then the normal priority rules would apply, and SP-B's security interest would become senior to SP-A's security interest. See Sections 9-322(a)(2), 9-515(c).

6. **Unusual Situations.** The appropriateness of the rule of subsection (a) is most apparent when it works to subordinate security interests having priority under the basic priority rules of Section 9-322(a) or the purchase-money priority rules of Section 9-324. The rule also works properly when applied to the security interest of a buyer under Section 2-711(3) or a lessee under Section 2A-508(5). However, subsection (a) may provide an inappropriate resolution of the "double debtor" problem in some of the wide variety of other contexts in which the problem may arise. Although subsection (b) limits the application of subsection (a) to those cases in which subordination is known to be appropriate, courts should apply the rule in other settings, if necessary to promote the underlying purposes and policies of the Uniform Commercial Code. See Section 1-102(1).

§ 9-326. PRIORITY OF SECURITY INTERESTS CREATED BY NEW DEBTOR.

(a) [Subordination of security interest created by new debtor.] Subject to subsection (b), a security interest created by a new debtor which is perfected by a filed financing statement that is effective solely under Section 9-508 in collateral in which a new debtor has or acquires rights is subordinate to a security interest in the same collateral which is perfected other than by a filed financing statement that is effective solely under Section 9-508.

(b) [Priority under other provisions; multiple original debtors.] The other provisions of this part determine the priority among conflicting security interests in the same collateral perfected by filed financing statements that are effective solely under Section 9-508. However, if the security agreements to which a new debtor became bound as debtor were not entered into by the same original debtor, the conflicting security interests rank according to priority in time of the new debtor's having become bound.

ANALYSIS

The priority which a financing statement filed as to the assets of the old debtor gives in the assets acquired by the debtor after the new debtor becomes bound to the old debtor's security agreement does not trump a security interest in those new assets of the new debtor perfected in another manner (*e.g.* by filing as to new debtor). This result follows even if the filing as to new debtor is later in time. *See* new §§ 9-203(d) & (e) and *Secured Transactions* § 1A.05.

Official Comment

1. **Source.** New.

2. **Subordination of Security Interests Created by New Debtor.** This section addresses the priority contests that may arise when a new debtor becomes bound by the security agreement of an original debtor and each debtor has a secured creditor.

Subsection (a) subordinates the original debtor's secured party's security interest perfected against the new debtor solely under Section 9-508. The security interest is subordinated to security interests in the same collateral perfected by another method, e.g., by filing against the new debtor. As used in this section, "a filed financing statement that is effective solely under Section 9-508" refers to a financing statement filed against the *original debtor* that continues to be effective under Section 9-508. It does not encompass a new initial financing statement providing the name of the new debtor, even if the initial financing statement is filed to maintain the effectiveness of a financing statement under the circumstances described in Section 9-508(b). Nor does it encompass a financing statement filed against the original debtor which remains effective against collateral transferred by the original debtor to the new debtor. See Section 9-508(c). Concerning priority contests involving transferred collateral, see Sections 9-325 and 9-507.

Example 1: SP-X holds a perfected-by-filing security interest in X Corp's existing and after-acquired inventory, and SP-Z holds a perfected-by-possession security interest in an item of Z Corp's inventory. Z Corp becomes bound as debtor by X Corp's security agreement (e.g., Z Corp buys X Corp's assets and assumes its security agreement). See Section 9-203(d). Under Section 9-508, SP-X's financing statement is effective to perfect a security interest in the item of inventory in which Z Corp has rights. However, subsection (a) provides that SP-X's security interest is subordinate to SP-Z's, regardless of whether SP-X's financing statement was filed before SP-Z perfected its security interest.

Example 2: SP-X holds a perfected-by-filing security interest in X Corp's existing and after-acquired inventory, and SP-Z holds a perfected-by-filing security interest in Z Corp's existing and after-acquired inventory. Z Corp becomes bound as debtor by X Corp's security agreement. Subsequently, Z Corp acquires a new item of inventory. Under Section 9-508, SP-X's financing statement is effective to perfect a security interest in the new item of inventory in which Z Corp has rights. However, because SP-Z's security interest was perfected by another method, subsection (a) provides that SP-X's security interest is subordinate to SP-Z's, regardless of which financing statement was filed first. This would be the case even if SP-Z filed after Z Corp became bound by X Corp's security agreement.

3. **Other Priority Rules.** Subsection (b) addresses the priority among security interests created by the original debtor (X Corp). By invoking the other priority rules of this subpart, as applicable, subsection (b) preserves the relative priority of security interests created by the original debtor.

Example 3: Under the facts of Example 2, SP-Y also holds a perfected-by-filing security interest in X Corp's existing and after-acquired inventory. SP-Y filed after SP-X. Inasmuch as both SP-X's and SP-Y's security interests in inventory acquired by Z Corp after it became bound are perfected solely under Section 9-508, the normal priority rules determine their relative priorities. Under the "first-to-file-or-perfect" rule of Section 9-322(a)(1), SP-X has priority over SP-Y.

Example 4: Under the facts of Example 3, after Z Corp became bound by X Corp's security agreement, SP-Y promptly filed a new initial financing statement against Z Corp. At that time, SP-X's security interest was perfected only by virtue of its original filing against X Corp which was "effective solely under Section 9-508." Because SP-Y's security interest no longer is perfected by a financing statement that is "effective solely under Section 9-508," this section does not apply to the priority contest. Rather, the normal priority rules apply. Under Section 9-322, because SP-Y's financing statement was filed *against Z Corp*, the new debtor, before SP-X's, SP-Y's security interest is senior to that of SP-X. Similarly, the normal priority rules would govern priority between SP-Y and SP-Z.

The second sentence of subsection (b) effectively limits the applicability of the first sentence to situations in which a new debtor has become bound by more than one security agreement entered into by the *same* original debtor. When the new debtor has become bound by security agreements entered into by *different* original debtors, the second sentence provides that priority is based on priority in time of the new debtor's becoming bound.

Example 5: Under the facts of Example 2, SP-W holds a perfected-by-filing security interest in W Corp's existing and after-acquired inventory. After Z Corp became bound by X Corp's security agreement in favor of SP-X, Z Corp became bound by W Corp's security agreement. Under subsection (b), SP-W's security interest in inventory acquired by Z Corp is subordinate to that of SP-X, because Z Corp became bound under SP-X's security agreement before it became bound under SP-W's security agreement. This is the result regardless of which financing statement (SP-X's or SP-W's) was filed first.

The second sentence of subsection (b) reflects the generally accepted view that priority based on the first-to-file rule is inappropriate for resolving priority disputes when the filings were made against different debtors. Like subsection (a) and the first sentence of subsection (b), however, the second sentence of subsection (b) relates only to priority conflicts among security interests perfected by filed financing statements that are "effective solely under Section 9-508."

Example 6: Under the facts of Example 5, after Z Corp became bound by W Corp's security agreement, SP-W promptly filed a new initial financing statement against Z Corp. At that time, SP-X's security interest was perfected only pursuant to its original filing against X Corp which was "effective solely under Section 9-508." Because SP-W's security interest is not perfected by a financing statement that is "effective solely under Section 9-508," this section does not apply to the priority contest. Rather, the normal priority rules apply. Under Section 9-322, because SP-W's financing statement was the first to be filed *against Z Corp*, the new debtor, SP-W's security interest is senior to that of SP-X. Similarly, the normal priority rules would govern priority between SP-W and SP-Z.

§ 9-327. PRIORITY OF SECURITY INTERESTS IN DEPOSIT ACCOUNT. The following rules govern priority among conflicting security interests in the same deposit account:

(1) A security interest held by a secured party having control of the deposit account under Section 9-104 has priority over a conflicting security interest held by a secured party that does not have control.

(2) Except as otherwise provided in paragraphs (3) and (4), security interests perfected by control under Section 9-314 rank according to priority in time of obtaining control.

(3) Except as otherwise provided in paragraph (4), a security interest held by the bank with which the deposit account is maintained has priority over a conflicting security interest held by another secured party.

(4) A security interest perfected by control under Section 9-104(a)(3) has priority over a security interest held by the bank with which the deposit account is maintained.

ANALYSIS

The only ways of assuredly denying priority to the bank at which the account is maintained are to move the funds to an account in the name of the other secured party or to obtain a subordination from the bank. Apparently, the account may be a joint account of the debtor and the other secured party. *See* Official Comment 3; *see also Secured Transactions* § 6D.02[7].

Official Comment

1. **Source.** New; derived from former Section 9-115(5).

2. **Scope of This Section.** This section contains the rules governing the priority of conflicting security interests in deposit accounts. It overrides conflicting priority rules. See Sections 9-322(f)(1), 9-324(a), (b), (d), (f). This section does not apply to accounts evidenced by an instrument (e.g., certain certificates of deposit), which by definition are not "deposit accounts."

3. **Control.** Under paragraph (1), security interests perfected by control (Sections 9-314, 9-104) take priority over those perfected otherwise, e.g., as identifiable cash proceeds under Section 9-315. Secured parties for whom the deposit account is an integral part of the credit decision will, at a minimum, insist upon the right to immediate access to the deposit account upon the debtor's default (i.e., control). Those secured parties for whom the deposit account is less essential will not take control, thereby running the risk that the debtor will dispose of funds on deposit (either outright or for collateral purposes) after default but before the account can be frozen by court order or the secured party can obtain control.

Paragraph (2) governs the case (expected to be very rare) in which a bank enters into a Section 9-104(a)(2) control agreement with more than one secured party. It provides that the security interests rank according to time of obtaining control. If the bank is solvent and the control agreements are well drafted, the bank will be liable to each secured party, and the priority rule will have no practical effect.

4. **Priority of Bank.** Under paragraph (3), the security interest of the bank with which the deposit account is maintained normally takes priority over all other conflicting security interests in the deposit account, regardless of whether the deposit account constitutes the competing secured party's original collateral or its proceeds. A rule of this kind enables banks to extend credit to their depositors without the need to examine either the public record or their own records to determine whether another party might have a security interest in the deposit account.

A secured party who takes a security interest in the deposit account as original collateral can protect itself against the results of this rule in one of two ways. It can take control of the deposit account by becoming the bank's customer. Under paragraph (4), this arrangement operates to subordinate the bank's security interest. Alternatively, the secured party can obtain a subordination agreement from the bank. See Section 9-339.

A secured party who claims the deposit account as proceeds of other collateral can reduce the risk of becoming junior by obtaining the debtor's agreement to deposit proceeds into a specific cash-collateral account and obtaining the agreement of that bank to subordinate all its claims to those of the secured party. But if the debtor violates its agreement and deposits funds into a deposit account other than the cash-collateral account, the secured party risks being subordinated.

5. **Priority in Proceeds of, and Funds Transferred from, Deposit Account.** The priority afforded by this section does not extend to proceeds of a deposit account. Rather, Section 9-322(c) through (e) and the provisions referred to in Section 9-322(f) govern priorities in proceeds of a deposit account. Section 9-315(d) addresses continuation of perfection in proceeds of deposit accounts. As to funds transferred from a deposit account that serves as collateral, see Section 9-332.

§ 9-328. PRIORITY OF SECURITY INTERESTS IN INVESTMENT PROPERTY. The following rules govern priority among conflicting security interests in the same investment property:

(1) A security interest held by a secured party having control of investment property under Section 9-106 has priority over a security interest held by a secured party that does not have control of the investment property.

(2) Except as otherwise provided in paragraphs (3) and (4), conflicting security interests held by secured parties each of which has control under Section 9-106 rank according to priority in time of:

(A) if the collateral is a security, obtaining control;

(B) if the collateral is a security entitlement carried in a securities account and:

(i) if the secured party obtained control under Section 8-106(d)(1), the secured party's becoming the person for which the securities account is maintained;

(ii) if the secured party obtained control under Section 8-106(d)(2), the securities intermediary's agreement to comply with the secured party's entitlement orders with respect to security entitlements carried or to be carried in the securities account; or

(iii) if the secured party obtained control through another person under Section 8-106(d)(3), the time on which priority would be based under this paragraph if the other person were the secured party; or

(C)   if the collateral is a commodity contract carried with a commodity intermediary, the satisfaction of the requirement for control specified in Section 9-106(b)(2) with respect to commodity contracts carried or to be carried with the commodity intermediary.

(3)   A security interest held by a securities intermediary in a security entitlement or a securities account maintained with the securities intermediary has priority over a conflicting security interest held by another secured party.

(4)   A security interest held by a commodity intermediary in a commodity contract or a commodity account maintained with the commodity intermediary has priority over a conflicting security interest held by another secured party.

(5)   A security interest in a certificated security in registered form which is perfected by taking delivery under Section 9-313(a) and not by control under Section 9-314 has priority over a conflicting security interest perfected by a method other than control.

(6)   Conflicting security interests created by a broker, securities intermediary, or commodity intermediary which are perfected without control under Section 9-106 rank equally.

(7)   In all other cases, priority among conflicting security interests in investment property is governed by Sections 9-322 and 9-323.

ANALYSIS

The priority rules as to investment property added to the Code in 1994 with the addition of § 9-115 are rewritten, but the most important point remains unchanged. If an investor grants a security interest to his broker in a securities entitlement maintained with the broker, the broker has control under § 8-106(e) and priority over other security interests under new § 9-328(3).

Official Comment

1. **Source.** Former Section 9-115(5).

2. **Scope of This Section.** This section contains the rules governing the priority of conflicting security interests in investment property. Paragraph (1) states the most important general rule-that a secured party who obtains control

has priority over a secured party who does not obtain control. Paragraphs (2) through (4) deal with conflicting security interests each of which is perfected by control. Paragraph (5) addresses the priority of a security interest in a certificated security which is perfected by delivery but not control. Paragraph (6) deals with the relatively unusual circumstance in which a broker, securities intermediary, or commodity intermediary has created conflicting security interests none of which is perfected by control. Paragraph (7) provides that the general priority rules of Sections 9-322 and 9-323 apply to cases not covered by the specific rules in this section. The principal application of this residual rule is that the usual first in time of filing rule applies to conflicting security interests that are perfected only by filing. Because the control priority rule of paragraph (1) provides for the ordinary cases in which persons purchase securities on margin credit from their brokers, there is no need for special rules for purchase-money security interests. See also Section 9-103 (limiting purchase-money collateral to goods and software).

3. **General Rule: Priority of Security Interest Perfected by Control.** Under paragraph (1), a secured party who obtains control has priority over a secured party who does not obtain control. The control priority rule does not turn on either temporal sequence or awareness of conflicting security interests. Rather, it is a structural rule, based on the principle that a lender should be able to rely on the collateral without question if the lender has taken the necessary steps to assure itself that it is in a position where it can foreclose on the collateral without further action by the debtor. The control priority rule is necessary because the perfection rules provide considerable flexibility in structuring secured financing arrangements. For example, at the "retail" level, a secured lender to an investor who wants the full measure of protection can obtain control, but the creditor may be willing to accept the greater measure of risk that follows from perfection by filing. Similarly, at the "wholesale" level, a lender to securities firms can leave the collateral with the debtor and obtain a perfected security interest under the automatic perfection rule of Section 9-309(a)(10), but a lender who wants to be entirely sure of its position will want to obtain control. The control priority rule of paragraph (1) is an essential part of this system of flexibility. It is feasible to provide more than one method of perfecting security interests only if the rules ensure that those who take the necessary steps to obtain the full measure of protection do not run the risk of subordination to those who have not taken such steps. A secured party who is unwilling to run the risk that the debtor has granted or will grant a conflicting control security interest should not make a loan without obtaining control of the collateral.

As applied to the retail level, the control priority rule means that a secured party who obtains control has priority over a conflicting security interest perfected by filing without regard to inquiry into whether the control secured party was aware of the filed security interest. Prior to the 1994 revisions to

Articles 8 and 9, Article 9 did not permit perfection of security interests in securities by filing. Accordingly, parties who deal in securities never developed a practice of searching the UCC files before conducting securities transactions. Although filing is now a permissible method of perfection, in order to avoid disruption of existing practices in this business it is necessary to give perfection by filing a different and more limited effect for securities than for some other forms of collateral. The priority rules are not based on the assumption that parties who perfect by the usual method of obtaining control will search the files. Quite the contrary, the control priority rule is intended to ensure that, with respect to investment property, secured parties who do obtain control are entirely unaffected by filings. To state the point another way, perfection by filing is intended to affect only general creditors or other secured creditors who rely on filing. The rule that a security interest perfected by filing can be primed by a control security interest, without regard to awareness, is a consequence of the system of perfection and priority rules for investment property. These rules are designed to take account of the circumstances of the securities markets, where filing is not given the same effect as for some other forms of property. No implication is made about the effect of filing with respect to security interests in other forms of property, nor about other Article 9 rules, e.g., Section 9-330, which govern the circumstances in which security interests in other forms of property perfected by filing can be primed by subsequent perfected security interests.

The following examples illustrate the application of the priority rule in paragraph (1):

Example 1: Debtor borrows from Alpha and grants Alpha a security interest in a variety of collateral, including all of Debtor's investment property. At that time Debtor owns 1000 shares of XYZ Co. stock for which Debtor has a certificate. Alpha perfects by filing. Later, Debtor borrows from Beta and grants Beta a security interest in the 1000 shares of XYZ Co. stock. Debtor delivers the certificate, properly indorsed, to Beta. Alpha and Beta both have perfected security interests in the XYZ Co. stock. Beta has control, see Section 8-106(b)(1), and hence has priority over Alpha.

Example 2: Debtor borrows from Alpha and grants Alpha a security interest in a variety of collateral, including all of Debtor's investment property. At that time Debtor owns 1000 shares of XYZ Co. stock, held through a securities account with Able & Co. Alpha perfects by filing. Later, Debtor borrows from Beta and grants Beta a security interest in the 1000 shares of XYZ Co. stock. Debtor instructs Able to have the 1000 shares transferred through the clearing corporation to Custodian Bank, to be credited to Beta's account with Custodian Bank. Alpha and Beta both have perfected security interests in the XYZ Co. stock. Beta has control, see Section 8-106(d)(1), and hence has priority over Alpha.

Example 3: Debtor borrows from Alpha and grants Alpha a security interest in a variety of collateral, including all of Debtor's investment property. At that time Debtor owns 1000 shares of XYZ Co. stock, which is held through a securities account with Able & Co. Alpha perfects by filing. Later, Debtor borrows from Beta and grants Beta a security interest in the 1000 shares of XYZ Co. stock. Debtor, Able, and Beta enter into an agreement under which Debtor will continue to receive dividends and distributions, and will continue to have the right to direct dispositions, but Beta will also have the right to direct dispositions and receive the proceeds. Alpha and Beta both have perfected security interests in the XYZ Co. stock (more precisely, in the Debtor's security entitlement to the financial asset consisting of the XYZ Co. stock). Beta has control, see Section 8-106(d)(2), and hence has priority over Alpha.

Example 4: Debtor borrows from Alpha and grants Alpha a security interest in a variety of collateral, including all of Debtor's investment property. At that time Debtor owns 1000 shares of XYZ Co. stock, held through a securities account with Able & Co. Alpha perfects by filing. Debtor's agreement with Able & Co. provides that Able has a security interest in all securities carried in the account as security for any obligations of Debtor to Able. Debtor incurs obligations to Able and later defaults on the obligations to Alpha and Able. Able has control by virtue of the rule of Section 8-106(e) that if a customer grants a security interest to its own intermediary, the intermediary has control. Since Alpha does not have control, Able has priority over Alpha under the general control priority rule of paragraph (1).

4. **Conflicting Security Interests Perfected by Control: Priority of Securities Intermediary or Commodity Intermediary.** Paragraphs (2) through (4) govern the priority of conflicting security interests each of which is perfected by control. The following example explains the application of the rules in paragraphs (3) and (4):

Example 5: Debtor holds securities through a securities account with Able & Co. Debtor's agreement with Able & Co. provides that Able has a security interest in all securities carried in the account as security for any obligations of Debtor to Able. Debtor borrows from Beta and grants Beta a security interest in 1000 shares of XYZ Co. stock carried in the account. Debtor, Able, and Beta enter into an agreement under which Debtor will continue to receive dividends and distributions and will continue to have the right to direct dispositions, but Beta will also have the right to direct dispositions and receive the proceeds. Debtor incurs obligations to Able and later defaults on the obligations to Beta and Able. Both Beta and Able have control, so the general control priority rule of paragraph (1) does not apply. Compare Example 4. Paragraph (3) provides that a security interest held by a securities intermediary in positions of its own customer has priority over a conflicting security interest of an external lender, so Able has priority over Beta. (Paragraph (4) contains a parallel rule for commodity intermediaries.) The agreement among Able, Beta, and Debtor could, of course, determine the relative priority of the security interests of Able and Beta, see Section 9-339, but the fact that the intermediary has agreed to act on the instructions of a secured party such as Beta does not itself imply any agreement by the intermediary to subordinate.

5. Conflicting Security Interests Perfected by Control: Temporal Priority. Former Section 9-115 introduced into Article 9 the concept of conflicting security interests that rank equally. Paragraph (2) of this section governs priority in those circumstances in which more than one secured party (other than a broker, securities intermediary, or commodity intermediary) has control. It replaces the equal-priority rule for conflicting security interests in investment property with a temporal rule. For securities, both certificated and uncertificated, under paragraph (2)(A) priority is based on the time that control is obtained. For security entitlements carried in securities accounts, the treatment is more complex. Paragraph (2)(B) bases priority on the timing of the steps taken to achieve control. The following example illustrates the application of paragraph (2).

Example 6: Debtor borrows from Alpha and grants Alpha a security interest in a variety of collateral, including all of Debtor's investment property. At that time Debtor owns a security entitlement that includes 1000 shares of XYZ Co. stock that Debtor holds through a securities account with Able & Co. Debtor, Able, and Alpha enter into an agreement under which Debtor will continue to receive dividends and distributions, and will continue to have the right to direct dispositions, but Alpha will also have the right to direct dispositions and receive the proceeds. Later, Debtor borrows from Beta and grants Beta a security interest all its investment property, existing and after-acquired. Debtor, Able, and Beta enter into an agreement under which Debtor will continue to receive dividends and distributions, and will continue to have the right to direct dispositions, but Beta will also have the right to direct dispositions and receive the proceeds. Alpha and Beta both have perfected-by-control security interests in the security entitlement to the XYZ Co. stock by virtue of their agreements with Able. See Sections 9-314(a), 9-106(a), 8-106(d)(2). Under paragraph (2)(B)(ii), the priority of each security interest dates from the time of the secured party's agreement with Able. Because Alpha's agreement was first in time, Alpha has priority. This priority applies equally to security entitlements to financial assets credited to the account after the agreement was entered into.

The priority rule is analogous to "first-to-file" priority under Section 9-322 with respect to after-acquired collateral. Paragraphs (2)(B)(i) and (2)(B)(iii) provide similar rules for security entitlements as to which control is obtained by other methods, and paragraph (2)(C) provides a similar rule for commodity contracts carried in a commodity account. Section 8-510 also has been revised to provide a temporal priority conforming to paragraph (2)(B).

6. Certificated Securities. A long-standing practice has developed whereby secured parties whose collateral consists of a security evidenced by a security certificate take possession of the security certificate. If the security certificate is in bearer form, the secured party's acquisition of possession constitutes "delivery" under Section 8-301(a)(1), and the delivery constitutes "control" under Section 8-106(a). Comment 5 discusses the priority of security interests perfected by control of investment property.

If the security certificate is in registered form, the secured party will not achieve control over the security unless the security certificate contains an appropriate indorsement or is (re)registered in the secured party's name. See Section 8-106(b). However, the secured party's acquisition of possession constitutes "delivery" of the security certificate under Section 8-301 and serves to perfect the security interest under Section 9-313(a), even if the security certificate has not been appropriately indorsed and has not been (re)registered in the secured party's name. A security interest perfected by this method has priority over a security interest perfected other than by control (e.g., by filing). See paragraph (5).

The priority rule stated in paragraph (5) may seem anomalous, in that it can afford less favorable treatment to purchasers who buy collateral outright that to those who take a security interest in it. For example, a buyer of a security certificate would cut off a security interest perfected by filing only if the buyer achieves the status of a protected purchaser under Section 8-303. The buyer would not be a protected purchaser, for example, if it does not obtain "control" under Section 8-106 (e.g., if it fails to obtain a proper indorsement of the certificate) or if it had notice of an adverse claim under Section 8-105. The apparent anomaly disappears, however, when one understands the priority rule not as one intended to protect careless or guilty parties, but as one that eliminates the need to conduct a search of the public records only insofar as necessary to serve the needs of the securities markets.

7. **Secured Financing of Securities Firms.** Priority questions concerning security interests granted by brokers and securities intermediaries are governed by the general control-beats-non-control priority rule of paragraph (1), as supplemented by the special rules set out in paragraphs (2) (temporal priority-first to control), (3) (special priority for securities intermediary), and (6) (equal priority for non-control). The following examples illustrate the priority rules as applied to this setting. (In all cases it is assumed that the debtor retains sufficient other securities to satisfy all customers' claims. This section deals with the relative rights of secured lenders to a securities firm. Disputes between a secured lender and the firm's own customers are governed by Section 8-511.)

Example 7: Able & Co., a securities dealer, enters into financing arrangements with two lenders, Alpha Bank and Beta Bank. In each case the agreements provide that the lender will have a security interest in the securities identified on lists provided to the lender on a daily basis, that the debtor will deliver the securities to the lender on demand, and that the debtor will not list as collateral any securities which the debtor has pledged to any other lender. Upon Able's insolvency it is discovered that Able has listed the same securities on the collateral lists provided to both Alpha and Beta. Alpha and Beta both have perfected security interests under the automatic-perfection rule of Section 9-309(10). Neither Alpha nor Beta has control. Paragraph (6) provides that the security interests of Alpha and Beta rank equally, because each of them has a non-control security interest granted by a securities firm. They share pro-rata.

Example 8: Able enters into financing arrangements, with Alpha Bank and Beta Bank as in Example 7. At some point, however, Beta decides that it is unwilling to continue to provide financing on a non-control basis. Able directs the clearing corporation where it holds its principal inventory of securities to move specified securities into Beta's account. Upon Able's insolvency it is discovered that a list of collateral provided to Alpha includes securities that had been moved to Beta's account. Both Alpha and Beta have perfected security interests; Alpha under the automatic-perfection rule of Section 9-309(10), and Beta under that rule and also the perfection-by-control rule in Section 9-314(a). Beta has control but Alpha does not. Beta has priority over Alpha under paragraph (1).

Example 9: Able & Co. carries its principal inventory of securities through Clearing Corporation, which offers a "shared control" facility whereby a participant securities firm can enter into an arrangement with a lender under which the securities firm will retain the power to trade and otherwise direct dispositions of securities carried in its account, but Clearing Corporation agrees that, at any time the lender so directs, Clearing Corporation will transfer any securities from the firm's account to the lender's account or otherwise dispose of them as directed by the lender. Able enters into financing arrangements with two lenders, Alpha and Beta, each of which obtains such a control agreement from Clearing Corporation. The agreement with each lender provides that Able will designate specific securities as collateral on lists provided to the lender on a daily or other periodic basis, and that it will not pledge the same securities to different lenders. Upon Able's insolvency, it is discovered that Able has listed the same securities on the collateral lists provided to both Alpha and Beta. Both Alpha and Beta have control over the disputed securities. Paragraph (2) awards priority to whichever secured party first entered into the agreement with Clearing Corporation.

8. **Relation to Other Law.** Section 1-103 provides that "unless displaced by particular provisions of this Act, the principles of law and equity . . . shall supplement its provisions." There may be circumstances in which a secured party's action in acquiring a security interest that has priority under this section constitutes conduct that is wrongful under other law. Though the possibility of such resort to other law may provide an appropriate "escape valve" for cases of egregious conduct, care must be taken to ensure that this does not impair the certainty and predictability of the priority rules. Whether a court may appropriately look to other law to impose liability upon or estop a secured party from asserting its Article 9 priority depends on an assessment

of the secured party's conduct under the standards established by such other law as well as a determination of whether the particular application of such other law is displaced by the UCC.

Some circumstances in which other law is clearly displaced by the UCC rules are readily identifiable. Common law "first in time, first in right" principles, or correlative tort liability rules such as common law conversion principles under which a purchaser may incur liability to a person with a prior property interest without regard to awareness of that claim, are necessarily displaced by the priority rules set out in this section since these rules determine the relative ranking of security interests in investment property. So too, Article 8 provides protections against adverse claims to certain purchasers of interests in investment property. In circumstances where a secured party not only has priority under Section 9-328, but also qualifies for protection against adverse claims under Section 8-303, 8-502, or 8-510, resort to other law would be precluded.

In determining whether it is appropriate in a particular case to look to other law, account must also be taken of the policies that underlie the commercial law rules on securities markets and security interests in securities. A principal objective of the 1994 revision of Article 8 and the provisions of Article 9 governing investment property was to ensure that secured financing transactions can be implemented on a simple, timely, and certain basis. One of the circumstances that led to the revision was the concern that uncertainty in the application of the rules on secured transactions involving securities and other financial assets could contribute to systemic risk by impairing the ability of financial institutions to provide liquidity to the markets in times of stress. The control priority rule is designed to provide a clear and certain rule to ensure that lenders who have taken the necessary steps to establish control do not face a risk of subordination to other lenders who have not done so.

The control priority rule does not turn on an inquiry into the state of a secured party's awareness of potential conflicting claims because a rule under which a person's rights depended on that sort of after-the-fact inquiry could introduce an unacceptable measure of uncertainty. If an inquiry into awareness could provide a complete and satisfactory resolution of the problem in all cases, the priority rules of this section would have incorporated that test. The fact that they do not necessarily means that resort to other law based solely on that factor is precluded, though the question whether a control secured party induced or encouraged its financing arrangement with actual knowledge that the debtor would be violating the rights of another secured party may, in some circumstances, appropriately be treated as a factor in determining whether the control party's action is the kind of egregious conduct for which resort to other law is appropriate.

§ 9-329. PRIORITY OF SECURITY INTERESTS IN LETTER-OF-CREDIT RIGHT. The following rules govern

priority among conflicting security interests in the same letter-of-credit right:

(1) A security interest held by a secured party having control of the letter-of-credit right under Section 9-107 has priority to the extent of its control over a conflicting security interest held by a secured party that does not have control.

(2) Security interests perfected by control under Section 9-314 rank according to priority in time of obtaining control.

Official Comment

1. **Source.** New; loosely modeled after former Section 9-115(5).

2. **General Rule.** Paragraph (1) awards priority to a secured party who perfects a security interest directly in letter-of-credit rights (i.e., one that takes an assignment of proceeds and obtains consent of the issuer or any nominated person under Section 5-114(c)) over another conflicting security interest (i.e., one that is perfected automatically in the letter-of-credit rights as supporting obligations under Section 9-308(d)). This is consistent with international letter-of-credit practice and provides finality to payments made to recognized assignees of letter-of-credit proceeds. If an issuer or nominated person recognizes multiple security interests in a letter-of-credit right, resulting in multiple parties having control (Section 9-107), under paragraph (2) the security interests rank according to the time of obtaining control.

3. **Drawing Rights; Transferee Beneficiaries.** Drawing under a letter of credit is personal to the beneficiary and requires the beneficiary to perform the conditions for drawing under the letter of credit. Accordingly, a beneficiary's grant of a security interest in a letter of credit includes the beneficiary's "letter-of-credit right" as defined in Section 9-102 and the right to "proceeds of [the] letter of credit" as defined in Section 5-114(a), but does not include the right to demand payment under the letter of credit.

Section 5-114(e) provides that the "[r]ights of a transferee beneficiary or nominated person are independent of the beneficiary's assignment of the proceeds of a letter of credit and are superior to the assignee's right to the proceeds." To the extent the rights of a transferee beneficiary or nominated person are independent and superior, this Article does not apply. See Section 9-109(c).

Under Article 5, there is in effect a novation upon the transfer with the issuer becoming bound on a new, independent obligation to the transferee. The rights of nominated persons and transferee beneficiaries under a letter of credit include the right to demand payment from the issuer. Under Section 5-114(e), their rights to payment are independent of their obligations to the beneficiary (or original beneficiary) and superior to the rights of assignees of letter of credit proceeds (Section 5-114(c)) and others claiming a security interest in the beneficiary's (or original beneficiary's) letter of credit rights.

A transfer of drawing rights under a transferable letter of credit establishes independent Article 5 rights in the transferee and does not create or perfect an Article 9 security interest in the transferred drawing rights. The definition of "letter-of-credit right" in Section 9-102 excludes a beneficiary's drawing rights. The exercise of drawing rights by a transferee beneficiary may breach a contractual obligation of the transferee to the original beneficiary concerning when and how much the transferee may draw or how it may use the funds received under the letter of credit. If, for example, drawing rights are transferred to support a sale or loan from the transferee to the original beneficiary, then the transferee would be obligated to the original beneficiary under the sale or loan agreement to account for any drawing and for the use of any funds received. The transferee's obligation would be governed by the applicable law of contracts or restitution.

4. **Secured Party-Transferee Beneficiaries.** As described in Comment 3, drawing rights under letters of credit are transferred in many commercial contexts in which the transferee is not a secured party claiming a security interest in an underlying receivable supported by the letter of credit. Consequently, a transfer of a letter of credit is not a method of "perfection" of a security interest. The transferee's independent right to draw under the letter of credit and to receive and retain the value thereunder (in effect, priority) is not based on Article 9 but on letter-of-credit law and the terms of the letter of credit. Assume, however, that a secured party does hold a security interest in a receivable that is owned by a beneficiary-debtor and supported by a transferable letter of credit. Assume further that the beneficiary-debtor causes the letter of credit to be transferred to the secured party, the secured party draws under the letter of credit, and, upon the issuer's payment to the secured party-transferee, the underlying account debtor's obligation to the original beneficiary-debtor is satisfied. In this situation, the payment to the secured party-transferee is proceeds of the receivable collected by the secured party-transferee. Consequently, the secured party-transferee would have certain duties to the debtor and third parties under Article 9. For example, it would be obliged to collect under the letter of credit in a commercially reasonable manner and to remit any surplus pursuant to Sections 9-607 and 9-608.

This scenario is problematic under letter-of-credit law and practice, inasmuch as a transferee beneficiary collects in its own right arising from its own performance. Accordingly, under Section 5-114, the independent and superior rights of a transferee control over any inconsistent duties under Article 9. A transferee beneficiary may take a transfer of drawing rights to avoid reliance on the original beneficiary's credit and collateral, and it may consider any Article 9 rights superseded by its Article 5 rights. Moreover, it will not always be clear (i) whether a transferee beneficiary has a security interest in the underlying collateral, (ii) whether any security interest is senior to the rights of others, or (iii) whether the transferee beneficiary is aware that it holds a security interest. There will be clear cases in which the role of a transferee beneficiary as such is merely incidental to a conventional secured financing. There also will be cases in which the existence of a security interest may have little to do with the position of a transferee beneficiary as such. In dealing with these cases and less clear cases involving the possible application of Article 9 to a nominated person or a transferee beneficiary, the right to demand payment under a letter of credit should be distinguished from letter-of-credit rights. The courts also should give appropriate consideration to the policies and provisions of Article 5 and letter-of-credit practice as well as Article 9.

§ 9-330. PRIORITY OF PURCHASER OF CHATTEL PAPER OR INSTRUMENT.

(a) [Purchaser's priority: security interest claimed merely as proceeds.] A purchaser of chattel paper has priority over a security interest in the chattel paper which is claimed merely as proceeds of inventory subject to a security interest if:

(1)   in good faith and in the ordinary course of the purchaser's business, the purchaser gives new value and takes possession of the chattel paper or obtains control of the chattel paper under Section 9-105; and

(2)   the chattel paper does not indicate that it has been assigned to an identified assignee other than the purchaser.

(b) [Purchaser's priority: other security interests.] A purchaser of chattel paper has priority over a security interest in the chattel paper which is claimed other than merely as proceeds of inventory subject to a security interest if the purchaser gives new value and takes possession of the chattel paper or obtains control of the chattel paper under Section 9-105 in good faith, in the ordinary course of the purchaser's business, and without knowledge that the purchase violates the rights of the secured party.

ANALYSIS

This section does not resolve the issue of whether fractionalization is appropriate when a transferee takes chattel paper or an instrument partly for new value and partly in satisfaction of an existing debt. If a purchaser pays $10,000 in cash for chattel paper and also forgives a $10,000 debt should it have priority over an earlier filed interest to the extent of 50% of the value of the chattel paper? *See Secured Transactions* § 28.06[5][e].

(c) [Chattel paper purchaser's priority in proceeds.] Except as otherwise provided in Section 9-327, a purchaser having priority in chattel paper under subsection (a) or (b) also has priority in proceeds of the chattel paper to the extent that:

(1)   Section 9-322 provides for priority in the proceeds; or

(2)   the proceeds consist of the specific goods covered by the chattel paper or cash proceeds of the specific goods, even if the purchaser's security interest in the proceeds is unperfected.

(d) [Instrument purchaser's priority.] Except as otherwise provided in Section 9-331(a), a purchaser of an instrument has priority over a security interest in the instrument perfected by a method other than possession if the purchaser gives value and takes possession of the instrument in good faith and without knowledge that the purchase violates the rights of the secured party.

ANALYSIS

In general, Revised Article 9 accommodates existing and emerging patterns of finance. Certainly that is the case with the role given to legending and the attempt to recognize electronic chattel paper under this section. But there may be a question as to whether Revised Article 9 accommodates existing patterns with respect to the sale of instruments, particularly promissory notes.

Under Revised Article 9, a security interest in an instrument, negotiable or non-negotiable, may for the first time be perfected by filing. New § 9-312(a). The priority accorded to purchasers of notes who take possession under § 9-330(d) is therefore much more important than it was under old § 9-308. The principal financer of a business will routinely take an interest in all of the firm's instruments and file to perfect its interest. Qualifying for priority under new § 9-330(d) is the only way recognized by Revised Article 9 that a purchaser of a negotiable instrument may prevail over that earlier-filed creditor without demonstrating that it is a holder in due course, entitled to the victory under §§ 3-305 and 9-331, or that the principal financer authorized the sale of the note free of the original floating lien interest under new § 9-315. More importantly, new § 9-330(d) is the only route recognized by the revised Article 9 for a purchaser of a non-negotiable instrument to prevail over the first-filed creditor who has not authorized the sale free of its interest. Notes are often purchased based on the seller's possession of the paper without a search of the record.

Will new § 9-330(d) give sufficient protection to purchasers to allow such sales to continue? In contrast to old § 9-308, new § 9-330(d) does not require the purchaser of the instrument to give new value. Any value under § 1-201(44) should suffice. The purchaser of an instrument will be protected even if it takes it in payment of, or as security for, an existing debt. The holder of an unsecured debt can jump over a filed secured creditor under new § 9-330(d) by purchasing an instrument from the debtor in payment of the existing debt claim.

But the purchaser of the instrument must take in "good faith," which is now defined in new § 9-102(a)(43) to include "observance of reasonable commercial standards of fair dealing." Will purchasers of non-negotiable notes be willing to invest large sums and continue to buy based on possession confident that they can meet this standard or will they insist on searching for filings against instruments? Official Comments 6 and 7 to this provision are designed to give assurances that a purchaser of chattel paper or instruments (in contrast to a purchaser of accounts) is not required to search for filings in order to be in good faith. *Compare* Official Comment 5 to new § 9-331.

(e)   [Holder of purchase-money security interest gives new value.] For purposes of subsections (a) and (b), the holder of a purchase-money security interest in inventory gives new value for chattel paper constituting proceeds of the inventory.

(f)   [Indication of assignment gives knowledge.] For purposes of subsections (b) and (d), if chattel paper or an instrument indicates that it has been assigned to an identified secured party other than the purchaser, a purchaser of the chattel paper or instrument has knowledge that the purchase violates the rights of the secured party.

Official Comment

1. **Source.** Former Section 9-308.

2. **Non-Temporal Priority.** This Article permits a security interest in chattel paper or instruments to be perfected either by filing or by the secured party's taking possession. This section enables secured parties and other purchasers of chattel paper (both electronic and tangible) and instruments to obtain priority over earlier-perfected security interests.

3. **Chattel Paper.** Subsections (a) and (b) follow former Section 9-308 in distinguishing between earlier-perfected security interests in chattel paper that is claimed merely as proceeds of inventory subject to a security interest and chattel paper that is claimed other than merely as proceeds. Like former Section 9-308, this section does not elaborate upon the phrase "merely as proceeds." For an elaboration, see PEB Commentary No. 8.

This section makes explicit the "good faith" requirement and retains the requirements of "the ordinary course of the purchaser's business" and the giving of "new value" as conditions for priority. Concerning the last, this Article deletes former Section 9-108 and adds to Section 9-102 a completely different definition of the term "new value." Under subsection (e), the holder of a purchase-money security interest in inventory is deemed to give "new value" for chattel paper constituting the proceeds of the inventory. Accordingly, the purchase-money secured party may qualify for priority in the chattel paper under subsection (a) or (b), whichever is applicable, even if it does not make an additional advance against the chattel paper.

If a possessory security interest in tangible chattel paper or a perfected-by-control security interest in electronic chattel paper does not qualify for priority under this section, it may be subordinate to a perfected-by-filing security interest under Section 9-322(a)(1).

4. **Possession.** The priority afforded by this section turns in part on whether a purchaser "takes possession" of tangible chattel paper. Similarly, the governing law provisions in Section 9-301 address both "possessory" and "nonpossessory" security interests. Two common practices have raised particular concerns. First, in some cases the parties create more than one copy or counterpart of chattel paper evidencing a single secured obligation or lease. This practice raises questions as to which counterpart is the "original" and whether it is necessary for a purchaser to take possession of all counterparts in order to "take possession" of the chattel paper. Second, parties sometimes enter into a single "master" agreement. The master agreement contemplates that the parties will enter into separate "schedules" from time to time, each evidencing chattel paper. Must a purchaser of an obligation or lease evidenced by a single schedule also take possession of the master agreement as well as the schedule in order to "take possession" of the chattel paper?

The problem raised by the first practice is easily solved. The parties may in the terms of their agreement and by designation on the chattel paper identify only one counterpart as the original chattel paper for purposes of taking possession of the chattel paper. Concerns about the second practice also are easily solved by careful drafting. Each schedule should provide that it incorporates the terms of the master agreement, not the other way around. This will make it clear that each schedule is a "stand alone" document.

5. **Chattel Paper Claimed Merely as Proceeds.** Subsection (a) revises the rule in former Section 9-308(b) to eliminate reference to what the purchaser knows. Instead, a purchaser who meets the possession or control, ordinary course, and new value requirements takes priority over a competing security interest unless the chattel paper itself indicates that it has been assigned to an identified assignee other than the purchaser. Thus subsection (a) recognizes the common practice of placing a "legend" on chattel paper to indicate that it has been assigned. This approach, under which the chattel paper purchaser who gives new value in ordinary course can rely on possession of unlegended, tangible chattel paper without any concern for other facts that it may know, comports with the expectations of both inventory and chattel paper financers.

6. **Chattel Paper Claimed Other Than Merely as Proceeds.** Subsection (b) eliminates the requirement that the purchaser take without knowledge that the "specific paper" is subject to the security interest and substitutes for it the requirement that the purchaser take "without knowledge that the purchase violates the rights of the secured party." This standard derives from the definition of "buyer in ordinary course of business" in Section 1-201(9). The source of the purchaser's knowledge is irrelevant. Note, however, that "knowledge" means "actual knowledge." Section 1-201(25).

In contrast to a junior secured party in accounts, who may be required in some special circumstances to undertake a search under the "good faith" requirement, see Comment 5 to Section 9-331, a purchaser of chattel paper under this section is not required as a matter of good faith to make a search in order to determine the existence of prior security interests. There may be circumstances where the purchaser undertakes a search nevertheless, either on its own volition or because other considerations make it advisable to do so, e.g., where the purchaser also is purchasing accounts. Without more, a purchaser of chattel paper who has seen a financing statement covering the chattel paper or who knows that the chattel paper is encumbered with a security interest, does not have knowledge that its purchase violates the secured party's rights. However, if a purchaser sees a statement in a financing statement to the effect that a purchase of chattel paper from the debtor would violate the rights of the filed secured party, the purchaser would have such knowledge. Likewise, under new subsection (f), if the chattel paper itself indicates that it had been assigned to an identified secured party other than the purchaser, the purchaser would have wrongful knowledge for purposes of subsection (b), thereby preventing the purchaser from qualifying for priority under that subsection, even if the purchaser did not have actual knowledge. In the case of tangible chattel paper, the indication normally would consist of a written legend on the chattel paper. In the case of electronic chattel paper, this Article leaves to developing market and technological practices the manner in which the chattel paper would indicate an assignment.

7. **Instruments.** Subsection (d) contains a special priority rule for instruments. Under this subsection, a purchaser of an instrument has priority over a security interest perfected by a method other than possession (e.g., by filing, temporarily under Section 9-312(e) or (g), as proceeds under Section 9-315(d), or automatically upon attachment under Section 9-309(4) if the security interest arises out of a sale of the instrument) if the purchaser gives value and takes possession of the instrument in good faith and without knowledge that the purchase violates the rights of the secured party. Generally, to the extent subsection (d) conflicts with Section 3-306, subsection (d) governs. See Section 3-102(b). For example, notice of a conflicting security interest precludes a purchaser from becoming a holder in due course under Section 3-302 and thereby taking free of all claims to the instrument under Section 3-306. However, a purchaser who takes even with knowledge of the security interest qualifies for priority under subsection (d) if it takes without knowledge that the purchase violates the rights of the holder of the security interest. Likewise, a purchaser qualifies for priority under subsection (d) if it takes for "value" as defined in Section 1-201, even if it does not take for "value" as defined in Section 3-303.

Subsection (d) is subject to Section 9-331(a), which provides that Article 9 does not limit the rights of a holder in due course under Article 3. Thus, in the rare case in which the purchaser of an instrument qualifies for priority under subsection (d), but another person has the rights of a holder in due course of the instrument, the other person takes free of the purchaser's claim. See Section 3-306.

The rule in subsection (d) is similar to the rules in subsections (a) and (b), which govern priority in chattel paper. The observations in Comment 6 concerning the requirement of good faith and the phrase "without knowledge that the purchase violates the rights of the secured party" apply equally to purchasers of instruments. However, unlike a purchaser of chattel paper, to qualify for priority under this section a purchaser of an instrument need only give "value" as defined in Section 1-201; it need not give "new value." Also, the purchaser need not purchase the instrument in the ordinary course of its business.

Subsection (d) applies to checks as well as notes. For example, to collect and retain checks that are proceeds (collections) of accounts free of a senior secured party's claim to the same checks, a junior secured party must satisfy the good-faith requirement (honesty in fact and the observance of reasonable commercial standards of fair dealing) of this subsection. This is the same good-faith requirement applicable to holders in due course. See Section 9-331, Comment 5.

8. **Priority in Proceeds of Chattel Paper.** Subsection (c) sets forth the two circumstances under which the priority afforded to a purchaser of chattel paper under subsection (a) or (b) extends also to proceeds of the chattel paper. The first is if the purchaser would have priority under the normal priority rules applicable to proceeds. The second, which the following Comments discuss in greater detail, is if the proceeds consist of the specific goods covered by the chattel paper. Former Article 9 generally was silent as to the priority of a security interest in proceeds when a purchaser qualifies for priority under Section 9-308 (but see former Section 9-306(5)(b), concerning returned and repossessed goods).

9. **Priority in Returned and Repossessed Goods.** Returned and repossessed goods may constitute proceeds of chattel paper. The following Comments explain the treatment of returned and repossessed goods as proceeds of chattel paper. The analysis is consistent with that of PEB Commentary No. 5, which these Comments replace, and is based upon the following example:

Example: SP-1 has a security interest in all the inventory of a dealer in goods (Dealer); SP-1's security interest is perfected by filing. Dealer sells some of its inventory to a buyer in the ordinary course of business (BIOCOB) pursuant to a conditional sales contract (chattel paper) that does not indicate that it has been assigned to SP-1. SP-2 purchases the chattel paper from Dealer and takes possession of the paper in good faith, in the ordinary course of business, and without knowledge that the purchase violates the rights of SP-1. Subsequently, BIOCOB returns the goods to Dealer because they are defective. Alternatively, Dealer acquires possession of the goods following BIOCOB's default.

10. **Assignment of Non-Lease Chattel Paper.**

a. **Loan by SP-2 to Dealer Secured by Chattel Paper (or Functional Equivalent Pursuant to Recourse Arrangement).**

(1) **Returned Goods.** If BIOCOB returns the goods to Dealer for repairs, Dealer is merely a bailee and acquires thereby no meaningful rights in the goods to which SP-1's security interest could attach. (Although SP-1's security interest could attach to Dealer's interest as a bailee, that interest is not likely to be of any particular value to SP-1.) Dealer is the owner of the *chattel paper* (i.e., the owner of a right to payment secured by a security interest in the goods); SP-2 has a security interest in the chattel paper, as does SP-1 (as proceeds of the goods under Section 9-315). Under Section 9-330, SP-2's security interest in the chattel paper is senior to that of SP-1. SP-2 enjoys this priority regardless of whether, or when, SP-2 filed a financing statement covering the chattel paper. Because chattel paper and goods represent different types of collateral, Dealer does not have any meaningful interest in *goods* to which either SP-1's or SP-2's security interest could attach in order to secure Dealer's obligations to either creditor. See Section 9-102 (defining "chattel paper" and "goods").

Now assume that BIOCOB returns the goods to Dealer under circumstances whereby Dealer once again becomes the owner of the goods. This would be the case, for example, if the goods were defective and BIOCOB was entitled to reject or revoke acceptance of the goods. See Sections 2-602 (rejection), 2-608 (revocation of acceptance). Unless BIOCOB has waived its defenses as against assignees of the chattel paper, SP-1's and SP-2's rights against BIOCOB would be subject to BIOCOB's claims and defenses. See Sections 9-403, 9-404. SP-1's security interest would attach again because the returned goods would be proceeds of the chattel paper. Dealer's acquisition of the goods easily can be characterized as "proceeds" consisting of an "in kind" collection on or distribution on account of the chattel paper. See Section 9-102 (definition of "proceeds"). Assuming that SP-1's security interest is perfected by filing against the goods and that the filing is made in the same office where a filing would be made against the chattel paper, SP-1's security interest in the goods would remain perfected beyond the 20-day period of automatic perfection. See Section 9-315(e).

Because Dealer's newly reacquired interest in the goods is proceeds of the chattel paper, SP-2's security interest also would attach in the goods as proceeds. If SP-2 had perfected its security interest in the chattel paper by filing (again, assuming that filing against the chattel paper was made in the same office where a filing would be made against the goods), SP-2's security interest in the reacquired goods would be perfected beyond 20 days. See Section 9-315(e). However, if SP-2 had relied only on its possession of the chattel paper for perfection and had not filed against the chattel paper or the goods, SP-2's security interest would be unperfected after the 20-day period. See Section 9-315(e). Nevertheless, SP-2's unperfected security interest in the goods would be senior to SP-1's security interest under Section 9-330(c). The result in this priority contest is not affected by SP-2's acquiescence or non-acquiescence in the return of the goods to Dealer.

(2) **Repossessed Goods.** As explained above, Dealer owns the chattel paper covering the goods, subject to security interests in favor of SP-1 and SP-2. In Article 9 parlance, Dealer has an interest in chattel paper, not goods. If Dealer, SP-1, or SP-2 repossesses the goods upon BIOCOB's default, whether the repossession is rightful or wrongful as among Dealer, SP-1, or SP-2, Dealer's interest will not change. The location of goods and the party who possesses them does not affect the fact that Dealer's interest is in chattel paper, not goods. The goods continue to be owned by BIOCOB. SP-1's security interest in the goods does not attach until such time as Dealer reacquires an interest (other than a bare possessory interest) in the goods. For example, Dealer might buy the goods at a foreclosure sale from SP-2 (whose security interest in the chattel paper is senior to that of SP-1); that disposition would cut off BIOCOB's rights in the goods. Section 9-617.

In many cases the matter would end upon sale of the goods to Dealer at a foreclosure sale and there would be no priority contest between SP-1 and SP-2; Dealer would be unlikely to buy the goods under circumstances whereby SP-2 would retain its security interest. There can be exceptions, however. For example, Dealer may be obliged to purchase the goods from SP-2 and SP-2 may be obliged to convey the goods to Dealer, but Dealer may fail to pay SP-2. Or, one could imagine that SP-2, like SP-1, has a general security interest in the inventory of Dealer. In the latter case, SP-2 should not receive the benefit of any special priority rule, since its interest in no way derives from priority under Section 9-330. In the former case, SP-2's security interest in the goods reacquired by Dealer is senior to SP-1's security interest under Section 9-330.

b. **Dealer's Outright Sale of Chattel Paper to SP-2.** Article 9 also applies to a transaction whereby SP-2 buys the chattel paper in an outright sale transaction without recourse against Dealer. Sections 1-201(37), 9-109(a). Although Dealer does not, in such a transaction, retain any residual ownership interest in the chattel paper, the chattel paper constitutes proceeds of the goods to which SP-1's security interest will attach and continue following the sale of the goods. Section 9-315(a). Even though Dealer has not retained any interest in the chattel paper, as discussed above BIOCOB subsequently may return the goods to Dealer under circumstances whereby Dealer reacquires an interest in the goods. The priority contest between SP-1 and SP-2 will be resolved as discussed above; Section 9-330 makes no distinction among purchasers of chattel paper on the basis of whether the purchaser is an outright buyer of chattel paper or one whose security interest secures an obligation of Dealer.

11. **Assignment of Lease Chattel Paper.** As defined in Section 9-102, "chattel paper" includes not only writings that evidence security interests in specific goods but also those that evidence true leases of goods.

The analysis with respect to lease chattel paper is similar to that set forth above with respect to non-lease chattel paper. It is complicated, however, by the fact that, unlike the case of chattel paper arising out of a sale, Dealer retains a residual interest in the *goods*. See Section 2A-103(1)(q) (defining "lessor's residual interest"); *In re Leasing Consultants, Inc.*, 486 F.2d 367 (2d Cir. 1973) (lessor's residual interest under true lease is an interest in goods and is a separate type of collateral from lessor's interest in the lease). If Dealer leases goods to a "lessee in ordinary course of business" (LIOCOB), then LIOCOB takes its interest under the lease (i.e., its "leasehold interest") free of the security interest of SP-1. See Sections 2A-307(3), 2A-103(1)(m) (defining "leasehold interest"), (1)(o) (defining "lessee in ordinary course of business"). SP-1 would, however, retain its security interest in the residual interest. In addition, SP-1 would acquire an interest in the lease chattel paper as proceeds. If Dealer then assigns the lease chattel paper to SP-2, Section 9-330 gives SP-2 priority over SP-1 with respect to the chattel paper, *but not* with respect to the residual interest in the *goods*. Consequently, assignees of lease chattel paper typically take a security interest in and file against the lessor's residual interest in goods, expecting their priority in the goods to be governed by the first-to-file-or-perfect rule of Section 9-322.

If the goods are returned to Dealer, other than upon expiration of the lease term, then the security interests of both SP-1 and SP-2 normally would attach to the goods as proceeds of the chattel paper. (If the goods are returned to Dealer at the expiration of the lease term and the lessee has made all payments due under the lease, however, then Dealer no longer has any rights under the chattel paper. Dealer's interest in the goods consists solely of its residual interest, as to which SP-2 has no claim.) This would be the case, for example, when the lessee rescinds the lease or when the lessor recovers possession in the exercise of its remedies under Article 2A. See, e.g., Section 2A-525. If SP-2 enjoyed priority in the chattel paper under Section 9-330, then SP-2 likewise would enjoy priority in the returned goods as proceeds. This does not mean that SP-2 necessarily is entitled to the entire value of the returned goods. The value of the goods represents the sum of the present value of (i) the value of their use for the term of the lease and (ii) the value of the residual interest. SP-2 has priority in the former, but SP-1 ordinarily would have priority in the latter. Thus, an allocation of a portion of the value of the goods to each component may be necessary. Where, as here, one secured party has a security interest in the lessor's residual interest and another has a priority security interest in the chattel paper, it may be advisable for the conflicting secured parties to establish a method for making such an allocation and otherwise to determine their relative rights in returned goods by agreement.

§ 9-331. PRIORITY OF RIGHTS OF PURCHASERS OF INSTRUMENTS, DOCUMENTS, AND SECURITIES UNDER OTHER ARTICLES; PRIORITY OF INTERESTS IN FINANCIAL ASSETS AND SECURITY ENTITLEMENTS UNDER ARTICLE 8.

(a) [Rights under Articles 3, 7, and 8 not limited.] This article does not limit the rights of a holder in due course of a negotiable instrument, a holder to which a negotiable document of title has been duly negotiated, or a protected purchaser of a security. These holders or purchasers take priority over an earlier security interest, even if perfected, to the extent provided in Articles 3, 7, and 8.

(b) [Protection under Article 8.] This article does not limit the rights of or impose liability on a person to the extent that the person is protected against the assertion of an adverse claim under Article 8.

ANALYSIS

For discussion of Article 8 provisions providing protection against adverse claims, see *Secured Transactions* § 6D.03.

(c) [Filing not notice.] Filing under this article does not constitute notice of a claim or defense to the holders, or purchasers, or persons described in subsections (a) and (b).

Official Comment

1. **Source.** Former Section 9-309.

2. **"Priority."** In some provisions, this Article distinguishes between claimants that take collateral free of a security interest (in the sense that the security interest no longer encumbers the collateral) and those that take an interest in the collateral that is senior to a surviving security interest. See, e.g., Section 9-317. Whether a holder or purchaser referred to in this section takes free or is senior to a security interest depends on the whether the purchaser is a buyer of the collateral or takes a security interest in it. The term "priority" is meant to encompass both scenarios, as it does in Section 9-330.

3. **Rights Acquired by Purchasers.** The rights to which this section refers are set forth in Sections 3-305 and 3-306 (holder in due course), 7-502 (holder to whom a negotiable document of title has been duly negotiated), and 8-303 (protected purchaser). The holders and purchasers referred to in this section do not always take priority over a security interest. See, e.g., Section 7-503 (affording paramount rights to certain owners and secured parties as against holder to whom a negotiable document of title has been duly negotiated). Accordingly, this section adds the clause, "to the extent provided in Articles 3, 7, and 8" to former Section 9-309.

4. **Financial Assets and Security Entitlements.** New subsection (b) provides explicit protection for those who deal with financial assets and security entitlements and who are immunized from liability under Article 8. See, e.g., Sections 8-502, 8-503(e), 8-510, 8-511. The new subsection makes explicit in Article 9 what is implicit in former Article 9 and explicit in several provisions of Article 8. It does not change the law.

5. **Collections by Junior Secured Party.** Under this section, a secured party with a junior security interest in receivables (accounts, chattel paper, promissory notes, or payment intangibles) may collect and retain the proceeds of those receivables free of the claim of a senior secured party to the same receivables, if the junior secured party is a holder in due course of the

proceeds. In order to qualify as a holder in due course, the junior must satisfy the requirements of Section 3-302, which include taking in "good faith." This means that the junior not only must act "honestly" but also must observe "reasonable commercial standards of fair dealing" under the particular circumstances. See Section 9-102(a). Although "good faith" does not impose a general duty of inquiry, e.g., a search of the records in filing offices, there may be circumstances in which "reasonable commercial standards of fair dealing" would require such a search.

Consider, for example, a junior secured party in the business of financing or buying accounts who fails to undertake a search to determine the existence of prior security interests. Because a search, under the usages of trade of that business, would enable it to know or learn upon reasonable inquiry that collecting the accounts violated the rights of a senior secured party, the junior may fail to meet the good-faith standard. See *Utility Contractors Financial Services, Inc. v. Amsouth Bank, NA*, 985 F.2d 1554 (11th Cir. 1993). Likewise, a junior secured party who collects accounts when it knows or should know under the particular circumstances that doing so would violate the rights of a senior secured party, because the debtor had agreed not to grant a junior security interest in, or sell, the accounts, may not meet the good-faith test. Thus, if a junior secured party conducted or should have conducted a search and a financing statement filed on behalf of the senior secured party states such a restriction, the junior's collection would not meet the good-faith standard. On the other hand, if there was a course of performance between the senior secured party and the debtor which placed no such restrictions on the debtor and allowed the debtor to collect and use the proceeds without any restrictions, the junior secured party may then satisfy the requirements for being a holder in due course. This would be more likely in those circumstances where the junior secured party was providing additional financing to the debtor on an on-going basis by lending against or buying the accounts and had no notice of any restrictions against doing so. Generally, the senior secured party would not be prejudiced because the practical effect of such payment to the junior secured party is little different than if the debtor itself had made the collections and subsequently paid the secured party from the debtor's general funds. Absent collusion, the junior secured party would take the funds free of the senior security interests. See Section 9-332. In contrast, the senior secured party is likely to be prejudiced if the debtor is going out of business and the junior secured party collects the accounts by notifying the account debtors to make payments directly to the junior. Those collections may not be consistent with "reasonable commercial standards of fair dealing."

Whether the junior secured party qualifies as a holder in due course is fact-sensitive and should be decided on a case-by-case basis in the light of those circumstances. Decisions such as *Financial Management Services Inc. v. Familian*, 905 P.2d 506 (Ariz. App. Div. 1995) (finding holder in due course status) could be determined differently under this application of the good-faith requirement.

The concepts addressed in this Comment are also applicable to junior secured parties as purchasers of instruments under Section 9-330(d). See Section 9-330, Comment 7.

§ 9-332. TRANSFER OF MONEY; TRANSFER OF FUNDS FROM DEPOSIT ACCOUNT.

(a) [Transferee of money.] A transferee of money takes the money free of a security interest unless the transferee acts in collusion with the debtor in violating the rights of the secured party.

(b) [Transferee of funds from deposit account.] A transferee of funds from a deposit account takes the funds free of a security interest in the deposit account unless the transferee acts in collusion with the debtor in violating the rights of the secured party.

ANALYSIS

Subsection (b) gives super-negotiability to transfers of funds from the debtor's bank account --the transferee wins unless it acts in collusion. But subsection (b) only allows the transferee to take "free of a security interest in the deposit account." Does this language refer to an original interest in the deposit account, or does it also embrace an interest in the deposit account as proceeds of other collateral? The apparent extensions to proceeds interests could undermine historic restrictions on the negotiability of payment by check.

> *Example A*: First Bank holds a security interest in the deposit account of Debtor Co. as proceeds of the accounts of Debtor Co. Debtor Co. issues a check on the account to Payee, an unsecured creditor, who does not qualify as a holder in due course because it knows of the interest of First Bank. Under old Article 9, Payee could argue that it nevertheless takes free under Comment 3(c) to old § 9-306. But that comment only protects payments "in ordinary course" and was not followed by all courts. *See Secured Transactions* § 7A.15[2][e]. But assuming that new § 9-322(b) applies to proceeds interests, Payee wins under Revised Article 9 so long as it does not act in collusion with Debtor Co. to violate the rights of First Bank.

Example B: Same as above except that Payee holds a junior security interest in the deposit account of Debtor Co. as proceeds of the accounts of Debtor Co. Allowing Payee to take free under new § 9-332(b) seems inconsistent in the analysis in Official Comment 5 to new § 9-331. Perhaps that analysis applies when the proceeds are taken directly from the account debtors while new § 9-332 applies only when the funds pass through the debtor's bank account. Should the rights of the junior creditor be different depending on the routing of the funds?

Official Comment

1. **Source.** New.

2. **Scope of This Section.** This section affords broad protection to transferees who take funds from a deposit account and to those who take money. The term "transferee" is not defined; however, the debtor itself is not a transferee. Thus this section does not cover the case in which a debtor withdraws money (currency) from its deposit account or the case in which a bank debits an encumbered account and credits another account it maintains for the debtor.

A transfer of funds from a deposit account, to which subsection (b) applies, normally will be made by check, by funds transfer, or by debiting the debtor's deposit account and crediting another depositor's account.

Example 1: Debtor maintains a deposit account with Bank A. The deposit account is subject to a perfected security interest in favor of Lender. Debtor draws a check on the account, payable to Payee. Inasmuch as the check is not the proceeds of the deposit account (it is an order to pay funds from the deposit account), Lender's security interest in the deposit account does not give rise to a security interest in the check. Payee deposits the check into its own deposit account, and Bank A pays it. Unless Payee acted in collusion with Debtor in violating Lender's rights, Payee takes the funds (the credits running in favor of Payee) free of Lender's security interest. This is true regardless of whether Payee is a holder in due course of the check and even if Payee gave no value for the check.

Example 2: Debtor maintains a deposit account with Bank A. The deposit account is subject to a perfected security interest in favor of Lender. At Bank B's suggestion, Debtor moves the funds from the account at Bank A to Debtor's deposit account with Bank B. Unless Bank B acted in collusion with Debtor in violating Lender's rights, Bank B takes the funds (the credits running in favor of Bank B) free from Lender's security interest. See subsection (b). However, inasmuch as the deposit account maintained with Bank B constitutes the proceeds of the deposit account at Bank A, Lender's security interest would attach to that account as proceeds. See Section 9-315.

Subsection (b) also would apply if, in the example, Bank A debited Debtor's deposit account in exchange for the issuance of Bank A's cashier's check. Lender's security interest would attach to the cashier's check as proceeds of the deposit account, and the rules applicable to instruments would govern any competing claims to the cashier's check. See, e.g., Sections 3-306, 9-322, 9-330, 9-331.

If Debtor withdraws money (currency) from an encumbered deposit account and transfers the money to a third party, then subsection (a), to the extent not displaced by federal law relating to money, applies. It contains the same rule as subsection (b).

Subsection (b) applies to *transfers of funds from* a deposit account; it does not apply to *transfers of the deposit account* itself or of an interest therein. For example, this section does not apply to the creation of a security interest in a deposit account. Competing claims to the deposit account itself are dealt with by other Article 9 priority rules. See Sections 9-317(a), 9-327, 9-340, 9-341. Similarly, a corporate merger normally would not result in a transfer of funds from a deposit account. Rather, it might result in a transfer of the deposit account itself. If so, the normal rules applicable to transferred collateral would apply; this section would not.

3. **Policy.** Broad protection for transferees helps to ensure that security interests in deposit accounts do not impair the free flow of funds. It also minimizes the likelihood that a secured party will enjoy a claim to whatever the transferee purchases with the funds. Rules concerning recovery of payments traditionally have placed a high value on finality. The opportunity to upset a completed transaction, or even to place a completed transaction in jeopardy by bringing suit against the transferee of funds, should be severely limited. Although the giving of value usually is a prerequisite for receiving the ability to take free from third-party claims, where payments are concerned the law is even more protective. Thus, Section 3-418(c) provides that, even where the law of restitution otherwise would permit recovery of funds paid by mistake, no recovery may be had from a person "who in good faith changed position in reliance on the payment." Rather than adopt this standard, this section eliminates all reliance requirements whatsoever. Payments made by mistake are relatively rare, but payments of funds from encumbered deposit accounts (e.g., deposit accounts containing collections from accounts receivable) occur with great regularity. In the mine run of cases, unlike payment by mistake, no one would object to these payments. In the vast proportion of cases, the transferee probably would be able to show a change of position in reliance on the payment. This section does not put the transferee to the burden of having to make this proof.

4. **"Bad Actors."** To deal with the question of the "bad actor," this section borrows "collusion" language from Article 8. See, e.g., Sections 8-115, 8-503(e). This is the most protective (i.e., least stringent) of the various standards now found in the UCC. Compare, e.g., Section 1-201(9) ("without

knowledge that the sale . . . is in violation of the . . . security interest"); Section 1-201(19) ("honesty in fact in the conduct or transaction concerned"); Section 3-302(a)(2)(v) ("without notice of any claim").

5. **Transferee Who Does Not Take Free.** This section sets forth the circumstances under which certain transferees of money or funds take free of security interests. It does not determine the rights of a transferee who does not take free of a security interest.

Example 3: The facts are as in Example 2, but, in wrongfully moving the funds from the deposit account at Bank A to Debtor's deposit account with Bank B, Debtor acts in collusion with Bank B. Bank B does not take the funds free of Lender's security interest under this section. If Debtor grants a security interest to Bank B, Section 9-327 governs the relative priorities of Lender and Bank B. Under Section 9-327(3), Bank B's security interest in the Bank B deposit account is senior to Lender's security interest in the deposit account as proceeds. However, Bank B's senior security interest does not protect Bank B against any liability to Lender that might arise from Bank B's wrongful conduct.

§ 9-333. PRIORITY OF CERTAIN LIENS ARISING BY OPERATION OF LAW.

(a) ["Possessory lien."] In this section, "possessory lien" means an interest, other than a security interest or an agricultural lien:

(1) which secures payment or performance of an obligation for services or materials furnished with respect to goods by a person in the ordinary course of the person's business;

(2) which is created by statute or rule of law in favor of the person; and

(3) whose effectiveness depends on the person's possession of the goods.

(b) [Priority of possessory lien.] A possessory lien on goods has priority over a security interest in the goods unless the lien is created by a statute that expressly provides otherwise.

Official Comment

1. **Source.** Former Section 9-310.

2. **"Possessory Liens."** This section governs the relative priority of security interests arising under this Article and "possessory liens," i.e., common-law and statutory liens whose effectiveness depends on the lienor's possession of goods with respect to which the lienor provided services or furnished materials in the ordinary course of its business. As under former Section 9-310, the possessory lien has priority over a security interest unless the

possessory lien is created by a statute that expressly provides otherwise. If the statute creating the possessory lien is silent as to its priority relative to a security interest, this section provides a rule of interpretation that the possessory lien takes priority, even if the statute has been construed judicially to make the possessory lien subordinate.

§ 9-334. PRIORITY OF SECURITY INTERESTS IN FIXTURES AND CROPS.

(a)　[Security interest in fixtures under this article.] A security interest under this article may be created in goods that are fixtures or may continue in goods that become fixtures. A security interest does not exist under this article in ordinary building materials incorporated into an improvement on land.

(b)　[Security interest in fixtures under real-property law.] This article does not prevent creation of an encumbrance upon fixtures under real property law.

(c)　[General rule: subordination of security interest in fixtures.] In cases not governed by subsections (d) through (h), a security interest in fixtures is subordinate to a conflicting interest of an encumbrancer or owner of the related real property other than the debtor.

(d)　[Fixtures purchase-money priority.] Except as otherwise provided in subsection (h), a perfected security interest in fixtures has priority over a conflicting interest of an encumbrancer or owner of the real property if the debtor has an interest of record in or is in possession of the real property and:

(1)　the security interest is a purchase-money security interest;

(2)　the interest of the encumbrancer or owner arises before the goods become fixtures; and

(3)　the security interest is perfected by a fixture filing before the goods become fixtures or within 20 days thereafter.

(e)　[Priority of security interest in fixtures over interests in real property.] A perfected security interest in fixtures has priority over a conflicting interest of an encumbrancer or owner of the real property if:

(1)　the debtor has an interest of record in the real property or is in possession of the real property and the security interest:

(A)　is perfected by a fixture filing before the interest of the encumbrancer or owner is of record; and

(B)   has priority over any conflicting interest of a predecessor in title of the encumbrancer or owner;

(2)   before the goods become fixtures, the security interest is perfected by any method permitted by this article and the fixtures are readily removable:

(A)   factory or office machines;

(B)   equipment that is not primarily used or leased for use in the operation of the real property; or

(C)   replacements of domestic appliances that are consumer goods;

ANALYSIS

The priority of the Article 9 financer in readily removable equipment not primarily used or leased for use in the operation of the real property under § 9-334(e)(2) is new with Revised Article 9. It does not appear that this addition will change the results of many cases since such equipment is routinely classified as a non-fixture under the old Article 9. *See Secured Transactions* § 3A.06[2]. Moreover, the new category overlaps to some extent with readily removable factory or office machines, a category already recognized by old § 9-313.

(3)   the conflicting interest is a lien on the real property obtained by legal or equitable proceedings after the security interest was perfected by any method permitted by this article; or

(4)   the security interest is:

(A)   created in a manufactured home in a manufactured-home transaction; and

(B)   perfected pursuant to a statute described in Section 9-311(a)(2).

(f)   [Priority based on consent, disclaimer, or right to remove.] A security interest in fixtures, whether or not perfected, has priority over a conflicting interest of an encumbrancer or owner of the real property if:

(1)   the encumbrancer or owner has, in an authenticated record, consented to the security interest or disclaimed an interest in the goods as fixtures; or

(2)   the debtor has a right to remove the goods as against the encumbrancer or owner.

(g)   [Continuation of subsection (f) priority.] The priority of the security interest under subsection (f)(2) continues for a reasonable time if the debtor's right to remove the goods as against the encumbrancer or owner terminates.

(h)   [Priority of construction mortgage.] A mortgage is a construction mortgage to the extent that it secures an obligation incurred for the construction of an improvement on land, including the acquisition cost of the land, if a recorded record of the mortgage so indicates. Except as otherwise provided in subsections (e) and (f), a security interest in fixtures is subordinate to a construction mortgage if a record of the mortgage is recorded before the goods become fixtures and the goods become fixtures before the completion of the construction. A mortgage has this priority to the same extent as a construction mortgage to the extent that it is given to refinance a construction mortgage.

(i)   [Priority of security interest in crops.] A perfected security interest in crops growing on real property has priority over a conflicting interest of an encumbrancer or owner of the real property if the debtor has an interest of record in or is in possession of the real property.

ANALYSIS

Growing crops are goods under old § 9-105(1)(h) and new § 9-102(a)(44). There is, therefore, no doubt that a security interest can be created in growing crops under Article 9. But, in some states, real estate mortgages can also cover crops, and old Article 9 had no provision regulating priority conflicts between Article 9 crop interests and real estate crop interests. *See Secured Transactions* § 16.04. New § 9-334(i) gives the priority to the Article 9 interests when the debtor has an interest of record or is in possession of the real property. Persons searching the real estate title to farm land must therefore look for U.C.C. filings against persons with an interest of record or in possession of the real estate. Under Revised Article 9, neither the security agreement nor the financing statement is required any longer to contain a description of the land on which the crops are growing. *See* new §§ 9-203, 9-502, 9-516. After uncovering a filing against crop collateral, the real estate searcher will have to investigate to determine if the crops are growing on the land with respect to which the search is being conducted.

(j) [Subsection (i) prevails.] Subsection (i) prevails over any inconsistent provisions of the following statutes:

[List here any statutes containing provisions inconsistent with subsection (i).]

Legislative Note: States that amend statutes to remove provisions inconsistent with subsection (i) need not enact subsection (j).

Official Comment

1. **Source.** Former Section 9-313.

2. **Scope of This Section.** This section contains rules governing the priority of security interests in fixtures and crops as against persons who claim an interest in real property. Priority contests with other Article 9 security interests are governed by the other priority rules of this Article. The provisions with respect to fixtures follow those of former Section 9-313. However, they have been rewritten to conform to Section 2A-309 and to prevailing style conventions. Subsections (i) and (j), which apply to crops, are new.

3. **Security Interests in Fixtures.** Certain goods that are the subject of personal-property (chattel) financing become so affixed or otherwise so related to real property that they become part of the real property. These goods

are called "fixtures." See Section 9-102 (definition of "fixtures"). Some fixtures retain their personal-property nature: a security interest under this Article may be created in fixtures and may continue in goods that become fixtures. See subsection (a). However, if the goods are ordinary building materials incorporated into an improvement on land, no security interest in them exists. Rather, the priority of claims to the building materials are determined by the law governing claims to real property. (Of course, the fact that no security interest exists in ordinary building materials incorporated into an improvement on land does not prejudice any rights the secured party may have against the debtor or any other person who violated the secured party's rights by wrongfully incorporating the goods into real property.)

Thus, this section recognizes three categories of goods: (1) those that retain their chattel character entirely and are not part of the real property; (2) ordinary building materials that have become an integral part of the real property and cannot retain their chattel character for purposes of finance; and (3) an intermediate class that has become real property for certain purposes, but as to which chattel financing may be preserved.

To achieve priority under certain provisions of this section, a security interest must be perfected by making a "fixture filing" (defined in Section 9-102) in the real-property records. Because the question whether goods have become fixtures often is a difficult one under applicable real-property law, a secured party may make a fixture filing as a precaution. Courts should not infer from a fixture filing that the secured party concedes that the goods are or will become fixtures.

4. **Priority in Fixtures: General.** In considering priority problems under this section, one must first determine whether real-property claimants per se have an interest in the crops or fixtures as part of real property. If not, it is immaterial, so far as concerns real property parties as such, whether a security interest arising under this Article is perfected or unperfected. In no event does a real-property claimant (e.g., owner or mortgagee) acquire an interest in a "pure" chattel just because a security interest therein is unperfected. If on the other hand real-property law gives real-property parties an interest in the goods, a conflict arises and this section states the priorities.

5. **Priority in Fixtures: Residual Rule.** Subsection (c) states the residual priority rule, which applies only if one of the other rules does not: A security interest in fixtures is subordinate to a conflicting interest of an encumbrancer or owner of the related real property other than the debtor.

6. **Priority in Fixtures: First to File or Record.** Subsection (e)(1), which follows former Section 9-313(4)(b), contains the usual priority rule of conveyancing, that is, the first to file or record prevails. In order to achieve priority under this rule, however, the security interest must be perfected by a "fixture filing" (defined in Section 9-102), i.e., a filing for record in the

real property records and indexed therein, so that it will be found in a real-property search.. The condition in subsection (e)(1)(B), that the security interest must have had priority over any conflicting interest of a predecessor in title of the conflicting encumbrancer or owner, appears to limit to the first-in-time principle. However, this apparent limitation is nothing other than an expression of the usual rule that a person must be entitled to transfer what he has. Thus, if the fixture security interest is subordinate to a mortgage, it is subordinate to an interest of an assignee of the mortgage, even though the assignment is a later recorded instrument. Similarly if the fixture security interest is subordinate to the rights of an owner, it is subordinate to a subsequent grantee of the owner and likewise subordinate to a subsequent mortgagee of the owner.

7. **Priority in Fixtures: Purchase-Money Security Interests.** Subsection (d), which follows former Section 9-313(4)(a), contains the principal exception to the first-to-file-or-record rule of subsection (e)(1). It affords priority to purchase-money security interests in fixtures as against *prior* recorded real-property interests, provided that the purchase-money security interest is filed as a fixture filing in the real-property records before the goods become fixtures or within 20 days thereafter. This priority corresponds to the purchase-money priority under Section 9-324(a). (Like other 10-day periods in former Article 9, the 10-day period in this section has been changed to 20 days.)

It should be emphasized that this purchase-money priority with the 20-day grace period for filing is limited to rights against real-property interests that arise *before* the goods become fixtures. There is no such priority with the 20-day grace period as against real-property interests that arise subsequently. The fixture security interest can defeat subsequent real-property interests only if it is filed first and prevails under the usual conveyancing rule in subsection (e)(1) or one of the other rules in this section.

8. **Priority in Fixtures: Readily Removable Goods.** Subsection (e)(2), which derives from Section 2A-309 and former Section 9-313(4)(d), contains another exception to the usual first-to-file-or-rule. It affords priority to the holders of security interests in certain types of readily removable goods-factory and office machines, equipment that is not primarily used or leased for use in the operation of the real property, and (as discussed below) certain replacements of domestic appliances. This rule is made necessary by the confusion in the law as to whether certain machinery, equipment, and appliances become fixtures. It protects a secured party who, perhaps in the mistaken belief that the readily removable goods will not become fixtures, makes a UCC filing (or otherwise perfects under this Article) rather than making a fixture filing.

Frequently, under applicable law, goods of the type described in subsection (e)(2) will not be considered to have become part of the real property. In those cases, the fixture security interest does not conflict with a real-property interest, and resort to this section is unnecessary. However, if the goods have become part of the real property, subsection (e)(2) enables a fixture secured party to take priority over a conflicting real-property interest if the fixture security interest is perfected by a fixture filing or by any other method permitted by this Article. If perfection is by fixture filing, the fixture security interest would have priority over subsequently recorded real-property interests under subsection (e)(1) and, if the fixture security interest is a purchase-money security interest (a likely scenario), it would also have priority over most real property interests under the purchase-money priority of subsection (d). Note, however, that unlike the purchase-money priority rule in subsection (d), the priority rules in subsection (e) override the priority given to a construction mortgage under subsection (h).

The rule in subsection (e)(2) is limited to readily removable replacements of domestic appliances. It does not apply to original installations. Moreover, it is limited to appliances that are "consumer goods" (defined in Section 9-102) in the hands of the debtor. The principal effect of the rule is to make clear that a secured party financing occasional replacements of domestic appliances in noncommercial, owner-occupied contexts need not concern itself with real-property descriptions or records; indeed, for a purchase-money replacement of consumer goods, perfection without any filing will be possible. See Section 9-309(1).

9. **Priority in Fixtures: Judicial Liens.** Subsection (e)(3), which follows former Section 9-313(4)(d), adopts a first-in-time rule applicable to conflicts between a fixture security interest and a lien on the real property obtained by legal or equitable proceedings. Such a lien is subordinate to an earlier-perfected security interest, regardless of the method by which the security interest was perfected. Judgment creditors generally are not reliance creditors who search real-property records. Accordingly, a perfected fixture security interest takes priority over a subsequent judgment lien or other lien obtained by legal or equitable proceedings, even if no evidence of the security interest appears in the relevant real-property records. Subsection (e)(3) thus protects a perfected fixture security interest from avoidance by a trustee in bankruptcy under Bankruptcy Code Section 544(a), regardless of the method of perfection.

10. **Priority in Fixtures: Manufactured Homes.** A manufactured home may become a fixture. New subsection (e)(4) contains a special rule granting priority to certain security interests created in a "manufactured home" as part of a "manufactured-home transaction" (both defined in Section 9-102). Under this rule, a security interest in a manufactured home that becomes a fixture has priority over a conflicting interest of an encumbrancer or owner of the real property if the security interest is perfected under a certificate-of-title statute (see Section 9-311). Subsection (e)(4) is only one of the priority rules

applicable to security interests in a manufactured home that becomes a fixture. Thus, a security interest in a manufactured home which does not qualify for priority under this subsection may qualify under another.

11. **Priority in Fixtures: Construction Mortgages.** The purchase-money priority presents a difficult problem in relation to construction mortgages. The latter ordinarily will have been recorded even before the commencement of delivery of materials to the job, and therefore would take priority over fixture security interests were it not for the purchase-money priority. However, having recorded first, the holder of a construction mortgage reasonably expects to have first priority in the improvement built using the mortgagee's advances. Subsection (g) expressly gives priority to the construction mortgage recorded before the filing of the purchase-money security interest in fixtures. A refinancing of a construction mortgage has the same priority as the construction mortgage itself. The phrase "an obligation incurred for the construction of an improvement" covers both optional advances and advances pursuant to commitment. Both types of advances have the same priority under subsection (g).

The priority under this subsection applies only to goods that become fixtures during the construction period leading to the completion of the improvement. The construction priority will not apply to additions to the building made long after completion of the improvement, even if the additions are financed by the real-property mortgagee under an open-end clause of the construction mortgage. In such case, subsections (d), (e), and (f) govern.

Although this subsection affords a construction mortgage priority over a purchase-money security interest that otherwise would have priority under subsection (d), the subsection is subject to the priority rules in subsections (e) and (f). Thus, a construction mortgage may be junior to a fixture security interest perfected by a fixture filing before the construction mortgage was recorded. See subsection (e)(1).

12. **Crops.** Growing crops are "goods" in which a security interest may be created and perfected under this Article. In some jurisdictions, a mortgage of real property may cover crops, as well. In the event that crops are encumbered by both a mortgage and an Article 9 security interest, subsection (i) provides that the security interest has priority. States whose real-property law provides otherwise should either amend that law directly or override it by enacting subsection (j).

§ 9-335. ACCESSIONS.

(a) **[Creation of security interest in accession.]** A security interest may be created in an accession and continues in collateral that becomes an accession.

(b) [Perfection of security interest.] If a security interest is perfected when the collateral becomes an accession, the security interest remains perfected in the collateral.

(c) [Priority of security interest.] Except as otherwise provided in subsection (d), the other provisions of this part determine the priority of a security interest in an accession.

(d) [Compliance with certificate-of-title statute.] A security interest in an accession is subordinate to a security interest in the whole which is perfected by compliance with the requirements of a certificate-of-title statute under Section 9-311(b).

(e) [Removal of accession after default.] After default, subject to Part 6, a secured party may remove an accession from other goods if the security interest in the accession has priority over the claims of every person having an interest in the whole.

(f) [Reimbursement following removal.] A secured party that removes an accession from other goods under subsection (e) shall promptly reimburse any holder of a security interest or other lien on, or owner of, the whole or of the other goods, other than the debtor, for the cost of repair of any physical injury to the whole or the other goods. The secured party need not reimburse the holder or owner for any diminution in value of the whole or the other goods caused by the absence of the accession removed or by any necessity for replacing it. A person entitled to reimbursement may refuse permission to remove until the secured party gives adequate assurance for the performance of the obligation to reimburse.

ANALYSIS

Under this provision, accessions are governed by the same rules of priority applicable to other collateral except that an interest in an accession united to a certificated asset is subordinate to an interest in the certificated asset perfected by compliance with the certificate statute. The priority recognized by old § 9-314 for pre-annexation accessions interests as such is repealed.

Example A: Financer A holds a first-filed security interest in all of Debtor's equipment, including after-acquired equipment. Debtor acquires steamers from Supplier B with Supplier B retaining a security interest in the steamers. Supplier B does not file. The steamers are affixed to carpet dyeing equipment so as to constitute accessions. Financer A does not make any new advances.

Under old § 9-314(1), Supplier B had priority as to the steamers simply because its security interest attached to the steamers before they were affixed to the carpet dyeing equipment. *See Secured Transactions* §§ 7A.30, 17.04. But under new §§ 9-322 and 9-335(c) Financer A wins as first-filed. Supplier B could overcome that priority by meeting the requirements for a purchase-money priority under new § 9-324(a).

Official Comment

1. **Source.** Former Section 9-314.

2. **"Accession."** This section applies to an "accession," as defined in Section 9-102, regardless of the cost or difficulty of removing the accession from the other goods, and regardless of whether the original goods have come to form an integral part of the other goods. This section does not apply to goods whose identity has been lost. Goods of that kind are "commingled goods" governed by Section 9-336. Neither this section nor the following one addresses the case of collateral that changes form without the addition of other goods.

3. **"Accession" vs. "Other Goods."** This section distinguishes among the "accession," the "other goods," and the "whole." The last term refers to the combination of the "accession" and the "other goods." If one person's collateral becomes physically united with another person's collateral, each is an "accession."

Example 1: SP-1 holds a security interest in the debtor's tractors (which are not subject to a certificate-of-title statute), and SP-2 holds a security interest in a particular tractor engine. The engine is installed in a tractor. From the perspective of SP-1, the tractor becomes an "accession" and the engine is the "other goods." From the perspective of SP-2, the engine is the "accession" and the tractor is the "other goods." The completed tractor-tractor cum engine-constitutes the "whole."

4. **Scope.** This section governs only a few issues concerning accessions. Subsection (a) contains rules governing continuation of a security interest in an accession. Subsection (b) contains a rule governing continued perfection of a security interest in goods that become an accession. Subsection (d) contains a special priority rule governing accessions that become part of a whole covered by a certificate of title. Subsections (e) and (f) govern enforcement of a security interest in an accession.

5. **Matters Left to Other Provisions of This Article: Attachment and Perfection.** Other provisions of this Article often govern accession-related issues. For example, this section does not address whether a secured party acquires a security interest in the whole if its collateral becomes an accession. Normally this will turn on the description of the collateral in the security agreement.

Example 2: Debtor owns a computer subject to a perfected security interest in favor of SP-1. Debtor acquires memory and installs it in the computer. Whether SP-1's security interest attaches to the memory depends on whether the security agreement covers it.

Similarly, this section does not determine whether perfection against collateral that becomes an accession is effective to perfect a security interest in the whole. Other provisions of this Article, including the requirements for indicating the collateral covered by a financing statement, resolve that question.

6. **Matters Left to Other Provisions of This Article: Priority.** With one exception, concerning goods covered by a certificate of title (see subsection (d)), the other provisions of this Part, including the rules governing purchase-money security interests, determine the priority of most security interests in an accession, including the relative priority of a security interest in an accession and a security interest in the whole. See subsection (c).

Example 3: Debtor owns an office computer subject to a security interest in favor of SP-1. Debtor acquires memory and grants a perfected security interest in the memory to SP-2. Debtor installs the memory in the computer, at which time (one assumes) SP-1's security interest attaches to the memory. The first-to-file-or-perfect rule of Section 9-322 governs priority in the memory. If, however, SP-2's security interest is a purchase-money security interest, Section 9-324(a) would afford priority in the memory to SP-2, regardless of which security interest was perfected first.

7. **Goods Covered by Certificate of Title.** This section does govern the priority of a security interest in an accession that is or becomes part of a whole that is subject to a security interest perfected by compliance with a certificate-of-title statute. Subsection (d) provides that a security interest in the whole, perfected by compliance with a certificate-of-title statute, takes priority over a security interest in the accession. It enables a secured party to rely upon a certificate of title without having to check the UCC files to determine whether any components of the collateral may be encumbered. The subsection imposes a corresponding risk upon those who finance goods that may become part of goods covered by a certificate of title. In doing so, it reverses the priority that appeared reasonable to most pre-UCC courts.

Example 4: Debtor owns an automobile subject to a security interest in favor of SP-1. The security interest is perfected by notation on the certificate of title. Debtor buys tires subject to a perfected-by-filing purchase-money security interest in favor of SP-2 and mounts the tires on the automobile's wheels. If the security interest in the automobile attaches to the tires, then SP-1 acquires priority over SP-2. The same result would obtain if SP-1's security interest attached to the automobile and was perfected after the tires had been mounted on the wheels.

§ 9-336. COMMINGLED GOODS.

(a) ["Commingled goods."] In this section, "commingled goods" means goods that are physically united with other goods in such a manner that their identity is lost in a product or mass.

(b) [No security interest in commingled goods as such.] A security interest does not exist in commingled goods as such. However, a security interest may attach to a product or mass that results when goods become commingled goods.

(c) [Attachment of security interest to product or mass.] If collateral becomes commingled goods, a security interest attaches to the product or mass.

(d) [Perfection of security interest.] If a security interest in collateral is perfected before the collateral becomes commingled goods, the security interest that attaches to the product or mass under subsection (c) is perfected.

(e) [Priority of security interest.] Except as otherwise provided in subsection (f), the other provisions of this part determine the priority of a security interest that attaches to the product or mass under subsection (c).

(f) [Conflicting security interests in product or mass.] If more than one security interest attaches to the product or mass under subsection (c), the following rules determine priority:

(1) A security interest that is perfected under subsection (d) has priority over a security interest that is unperfected at the time the collateral becomes commingled goods.

(2) If more than one security interest is perfected under subsection (d), the security interests rank equally in proportion to value of the collateral at the time it became commingled goods.

ANALYSIS

Surprisingly few reported cases have been decided under old § 9-315, the commingled goods provision of the old Article 9. *See Secured*

Transactions § 7A.31. However, this section may acquire a higher profile. Old § 9-315 applied only when collateral became part of a product or mass as a result of manufacturing, processing, assembly or commingling. This new provision uses the more general language "physically united." There is no indication that this generalization is intended to override the cases which hold that a security interest in feed fed to cattle does not continue in the cattle as commingled goods, but the change in wording would allow for this issue to be relitigated. Moreover, new § 9-315(b)(1) allows for goods proceeds to be identified despite their commingling with other goods under this section. A financer attempting to trace inventory or farm products to the receivables collateral in which it held its original interest could be aided by new § 9-315.

> *Example A*: First Bank holds a perfected security interest in the accounts of a manufacturer of modular homes. Collections from the accounts are used to purchase Shipment X of new materials. First Bank acquires a perfected proceeds interest in the new materials in Shipment X. Later, the manufacturer obtains an unsecured advance from Second Bank and uses that advance to finance Shipment Y of new materials. The items in the two shipments are physically united so that it is no longer possible to trace a particular item to a particular shipment.

The commingling of goods proceeds with non-proceeds does not extinguish the proceeds interest of First Bank in the commingled items. Under new § 9-336(c) and (d), First Bank holds a perfected interest in the commingled mass.

> *Example B*: Same facts as above except that Second Bank perfects an interest in the materials in Shipment B before the commingling. The first-to-file rule does not control. First Bank and Second Bank share interests in the commingled items in accord with the ratio formula of new § 9-336(f).

Official Comment

1. **Source.** Former Section 9-315.

2. **"Commingled Goods."** Subsection (a) defines "commingled goods." It is meant to include not only goods whose identity is lost through manufacturing or production (e.g., flour that has become part of baked goods) but also goods whose identity is lost by commingling with other goods from which they cannot be distinguished (e.g., ball bearings).

3. Consequences of Becoming "Commingled Goods." By definition, the identity of the original collateral cannot be determined once the original collateral becomes commingled goods. Consequently, the security interest in the specific original collateral alone is lost once the collateral becomes commingled goods, and no security interest in the original collateral can be created thereafter except as a part of the resulting product or mass. See subsection (b).

Once collateral becomes commingled goods, the secured party's security interest is transferred from the original collateral to the product or mass. See subsection (c). If the security interest in the original collateral was perfected, the security interest in the product or mass is a perfected security interest. See subsection (d). This perfection continues until lapse.

4. Priority of Perfected Security Interests That Attach Under This Section. This section governs the priority of competing security interests in a product or mass only when both security interests arise under this section. In that case, if both security interests are perfected by operation of this section (see subsections (c) and (d)), then the security interests rank equally, in proportion to the value of the collateral at the time it became commingled goods. See subsection (f)(2).

Example 1: SP-1 has a perfected security interest in Debtor's eggs, which have a value of $300 and secure a debt of $400, and SP-2 has a perfected security interest in Debtor's flour, which has a value of $500 and secures a debt of $600. Debtor uses the flour and eggs to make cakes, which have a value of $1000. The two security interests rank equally and share in the ratio of 3:5. Applying this ratio to the entire value of the product, SP-1 would be entitled to $375 (i.e., 3/8 x $1000), and SP-2 would be entitled to $625 (i.e., 5/8 x $1000).

Example 2: Assume the facts of Example 1, except that SP-1's collateral, worth $300, secures a debt of $200. Recall that, if the cake is worth $1000, then applying the ratio of 3:5 would entitle SP-1 to $375 and SP-2 to $625. However, SP-1 is not entitled to collect from the product more than it is owed. Accordingly, SP-1's share would be only $200, SP-2 would receive the remaining value, up to the amount it is owed ($600).

Example 3: Assume that the cakes in the previous examples have a value of only $600. Again, the parties share in the ratio of 3:5. If, as in Example 1, SP-1 is owed $400, then SP-1 is entitled to $225 (i.e., 3/8 x $600), and SP-2 is entitled to $375 (i.e., 5/8 x $600). Debtor receives nothing. If, however, as in Example 2, SP-1 is owed only $200, then SP-2 receives $400.

The results in the foregoing examples remain the same, regardless of whether SP-1 or SP-2 (or each) has a purchase-money security interest.

5. Perfection: Unperfected Security Interests. The rule explained in the preceding Comment applies only when both security interests in original collateral are perfected when the goods become commingled goods. If a security interest in original collateral is unperfected at the time the collateral becomes commingled goods, subsection (f)(1) applies.

Example 4: SP-1 has a perfected security interest in the debtor's eggs, and SP-2 has an unperfected security interest in the debtor's flour. Debtor uses the flour and eggs to make cakes. Under subsection (c), both security interests attach to the cakes. But since SP-1's security interest was perfected at the time of commingling and SP-2's was not, only SP-1's security interest in the cakes is perfected. See subsection (d). Under subsection (f)(1) and Section 9-322(a)(2), SP-1's perfected security interest has priority over SP-2's unperfected security interest.

If both security interests are unperfected, the rule of Section 9-322(a)(3) would apply.

6. **Multiple Security Interests.** On occasion, a single input may be encumbered by more than one security interest. In those cases, the multiple secured parties should be treated like a single secured party for purposes of determining their collective share under subsection (f)(2). The normal priority rules would determine how that share would be allocated between them. Consider the following example, which is a variation on Example 1 above:

Example 5: SP-1A has a perfected, first-priority security interest in Debtor's eggs. SP-1B has a perfected, second-priority security interest in the same collateral. The eggs have a value of $300. Debtor owes $200 to SP-1A and $200 to SP-1B. SP-2 has a perfected security interest in Debtor's flour, which has a value of $500 and secures a debt of $600. Debtor uses the flour and eggs to make cakes, which have a value of $1000.

For purposes of subsection (f)(2), SP-1A and SP-1B should be treated like a single secured party. The collective security interest would rank equally with that of SP-2. Thus, the secured parties would share in the ratio of 3 (for SP-1A and SP-1B combined) to 5 (for SP-2). Applying this ratio to the entire value of the product, SP-1A and SP-1B in the aggregate would be entitled to $375 (i.e., 3/8 x $1000), and SP-2 would be entitled to $625 (i.e., 5/8 x $1000).

SP-1A and SP-1B would share the $300 in accordance with their priority, as established under other rules. Inasmuch as SP-1A has first priority, it would receive $200, and SP-1B would receive $100.

7. **Priority of Security Interests That Attach Other Than by Operation of This Section.** Under subsection (e), the normal priority rules determine the priority of a security interest that attaches to the product or mass other than by operation of this section. For example, assume that SP-1 has a perfected security interest in Debtor's existing and after-acquired baked goods, and SP-2 has a perfected security interest in Debtor's flour. When the flour is processed into cakes, subsections (c) and (d) provide that SP-2 acquires a perfected security interest in the cakes. If SP-1 filed against the baked goods before SP-2 filed against the flour, then SP-1 will enjoy priority

in the cakes. See Section 9-322 (first-to-file-or perfect). But if SP-2 filed against the flour before SP-1 filed against the baked goods, then SP-2 will enjoy priority in the cakes to the extent of its security interest.

§ 9-337. PRIORITY OF SECURITY INTERESTS IN GOODS COVERED BY CERTIFICATE OF TITLE. If, while a security interest in goods is perfected by any method under the law of another jurisdiction, this State issues a certificate of title that does not show that the goods are subject to the security interest or contain a statement that they may be subject to security interests not shown on the certificate:

(1) a buyer of the goods, other than a person in the business of selling goods of that kind, takes free of the security interest if the buyer gives value and receives delivery of the goods after issuance of the certificate and without knowledge of the security interest; and

(2) the security interest is subordinate to a conflicting security interest in the goods that attaches, and is perfected under Section 9-311(b), after issuance of the certificate and without the conflicting secured party's knowledge of the security interest.

Official Comment

1. **Source.** Derived from former Section 9-103(2)(d).

2. **Protection for Buyers and Secured Parties.** This section affords protection to certain good-faith purchasers for value who are likely to have relied on a "clean" certificate of title, i.e., one that neither shows that the goods are subject to a particular security interest nor contains a statement that they may be subject to security interests not shown on the certificate. Under this section, a buyer can take free of, and the holder of a conflicting security interest can acquire priority over, a security interest that is perfected by any method under the law of another jurisdiction. The fact that the security interest has been reperfected by possession under Section 9-313 does not of itself disqualify the holder of a conflicting security interest from protection under paragraph (2).

§ 9-338. PRIORITY OF SECURITY INTEREST OR AG-RICULTURAL LIEN PERFECTED BY FILED FINANC-ING STATEMENT PROVIDING CERTAIN INCOR-RECT INFORMATION. If a security interest or agricultural lien is perfected by a filed financing statement providing information described in Section 9-516(b)(5) which is incorrect at the time the financing statement is filed:

(1) the security interest or agricultural lien is subordinate to a conflicting perfected security interest in the collateral to the extent that the holder of the conflicting security interest gives value in reasonable reliance upon the incorrect information; and

(2) a purchaser, other than a secured party, of the collateral takes free of the security interest or agricultural lien to the extent that, in reasonable reliance upon the incorrect information, the purchaser gives value and, in the case of chattel paper, documents, goods, instruments, or a security certificate, receives delivery of the collateral.

ANALYSIS

Revised Article 9 conducts a war on lien creditors — particularly the trustee in bankruptcy. If a financing statement is accepted by a filing office even though it contains any incorrect information required by § 9-516(b)(5) (the mailing address of the debtor, whether the debtor is an individual or organization, and the type, jurisdiction and identifying number of an organizational debtor), then the security interest is nevertheless perfected. This new § 9-338 protects buyers and other secured creditors who relied on the incorrect information. The negative inference is that other creditors are not protected. That inference is fully supported by § 9-516. A creditor extending unsecured credit in reliance on information supplied by a credit reporting agency misled by the incorrect § 9-516(b)(5) information is not protected. Even if that creditor obtains a judgment and levies on the collateral, it would be inferior to the secured creditor whose financing statement contained the wrong information. Even if the debtor files for bankruptcy, the security interest cannot be invalidated under Bankruptcy Code § 544(a). Moreover, it is not the job of the filing office to verify the accuracy of the information required by § 9-516(5). The office is authorized to reject a statement only because it does not have one of the required entries.

Official Comment

1. **Source.** New.

2. **Effect of Incorrect Information in Financing Statement.** Section 9-520(a) requires the filing office to reject financing statements that do not contain information concerning the debtor as specified in Section 9-516(b)(5). A error in this information does not render the financing statement ineffective.

On rare occasions, a subsequent purchaser of the collateral (i.e., a buyer or secured party) may rely on the misinformation to its detriment. This section subordinates a security interest or agricultural lien perfected by an effective, but flawed, financing statement to the rights of a buyer or holder of a perfected security interest to the extent that, in reasonable reliance on the incorrect information, the purchaser gives value and, in the case of tangible collateral, receives delivery of the collateral. A purchaser who has not made itself aware of the information in the filing office with respect to the debtor cannot act in "reasonable reliance" upon incorrect information.

3. **Relationship to Section 9-507.** This section applies to financing statements that contain information that is incorrect at the time of filing and imposes a small risk of subordination on the filer. In contrast, Section 9-507 deals with financing statements containing information that is correct at the time of filing but which becomes incorrect later. Except as provided in Section 9-507 with respect to changes in the debtor's name, an otherwise effective financing statement does not become ineffective if the information contained in it becomes inaccurate.

§ 9-339. PRIORITY SUBJECT TO SUBORDINATION.

This article does not preclude subordination by agreement by a person entitled to priority.

Official Comment

1. **Source.** Former Section 9-316.

2. **Subordination by Agreement.** The preceding sections deal elaborately with questions of priority. This section makes it entirely clear that a person entitled to priority may effectively agree to subordinate its claim. Only the person entitled to priority may make such an agreement: a person's rights cannot be adversely affected by an agreement to which the person is not a party.

[SUBPART 4. RIGHTS OF BANK]

§ 9-340. EFFECTIVENESS OF RIGHT OF RECOUPMENT OR SET-OFF AGAINST DEPOSIT ACCOUNT.

(a) [Exercise of recoupment or set-off.] Except as otherwise provided in subsection (c), a bank with which a deposit account is maintained may exercise any right of recoupment or set-off against a secured party that holds a security interest in the deposit account.

(b) [Recoupment or setoff not affected by security interest.] Except as otherwise provided in subsection (c), the application of this article to a security interest in a deposit account does not affect a right of recoupment or set-off of the secured party as to a deposit account maintained with the secured party.

(c) [When set-off ineffective.] The exercise by a bank of a set-off against a deposit account is ineffective against a secured party that holds a security interest in the deposit account which is perfected by control under Section 9-104(a)(3), if the set-off is based on a claim against the debtor.

ANALYSIS

Under old Article 9, most opinions have given priority to a secured creditor with a perfected proceeds interest in a bank account over the set-off right asserted by the depositary bank. *See Secured Transactions* § 3.15[2]. Under this new § 9-340 the bank set-off will have priority except where the secured creditor controls the deposit account by becoming the bank's customer with respect to the account. The designation of the creditor as customer could well destroy the mutuality required for the set-off right to exist in first place. This change preferring the right of set-off was required to convince the bankers to accept original Article 9 security interests in deposit accounts. If the depositary bank is itself the secured creditor, it wins under new § 9-327(3). If it is not the secured creditor, it wins under new § 9-340. The non-bank secured creditor can be assured of prevailing as to the deposit account against the bank at which the account is maintained only if 1) the bank is not a creditor of the debtor; 2) the non-bank is named as a customer with respect to the account; or 3) the bank agrees to subordinate to the non-bank secured creditor.

Official Comment

1. **Source.** New; subsection (b) is based on a nonuniform Illinois amendment.

2. **Set-off vs. Security Interest.** This section resolves the conflict between a security interest in a deposit account and the bank's rights of recoupment and set-off.

Subsection (a) states the general rule and provides that the bank may effectively exercise rights of recoupment and set-off against the secured party.

Subsection (c) contains an exception: if the secured party has control under Section 9-104(a)(3) (i.e., if it has become the bank's customer), then any set-off exercised by the bank against a debt owed by the debtor (as opposed to a debt owed to the bank by the secured party) is ineffective. The bank may, however, exercise its recoupment rights effectively. This result is consistent with the priority rule in Section 9-327(4), under which the security interest of a bank in a deposit account is subordinate to that of a secured party who has control under Section 9-104(a)(3).

This section deals with rights of set-off and recoupment that a bank may have under other law. It does not create a right of set-off or recoupment, nor is it intended to override any limitations or restrictions that other law imposes on the exercise of those rights.

3. **Preservation of Set-Off Right.** Subsection (b) makes clear that a bank may hold both a right of set-off against, and an Article 9 security interest in, the same deposit account. By holding a security interest in a deposit account, a bank does not impair any right of set-off it would otherwise enjoy. This subsection does not pertain to accounts evidenced by an instrument (e.g., certain certificates of deposit), which are excluded from the definition of "deposit accounts."

§ 9-341. BANK'S RIGHTS AND DUTIES WITH RESPECT TO DEPOSIT ACCOUNT.
Except as otherwise provided in Section 9-340(c), and unless the bank otherwise agrees in an authenticated record, a bank's rights and duties with respect to a deposit account maintained with the bank are not terminated, suspended, or modified by:

(1) the creation, attachment, or perfection of a security interest in the deposit account;

(2) the bank's knowledge of the security interest; or

(3) the bank's receipt of instructions from the secured party.

Official Comment

1. **Source.** New.

2. **Free Flow of Funds.** This section is designed to prevent security interests in deposit accounts from impeding the free flow of funds through the payment system. Subject to two exceptions, it leaves the bank's rights and duties with respect to the deposit account and the funds on deposit unaffected by the creation or perfection of a security interest or by the bank's knowledge of the security interest. In addition, the section permits the bank to ignore the instructions of the secured party unless it had agreed to honor them or unless other law provides to the contrary. A secured party who wishes

to deprive the debtor of access to funds on deposit or to appropriate those funds for itself needs to obtain the agreement of the bank, utilize the judicial process, or comply with procedures set forth in other law. Section 4-303(a), concerning the effect of notice on a bank's right and duty to pay items, is not to the contrary. That section addresses only whether an otherwise effective notice comes too late; it does not determine whether a timely notice is otherwise effective.

3. **Operation of Rule.** The general rule of this section is subject to Section 9-340(c), under which a bank's right of set-off may not be exercised against a deposit account in the secured party's name if the right is based on a claim against the debtor. This result reflects current law in many jurisdictions and does not appear to have unduly disrupted banking practices or the payments system. The more important function of this section, which is not impaired by Section 9-340, is the bank's right to follow the debtor's (customer's) instructions (e.g., by honoring checks, permitting withdrawals, etc.) until such time as the depository institution is served with judicial process or receives instructions with respect to the funds on deposit from a secured party who has control over the deposit account.

4. **Liability of Bank.** This Article does not determine whether a bank that pays out funds from an encumbered deposit is liable to the holder of a security interest. Although the fact that a secured party has control over the deposit account and the manner by which control was achieved may be relevant to the imposition of liability, whatever rule applies generally when a bank pays out funds in which a third party has an interest would determine liability to a secured party. Often, this rule is found in a non-UCC adverse claim statute.

5. **Certificates of Deposit.** This section does not address the obligations of banks that issue instruments evidencing deposits (e.g., certain certificates of deposit).

§ 9-342. BANK'S RIGHT TO REFUSE TO ENTER INTO OR DISCLOSE EXISTENCE OF CONTROL AGREE-MENT.

This article does not require a bank to enter into an agreement of the kind described in Section 9-104(a)(2), even if its customer so requests or directs. A bank that has entered into such an agreement is not required to confirm the existence of the agreement to another person unless requested to do so by its customer.

Official Comment

1. **Source.** New; derived from Section 8-106(g).

2. **Protection for Bank.** This section protects banks from the need to enter into agreements against their will and from the need to respond to inquiries from persons other than their customers.

PART 4   RIGHTS OF THIRD PARTIES

§ 9-401.   ALIENABILITY OF DEBTOR'S RIGHTS.

(a) **[Other law governs alienability; exceptions.]** Except as otherwise provided in subsection (b) and Sections 9-406, 9-407, 9-408, and 9-409, whether a debtor's rights in collateral may be voluntarily or involuntarily transferred is governed by law other than this article.

(b) **[Agreement does not prevent transfer.]** An agreement between the debtor and secured party which prohibits a transfer of the debtor's rights in collateral or makes the transfer a default does not prevent the transfer from taking effect.

ANALYSIS

Revised Article 9 does not carry forward the affirmative declaration of old § 9-311 permitting involuntary alienation of the collateral by attachment, levy, garnishment or other appropriate legal process. The drafters of the original Article 9 felt that this declaration was an appropriate response to the charge that security interests, in general, and floating liens in particular could be used to shield improperly a debtor's assets from the claims of the debtor's unsecured creditors. *See Secured Transactions* § 7.02[5]. The drafters of the Revised Article 9 feel no similar compulsion. Whether the existence of a security interest prevents another creditor from using the remedies of the law of creditors' rights is differed to "applicable law other than this article." That other law (if any can be found) is likely to be the law of creditors' rights addressing the particular remedy in the particular state or perhaps even the law of fraudulent conveyance. Official Comment 4 acknowledges that a debtor may have a substantial equity in collateral, but differs the resolution of the problem to the courts. The revisers are either prepared to accept such a shielding of the debtor's assets or are unable to say that they reject such shielding affirmatively. Revised Article 9 makes life as difficult as possible for unsecured creditors.

Official Comment

1. **Source.** Former Section 9-311.

2. **Scope of This Part.** This Part deals with several issues affecting third parties (i.e., parties other than the debtor and the secured party). These issues are not addressed in Part 3, Subpart 3, which deals with priorities. This Part primarily addresses the rights and duties of account debtors and other persons obligated on collateral who are not, themselves, parties to a secured transaction.

3. **Governing Law.** There was some uncertainty under former Article 9 as to which jurisdiction's law (usually, which jurisdiction's version of Article 9) applied to the matters that this Part addresses. Part 3, Subpart 1, does not determine the law governing these matters because they do not relate to perfection, the effect of perfection or nonperfection, or priority. However, it might be inappropriate for a designation of applicable law by a debtor and secured party under Section 1-105 to control the law applicable to an independent transaction or relationship between the debtor and an account debtor.

Consider an example under Section 9-408.

Example 1: State X has adopted this Article; former Article 9 is the law of State Y. A general intangible (e.g., a franchise agreement) between a debtor-franchisee, D, and an account debtor-franchisor, AD, is governed by the law of State Y. D grants to SP a security interest in its rights under the franchise agreement. The franchise agreement contains a term prohibiting D's assignment of its rights under the agreement. D and SP agree that their secured transaction is governed by the law of State X. Under State X's Section 9-408, the restriction on D's assignment is ineffective to prevent the creation, attachment, or perfection of SP's security interest. State Y's former Section 9-318(4), however, does not address restrictions on the creation of security interests in general intangibles other than general intangibles for money due or to become due. Accordingly, it does not address restrictions on the assignment to SP of D's rights under the franchise agreement. The non-Article-9 law of State Y, which does address restrictions, provides that the prohibition on assignment is effective.

This Article does not provide a specific answer to the question of which State's law applies to the restriction on assignment in the example. However, assuming that under non-UCC choice-of-law principles the effectiveness of the restriction would be governed by the law of State Y, which governs the franchise agreement, the fact that State X's Article 9 governs the secured transaction between SP and D would not override the otherwise applicable law governing the agreement. Of course, to the extent that jurisdictions eventually adopt identical versions of this Article and courts interpret it consistently, the inability to identify the applicable law in circumstances such as those in the example may be inconsequential.

4. **Inalienability Under Other Law.** Subsection (a) addresses the question whether property necessarily is transferable by virtue of its inclusion (i.e.,

its eligibility as collateral) within the scope of Article 9. It gives a negative answer, subject to the identified exceptions. The substance of subsection (a) was implicit under former Article 9.

5. **Negative Pledge Covenant.** Subsection (b) is an exception to the general rule in subsection (a). It makes clear that in secured transactions under this Article the debtor has rights in collateral (whether legal title or equitable) which it can transfer and which its creditors can reach. It is best explained with an example.

Example 2: A debtor, D, grants to SP a security interest to secure a debt in excess of the value of the collateral. D agrees with SP that it will not create a subsequent security interest in the collateral and that any security interest purportedly granted in violation of the agreement will be void. Subsequently, in violation of its agreement with SP, D purports to grant a security interest in the same collateral to another secured party.

Subsection (b) validates D's creation of the subsequent (prohibited) security interest, which might even achieve priority over the earlier security interest. See Comment 7. However, unlike some other provisions of this Part, such as Section 9-406, subsection (b) does not provide that the agreement restricting assignment itself is "ineffective." Consequently, the debtor's breach may create a default.

6. **Rights of Lien Creditors.** Difficult problems may arise with respect to attachment, levy, and other judicial procedures under which a debtor's creditors may reach collateral subject to a security interest. For example, an obligation may be secured by collateral worth many times the amount of the obligation. If a lien creditor has caused all or a portion of the collateral to be seized under judicial process, it may be difficult to determine the amount of the debtor's "equity" in the collateral that has been seized. The section leaves resolution of this problem to the courts. The doctrine of marshaling may be appropriate.

7. **Sale of Receivables.** If a debtor sells an account, chattel paper, payment intangible, or promissory note outright, as against the buyer the debtor has no remaining rights to transfer. If, however, the buyer fails to perfect its interest, then solely insofar as the rights of certain third parties are concerned, the debtor is deemed to retain its rights and title. See Section 9-318. The debtor has the power to convey these rights to a subsequent purchaser. If the subsequent purchaser (buyer or secured lender) perfects its interest, it will achieve priority over the earlier, unperfected purchaser. See Section 9-322(a)(1).

§ 9-402. SECURED PARTY NOT OBLIGATED ON CONTRACT OF DEBTOR OR IN TORT. The existence of a security interest, agricultural lien, or authority given to a

debtor to dispose of or use collateral, without more, does not subject a secured party to liability in contract or tort for the debtor's acts or omissions.

Official Comment

1. **Source.** Former Section 9-317.

2. **Nonliability of Secured Party.** This section, like former Section 9-317, rejects theories on which a secured party might be held liable on a debtor's contracts or in tort merely because a security interest exists or because the debtor is entitled to dispose of or use collateral. This section expands former Section 9-317 to cover agricultural liens.

§ 9-403. AGREEMENT NOT TO ASSERT DEFENSES AGAINST ASSIGNEE.

(a) **["Value."]** In this section, "value" has the meaning provided in Section 3-303(a).

(b) **[Agreement not to assert claim or defense.]** Except as otherwise provided in this section, an agreement between an account debtor and an assignor not to assert against an assignee any claim or defense that the account debtor may have against the assignor is enforceable by an assignee that takes an assignment:

(1)   for value;

(2)   in good faith;

(3)   without notice of a claim of a property or possessory right to the property assigned; and

(4)   without notice of a defense or claim in recoupment of the type that may be asserted against a person entitled to enforce a negotiable instrument under Section 3-305(a).

(c) **[When subsection (b) not applicable.]** Subsection (b) does not apply to defenses of a type that may be asserted against a holder in due course of a negotiable instrument under Section 3-305(b).

(d) **[Omission of required statement in consumer transaction.]** In a consumer transaction, if a record evidences the account debtor's obligation, law other than this article requires that the record include a statement to the effect that the rights of an assignee are subject to claims or defenses that the account debtor could assert against the original obligee, and the record does not include such a statement:

(1)   the record has the same effect as if the record included such a statement; and

(2)   the account debtor may assert against an assignee those claims and defenses that would have been available if the record included such a statement.

ANALYSIS

The FTC's Holder in Due Course Regulations, 16 C.F.R. §§ 433.1–433.3 require the legend preserving consumer claims and defenses to be present as a controlling contract term in two types of consumer credit contracts: "financed sales" and "purchase-money loans." Both of these terms have technical definitions under the regulation. *See Secured Transactions* § 20.10[3]. In a financed sale, the seller of the goods and services takes a note or contract from the consumer and then sells that paper to a third-party financer. Omission of the regulatorily-mandated legend is not likely to allow an institutional third-party financer to qualify as a holder in due course. The institutional financer is likely to be charged with knowledge that the seller has violated the FTC regulation by omitting the legend and will have an uphill battle in convincing a court that it has acted in good faith. This new § 9-403(d), added as part of the last minute consumer/creditor compromise, could conceivably have more impact on purchase-money loan transactions where a third party financer lends to the consumer and then sells the note to still another financer. The purchaser of the note may in some circumstances be able to credibly assert that it had no awareness that the FTC Regulation was being violated. When they apply, new §§ 9-403(d) and 9-404(d) deem the legend to be present whenever it is required to be present by the FTC Regulation. In that event § 3-106(d) establishes that even the innocent financer purchasing the note cannot be a holder in due course. Consumer advocates could save having to litigate holder-in-due course status on a case-by-case basis. However, these last-minute provisions seem to be poor vehicles for this consumer protection initiative because they apply only when a record evidences an account debtor's obligation. The obligor on a note which qualifies as an Article 9 instrument is not an account debtor. *See* new § 9-102(a)(3). Thus, it would not seem that these provisions deeming the legend to be present would apply by their terms when notes, as opposed to installment contracts, are used in the transaction.

(e) [Rule for individual under other law.] This section is subject to law other than this article which establishes a different rule for an account debtor who is an individual and who incurred the obligation primarily for personal, family, or household purposes.

(f) [Other law not displaced.] Except as otherwise provided in subsection (d), this section does not displace law other than this article which gives effect to an agreement by an account debtor not to assert a claim or defense against an assignee.

Official Comment

1. **Source.** Former Section 9-206.

2. **Scope and Purpose.** Subsection (b), like former Section 9-206, generally validates an agreement between an account debtor and an assignor that the account debtor will not assert against an assignee claims and defenses that it may have against the assignor. These agreements are typical in installment sale agreements and leases. However, this section expands former Section 9-206 to apply to all account debtors; it is not limited to account debtors that have bought or leased goods. This section applies only to the obligations of an "account debtor," as defined in Section 9-102. Thus, it does not determine the circumstances under which and the extent to which a person who is obligated on a negotiable instrument is disabled from asserting claims and defenses. Rather, Article 3 must be consulted. See, e.g., Sections 3-305, 3-306. Article 3 governs even when the negotiable instrument constitutes part of chattel paper. See Section 9-102 (an obligor on a negotiable instrument constituting part of chattel paper is not an "account debtor").

3. **Conditions of Validation; Relationship to Article 3.** Subsection (b) validates an account debtor's agreement only if the assignee takes an assignment for value, in good faith, and without notice of conflicting claims to the property assigned or of certain claims or defenses of the assignor. Like former Section 9-206, this section is designed to put the assignee in a position that is no better and no worse than that of a holder in due course of an negotiable instrument under Article 3. However, former Section 9-206 left open certain issues, e.g., whether the section incorporated the special Article 3 definition of "value" in Section 3-303 or the generally applicable definition in Section 1-201(44). Subsection (a) addresses this question; it provides that "value" has the meaning specified in Section 3-303(a). Similarly, subsection (c) provides that subsection (b) does not validate an agreement with respect to defenses that could be asserted against a holder in due course under Section 9-305(b) (the so-called "real" defenses). In 1990, the definition of "holder in due course" (Section 3-302) and the articulation of the rights of a holder in due course (Sections 3-305 and 3-306) were revised substantially. This section tracks more closely the rules of Sections 3-302, 3-305, and 3-306.

4. **Relationship to Terms of Assigned Property.** Former Section 9-206(2), concerning warranties accompanying the sale of goods, has been deleted as unnecessary. This Article does not regulate the terms of the account, chattel paper, or general intangible that is assigned, except insofar as the account, chattel paper, or general intangible itself creates a security interest (as often is the case with chattel paper). Thus, Article 2, and not this Article, determines whether a seller of goods makes or effectively disclaims warranties, even if the sale is secured. Similarly, other law, and not this Article, determines the effectiveness of an account debtor's undertaking to pay notwithstanding, and not to assert, any defenses or claims against an assignor–e.g., a "hell or high water" provision in the underlying agreement that is assigned. If other law gives effect to this undertaking, then, under principles of *nemo dat,* the undertaking would be enforceable by the assignee (secured party). If other law prevents the assignor from enforcing the undertaking, this section nevertheless might permit the assignee to do so. The right of the assignee to enforce would depend upon whether, under the particular facts, the account debtor's undertaking fairly could be construed as an agreement that falls within the scope of this section and whether the assignee meets the requirements of this section.

5. **Relationship to Federal Trade Commission Rule.** Subsection (d) is new. It applies to rights evidenced by a record that is required to contain, but does not contain, the notice set forth in Federal Trade Commission Rule 433, 16 C.F.R. Part 433 (the "Holder-in-Due-Course Regulations"). Under this subsection, an assignee of such a record takes subject to the consumer account debtor's claims and defenses to the same extent as it would have if the writing had contained the required notice. Thus, subsection (d) effectively renders waiver-of-defense clauses ineffective in the transactions with consumers to which it applies.

6. **Relationship to Other Law.** Like former Section 9-206(1), this section takes no position on the enforceability of waivers of claims and defenses by consumer account debtors, leaving that question to other law. However, the reference to "law other than this article" in subsection (e) encompasses administrative rules and regulations; the reference in former Section 9-206(1) that it replaces ("statute or decision") arguably did not.

This section does not displace other law that gives effect to a non-consumer account debtor's agreement not to assert defenses against an assignee, even if the agreement would not qualify under subsection (b). See subsection (f). It validates, but does not invalidate, agreements made by a non-consumer account debtor. This section also does not displace other law to the extent that the other law permits an assignee, who takes an assignment with notice of a claim of a property or possessory right, a defense, or a claim in recoupment, to enforce an account debtor's agreement not to assert claims and defenses against the assign*or* (e.g., a "hell-or-high-water" agreement). See Comment 4. It also does not displace an assignee's right to assert that an account debtor is estopped from asserting a claim or defense. Nor does this section displace other law with respect to waivers of potential future claims and defenses that are the subject of an agreement between the account debtor and the assign*ee*. Finally, it does not displace Section 1-107, concerning waiver of a breach that allegedly already has occurred.

§ 9-404. RIGHTS ACQUIRED BY ASSIGNEE; CLAIMS AND DEFENSES AGAINST ASSIGNEE.

(a) [Assignee's rights subject to terms, claims, and defenses; exceptions.] Unless an account debtor has made an enforceable agreement not to assert defenses or claims, and subject to subsections (b) through (e), the rights of an assignee are subject to:

(1) all terms of the agreement between the account debtor and assignor and any defense or claim in recoupment arising from the transaction that gave rise to the contract; and

(2) any other defense or claim of the account debtor against the assignor which accrues before the account debtor receives a notification of the assignment authenticated by the assignor or the assignee.

(b) [Account debtor's claim reduces amount owed to assignee.] Subject to subsection (c) and except as otherwise provided in subsection (d), the claim of an account debtor against an assignor may be asserted against an assignee under subsection (a) only to reduce the amount the account debtor owes.

(c) [Rule for individual under other law.] This section is subject to law other than this article which establishes a different rule for an account debtor who is an individual and who incurred the obligation primarily for personal, family, or household purposes.

(d) [Omission of required statement in consumer transaction.] In a consumer transaction, if a record evidences the account debtor's obligation, law other than this article requires that the record include a statement to the effect that the account debtor's recovery against an assignee with respect to claims and defenses against the assignor may not exceed amounts paid by the account debtor under the record, and the record does not include such a statement, the extent to which a claim of an account debtor against the assignor may be asserted against an assignee is determined as if the record included such a statement.

(e) [Inapplicability to health-care-insurance receivable.] This section does not apply to an assignment of a health-care-insurance receivable.

Official Comment

1. **Source.** Former Section 9-318(1).

2. **Purpose; Rights of Assignee in General.** Subsection (a), like former Section 9-318(1), provides that an assignee generally takes an assignment subject to defenses and claims of an account debtor. Under subsection (a)(1), if the account debtor's defenses on an assigned claim arise from the transaction that gave rise to the contract with the assignor, it makes no difference whether the defense or claim accrues before or after the account debtor is notified of the assignment. Under subsection (a)(2), the assignee takes subject to other defenses or claims only if they accrue before the account debtor has been notified of the assignment. Of course, an account debtor may waive its right to assert defenses or claims against an assignee under Section 9-403 or other applicable law. Subsection (a) tracks Section 3-305(a)(3) more closely than its predecessor.

3. **Limitation on Affirmative Claims.** Subsection (b) is new. It limits the claim that the account debtor may assert against an assignee. Borrowing from Section 3-305(a)(3) and cases construing former Section 9-318, subsection (b) generally does not afford the account debtor the right to an affirmative recovery from an assignee.

4. **Consumer Account Debtors; Relationship to Federal Trade Commission Rule.** Subsections (c) and (d) also are new. Subsection (c) makes clear that the rules of this section are subject to other law establishing special rules for consumer account debtors. An "account debtor who is an individual" as used in subsection (c) includes individuals who are jointly or jointly and severally obligated. Subsection (d) applies to rights evidenced by a record that is required to contain, but does not contain, the notice set forth in Federal Trade Commission Rule 433, 16 C.F.R. Part 433 (the "Holder-in-Due-Course Regulations"). Under subsection (d), a consumer account debtor has the same right to an affirmative recovery from an assignee of such a record as the consumer would have had against the assignee had the record contained the required notice.

5. **Scope; Application to "Account Debtor."** This section deals only with the rights and duties of "account debtors"-and for the most part only with account debtors on accounts, chattel paper, and payment intangibles. Subsection (e) provides that the obligation of an insurer with respect to a health-care-insurance receivable is governed by other law. References in this section to an "account debtor" include account debtors on collateral that is proceeds. Neither this section nor any other provision of this Article, including Sections

9-408 and 9-409, provides analogous regulation of the rights and duties of other obligors on collateral, such as the maker of a negotiable instrument (governed by Article 3), the issuer of or nominated person under a letter of credit (governed by Article 5), or the issuer of a security (governed by Article 8). Article 9 leaves those rights and duties untouched; however, Section 9-409 deals with the special case of letters of credit. When chattel paper is composed in part of a negotiable instrument, the obligor on the instrument is not an "account debtor," and Article 3 governs the rights of the assignee of the chattel paper with respect to the issues that this section addresses. See, e.g., Section 3-601 (dealing with discharge of an obligation to pay a negotiable instrument).

§ 9-405. MODIFICATION OF ASSIGNED CONTRACT.

(a) [Effect of modification on assignee.] A modification of or substitution for an assigned contract is effective against an assignee if made in good faith. The assignee acquires corresponding rights under the modified or substituted contract. The assignment may provide that the modification or substitution is a breach of contract by the assignor. This subsection is subject to subsections (b) through (d).

(b) [Applicability of subsection (a).] Subsection (a) applies to the extent that:

(1)   the right to payment or a part thereof under an assigned contract has not been fully earned by performance; or

(2)   the right to payment or a part thereof has been fully earned by performance and the account debtor has not received notification of the assignment under Section 9-406(a).

(c) [Rule for individual under other law.] This section is subject to law other than this article which establishes a different rule for an account debtor who is an individual and who incurred the obligation primarily for personal, family, or household purposes.

(d) [Inapplicability to health-care-insurance receivable.] This section does not apply to an assignment of a health-care-insurance receivable.

Official Comment

1. **Source.** Former Section 9-318(2).

2. **Modification of Assigned Contract.** The ability of account debtors and assignors to modify assigned contracts can be important, especially in the

case of government contracts and complex contractual arrangements (e.g., construction contracts) with respect to which modifications are customary. Subsections (a) and (b) provide that good-faith modifications of assigned contracts are binding against an assignee to the extent that (i) the right to payment has not been fully earned or (ii) the right to payment has been earned and notification of the assignment has not been given to the account debtor. Former Section 9-318(2) did not validate modifications of fully-performed contracts under any circumstances, whether or not notification of the assignment had been given to the account debtor. Subsection (a) protects the interests of assignees by (i) limiting the effectiveness of modifications to those made in good faith, (ii) affording the assignee with corresponding rights under the contract as modified, and (iii) recognizing that the modification may be a breach of the assignor's agreement with the assignee.

3. **Consumer Account Debtors.** Subsection (c) is new. It makes clear that the rules of this section are subject to other law establishing special rules for consumer account debtors.

4. **Account Debtors on Health-Care-Insurance Receivables.** Subsection (d) also is new. It provides that this section does not apply to an assignment of a heath-care-insurance receivable. The obligation of an insurer with respect to a health-care-insurance receivable is governed by other law.

§ 9-406. DISCHARGE OF ACCOUNT DEBTOR; NOTIFICATION OF ASSIGNMENT; IDENTIFICATION AND PROOF OF ASSIGNMENT; RESTRICTIONS ON ASSIGNMENT OF ACCOUNTS, CHATTEL PAPER, PAYMENT INTANGIBLES, AND PROMISSORY NOTES INEFFECTIVE.

(a) **[Discharge of account debtor; effect of notification.]** Subject to subsections (b) through (i), an account debtor on an account, chattel paper, or a payment intangible may discharge its obligation by paying the assignor until, but not after, the account debtor receives a notification, authenticated by the assignor or the assignee, that the amount due or to become due has been assigned and that payment is to be made to the assignee. After receipt of the notification, the account debtor may discharge its obligation by paying the assignee and may not discharge the obligation by paying the assignor.

TEXT, OFFICIAL COMMENTS AND ANALYSIS § 9-406

ANALYSIS

This subsection, like the other rules of this part applying only to "account debtors," does not apply to an obligor on an instrument, negotiable or non-negotiable, because such an obligor is not an "account debtor" as the term is defined in new § 9-102(a)(3). To this extent, the law is not changed. In addition, the provision does not apply to an obligor on a general intangible which is not a payment intangible. For example, an obligor on a license who has an obligation to pay that is not the obligor's primary obligation would not be covered by new § 9-406(a). But that obligor was covered by old § 9-318(3).

(b) [When notification ineffective.] Subject to subsection (h), notification is ineffective under subsection (a):

(1)   if it does not reasonably identify the rights assigned;

(2)   to the extent that an agreement between an account debtor and a seller of a payment intangible limits the account debtor's duty to pay a person other than the seller and the limitation is effective under law other than this article; or

(3)   at the option of an account debtor, if the notification notifies the account debtor to make less than the full amount of any installment or other periodic payment to the assignee, even if:

(A)   only a portion of the account, chattel paper, or general intangible has been assigned to that assignee;

(B)   a portion has been assigned to another assignee; or

(C)   the account debtor knows that the assignment to that assignee is limited.

(c) [Proof of assignment.] Subject to subsection (h), if requested by the account debtor, an assignee shall seasonably furnish reasonable proof that the assignment has been made. Unless the assignee complies, the account debtor may discharge its obligation by paying the assignor, even if the account debtor has received a notification under subsection (a).

(d) [Term restricting assignment generally ineffective.] Except as otherwise provided in subsection (e) and Sections 2A-303 and 9-407, and subject to subsection (h), a term in an agreement between an account debtor and an assignor or in a promissory note is ineffective to the extent that it:

(1)   prohibits, restricts, or requires the consent of the account debtor or person obligated on the promissory note to the assignment or transfer of, or the creation, attachment, perfection, or enforcement of a security interest in, the account, chattel paper, payment intangible, or promissory note; or

(2)   provides that the creation, attachment, perfection, or enforcement of the security interest may give rise to a default, breach, right of recoupment, claim, defense, termination, right of termination, or remedy under the account, chattel paper, payment intangible, or promissory note.

ANALYSIS

New subsection 9-406(d) makes contract provisions prohibiting security interests ineffective and allows the security interest to bind the account debtor or the obligor on the note. In contrast, new § 9-408(a) makes the contract provisions which it affects ineffective to prevent creation or perfection of the security interest, but does not allow this resulting security interest to bind the account debtor or the obligor on a note. The best way to make sense out of the relationship between the sections seems to be to assume that new § 9-406(d) applies when new § 9-408(a) is inapplicable.

Example A: Seller sells beer on open account to Buyer. The sales contract provides that seller may not assign or grant a security interest in his right under the contract. Seller nevertheless assigns the account to Bank One. Bank One notifies Buyer, the account debtor, of the assignment and demands that payment be made to it. Section 9-408(a) is inapplicable because the asset assigned is an account, not a health-care insurance receivable or general intangible. The contract provision is ineffective under new § 9-406(d) and Buyer is bound to pay Bank One under 9-406(a).

Example B: Lender advances funds to Borrower, who signs a promissory note evidencing its obligation to pay the loan. The note provides that it may not be assigned nor may security interests be created in it. Nevertheless, Lender grants a security interest in the note to Valley Finance, which perfects by filing. When Lender defaults on its obligation to Valley Finance, Valley Finance demands that Borrower make payments due on the note to it. New § 9-408(a) does not apply because the note was transferred in a security transaction, not in an outright sale. The provisions prohibiting a security interest are ineffective under § 9-406(d). Borrower is obligated to pay Valley Finance under new § 9-607.

Example C: Same facts as above except that the note is sold outright by Lender to Valley Finance. Now the controlling provision is new § 9-408 because a sale of a note creates the "security interest" in favor of Valley Finance. The restriction on creation of security interests is ineffective. Valley Finance has a perfected interest in the note and in the event of the bankruptcy of Lender, it has an interest in the payments made by Borrower which remains effective under Section 552 of the Bankruptcy Code. However, Borrower is not itself obligated in the event of Lender's default to pay Valley Finance because the security interest does not bind it under new § 9-408(d).

Example D: Software Inc. licenses the use of a program by Debtor Co. The license provides that no security interests can be created in the rights of Debtor Co. These rights of the licensee qualify as an Article 9 general intangible. The licensee is an account debtor because new § 9-102(a)(3) sweeps obligors on a general intangible within that category even though their primary obligation is not a payment of money. New § 9-406(d) nevertheless does not apply if Debtor Co. grants a security interest in its license rights because (1) it would be both the assignor and the account debtor in the transaction; and (2) new § 9-408(a) is obviously designed to control the transaction and would be undermined if new § 9-406(d) applied.

(e) [Inapplicability of subsection (d) to certain sales.]
Subsection (d) does not apply to the sale of a payment intangible or promissory note.

(f) **[Legal restrictions on assignment generally ineffective.]** Except as otherwise provided in Sections 2A-303 and 9-407 and subject to subsections (h) and (i), a rule of law, statute, or regulation that prohibits, restricts, or requires the consent of a government, governmental body or official, or account debtor to the assignment or transfer of, or creation of a security interest in, an account or chattel paper is ineffective to the extent that the rule of law, statute, or regulation:

(1) prohibits, restricts, or requires the consent of the government, governmental body or official, or account debtor to the assignment or transfer of, or the creation, attachment, perfection, or enforcement of a security interest in the account or chattel paper; or

(2) provides that the creation, attachment, perfection, or enforcement of the security interest may give rise to a default, breach, right of recoupment, claim, defense, termination, right of termination, or remedy under the account or chattel paper.

(g) **[Subsection (b)(3) not waivable.]** Subject to subsection (h), an account debtor may not waive or vary its option under subsection (b)(3).

(h) **[Rule for individual under other law.]** This section is subject to law other than this article which establishes a different rule for an account debtor who is an individual and who incurred the obligation primarily for personal, family, or household purposes.

(i) **[Inapplicability to health-care-insurance receivable.]** This section does not apply to an assignment of a health-care-insurance receivable.

(j) **[Section prevails over specified inconsistent law.]** This section prevails over any inconsistent provisions of the following statutes, rules, and regulations:

[List here any statutes, rules, and regulations containing provisions inconsistent with this section.]

Legislative Note: States that amend statutes, rules, and regulations to remove provisions inconsistent with this section need not enact subsection (j)

Official Comment

1. **Source.** Former Section 9-318(3), (4).

2. **Account Debtor's Right to Pay Assignor Until Notification.** Subsection (a) provides the general rule concerning an account debtor's right to pay

the assignor until the account debtor receives appropriate notification. The revision makes clear that once the account debtor receives the notification, the account debtor cannot discharge its obligation by paying the assignor. It also makes explicit that payment to the assignor before notification, or payment to the assignee after notification, discharges the obligation. No change in meaning from former Section 9-318 is intended. Nothing in this section conditions the effectiveness of a notification on the identity of the person who gives it. An account debtor that doubts whether the right to payment has been assigned may avail itself of the procedures in subsection (c). See Comment 4.

An effective notification under subsection (a) must be authenticated. This requirement normally could be satisfied by sending notification on the notifying person's letterhead or on a form on which the notifying person's name appears. In each case the printed name would be a symbol adopted by the notifying person for the purpose of identifying the person and adopting the notification. See Section 9-102 (defining "authenticate").

Subsection (a) applies only to account debtors on accounts, chattel paper, and payment intangibles. (Section 9-102 defines the term "account debtor" more broadly, to include those obligated on all general intangibles.) Although subsection (a) is more precise than its predecessor, it probably does not change the rule that applied under former Article 9. Former Section 9-318(3) referred to the account debtor's obligation to "pay," indicating that the subsection was limited to account debtors on accounts, chattel paper, and other payment obligations.

3. **Limitations on Effectiveness of Notification.** Subsection (b) contains some special rules concerning the effectiveness of a notification under subsection (a).

Subsection (b)(1) tracks former Section 9-318(3) by making ineffective a notification that does not reasonably identify the rights assigned. A reasonable identification need not identify the right to payment with specificity, but what is reasonable also is not left to the arbitrary decision of the account debtor. If an account debtor has doubt as to the adequacy of a notification, it may not be safe in disregarding the notification unless it notifies the assignee with reasonable promptness as to the respects in which the account debtor considers the notification defective.

Subsection (b)(2), which is new, applies only to sales of payment intangibles. It makes a notification ineffective to the extent that other law gives effect to an agreement between an account debtor and a seller of a payment intangible that limits the account debtor's duty to pay a person other than the seller. Payment intangibles are substantially less fungible than accounts and chattel paper. In some (e.g., commercial bank loans), account debtors customarily and legitimately expect that they will not be required to pay any person other than the financial institution that has advanced funds.

It has become common in financing transactions to assign interests in a single obligation to more than one assignee. Requiring an account debtor that owes a single obligation to make multiple payments to multiple assignees would be unnecessarily burdensome. Thus, under subsection (b)(3), an account debtor that is notified to pay an assignee less than the full amount of any installment or other periodic payment has the option to treat the notification as ineffective, ignore the notice, and discharge the assigned obligation by paying the assignor. Some account debtors may not realize that the law affords them the right to ignore certain notices of assignment with impunity. By making the notification ineffective at the account debtor's option, subsection (b)(3) permits an account debtor to pay the assignee in accordance with the notice and thereby to satisfy its obligation *pro tanto*. Under subsection (g), the rights and duties created by subsection (b)(3) cannot be waived or varied.

4. **Proof of Assignment.** Subsection (c) links payment with discharge, as in subsection (a). It follows former Section 9-318(3) in referring to the right of the account debtor to pay the assignor if the requested proof of assignment is not seasonably forthcoming. Even if the proof is not forthcoming, the notification of assignment would remain effective, so that, in the absence of reasonable proof of the assignment, the account debtor could discharge the obligation by paying either the assignee or the assignor. Of course, if the assignee did not in fact receive an assignment, the account debtor cannot discharge its obligation by paying a putative assignee who is a stranger. The observations in Comment 3 concerning the reasonableness of an identification of a right to payment also apply here. An account debtor that questions the adequacy of proof submitted by an assignor would be well advised to promptly inform the assignor of the defects.

An account debtor may face another problem if its obligation becomes due while the account debtor is awaiting reasonable proof of the assignment that it has requested from the assignee. This section does not excuse the account debtor from timely compliance with its obligations. Consequently, an account debtor that has received a notification of assignment and who has requested reasonable proof of the assignment may discharge its obligation by paying the assignor at the time (or even earlier if reasonably necessary to avoid risk of default) when a payment is due, even if the account debtor has not yet received a response to its request for proof. On the other hand, after requesting reasonable proof of the assignment, an account debtor may not discharge its obligation by paying the assignor substantially in advance of the time that the payment is due unless the assignee has failed to provide the proof seasonably.

5. **Contractual Restrictions on Assignment.** Former Section 9-318(4) rendered ineffective an agreement between an account debtor and an assignor which prohibited assignment of an account (whether outright or to secure an obligation) or prohibited a security assignment of a general intangible for the payment of money due or to become due. Subsection (d) essentially

follows former Section 9-318(4), but expands the rule of free assignability to chattel paper (subject to Sections 2A-303 and 9-407) and promissory notes and explicitly overrides both restrictions and prohibitions of assignment. The policies underlying the ineffectiveness of contractual restrictions under this section build on common-law developments that essentially have eliminated legal restrictions on assignments of rights to payment as security and other assignments of rights to payment such as accounts and chattel paper. Any that might linger for accounts and chattel paper are addressed by new subsection (f). See Comment 6.

Former Section 9-318(4) did not apply to a sale of a payment intangible (as described in the former provision, "a general intangible for money due or to become due") but did apply to an assignment of a payment intangible for security. Subsection (e) continues this approach and also makes subsection (d) inapplicable to sales of promissory notes. Section 9-408 addresses anti-assignment clauses with respect to sales of payment intangibles and promissory notes.

Like former Section 9-318(4), subsection (d) provides that anti-assignment clauses are "ineffective." The quoted term means that the clause is of no effect whatsoever; the clause does not prevent the assignment from taking effect between the parties and the prohibited assignment does not constitute a default under the agreement between the account debtor and assignor. However, subsection (d) does not override terms that do not directly prohibit, restrict, or require consent to an assignment but which might, nonetheless, present a practical impairment of the assignment. Properly read, however, subsection (d) reaches only covenants that prohibit, restrict, or require consents to assignments; it does not override all terms that might "impair" an assignment in fact.

Example: Buyer enters into an agreement with Seller to buy equipment that Seller is to manufacture according to Buyer's specifications. Buyer agrees to make a series of prepayments during the construction process. In return, Seller agrees to set aside the prepaid funds in a special account and to use the funds solely for the manufacture of the designated equipment. Seller also agrees that it will not assign any of its rights under the sale agreement with Buyer. Nevertheless, Seller grants to Secured Party a security interest in its accounts. Seller's anti-assignment agreement is ineffective under subsection (d); its agreement concerning the use of prepaid funds, which is not a restriction or prohibition on assignment, is not. However, if Secured Party notifies Buyer to make all future payments directly to Secured Party, Buyer will be obliged to do so under subsection (a) if it wishes the payments to discharge its obligation. Unless Secured Party releases the funds to Seller so that Seller can comply with its use-of-funds covenant, Seller will be in breach of that covenant.

In the example, there appears to be a plausible business purpose for the use-of-funds covenant. However, a court may conclude that a covenant with no business purpose other than imposing an impediment to an assignment actually is a direct restriction that is rendered ineffective by subsection (d).

6. **Legal Restrictions on Assignment.** Former Section 9-318(4), like subsection (d) of this section, addressed only contractual restrictions on assignment. The former section was grounded on the reality that legal, as opposed to contractual, restrictions on assignments of rights to payment had largely disappeared. New subsection (f) codifies this principle of free assignability for accounts and chattel paper. For the most part the discussion of contractual restrictions in Comment 5 applies as well to legal restrictions rendered ineffective under subsection (f).

7. **Multiple Assignments.** This section, like former Section 9-318, is not a complete codification of the law of assignments of rights to payment. In particular, it is silent concerning many of the ramifications for an account debtor in cases of multiple assignments of the same right. For example, an assignor might assign the same receivable to multiple assignees (which assignments could be either inadvertent or wrongful). Or, the assignor could assign the receivable to assignee-1, which then might re-assign it to assignee-2, and so forth. The rights and duties of an account debtor in the face of multiple assignments and in other circumstances not resolved in the statutory text are left to the common-law rules. See, e.g., Restatement (2d), Contracts §§ 338(3), 339. The failure of former Article 9 to codify these rules does not appear to have caused problems.

8. **Consumer Account Debtors.** Subsection (h) is new. It makes clear that the rules of this section are subject to other law establishing special rules for consumer account debtors.

9. **Account Debtors on Health-Care-Insurance Receivables.** Subsection (i) also is new. The obligation of an insurer with respect to a health-care-insurance receivable is governed by other law. Section 9-408 addresses contractual and legal restrictions on the assignment of a health-care-insurance receivable.

§ 9-407. RESTRICTIONS ON CREATION OR ENFORCEMENT OF SECURITY INTEREST IN LEASEHOLD INTEREST OR IN LESSOR'S RESIDUAL INTEREST.

(a) [Term restricting assignment generally ineffective.] Except as otherwise provided in subsection (b), a term in a lease agreement is ineffective to the extent that it:

(1) prohibits, restricts, or requires the consent of a party to the lease to the creation, attachment, perfection, or enforcement of a security interest in an interest of a party under the lease contract or in the lessor's residual interest in the goods; or

(2) provides that the creation, attachment, perfection, or enforcement of the security interest may give rise to a default, breach, right of recoupment, claim, defense, termination, right of termination, or remedy under the lease.

(b) [Effectiveness of certain terms.] Except as otherwise provided in Section 2A-303(7), a term described in subsection (a)(2) is effective to the extent that there is:

(1) a transfer by the lessee of the lessee's right of possession or use of the goods in violation of the term; or

(2) a delegation of a material performance of either party to the lease contract in violation of the term.

(c) [Security interest not material impairment.] The creation, attachment, perfection, or enforcement of a security interest in the lessor's interest under the lease contract or the lessor's residual interest in the goods is not a transfer that materially impairs the lessee's prospect of obtaining return performance or materially changes the duty of or materially increases the burden or risk imposed on the lessee within the purview of Section 2A-303(4) unless, and then only to the extent that, enforcement actually results in a delegation of material performance of the lessor.

Official Comment

1. **Source.** Section 2A-303.

2. **Restrictions on Assignment Generally Ineffective.** Under subsection (a), as under former Section 2A-303(3), a term in a lease agreement which prohibits or restricts the creation of a security interest generally is ineffective. This reflects the general policy of Section 9-406(d) and former Section 9-318(4). This section has been conformed in several respects to analogous provisions in Sections 9-406, 9-408, and 9-409, including the substitution of "ineffective" for "not enforceable" and the substitution of "creation, attachment, perfection, or enforcement of a security interest" for "creation or enforcement of a security interest."

3. **Exceptions for Certain Transfers and Delegations.** Subsection (b) provides exceptions to the general ineffectiveness of restrictions under subsection (a). A term that otherwise is ineffective under subsection (a)(2) is effective to the extent that a lessee transfers its right to possession and use of goods or if either party delegates material performance of the lease contract in violation of the term. However, under subsection (c), as under former Section 2A-303(3), a lessor's creation of a security interest in its interest in a lease contract or its residual interest in the leased goods is not a material impairment under Section 2A-303(4) (former Section 2A-303(5)), absent an actual delegation of the lessor's material performance. The terms

of the lease contract determine whether the lessor, in fact, has any remaining obligations to perform. If it does, it is then necessary to determine whether there has been an actual delegation of "material performance." See Section 2A-303, Comments 3 and 4.

§ 9-408. RESTRICTIONS ON ASSIGNMENT OF PROMISSORY NOTES, HEALTH-CARE-INSURANCE RECEIVABLES, AND CERTAIN GENERAL INTANGIBLES INEFFECTIVE.

(a) [Term restricting assignment generally ineffective.] Except as otherwise provided in subsection (b), a term in a promissory note or in an agreement between an account debtor and a debtor which relates to a health-care-insurance receivable or a general intangible, including a contract, permit, license, or franchise, and which term prohibits, restricts, or requires the consent of the person obligated on the promissory note or the account debtor to, the assignment or transfer of, or creation, attachment, or perfection of a security interest in, the promissory note, health-care-insurance receivable, or general intangible, is ineffective to the extent that the term:

(1) would impair the creation, attachment, or perfection of a security interest; or

(2) provides that the creation, attachment, or perfection of the security interest may give rise to a default, breach, right of recoupment, claim, defense, termination, right of termination, or remedy under the promissory note, health-care-insurance receivable, or general intangible.

(b) [Applicability of subsection (a) to sales of certain rights to payment.] Subsection (a) applies to a security interest in a payment intangible or promissory note only if the security interest arises out of a sale of the payment intangible or promissory note.

(c) [Legal restrictions on assignment generally ineffective.] A rule of law, statute, or regulation that prohibits, restricts, or requires the consent of a government, governmental body or official, person obligated on a promissory note, or account debtor to the assignment or transfer of, or creation of a security interest in, a promissory note, health-care-insurance receivable, or general intangible, including a contract, permit, license, or franchise between an account debtor and a debtor, is ineffective to the extent that the rule of law, statute, or regulation:

(1) would impair the creation, attachment, or perfection of a security interest; or

(2) provides that the creation, attachment, or perfection of the security interest may give rise to a default, breach, right of recoupment, claim, defense, termination, right of termination, or remedy under the promissory note, health-care-insurance receivable, or general intangible.

(d) [Limitation on ineffectiveness under subsections (a) and (c).] To the extent that a term in a promissory note or in an agreement between an account debtor and a debtor which relates to a health-care-insurance receivable or general intangible or a rule of law, statute, or regulation described in subsection (c) would be effective under law other than this article but is ineffective under subsection (a) or (c), the creation, attachment, or perfection of a security interest in the promissory note, health-care-insurance receivable, or general intangible:

(1) is not enforceable against the person obligated on the promissory note or the account debtor;

(2) does not impose a duty or obligation on the person obligated on the promissory note or the account debtor;

(3) does not require the person obligated on the promissory note or the account debtor to recognize the security interest, pay or render performance to the secured party, or accept payment or performance from the secured party;

(4) does not entitle the secured party to use or assign the debtor's rights under the promissory note, health-care-insurance receivable, or general intangible, including any related information or materials furnished to the debtor in the transaction giving rise to the promissory note, health-care-insurance receivable, or general intangible;

(5) does not entitle the secured party to use, assign, possess, or have access to any trade secrets or confidential information of the person obligated on the promissory note or the account debtor; and

(6) does not entitle the secured party to enforce the security interest in the promissory note, health-care-insurance receivable, or general intangible.

(e) [Section prevails over specified inconsistent law.] This section prevails over any inconsistent provisions of the following statutes, rules, and regulations:

[List here any statutes, rules, and regulations containing provisions inconsistent with this section.]

Legislative Note: States that amend statutes, rules, and regulations to remove provisions inconsistent with this section need not enact subsection (e).

ANALYSIS

This provision reflects the policy judgment that a debtor should always have the power to create a security interest in its franchises and licenses and to sell its payment intangibles or promissory notes. At least the security interest or the sale should be effective in the debtor's bankruptcy case, even though it does not bind the franchisor, licensor, or obligor on the payment intangible or promissory note that is otherwise protected by a contract provision, statute or regulation. If a broadcast license is sold with FCC approval or a software licensor consents to an assignment of the license in the debtor's bankruptcy, then the financer has a priority claim to the proceeds *vis-a-vis* the debtor's trustee or debtor in possession.

Official Comment

1. **Source.** New.

2. **Free Assignability.** This section makes ineffective any attempt to restrict the assignment of a general intangible, health-care-insurance receivable, or promissory note, whether the restriction appears in the terms of a promissory note or the agreement between an account debtor and a debtor (subsection (a)) or in a rule of law, including a statute or governmental rule or regulation (subsection (c)). This result allows the creation, attachment, and perfection of a security interest in a general intangible, such as an agreement for the nonexclusive license of software, as well as sales of certain receivables, such as a health-care-insurance receivable (which is an "account"), payment intangible, or promissory note, without giving rise to a default or breach by the assignor or from triggering a remedy of the account debtor or person obligated on a promissory note. This enhances the ability of certain debtors to obtain credit. On the other hand, subsection (d) protects the other party-the "account debtor" on a general intangible or the person obligated on a promissory note-from adverse effects arising from the security interest. It leaves the account debtor's or obligated person's rights and obligations unaffected in all material respects if a restriction rendered ineffective by subsection (a) or (c) would be effective under law other than Article 9.

Example 1: A term of an agreement for the nonexclusive license of computer software prohibits the licensee from assigning any of its rights as licensee with respect to the software. The agreement also provides that an attempt to assign rights in violation of the restriction is a default entitling the licensor to terminate the license agreement. The licensee, as debtor, grants to a secured party a security interest in its rights under the license and in the computers in which it is installed. Under this section, the term prohibiting assignment and providing for a default upon an attempted assignment is ineffective to prevent the creation, attachment, or perfection of the security interest or entitle the licensor to terminate the license agreement. However, under subsection (d), the secured party (absent the licensor's agreement) is not entitled to enforce the license or to use, assign, or otherwise enjoy the benefits of the licensed software, and the licensor need not recognize (or pay any attention to) the secured party. Even if the secured party takes possession of the computers on the debtor's default, the debtor would remain free to remove the software from the computer, load it on another computer, and continue to use it, if the license so permits. If the debtor does not remove the software, other law may require the secured party to remove it before disposing of the computer. Disposition of the software with the computer could violate an effective prohibition on enforcement of the security interest. See subsection (d).

3. **Nature of Debtor's Interest.** Neither this section nor any other provision of this Article determines whether a debtor has a property interest. The definition of the term "security interest" provides that it is an "interest in personal property." See Section 1-201(37). Ordinarily, a debtor can create a security interest in collateral only if it has "rights in the collateral." See Section 9-203(b). Other law determines whether a debtor has a property interest ("rights in the collateral") and the nature of that interest. For example, the nonexclusive license addressed in Example 1 may not create any property interest whatsoever in the intellectual property (e.g., copyright) that underlies the license and that effectively enables the licensor to grant the license. The debtor's property interest may be confined solely to its interest in the promises made by the licensor in the license agreement (e.g., a promise not to sue the debtor for its use of the software).

4. **Scope: Sales of Payment Intangibles and Other General Intangibles; Assignments Unaffected by this Section.** Subsections (a) and (c) render ineffective restrictions on assignments only "to the extent" that the assignments restrict the "creation, attachment, or perfection of a security interest," including sales of payment intangibles and promissory notes. This section does not render ineffective a restriction on an assignment that does not create a security interest. For example, if the debtor in Comment 2, Example 1 purported to assign the license to another entity that would use the computer software itself, other law would govern the effectiveness of the anti-assignment provisions.

Subsection (a) applies to a security interest in payment intangibles only if the security interest arises out of sale of the payment intangibles. Contractual restrictions directed to security interests in payment intangibles which secure an obligation are subject to Section 9-406(d). Subsection (a) also deals with sales of promissory notes which also create security interests. See Section 9-109(a). Subsection (c) deals with all security interests in payment intangibles or promissory notes, whether or not arising out of a sale.

Subsection (a) does not render ineffective any term, and subsection (c) does not render ineffective any law, statute or regulation, that restricts outright sales of general intangibles other than payment intangibles. They deal only with restrictions on security interests. The only sales of general intangibles that create security interests are sales of payment intangibles.

5. **Terminology: "Account Debtor"; "Person Obligated on a Promissory Note."** This section uses the term "account debtor" as it is defined in Section 9-102. The term refers to the party, other than the debtor, to a general intangible, including a permit, license, franchise, or the like, and the person obligated on a health-care-insurance receivable, which is a type of account. The definition of "account debtor" does not limit the term to persons who are obligated to *pay* under a general intangible. Rather, the term includes all persons who are obligated on a general intangible, including those who are obligated to render performance in exchange for payment. In some cases, e.g., the creation of a security interest in a franchisee's rights under a franchise agreement, the principal payment obligation may be owed *by* the debtor (franchisee) *to* the account debtor (franchisor). This section also refers to a "person obligated on a promissory note," inasmuch as those persons do not fall within the definition of "account debtor."

Example 2: A licensor and licensee enter into an agreement for the nonexclusive license of computer software. The licensee's interest in the license agreement is a general intangible. If the licensee grants to a secured party a security interest in its rights under the license agreement, the licensee is the debtor and the licensor is the account debtor. On the other hand, if the licensor grants to a secured party a security interest in its right to payment (an account) under the license agreement, the licensor is the debtor and the licensee is the account debtor. (This section applies to the security interest in the general intangible but not to the security interest in the account, which is not a health-care-insurance receivable.)

6. **Effects on Account Debtors and Persons Obligated on Promissory Notes.** Subsections (a) and (c) affect two classes of persons. These subsections affect account debtors on general intangibles and health-care-insurance receivables and persons obligated on promissory notes. Subsection (c) also affects governmental entities that enact or determine rules of law. *However, subsection (d) ensures that these affected persons are not affected adversely.* That provision removes any burdens or adverse effects on these persons for which any rational basis could exist to restrict the effectiveness of an

assignment or to exercise any remedies. For this reason, the effects of subsections (a) and (c) are immaterial insofar as those persons are concerned.

Subsection (a) does not override terms that do not directly prohibit, restrict, or require consent to an assignment but which might, nonetheless, present a practical impairment of the assignment. Properly read, however, this section, like Section 9-406(d), reaches only covenants that prohibit, restrict, or require consents to assignments; it does not override all terms that might "impair" an assignment in fact.

Example 3: A licensor and licensee enter into an agreement for the nonexclusive license of valuable business software. The license agreement includes terms (i) prohibiting the licensee from assigning its rights under the license, (ii) prohibiting the licensee from disclosing to anyone certain information relating to the software and the licensor, and (iii) deeming prohibited assignments and prohibited disclosures to be defaults. The licensee wishes to obtain financing and, in exchange, is willing to grant a security interest in its rights under the license agreement. The secured party, reasonably, refuses to extend credit unless the licensee discloses the information that it is prohibited from disclosing under the license agreement. The secured party cannot determine the value of the proposed collateral in the absence of this information. Under this section, the terms of the license prohibiting the assignment (grant of the security interest) and making the assignment a default are ineffective. However, the nondisclosure covenant is not a term that prohibits the assignment or creation of a security interest in the license. Consequently, the nondisclosure term is enforceable even though the *practical* effect is to restrict the licensee's ability to use its rights under the license agreement as collateral.

The nondisclosure term also would be effective in the factual setting of Comment 2, Example 1. If the secured party's possession of the computers loaded with software would put it in a position to discover confidential information that the debtor was prohibited from disclosing, the licensor should be entitled to enforce its rights against the secured party. Moreover, the licensor could have required the debtor to obtain the secured party's agreement that (i) it would immediately return all copies of software loaded on the computers and that (ii) it would not examine or otherwise acquire any information contained in the software. This section does not prevent an account debtor from protecting by agreement its independent interests that are unrelated to the "creation, attachment, or perfection" of a security interest. In Example 1, moreover, the secured party is not in possession of copies of software by virtue of its security interest or in connection with enforcing its security interest *in the debtor's license of the software*. Its possession is incidental to its possession of the computers, in which it has a security interest. Enforcing against the secured party a restriction relating to the software in no way interferes with its security interest in the computers.

7. Effect in Assignor's Bankruptcy. This section could have a substantial effect if the assignor enters bankruptcy. Roughly speaking, Bankruptcy Code Section 552 invalidates security interests in property acquired after a bankruptcy petition is filed, except to the extent that the postpetition property constitutes proceeds of prepetition collateral.

Example 4: A debtor is the owner of a cable television franchise that, under applicable law, cannot be assigned without the consent of the municipal franchisor. A lender wishes to extend credit to the debtor, provided that the credit is secured by the debtor's "going business" value. To secure the loan, the debtor grants a security interest in all its existing and after-acquired property. The franchise represents the principal value of the business. The municipality refuses to consent to any assignment for collateral purposes. If other law were given effect, the security interest in the franchise would not attach; and if the debtor were to enter bankruptcy and sell the business, the secured party would receive but a fraction of the business's value. Under this section, however, the security interest would attach to the franchise. As a result, the security interest would attach to the proceeds of any sale of the franchise while a bankruptcy is pending. However, this section would protect the interests of the municipality by preventing the secured party from enforcing its security interest to the detriment of the municipality.

8. Effect Outside of Bankruptcy. The principal effects of this section will take place outside of bankruptcy. Compared to the relatively few debtors that enter bankruptcy, there are many more that do not. By making available previously unavailable property as collateral, this section should enable debtors to obtain additional credit. For purposes of determining whether to extend credit, under some circumstances a secured party may ascribe value to the collateral to which its security interest has attached, even if this section precludes the secured party from enforcing the security interest without the agreement of the account debtor or person obligated on the promissory note. This may be the case where the secured party sees a likelihood of obtaining that agreement in the future. This may also be the case where the secured party anticipates that the collateral will give rise to a type of proceeds as to which this section would not apply.

Example 5: Under the facts of Example 4, the debtor does not enter bankruptcy. Perhaps in exchange for a fee, the municipality agrees that the debtor may transfer the franchise to a buyer. As consideration for the transfer, the debtor receives from the buyer its check for part of the purchase price and its promissory note for the balance. The security interest attaches to the check and promissory note as proceeds. See Section 9-315(a)(2). This section does not apply to the security interest in the check, which is not a promissory note, health-care-insurance receivable, or general intangible. Nor does it apply to the security interest in the promissory note, inasmuch as it was not sold to the secured party.

9. **Contrary Federal Law.** This section does not override federal law to the contrary. However, it does reflect an important policy judgment that should provide a template for future federal law reforms.

§ 9-409. RESTRICTIONS ON ASSIGNMENT OF LETTER-OF-CREDIT RIGHTS INEFFECTIVE.

(a) [Term or law restricting assignment generally ineffective.] A term in a letter of credit or a rule of law, statute, regulation, custom, or practice applicable to the letter of credit which prohibits, restricts, or requires the consent of an applicant, issuer, or nominated person to a beneficiary's assignment of or creation of a security interest in a letter-of-credit right is ineffective to the extent that the term or rule of law, statute, regulation, custom, or practice:

(1)   would impair the creation, attachment, or perfection of a security interest in the letter-of-credit right; or

(2)   provides that the creation, attachment, or perfection of the security interest may give rise to a default, breach, right of recoupment, claim, defense, termination, right of termination, or remedy under the letter-of-credit right.

(b) [Limitation on ineffectiveness under subsection (a).] To the extent that a term in a letter of credit is ineffective under subsection (a) but would be effective under law other than this article or a custom or practice applicable to the letter of credit, to the transfer of a right to draw or otherwise demand performance under the letter of credit, or to the assignment of a right to proceeds of the letter of credit, the creation, attachment, or perfection of a security interest in the letter-of-credit right:

(1)   is not enforceable against the applicant, issuer, nominated person, or transferee beneficiary;

(2)   imposes no duties or obligations on the applicant, issuer, nominated person, or transferee beneficiary; and

(3)   does not require the applicant, issuer, nominated person, or transferee beneficiary to recognize the security interest, pay or render performance to the secured party, or accept payment or other performance from the secured party.

Official Comment

1. **Source.** New.

2. **Purpose and Relevance.** This section, patterned on Section 9-408, limits the effectiveness of attempts to restrict the creation, attachment, or perfection of a security interest in letter-of-credit rights, whether the restriction appears in the letter of credit or a rule of law, custom, or practice applicable to the letter of credit. It protects the creation, attachment, and perfection of a security interest while preventing these events from giving rise to a default or breach by the assignor or from triggering a remedy or defense of the issuer or other person obligated on a letter of credit. Letter-of-credit rights are a type of supporting obligation. See Section 9-102. Under Sections 9-203 and 9-308, a security interest in a supporting obligation attaches and is perfected automatically if the security interest in the supported obligation attaches and is perfected. See Section 9-107, Comment 5. The automatic attachment and perfection under Article 9 would be anomalous or misleading if, under other law (e.g., Article 5), a restriction on transfer or assignment were effective to block attachment and perfection.

3. **Relationship to Letter-of-Credit Law.** Although restrictions on an assignment of a letter of credit are ineffective to prevent creation, attachment, and perfection of a security interest, subsection (b) protects the issuer and other parties from any adverse effects of the security interest by preserving letter-of-credit law and practice that limits the right of a beneficiary to transfer its right to draw or otherwise demand performance (Section 5-112) and limits the obligation of an issuer or nominated person to recognize a beneficiary's assignment of letter-of-credit proceeds (Section 5-114). Thus, this section's treatment of letter-of-credit rights differs from this Article's treatment of instruments and investment property. Moreover, under Section 9-109(c)(4), this Article does not apply to the extent that the rights of a transferee beneficiary or nominated person are independent and superior under Section 5-114, thereby preserving the "independence principle" of letter-of-credit law.

PART 5   FILING

[SUBPART 1.   FILING OFFICE; CONTENTS AND EFFECTIVENESS OF FINANCING STATEMENT]

§ 9-501.   FILING OFFICE.

(a)   [Filing offices.] Except as otherwise provided in subsection (b), if the local law of this State governs perfection of a security interest or agricultural lien, the office in which to file a financing statement to perfect the security interest or agricultural lien is:

(1)   the office designated for the filing or recording of a record of a mortgage on the related real property, if:

(A)   the collateral is as-extracted collateral or timber to be cut; or

(B)   the financing statement is filed as a fixture filing and the collateral is goods that are or are to become fixtures; or

(2)   the office of [ ] [or any office duly authorized by [ ]], in all other cases, including a case in which the collateral is goods that are or are to become fixtures and the financing statement is not filed as a fixture filing.

(b)   [Filing office for transmitting utilities.] The office in which to file a financing statement to perfect a security interest in collateral, including fixtures, of a transmitting utility is the office of [ ]. The financing statement also constitutes a fixture filing as to the collateral indicated in the financing statement which is or is to become fixtures.

Legislative Note: The State should designate the filing office where the brackets appear. The filing office may be that of a governmental official (e.g., the Secretary of State) or a private party that maintains the State's filing system.

ANALYSIS

Under Revised Article 9, the only local filings will be real estate related filings (as extracted collateral, timber to be cut or fixture filings). As to the havoc caused by local filing requirements under old Article 9, see *Secured Transactions* Chapter 6. Time will tell whether all state legislatures will be able to accept the idea that non-real estate related filings must be at the state level.

Official Comment

1. **Source.** Derived from former Section 9-401.

2. **Where to File.** Subsection (a) indicates where in a given State a financing statement is to be filed. Former Article 9 afforded each State three alternative approaches, depending on the extent to which the State desires central filing (usually with the Secretary of State), local filing (usually with a county office), or both. As Comment 1 to former Section 9-401 observed, "The principal advantage of state-wide filing is ease of access to the credit information which the files exist to provide. Consider for example the national distributor who wishes to have current information about the credit standing of the thousands of persons he sells to on credit. The more completely the files are centralized on a state-wide basis, the easier and cheaper it becomes to procure credit information; the more the files are scattered in local filing units, the more burdensome and costly." Local filing increases the net costs of secured transactions also by increasing uncertainty and the number of required filings. Any benefit that local filing may have had in the 1950's is now insubstantial. Accordingly, this Article dictates central filing for most situations, while retaining local filing for real-estate-related collateral and special filing provisions for transmitting utilities.

3. **Minerals and Timber.** Under subsection (a)(1), a filing in the office where a record of a mortgage on the related real property would be filed will perfect a security interest in as-extracted collateral. Inasmuch as the security interest does not attach until extraction, the filing continues to be effective after extraction. A different result occurs with respect to timber to be cut, however. Unlike as-extracted collateral, standing timber may be goods before it is cut. See Section 9-102 (defining "goods"). Once cut, however, it is no longer timber *to be* cut, and the filing in the real-property-mortgage office ceases to be effective. The timber then becomes ordinary goods, and filing in the office specified in subsection (a)(2) is necessary for perfection. Note also that after the timber is cut the law of the debtor's location, not the location of the timber, governs perfection under Section 9-301.

4. **Fixtures.** There are two ways in which a secured party may file a financing statement to perfect a security interest in goods that are or are to become fixtures. It may file in the Article 9 records, as with most other goods. See subsection (a)(2). Or it may file the financing statement as a "fixture filing," defined in Section 9-102, in the office in which a record of a mortgage on the related real property would be filed. See subsection (a)(1)(B).

5. **Transmitting Utilities.** The usual filing rules do not apply well for a transmitting utility (defined in Section 9-102). Many pre-UCC statutes provided special filing rules for railroads and in some cases for other public utilities, to avoid the requirements for filing with legal descriptions in every county in which such debtors had property. Former Section 9-401(5) recreated and broadened these provisions, and subsection (b) follows this approach. The nature of the debtor will inform persons searching the record as to where to make a search.

§ 9-502. CONTENTS OF FINANCING STATEMENT; RECORD OF MORTGAGE AS FINANCING STATEMENT; TIME OF FILING FINANCING STATEMENT.

(a) [Sufficiency of financing statement.] Subject to subsection (b), a financing statement is sufficient only if it:

(1)   provides the name of the debtor;

(2)   provides the name of the secured party or a representative of the secured party; and

(3)   indicates the collateral covered by the financing statement.

ANALYSIS

A secured creditor could be misled by this subsection. As a practical matter, the *other requirements* for a financing statement (*e.g.*, name and mailing address of the secured party, mailing address of debtor, whether debtor is an individual or organization, the type and jurisdiction of the organization and its identification number, if it has one) are stated in new § 9-516(b). The requirements in new § 9-516(b) come into play only if the filing office refuses to accept a financing statement because of their omission. But under new § 9-520(a), the filing office is directed to reject a filing that fails to satisfy the additional requirements of § 9-516(b). To understand what Revised Article 9 changes, one must compare new §§ 9-502 and 9-516 with old § 9-402. There is no longer any requirement that the debtor sign the financing statement, only that the debtor authorize the filing under new § 9-509. There is no longer a need for a description of the real estate in the case of growing crops. If the statement is rejected by the filing office (as it should be) because it fails to contain the debtor's mailing address or the new information required by § 9-516(b)(5)(B) & (C), it will be ineffective. Thus, the only sane course is for the creditor to assure that the statement contains the creditor's name and mailing address (as with UCC-1's under old Article 9), as well as gives an indication as to whether the debtor is an individual or organization and, in the case of an organization, the type, jurisdiction and organizational ID number of the entity (all information not required at all under the uniform version of old Article 9).

(b) [Real-property-related financing statements.] Except as otherwise provided in Section 9-501(b), to be sufficient, a financing statement that covers as-extracted collateral or timber to be cut, or which is filed as a fixture filing and covers goods that are or are to become fixtures, must satisfy subsection (a) and also:

(1)   indicate that it covers this type of collateral;

(2)   indicate that it is to be filed [for record] in the real property records;

(3)   provide a description of the real property to which the collateral is related [sufficient to give constructive notice of a mortgage under the law of this State if the description were contained in a record of the mortgage of the real property]; and

(4)   if the debtor does not have an interest of record in the real property, provide the name of a record owner.

(c) [Record of mortgage as financing statement.] A record of a mortgage is effective, from the date of recording, as a financing statement filed as a fixture filing or as a financing statement covering as-extracted collateral or timber to be cut only if:

(1)   the record indicates the goods or accounts that it covers;

(2)   the goods are or are to become fixtures related to the real property described in the record or the collateral is related to the real property described in the record and is as-extracted collateral or timber to be cut;

(3)   the record satisfies the requirements for a financing statement in this section other than an indication that it is to be filed in the real property records; and

(4)   the record is [duly] recorded.

(d) [Filing before security agreement or attachment.] A financing statement may be filed before a security agreement is made or a security interest otherwise attaches.

Legislative Note: Language in brackets is optional. Where the State has any special recording system for real property other than the usual grantor-grantee index (as, for instance, a tract system or a title registration or Torrens system) local adaptations of subsection (b) and Section 9-519(d) and (e) may be necessary. See, e.g., Mass. Gen. Laws Chapter 106, Section 9-410.

Official Comment

1. **Source.** Former Section 9-402(1), (5), (6).

2. **"Notice Filing."** This section adopts the system of "notice filing." What is required to be filed is not, as under pre-UCC chattel mortgage and conditional sales acts, the security agreement itself, but only a simple record providing a limited amount of information (financing statement). The financing statement may be filed before the security interest attaches or thereafter. See subsection (d). See also Section 9-308(a) (contemplating situations in which a financing statement is filed before a security interest attaches).

The notice itself indicates merely that a person may have a security interest in the collateral indicated. Further inquiry from the parties concerned will be necessary to disclose the complete state of affairs. Section 9-210 provides a statutory procedure under which the secured party, at the debtor's request, may be required to make disclosure. However, in many cases, information may be forthcoming without the need to resort to the formalities of that section.

Notice filing has proved to be of great use in financing transactions involving inventory, accounts, and chattel paper, because it obviates the necessity of refiling on each of a series of transactions in a continuing arrangement under which the collateral changes from day to day. However, even in the case of filings that do not necessarily involve a series of transactions (e.g., a loan secured by a single item of equipment), a financing statement is effective to encompass transactions under a security agreement not in existence and not contemplated at the time the notice was filed, if the indication of collateral in the financing statement is sufficient to cover the collateral concerned. Similarly, a financing statement is effective to cover after-acquired property of the type indicated and to perfect with respect to future advances under security agreements, regardless of whether after-acquired property or future advances are mentioned in the financing statement and even if not in the contemplation of the parties at the time the financing statement was authorized to be filed.

3. **Debtor's Signature; Required Authorization.** Subsection (a) sets forth the simple formal requirements for an effective financing statement. These requirements are: (1) the debtor's name; (2) the name of a secured party or representative of the secured party; and (3) an indication of the collateral.

Whereas former Section 9-402(1) required the debtor's signature to appear on a financing statement, this Article contains no signature requirement. The elimination of the signature requirement facilitates paperless filing. (However, as PEB Commentary No. 15 indicates, a paperless financing statement was sufficient under former Article 9.) Elimination of the signature requirement also makes the exceptions provided by former Section 9-402(2) unnecessary.

The fact that this Article does not require that an authenticating symbol be contained in the public record does not mean that all filings are authorized. Rather, Section 9-509(a) entitles a person to file an initial financing statement, an amendment that adds collateral, or an amendment that adds a debtor only if the debtor authorizes the filing, and Section 9-509(d) entitles a person other than the debtor to file a termination statement only if the secured party of record authorizes the filing. Of course, a filing has legal effect only to the extent it is authorized. See Section 9-510.

Law other than this Article, including the law with respect to ratification of past acts, generally determines whether a person has the requisite authority to file a record under this Article. See Section 1-103. However, under Section 9-509(b), the debtor's authentication of (or becoming bound by) a security agreement *ipso facto* constitutes the debtor's authorization of the filing of a financing statement covering the collateral described in the security agreement. The secured party need not obtain a separate authorization.

Section 9-625 provides a remedy for unauthorized filings. Making an unauthorized filing also may give rise to civil or criminal liability under other law. In addition, this Article contains provisions that assist in the discovery of unauthorized filings and the amelioration of their practical effect. For example, Section 9-518 provides a procedure whereby a person may add to the public record a statement to the effect that a financing statement indexed under the person's name was wrongfully filed, and Section 9-509(d) entitles any person to file a termination statement if the secured party of record fails to comply with its obligation to file or send one to the debtor, the debtor authorizes the filing, and the termination statement so indicates. However, the filing office is neither obligated nor permitted to inquire into issues of authorization. See Section 9-520(a).

4. **Certain Other Requirements.** Subsection (a) deletes other provisions of former Section 9-402(1) because they seems unwise (real-property description for financing statements covering crops), unnecessary (adequacy of copies of financing statements), or both (copy of security agreement as financing statement). In addition, the filing office must reject a financing statement lacking certain other information formerly required as a condition of perfection (e.g., an address for the debtor or secured party). See Sections 9-516(b), 9-520(a). However, if the filing office accepts the record, it is effective nevertheless. See Section 9-520(c).

5. **Real-Property-Related Filings.** Subsection (b) contains the requirements for financing statements filed as fixture filings and financing statements covering timber to be cut or minerals and minerals-related accounts constituting as-extracted collateral. A description of the related real property must

be sufficient to reasonably identify it. See Section 9-108. This formulation rejects the view that the real property description must be by metes and bounds, or otherwise conforming to traditional real-property practice in conveyancing, but, of course, the incorporation of such a description by reference to the recording data of a deed, mortgage or other instrument containing the description should suffice under the most stringent standards. The proper test is that a description of real property must be sufficient so that the financing statement will fit into the real-property search system and be found by a real-property searcher. Under the optional language in subsection (b)(3), the test of adequacy of the description is whether it would be adequate in a record of a mortgage of the real property. As suggested in the Legislative Note, more detail may be required if there is a tract indexing system or a land registration system.

If the debtor does not have an interest of record in the real property, a real-property-related financing statement must show the name of a record owner, and Section 9-519(d) requires the financing statement to be indexed in the name of that owner. This requirement also enables financing statements covering as-extracted collateral or timber to be cut and financing statements filed as fixture filings to fit into the real-property search system.

6. **Record of Mortgage Effective as Financing Statement.** Subsection (c) explains when a record of a mortgage is effective as a financing statement filed as a fixture filing or to cover timber to be cut or as-extracted collateral. Use of the term "record of a mortgage" recognizes that in some systems the record actually filed is not the record pursuant to which a mortgage is created. Moreover, "mortgage" is defined in Section 9-102 as an "interest in real property," not as the record that creates or evidences the mortgage or the record that is filed in the public recording systems. A record creating a mortgage may also create a security interest with respect to fixtures (or other goods) in conformity with this Article. A single agreement creating a mortgage on real property and a security interest in chattels is common and useful for certain purposes. Under subsection (c), the recording of the record evidencing a mortgage (if it satisfies the requirements for a financing statement) constitutes the filing of a financing statement as to the fixtures (but not, of course, as to other goods). Section 9-515(g) makes the usual five-year maximum life for financing statements inapplicable to mortgages that operate as fixture filings under Section 9-502(c). Such mortgages are effective for the duration of the real-property recording.

Of course, if a combined mortgage covers chattels that are not fixtures, a regular financing statement filing is necessary with respect to the chattels, and subsection (c) is inapplicable. Likewise, a financing statement filed as a "fixture filing" is not effective to perfect a security interest in personal property other than fixtures.

In some cases it may be difficult to determine whether goods are or will become fixtures. Nothing in this Part prohibits the filing of a "precautionary" fixture filing, which would provide protection in the event goods are determined to be fixtures. The fact of filing should not be a factor in the determining whether goods are fixtures. Cf. Section 9-505(b).

§ 9-503. NAME OF DEBTOR AND SECURED PARTY.

(a) [Sufficiency of debtor's name.] A financing statement sufficiently provides the name of the debtor:

(1) if the debtor is a registered organization, only if the financing statement provides the name of the debtor indicated on the public record of the debtor's jurisdiction of organization which shows the debtor to have been organized;

(2) if the debtor is a decedent's estate, only if the financing statement provides the name of the decedent and indicates that the debtor is an estate;

(3) if the debtor is a trust or a trustee acting with respect to property held in trust, only if the financing statement:

(A) provides the name specified for the trust in its organic documents or, if no name is specified, provides the name of the settlor and additional information sufficient to distinguish the debtor from other trusts having one or more of the same settlors; and

(B) indicates, in the debtor's name or otherwise, that the debtor is a trust or is a trustee acting with respect to property held in trust; and

(4) in other cases:

(A) if the debtor has a name, only if it provides the individual or organizational name of the debtor; and

(B) if the debtor does not have a name, only if it provides the names of the partners, members, associates, or other persons comprising the debtor.

(b) [Additional debtor-related information.] A financing statement that provides the name of the debtor in accordance with subsection (a) is not rendered ineffective by the absence of:

(1) a trade name or other name of the debtor; or

(2) unless required under subsection (a)(4)(B), names of partners, members, associates, or other persons comprising the debtor.

(c) [Debtor's trade name insufficient.] A financing statement that provides only the debtor's trade name does not sufficiently provide the name of the debtor.

(d) [Representative capacity.] Failure to indicate the representative capacity of a secured party or representative of a secured party does not affect the sufficiency of a financing statement.

(e) [Multiple debtors and secured parties.] A financing statement may provide the name of more than one debtor and the name of more than one secured party.

ANALYSIS

For the case law on trade name filings under the old Article 9, see *Secured Transactions* § 22.02. New § 9-503(c) would override cases in the Fifth and Eleventh Circuits upholding trade name filings in circumstances where the courts believed that a searcher should have searched under the trade name. This provision must be read together with § 9-506 as to what constitutes a seriously misleading mistake as to the debtor's name.

Official Comment

1. **Source.** Subsections (a)(4)(A), (b), and (c) derive from former Section 9-402(7); otherwise, new.

2. **Debtor's Name.** The requirement that a financing statement provide the debtor's name is particularly important. Financing statements are indexed under the name of the debtor, and those who wish to find financing statements search for them under the debtor's name. Subsection (a) explains what the debtor's name is for purposes of a financing statement. If the debtor is a "registered organization" (defined in Section 9-102 so as to ordinarily include corporations, limited partnerships, and limited liability companies), then the debtor's name is the name shown on the public records of the debtor's "jurisdiction of organization" (also defined in Section 9-102). Subsections (a)(2) and (a)(3) contain special rules for decedent's estates and common-law trusts. (Subsection (a)(1) applies to business trusts that are registered organizations.)

Subsection (a)(4)(A) essentially follows the first sentence of former Section 9-402(7). Section 1-201(28) defines the term "organization," which appears in subsection (a)(4), very broadly, to include all legal and commercial entities as well as associations that lack the status of a legal entity. Thus, the term includes corporations, partnerships of all kinds, business trusts, limited liability companies, unincorporated associations, personal trusts, governments, and estates. If the organization has a name, that name is the correct name to put on a financing statement. If the organization does not have a name, then the financing statement should name the individuals or other entities who comprise the organization.

Together with subsections (b) and (c), subsection (a) reflects the view prevailing under former Article 9 that the actual individual or organizational name of the debtor on a financing statement is both necessary and sufficient, whether or not the financing statement provides trade or other names of the debtor and, if the debtor has a name, whether or not the financing statement provides the names of the partners, members, or associates who comprise the debtor.

Note that, even if the name provided in an initial financing statement is correct, the filing office nevertheless must reject the financing statement if does not identify an individual debtor's last name (e.g., if it is not clear whether the debtor's name is Perry Mason or Mason Perry). See Section 9-516(b)(3)(C).

3. **Secured Party's Name.** New subsection (d) makes clear that when the secured party is a representative, a financing statement is sufficient if it names the secured party, whether or not it indicates any representative capacity. Similarly, a financing statement that names a representative of the secured party is sufficient, even if it does not indicate the representative capacity.

Example: Debtor creates a security interest in favor of Bank X, Bank Y, and Bank Z, but not to their representative, the collateral agent (Bank A). The collateral agent is not itself a secured party. See Section 9-102. Under Sections 9-502(a) and 9-503(d), however, a financing statement is effective if it names as secured party Bank A and not the actual secured parties, even if it omits Bank A's representative capacity.

Each person whose name is provided in an initial financing statement as the name of the secured party or representative of the secured party is a secured party of record. See Section 9-511.

4. **Multiple Names.** Subsection (e) makes explicit what is implicit under former Article 9: a financing statement may provide the name of more than one debtor and secured party. See Section 1-102(5)(a) (words in the singular include the plural). With respect to records relating to more than one debtor, see Section 9-520(d). With respect to financing statements providing the name of more than one secured party, see Sections 9-509(e) and 9-510(b).

§ 9-504. INDICATION OF COLLATERAL. A financing statement sufficiently indicates the collateral that it covers only if the financing statement provides:

(1) a description of the collateral pursuant to Section 9-108; or

(2) an indication that the financing statement covers all assets or all personal property.

ANALYSIS

The drafting attention with respect to this provision has been on the approval of super-generic descriptions ("all assets," "all personal property") for financing statements in new § 9-504(2). The text itself states that a secured party has the alternatives of describing the collateral or indicating that all assets or all personal property are covered. However, Official Comment 2 to this section creates some uncertainty as to whether super-generic descriptions will always be acceptable. By stating that the provision is designed to accommodate creditors when they create an interest in all, or substantially all, of a debtor's assets, the Commentary opens the door to courts refusing to permit super-generic descriptions when the security agreement claims only one or some narrower category of the debtor's assets. *See* U.C.C. § 1-102 and Official Comment 1 thereto (each section should be read in light of its purpose). However, this Commentary also seems to recognize that a financing statement may cover a broader range of assets than a security agreement with the security agreement, defining the actual reach of the creditor's security interests. Moreover, other Commentary in the Revision blesses super-generic description in a financing statement without limitation. *See* new § 9-101, comment 4(h); new § 9-108 comment 2. In addition, new § 9-502(d) continues the authorization for filings before "a security agreement is made or a security interest otherwise attaches." If a court decides to read implied restrictions into new § 9-504, how would it handle a prospective filing made before the parties have agreed to what the collateral will be? Would super-generics be permissible so long as the parties contemplated the possibility of later covering all assets, or only when an existing agreement covers all assets?

This issue of when to permit the super-generic descriptions is very important. If the courts stay with the text of Section 9-504 itself, avoid complications as to prospective filings and hold that such descriptions are always sufficient, financers will be tempted to pre-print forms always using the super-generic language, thus providing no public information for the searcher as to what the security arrangement actually covers. In addition, universal approval of super-generics could work together with the priority rule in new § 9-317(a)(2) allowing secured creditors to trump lien creditors based on filing alone to encourage filings against debtors to assure priority over lien creditors years later even though no financing is currently planned or anticipated. This approval may also work with new § 9-512 which will allow a filer to sell or assign its priority by filing an amendment changing the name of the secured creditor.

Institutional creditors may get in the habit of making advance "preemptive" filings against all assets of debtor firms. They only need the debtor's authorization to make filing and they can argue that the authorization and filing do not themselves create any interest. Debtors who are not well-advised may give the authorization thinking that their cooperation will impress the big-time finance. Or debtors may authorize a friend to file planning for the friend to later sell its priority to financer, which will have priority over intervening lien creditors and secured creditors unable to trump the friend's priority. *See* the text analysis to new § 9-317.

Ironically, at the same time that this provision blesses super-generic descriptions, it tightens the requirements for other descriptions. Old § 9-402(1) gave the creditor the option of "indicating the types" or "describing the items" of collateral. Properly construed, this language did not demand an identifying description of the collateral in a financing statement. "Accounts" or "Equipment" were sufficient, if inartful, under the old Article 9 because they indicated the type of collateral. *See Secured Transactions* § 6C.05[7][d]. The revised article eliminates the option of "indicating the types." All collateral designations must be identifying under new § 9-108. "Accounts" or "Equipment" arguably will not do, though "all accounts" or "all equipment" should be sufficient. One could even argue that this change supports reading new § 9-504(1) as permitting super-generics only when they are descriptive of the security interest actually held by the creditor.

Official Comment

1. **Source.** Former Section 9-402(1).

2. **Indication of Collateral.** To comply with Section 9-502(a), a financing statement must "indicate" the collateral it covers. This section explains what suffices for an indication.

Paragraph (1) provides that a "description" of the collateral (as the term is explained in Section 9-108) suffices as an indication for purposes of the sufficiency of a financing statement.

Debtors sometimes create a security interest in all, or substantially all, of their assets. To accommodate this practice, paragraph (2) expands the class of sufficient collateral references to embrace "an indication that the financing statement covers all assets or all personal property." If the property in question belongs to the debtor and is personal property, any searcher will know that the property is covered by the financing statement. Of course, regardless of its breadth, a financing statement has no effect with respect to property indicated but to which a security interest has not attached. Note that a broad statement of this kind (e.g., "all debtor's personal property") would not be a sufficient "description" for purposes of a security agreement. See Sections 9-203(b)(3)(A), 9-108. It follows that a somewhat narrower description than "all assets," e.g., "all assets other than automobiles," is sufficient for purposes of this section, even if it does not suffice for purposes of a security agreement.

§ 9-505. FILING AND COMPLIANCE WITH OTHER STATUTES AND TREATIES FOR CONSIGNMENTS, LEASES, OTHER BAILMENTS, AND OTHER TRANSACTIONS.

(a) **[Use of terms other than "debtor" and "secured party."]** A consignor, lessor, or other bailor of goods, a licensor, or a buyer of a payment intangible or promissory note may file a financing statement, or may comply with a statute or treaty described in Section 9-311(a), using the terms "consignor", "consignee", "lessor", "lessee", "bailor", "bailee", "licensor", "licensee", "owner", "registered owner", "buyer", "seller", or words of similar import, instead of the terms "secured party" and "debtor".

(b) **[Effect of financing statement under subsection (a).]** This part applies to the filing of a financing statement under subsection (a) and, as appropriate, to compliance that is equivalent to filing a financing statement under Section 9-311(b), but the filing or compliance is not of itself a factor in determining whether the collateral secures an obligation. If it is determined for another reason that the collateral secures an obligation, a security interest held by the consignor, lessor, bailor, licensor, owner, or buyer which attaches to the collateral is perfected by the filing or compliance.

Official Comment

1. **Source.** Former Section 9-408.

2. **Precautionary Filing.** Occasionally, doubts arise concerning whether a transaction creates a relationship to which this Article or its filing provisions apply. For example, questions may arise over whether a "lease" of equipment in fact creates a security interest or whether the "sale" of payment intangibles in fact secures an obligation, thereby requiring action to perfect the security interest. This section, which derives from former Section 9-408, affords the option of filing of a financing statement with appropriate changes of terminology but without affecting the substantive question of classification of the transaction.

3. **Changes from Former Section 9-408.** This section expands the rule of Section 9-408 to embrace more generally other bailments and transactions, as well as sales transactions, primarily sales of payment intangibles and promissory notes. It provides the same benefits for compliance with a statute or treaty described in Section 9-311(a) that former Section 9-408 provided

for filing, in connection with the use of terms such as "lessor," "consignor," etc. The references to "owner" and "registered owner" are intended to address, for example, the situation where a putative lessor is the registered owner of an automobile covered by a certificate of title and the transaction is determined to create a security interest. Although this section provides that the security interest is perfected, the relevant certificate-of-title statute may expressly provide to the contrary or may be ambiguous. If so, it may be necessary or advisable to amend the certificate-of-title statute to ensure that perfection of the security interest will be achieved.

As does Section 1-201, former Article 9 referred to transactions, including leases and consignments, "intended as security." This misleading phrase created the erroneous impression that the parties to a transaction can dictate how the law will classify it (e.g., as a bailment or as a security interest) and thus affect the rights of third parties. This Article deletes the phrase wherever it appears. Subsection (b) expresses the principle more precisely by referring to a security interest that "secures an obligation."

4. **Consignments.** Although a "true" consignment is a bailment, the filing and priority provisions of former Article 9 applied to "true" consignments. See former Sections 2-326(3), 9-114. A consignment "intended as security" created a security interest that was in all respects subject to former Article 9. This Article subsumes most true consignments under the rubric of "security interest." See Sections 9-102 (definition of "consignment"), 9-109(a)(4), 1-201(37) (definition of "security interest"). Nevertheless, it maintains the distinction between a (true) "consignment," as to which only certain aspects of Article 9 apply, and a so-called consignment that actually "secures an obligation," to which Article 9 applies in full. The revisions to this section reflect the change in terminology.

§ 9-506. EFFECT OF ERRORS OR OMISSIONS.

(a) **[Minor errors and omissions.]** A financing statement substantially satisfying the requirements of this part is effective, even if it has minor errors or omissions, unless the errors or omissions make the financing statement seriously misleading.

(b) **[Financing statement seriously misleading.]** Except as otherwise provided in subsection (c), a financing statement that fails sufficiently to provide the name of the debtor in accordance with Section 9-503(a) is seriously misleading.

(c) **[Financing statement not seriously misleading.]** If a search of the records of the filing office under the debtor's correct name, using the filing office's standard search logic, if any, would disclose a financing statement that fails sufficiently to provide the name of the debtor in accordance with Section 9-503(a), the name provided does not make the financing statement seriously misleading.

ANALYSIS

This test reflects the reasoning of the perceptive cases dealing with name sufficiency under the old Article 9. *See Secured Transactions* § 6C.02[4].

(d) ["Debtor's correct name."] For purposes of Section 9-508(b), the "debtor's correct name" in subsection (c) means the correct name of the new debtor.

Official Comment

1. **Source.** Former Section 9-402(8).

2. **Errors.** Like former Section 9-402(8), subsection (a) is in line with the policy of this Article to simplify formal requisites and filing requirements. It is designed to discourage the fanatical and impossibly refined reading of statutory requirements in which courts occasionally have indulged themselves. Subsection (a) provides the standard applicable to indications of collateral. Subsections (b) and (c), which are new, concern the effectiveness of financing statements in which the debtor's name is incorrect. Subsection (b) contains the general rule: a financing statement that fails sufficiently to provide the debtor's name in accordance with Section 9-503(a) is seriously misleading as a matter of law. Subsection (c) provides an exception: If the financing statement nevertheless would be discovered in a search under the debtor's correct name, using the filing office's standard search logic, if any, then as a matter of law the incorrect name does not make the financing statement seriously misleading. A financing statement that is seriously misleading under this section is ineffective even if it is disclosed by (i) using a search logic other than that of the filing office to search the official records, or (ii) using the filing office's standard search logic to search a data base other than that of the filing office.

In addition to requiring the debtor's name and an indication of the collateral, Section 9-502(a) requires a financing statement to provide the name of the secured party or a representative of the secured party. Inasmuch as searches are not conducted under the secured party's name, and no filing is needed to continue the perfected status of security interest after it is assigned, an error in the name of the secured party or its representative will not be seriously misleading. However, in an appropriate case, an error of this kind may give rise to an estoppel in favor of a particular holder of a conflicting claim to the collateral. See Section 1-103.

3. **New Debtors.** Subsection (d) provides that, in determining the extent to which a financing statement naming an original debtor is effective against a new debtor, the sufficiency of financing statement should be tested against the name of the new debtor.

§ 9-507. EFFECT OF CERTAIN EVENTS ON EFFECTIVENESS OF FINANCING STATEMENT.

(a) **[Disposition.]** A filed financing statement remains effective with respect to collateral that is sold, exchanged, leased, licensed, or otherwise disposed of and in which a security interest or agricultural lien continues, even if the secured party knows of or consents to the disposition.

(b) **[Information becoming seriously misleading.]** Except as otherwise provided in subsection (c) and Section 9-508, a financing statement is not rendered ineffective if, after the financing statement is filed, the information provided in the financing statement becomes seriously misleading under Section 9-506.

(c) **[Change in debtor's name.]** If a debtor so changes its name that a filed financing statement becomes seriously misleading under Section 9-506:

(1) the financing statement is effective to perfect a security interest in collateral acquired by the debtor before, or within four months after, the change; and

(2) the financing statement is not effective to perfect a security interest in collateral acquired by the debtor more than four months after the change, unless an amendment to the financing statement which renders the financing statement not seriously misleading is filed within four months after the change.

ANALYSIS

The general rule of new § 9-507(b) is that post-filing changes that do not involve the debtor's name do not matter. For example, a change in address of the debtor or secured party would not itself impair a filing. The same would be true of a change in the organizational number of the debtor required by new § 9-516(b)(5). What if the debtor's usage of the collateral changes so as to change its classification in the Article 9 scheme of defined types? For example, after a filing against inventory alone, the debtor appliance store removes an air-conditioner from its inventory and uses it as equipment to cool its own store. Is the information in the filing now "seriously misleading" or simply inapplicable to the air-conditioner? Apparently, the revisers also intended for this type of post-filing change to have no effect, though one could wonder if the statutory language is sufficient to produce the intended result.

Official Comment

1. **Source.** Former Section 9-402(7).

2. **Scope of Section.** This section deals with situations in which the information in a proper financing statement becomes inaccurate after the financing statement is filed. Compare Section 9-338, which deals with situations in which a financing statement contains a particular kind of information concerning the debtor (i.e., the information described in Section 9-516(b)(5)) that is incorrect at the time it is filed.

3. **Post-Filing Disposition of Collateral.** Under subsection (a), a financing statement remains effective even if the collateral is sold or otherwise disposed of. This subsection clarifies the third sentence of former Section 9-402(7) by providing that a financing statement remains effective following the disposition of collateral only when the security interest or agricultural lien continues in that collateral. This result is consistent with the conclusion of PEB Commentary No. 3. Normally, a security interest does continue after disposition of the collateral. See Section 9-315(a). Law other than this Article determines whether an agricultural lien survives disposition of the collateral.

As a consequence of the disposition, the collateral may be owned by a person other than the debtor against whom the financing statement was filed. Under subsection (a), the secured party remains perfected even if it does not correct the public record. For this reason, any person seeking to determine whether a debtor owns collateral free of security interests must inquire as to the debtor's source of title and, if circumstances seem to require it, search in the name of a former owner. Subsection (a) addresses only the sufficiency of the information contained in the financing statement. A disposition of collateral may result in loss of perfection for other reasons. See Section 9-316.

Example: Dee Corp. is an Illinois corporation. It creates a security interest in its equipment in favor of Secured Party. Secured Party files a proper financing statement in Illinois. Dee Corp. sells an item of equipment to Bee Corp., a Pennsylvania corporation, subject to the security interest. The security interest continues, see Section 9-315(a), and remains perfected, see Section 9-507(a), notwithstanding that the financing statement is filed under "D" (for Dee Corp.) and not under "B." However, because Bee Corp. is located in Pennsylvania and not Illinois, see Section 9-307, unless Secured Party perfects under Pennsylvania law within one year after the transfer, its security interest will become unperfected and will be deemed to have been unperfected against purchasers of the collateral. See Section 9-316.

4. **Other Post-Filing Changes.** Subsection (b) provides that, as a general matter, post-filing changes that render a financing statement inaccurate and seriously misleading have no effect on a financing statement. The financing statement remains effective. It is subject to two exceptions: Section 9-508 and Section 9-507(c). Section 9-508 addresses the effectiveness of a financing statement filed against an original debtor when a new debtor becomes bound by the original debtor's security agreement. It is discussed in the Comments to that section. Section 9-507(c) addresses a "pure" change of the debtor's name, i.e., a change that does not implicate a new debtor. It clarifies former Section 9-402(7). If a name change renders a filed financing statement seriously misleading, the financing statement is not effective as to collateral acquired more than four months after the change, unless before the expiration of the four months an amendment is filed that specifies the debtor's new correct name (or provides an incorrect name that renders the financing statement not seriously misleading under Section 9-506). As under former Section 9-402(7), the original financing statement would continue to be effective with respect to collateral acquired before the name change as well as collateral acquired within the four-month period.

§ 9-508. EFFECTIVENESS OF FINANCING STATEMENT IF NEW DEBTOR BECOMES BOUND BY SECURITY AGREEMENT.

(a) [Financing statement naming original debtor.] Except as otherwise provided in this section, a filed financing statement naming an original debtor is effective to perfect a security interest in collateral in which a new debtor has or acquires rights to the extent that the financing statement would have been effective had the original debtor acquired rights in the collateral.

(b) [Financing statement becoming seriously misleading.] If the difference between the name of the original debtor and that of the new debtor causes a filed financing statement that is effective under subsection (a) to be seriously misleading under Section 9-506:

(1) the financing statement is effective to perfect a security interest in collateral acquired by the new debtor before, and within four months after, the new debtor becomes bound under Section 9-203(d); and

(2) the financing statement is not effective to perfect a security interest in collateral acquired by the new debtor more than four months after the new debtor becomes bound under Section

9-203(d) unless an initial financing statement providing the name of the new debtor is filed before the expiration of that time.

(c) [When section not applicable.] This section does not apply to collateral as to which a filed financing statement remains effective against the new debtor under Section 9-507(a).

Official Comment

1. **Source.** New.

2. **The Problem.** Section 9-203(d) and (e) and this section deal with situations where one party (the "new debtor") becomes bound as debtor by a security agreement entered into by another person (the "original debtor"). These situations often arise as a consequence of changes in business structure. For example, the original debtor may be an individual debtor who operates a business as a sole proprietorship and then incorporates it. Or, the original debtor may be a corporation that is merged into another corporation. Under both former Article 9 and this Article, collateral that is transferred in the course of the incorporation or merger normally would remain subject to a perfected security interest. See Sections 9-315(a), 9-507(a). Former Article 9 was less clear with respect to whether an after-acquired property clause in a security agreement signed by the original debtor would be effective to create a security interest in property acquired by the new corporation or the merger survivor and, if so, whether a financing statement filed against the original debtor would be effective to perfect the security interest. This section and Sections 9-203(d) and (e) are a clarification.

3. **How New Debtor Becomes Bound.** Normally, a security interest is unenforceable unless the debtor has authenticated a security agreement describing the collateral. See Section 9-203(b). New Section 9-203(e) creates an exception, under which a security agreement entered into by one person is effective with respect to the property of another. This exception comes into play if a "new debtor" becomes bound as debtor by a security agreement entered into by another person (the "original debtor"). (The quoted terms are defined in Section 9-102.) If a new debtor does become bound, then the security agreement entered into by the original debtor satisfies the security-agreement requirement of Section 9-203(b)(3) as to existing or after-acquired property of the new debtor to the extent the property is described in the security agreement. In that case, no other agreement is necessary to make a security interest enforceable in that property. See Section 9-203(e).

Section 9-203(d) explains when a new debtor becomes bound by an original debtor's security agreement. Under Section 9-203(d)(1), a new debtor becomes bound as debtor if, by contract or operation of other law, the security agreement becomes effective to create a security interest in the new debtor's property. For example, if the applicable corporate law of mergers provides that when A Corp merges into B Corp, B Corp becomes a debtor under A Corp's security agreement, then B Corp would become bound as debtor following such a merger. Similarly, B Corp would become bound as debtor if B Corp contractually assumes A's obligations under the security agreement.

Under certain circumstances, a new debtor becomes bound for purposes of this Article even though it would not be bound under other law. Under Section 9-203(d)(2), a new debtor becomes bound when, by contract or operation of other law, it (i) becomes obligated not only for the secured obligation but also generally for the obligations of the original debtor and (ii) acquires or succeeds to substantially all the assets of the original debtor. For example, some corporate laws provide that, when two corporations merge, the surviving corporation succeeds to the assets of its merger partner and "has all liabilities" of both corporations. In the case where, for example, A Corp merges into B Corp (and A Corp ceases to exist), some people have questioned whether A Corp's grant of a security interest in its existing and after-acquired property becomes a "liability" of B Corp, such that B Corp's existing and after-acquired property becomes subject to a security interest in favor of A Corp's lender. Even if corporate law were to give a negative answer, under Section 9-203(d)(2), B Corp would become bound for purposes of Section 9-203(e) and this section. The "substantially all of the assets" requirement of Section 9-203(d)(2) excludes sureties and other secondary obligors as well as persons who become obligated through veil piercing and other non-successorship doctrines. In most cases, it will exclude successors to the assets and liabilities of a division of a debtor.

4. **When Financing Statement Effective Against New Debtor.** Subsection (a) provides that a filing against the original debtor is effective to perfect a security interest in collateral that a new debtor has at the time it becomes bound by the original debtor's security agreement and collateral that it acquires before the expiration of four months after the new debtor becomes bound. Under subsection (b), however, if the filing against the original debtor is seriously misleading as to the new debtor's name, the filing is effective as to collateral acquired by the new debtor after the four-month period only if a person files during the four-month period an initial financing statement providing the name of the new debtor. Compare Section 9-507(c) (four-month period of effectiveness with respect to collateral acquired by a debtor after the debtor changes its name).

5. **Transferred Collateral.** This section does not apply to collateral transferred by the original debtor to a new debtor. Under those circumstances, the filing against the original debtor continues to be effective until it lapses. See subsection (c); Section 9-507(a).

6. **Priority.** Section 9-326 governs the priority contest between a secured creditor of the original debtor and a secured creditor of the new debtor.

§ 9-509. PERSONS ENTITLED TO FILE A RECORD.

(a) **[Person entitled to file record.]** A person may file an initial financing statement, amendment that adds collateral covered by a financing statement, or amendment that adds a debtor to a financing statement only if:

(1)   the debtor authorizes the filing in an authenticated record; or

(2)   the person holds an agricultural lien that has become effective at the time of filing and the financing statement covers only collateral in which the person holds an agricultural lien.

(b)   [Security agreement as authorization.] By authenticating or becoming bound as debtor by a security agreement, a debtor or new debtor authorizes the filing of an initial financing statement, and an amendment, covering:

(1)   the collateral described in the security agreement; and

(2)   property that becomes collateral under Section 9-315(a)(2), whether or not the security agreement expressly covers proceeds.

ANALYSIS

Apart from establishing that authenticating a security agreement authorizes a filing as to the described collateral and its proceeds, new § 9-509 does not specify what is required to authorize a filing. Comment 3 to new § 9-502 states that pursuant to other law, "including the law with respect to ratification of past acts," which determines whether a person is authorized to file. Section 26 of the Restatement (Second) of Agency rejects any general "equal dignity" rule requiring the authorization to be expressed in the same form required for the authorized act. Apparently, the authorization of filing may be oral or electronic as well as written. But an unauthorized filing is ineffective under new § 9-510(a). When the filing comes after the authentication of the security agreement, the requirement of debtor authorization of the filing is automatically satisfied as to the collateral covered by the agreement. The critical step is for the creditor to be able to prove that an authentication of the security agreement occurred under new § 9-102(a)(7) *before* it filed. Comment 3 to new § 9-502 suggests that post-filing ratification by the debtor could provide the authorization. But post-filing ratification could open the door to collusion between a debtor and a preferred creditor. One can even imagine a creditor filing in the hopes of later obtaining a ratification. Apart from the ratification issue, arguments will arise as to prospective filings before authentication of the security agreement. As to such prospective filing, the creditor will be well-advised to obtain the authorization in a form so that the authorization can subsequently be proved without doubt. If it fails to do so, proof that the prospective filing was orally authorized would appear to be sufficient. But there may be circumstances for skepticism as to testimony as to what was orally authorized.

(c) [Acquisition of collateral as authorization.] By acquiring collateral in which a security interest or agricultural lien continues under Section 9-315(a)(1), a debtor authorizes the filing of an initial financing statement, and an amendment, covering the collateral and property that becomes collateral under Section 9-315(a)(2).

(d) [Person entitled to file certain amendments.] A person may file an amendment other than an amendment that adds collateral covered by a financing statement or an amendment that adds a debtor to a financing statement only if:

(1)   the secured party of record authorizes the filing; or

(2)   the amendment is a termination statement for a financing statement as to which the secured party of record has failed to file or send a termination statement as required by Section 9-513(a) or (c), the debtor authorizes the filing, and the termination statement indicates that the debtor authorized it to be filed.

(e) [Multiple secured parties of record.] If there is more than one secured party of record for a financing statement, each secured party of record may authorize the filing of an amendment under subsection (d).

ANALYSIS

Old Article 9 recognized six types of filings: the initial financing statement, a.k.a. UCC-1, amendment, continuation, assignment, release and termination statements. Each of these filings had its own distinct role and requirements. *See Secured Transactions* Ch. 6B. Under Revised Article 9, the scheme for classifying filings is different. The two broadest categories are the initial financing statement (discussed in new §§ 9-502 through 9-504) and the amendment (described in new § 9-512). *See* the model national forms in new § 9-521. There are two specialized forms of amendments: continuation statements (*see* new § 9-102(a)(27)) and termination statements (*see*

new § 9-102(a)(79)). Under old Article 9 continuations and termina-
tions were distinct from amendments. Under Revised Article 9, they
are types of amendments. But they do not by any means exhaust the
amendment category. Amendments may also assign (new § 9-514) and
release (new § 9-512(a)) or otherwise change the information on the
initial statement (new § 9-512(a)). They may even change the name
of the secured party, thus transferring the priority of the original
secured party. *See* new § 9-512(e)(2). Moreover, the original secured
party may itself authorize such an amendment under Revised Article
9. *See* new § 9-509(d). The following chart attempts to diagram the
classification scheme and indicate who is entitled to authorize the
filing.

Filing		Person Who Authorizes Filing
I. Initial Financing Statement	–	Debtor
II. Amendments		
A. Continuation Statements	–	Secured Party of Record
B. Termination Statement	–	Secured Party of Record except for § 9-509(c) situation
C. Amendments Adding Collateral or Debtor	–	Debtor
D. Other Amendments (*e.g.* changing addresses, debtor's identification number)	–	Secured Party of Record except for § 9-509(c) situation

Official Comment

1. **Source.** New.

2. **Scope and Approach of This Section.** This section collects in one place
most of the rules determining whether a record may be filed. Section 9-510
explains the extent to which a filed record is effective. Under these sections,
the identity of the person who effects a filing is immaterial. The filing scheme
contemplated by this Part does not contemplate that the identity of a "filer"
will be a part of the searchable records. This is consistent with, and a necessary aspect of, eliminating signatures or other evidence of authorization from
the system. (Note that the 1972 amendments to this Article eliminated the
requirement that a financing statement contain the signature of the secured
party.) As long as the appropriate person authorizes the filing, or, in the case
of a termination statement, the debtor is entitled to the termination, it is
insignificant whether the secured party or another person files any given
record. The question of authorization is one for the court, not the filing office.
However, a filing office may choose to employ authentication procedures in
connection with electronic communications, e.g., to verify the identity of a
filer who seeks to charge the filing fee.

3. **Unauthorized Filings.** Records filed in the filing office do not require signatures for their effectiveness. Subsection (a)(1) substitutes for the debtor's signature on a financing statement the requirement that the debtor authorize in an authenticated record the filing of an initial financing statement or an amendment that adds collateral. Also, under subsection (a)(1), if an amendment adds a debtor, the debtor who is added must authorize the amendment. A person who files an unauthorized record in violation of subsection (a)(1) is liable under Section 9-625 for actual and statutory damages. Of course, a filed financing statement is ineffective to perfect a security interest if the filing is not authorized. See Section 9-510(a). Law other than this Article, including the law with respect to ratification of past acts, generally determines whether a person has the requisite authority to file a record under this section. See Sections 1-103, 9-502, Comment 3.

4. *Ipso Facto* **Authorization.** Under subsection (b), the authentication of a security agreement *ipso facto* constitutes the debtor's authorization of the filing of a financing statement covering the collateral described in the security agreement. The secured party need not obtain a separate authorization. Similarly, a new debtor's becoming bound by a security agreement *ipso facto* constitutes the new debtor's authorization of the filing of a financing statement covering the collateral described in the security agreement by which the new debtor has become bound. And, under subsection (c), the acquisition of collateral in which a security interest continues after disposition under Section 9-315(a)(1) *ipso facto* constitutes an authorization to file an initial financing statement against the person who acquired the collateral. The authorization to file an initial financing statement also constitutes an authorization to file a record covering actual proceeds of the original collateral, even if the security agreement is silent as to proceeds.

Example 1: Debtor authenticates a security agreement creating a security interest in Debtor's inventory in favor of Secured Party. Secured Party files a financing statement covering inventory and accounts. The financing statement is authorized insofar as it covers inventory and unauthorized insofar as it covers accounts. (Note, however, that the financing statement will be effective to perfect a security interest in accounts constituting proceeds of the inventory to the same extent as a financing statement covering only inventory.)

Example 2: Debtor authenticates a security agreement creating a security interest in Debtor's inventory in favor of Secured Party. Secured Party files a financing statement covering inventory. Debtor sells some inventory, deposits the buyer's payment into a deposit account, and withdraws the funds to purchase equipment. As long as the equipment can be traced to the inventory, the security interest continues in the equipment. See Section 9-315(a)(2). However, because the equipment was acquired with cash proceeds, the financing statement becomes ineffective to perfect the security interest in the equipment on the 21st day after the security interest attaches to the equipment unless Secured Party continues perfection beyond the 20-day period by filing a financing statement against the equipment or amending the filed financing statement to cover equipment. See Section 9-315(d). Debtor's authentication of the security agreement authorizes the filing of an initial financing statement or amendment covering the equipment, which is "property that becomes collateral under Section 9-315(a)(2)." See Section 9-509(b)(2).

5. **Agricultural Liens.** Under subsection (a)(2), the holder of an agricultural lien may file a financing statement covering collateral subject to the lien without obtaining the debtor's authorization. Because the lien arises as matter of law, the debtor's consent is not required. A person who files an unauthorized record in violation of this subsection is liable under Section 9-625(e) for a statutory penalty and damages.

6. **Amendments; Termination Statements Authorized by Debtor.** Most amendments may not be filed unless the secured party of record, as determined under Section 9-511, authorizes the filing. See subsection (d)(1). However, under subsection (d)(2), the authorization of the secured party of record is not required for the filing of a termination statement if the secured party of record failed to send or file a termination statement as required by Section 9-513, the debtor authorizes it to be filed, and the termination statement so indicates.

7. **Multiple Secured Parties of Record.** Subsection (e) deals with multiple secured parties of record. It permits each secured party of record to authorize the filing of amendments. However, Section 9-510(b) protects the rights and powers of one secured party of record from the effects of filings made by another secured party of record. See Section 9-510, Comment 3.

8. **Successor to Secured Party of Record.** A person may succeed to the powers of the secured party of record by operation of other law, e.g., the law of corporate mergers. In that case, the successor has the power to authorize filings within the meaning of this section.

§ 9-510. EFFECTIVENESS OF FILED RECORD.

(a) **[Filed record effective if authorized.]** A filed record is effective only to the extent that it was filed by a person that may file it under Section 9-509.

(b) **[Authorization by one secured party of record.]** A record authorized by one secured party of record does not affect the financing statement with respect to another secured party of record.

(c) **[Continuation statement not timely filed.]** A continuation statement that is not filed within the six-month period prescribed by Section 9-515(d) is ineffective.

Official Comment

1. **Source.** New.

2. **Ineffectiveness of Unauthorized or Overbroad Filings.** Subsection (a) provides that a filed financing statement is effective only to the extent it was filed by a person entitled to file it.

Example 1: Debtor authorizes the filing of a financing statement covering inventory. Under Section 9-509, the secured party may file a financing statement covering only inventory; it may not file a financing statement covering other collateral. The secured party files a financing statement covering inventory and equipment. This section provides that the financing statement is effective only to the extent the secured party may file it. Thus, the financing statement is effective to perfect a security interest in inventory but ineffective to perfect a security interest in equipment.

3. **Multiple Secured Parties of Record.** Section 9-509(e) permits any secured party of record to authorize the filing of most amendments. Subsection (b) of this section prevents a filing authorized by one secured party of record from affecting the rights and powers of another secured party of record without the latter's consent.

Example 2: Debtor creates a security interest in favor of A and B. The filed financing statement names A and B as the secured parties. An amendment deleting some collateral covered by the financing statement is filed pursuant to B's authorization. Although B's security interest in the deleted collateral becomes unperfected, A's security interest remains perfected in all the collateral.

Example 3: Debtor creates a security interest in favor of A and B. The financing statement names A and B as the secured parties. A termination statement is filed pursuant to B's authorization. Although the effectiveness of the financing statement terminates with respect to B's security interest, A's rights are unaffected. That is, the financing statement continues to be effective to perfect A's security interest.

4. **Continuation Statements.** A continuation statement may be filed only within the six months immediately before lapse. See Section 9-515(d). The filing office is obligated to reject a continuation statement that is filed outside the six-month period. See Sections 9-520(a), 9-516(b)(7). Subsection (c) provides that if the filing office fails to reject a continuation statement that is not filed in a timely manner, the continuation statement is ineffective nevertheless.

§ 9-511. SECURED PARTY OF RECORD.

(a) **[Secured party of record.]** A secured party of record with respect to a financing statement is a person whose name is provided as the name of the secured party or a representative of the secured party in an initial financing statement that has been filed.

If an initial financing statement is filed under Section 9-514(a), the assignee named in the initial financing statement is the secured party of record with respect to the financing statement.

(b) [Amendment naming secured party of record.] If an amendment of a financing statement which provides the name of a person as a secured party or a representative of a secured party is filed, the person named in the amendment is a secured party of record. If an amendment is filed under Section 9-514(b), the assignee named in the amendment is a secured party of record.

(c) [Amendment deleting secured party of record.] A person remains a secured party of record until the filing of an amendment of the financing statement which deletes the person.

Official Comment

1. **Source.** New.

2. **Secured Party of Record.** This new section explains how the secured party of record is to be determined. If SP-1 is named as the secured party in an initial financing statement, it is the secured party of record. Similarly, if an initial financing statement reflects a total assignment from SP-0 to SP-1, then SP-1 is the secured party of record. See subsection (a). If, subsequently, an amendment is filed assigning SP-1's status to SP-2, then SP-2 becomes the secured party of record in place of SP-1. The same result obtains if a subsequent amendment deletes the reference to SP-1 and substitutes therefor a reference to SP-2. If, however, a subsequent amendment adds SP-2 as a secured party but does not purport to remove SP-1 as a secured party, then SP-2 and SP-1 each is a secured party of record. See subsection (b). An amendment purporting to remove the only secured party of record without providing a successor is ineffective. See Section 9-512(e). At any point in time, all effective records that comprise a financing statement must be examined to determine the person or persons that have the status of secured party of record.

3. **Successor to Secured Party of Record.** Application of other law may result in a person succeeding to the powers of a secured party of record. For example, if the secured party of record (A) merges into another corporation (B) and the other corporation (B) survives, other law may provide that B has all of A's powers. In that case, B is authorized to take all actions under this Part that A would have been authorized to take. Similarly, acts taken by a person who is authorized under generally applicable principles of agency to act on behalf of the secured party of record are effective under this Part.

§ 9-512. AMENDMENT OF FINANCING STATEMENT.
[Alternative A]
(a) [Amendment of information in financing statement.] Subject to Section 9-509, a person may add or delete collateral

covered by, continue or terminate the effectiveness of, or, subject to subsection (e), otherwise amend the information provided in, a financing statement by filing an amendment that:

(1)   identifies, by its file number, the initial financing statement to which the amendment relates; and

(2)   if the amendment relates to an initial financing statement filed [or recorded] in a filing office described in Section 9-501(a)(1), provides the information specified in Section 9-502(b).

[Alternative B]

(a)   [Amendment of information in financing statement.] Subject to Section 9-509, a person may add or delete collateral covered by, continue or terminate the effectiveness of, or, subject to subsection (e), otherwise amend the information provided in, a financing statement by filing an amendment that:

(1)   identifies, by its file number, the initial financing statement to which the amendment relates; and

(2)   if the amendment relates to an initial financing statement filed [or recorded] in a filing office described in Section 9-501(a)(1), provides the date [and time] that the initial financing statement was filed [or recorded] and the information specified in Section 9-502(b).

ANALYSIS

The authorization to "otherwise amend the information" in the statement includes authority to change the name of the secured party. New § 9-512(e) confirms this capacity. Thus, a filer may under Revised Article 9 sell or otherwise transfer its priority. This is an important clarification of a disputed point under old Article 9. *See Secured Transactions* § 6B.05[3][b].

[End of Alternatives]

(b)   [Period of effectiveness not affected.] Except as otherwise provided in Section 9-515, the filing of an amendment does not extend the period of effectiveness of the financing statement.

(c)   [Effectiveness of amendment adding collateral.] A financing statement that is amended by an amendment that adds collateral is effective as to the added collateral only from the date of the filing of the amendment.

(d) [Effectiveness of amendment adding debtor.] A financing statement that is amended by an amendment that adds a debtor is effective as to the added debtor only from the date of the filing of the amendment.

(e) [Certain amendments ineffective.] An amendment is ineffective to the extent it:

(1) purports to delete all debtors and fails to provide the name of a debtor to be covered by the financing statement; or

(2) purports to delete all secured parties of record and fails to provide the name of a new secured party of record.

Legislative Note: States whose real-estate filing offices require additional information in amendments and cannot search their records by both the name of the debtor and the file number should enact Alternative B to Sections 9-512(a), 9-518(b), 9-519(f) and 9-522(a).

Official Comment

1. **Source.** Former 9-402(4).

2. **Changes to Financing Statements.** This section addresses changes to financing statements, including addition and deletion of collateral. Although termination statements, assignments, and continuation statements are types of amendment, this Article follows former Article 9 and contains separate sections containing additional provisions applicable to particular types of amendments. See Section 9-513 (termination statements); 9-514 (assignments); 9-515 (continuation statements). One should not infer from this separate treatment that this Article requires a separate amendment to accomplish each change. Rather, a single amendment would be legally sufficient to, e.g., add collateral and continue the effectiveness of the financing statement.

3. **Amendments.** An amendment under this Article may identify only the information contained in a financing statement that is to be changed; alternatively, it may take the form of an amended and restated financing statement. The latter would state, for example, that the financing statement "is amended and restated to read as follows: . . ." References in this Part to an "amended financing statement" are to a financing statement as amended by an amendment using either technique.

This section revises former Section 9-402(4) to permit secured parties of record to make changes in the public record without the need to obtain the debtor's signature. However, the filing of an amendment that adds collateral or adds a debtor must be authorized by the debtor or it will not be effective. See Sections 9-509(a), 9-510(a).

4. **Amendment Adding Debtor.** An amendment that adds a debtor is effective, provided that the added debtor authorizes the filing. See Section

9-509(a). However, filing an amendment adding a debtor to a previously filed financing statement affords no advantage over filing an initial financing statement against that debtor and may be disadvantageous. With respect to the added debtor, for purposes of determining the priority of the security interest, the time of filing is the time of the filing of the amendment, not the time of the filing of the initial financing statement. See subsection (d). However, the effectiveness of the financing statement lapses with respect to added debtor at the time it lapses with respect to the original debtor. See subsection (b).

5. **Deletion of All Debtors or Secured Parties of Record.** Subsection (e) assures that there will be a debtor and secured party of record for every financing statement.

Example: A filed financing statement names A and B as secured parties of record and covers inventory and equipment. An amendment deletes equipment and purports to delete A and B as secured parties of record without adding a substitute secured party. The amendment is ineffective to the extent it purports to delete the secured parties of record but effective with respect to the deletion of collateral. As a consequence, the financing statement, as amended, covers only inventory, but A and B remain as secured parties of record.

§ 9-513. TERMINATION STATEMENT.

(a) **[Consumer goods.]** A secured party shall cause the secured party of record for a financing statement to file a termination statement for the financing statement if the financing statement covers consumer goods and:

(1) there is no obligation secured by the collateral covered by the financing statement and no commitment to make an advance, incur an obligation, or otherwise give value; or

(2) the debtor did not authorize the filing of the initial financing statement.

(b) **[Time for compliance with subsection (a).]** To comply with subsection (a), a secured party shall cause the secured party of record to file the termination statement:

(1) within one month after there is no obligation secured by the collateral covered by the financing statement and no commitment to make an advance, incur an obligation, or otherwise give value; or

(2) if earlier, within 20 days after the secured party receives an authenticated demand from a debtor.

(c) [Other collateral.] In cases not governed by subsection (a), within 20 days after a secured party receives an authenticated demand from a debtor, the secured party shall cause the secured party of record for a financing statement to send to the debtor a termination statement for the financing statement or file the termination statement in the filing office if:

(1) except in the case of a financing statement covering accounts or chattel paper that has been sold or goods that are the subject of a consignment, there is no obligation secured by the collateral covered by the financing statement and no commitment to make an advance, incur an obligation, or otherwise give value;

(2) the financing statement covers accounts or chattel paper that has been sold but as to which the account debtor or other person obligated has discharged its obligation;

(3) the financing statement covers goods that were the subject of a consignment to the debtor but are not in the debtor's possession; or

(4) the debtor did not authorize the filing of the initial financing statement.

(d) [Effect of filing termination statement.] Except as otherwise provided in Section 9-510, upon the filing of a termination statement with the filing office, the financing statement to which the termination statement relates ceases to be effective.

ANALYSIS

Revised Article 9 could exacerbate the problem of unauthorized "bogus" U.C.C. filings since a filing will no longer be required to have even the purported signature of the debtor. However, new § 9-513 does recognize the debtor's right to demand termination of such filings and to recover the $500 penalty of new § 9-625(e)(4) if the termination is not provided. This would be in addition to the $500 penalty for filing without authorization in the first place. *See* new § 9-625(e)(3). In addition, the filer would be liable for the named debtor's actual loss under new § 9-625(b). Moreover, the named debtor is authorized by § 9-509(c)(2) to file a termination when the required termination is not provided. Since most bogus filings are politically motivated or in response to criminal prosecutions, no one pretends that these measures will completely solve the problem.

Official Comment

1. **Source.** Former Section 9-404.

2. **Duty to File or Send.** This section specifies when a secured party must cause the secured party of record to file or send to the debtor a termination statement for a financing statement. Because most financing statements expire in five years unless a continuation statement is filed (Section 9-515), no compulsion is placed on the secured party to file a termination statement unless demanded by the debtor, except in the case of consumer goods. Because many consumers will not realize the importance to them of clearing the public record, an affirmative duty is put on the secured party in that case. But many purchase-money security interests in consumer goods will not be filed, except for motor vehicles. See Section 9-309(1). Under Section 9-311(b), compliance with a certificate-of-title statute is "equivalent to the filing of a financing statement under this article." Thus, this section applies to a certificate of title unless the section is superseded by a certificate-of-title statute that contains a specific rule addressing a secured party's duty to cause a notation of a security interest to be removed from a certificate of title. In the context of a certificate of title, however, the secured party could comply with this section by causing the removal itself or providing the debtor with documentation sufficient to enable the debtor to effect the removal.

Subsections (a) and (b) apply to a financing statement covering consumer goods. Subsection (c) applies to other financing statements. Subsection (a) and (c) each makes explicit what was implicit under former Article 9: If the debtor did not authorize the filing of a financing statement in the first place, the secured party of record should file or send a termination statement. The liability imposed upon a secured party that fails to comply with subsection (a) or (c) is identical to that imposed for the filing of an unauthorized financing statement or amendment. See Section 9-625(e).

3. **"Bogus" Filings.** A secured party's duty to send a termination statement arises when the secured party "receives" an authenticated demand from the debtor. In the case of an unauthorized financing statement, the person named as debtor in the financing statement may have no relationship with the named secured party and no reason to know the secured party's address. Inasmuch as the address in the financing statement is "held out by [the person named as secured party in the financing statement] as the place for receipt of such communications [i.e., communications relating to security interests]," the putative secured party is deemed to have "received" a notification delivered to that address. See Section 1-201(26). If a termination statement is not forthcoming, the person named as debtor itself may authorize the filing of a termination statement, which will be effective if it indicates that the person authorized it to be filed. See Sections 9-509(d)(2), 9-510(c).

4. **Buyers of Receivables.** Applied literally, former Section 9-404(1) would have required many buyers of receivables to file a termination statement

immediately upon filing a financing statement because "there is no outstanding secured obligation and no commitment to make advances, incur obligations, or otherwise give value." Subsections (c)(1) and (2) remedy this problem. While the security interest of a buyer of accounts or chattel paper (B-1) is perfected, the debtor is not deemed to retain an interest in the sold receivables and thus could transfer no interest in them to another buyer (B-2) or to a lien creditor (LC). However, for purposes of determining the rights of the debtor's creditors and certain purchasers of accounts or chattel paper from the debtor, while B-1's security interest is unperfected, the debtor-seller is deemed to have rights in the sold receivables, and a competing security interest or judicial lien may attach to those rights. See Sections 9-318, 9-109, Comment 5. Suppose that B-1's security interest in certain accounts and chattel paper is perfected by filing, but the effectiveness of the financing statement lapses. Both before and after lapse, B-1 collects some of the receivables. After lapse, LC acquires a lien on the accounts and chattel paper. B-1's unperfected security interest in the accounts and chattel paper is subordinate to LC's rights. See Section 9-317(a)(2). But collections on accounts and chattel paper are not "accounts" or "chattel paper." Even if B-1's security interest in the accounts and chattel paper is or becomes unperfected, neither the debtor nor LC acquires rights to the collections that B-1 collects (and owns) before LC acquires a lien.

5. **Effect of Filing.** Subsection (d) states the effect of filing a termination statement: the related financing statement ceases to be effective. If one of several secured parties of record files a termination statement, subsection (d) applies only with respect to the rights of the person who authorized the filing of the termination statement. See Section 9-510(b). The financing statement remains effective with respect to the rights of the others. However, even if a financing statement is *terminated* (and thus no longer is effective) with respect to all secured parties of record, the financing statement, including the termination statement, will remain of record until at least one year after it *lapses* with respect to all secured parties of record. See Section 9-519(g).

§ 9-514. ASSIGNMENT OF POWERS OF SECURED PARTY OF RECORD.

(a) [Assignment reflected on initial financing statement.] Except as otherwise provided in subsection (c), an initial financing statement may reflect an assignment of all of the secured party's power to authorize an amendment to the financing statement by providing the name and mailing address of the assignee as the name and address of the secured party.

(b) [Assignment of filed financing statement.] Except as otherwise provided in subsection (c), a secured party of record may assign of record all or part of its power to authorize an amendment to a financing statement by filing in the filing office an amendment of the financing statement which:

(1)　identifies, by its file number, the initial financing statement to which it relates;

(2)　provides the name of the assignor; and

(3)　provides the name and mailing address of the assignee.

(c)　**[Assignment of record of mortgage.]** An assignment of record of a security interest in a fixture covered by a record of a mortgage which is effective as a financing statement filed as a fixture filing under Section 9-502(c) may be made only by an assignment of record of the mortgage in the manner provided by law of this State other than [the Uniform Commercial Code].

Official Comment

1. **Source.** Former Section 9-405.

2. **Assignments.** This section provides a permissive device whereby a secured party of record may effectuate an assignment of its power to affect a financing statement. It may also be useful for a secured party who has assigned all or part of its security interest or agricultural lien and wishes to have the fact noted of record, so that inquiries concerning the transaction would be addressed to the assignee. See Section 9-502, Comment 2. Upon the filing of an assignment, the assignee becomes the "secured party of record" and may authorize the filing of a continuation statement, termination statement, or other amendment. Note that under Section 9-310(c) no filing of an assignment is required as a condition of continuing the perfected status of the security interest against creditors and transferees of the original debtor. However, if an assignment is not filed, the assignor remains the secured party of record, with the power (even if not the right) to authorize the filing of effective amendments. See Sections 9-511(c), 9-509(d).

Where a record of a mortgage is effective as a financing statement filed as a fixture filing (Section 9-502(c)), then an assignment of record of the security interest may be made only in the manner in which an assignment of record of the mortgage may be made under local real-property law.

3. **Comparison to Prior Law.** Most of the changes reflected in this section are for clarification or to embrace medium-neutral drafting. As a general matter, this section preserves the opportunity given by former Section 9-405 to assign a security interest of record in one of two different ways. Under subsection (a), a secured party may assign all of its power to affect a financing statement by naming an assignee in the initial financing statement. The secured party of record may accomplish the same result under subsection (b)

by making a subsequent filing. Subsection (b) also may be used for an assignment of only some of the secured party of record's power to affect a financing statement, e.g., the power to affect the financing statement as it relates to particular items of collateral or as it relates to an undivided interest in a security interest in all the collateral. An initial financing statement may not be used to change the secured party of record under these circumstances. However, an amendment adding the assignee as a secured party of record may be used.

§ 9-515. DURATION AND EFFECTIVENESS OF FINANCING STATEMENT; EFFECT OF LAPSED FINANCING STATEMENT.

(a) **[Five-year effectiveness.]** Except as otherwise provided in subsections (b), (e), (f), and (g), a filed financing statement is effective for a period of five years after the date of filing.

ANALYSIS

Old § 9-403(2) provided that a statement was effective for "five years from the date of filing." Revised § 9-515(a) sets the time as "five years after the date of the filing." This change seems calculated to assure that continuations on the fifth anniversary date of the original filing are effective (*e.g.*, original filing Feb. 1, 2002; continuation on Feb. 1, 2007). Almost all of the decisions under old Article 9 have so held. *See Secured Transactions* § 6B.03[1][a][ii].

(b) **[Public-finance or manufactured-home transaction.]** Except as otherwise provided in subsections (e), (f), and (g), an initial financing statement filed in connection with a public-finance transaction or manufactured-home transaction is effective for a period of 30 years after the date of filing if it indicates that it is filed in connection with a public-finance transaction or manufactured-home transaction.

(c) **[Lapse and continuation of financing statement.]** The effectiveness of a filed financing statement lapses on the expiration of the period of its effectiveness unless before the lapse a continuation statement is filed pursuant to subsection (d). Upon lapse, a financing statement ceases to be effective and any security interest or agricultural lien that was perfected by the financing statement becomes unperfected, unless the security interest is perfected otherwise. If the security interest or agricultural lien becomes unperfected upon lapse, it is deemed never to have been perfected as against a purchaser of the collateral for value.

(d) [When continuation statement may be filed.] A continuation statement may be filed only within six months before the expiration of the five-year period specified in subsection (a) or the 30-year period specified in subsection (b), whichever is applicable.

ANALYSIS

The six-month window is not as absolute as under old Article 9. If the filing office, in violation of its duty, takes a continuation filed outside the six-month window, the continuation is effective. *See* new §§ 9-516(b)(7) and 9-520(c), and *Secured Transactions* § 6B.03[1][a][i].

(e) [Effect of filing continuation statement.] Except as otherwise provided in Section 9-510, upon timely filing of a continuation statement, the effectiveness of the initial financing statement continues for a period of five years commencing on the day on which the financing statement would have become ineffective in the absence of the filing. Upon the expiration of the five-year period, the financing statement lapses in the same manner as provided in subsection (c), unless, before the lapse, another continuation statement is filed pursuant to subsection (d). Succeeding continuation statements may be filed in the same manner to continue the effectiveness of the initial financing statement.

(f) [Transmitting utility financing statement.] If a debtor is a transmitting utility and a filed financing statement so indicates, the financing statement is effective until a termination statement is filed.

(g) [Record of mortgage as financing statement.] A record of a mortgage that is effective as a financing statement filed as a fixture filing under Section 9-502(c) remains effective as a financing statement filed as a fixture filing until the mortgage is released or satisfied of record or its effectiveness otherwise terminates as to the real property.

Official Comment

1. **Source.** Former Section 9-403(2), (3), (6).

2. **Period of Financing Statement's Effectiveness.** Subsection (a) states the general rule: a financing statement is effective for a five-year period unless its effectiveness is continued under this section or terminated under Section 9-513. Subsection (b) provides that if the financing statement relates to a public-finance transaction or a manufactured-home transaction and so indicates, the financing statement is effective for 30 years. These financings typically extend well beyond the standard, five-year period. Under subsection (f), a financing statement filed against a transmitting utility remains effective indefinitely, until a termination statement is filed. Likewise, under subsection (g), a mortgage effective as a fixture filing remains effective until its effectiveness terminates under real-property law.

3. **Lapse.** When the period of effectiveness under subsection (a) or (b) expires, the effectiveness of the financing statement lapses. The last sentence of subsection (c) addresses the effect of lapse. The deemed retroactive unperfection applies only with respect to purchasers for value; unlike former Section 9-403(2), it does not apply with respect to lien creditors.

Example 1: SP-1 and SP-2 both hold security interests in the same collateral. Both security interests are perfected by filing. SP-1 filed first and has priority under Section 9-322(a)(1). The effectiveness of SP-1's filing lapses. As long as SP-2's security interest remains perfected thereafter, SP-2 is entitled to priority over SP-1's security interest, which is deemed never to have been perfected as against a purchaser for value (SP-2). See Section 9-322(a)(2).

Example 2: SP holds a security interest perfected by filing. On July 1, LC acquires a judicial lien on the collateral. Two weeks later, the effectiveness of the financing statement lapses. Although the security interest becomes unperfected upon lapse, it was perfected when LC acquired its lien. Accordingly, notwithstanding the lapse, the perfected security interest has priority over the rights of LC, who is not a purchaser. See Section 9-317(a)(2).

4. **Effect of Debtor's Bankruptcy.** Under former Section 9-403(2), lapse was tolled if the debtor entered bankruptcy or another insolvency proceeding. Nevertheless, being unaware that insolvency proceedings had been commenced, filing offices routinely removed records from the files as if lapse had not been tolled. Subsection (c) deletes the former tolling provision and thereby imposes a new burden on the secured party: to be sure that a financing statement does not lapse during the debtor's bankruptcy. The secured party can prevent lapse by filing a continuation statement, even without first obtaining relief from the automatic stay. See Bankruptcy Code Section 362(b)(3). Of course, if the debtor enters bankruptcy before lapse, the provisions of this Article with respect to lapse would be of no effect to the extent that federal bankruptcy law dictates a contrary result (e.g., to the extent that the Bankruptcy Code determines rights as of the date of the filing of the bankruptcy petition).

5. **Continuation Statements.** Subsection (d) explains when a continuation statement may be filed. A continuation statement filed at a time other than that prescribed by subsection (d) is ineffective, see Section 9-510(c), and the filing office may not accept it. See Sections 9-520(a), 9-516(b). Subsection (e) specifies the effect of a continuation statement and provides for successive continuation statements.

§ 9-516. WHAT CONSTITUTES FILING; EFFECTIVENESS OF FILING.

(a)　[What constitutes filing.] Except as otherwise provided in subsection (b), communication of a record to a filing office and tender of the filing fee or acceptance of the record by the filing office constitutes filing.

(b)　[Refusal to accept record; filing does not occur.] Filing does not occur with respect to a record that a filing office refuses to accept because:

(1)　the record is not communicated by a method or medium of communication authorized by the filing office;

ANALYSIS

These are key provisions relating to electronic filings. "Communication of a record" will constitute a filing under new § 9-516(a) provided that the method of communication has been authorized by the filing office under new § 9-516(b)(1). Thus, electronic filing is permissible wherever it is authorized by the filing office. That authorization may occur by rule under new § 9-526 which encourages, but does not require, the filing office to permit electronic filing. Electronic filing will also be effective whenever a filing office fails to reject a filing in that form even in the absence of a general authorization of the rule or otherwise. Failure to satisfy § 9-516(b) form requirements vitiates a filing only if the filing office refuses to accept it. *See* new § 9-520(c).

(2)　an amount equal to or greater than the applicable filing fee is not tendered;

(3)　the filing office is unable to index the record because:

(A)　in the case of an initial financing statement, the record does not provide a name for the debtor;

(B)   in the case of an amendment or correction statement, the record:

(i)   does not identify the initial financing statement as required by Section 9-512 or 9-518, as applicable; or

(ii)   identifies an initial financing statement whose effectiveness has lapsed under Section 9-515;

(C)   in the case of an initial financing statement that provides the name of a debtor identified as an individual or an amendment that provides a name of a debtor identified as an individual which was not previously provided in the financing statement to which the record relates, the record does not identify the debtor's last name; or

(D)   in the case of a record filed [or recorded] in the filing office described in Section 9-501(a)(1), the record does not provide a sufficient description of the real property to which it relates;

(4)   in the case of an initial financing statement or an amendment that adds a secured party of record, the record does not provide a name and mailing address for the secured party of record;

(5)   in the case of an initial financing statement or an amendment that provides a name of a debtor which was not previously provided in the financing statement to which the amendment relates, the record does not:

(A)   provide a mailing address for the debtor;

(B)   indicate whether the debtor is an individual or an organization; or

(C)   if the financing statement indicates that the debtor is an organization, provide:

(i)   a type of organization for the debtor;

(ii)   a jurisdiction of organization for the debtor; or

(iii)   an organizational identification number for the debtor or indicate that the debtor has none;

(6)   in the case of an assignment reflected in an initial financing statement under Section 9-514(a) or an amendment filed under Section 9-514(b), the record does not provide a name and mailing address for the assignee; or

ANALYSIS

These additional content requirements for a financing statement are operative only if the filing office rejects the filing for failure to satisfy these requirements as it is so directed to do by new § 9-520(a). *See* new § 9-520(c). Imagine that a central filing made in California against the debtor "Jim Smith," that does not supply an address. According to the Revision, that filing is effective if it is accepted by the filing office. If the filing office is not alert to reject what it should reject, the job of searching to verify what a debtor says about its assets could become more complicated indeed.

(7)   in the case of a continuation statement, the record is not filed within the six-month period prescribed by Section 9-515(d).

(c)   [Rules applicable to subsection (b).] For purposes of subsection (b):

(1)   a record does not provide information if the filing office is unable to read or decipher the information; and

(2)   a record that does not indicate that it is an amendment or identify an initial financing statement to which it relates, as required by Section 9-512, 9-514, or 9-518, is an initial financing statement.

(d)   [Refusal to accept record; record effective as filed record.] A record that is communicated to the filing office with tender of the filing fee, but which the filing office refuses to accept for a reason other than one set forth in subsection (b), is effective as a filed record except as against a purchaser of the collateral which gives value in reasonable reliance upon the absence of the record from the files.

Official Comment

1. **Source.** Subsection (a): former Section 9-403(1); the remainder is new.

2. **What Constitutes Filing.** Subsection (a) deals generically with what constitutes filing of a record, including an initial financing statement and amendments of all kinds (e.g., assignments, termination statements, and continuation statements). It follows former Section 9-403(1), under which either acceptance of a record by the filing office or presentation of the record and tender of the filing fee constitutes filing.

3. **Effectiveness of Rejected Record.** Subsection (b) provides an exclusive list of grounds upon which the filing office may reject a record. See Section 9-520(a). Although some of these grounds would also be grounds for rendering a filed record ineffective (e.g., an initial financing statement does not provide a name for the debtor), many others would not be (e.g., an initial financing statement does not provide a mailing address for the debtor or secured party of record). Neither this section nor Section 9-520 requires or authorizes the filing office to determine, or even consider, the accuracy of information provided in a record. For example, the State A filing office may not reject under subsection (b)(5)(C) an initial financing statement indicating that the debtor is a State A corporation and providing a three-digit organizational identification number, even if all State A organizational identification numbers contain at least five digits and two letters.

A financing statement or other record that is communicated to the filing office but which the filing office refuses to accept provides no public notice, regardless of the reason for the rejection. However, this section distinguishes between records that the filing office rightfully rejects and those that it wrongfully rejects. A filer is able to prevent a rightful rejection by complying with the requirements of subsection (b). No purpose is served by giving effect to records that justifiably never find their way into the system, and subsection (b) so provides.

Subsection (d) deals with the filing office's unjustified refusal to accept a record. Here, the filer is in no position to prevent the rejection and as a general matter should not be prejudiced by it. Although wrongfully rejected records generally are effective, subsection (d) contains a special rule to protect a third-party purchaser of the collateral (e.g., a buyer or competing secured party) who gives value in reliance upon the apparent absence of the record from the files. As against a person who searches the public record and reasonably relies on what the public record shows, subsection (d) imposes upon the filer the risk that a record failed to make its way into the filing system because of the filing office's wrongful rejection of it. (Compare Section 9-517, under which a mis-indexed financing statement is fully effective.) This risk is likely to be small, particularly when a record is presented electronically, and the filer can guard against this risk by conducting a post-filing search of the records. Moreover, Section 9-520(b) requires the filing office to give prompt notice of its refusal to accept a record for filing.

4. **Method or Medium of Communication.** Rejection pursuant to subsection (b)(1) for failure to communicate a record properly should be understood to mean noncompliance with procedures relating to security, authentication, or other communication-related requirements that the filing office may impose. Subsection (b)(1) does not authorize a filing office to impose additional substantive requirements. See Section 9-520, Comment 2.

5. **Address for Secured Party of Record.** Under subsection (b)(4) and• Section 9-520(a), the lack of a mailing address for the secured party of record requires the filing office to reject an initial financing statement. The failure to include an address for the secured party of record no longer renders a financing statement ineffective. See Section 9-502(a). The function of the address is not to identify the secured party of record but rather to provide an address to which others can send required notifications, e.g., of a purchase-money security interest in inventory or of the disposition of collateral. Inasmuch as the address shown on a filed financing statement is an "address that is reasonable under the circumstances," a person required to send a notification to the secured party may satisfy the requirement by sending a notification to that address, even if the address is or becomes incorrect. See Section 9-102 (definition of "send"). Similarly, because the address is "held out by [the secured party] as the place for receipt of such communications [i.e., communications relating to security interests]," the secured party is deemed to have received a notification delivered to that address. See Section 1-201(26).

6. **Uncertainty Concerning Individual Debtor's Last Name.** Subsection (b)(3)(C) requires the filing office to reject an initial financing statement or amendment adding an individual debtor if the office cannot index the record because it does not identify the debtor's last name (e.g., it is unclear whether the debtor's name is Elton John or John Elton).

7. **Inability of Filing Office to Read or Decipher Information.** Under subsection (c)(1), if the filing office cannot read or decipher information, the information is not provided by a record for purposes of subsection (b).

8. **Classification of Records.** For purposes of subsection (b), a record that does not indicate it is an amendment or identify an initial financing statement to which it relates is deemed to be an initial financing statement. See subsection (c)(2).

9. **Effectiveness of Rejectable But Unrejected Record.** Section 9-520(a) requires the filing office to refuse to accept an initial financing statement for a reason set forth in subsection (b). However, if the filing office accepts such a financing statement nevertheless, the financing statement generally is effective if it complies with the requirements of Section 9-502(a) and (b). See Section 9-520(c). Similarly, an otherwise effective financing statement generally remains so even though the information in the financing statement becomes incorrect. See Section 9-507(b). (Note that if the information required by subsection (b)(5) is incorrect when the financing statement is filed, Section 9-338 applies.)

§ 9-517. EFFECT OF INDEXING ERRORS.
The failure of the filing office to index a record correctly does not affect the effectiveness of the filed record.

Official Comment

1. **Source.** New.

2. **Effectiveness of Mis-Indexed Records.** This section provides that the filing office's error in mis-indexing a record does not render ineffective an otherwise effective record. As did former Section 9-401, this section imposes the risk of filing-office error on those who search the files rather than on those who file.

§ 9-518. CLAIM CONCERNING INACCURATE OR WRONGFULLY FILED RECORD.

(a) [Correction statement.] A person may file in the filing office a correction statement with respect to a record indexed there under the person's name if the person believes that the record is inaccurate or was wrongfully filed.

[Alternative A]

(b) [Sufficiency of correction statement.] A correction statement must:

(1) identify the record to which it relates by the file number assigned to the initial financing statement to which the record relates;

(2) indicate that it is a correction statement; and

(3) provide the basis for the person's belief that the record is inaccurate and indicate the manner in which the person believes the record should be amended to cure any inaccuracy or provide the basis for the person's belief that the record was wrongfully filed.

[Alternative B]

(b) [Sufficiency of correction statement.] A correction statement must:

(1) identify the record to which it relates by:

(A) the file number assigned to the initial financing statement to which the record relates; and

(B) if the correction statement relates to a record filed [or recorded] in a filing office described in Section 9-501(a)(1), the date [and time] that the initial financing statement was filed [or recorded] and the information specified in Section 9-502(b);

(2) indicate that it is a correction statement; and

(3)   provide the basis for the person's belief that the record is inaccurate and indicate the manner in which the person believes the record should be amended to cure any inaccuracy or provide the basis for the person's belief that the record was wrongfully filed.

[End of Alternatives]

(c)   [Record not affected by correction statement.] The filing of a correction statement does not affect the effectiveness of an initial financing statement or other filed record.

Legislative Note: States whose real-estate filing offices require additional information in amendments and cannot search their records by both the name of the debtor and the file number should enact Alternative B to Sections 9-512(a), 9-518(b), 9-519(f) and 9-522(a).

Official Comment

1. **Source.** New.

2. **Correction Statements.** Former Article 9 did not afford a nonjudicial means for a debtor to correct a financing statement or other record that was inaccurate or wrongfully filed. Subsection (a) affords the debtor the right to file a correction statement. Among other requirements, the correction statement must provide the basis for the debtor's belief that the public record should be corrected. See subsection (b). These provisions, which resemble the analogous remedy in the Fair Credit Reporting Act, 15 U.S.C. § 1681i, afford an aggrieved person the opportunity to state its position on the public record. They do not permit an aggrieved person to change the legal effect of the public record. Thus, although a filed correction statement becomes part of the "financing statement," as defined in Section 9-102, the filing does not affect the effectiveness of the initial financing statement or any other filed record. See subsection (c).

This section does not displace other provisions of this Article that impose liability for making unauthorized filings or failing to file or send a termination statement. See Section 9-625(e). Nor does it displace any available judicial remedies.

3. **Resort to Other Law.** This Article cannot provide a satisfactory or complete solution to problems caused by misuse of the public records. The problem of "bogus" filings is not limited to the UCC filing system but extends to the real-property records, as well. A summary judicial procedure for correcting the public record and criminal penalties for those who misuse the filing and recording systems are likely to be more effective and put less strain on the filing system than provisions authorizing or requiring action by filing and recording offices.

[SUBPART 2. DUTIES AND OPERATION OF FILING OFFICE]

ANALYSIS

Old Article 9 says very little about the operation of the filing office. Extended delays in indexing have been common in some jurisdictions as are variances as to what a particular office will accept as a filing. Sections 9-519 through 9-520 are designed to streamline the operation of filing offices by precisely describing the duties of the filing offices, specifying time-limits for performance of those duties, recognizing national uniform forms for the initial financing statement and for amendments and encouraging adoption of filing office rules modelled after those promulgated by the International Association of Corporate Administrators.

§ 9-519. NUMBERING, MAINTAINING, AND INDEXING RECORDS; COMMUNICATING INFORMATION PROVIDED IN RECORDS.

(a) [Filing office duties.] For each record filed in a filing office, the filing office shall:

(1) assign a unique number to the filed record;

(2) create a record that bears the number assigned to the filed record and the date and time of filing;

(3) maintain the filed record for public inspection; and

(4) index the filed record in accordance with subsections (c), (d), and (e).

(b) [File number.] A file number [assigned after January 1, 2002,] must include a digit that:

(1) is mathematically derived from or related to the other digits of the file number; and

(2) aids the filing office in determining whether a number communicated as the file number includes a single-digit or transpositional error.

(c) [Indexing: general.] Except as otherwise provided in subsections (d) and (e), the filing office shall:

(1) index an initial financing statement according to the name of the debtor and index all filed records relating to the initial financing statement in a manner that associates with one another an initial financing statement and all filed records relating to the initial financing statement; and

(2) index a record that provides a name of a debtor which was not previously provided in the financing statement to which the record relates also according to the name that was not previously provided.

(d) [Indexing: real-property-related financing statement.] If a financing statement is filed as a fixture filing or covers as-extracted collateral or timber to be cut, [it must be filed for record and] the filing office shall index it:

(1) under the names of the debtor and of each owner of record shown on the financing statement as if they were the mortgagors under a mortgage of the real property described; and

(2) to the extent that the law of this State provides for indexing of records of mortgages under the name of the mortgagee, under the name of the secured party as if the secured party were the mortgagee thereunder, or, if indexing is by description, as if the financing statement were a record of a mortgage of the real property described.

(e) [Indexing: real-property-related assignment.] If a financing statement is filed as a fixture filing or covers as-extracted collateral or timber to be cut, the filing office shall index an assignment filed under Section 9-514(a) or an amendment filed under Section 9-514(b):

(1) under the name of the assignor as grantor; and

(2) to the extent that the law of this State provides for indexing a record of the assignment of a mortgage under the name of the assignee, under the name of the assignee.

[Alternative A]

(f) [Retrieval and association capability.] The filing office shall maintain a capability:

(1) to retrieve a record by the name of the debtor and by the file number assigned to the initial financing statement to which the record relates; and

(2)   to associate and retrieve with one another an initial financing statement and each filed record relating to the initial financing statement.

[Alternative B]

(f)   [Retrieval and association capability.] The filing office shall maintain a capability:

(1)   to retrieve a record by the name of the debtor and:

(A)   if the filing office is described in Section 9-501(a)(1), by the file number assigned to the initial financing statement to which the record relates and the date [and time] that the record was filed [or recorded]; or

(B)   if the filing office is described in Section 9-501(a)(2), by the file number assigned to the initial financing statement to which the record relates; and

(2)   to associate and retrieve with one another an initial financing statement and each filed record relating to the initial financing statement.

[End of Alternatives]

(g)   [Removal of debtor's name.] The filing office may not remove a debtor's name from the index until one year after the effectiveness of a financing statement naming the debtor lapses under Section 9-515 with respect to all secured parties of record.

(h)   [Timeliness of filing office performance.] The filing office shall perform the acts required by subsections (a) through (e) at the time and in the manner prescribed by filing-office rule, but not later than two business days after the filing office receives the record in question.

(i)   [Inapplicability to real-property-related filing office.] [Subsection] [Subsections] [(b)] [and] [(h)] [does] [do] not apply to a filing office described in Section 9-501(a)(1).]

Legislative Notes:

1. States whose filing offices currently assign file numbers that include a verification number, commonly known as a "check digit," or can implement this requirement before the effective date of this Article should omit the bracketed language in subsection (b).

2. In States in which writings will not appear in the real property records and indices unless actually recorded the bracketed language in subsection (d) should be used.

3. States whose real-estate filing offices require additional information in amendments and cannot search their records by both the name of the debtor and the file number should enact Alternative B to Sections 9-512(a), 9-518(b), 9-519(f) and 9-522(a).

4. A State that elects not to require real-estate filing offices to comply with either or both of subsections (b) and (h) may adopt an applicable variation of subsection (i) and add "Except as otherwise provided in subsection (i)," to the appropriate subsection or subsections.

ANALYSIS

A filing officer that fails to meet the two business day time limit would presumably be guilty of negligence in the performance of his or her duties, except when the delay is excused by new § 9-524. Parties who can show damages proximately caused by the negligence should be entitled to recover their damages in the absence of local legislation or rule of law immunizing the filing officer from liability.

Official Comment

1. **Source.** Former Sections 9-403(4), (7), 9-405(2).

2. **Filing Office's Duties.** Subsections (a) through (e) set forth the duties of the filing office with respect to filed records. Subsection (h), which is new, imposes a minimum standard of performance for those duties. Prompt indexing is crucial to the effectiveness of any filing system. An accepted but un-indexed record affords no public notice. Subsection (f) requires the filing office to maintain appropriate storage and retrieval facilities, and subsection (g) contains minimum requirements for the retention of records.

3. **File Number.** Subsection (a)(1) requires the filing office to assign a unique number to each filed record. That number is the "file number" only if the record is an initial financing statement. See Section 9-102.

4. **Time of Filing.** Subsection (a)(2) and Section 9-523 refer to the "date and time" of filing. The statutory text does not contain any instructions to a filing office as to how the time of filing is to be determined. The method of determining or assigning a time of filing is an appropriate matter for filling-office rules to address.

5. **Related Records.** Subsections (c) and (f) are designed to ensure that an initial financing statement and all filed records relating to it are associated with one another, indexed under the name of the debtor, and retrieved together. To comply with subsection (f), a filing office (other than a real-property recording office in a State that enacts subsection (f), Alternative B) must be capable of retrieving records in each of two ways: by the name of the debtor and by the file number of the initial financing statement to which the record relates.

6. **Prohibition on Deleting Names from Index.** This Article contemplates that the filing office will not delete the name of a debtor from the index until at least one year passes after the effectiveness of the financing statement lapses as to all secured parties of record. See subsection (g). This rule applies even if the filing office accepts an amendment purporting to delete or modify the name of a debtor or terminate the effectiveness of the financing statement. If an amendment provides a modified name for a debtor, the amended name should be added to the index, see subsection (c)(2), but the pre-amendment name should remain in the index.

Compared to former Article 9, the rule in subsection (g) increases the amount of information available to those who search the public records. The rule also contemplates that searchers-not the filing office-will determine the significance and effectiveness of filed records.

§ 9-520. ACCEPTANCE AND REFUSAL TO ACCEPT RECORD.

(a)   [Mandatory refusal to accept record.] A filing office shall refuse to accept a record for filing for a reason set forth in Section 9-516(b) and may refuse to accept a record for filing only for a reason set forth in Section 9-516(b).

ANALYSIS

The filing office may reject only for the reasons stated in Section 9-516(b). That section says nothing about the indication of the collateral required by Section 9-502(a)(3) for an effective statement. The filing office is not to concern itself with the adequacy of, or even the presence of the collateral description. However, a financing statement can be effective under new § 9-502(3) only to the extent that it indicates the collateral is covered.

(b) [Communication concerning refusal.] If a filing office refuses to accept a record for filing, it shall communicate to the person that presented the record the fact of and reason for the refusal and the date and time the record would have been filed had the filing office accepted it. The communication must be made at the time and in the manner prescribed by filing-office rule but [, in the case of a filing office described in Section 9-501(a)(2),] in no event more than two business days after the filing office receives the record.

(c) [When filed financing statement effective.] A filed financing statement satisfying Section 9-502(a) and (b) is effective, even if the filing office is required to refuse to accept it for filing under subsection (a). However, Section 9-338 applies to a filed financing statement providing information described in Section 9-516(b)(5) which is incorrect at the time the financing statement is filed.

(d) [Separate application to multiple debtors.] If a record communicated to a filing office provides information that relates to more than one debtor, this part applies as to each debtor separately.

Legislative Note: A State that elects not to require real-property filing offices to comply with subsection (b) should include the bracketed language.

Official Comment

1. **Source.** New.

2. **Refusal to Accept Record for Filing.** In some States, filing offices considered themselves obligated by former Article 9 to review the form and content of a financing statement and to refuse to accept those that they determine are legally insufficient. Some filing offices imposed requirements for or conditions to filing that do not appear in the statute. Under this section, the filing office is not expected to make legal judgments and is not permitted to impose additional conditions or requirements.

Subsection (a) both prescribes and limits the bases upon which the filing office must and may reject records by reference to the reasons set forth in Section 9-516(b). For the most part, the bases for rejection are limited to those that prevent the filing office from dealing with a record that it receives-because some the requisite information (e.g., the debtor's name) is missing or cannot be deciphered, because the record is not communicated by a method (e.g., it is MIME-rather than UU-encoded) or medium (e.g., it is written rather than electronic) that the filing office accepts, or because the filer fails to tender an amount equal to or greater than the filing fee.

3. **Consequences of Accepting Rejectable Record.** Section 9-516(b) includes among the reasons for rejecting an initial financing statement the failure to give certain information that is not required as a condition of effectiveness. In conjunction with Section 9-516(b)(5), this section requires the filing office to refuse to accept a financing statement that is legally sufficient to perfect a security interest under Section 9-502 but does not contain a mailing address for the debtor, does not disclose whether the debtor is an individual or an organization (e.g., a partnership or corporation) or, if the debtor is an organization, does not give certain specified information concerning the organization. The information required by Section 9-516(b)(5) assists searchers in weeding out "false positives," i.e., records that a search reveals but which do not pertain to the debtor in question. It assists filers by helping to ensure that the debtor's name is correct and that the financing statement is filed in the proper jurisdiction.

If the filing office accepts a financing statement that does not give this information at all, the filing is fully effective. Section 9-520(c). The financing statement also generally is effective if the information is given but is incorrect; however, Section 9-338 affords protection to buyers and holders of a perfected security interests who gives value in reasonable reliance upon the incorrect information.

4. **Filing Office's Duties with Respect to Rejected Record.** Subsection (b) requires the filing office to communicate the fact of rejection and the reason therefor within a fixed period of time. Inasmuch as a rightfully rejected record is ineffective and a wrongfully rejected record is not fully effective, prompt communication concerning any rejection is important.

5. **Partial Effectiveness of Record.** Under subsection (d), the provisions of this Part apply to each debtor separately. Thus, a filing office may reject an initial financing statement or other record as to one named debtor but accept it as to the other.

Example: An initial financing statement is communicated to the filing office. The financing statement names two debtors, John Smith and Jane Smith. It contains all of the information described in Section 9-516(b)(5) with respect to John but lacks some of the information with respect to Jane. The filing office must accept the financing statement with respect to John, reject it with respect to Jane, and notify the filer of the rejection.

§ 9-521. UNIFORM FORM OF WRITTEN FINANCING STATEMENT AND AMENDMENT.

(a) **[Initial financing statement form.]** A filing office that accepts written records may not refuse to accept a written initial financing statement in the following form and format except for a reason set forth in Section 9-516(b):

UCC FINANCING STATEMENT

FOLLOW INSTRUCTIONS (front and back) CAREFULLY

A. NAME & PHONE OF CONTACT AT FILER (optional)

B. SEND ACKNOWLEDGMENT TO: (Name and Address)

THE ABOVE SPACE IS FOR FILING OFFICE USE ONLY

1. DEBTOR'S EXACT FULL LEGAL NAME - insert only one debtor name (1a or 1b) - do not abbreviate or combine names

1a. ORGANIZATION'S NAME					
OR 1b. INDIVIDUAL'S LAST NAME		FIRST NAME		MIDDLE NAME	SUFFIX
1c. MAILING ADDRESS		CITY		STATE	POSTAL CODE	COUNTRY

| 1d. TAX ID #: SSN OR EIN | ADD'L INFO RE ORGANIZATION DEBTOR | 1e. TYPE OF ORGANIZATION | 1f. JURISDICTION OF ORGANIZATION | 1g. ORGANIZATIONAL ID #, if any | NONE |

2. ADDITIONAL DEBTOR'S EXACT FULL LEGAL NAME - insert only one debtor name (2a or 2b) - do not abbreviate or combine names

2a. ORGANIZATION'S NAME					
OR 2b. INDIVIDUAL'S LAST NAME		FIRST NAME		MIDDLE NAME	SUFFIX
2c. MAILING ADDRESS		CITY		STATE	POSTAL CODE	COUNTRY

| 2d. TAX ID #: SSN OR EIN | ADD'L INFO RE ORGANIZATION DEBTOR | 2e. TYPE OF ORGANIZATION | 2f. JURISDICTION OF ORGANIZATION | 2g. ORGANIZATIONAL ID #, if any | NONE |

3. SECURED PARTY'S NAME (or NAME of TOTAL ASSIGNEE of ASSIGNOR S/P) - insert only one secured party name (3a or 3b)

3a. ORGANIZATION'S NAME					
OR 3b. INDIVIDUAL'S LAST NAME		FIRST NAME		MIDDLE NAME	SUFFIX
3c. MAILING ADDRESS		CITY		STATE	POSTAL CODE	COUNTRY

4. This FINANCING STATEMENT covers the following collateral:

5. ALTERNATIVE DESIGNATION (if applicable):	LESSEE/LESSOR	CONSIGNEE/CONSIGNOR	BAILEE/BAILOR	SELLER/BUYER	AG. LIEN	NON-UCC FILING
6. This FINANCING STATEMENT is to be filed [for record] (or recorded) in the REAL ESTATE RECORDS. Attach Addendum [if applicable]		7. Check to REQUEST SEARCH REPORT(S) on Debtor(s) [ADDITIONAL FEE] [optional]			All Debtors	Debtor 1	Debtor 2
8. OPTIONAL FILER REFERENCE DATA						

NATIONAL UCC FINANCING STATEMENT (FORM UCC1) (REV. 07/29/98)

UCC FINANCING STATEMENT ADDENDUM

FOLLOW INSTRUCTIONS (front and back) CAREFULLY

9. NAME OF FIRST DEBTOR (1a or 1b) ON RELATED FINANCING STATEMENT

9a. ORGANIZATION'S NAME

OR

9b. INDIVIDUAL'S LAST NAME | FIRST NAME | MIDDLE NAME, SUFFIX

10. MISCELLANEOUS:

THE ABOVE SPACE IS FOR FILING OFFICE USE ONLY

11. ADDITIONAL DEBTOR'S EXACT FULL LEGAL NAME - insert only one name (11a or 11b) - do not abbreviate or combine names

11a. ORGANIZATION'S NAME

OR

11b. INDIVIDUAL'S LAST NAME | FIRST NAME | MIDDLE NAME | SUFFIX

11c. MAILING ADDRESS | CITY | STATE | POSTAL CODE | COUNTRY

11d. TAX ID #: SSN OR EIN | ADD'L INFO RE ORGANIZATION DEBTOR | 11e. TYPE OF ORGANIZATION | 11f. JURISDICTION OF ORGANIZATION | 11g. ORGANIZATIONAL ID #, if any [ ] NONE

12. [ ] ADDITIONAL SECURED PARTY'S or [ ] ASSIGNOR S/P'S NAME - insert only one name (12a or 12b)

12a. ORGANIZATION'S NAME

OR

12b. INDIVIDUAL'S LAST NAME | FIRST NAME | MIDDLE NAME | SUFFIX

12c. MAILING ADDRESS | CITY | STATE | POSTAL CODE | COUNTRY

13. This FINANCING STATEMENT covers [ ] timber to be cut or [ ] as-extracted collateral, or is filed as a [ ] fixture filing.

14. Description of real estate:

15. Name and address of a RECORD OWNER of above-described real estate (if Debtor does not have a record interest):

16. Additional collateral description:

17. Check only if applicable and check only one box.
Debtor is a [ ] Trust or [ ] Trustee acting with respect to property held in trust or [ ] Decedent's Estate

18. Check only if applicable and check only one box.
[ ] Debtor is a TRANSMITTING UTILITY
[ ] Filed in connection with a Manufactured-Home Transaction — effective 30 years
[ ] Filed in connection with a Public-Finance Transaction — effective 30 years

NATIONAL UCC FINANCING STATEMENT ADDENDUM (FORM UCC1Ad) (REV. 07/29/98)

(b) [Amendment form.] A filing office that accepts written records may not refuse to accept a written record in the following form and format except for a reason set forth in Section 9-516(b):

UCC FINANCING STATEMENT AMENDMENT

FOLLOW INSTRUCTIONS (front and back) CAREFULLY

A. NAME & PHONE OF CONTACT AT FILER [optional]

B. SEND ACKNOWLEDGMENT TO: (Name and Address)

THE ABOVE SPACE IS FOR FILING OFFICE USE ONLY

1a. INITIAL FINANCING STATEMENT FILE #

1b. This FINANCING STATEMENT AMENDMENT is to be filed [for record] (or recorded) in the REAL ESTATE RECORDS.

2. ☐ TERMINATION: Effectiveness of the Financing Statement identified above is terminated with respect to security interest(s) of the Secured Party authorizing this Termination Statement.

3. ☐ CONTINUATION: Effectiveness of the Financing Statement identified above with respect to security interest(s) of the Secured Party authorizing this Continuation Statement is continued for the additional period provided by applicable law.

4. ☐ ASSIGNMENT (full or partial): Give name of assignee in item 7a or 7b and address of assignee in item 7c; and also give name of assignor in item 9.

5. AMENDMENT (PARTY INFORMATION): This Amendment affects ☐ Debtor or ☐ Secured Party of record. Check only one of these two boxes.
Also check one of the following three boxes and provide appropriate information in items 6 and/or 7.

☐ CHANGE name and/or address: Give current record name in item 6a or 6b; also give new name (if name change) in item 7a or 7b and/or new address (if address change) in item 7c. ☐ DELETE name: Give record name to be deleted in item 6a or 6b. ☐ ADD name: Complete item 7a or 7b, and also item 7c; also complete items 7d-7g (if applicable).

6. CURRENT RECORD INFORMATION:

6a. ORGANIZATION'S NAME			
OR 6b. INDIVIDUAL'S LAST NAME	FIRST NAME	MIDDLE NAME	SUFFIX

7. CHANGED (NEW) OR ADDED INFORMATION:

7a. ORGANIZATION'S NAME			
OR 7b. INDIVIDUAL'S LAST NAME	FIRST NAME	MIDDLE NAME	SUFFIX
7c. MAILING ADDRESS	CITY	STATE POSTAL CODE	COUNTRY

7d. TAX ID #: SSN OR EIN	ADD'L INFO RE ORGANIZATION DEBTOR	7e. TYPE OF ORGANIZATION	7f. JURISDICTION OF ORGANIZATION	7g. ORGANIZATIONAL ID #, if any
				☐ NONE

8. AMENDMENT (COLLATERAL CHANGE): check only one box.

Describe collateral ☐ deleted or ☐ added, or give entire ☐ restated collateral description, or describe collateral ☐ assigned.

9. NAME OF SECURED PARTY OF RECORD AUTHORIZING THIS AMENDMENT (name of assignor, if this is an Assignment). If this is an Amendment authorized by a Debtor which adds collateral or adds the authorizing Debtor, or if this is a Termination authorized by a Debtor, check here ☐ and enter name of DEBTOR authorizing this Amendment.

9a. ORGANIZATION'S NAME			
OR 9b. INDIVIDUAL'S LAST NAME	FIRST NAME	MIDDLE NAME	SUFFIX

10. OPTIONAL FILER REFERENCE DATA

NATIONAL UCC FINANCING STATEMENT AMENDMENT (FORM UCC3) (REV. 07/29/98)

UCC FINANCING STATEMENT AMENDMENT ADDENDUM

FOLLOW INSTRUCTIONS (front and back) CAREFULLY

11. INITIAL FINANCING STATEMENT FILE # (same as Item 1a on Amendment form)

12. NAME OF PARTY AUTHORIZING THIS AMENDMENT (same as Item 9 on Amendment form)

12a. ORGANIZATION'S NAME

OR

12b. INDIVIDUAL'S LAST NAME | FIRST NAME | MIDDLE NAME, SUFFIX

13. Use this space for additional information

THE ABOVE SPACE IS FOR FILING OFFICE USE ONLY

NATIONAL UCC FINANCING STATEMENT AMENDMENT ADDENDUM (FORM UCC3Ad) (REV. 07/29/98)

Official Comment

1. **Source.** New.

2. **"Safe Harbor" Written Forms.** Although Section 9-520 limits the bases upon which the filing office can refuse to accept records, this section provide sample written forms that must be accepted in every filing office in the country, as long as the filing office's rules permit it to accept written communications. By completing one of the forms in this section, a secured party can be certain that the filing office is obligated to accept it.

The forms in this section are based upon national financing statement forms that were in use under former Article 9. Those forms were developed over an extended period and reflect the comments and suggestions of filing officers, secured parties and their counsel, and service companies. The formatting of those forms and of the ones in this section has been designed to reduce error by both filers and filing offices.

A filing office that accepts written communications may not reject, on grounds of form or format, a filing using these forms. Although filers are not required to use the forms, they are encouraged and can be expected to do so, inasmuch as the forms are well designed and avoid the risk of rejection on the basis of form or format. As their use expands, the forms will rapidly become familiar to both filers and filing-office personnel. Filing offices may and should encourage the use of these forms by declaring them to be the "standard" (but not exclusive) forms for each jurisdiction, albeit without in any way suggesting that alternative forms are unacceptable.

The multi-purpose form in subsection (b) covers changes with respect to the debtor, the secured party, the collateral, and the status of the financing statement (termination and continuation). A single form may be used for several different types of amendments at once (e.g., both to change a debtor's name and continue the effectiveness of the financing statement).

§ 9-522. MAINTENANCE AND DESTRUCTION OF RECORDS.

[Alternative A]

(a) [Post-lapse maintenance and retrieval of information.] The filing office shall maintain a record of the information provided in a filed financing statement for at least one year after the effectiveness of the financing statement has lapsed under Section 9-515 with respect to all secured parties of record. The record must be retrievable by using the name of the debtor and by using the file number assigned to the initial financing statement to which the record relates.

[Alternative B]

(a) [Post-lapse maintenance and retrieval of informa-tion.] The filing office shall maintain a record of the information provided in a filed financing statement for at least one year after the effectiveness of the financing statement has lapsed under Section 9-515 with respect to all secured parties of record. The record must be retrievable by using the name of the debtor and:

(1) if the record was filed [or recorded] in the filing office described in Section 9-501(a)(1), by using the file number assigned to the initial financing statement to which the record relates and the date [and time] that the record was filed [or recorded]; or

(2) if the record was filed in the filing office described in Section 9-501(a)(2), by using the file number assigned to the initial financing statement to which the record relates.

[End of Alternatives]

(b) [Destruction of written records.] Except to the extent that a statute governing disposition of public records provides otherwise, the filing office immediately may destroy any written record evidencing a financing statement. However, if the filing office destroys a written record, it shall maintain another record of the financing statement which complies with subsection (a).

Legislative Note: States whose real-estate filing offices require addi-tional information in amendments and cannot search their records by both the name of the debtor and the file number should enact Alternative B to Sections 9-512(a), 9-518(b), 9-519(f) and 9-522(a).

Official Comment

1. **Source.** Former Section 9-403(3), revised substantially.

2. **Maintenance of Records.** Section 9-523 requires the filing office to provide information concerning certain lapsed financing statements. Accord-ingly, subsection (a) requires the filing office to maintain a record of the information in a financing statement for at least one year after lapse. During that time, the filing office may not delete any information with respect to a filed financing statement; it may only add information. This approach relieves the filing office from any duty to determine whether to substitute or delete information upon receipt of an amendment. It also assures searchers that they will receive all information with respect to financing statements filed against a debtor and thereby be able themselves to determine the state of the public record.

The filing office may maintain this information in any medium. Subsection (b) permits the filing office immediately to destroy written records evidencing a financing statement, provided that the filing office maintains another record of the information contained in the financing statement as required by subsection (a).

§ 9-523. INFORMATION FROM FILING OFFICE; SALE OR LICENSE OF RECORDS.

(a) [Acknowledgment of filing written record.] If a person that files a written record requests an acknowledgment of the filing, the filing office shall send to the person an image of the record showing the number assigned to the record pursuant to Section 9-519(a)(1) and the date and time of the filing of the record. However, if the person furnishes a copy of the record to the filing office, the filing office may instead:

(1) note upon the copy the number assigned to the record pursuant to Section 9-519(a)(1) and the date and time of the filing of the record; and

(2) send the copy to the person.

(b) [Acknowledgment of filing other record.] If a person files a record other than a written record, the filing office shall communicate to the person an acknowledgment that provides:

(1) the information in the record;

(2) the number assigned to the record pursuant to Section 9-519(a)(1); and

(3) the date and time of the filing of the record.

(c) [Communication of requested information.] The filing office shall communicate or otherwise make available in a record the following information to any person that requests it:

(1) whether there is on file on a date and time specified by the filing office, but not a date earlier than three business days before the filing office receives the request, any financing statement that:

(A) designates a particular debtor [or, if the request so states, designates a particular debtor at the address specified in the request];

(B) has not lapsed under Section 9-515 with respect to all secured parties of record; and

(C) if the request so states, has lapsed under Section 9-515 and a record of which is maintained by the filing office under Section 9-522(a);

(2) the date and time of filing of each financing statement; and

(3) the information provided in each financing statement.

(d) [Medium for communicating information.] In complying with its duty under subsection (c), the filing office may communicate information in any medium. However, if requested, the filing office shall communicate information by issuing [its written certificate] [a record that can be admitted into evidence in the courts of this State without extrinsic evidence of its authenticity].

(e) [Timeliness of filing office performance.] The filing office shall perform the acts required by subsections (a) through (d) at the time and in the manner prescribed by filing-office rule, but not later than two business days after the filing office receives the request.

(f) [Public availability of records.] At least weekly, the [insert appropriate official or governmental agency] [filing office] shall offer to sell or license to the public on a nonexclusive basis, in bulk, copies of all records filed in it under this part, in every medium from time to time available to the filing office.

Legislative Notes:

1. States whose filing office does not offer the additional service of responding to search requests limited to a particular address should omit the bracketed language in subsection (c)(1)(A).

2. A State that elects not to require real-estate filing offices to comply with either or both of subsections (e) and (f) should specify in the appropriate subsection(s) only the filing office described in Section 9-501(a)(2).

ANALYSIS

Deep in their corporate hearts, the revisers believe that private agencies will normally do a better job of information storage and retrieval than public officials. The provision does not require a public bidding procedure. A filing office which does not want competition could apparently set a prohibitive price.

Official Comment

1. **Source.** Former Section 9-407; subsections (d) and (e) are new.

2. **Filing Office's Duty to Provide Information.** Former Section 9-407, dealing with obtaining information from the filing office, was bracketed to suggest to legislatures that its enactment was optional. Experience has shown that the method by which interested persons can obtain information concerning the public records should be uniform. Accordingly, the analogous provisions of this Article are not in brackets.

Most of the other changes from former Section 9-407 are for clarification, to embrace medium-neutral drafting, or to impose standards of performance on the filing office.

3. **Acknowledgments of Filing.** Subsections (a) and (b) require the filing office to acknowledge the filing of a record. Under subsection (a), the filing office is required to acknowledge the filing of a written record only upon request of the filer. Subsection (b) requires the filing office to acknowledge the filing of a non-written record even in the absence of a request from the filer.

4. **Response to Search Request.** Subsection (c)(3) requires the filing office to provide "the information contained in each financing statement" to a person who requests it. This requirement can be satisfied by providing copies, images, or reports. The requirement does not in any manner inhibit the filing office from also offering to provide less than all of the information (presumably for a lower fee) to a person who asks for less. Thus, subsection (c) accommodates the practice of providing only the type of record (e.g., initial financing statement, continuation statement), number assigned to the record, date and time of filing, and names and addresses of the debtor and secured party when a requesting person asks for no more (i.e., when the person does not ask for copies of financing statements). In contrast, the filing office's obligation under subsection (b) to provide an acknowledgment containing "the information contained in the record" is not defined by a customer's request. Thus unless the filer stipulates otherwise, to comply with subsection (b) the filing office's acknowledgment must contain all of the information in a record.

Subsection (c) assures that a minimum amount of information about filed records will be available to the public. It does not preclude a filing office from offering additional services.

5. **Lapsed and Terminated Financing Statements.** This section reflects the policy that terminated financing statements will remain part of the filing office's data base. The filing office may remove from the data base only lapsed financing statements, and then only when at least a year has passed after lapse. See Section 9-519(g). Subsection (c)(1)(C) requires a filing office to conduct a search and report as to lapsed financing statements that have not been removed from the data base, when requested.

6. **Search by Debtor's Address.** Subsection (c)(1)(A) contemplates that, by making a single request, a searcher will receive the results of a search of the entire public record maintained by any given filing office. Addition of the bracketed language in subsection (c)(1)(A) would permit a search report limited to financing statements showing a particular address for the debtor, but only if the search request is so limited. With or without the bracketed language, this subsection does not permit the filing office to compel a searcher to limit a request by address.

7. **Medium of Communication; Certificates.** Former Article 9 provided that the filing office respond to a request for information by providing a certificate. The principle of medium-neutrality would suggest that the statute not require a written certificate. Subsection (d) follows this principle by permitting the filing office to respond by communicating "in any medium." By permitting communication "in any medium," subsection (d) is not inconsistent with a system in which persons other than filing office staff conduct searches of the filing office's (computer) records.

Some searchers find it necessary to introduce the results of their search into evidence. Because official written certificates might be introduced into evidence more easily than official communications in another medium, subsection (d) affords States the option of requiring the filing office to issue written certificates upon request. The alternative bracketed language in subsection (d) recognizes that some States may prefer to permit the filing office to respond in another medium, as long as the response can be admitted into evidence in the courts of that State without extrinsic evidence of its authenticity.

8. **Performance Standard.** The utility of the filing system depends on the ability of searchers to get current information quickly. Accordingly, subsection (e) requires that the filing office respond to a request for information no later than two business days after it receives the request. The information contained in the response must be current as of a date no earlier than three business days before the filing office receives the request. See subsection (c)(1). The failure of the filing office to comply with performance standards, such as subsection (e), has no effect on the private rights of persons affected by the filing of records.

9. **Sales of Records in Bulk.** Subsection (f), which is new, mandates that the appropriate official or the filing office sell or license the filing records to the public in bulk, on a nonexclusive basis, in every medium available to the filing office. The details of implementation are left to filing-office rules.

§ 9-524. DELAY BY FILING OFFICE. Delay by the filing office beyond a time limit prescribed by this part is excused if:

(1) the delay is caused by interruption of communication or computer facilities, war, emergency conditions, failure of equipment, or other circumstances beyond control of the filing office; and

(2) the filing office exercises reasonable diligence under the circumstances.

Official Comment

Source. New; derived from Section 4-109.

§ 9-525. FEES.

(a) [Initial financing statement: general.] Except as otherwise provided in subsection (e), the fee for filing and indexing a record under this part, other than an initial financing statement of the kind described in Section 9-502(c), is [the amount specified in subsection (c), if applicable, plus]:

(1) $ ___[X]___ if the record is communicated in writing and consists of one or two pages;

(2) $ ___[2X]___ if the record is communicated in writing and consists of more than two pages; and

(3) $ ___[1/2X]__ if the record is communicated by another medium authorized by filing-office rule.

(b) [Initial financing statement: Section 9-502(c).] Except as otherwise provided in subsection (e), the fee for filing and indexing an initial financing statement of the kind described in Section 9-502(c) is [the amount specified in subsection (c), if applicable, plus]:

(1) $ _____ if the financing statement indicates that it is filed in connection with a public-finance transaction;

(2) $ _____ if the financing statement indicates that it is filed in connection with a manufactured-home transaction.

[Alternative A]

(c) [Number of names.] The number of names required to be indexed does not affect the amount of the fee in subsections (a) and (b).

[Alternative B]

(c) [Number of names.] Except as otherwise provided in subsection (e), if a record is communicated in writing, the fee for each name more than two required to be indexed is $ ___.

[End of Alternatives]

(d) [Response to information request.] The fee for responding to a request for information from the filing office, including for [issuing a certificate showing] [communicating] whether there is on file any financing statement naming a particular debtor, is:

(1) $ __ if the request is communicated in writing; and

(2) $ __ if the request is communicated by another medium authorized by filing-office rule.

(e) [Record of mortgage.] This section does not require a fee with respect to a record of a mortgage which is effective as a financing statement filed as a fixture filing or as a financing statement covering as-extracted collateral or timber to be cut under Section 9-502(c). However, the recording and satisfaction fees that otherwise would be applicable to the record of the mortgage apply.

Legislative Notes:

1. To preserve uniformity, a State that places the provisions of this section together with statutes setting fees for other services should do so without modification.

2. A State should enact subsection (c), Alternative A, and omit the bracketed language in subsections (a) and (b) unless its indexing system entails a substantial additional cost when indexing additional names.

Official Comment

1. **Source.** Various sections of former Part 4.

2. **Fees.** This section contains all fee requirements for filing, indexing, and responding to requests for information. Uniformity in the fee structure (but not necessarily in the amount of fees) makes this Article easier for secured parties to use and reduces the likelihood that a filed record will be rejected for failure to pay at least the correct amount of the fee. See Section 9-516(b)(2).

The costs of processing electronic records are less than those with respect to written records. Accordingly, this section mandates a lower fee as an incentive to file electronically and imposes the additional charge (if any) for multiple debtors only with respect to written records. When written records are used, this Article encourages the use of the uniform forms in Section 9-521. The fee for filing these forms should be no greater than the fee for other written records.

To make the relevant information included in a filed record more accessible once the record is found, this section mandates a higher fee for longer written records than for shorter ones. Finally, recognizing that financing statements naming more than one debtor are most often filed against a husband and wife, any additional charge for multiple debtors applies to records filed with respect to more than two debtors, rather than with respect to more than one.

§ 9-526. FILING-OFFICE RULES.

(a) [Adoption of filing-office rules.] The [insert appropriate governmental official or agency] shall adopt and publish rules to implement this article. The filing-office rules must be[:

(1)] consistent with this article[; and

(2) adopted and published in accordance with the [insert any applicable state administrative procedure act]].

(b) [Harmonization of rules.] To keep the filing-office rules and practices of the filing office in harmony with the rules and practices of filing offices in other jurisdictions that enact substantially this part, and to keep the technology used by the filing office compatible with the technology used by filing offices in other jurisdictions that enact substantially this part, the [insert appropriate governmental official or agency], so far as is consistent with the purposes, policies, and provisions of this article, in adopting, amending, and repealing filing-office rules, shall:

(1) consult with filing offices in other jurisdictions that enact substantially this part; and

(2) consult the most recent version of the Model Rules promulgated by the International Association of Corporate Administrators or any successor organization; and

(3) take into consideration the rules and practices of, and the technology used by, filing offices in other jurisdictions that enact substantially this part.

Official Comment

1. **Source.** New; subsection (b) derives in part from the Uniform Consumer Credit Code (1974).

2. **Rules Required.** Operating a filing office is a complicated business, requiring many more rules and procedures than this Article can usefully provide. Subsection (a) requires the adoption of rules to carry out the provisions of Article 9. The filing-office rules must be consistent with the provisions of the statute and adopted in accordance with local procedures. The publication requirement informs secured parties about filing-office practices, aids secured parties in evaluating filing-related risks and costs, and promotes regularity of application within the filing office.

3. **Importance of Uniformity.** In today's national economy, uniformity of the policies and practices of the filing offices will reduce the costs of secured transactions substantially. The International Association of Corporate Administrators (IACA), referred to in subsection (b), is an organization whose membership includes filing officers from every State. These individuals are responsible for the proper functioning of the Article 9 filing system and have worked diligently to develop model filing-office rules, with a view toward efficiency and uniformity.

Although uniformity is an important desideratum, subsection (a) affords considerable flexibility in the adoption of filing-office rules. Each State may adopt a version of subsection (a) that reflects the desired relationship between the statewide filing office described in Section 9-501(a)(2) and the local filing offices described in Section 9-501(a)(1) and that takes into account the practices of its filing offices. Subsection (a) need not designate a single official or agency to adopt rules applicable to all filing offices, and the rules applicable to the statewide filing office need not be identical to those applicable to the local filing office. For example, subsection (a) might provide for the statewide filing office to adopt filing-office rules, and, if not prohibited by other law, the filing office might adopt one set of rules for itself and another for local offices. Or, subsection (a) might designate one official or agency to adopt rules for the statewide filing office and another to adopt rules for local filing offices.

§ 9-527.   DUTY TO REPORT. The [insert appropriate governmental official or agency] shall report [annually on or before __] to the [Governor and Legislature] on the operation of the filing office. The report must contain a statement of the extent to which:

(1)   the filing-office rules are not in harmony with the rules of filing offices in other jurisdictions that enact substantially this part and the reasons for these variations; and

(2)   the filing-office rules are not in harmony with the most recent version of the Model Rules promulgated by the International Association of Corporate Administrators, or any successor organization, and the reasons for these variations.

Official Comment

1. **Source.** New; derived in part from the Uniform Consumer Credit Code (1974).

2. **Duty to Report.** This section is designed to promote compliance with the standards of performance imposed upon the filing office and with the requirement that the filing office's policies, practices, and technology be consistent and compatible with the policies, practices, and technology of other filing offices.

PART 6   DEFAULT

[SUBPART 1.   DEFAULT AND ENFORCEMENT OF SECURITY INTEREST]

§ 9-601.   RIGHTS AFTER DEFAULT; JUDICIAL ENFORCEMENT; CONSIGNOR OR BUYER OF ACCOUNTS, CHATTEL PAPER, PAYMENT INTANGIBLES, OR PROMISSORY NOTES.

(a)   **[Rights of secured party after default.]** After default, a secured party has the rights provided in this part and, except as otherwise provided in Section 9-602, those provided by agreement of the parties. A secured party:

(1)   may reduce a claim to judgment, foreclose, or otherwise enforce the claim, security interest, or agricultural lien by any available judicial procedure; and

(2)   if the collateral is documents, may proceed either as to the documents or as to the goods they cover.

(b)   **[Rights and duties of secured party in possession or control.]** A secured party in possession of collateral or control of collateral under Section 9-104, 9-105, 9-106, or 9-107 has the rights and duties provided in Section 9-207.

(c)   **[Rights cumulative; simultaneous exercise.]** The rights under subsections (a) and (b) are cumulative and may be exercised simultaneously.

(d)   **[Rights of debtor and obligor.]** Except as otherwise provided in subsection (g) and Section 9-605, after default, a debtor and an obligor have the rights provided in this part and by agreement of the parties.

(e)   **[Lien of levy after judgment.]** If a secured party has reduced its claim to judgment, the lien of any levy that may be made upon the collateral by virtue of an execution based upon the judgment relates back to the earliest of:

(1)   the date of perfection of the security interest or agricultural lien in the collateral;

(2)   the date of filing a financing statement covering the collateral; or

(3)   any date specified in a statute under which the agricultural lien was created.

(f)   [Execution sale.] A sale pursuant to an execution is a foreclosure of the security interest or agricultural lien by judicial procedure within the meaning of this section. A secured party may purchase at the sale and thereafter hold the collateral free of any other requirements of this article.

(g)   [Consignor or buyer of certain rights to payment.] Except as otherwise provided in Section 9-607(c), this part imposes no duties upon a secured party that is a consignor or is a buyer of accounts, chattel paper, payment intangibles, or promissory notes.

Official Comment

1. **Source.** Former Section 9-501(1), (2), (5).

2. **Enforcement: In General.** The rights of a secured party to enforce its security interest in collateral after the debtor's default are an important feature of a secured transaction. (Note that the term "rights," as defined in Section 1-201, includes "remedies.") This Part provides those rights as well as certain limitations on their exercise for the protection of the defaulting debtor, other creditors, and other affected persons. However, subsections (a) and (d) make clear that the rights provided in this Part do not exclude other rights provided by agreement.

3. **When Remedies Arise.** Under subsection (a) the secured party's rights arise "[a]fter default." As did former Section 9-501, this Article leaves to the agreement of the parties the circumstances giving rise to a default. This Article does not determine whether a secured party's post-default conduct can constitute a waiver of default in the face of an agreement stating that such conduct shall not constitute a waiver. Rather, it continues to leave to the parties' agreement, as supplemented by law other than this Article, the determination whether a default has occurred or has been waived. See Section 1-103.

4. **Possession of Collateral; Section 9-207.** After a secured party takes possession of collateral following a default, there is no longer any distinction between a security interest that before default was nonpossessory and a security interest that was possessory before default, as under a common-law

pledge. This Part generally does not distinguish between the rights of a secured party with a nonpossessory security interest and those of a secured party with a possessory security interest. However, Section 9-207 addresses rights and duties with respect to collateral in a secured party's possession. Under subsection (b) of this section, Section 9-207 applies not only to possession before default but also to possession after default. Subsection (b) also has been conformed to Section 9-207, which, unlike former Section 9-207, applies to secured parties having control of collateral.

5. **Cumulative Remedies.** Former Section 9-501(1) provided that the secured party's remedies were cumulative, but it did not explicitly provide whether the remedies could be exercised simultaneously. Subsection (c) permits the simultaneous exercise of remedies if the secured party acts in good faith. The liability scheme of Subpart 2 affords redress to an aggrieved debtor or obligor. Moreover, permitting the simultaneous exercise of remedies under subsection (c) does not override any non-UCC law, including the law of tort and statutes regulating collection of debts, under which the simultaneous exercise of remedies in a particular case constitutes abusive behavior or harassment giving rise to liability.

6. **Judicial Enforcement.** Under subsection (a) a secured party may reduce its claim to judgment or foreclose its interest by any available procedure outside this Article under applicable law. Subsection (e) generally follows former Section 9-501(5). It makes clear that any judicial lien that the secured party may acquire against the collateral effectively is a continuation of the original security interest (if perfected) and not the acquisition of a new interest or a transfer of property on account of a preexisting obligation. Under former Section 9-501(5), the judicial lien was stated to relate back to the date of perfection of the security interest. Subsection (e), however, provides that the lien relates back to the earlier of the date of filing or the date of perfection. This provides a secured party who enforces a security interest by judicial process with the benefit of the "first-to-file-or-perfect" priority rule of Section 9-322(a)(1).

7. **Agricultural Liens.** Part 6 provides parallel treatment for the enforcement of agricultural liens and security interests. Because agricultural liens are statutory rather than consensual, this Article does draw a few distinctions between these liens and security interests. Under subsection (e), the statute creating an agricultural lien would govern whether and the date to which an execution lien relates back. Section 9-606 explains when a "default" occurs in the agricultural lien context.

8. **Execution Sales.** Subsection (f) also follows former Section 9-501(5). It makes clear that an execution sale is an appropriate method of foreclosure contemplated by this Part. However, the sale is governed by other law and not by this Article, and the limitations under Section 9-610 on the right of a secured party to purchase collateral do not apply.

9. **Sales of Receivables; Consignments.** Subsection (g) provides that, except as provided in Section 9-607(c), the duties imposed on secured parties do not apply to buyers of accounts, chattel paper, payment intangibles, or promissory notes. Although denominated "secured parties," these buyers own the entire interest in the property sold and so may enforce their rights without regard to the seller ("debtor") or the seller's creditors. Likewise, a true consignor may enforce its ownership interest under other law without regard to the duties that this Part imposes on secured parties. Note, however, that Section 9-615 governs cases in which a consignee's secured party (other than a consignor) is enforcing a security interest that is senior to the security interest (i.e., ownership interest) of a true consignor.

§ 9-602. WAIVER AND VARIANCE OF RIGHTS AND DUTIES.
Except as otherwise provided in Section 9-624, to the extent that they give rights to a debtor or obligor and impose duties on a secured party, the debtor or obligor may not waive or vary the rules stated in the following listed sections:

(1) Section 9-207(b)(4)(C), which deals with use and operation of the collateral by the secured party;

(2) Section 9-210, which deals with requests for an accounting and requests concerning a list of collateral and statement of account;

(3) Section 9-607(c), which deals with collection and enforcement of collateral;

(4) Sections 9-608(a) and 9-615(c) to the extent that they deal with application or payment of noncash proceeds of collection, enforcement, or disposition;

(5) Sections 9-608(a) and 9-615(d) to the extent that they require accounting for or payment of surplus proceeds of collateral;

(6) Section 9-609 to the extent that it imposes upon a secured party that takes possession of collateral without judicial process the duty to do so without breach of the peace;

(7) Sections 9-610(b), 9-611, 9-613, and 9-614, which deal with disposition of collateral;

(8) Section 9-615(f), which deals with calculation of a deficiency or surplus when a disposition is made to the secured party, a person related to the secured party, or a secondary obligor;

(9) Section 9-616, which deals with explanation of the calculation of a surplus or deficiency;

(10) Sections 9-620, 9-621, and 9-622, which deal with acceptance of collateral in satisfaction of obligation;

(11) Section 9-623, which deals with redemption of collateral;

(12) Section 9-624, which deals with permissible waivers; and

(13) Sections 9-625 and 9-626, which deal with the secured party's liability for failure to comply with this article.

ANALYSIS

The anti-waiver policy applies to the extent that the listed provisions give rights to a debtor or obligor or impose duties on a secured party. The stated list of provisions is much more extensive than under old § 9-503(3). Included are specified collection and repossession provisions as well as disposition duties. Under Revised Article 9 a secondary obligor may not prior to default waive the right to notification of disposition or the duty to make a commercially reasonable disposition. *See new* § 9-624. With respect to all rights and duties except the duty not to commit a breach of the peace, the agreement may set standards measuring the fulfillment of the statutory rights and duties. *See new* § 9-603. The agreement may not speak to what constitutes a breach of the peace in either consumer or commercial cases.

Article 9 does not rule on whether the specified list would still be subject to the general principle of § 1-102(3) barring disclaimer of obligations of good faith, diligence, reasonableness and care. Thus, a secured agreement could not disclaim a pledgee's obligation under new § 9-207(a) to use reasonable care in the custody and preservation of collateral in its possession. And it is difficult to imagine circumstance in which an agreement could waive the requirement that a creditor apply proceeds of a deposition to a secured obligation as required by Section 9-603(1)(C). *See* Official Comment 2 to this provision.

Official Comment

1. **Source.** Former Section 9-501(3).

2. **Waiver: In General.** Section 1-102(3) addresses which provisions of the UCC are mandatory and which may be varied by agreement. With exceptions relating to good faith, diligence, reasonableness, and care, immediate parties, as between themselves, may vary its provisions by agreement. However, in the context of rights and duties after default, our legal system traditionally has looked with suspicion on agreements that limit the debtor's rights and free the secured party of its duties. As stated in former Section 9-501, Comment 4, "no mortgage clause has ever been allowed to clog the equity of redemption." The context of default offers great opportunity for overreaching. The suspicious attitudes of the courts have been grounded in common sense. This section, like former Section 9-501(3), codifies this long-standing and deeply rooted attitude. The specified rights of the debtor and duties of the secured party may not be waived or varied except as stated. Provisions that are not specified in this section are subject to the general rules in Section 1-102(3).

3. **Nonwaivable Rights and Duties.** This section revises former Section 9-501(3) by restricting the ability to waive or modify additional specified rights and duties: (i) duties under Section 9-207(c)(4)(C), which deals with the use and operation of consumer goods, (ii) the right to a response to a request for an accounting, concerning a list of collateral, or concerning a statement of account (Section 9-210), (iii) the duty to collect collateral in a commercially reasonable manner (Section 9-607), (iv) the implicit duty to refrain from a breach of the peace in taking possession of collateral under Section 9-609, (v) the duty to apply noncash proceeds of collection or disposition in a commercially reasonable manner (Sections 9-608 and 9-615), (vi) the right to a special method of calculating a surplus or deficiency in certain dispositions to a secured party, a person related to secured party, or a secondary obligor (Section 9-615), (vii) the duty to give an explanation of the calculation of a surplus or deficiency (Section 9-616), (viii) the right to limitations on the effectiveness of certain waivers (Section 9-624), and (ix) the right to hold a secured party liable for failure to comply with this Article (Sections 9-625 and 9-626). For clarity and consistency, this Article uses the term "waive or vary" instead of "renounc[e] or modify[]," which appeared in former Section 9-504(3).

This section provides generally that the specified rights and duties "may not be waived or varied" However, it does not restrict the ability of parties to agree to settle, compromise, or renounce claims for past conduct that may have constituted a violation or breach of those rights and duties, even if the settlement involves an express "waiver."

4. **Waiver by Debtors and Obligors.** The restrictions on waiver contained in this section apply to obligors as well as debtors. This resolves a question under former Article 9 as to whether secondary obligors, assuming that they were "debtors" for purposes of former Part 5, were permitted to waive, under the law of suretyship, rights and duties under that Part.

5. **Certain Post-Default Waivers.** Section 9-624 permits post-default waivers in limited circumstances. These waivers must be made in agreements that are authenticated. Under Section 1-201, an " 'agreement' means the bargain of the parties in fact." In considering waivers under Section 9-624 and analogous agreements in other contexts, courts should carefully scrutinize putative agreements that appear in records that also address many additional or unrelated matters.

§ 9-603. AGREEMENT ON STANDARDS CONCERNING RIGHTS AND DUTIES.

(a) **[Agreed standards.]** The parties may determine by agreement the standards measuring the fulfillment of the rights of a debtor or obligor and the duties of a secured party under a rule stated in Section 9-602 if the standards are not manifestly unreasonable.

(b) **[Agreed standards inapplicable to breach of peace.]** Subsection (a) does not apply to the duty under Section 9-609 to refrain from breaching the peace.

Official Comment

1. **Source.** Former Section 9-501(3).

2. **Limitation on Ability to Set Standards.** Subsection (a), like former Section 9-501(3), permits the parties to set standards for compliance with the rights and duties under this Part if the standards are not "manifestly unreasonable." Under subsection (b), the parties are not permitted to set standards measuring fulfillment of the secured party's duty to take collateral without breaching the peace.

§ 9-604. PROCEDURE IF SECURITY AGREEMENT COVERS REAL PROPERTY OR FIXTURES.

(a) **[Enforcement: personal and real property.]** If a security agreement covers both personal and real property, a secured party may proceed:

(1) under this part as to the personal property without prejudicing any rights with respect to the real property; or

(2) as to both the personal property and the real property in accordance with the rights with respect to the real property, in which case the other provisions of this part do not apply.

(b) **[Enforcement: fixtures.]** Subject to subsection (c), if a security agreement covers goods that are or become fixtures, a secured party may proceed:

(1) under this part; or

(2) in accordance with the rights with respect to real property, in which case the other provisions of this part do not apply.

(c) [Removal of fixtures.] Subject to the other provisions of this part, if a secured party holding a security interest in fixtures has priority over all owners and encumbrancers of the real property, the secured party, after default, may remove the collateral from the real property.

(d) [Injury caused by removal.] A secured party that removes collateral shall promptly reimburse any encumbrancer or owner of the real property, other than the debtor, for the cost of repair of any physical injury caused by the removal. The secured party need not reimburse the encumbrancer or owner for any diminution in value of the real property caused by the absence of the goods removed or by any necessity of replacing them. A person entitled to reimbursement may refuse permission to remove until the secured party gives adequate assurance for the performance of the obligation to reimburse.

Official Comment

1. **Source.** Former Sections 9-501(4), 9-313(8).

2. **Real-Property-Related Collateral.** The collateral in many transactions consists of both real and personal property. In the interest of simplicity, speed, and economy, subsection (a), like former Section 9-501(4), permits (but does not require) the secured party to proceed as to both real and personal property in accordance with its rights and remedies with respect to the real property. Subsection (a) also makes clear that a secured party who exercises rights under Part 6 with respect to personal property does not prejudice any rights under real-property law.

This Article does not address certain other real-property-related problems. In a number of States, the exercise of remedies by a creditor who is secured by both real property and non-real property collateral is governed by special legal rules. For example, under some anti-deficiency laws, creditors risk loss of rights against personal property collateral if they err in enforcing their rights against the real property. Under a "one-form-of-action" rule (or rule against splitting a cause of action), a creditor who judicially enforces a real property mortgage and does not proceed in the same action to enforce a security interest in personalty may (among other consequences) lose the right to proceed against the personalty. Although statutes of this kind create impediments to enforcement of security interests, this Article does not override these limitations under other law.

3. **Fixtures.** Subsection (b) is new. It makes clear that a security interest in fixtures may be enforced either under real-property law or under any of the applicable provisions of Part 6, including sale or other disposition either before or after removal of the fixtures (see subsection (c)). Subsection (b) also serves to overrule cases holding that a secured party's only remedy after default is the removal of the fixtures from the real property. See, e.g., *Maplewood Bank & Trust v. Sears, Roebuck & Co.*, 625 A.2d 537 (N.J. Super. Ct. App. Div. 1993).

Subsection (c) generally follows former Section 9-313(8). It gives the secured party the right to remove fixtures under certain circumstances. A secured party whose security interest in fixtures has priority over owners and encumbrancers of the real property may remove the collateral from the real property. However, subsection (d) requires the secured party to reimburse any owner (other than the debtor) or encumbrancer for the cost of repairing any physical injury caused by the removal. This right to reimbursement is implemented by the last sentence of subsection (d), which gives the owner or encumbrancer a right to security or indemnity as a condition for giving permission to remove.

§ 9-605. UNKNOWN DEBTOR OR SECONDARY OBLIGOR. A secured party does not owe a duty based on its status as secured party:

(1) to a person that is a debtor or obligor, unless the secured party knows:

(A) that the person is a debtor or obligor;

(B) the identity of the person; and

(C) how to communicate with the person; or

ANALYSIS

The breadth of the rule announced in this section is questionable. Arguably, the secured creditor will not know how to communicate with a person if the whereabouts of the person are unknown and no mechanism of communication has been established. In this analysis, if the debtor or secondary obligor moves without leaving a forwarding address or providing a method by which he can be contacted, the secured party owes no duties to that person. There must be thousands (maybe millions) of cases each year where a debtor leaves the collateral behind (typically a car, boat, mobile home, motorcycle, or pawned item) and disappears. *The caption of the section should refer to the disappeared as well as the unknown.* It is understandable that the secured creditor would not be required to give notification of disposition. But the provision on its face also relieves the secured creditor of such obligations as the duty to make a commercially reasonable disposition (new § 9-610) or to apply the proceeds of disposition to the secured obligation (new § 9-615). This sanction is a tough penalty to impose on those creditors called "skips," particularly when the skip does not take the collateral along to parts unknown. Presumably, the rationale for relieving the creditor of any duty to make a reasonable disposition is that if the creditor could contact the debtor, it could negotiate for a post-default waiver of the disposition requirement under new Section 9-624(b). The duty to apply cash proceeds to the secured debt under new § 9-608(a)(1)(c) is for some unexplained reason not subject to the anti-waiver policy of new § 9-602. But it is difficult to imagine that there are many contexts in which such a waiver would meet the requirement of § 1-102(3). *See* Comment 2 to new § 9-602. In addition, in all these situations not knowing how to talk with the debtor only deprives the creditor of the opportunity to negotiate a post-violation settlement agreement. All of these inabilities to negotiate with the disappeared debtor—particularly a consumer debtor—provide a very thin justification for relieving the secured creditor of duties long believe to be rooted in elementary canons of decency. But the revisers are emphatically committed to insulating the creditor with respect to the disappeared debtor. (*See also* § 9-628(a) relieving the creditor of liability if it does not know how to communicate with a person.) On some facts, this provision will be too much for some courts to take. They will find a way to subvert it. Note the hydra-headed final sentence to Official Comment 2 to this provision which cannot decide the role that "other law" may have in "skip" situations.

(2) to a secured party or lienholder that has filed a financing statement against a person, unless the secured party knows:

(A)   that the person is a debtor; and

(B)   the identity of the person.

Official Comment

1. **Source.** New.

2. **Duties to Unknown Persons.** This section relieves a secured party from duties owed to a debtor or obligor, if the secured party does not know about the debtor or obligor. Similarly, it relieves a secured party from duties owed to a secured party or lienholder who has filed a financing statement against the debtor, if the secured party does not know about the debtor. For example, a secured party may be unaware that the original debtor has sold the collateral subject to the security interest and that the new owner has become the debtor. If so, the secured party owes no duty to the new owner (debtor) or to a secured party who has filed a financing statement against the new owner. This section should be read in conjunction with the exculpatory provisions in Section 9-628. Note that it relieves a secured party not only from duties arising under this Article but also from duties arising under other law by virtue of the secured party's status as such under this Article, unless the other law otherwise provides.

§ 9-606.   TIME OF DEFAULT FOR AGRICULTURAL LIEN.

For purposes of this part, a default occurs in connection with an agricultural lien at the time the secured party becomes entitled to enforce the lien in accordance with the statute under which it was created.

Official Comment

1. **Source.** New.

2. **Time of Default.** Remedies under this Part become available upon the debtor's "default." See Section 9-601. This section explains when "default" occurs in the agricultural-lien context. It requires one to consult the enabling statute to determine when the lienholder is entitled to enforce the lien.

§ 9-607.   COLLECTION AND ENFORCEMENT BY SECURED PARTY.

(a)   [Collection and enforcement generally.] If so agreed, and in any event after default, a secured party:

(1)   may notify an account debtor or other person obligated on collateral to make payment or otherwise render performance to or for the benefit of the secured party;

(2)   may take any proceeds to which the secured party is entitled under Section 9-315;

(3)   may enforce the obligations of an account debtor or other person obligated on collateral and exercise the rights of the debtor with respect to the obligation of the account debtor or other person

obligated on collateral to make payment or otherwise render performance to the debtor, and with respect to any property that secures the obligations of the account debtor or other person obligated on the collateral;

(4)   if it holds a security interest in a deposit account perfected by control under Section 9-104(a)(1), may apply the balance of the deposit account to the obligation secured by the deposit account; and

(5)   if it holds a security interest in a deposit account perfected by control under Section 9-104(a)(2) or (3), may instruct the bank to pay the balance of the deposit account to or for the benefit of the secured party.

(b)   [Nonjudicial enforcement of mortgage.] If necessary to enable a secured party to exercise under subsection (a)(3) the right of a debtor to enforce a mortgage nonjudicially, the secured party may record in the office in which a record of the mortgage is recorded:

(1)   a copy of the security agreement that creates or provides for a security interest in the obligation secured by the mortgage; and

(2)   the secured party's sworn affidavit in recordable form stating that:

(A)   a default has occurred; and

(B)   the secured party is entitled to enforce the mortgage nonjudicially.

(c)   [Commercially reasonable collection and enforcement.] A secured party shall proceed in a commercially reasonable manner if the secured party:

(1)   undertakes to collect from or enforce an obligation of an account debtor or other person obligated on collateral; and

(2)   is entitled to charge back uncollected collateral or otherwise to full or limited recourse against the debtor or a secondary obligor.

(d)   [Expenses of collection and enforcement.] A secured party may deduct from the collections made pursuant to subsection (c) reasonable expenses of collection and enforcement, including reasonable attorney's fees and legal expenses incurred by the secured party.

(e) [Duties to secured party not affected.] This section does not determine whether an account debtor, bank, or other person obligated on collateral owes a duty to a secured party.

ANALYSIS

Subsection (e) seems mysteriously to take back much of what the earlier subsections say. Read literally, it means that the rights recognized by the section are only *vis-a-vis* the debtor (and presumably any secondary obligor), not as against the person owing money to the debtor. This would mean that "other law" would determine whether the secured party could actually recover from the account debtor. No similar caveat appears in old § 9-502. Of course, the rights of the secured party are normally derivative of those of the debtor. The secured party will not in the absence of a valid waiver of defenses or other negotiability principle have the right to recover from the account debtor when the terms of the agreement between the debtor and the account debtor would not permit the debtor to make such a recovery. Hopefully, the courts will redeem the revisers and "read" subsection (e) as simply reaffirming the derivative nature of the creditor's rights rather than automatically denying the secured creditor status as an assignee with respect to all intangible rights. *See* Official Comment 6 to this provision.

> *Example A*: Debtor grants a perfected security interest in its accounts to First Bank. Debtor sells rope on open account to Customer X. Customer X has no defense to its liability to pay the purchase price of the accepted rope to Debtor. There is no waiver of defenses clause in the agreement. After Debtor defaults on its financing to First Bank, First Bank's interest in the account should allow it to recover the prepaid price from Customer X under new § 9-607(3).

> *Example B*: Same as above except Customer X has a breach of warranty claim on the rope against Debtor under U.C.C. § 2-714(2). Customer X may resist First Bank's claim for the unpaid price by asserting its warranty claim because that claim could have been asserted against the Debtor.

> *Example C*: Central Bank issues a letter of credit to support Customer X's obligation to pay the price of the rope to Debtor. First Bank holds a perfected interest in the letter of credit right as a supporting obligation. *See* new §§ 9-102(a)(77); 9-203(f); 9-308(d). Under letter of credit law, an assignee cannot

enforce the credit against the issuing bank which has not consented to the assignment. *See* U.C.C. § 5-114. Therefore, the security interest of First Bank in the letter-of-credit right does not give First Bank enforceable rights against Central Bank.

Example D: First Bank holds a security interest in Debtor's deposit account at Valley Bank. Debtor's default does not give First Bank rights against Valley Bank unless Valley Bank has agreed to those rights in an authenticated record. *See* new § 9-341.

Official Comment

1. **Source.** Former Section 9-502; subsections (b), (d), and (e) are new.

2. **Collections: In General.** Collateral consisting of rights to payment is not only the most liquid asset of a typical debtor's business but also is property that may be collected without any interruption of the debtor's business This situation is far different from that in which collateral is inventory or equipment, whose removal may bring the business to a halt. Furthermore, problems of valuation and identification, present with collateral that is tangible personal property, frequently are not as serious in the case of rights to payment and other intangible collateral. Consequently, this section, like former Section 9-502, recognizes that financing through assignments of intangibles lacks many of the complexities that arise after default in other types of financing. This section allows the assignee to liquidate collateral by collecting whatever may become due on the collateral, whether or not the method of collection contemplated by the security arrangement before default was direct (i.e., payment by the account debtor to the assignee, "notification" financing) or indirect (i.e., payment by the account debtor to the assignor, "nonnotification" financing).

3. **Scope.** The scope of this section is broader than that of former Section 9-502. It applies not only to collections from account debtors and obligors on instruments but also to enforcement more generally against all persons obligated on collateral. It explicitly provides for the secured party's enforcement of the debtor's rights in respect of the account debtor's (and other third parties') obligations and for the secured party's enforcement of supporting obligations with respect to those obligations. (Supporting obligations are components of the collateral under Section 9-203(f).) The rights of a secured party under subsection (a) include the right to enforce claims that the debtor may enjoy against others. For example, the claims might include a breach-of-warranty claim arising out of a defect in equipment that is collateral or a secured party's action for an injunction against infringement of a patent that

is collateral. Those claims typically would be proceeds of original collateral under Section 9-315.

4. Collection and Enforcement Before Default. Like Part 6 generally, this section deals with the rights and duties of secured parties following default. However, as did former Section 9-502 with respect to collection rights, this section also applies to the collection and enforcement rights of secured parties even if a default has not occurred, as long as the debtor has so agreed. It is not unusual for debtors to agree that secured parties are entitled to collect and enforce rights against account debtors prior to default.

5. Collections by Junior Secured Party. A secured party who holds a security interest in a right to payment may exercise the right to collect and enforce under this section, even if the security interest is subordinate to a conflicting security interest in the same right to payment. Whether the junior secured party has priority in the collected proceeds depends on whether the junior secured party qualifies for priority as a purchaser of an instrument (e.g., the account debtor's check) under Section 9-330(d), as a holder in due course of an instrument under Sections 3-305 and 9-331(a), or as a transferee of money under Section 9-332(a). See Sections 9-330, Comment 7, 9-331, Comment 5, and 9-332.

6. Relationship to Rights and Duties of Persons Obligated on Collateral. This section permits a secured party to collect and enforce obligations included in collateral in its capacity as a secured party. It is not necessary for a secured party first to become the owner of the collateral pursuant to a disposition or acceptance. However, the secured party's rights, as between it and the debtor, to collect from and enforce collateral against account debtors and others obligated on collateral under subsection (a) are subject to Section 9-341, Part 4, and other applicable law. *Neither this section nor former Section 9-502 should be understood to regulate the duties of an account debtor or other person obligated on collateral.* Subsection (e) makes this explicit. For example, the secured party may be unable to exercise the debtor's rights under an instrument if the debtor is in possession of the instrument, or under a non-transferable letter of credit if the debtor is the beneficiary. Unless a secured party has control over a letter-of-credit right and is entitled to receive payment or performance from the issuer or a nominated person under Article 5, its remedies with respect to the letter-of-credit right may be limited to the recovery of any identifiable proceeds from the debtor. This section establishes only the baseline rights of the secured party *vis-a-vis the debtor*-the secured party is entitled to enforce and collect after default or earlier if so agreed.

7. Deposit Account Collateral. Subsections (a)(4) and (5) set forth the self-help remedy for a secured party whose collateral is a deposit account. Subsection (a)(4) addresses the rights of a secured party that is the bank with which the deposit account is maintained. That secured party automatically has control of the deposit account under Section 9-104(a)(1). After default, and otherwise if so agreed, the bank/secured party may apply the funds on deposit to the secured obligation.

If a security interest of a third party is perfected by control (Section 9-104(a)(2) or (a)(3)), then after default, and otherwise if so agreed, the secured party may instruct the bank to pay out the funds in the account. If the third party has control under Section 9-104(a)(3), the depositary institution is obliged to obey the instruction because the secured party is its customer. See Section 4-401. If the third party has control under Section 9-104(a)(2), the control agreement determines the depositary institution's obligation to obey.

If a security interest in a deposit account is unperfected, or is perfected by filing by virtue of the proceeds rules of Section 9-315, the depositary institution ordinarily owes no obligation to obey the secured party's instructions. See Section 9-341. To reach the funds without the debtor's cooperation, the secured party must use an available judicial procedure.

8. **Rights Against Mortgagor of Real Property.** Subsection (b) addresses the situation in which the collateral consists of a mortgage note (or other obligation secured by a mortgage on real property). After the debtor's (mortgagee's) default, the secured party (assignee) may wish to proceed with a nonjudicial foreclosure of the mortgage securing the note but may be unable to do so because it has not become the assignee of record. The assignee/secured party may not have taken a recordable assignment at the commencement of the transaction (perhaps the mortgage note in question was one of hundreds assigned to the secured party as collateral). Having defaulted, the mortgagee may be unwilling to sign a recordable assignment. This section enables the secured party (assignee) to become the assignee of record by recording in the applicable real-property records the security agreement and an affidavit certifying default. Of course, the secured party's rights derive from those of its debtor. Subsection (b) would not entitle the secured party to proceed with a foreclosure unless the mortgagor also were in default or the debtor (mortgagee) otherwise enjoyed the right to foreclose.

9. **Commercial Reasonableness.** Subsection (c) provides that the secured party's collection and enforcement rights under subsection (a) must be exercised in a commercially reasonable manner. These rights include the right to settle and compromise claims against the account debtor. The secured party's failure to observe the standard of commercial reasonableness could render it liable to an aggrieved person under Section 9-625, and the secured party's recovery of a deficiency would be subject to Section 9-626. Subsection (c) does not apply if, as is characteristic of most sales of accounts, chattel paper, payment intangibles, and promissory notes, the secured party (buyer) has no right of recourse against the debtor (seller) or a secondary obligor. However, if the secured party does have a right of recourse, the commercial-reasonableness standard applies to collection and enforcement even though the assignment to the secured party was a "true" sale. The obligation to proceed in a commercially reasonable manner arises because the collection

process affects the extent of the seller's recourse liability, not because the seller retains an interest in the sold collateral (the seller does not).

10. **Attorney's Fees and Legal Expenses.** The phrase "reasonable attorney's fees and legal expenses," which appears in subsection (d), includes only those fees and expenses incurred in proceeding against account debtors or other third parties. The secured party's right to recover these expenses from the collections arises automatically under this section. The secured party also may incur other attorney's fees and legal expenses in proceeding against the debtor or obligor. Whether the secured party has a right to recover those fees and expenses depends on whether the debtor or obligor has agreed to pay them, as is the case with respect to attorney's fees and legal expenses under Sections 9-608(a)(1)(A) and 9-615(a)(1). The parties also may agree to allocate a portion of the secured party's overhead to collection and enforcement under subsection (d) or Section 9-608(a).

§ 9-608.　APPLICATION OF PROCEEDS OF COLLECTION OR ENFORCEMENT; LIABILITY FOR DEFICIENCY AND RIGHT TO SURPLUS.

(a)　[Application of proceeds, surplus, and deficiency if obligation secured.] If a security interest or agricultural lien secures payment or performance of an obligation, the following rules apply:

(1)　A secured party shall apply or pay over for application the cash proceeds of collection or enforcement under this section in the following order to:

(A)　the reasonable expenses of collection and enforcement and, to the extent provided for by agreement and not prohibited by law, reasonable attorney's fees and legal expenses incurred by the secured party;

(B)　the satisfaction of obligations secured by the security interest or agricultural lien under which the collection or enforcement is made; and

(C)　the satisfaction of obligations secured by any subordinate security interest in or other lien on the collateral subject to the security interest or agricultural lien under which the collection or enforcement is made if the secured party receives an authenticated demand for proceeds before distribution of the proceeds is completed.

(2)　If requested by a secured party, a holder of a subordinate security interest or other lien shall furnish reasonable proof of the interest or lien within a reasonable time. Unless the holder complies, the secured party need not comply with the holder's demand under paragraph (1)(C).

(3)　A secured party need not apply or pay over for application noncash proceeds of collection and enforcement under this section unless the failure to do so would be commercially unreasonable. A secured party that applies or pays over for application noncash proceeds shall do so in a commercially reasonable manner.

(4)　A secured party shall account to and pay a debtor for any surplus, and the obligor is liable for any deficiency.

(b)　[No surplus or deficiency in sales of certain rights to payment.] If the underlying transaction is a sale of accounts, chattel paper, payment intangibles, or promissory notes, the debtor is not entitled to any surplus, and the obligor is not liable for any deficiency.

Official Comment

1. **Source.** Subsection (a) is new; subsection (b) derives from former Section 9-502(2).

2. **Modifications of Prior Law.** Subsections (a) and (b) modify former Section 9-502(2) by explicitly providing for the application of proceeds recovered by the secured party in substantially the same manner as provided in Section 9-615(a) and (e) for dispositions of collateral.

3. **Surplus and Deficiency.** Subsections (a)(4) and (b) omit, as unnecessary, the references contained in former Section 9-502(2) to agreements varying the baseline rules on surplus and deficiency. The parties are always free to agree that an obligor will not be liable for a deficiency, even if the collateral secures an obligation, and that an obligor is liable for a deficiency, even if the transaction is a sale of receivables. For parallel provisions, see Section 9-615(d) and (e).

4. **Noncash Proceeds.** Subsection (a)(3) addresses the situation in which an enforcing secured party receives noncash proceeds.

Example: An enforcing secured party receives a promissory note from an account debtor who is unable to pay an account when it is due. The secured party accepts the note in exchange for extending the date on which the account debtor's obligation is due. The secured party may wish to credit its debtor (the assignor) with the principal amount of the note upon receipt of the note, but probably will prefer to credit the debtor only as and when the note is paid.

Under subsection (a)(3), the secured party is under no duty to apply the note or its value to the outstanding obligation unless its failure to do so would be commercially unreasonable. If the secured party does apply the note to the outstanding obligation, however, it must do so in a commercially reasonable manner. The parties may provide for the method of application of noncash proceeds by agreement, if the method is not manifestly unreasonable. See Section 9-603. This section does not explain when the failure to apply noncash proceeds would be commercially unreasonable; it leaves that determination to case-by-case adjudication. In the example, the secured party appears to have accepted the account debtor's note in order to increase the likelihood of payment and decrease the likelihood that the account debtor would dispute its obligation. Under these circumstances, it may well be commercially reasonable for the secured party to credit its debtor's obligations only as and when cash proceeds are collected from the account debtor, especially given the uncertainty that attends the account debtor's eventual payment. For an example of a secured party's receipt of noncash proceeds in which it may well be commercially unreasonable for the secured party to delay crediting its debtor's obligations with the value of noncash proceeds, see Section 9-615, Comment 3.

When the secured party is not required to "apply or pay over for application noncash proceeds," the proceeds nonetheless remain collateral subject to this Article. If the secured party were to dispose of them, for example, appropriate notification would be required (see Section 9-611), and the disposition would be subject to the standards provided in this Part (see Section 9-610). Moreover, a secured party in possession of the noncash proceeds would have the duties specified in Section 9-207.

5. **No Effect on Priority of Senior Security Interest.** The application of proceeds required by subsection (a) does not affect the priority of a security interest in collateral which is senior to the interest of the secured party who is collecting or enforcing collateral under Section 9-607. Although subsection (a) imposes a duty to apply proceeds to the enforcing secured party's expenses and to the satisfaction of the secured obligations owed to it and to subordinate secured parties, that duty applies only among the enforcing secured party and those persons. Concerning the priority of a junior secured party who collects and enforces collateral, see Section 9-607, Comment 5.

§ 9-609.　SECURED PARTY'S RIGHT TO TAKE POSSESSION AFTER DEFAULT.

(a)　[Possession; rendering equipment unusable; disposition on debtor's premises.] After default, a secured party:

(1)　may take possession of the collateral; and

(2)　without removal, may render equipment unusable and dispose of collateral on a debtor's premises under Section 9-610.

(b)　[Judicial and nonjudicial process.] A secured party may proceed under subsection (a):

(1)　pursuant to judicial process; or

(2) without judicial process, if it proceeds without breach of the peace.

(c) [Assembly of collateral.] If so agreed, and in any event after default, a secured party may require the debtor to assemble the collateral and make it available to the secured party at a place to be designated by the secured party which is reasonably convenient to both parties.

Official Comment

1. **Source.** Former Section 9-503.

2. **Secured Party's Right to Possession.** This section follows former Section 9-503 and earlier uniform legislation. It provides that the secured party is entitled to take possession of collateral after default.

3. **Judicial Process; Breach of Peace.** Subsection (b) permits a secured party to proceed under this section without judicial process if it does so "without breach of the peace." Although former Section 9-503 placed the same condition on a secured party's right to take possession of collateral, subsection (b) extends the condition to the right provided in subsection (a)(2) as well. Like former Section 9-503, this section does not define or explain the conduct that will constitute a breach of the peace, leaving that matter for continuing development by the courts. In considering whether a secured party has engaged in a breach of the peace, however, courts should hold the secured party responsible for the actions of others taken on the secured party's behalf, including independent contractors engaged by the secured party to take possession of collateral.

This section does not authorize a secured party who repossesses without judicial process to utilize the assistance of a law-enforcement officer. A number of cases have held that a repossessing secured party's use of a law-enforcement officer without benefit of judicial process constituted a failure to comply with former Section 9-503.

4. **Damages for Breach of Peace.** Concerning damages that may be recovered based on a secured party's breach of the peace in connection with taking possession of collateral, see Section 9-625, Comment 3.

5. **Multiple Secured Parties.** More than one secured party may be entitled to take possession of collateral under this section. Conflicting rights to possession among secured parties are resolved by the priority rules of this Article. Thus, a senior secured party is entitled to possession as against a junior claimant. Non-UCC law governs whether a junior secured party in possession of collateral is liable to the senior in conversion. Normally, a junior who refuses to relinquish possession of collateral upon the demand of a secured party having a superior possessory right to the collateral would be liable in conversion.

6. Secured Party's Right to Disable and Dispose of Equipment on Debtor's Premises. In the case of some collateral, such as heavy equipment, the physical removal from the debtor's plant and the storage of the collateral pending disposition may be impractical or unduly expensive. This section follows former Section 9-503 by providing that, in lieu of removal, the secured party may render equipment unusable or may dispose of collateral on the debtor's premises. Unlike former Section 9-503, however, this section explicitly conditions these rights on the debtor's default. Of course, this section does not validate unreasonable action by a secured party. Under Section 9-610, all aspects of a disposition must be commercially reasonable.

7. Debtor's Agreement to Assemble Collateral. This section follows former Section 9-503 also by validating a debtor's agreement to assemble collateral and make it available to a secured party at a place that the secured party designates. Similar to the treatment of agreements to permit collection prior to default under Section 9-607 and former 9-502, however, this section validates these agreements whether or not they are conditioned on the debtor's default. For example, a debtor might agree to make available to a secured party, from time to time, any instruments or negotiable documents that the debtor receives on account of collateral. A court should not infer from this section's validation that a debtor's agreement to assemble and make available collateral would not be enforceable under other applicable law.

8. Agreed Standards. Subject to the limitation imposed by Section 9-603(b), this section's provisions concerning agreements to assemble and make available collateral and a secured party's right to disable equipment and dispose of collateral on a debtor's premises are likely topics for agreement on standards as contemplated by Section 9-603.

§ 9-610. DISPOSITION OF COLLATERAL AFTER DEFAULT.

(a)   [Disposition after default.] After default, a secured party may sell, lease, license, or otherwise dispose of any or all of the collateral in its present condition or following any commercially reasonable preparation or processing.

(b)   [Commercially reasonable disposition.] Every aspect of a disposition of collateral, including the method, manner, time, place, and other terms, must be commercially reasonable. If commercially reasonable, a secured party may dispose of collateral by public or private proceedings, by one or more contracts, as a unit or in parcels, and at any time and place and on any terms.

(c)   [Purchase by secured party.] A secured party may purchase collateral:

(1)   at a public disposition; or

(2)   at a private disposition only if the collateral is of a kind that is customarily sold on a recognized market or the subject of widely distributed standard price quotations.

ANALYSIS

After much controversy within the Drafting Committee, the general principles governing the disposition process remain the same as under old § 9-504. *See Secured Transactions* § 8.06. For a new specialized rule as to the calculation of the deficiency in low price dispositions to the secured party, a person related to the secured party or a secondary obligor, see new § 9-615(f).

(d)   [Warranties on disposition.] A contract for sale, lease, license, or other disposition includes the warranties relating to title, possession, quiet enjoyment, and the like which by operation of law accompany a voluntary disposition of property of the kind subject to the contract.

(e)   [Disclaimer of warranties.] A secured party may disclaim or modify warranties under subsection (d):

(1)   in a manner that would be effective to disclaim or modify the warranties in a voluntary disposition of property of the kind subject to the contract of disposition; or

(2)   by communicating to the purchaser a record evidencing the contract for disposition and including an express disclaimer or modification of the warranties.

(f)   [Record sufficient to disclaim warranties.] A record is sufficient to disclaim warranties under subsection (e) if it indicates "There is no warranty relating to title, possession, quiet enjoyment, or the like in this disposition" or uses words of similar import.

Official Comment

1. **Source.** Former Section 9-504(1), (3).

2. **Commercially Reasonable Dispositions.** Subsection (a) follows former Section 9-504 by permitting a secured party to dispose of collateral in a commercially reasonable manner following a default. Although subsection (b) permits both public and private dispositions, "every aspect of a disposition . . . must be commercially reasonable." This section encourages private

dispositions on the assumption that they frequently will result in higher realization on collateral for the benefit of all concerned. Subsection (a) does not restrict dispositions to sales; collateral may be sold, leased, licensed, or otherwise disposed. Section 9-627 provides guidance for determining the circumstances under which a disposition is "commercially reasonable."

3. **Time of Disposition.** This Article does not specify a period within which a secured party must dispose of collateral. This is consistent with this Article's policy to encourage private dispositions through regular commercial channels. It may, for example, be prudent not to dispose of goods when the market has collapsed. Or, it might be more appropriate to sell a large inventory in parcels over a period of time instead of in bulk. Of course, under subsection (b) every aspect of a disposition of collateral must be commercially reasonable. This requirement explicitly includes the "method, manner, time, place and other terms." For example, if a secured party does not proceed under Section 9-620 and holds collateral for a long period of time without disposing of it, and if there is no good reason for not making a prompt disposition, the secured party may be determined not to have acted in a "commercially reasonable" manner. See also Section 1-203 (general obligation of good faith).

4. **Pre-Disposition Preparation and Processing.** Former Section 9-504(1) appeared to give the secured party the choice of disposing of collateral either "in its then condition or following any commercially reasonable preparation or processing." Some courts held that the "commercially reasonable" standard of former Section 9-504(3) nevertheless could impose an affirmative duty on the secured party to process or prepare the collateral prior to disposition. Subsection (a) retains the substance of the quoted language. Although courts should not be quick to impose a duty of preparation or processing on the secured party, subsection (a) does not grant the secured party the right to dispose of the collateral "in its then condition" under *all* circumstances. A secured party may not dispose of collateral "in its then condition" when, taking into account the costs and probable benefits of preparation or processing and the fact that the secured party would be advancing the costs at its risk, it would be commercially unreasonable to dispose of the collateral in that condition.

5. **Disposition by Junior Secured Party.** Disposition rights under subsection (a) are not limited to first-priority security interests. Rather, any secured party as to whom there has been a default enjoys the right to dispose of collateral under this subsection. The exercise of this right by a secured party whose security interest is subordinate to that of another secured party does not of itself constitute a conversion or otherwise give rise to liability in favor of the holder of the senior security interest. Section 9-615 addresses application of the proceeds of a disposition by a junior secured party. Under Section 9-615(a), a junior secured party owes no obligation to apply the proceeds of disposition to the satisfaction of obligations secured by a senior security interest. Section 9-615(g) builds on this general rule by protecting

certain juniors from claims of a senior concerning cash proceeds of the disposition. Even if a senior were to have a non-Article 9 claim to proceeds of a junior's disposition, Section 9-615(g) would protect a junior that acts in good faith and without knowledge that its actions violate the rights of a senior party. Because the disposition by a junior would not cut off a senior's security interest or other lien (see Section 9-617), in many (probably most) cases the junior's receipt of the cash proceeds would not violate the rights of the senior.

The holder of a senior security interest is entitled, by virtue of its priority, to take possession of collateral from the junior secured party and conduct its own disposition, provided that the senior enjoys the right to take possession of the collateral from the debtor. See Section 9-609. The holder of a junior security interest normally must notify the senior secured party of an impending disposition. See Section 9-611. Regardless of whether the senior receives a notification from the junior, the junior's disposition does not of itself discharge the senior's security interest. See Section 9-617. Unless the senior secured party has authorized the disposition free and clear of its security interest, the senior's security interest ordinarily will survive the disposition by the junior and continue under Section 9-315(a). If the senior enjoys the right to repossess the collateral from the debtor, the senior likewise may recover the collateral from the transferee.

When a secured party's collateral is encumbered by another security interest or other lien, one of the claimants may seek to invoke the equitable doctrine of marshaling. As explained by the Supreme Court, that doctrine "rests upon the principle that a creditor having two funds to satisfy his debt, may not by his application of them to his demand, defeat another creditor, who may resort to only one of the funds." *Meyer v. United States*, 375 U.S. 233, 236 (1963), quoting *Sowell v. Federal Reserve Bank*, 268 U.S. 449, 456-57 (1925). The purpose of the doctrine is "to prevent the arbitrary action of a senior lienor from destroying the rights of a junior lienor or a creditor having less security." Id. at 237. Because it is an equitable doctrine, marshaling "is applied only when it can be equitably fashioned as to all of the parties" having an interest in the property. Id. This Article leaves courts free to determine whether marshaling is appropriate in any given case. See Section 1-103.

6. **Security Interests of Equal Rank.** Sometimes two security interests enjoy the same priority. This situation may arise by contract, e.g., pursuant to "equal and ratable" provisions in indentures, or by operation of law. See Section 9-328(6). This Article treats a security interest having equal priority like a senior security interest in many respects. Assume, for example, that SP-X and SP-Y enjoy equal priority, SP-W is senior to them, and SP-Z is junior. If SP-X disposes of the collateral under this section, then (i) SP-W's and SP-Y's security interests survive the disposition but SP-Z's does not, see Section 9-617, and (ii) neither SP-W nor SP-Y is entitled to receive a distribution of proceeds, but SP-Z is. See Section 9-615(a)(3).

When one considers the ability to obtain possession of the collateral, a secured party with equal priority is unlike a senior secured party. As the senior secured party, SP-W should enjoy the right to possession as against SP-X. See Section 9-609, Comment 5. If SP-W takes possession and disposes of the collateral under this section, it is entitled to apply the proceeds to satisfy its secured claim. SP-Y, however, should not have such a right to take possession from SP-X; otherwise, once SP-Y took possession from SP-X, SP-X would have the right to get possession from SP-Y, which would be obligated to redeliver possession to SP-X, and so on. Resolution of this problem is left to the parties and, if necessary, the courts.

7. **Public vs. Private Dispositions.** This Part maintains two distinctions between "public" and other dispositions: (i) the secured party may buy at the former, but normally not at the latter (Section 9-610(c)), and (ii) the debtor is entitled to notification of "the time and place of a public disposition" and notification of "the time after which" a private disposition or other intended disposition is to be made (Section 9-613(1)(E)). It does not retain the distinction under former Section 9-504(4), under which transferees in a noncomplying public disposition could lose protection more easily than transferees in other noncomplying dispositions. Instead, Section 9-617(b) adopts a unitary standard. Although the term is not defined, as used in this Article, a "public disposition" is one at which the price is determined after the public has had a meaningful opportunity for competitive bidding. "Meaningful opportunity" is meant to imply that some form of advertisement or public notice must precede the sale (or other disposition) and that the public must have access to the sale (disposition).

8. **Investment Property.** Dispositions of investment property may be regulated by the federal securities laws. Although a "public" disposition of securities under this Article may implicate the registration requirements of the Securities Act of 1933, it need not do so. A disposition that qualifies for a "private placement" exemption under the Securities Act of 1933 nevertheless may constitute a "public" disposition within the meaning of this section. Moreover, the "commercially reasonable" requirements of subsection (b) need not prevent a secured party from conducting a foreclosure sale without the issuer's compliance with federal registration requirements.

9. **"Recognized Market."** A "recognized market," as used in subsection (c) and Section 9-611(d), is one in which the items sold are fungible and prices are not subject to individual negotiation. For example, the New York Stock Exchange is a recognized market. A market in which prices are individually negotiated or the items are not fungible is not a recognized market, even if the items are the subject of widely disseminated price guides or are disposed of through dealer auctions.

10. **Relevance of Price.** While not itself sufficient to establish a violation of this Part, a low price suggests that a court should scrutinize carefully all aspects of a disposition to ensure that each aspect was commercially

reasonable. Note also that even if the disposition is commercially reasonable, Section 9-615(f) provides a special method for calculating a deficiency or surplus if (i) the transferee in the disposition is the secured party, a person related to the secured party, or a secondary obligor, and (ii) the amount of proceeds of the disposition is significantly below the range of proceeds that a complying disposition to a person other than the secured party, a person related to the secured party, or a secondary obligor would have brought.

11. **Warranties.** Subsection (d) affords the transferee in a disposition under this section the benefit of any title, possession, quiet enjoyment, and similar warranties that would have accompanied the disposition by operation of non-Article 9 law had the disposition been conducted under other circumstances. For example, the Article 2 warranty of title would apply to a sale of goods, the analogous warranties of Article 2A would apply to a lease of goods, and any common-law warranties of title would apply to dispositions of other types of collateral. See, e.g., Restatement (2d), Contracts § 333 (warranties of assignor).

Subsection (e) explicitly provides that these warranties can be disclaimed either under other applicable law or by communicating a record containing an express disclaimer. The record need not be written, but an oral communication would not be sufficient. See Section 9-102 (definition of "record"). Subsection (f) provides a sample of wording that will effectively exclude the warranties in a disposition under this section, whether or not the exclusion would be effective under non-Article 9 law.

The warranties incorporated by subsection (d) are those relating to "title, possession, quiet enjoyment, and the like." Depending on the circumstances, a disposition under this section also may give rise to other statutory or implied warranties, e.g., warranties of quality or fitness for purpose. Law other than this Article determines whether such other warranties apply to a disposition under this section. Other law also determines issues relating to disclaimer of such warranties. For example, a foreclosure sale of a car by a car dealer could give rise to an implied warranty of merchantability (Section 2-314) unless effectively disclaimed or modified (Section 2-316).

This section's approach to these warranties conflicts with the former Comment to Section 2-312. This Article rejects the baseline assumption that commercially reasonable dispositions under this section are out of the ordinary commercial course or peculiar. The Comment to Section 2-312 has been revised accordingly.

§ 9-611. NOTIFICATION BEFORE DISPOSITION OF COLLATERAL.

(a) **["Notification date."]** In this section, "notification date" means the earlier of the date on which:

(1)   a secured party sends to the debtor and any secondary obligor an authenticated notification of disposition; or

(2)   the debtor and any secondary obligor waive the right to notification.

(b)   [Notification of disposition required.] Except as otherwise provided in subsection (d), a secured party that disposes of collateral under Section 9-610 shall send to the persons specified in subsection (c) a reasonable authenticated notification of disposition.

(c)   [Persons to be notified.] To comply with subsection (b), the secured party shall send an authenticated notification of disposition to:

(1)   the debtor;

(2)   any secondary obligor; and

(3)   if the collateral is other than consumer goods:

(A)   any other person from which the secured party has received, before the notification date, an authenticated notification of a claim of an interest in the collateral;

(B)   any other secured party or lienholder that, 10 days before the notification date, held a security interest in or other lien on the collateral perfected by the filing of a financing statement that:

(i)   identified the collateral;

(ii)   was indexed under the debtor's name as of that date; and

(iii)   was filed in the office in which to file a financing statement against the debtor covering the collateral as of that date; and

(C)   any other secured party that, 10 days before the notification date, held a security interest in the collateral perfected by compliance with a statute, regulation, or treaty described in Section 9-311(a).

(d)   [Subsection (b) inapplicable: perishable collateral; recognized market.] Subsection (b) does not apply if the collateral is perishable or threatens to decline speedily in value or is of a type customarily sold on a recognized market.

(e)   [Compliance with subsection (c)(3)(B).] A secured party complies with the requirement for notification prescribed by subsection (c)(3)(B) if:

(1)   not later than 20 days or earlier than 30 days before the notification date, the secured party requests, in a commercially reasonable manner, information concerning financing statements indexed under the debtor's name in the office indicated in subsection (c)(3)(B); and

(2)   before the notification date, the secured party:

(A)   did not receive a response to the request for information; or

(B)   received a response to the request for information and sent an authenticated notification of disposition to each secured party or other lienholder named in that response whose financing statement covered the collateral.

ANALYSIS

Revised Article 9 expands the classes of persons entitled to notification of disposition. Old § 9-504(3) requires that notification be given to debtors and (in cases not involving consumer goods) other secured parties providing written notice of their interest. "Debtor" is an ambiguous term under old Article 9. *See* the text analysis to new § 9-102(a)(28). The classes entitled to notification under new § 9-611(c) are:

● *debtors* — for this purpose, persons owning or having some other property interest in the collateral except other secured creditors, lienholders, consignees and buyers of accounts, chattel paper, payment intangibles or promissory notes. *See* new §§ 9-102(a)(28); 9-601(g).

● *secondary obligors* — sureties and others with rights of recourse. *See* new § 9-102(a)(71).

● *persons providing an authenticated notification of a claim of interest in the collateral*, most notably, lienholders or secured creditors excluded from the "debtor" class.

● *specified secured creditors of record determined under new §§ 9-611(c)(3)(B).*

Official Comment

1. **Source.** Former Section 9-504(3).

2. **Reasonable Notification.** This section requires a secured party who wishes to dispose of collateral under Section 9-610 to send "a reasonable

authenticated notification of disposition" to specified interested persons, subject to certain exceptions. The notification must be reasonable as to the manner in which it is sent, its timeliness (i.e., a reasonable time before the disposition is to take place), and its content. See Sections 9-612 (timeliness of notification), 9-613 (contents of notification generally), 9-614 (contents of notification in consumer-goods transactions).

3. **Notification to Debtors and Secondary Obligors.** This section imposes a duty to send notification of a disposition not only to the debtor but also to any secondary obligor. Subsections (b) and (c) resolve an uncertainty under former Article 9 by providing that secondary obligors (sureties) are entitled to receive notification of an intended disposition of collateral, regardless of who created the security interest in the collateral. If the surety created the security interest, it would be the debtor. If it did not, it would be a secondary obligor. (This Article also resolves the question of the secondary obligor's ability to waive, pre-default, the right to notification-waiver generally is not permitted. See Section 9-602.) Section 9-605 relieves a secured party from any duty to send notification to a debtor or secondary obligor unknown to the secured party.

Under subsection (b), the principal obligor (borrower) is not always entitled to notification of disposition.

Example: Behnfeldt borrows on an unsecured basis, and Bruno grants a security interest in her car to secure the debt. Behnfeldt is a primary obligor, not a secondary obligor. As such, she is not entitled to notification of disposition under this section.

4. **Notification to Other Secured Parties.** Prior to the 1972 amendments to Article 9, former Section 9-504(3) required the enforcing secured party to send reasonable notification of the disposition:

except in the case of consumer goods to any other person who has a security interest in the collateral and who has duly filed a financing statement indexed in the name of the debtor in this State or who is known by the secured party to have a security interest in the collateral.

The 1972 amendments eliminated the duty to give notice to secured parties other than those from whom the foreclosing secured party had received written notice of a claim of an interest in the collateral.

Many of the problems arising from dispositions of collateral encumbered by multiple security interests can be ameliorated or solved by informing all secured parties of an intended disposition and affording them the opportunity to work with one another. To this end, subsection (c)(3)(B) expands the duties of the foreclosing secured party to include the duty to notify (and the corresponding burden of searching the files to discover) certain competing secured parties. The subsection imposes a search burden that in some cases may be greater than the pre-1972 burden on foreclosing secured parties but certainly is more modest than that faced by a new secured lender.

To determine who is entitled to notification, the foreclosing secured party must determine the proper office for filing a financing statement as of a particular date, measured by reference to the "notification date," as defined in subsection (a). This determination requires reference to the choice-of-law provisions of Part 3. The secured party must ascertain whether any financing statements covering the collateral and indexed under the debtor's name, as the name existed as of that date, in fact were filed in that office. The foreclosing secured party generally need not notify secured parties whose effective financing statements have become more difficult to locate because of changes in the location of the debtor, proceeds rules, or changes in the debtor's name.

Under subsection (c)(3)(C), the secured party also must notify a secured party who has perfected a security interest by complying with a statute or treaty described in Section 9-311(a), such as a certificate-of-title statute.

Subsection (e) provides a "safe harbor" that takes into account the delays that may be attendant to receiving information from the public filing offices. It provides, generally, that the secured party will be deemed to have satisfied its notification duty under subsection (c)(3)(B) if it requests a search from the proper office at least 20 but not more than 30 days before sending notification to the debtor and if it also sends a notification to all secured parties (and other lienholders) reflected on the search report. The secured party's duty under subsection (c)(3)(B) also will be satisfied if the secured party requests but does not receive a search report before the notification is sent to the debtor. Thus, if subsection (e) applies, a secured party who is entitled to notification under subsection (c)(3)(B) has no remedy against a foreclosing secured party who does not send the notification. The foreclosing secured party has complied with the notification requirement. Subsection (e) has no effect on the requirements of the other paragraphs of subsection (c). For example, if the foreclosing secured party received a notification from the holder of a conflicting security interest in accordance with subsection (c)(3)(A) but failed to send to the holder a notification of the disposition, the holder of the conflicting security interest would have the right to recover any loss under Section 9-625(b).

5. **Authentication Requirement.** Subsections (b) and (c) explicitly provide that a notification of disposition must be "authenticated." Some cases read former Section 9-504(3) as validating oral notification.

6. **Second Try.** This Article leaves to judicial resolution, based upon the facts of each case, the question whether the requirement of "reasonable notification" requires a "second try," i.e., whether a secured party who sends notification and learns that the debtor did not receive it must attempt to locate the debtor and send another notification.

7. **Recognized Market; Perishable Collateral.** New subsection (d) makes it clear that there is no obligation to give notification of a disposition in the

case of perishable collateral or collateral customarily sold on a recognized market (e.g., marketable securities). Former Section 9-504(3) might be read (incorrectly) to relieve the secured party from its duty to notify a debtor but not from its duty to notify other secured parties in connection with dispositions of such collateral.

8. **Failure to Conduct Notified Disposition.** Nothing in this Article prevents a secured party from electing not to conduct a disposition after sending a notification. Nor does this Article prevent a secured party from electing to send a revised notification if its plans for disposition change. This assumes, however, that the secured party acts in good faith, the revised notification is reasonable, and the revised plan for disposition and any attendant delay are commercially reasonable.

9. **Waiver.** A debtor or secondary obligor may waive the right to notification under this section only by a post-default authenticated agreement. See Section 9-624(a).

§ 9-612. TIMELINESS OF NOTIFICATION BEFORE DISPOSITION OF COLLATERAL.

(a)   [Reasonable time is question of fact.] Except as otherwise provided in subsection (b), whether a notification is sent within a reasonable time is a question of fact.

(b)   [10-day period sufficient in non-consumer transaction.] In a transaction other than a consumer transaction, a notification of disposition sent after default and 10 days or more before the earliest time of disposition set forth in the notification is sent within a reasonable time before the disposition.

ANALYSIS

In business transactions, mailing the notification after default, but 10 days before the sale satisfies the timeliness requirement. Is it realistic to believe that a debtor or other interested person will have an opportunity to meaningfully promote the sale of business equipment or inventory when the notice is mailed to it 10 days before the scheduled sale? Interestingly enough, Revised Article 9 allows secured creditors 20 days to file for purchase-money priorities under new §§ 9-317, 9-324(e), and 9-334(d). Under new § 9-616 a secured creditor is given 14 days from its *receipt* of a request for an explanation of the surplus or deficiency to provide that explanation. Under new § 9-620, the debtor is given 20 days from the sending of a proposed retention in satisfaction to get its objection back to the creditor. Why is the safe-harbor as to notification of disposition so short? Because commercial agreements under old Article 9 have often stipulated that notice 10 or more days before the sale is timely? Because no interest group in the drafting process devotes itself to protecting *commercial* debtors? Because a fast disposition is often in the interest of all concerned? Remember: A debtor or secondary obligor, after default, can waive the right to notification of disposition if convinced that it is in his interest to do so. *See* new § 9-624.

Official Comment

1. **Source.** New.

2. **Reasonable Notification.** Section 9-611(b) requires the secured party to send a "reasonable authenticated notification." Under that section, as under former Section 9-504(3), one aspect of a reasonable notification is its timeliness. This generally means that the notification must be sent at a reasonable time in advance of the date of a public disposition or the date after which a private disposition is to be made. A notification that is sent so near to the disposition date that a notified person could not be expected to act on or take account of the notification would be unreasonable.

3. **Timeliness of Notification: Safe Harbor.** The 10-day notice period in subsection (b) is intended to be a "safe harbor" and not a minimum requirement. To qualify for the "safe harbor" the notification must be sent after default. A notification also must be sent in a commercially reasonable manner. See Section 9-611(b) ("reasonable authenticated notification"). Those requirements prevent a secured party from taking advantage of the "safe harbor" by, for example, giving the debtor a notification at the time of the original extension of credit or sending the notice by surface mail to a debtor overseas.

§ 9-613. CONTENTS AND FORM OF NOTIFICATION BEFORE DISPOSITION OF COLLATERAL: GENERAL. Except in a consumer-goods transaction, the following rules apply:

(1) The contents of a notification of disposition are sufficient if the notification:

(A) describes the debtor and the secured party;

(B) describes the collateral that is the subject of the intended disposition;

(C) states the method of intended disposition;

(D)   states that the debtor is entitled to an accounting of the unpaid indebtedness and states the charge, if any, for an accounting; and

(E)   states the time and place of a public sale or the time after which any other disposition is to be made.

(2)   Whether the contents of a notification that lacks any of the information specified in paragraph (1) are nevertheless sufficient is a question of fact.

(3)   The contents of a notification providing substantially the information specified in paragraph (1) are sufficient, even if the notification includes:

(A)   information not specified by that paragraph; or

(B)   minor errors that are not seriously misleading.

(4)   A particular phrasing of the notification is not required.

(5)   The following form of notification and the form appearing in Section 9-614(3), when completed, each provides sufficient information:

NOTIFICATION OF DISPOSITION OF COLLATERAL

To: [*Name of debtor, obligor, or other
                                 person to which the notification is sent*]

From: [*Name, address, and telephone number
                                 of secured party*]

Name of Debtor(s):   [*Include only if debtor(s) are not an
                                 addressee*]

[*For a public disposition:*]

We will sell [or lease or license, *as applicable*] the [*describe
collateral*] [to the highest qualified bidder] in public as follows:

Day and Date: _____
Time: _____
Place: _____

[*For a private disposition:*]

We will sell [or lease or license, *as applicable*] the [*describe
collateral*] privately sometime after [*day and date*].

You are entitled to an accounting of the unpaid indebtedness
secured by the property that we intend to sell [or lease or license,
as applicable] [for a charge of $_____]. You may request an
accounting by calling us at [*telephone number*]

[End of Form]

ANALYSIS

Those cases under old § 9-504 which state that the notification need
not state whether the disposition is public or private are overruled.
See Secured Transactions § 8.06[3][b]. The revision adds specification
as to the contents of the notification, but simultaneously applies the
"minor errors" doctrine to the contents issue and provides a "safe-
harbor" form for non-consumer goods transactions.

Official Comment

1. **Source.** New.

2. **Contents of Notification.** To comply with the "reasonable authenticated notification" requirement of Section 9-611(b), the contents of a notification must be reasonable. Except in a consumer-goods transaction, the contents of a notification that includes the information set forth in paragraph (1) are sufficient as a matter of law, unless the parties agree otherwise. (The reference to "time" of disposition means here, as it did in former Section 9-504(3), not only the hour of the day but also the date.) Although a secured party may choose to include additional information concerning the transaction or the debtor's rights and obligations, no additional information is required unless the parties agree otherwise. A notification that lacks some of the information set forth in paragraph (1) nevertheless may be sufficient if found to be reasonable by the trier of fact, under paragraph (2). A properly completed sample form of notification in paragraph (5) or in Section 9-614(a)(3) is an example of a notification that would contain the information set forth in paragraph (1). Under paragraph (4), however, no particular phrasing of the notification is required.

§ 9-614. CONTENTS AND FORM OF NOTIFICATION BEFORE DISPOSITION OF COLLATERAL: CONSUMER-GOODS TRANSACTION. In a consumer-goods transaction, the following rules apply:

(1) A notification of disposition must provide the following information:

(A) the information specified in Section 9-613(1);

(B) a description of any liability for a deficiency of the person to which the notification is sent;

(C) a telephone number from which the amount that must be paid to the secured party to redeem the collateral under Section 9-623 is available; and

(D) a telephone number or mailing address from which additional information concerning the disposition and the obligation secured is available.

(2) A particular phrasing of the notification is not required.

(3) The following form of notification, when completed, provides sufficient information:

[Name and address of secured party]

[Date]

NOTICE OF OUR PLAN TO SELL PROPERTY

[*Name and address of any obligor who is also a debtor*]

Subject: [*Identification of Transaction*]

We have your [*describe collateral*], because you broke promises in our agreement.

[*For a public disposition:*]

We will sell [*describe collateral*] at public sale. A sale could include a lease or license. The sale will be held as follows:

Day and Date:_____

Time:_____

Place:_____

You may attend the sale and bring bidders if you want.

[*For a private disposition:*]

We will sell [*describe collateral*] at private sale sometime after [*date*]. A sale could include a lease or license.

The money that we get from the sale (after paying our costs) will reduce the amount you owe. If we get less money than you owe, you [*will or will not, as applicable*] still owe us the difference. If we get more money than you owe, you will get the extra money, unless we must pay it to someone else.

You can get the property back at any time before we sell it by paying us the full amount you owe (not just the past due payments), including our expenses. To learn the exact amount you must pay, call us at [*telephone number*].

If you want us to explain to you in writing how we have figured the amount that you owe us, you may call us at [*telephone number*] [or write us at [*secured party's address*]] and request a written explanation. [We will charge you $_____ for the explanation if we sent you another written explanation of the amount you owe us within the last six months.]

If you need more information about the sale call us at [*telephone number*]] [or write us at [*secured party's address*]].

We are sending this notice to the following other people who have an interest in [*describe collateral*] or who owe money under your agreement:

[*Names of all other debtors and obligors, if any*]

[End of Form]

(4) A notification in the form of paragraph (3) is sufficient, even if additional information appears at the end of the form.

(5) A notification in the form of paragraph (3) is sufficient, even if it includes errors in information not required by paragraph (1), unless the error is misleading with respect to rights arising under this article.

(6) If a notification under this section is not in the form of paragraph (3), law other than this article determines the effect of including information not required by paragraph (1).

ANALYSIS

These more rigid requirements as to the contents of the notification apply only when the obligation is incurred for consumer purposes and the collateral is goods (or goods and software) used primarily for consumer purpose. *See* new § 9-102(a)(24). The more relaxed § 9-613 applies when a consumer obligation is secured by investment property. The "minor errors" doctrine does not apply to notifications with respect to consumer goods collateral, nor can the creditor defend on the grounds that a notification that failed to satisfy § 9-614(1) was nevertheless a reasonable one. A notification with an error as to required telephone numbers or mailing addresses will be nonconforming. Seemingly technical flaws can expose the creditor to the penalty of § 9-625(c)(2) (damages equal to the interest factor and 10% of the principal of the transaction). This sum can be very substantial in transactions involving cars, boats and mobile homes. Creditors will be well advised to use the safe-harbor form provided in new § 9-614(3) and to establish procedures to double-check the accuracy of information included on the blank. After the protracted controversy over consumer default remedies, this specialized notification provision is one of the few new consumer protection provisions to survive the last minute debtor/creditor compromise.

Official Comment

1. **Source.** New.

2. **Notification in Consumer-Goods Transactions.** Paragraph (1) sets forth the information required for a reasonable notification in a consumer-goods transaction. A notification that lacks any of the information set forth

in paragraph (1) is insufficient as a matter of law. Compare Section 9-613(2), under which the trier of fact may find a notification to be sufficient even if it lacks some information listed in paragraph (1) of that section.

3. **Safe-Harbor Form of Notification; Errors in Information.** Although paragraph (2) provides that a particular phrasing of a notification is not required, paragraph (3) specifies a safe-harbor form that, when properly completed, satisfies paragraph (1). Paragraphs (4), (5), and (6) contain special rules applicable to erroneous and additional information. Under paragraph (4), a notification in the safe-harbor form specified in paragraph (3) is not rendered insufficient if it contains additional information at the end of the form. Paragraph (5) provides that non-misleading errors in information contained in a notification are permitted if the safe-harbor form is used *and if the errors are in information not required by paragraph (1)*. Finally, if a notification is in a form other than the paragraph (3) safe-harbor form, other law determines the effect of including in the notification information other than that required by paragraph (1).

§ 9-615. APPLICATION OF PROCEEDS OF DISPOSITION; LIABILITY FOR DEFICIENCY AND RIGHT TO SURPLUS.

(a) [Application of proceeds.] A secured party shall apply or pay over for application the cash proceeds of disposition in the following order to:

(1)   the reasonable expenses of retaking, holding, preparing for disposition, processing, and disposing, and, to the extent provided for by agreement and not prohibited by law, reasonable attorney's fees and legal expenses incurred by the secured party;

(2)   the satisfaction of obligations secured by the security interest or agricultural lien under which the disposition is made;

(3)   the satisfaction of obligations secured by any subordinate security interest in or other subordinate lien on the collateral if:

(A)   the secured party receives from the holder of the subordinate security interest or other lien an authenticated demand for proceeds before distribution of the proceeds is completed; and

(B)   in a case in which a consignor has an interest in the collateral, the subordinate security interest or other lien is senior to the interest of the consignor; and

(4)   a secured party that is a consignor of the collateral if the secured party receives from the consignor an authenticated demand for proceeds before distribution of the proceeds is completed.

(b) [Proof of subordinate interest.] If requested by a secured party, a holder of a subordinate security interest or other lien shall furnish reasonable proof of the interest or lien within a reasonable time. Unless the holder does so, the secured party need not comply with the holder's demand under subsection (a)(3).

(c) [Application of noncash proceeds.] A secured party need not apply or pay over for application noncash proceeds of disposition under this section unless the failure to do so would be commercially unreasonable. A secured party that applies or pays over for application noncash proceeds shall do so in a commercially reasonable manner.

(d) [Surplus or deficiency if obligation secured.] If the security interest under which a disposition is made secures payment or performance of an obligation, after making the payments and applications required by subsection (a) and permitted by subsection (c):

(1)   unless subsection (a)(4) requires the secured party to apply or pay over cash proceeds to a consignor, the secured party shall account to and pay a debtor for any surplus; and

(2)   the obligor is liable for any deficiency.

(e) [No surplus or deficiency in sales of certain rights to payment.] If the underlying transaction is a sale of accounts, chattel paper, payment intangibles, or promissory notes:

(1)   the debtor is not entitled to any surplus; and

(2)   the obligor is not liable for any deficiency.

(f) [Calculation of surplus or deficiency in disposition to person related to secured party.] The surplus or deficiency following a disposition is calculated based on the amount of proceeds that would have been realized in a disposition complying with this part to a transferee other than the secured party, a person related to the secured party, or a secondary obligor if:

(1)   the transferee in the disposition is the secured party, a person related to the secured party, or a secondary obligor; and

(2)   the amount of proceeds of the disposition is significantly below the range of proceeds that a complying disposition to a person other than the secured party, a person related to the secured party, or a secondary obligor would have brought.

(g) [Cash proceeds received by junior secured party.] A secured party that receives cash proceeds of a disposition in good faith and without knowledge that the receipt violates the rights of the holder of a security interest or other lien that is not subordinate to the security interest or agricultural lien under which the disposition is made:

(1)   takes the cash proceeds free of the security interest or other lien;

(2)   is not obligated to apply the proceeds of the disposition to the satisfaction of obligations secured by the security interest or other lien; and

(3)   is not obligated to account to or pay the holder of the security interest or other lien for any surplus.

ANALYSIS

New § 9-617 continues the rule of old § 9-504(4): the disposition discharges security interests subordinate to the interest under which the disposition is made but senior secured interests continue in the collateral. The transferee buying or otherwise acquiring an interest in the collateral takes subject to security interests senior to the interest under which the disposition is made. New § 9-615(g), which had no express counterpart under old Article 9, could be construed as allowing the senior secured creditor to double-dip. By negative implication, it denies protection to the secured creditor who knows that receipt of the disposition proceeds violates the rights of the senior secured creditor.

Example A: First Bank has the senior secured interest in the equipment of Debtor Co. The security agreement provides that Debtor Co. may not sell the equipment without the written consent of First Bank and that, if any sales are made, the proceeds will be promptly paid to First Bank. Second Bank holds a second-priority interest in the same equipment. After default by Debtor Co., Second Bank repossesses the equipment. First Bank informs Second Bank of its priority interest and the terms of its security interest. If Second Bank then sells the equipment without the consent of First Bank, its retention of the proceeds would apparently be wrongful *vis a vis* First Bank even though First Bank retains a security interest in the equipment which it can enforce against the purchaser at the disposition sale.

Official Comment

1. **Source.** Former Section 9-504(1), (2).

2. **Application of Proceeds.** This section contains the rules governing application of proceeds and the debtor's liability for a deficiency following a disposition of collateral. Subsection (a) sets forth the basic order of application. The proceeds are applied first to the expenses of disposition, second to the obligation secured by the security interest that is being enforced, and third, in the specified circumstances, to interests that are subordinate to that security interest.

Subsections (a) and (d) also address the right of a consignor to receive proceeds of a disposition by a secured party whose interest is senior to that of the consignor. Subsection (a) requires the enforcing secured party to pay excess proceeds first to subordinate secured parties or lienholders whose interests are senior to that of a consignor and, finally, to a consignor. Inasmuch as a consignor is the owner of the collateral, secured parties and lienholders whose interests are junior to the consignor's interest will not be entitled to any proceeds. In like fashion, under subsection (d)(1) the debtor is not entitled to a surplus when the enforcing secured party is required to pay over proceeds to a consignor.

3. **Noncash Proceeds.** Subsection (c) addresses the application of noncash proceeds of a disposition, such as a note or lease. The explanation in Section 9-608, Comment 4, generally applies to this subsection.

Example: A secured party in the business of selling or financing automobiles takes possession of collateral (an automobile) following its debtor's default. The secured party decides to sell the automobile in a private disposition under Section 9-610 and sends appropriate notification under Section 9-611. After undertaking its normal credit investigation and in accordance with its normal credit policies, the secured party sells the automobile on credit, on terms typical of the credit terms normally extended by the secured party in the ordinary course of its business. The automobile stands as collateral for the remaining balance of the price. The noncash proceeds received by the secured party are chattel paper. The secured party may wish to credit its debtor (the assignor) with the principal amount of the chattel paper or may wish to credit the debtor only as and when the payments are made on the chattel paper by the buyer.

Under subsection (c), the secured party is under no duty to apply the noncash proceeds (here, the chattel paper) or their value to the secured obligation unless its failure to do so would commercially unreasonable. If a secured party elects to apply the chattel paper to the outstanding obligation, however, it must do so in a commercially reasonable manner. The facts in the example indicate that it would be commercially unreasonable for the secured party to fail to apply the value of the chattel paper to the original debtor's secured obligation. Unlike the example in Comment 4 to Section 9-608, the noncash proceeds received in this example are of the type that the secured party regularly generates in the ordinary course of its financing business in nonforeclosure transactions. The original debtor should not be exposed to delay or uncertainty in this situation. Of course, there will be many situations that fall between the examples presented in the Comment to Section 9-608 and in this Comment. This Article leaves their resolution to the court based on the facts of each case.

One would expect that where noncash proceeds are or may be material, the secured party and debtor would agree to more specific standards in an agreement entered into before or after default. The parties may agree to the method of application of noncash proceeds if the method is not manifestly unreasonable. See Section 9-603.

When the secured party is not required to "apply or pay over for application noncash proceeds," the proceeds nonetheless remain collateral subject to this Article. See Section 9-608, Comment 4.

4. **Surplus and Deficiency.** Subsection (d) deals with surplus and deficiency. It revises former Section 9-504(2) by imposing an explicit requirement that the secured party "pay" the debtor for any surplus, while retaining the secured party's duty to "account." Inasmuch as the debtor may not be an obligor, subsection (d) provides that the obligor (not the debtor) is liable for the deficiency. The special rule governing surplus and deficiency when receivables have been sold likewise takes into account the distinction between a debtor and an obligor. Subsection (d) also addresses the situation in which a consignor has an interest that is subordinate to the security interest being enforced.

5. **Collateral Under New Ownership.** When the debtor sells collateral subject to a security interest, the original debtor (creator of the security interest) is no longer a debtor inasmuch as it no longer has a property interest

in the collateral; the buyer is the debtor. See Section 9-102. As between the debtor (buyer of the collateral) and the original debtor (seller of the collateral), the debtor (buyer) normally would be entitled to the surplus following a disposition. Subsection (d) therefore requires the secured party to pay the surplus to the debtor (buyer), not to the original debtor (seller) with which it has dealt. But, because this situation typically arises as a result of the debtor's wrongful act, this Article does not expose the secured party to the risk of determining ownership of the collateral. If the secured party does not know about the buyer and accordingly pays the surplus to the original debtor, the exculpatory provisions of this Article exonerate the secured party from liability to the buyer. See Sections 9-605, 9-628(a), (b). If a debtor sells collateral *free* of a security interest, as in a sale to a buyer in ordinary course of business (see Section 9-320(a)), the property is no longer collateral and the buyer is not a debtor.

6. **Certain "Low-Price" Dispositions.** Subsection (f) provides a special method for calculating a deficiency or surplus when the secured party, a person related to the secured party (defined in Section 9-102), or a secondary obligor acquires the collateral at a foreclosure disposition. It recognizes that when the foreclosing secured party or a related party is the transferee of the collateral, the secured party sometimes lacks the incentive to maximize the proceeds of disposition. As a consequence, the disposition may comply with the procedural requirements of this Article (e.g., it is conducted in a commercially reasonable manner following reasonable notice) but nevertheless fetch a low price.

Subsection (f) adjusts for this lack of incentive. If the proceeds of a disposition of collateral to a secured party, a person related to the secured party, or a secondary obligor are "significantly below the range of proceeds that a complying disposition to a person other than the secured party, a person related to the secured party, or a secondary obligor would have brought," then instead of calculating a deficiency (or surplus) based on the actual net proceeds, the calculation is based upon the amount that would have been received in a commercially reasonable disposition to a person other than the secured party, a person related to the secured party, or a secondary obligor. Subsection (f) thus rejects the view that the secured party's receipt of such a price necessarily constitutes noncompliance with Part 6. However, such a price may suggest the need for greater judicial scrutiny. See Section 9-610, Comment 10.

7. **"Person Related To."** Section 9-102 defines "person related to." That term is a key element of the system provided in subsection (f) for low-price dispositions. One part of the definition applies when the secured party is an individual, and the other applies when the secured party is an organization. The definition is patterned closely on the corresponding definition in Section 1.301(32) of the Uniform Consumer Credit Code.

§ 9-616. EXPLANATION OF CALCULATION OF SURPLUS OR DEFICIENCY.

(a) [Definitions.] In this section:

(1) "Explanation" means a writing that:

(A) states the amount of the surplus or deficiency;

(B) provides an explanation in accordance with subsection (c) of how the secured party calculated the surplus or deficiency;

(C) states, if applicable, that future debits, credits, charges, including additional credit service charges or interest, rebates, and expenses may affect the amount of the surplus or deficiency; and

(D) provides a telephone number or mailing address from which additional information concerning the transaction is available.

(2) "Request" means a record:

(A) authenticated by a debtor or consumer obligor;

(B) requesting that the recipient provide an explanation; and

(C) sent after disposition of the collateral under Section 9-610.

(b) [Explanation of calculation.] In a consumer-goods transaction in which the debtor is entitled to a surplus or a consumer obligor is liable for a deficiency under Section 9-615, the secured party shall:

(1) send an explanation to the debtor or consumer obligor, as applicable, after the disposition and:

(A) before or when the secured party accounts to the debtor and pays any surplus or first makes written demand on the consumer obligor after the disposition for payment of the deficiency; and

(B) within 14 days after receipt of a request; or

(2) in the case of a consumer obligor who is liable for a deficiency, within 14 days after receipt of a request, send to the consumer obligor a record waiving the secured party's right to a deficiency.

(c) [Required information.] To comply with subsection (a)(1)(B), a writing must provide the following information in the following order:

(1)   the aggregate amount of obligations secured by the security interest under which the disposition was made, and, if the amount reflects a rebate of unearned interest or credit service charge, an indication of that fact, calculated as of a specified date:

(A)   if the secured party takes or receives possession of the collateral after default, not more than 35 days before the secured party takes or receives possession; or

(B)   if the secured party takes or receives possession of the collateral before default or does not take possession of the collateral, not more than 35 days before the disposition;

(2)   the amount of proceeds of the disposition;

(3)   the aggregate amount of the obligations after deducting the amount of proceeds;

(4)   the amount, in the aggregate or by type, and types of expenses, including expenses of retaking, holding, preparing for disposition, processing, and disposing of the collateral, and attorney's fees secured by the collateral which are known to the secured party and relate to the current disposition;

(5)   the amount, in the aggregate or by type, and types of credits, including rebates of interest or credit service charges, to which the obligor is known to be entitled and which are not reflected in the amount in paragraph (1); and

(6)   the amount of the surplus or deficiency.

(d)   [Substantial compliance.] A particular phrasing of the explanation is not required. An explanation complying substantially with the requirements of subsection (a) is sufficient, even if it includes minor errors that are not seriously misleading.

(e)   [Charges for responses.] A debtor or consumer obligor is entitled without charge to one response to a request under this section during any six-month period in which the secured party did not send to the debtor or consumer obligor an explanation pursuant to subsection (b)(1). The secured party may require payment of a charge not exceeding $25 for each additional response.

ANALYSIS

Along with the specialized notice of disposition for consumer goods mandated by new § 9-614, the new requirement for explanation of the calculation of a deficiency or surplus was one of the major victories for consumer advocates to emerge in the last minute debtor/creditor compromise. It prevents a creditor from simply demanding payment of a bottom-line figure from the debtor or obligor. (Imagine a federal tax code allowing the taxpayer to turn in to the IRS a single bottom-line figure as to the amount of the taxpayer's liability for the year. Not a bad idea, you say?) The required disclosures in subsection (c) and the remedies for a violation were the result of extensive negotiations between consumer representatives and lawyers representing the automobile finance companies. Violation of this provision does not expose the creditor to the penalty of new § 9-625(c)(2). *See* new § 9-628(d). A creditor who fails to provide a requested explanation as required by § 9-616(b)(2) is liable for a $500 penalty. *See* § 9-625(e)(6). A creditor who fails to provide a disclosure required by § 9-616(b)(1) is liable for a $500 penalty if the failure "is part of a pattern, or consistent with a practice, of noncompliance." *See* new § 9-625(e)(5). In each case, the creditor would also be liable for debtor's actual damages under new § 9-625(b), though it is difficult to imagine what these would be apart from the amount by which any deficiency claim is overstated and mistakenly paid by the debtor or obligor.

Official Comment

1. **Source.** New.

2. **Duty to Send Information Concerning Surplus or Deficiency.** This section reflects the view that, in every consumer-goods transaction, the debtor or obligor is entitled to know the amount of a surplus or deficiency and the basis upon which the surplus or deficiency was calculated. Under subsection (b)(1), a secured party is obligated to provide this information (an "explanation," defined in subsection (a)(1)) no later than the time that it accounts for and pays a surplus or the time of its first written attempt to collect the deficiency. The obligor need not make a request for an accounting in order to receive an explanation. A secured party who does not attempt to collect a deficiency in writing or account for and pay a surplus has no obligation to send an explanation under subsection (b)(1) and, consequently, cannot be liable for noncompliance.

A debtor or secondary obligor need not wait until the secured party commences written collection efforts in order to receive an explanation of how a deficiency or surplus was calculated. Subsection (b)(2) obliges the secured party to send an explanation within 14 days after it receives a "request" (defined in subsection (a)(2)).

3. **Explanation of Calculation of Surplus or Deficiency.** Subsection (c) contains the requirements for how a calculation of a surplus or deficiency must be explained in order to satisfy subsection (a)(1)(B). It gives a secured

party some discretion concerning rebates of interest or credit service charges. The secured party may include these rebates in the aggregate amount of obligations secured, under subsection (c)(1), or may include them with other types of rebates and credits under subsection (c)(5). Rebates of interest or credit service charges are the only types of rebates for which this discretion is provided. If the secured party provides an explanation that includes rebates of pre-computed interest, its explanation must so indicate. The expenses and attorney's fees to be described pursuant to subsection (c)(4) are those relating to the most recent disposition, not those that may have been incurred in connection with earlier enforcement efforts and which have been resolved by the parties.

4. **Liability for Noncompliance.** A secured party who fails to comply with subsection (b)(2) is liable for any loss caused plus $500. See Section 9-625(b), (c), (e)(6). A secured party who fails to send an explanation under subsection (b)(1) is liable for any loss caused plus, if the noncompliance was "part of a pattern, or consistent with a practice of noncompliance," $500. See Section 9-625(b), (c), (e)(5). However, a secured party who fails to comply with this section is not liable for statutory minimum damages under Section 9-625(c)(2). See Section 9-628(d).

§ 9-617. RIGHTS OF TRANSFEREE OF COLLATERAL.

(a) [Effects of disposition.] A secured party's disposition of collateral after default:

(1) transfers to a transferee for value all of the debtor's rights in the collateral;

(2) discharges the security interest under which the disposition is made; and

(3) discharges any subordinate security interest or other subordinate lien [other than liens created under [cite acts or statutes providing for liens, if any, that are not to be discharged]].

(b) [Rights of good-faith transferee.] A transferee that acts in good faith takes free of the rights and interests described in subsection (a), even if the secured party fails to comply with this article or the requirements of any judicial proceeding.

(c) [Rights of other transferee.] If a transferee does not take free of the rights and interests described in subsection (a), the transferee takes the collateral subject to:

(1) the debtor's rights in the collateral;

(2) the security interest or agricultural lien under which the disposition is made; and

(3)   any other security interest or other lien.

Official Comment

1. **Source.** Former Section 9-504(4).

2. **Title Taken by Good-Faith Transferee.** Subsection (a) sets forth the rights acquired by persons who qualify under subsection (b)-transferees who act in good faith. Such a person is a "transferee," inasmuch as a buyer at a foreclosure sale does not meet the definition of "purchaser" in Section 1-201 (the transfer is not, *vis-a-vis* the debtor, "voluntary"). By virtue of the expanded definition of the term "debtor" in Section 9-102, subsection (a) makes clear that the ownership interest of a person who bought the collateral subject to the security interest is terminated by a subsequent disposition under this Part. Such a person is a debtor under this Article. Under former Article 9, the result arguably was the same, but the statute was less clear. Under subsection (a), a disposition normally discharges the security interest being foreclosed and any subordinate security interests and other liens.

A disposition has the effect specified in subsection (a), even if the secured party fails to comply with this Article. An aggrieved person (e.g., the holder of a subordinate security interest to whom a notification required by Section 9-611 was not sent) has a right to recover any loss under Section 9-625(b).

3. **Unitary Standard in Public and Private Dispositions.** Subsection (b) now contains a unitary standard that applies to transferees in both private and public dispositions—acting in good faith. However, this change from former Section 9-504(4) should not be interpreted to mean that a transferee acts in good faith even though it has knowledge of defects or buys in collusion, standards applicable to public dispositions under the former section. Properly understood, those standards were specific examples of the absence of good faith.

4. **Title Taken by Nonqualifying Transferee.** Subsection (c) specifies the consequences for a transferee who does not qualify for protection under subsections (a) and (b) (i.e., a transferee who does not act in good faith). The transferee takes subject to the rights of the debtor, the enforcing secured party, and other security interests or other liens.

§ 9-618. RIGHTS AND DUTIES OF CERTAIN SECONDARY OBLIGORS.

(a)   **[Rights and duties of secondary obligor.]** A secondary obligor acquires the rights and becomes obligated to perform the duties of the secured party after the secondary obligor:

(1)   receives an assignment of a secured obligation from the secured party;

(2)   receives a transfer of collateral from the secured party and agrees to accept the rights and assume the duties of the secured party; or

(3)   is subrogated to the rights of a secured party with respect to collateral.

(b)   [Effect of assignment, transfer, or subrogation.] An assignment, transfer, or subrogation described in subsection (a):

(1)   is not a disposition of collateral under Section 9-610; and

(2)   relieves the secured party of further duties under this article.

ANALYSIS

The most likely application of this provision: Appliance store sells its chattel paper to financer on a with recourse basis. After account debtor defaults, financer demands and receives full payment from the appliance store. The appliance store is now the secured creditor; the financer is out of the picture. The same results should follow under old § 9-504(5).

Official Comment

1. **Source.** Former Section 9-504(5).

2. **Scope of This Section.** Under this section, assignments of secured obligations and other transactions (regardless of form) that function like assignments of secured obligations are not dispositions to which Part 6 applies. Rather, they constitute assignments of rights and (occasionally) delegations of duties. Application of this section may require an investigation into the agreement of the parties, which may not be reflected in the words of the repurchase agreement (e.g., when the agreement requires a recourse party to "purchase the collateral" but contemplates that the purchaser will then conduct an Article 9 foreclosure disposition).

This section, like former Section 9-504(5), does not constitute a general and comprehensive rule for allocating rights and duties upon assignment of a secured obligation. Rather, it applies only in situations involving a secondary obligor described in subsection (a). In other contexts, the agreement of the parties and applicable law other than Article 9 determine whether the assignment imposes upon the assignee any duty to the debtor and whether the assignor retains its duties to the debtor after the assignment.

Subsection (a)(1) applies when there has been an assignment of an obligation that is secured at the time it is assigned. Thus, if a secondary obligor acquires the collateral at a disposition under Section 9-610 and simultaneously or subsequently discharges the unsecured deficiency claim, subsection (a)(1) is not implicated. Similarly, subsection (a)(3) applies only when the secondary obligor is subrogated to the secured party's rights with respect to collateral. Thus, this subsection will not be implicated if a secondary obligor discharges the debtor's unsecured obligation for a post-disposition deficiency. Similarly, if the secured party disposes of some of the collateral and the secondary obligor thereafter discharges the remaining obligation, subsection (a) applies only with respect to rights and duties concerning the remaining collateral, and, under subsection (b), the subrogation is not a disposition *of the remaining collateral.*

As discussed more fully in Comment 3, a secondary obligor may receive a transfer of collateral in a disposition under Section 9-610 in exchange for a payment that is applied against the secured obligation. However, a secondary obligor who pays and receives a transfer of collateral does not necessarily become subrogated to the rights of the secured party as contemplated by subsection (a)(3). Only to the extent the secondary obligor makes a payment in satisfaction of its secondary obligation would it become subrogated. To the extent its payment constitutes the price of the collateral in a Section 9-610 disposition by the secured party, the secondary obligor would not be subrogated. Thus, if the amount paid by the secondary obligor for the collateral in a Section 9-610 disposition is itself insufficient to discharge the secured obligation, but the secondary obligor makes an additional payment that satisfies the remaining balance, the secondary obligor would be subrogated to the secured party's deficiency claim. However, the duties of the secured party *as such* would have come to an end with respect to that collateral. In some situations the capacity in which the payment is made may be unclear. Accordingly, the parties should in their relationship provide clear evidence of the nature and circumstances of the payment by the secondary obligor.

3. **Transfer of Collateral to Secondary Obligor.** It is possible for a secured party to transfer collateral to a secondary obligor in a transaction that is a disposition under Section 9-610 and that establishes a surplus or deficiency under Section 9-615. Indeed, this Article includes a special rule, in Section 9-615(f), for establishing a deficiency in the case of some dispositions to, *inter alia*, secondary obligors. This Article rejects the view, which some may have ascribed to former Section 9-504(5), that a transfer of collateral to a recourse party can *never* constitute a disposition of collateral which discharges a security interest. Inasmuch as a secured party could itself buy collateral at its own public sale, it makes no sense to prohibit a recourse party ever from buying at the sale.

4. **Timing and Scope of Obligations.** Under subsection (a), a recourse party acquires rights and incurs obligations only "after" one of the specified circumstances occurs. This makes clear that when a successor assignee,

transferee, or subrogee becomes obligated it does not assume any liability for earlier actions or inactions of the secured party whom it has succeeded unless it agrees to do so. Once the successor becomes obligated, however, it is responsible for complying with the secured party's duties thereafter. For example, if the successor is in possession of collateral, then it has the duties specified in Section 9-207.

Under subsection (b), the same event (assignment, transfer, or subrogation) that gives rise to rights to, and imposes obligations on, a successor relieves its predecessor of any further duties under this Article. For example, if the security interest is enforced after the secured obligation is assigned, the assignee-but not the assignor-has the duty to comply with this Part. Similarly, the assignment does not excuse the assignor from liability for failure to comply with duties that arose before the event or impose liability on the assignee for the assignor's failure to comply.

§ 9-619. TRANSFER OF RECORD OR LEGAL TITLE.

(a)   ["Transfer statement."] In this section, "transfer state-ment" means a record authenticated by a secured party stating:

(1)   that the debtor has defaulted in connection with an obliga-tion secured by specified collateral;

(2)   that the secured party has exercised its post-default reme-dies with respect to the collateral;

(3)   that, by reason of the exercise, a transferee has acquired the rights of the debtor in the collateral; and

(4)   the name and mailing address of the secured party, debtor, and transferee.

(b)   [Effect of transfer statement.] A transfer statement entitles the transferee to the transfer of record of all rights of the debtor in the collateral specified in the statement in any official filing, recording, registration, or certificate-of-title system covering the collateral. If a transfer statement is presented with the applicable fee and request form to the official or office responsible for maintain-ing the system, the official or office shall:

(1)   accept the transfer statement;

(2)   promptly amend its records to reflect the transfer; and

(3)   if applicable, issue a new appropriate certificate of title in the name of the transferee.

(c)   [Transfer not a disposition; no relief of secured par-ty's duties.] A transfer of the record or legal title to collateral to a secured party under subsection (b) or otherwise is not of itself a disposition of collateral under this article and does not of itself relieve the secured party of its duties under this article.

Official Comment

1. **Source.** New.

2. **Transfer of Record or Legal Title.** Potential buyers of collateral that is covered by a certificate of title (e.g., an automobile) or is subject to a registration system (e.g., a copyright) typically require as a condition of their purchase that the certificate or registry reflect their ownership. In many cases, this condition can be met only with the consent of the record owner. If the record owner is the debtor and, as may be the case after the default, the debtor refuses to cooperate, the secured party may have great difficulty disposing of the collateral.

Subsection (b) provides a simple mechanism for obtaining record or legal title, for use primarily when other law does not provide one. Of course, use of this mechanism will not be effective to clear title to the extent that subsection (b) is preempted by federal law. Subsection (b) contemplates a transfer of record or legal title to a third party, following a secured party's exercise of its disposition or acceptance remedies under this Part, as well as a transfer by a debtor to a secured party prior to the secured party's exercise of those remedies. Under subsection (c), a transfer of record or legal title (under subsection (b) or under other law) to a secured party prior to the exercise of those remedies merely puts the secured party in a position to pass legal or record title to a transferee at foreclosure. A secured party who has obtained record or legal title retains its duties with respect to enforcement of its security interest, and the debtor retains its rights as well.

3. **Title-Clearing Systems Under Other Law.** Applicable non-UCC law (e.g., a certificate-of-title statute, federal registry rules, or the like) may provide a means by which the secured party may obtain or transfer record or legal title for the purpose of a disposition of the property under this Article. The mechanism provided by this section is in addition to any title-clearing provision under law other than this Article.

§ 9-620. ACCEPTANCE OF COLLATERAL IN FULL OR PARTIAL SATISFACTION OF OBLIGATION; COMPULSORY DISPOSITION OF COLLATERAL.

(a) **[Conditions to acceptance in satisfaction.]** Except as otherwise provided in subsection (g), a secured party may accept collateral in full or partial satisfaction of the obligation it secures only if:

(1)   the debtor consents to the acceptance under subsection (c);

(2)   the secured party does not receive, within the time set forth in subsection (d), a notification of objection to the proposal authenticated by:

(A)   a person to which the secured party was required to send a proposal under Section 9-621; or

(B)   any other person, other than the debtor, holding an interest in the collateral subordinate to the security interest that is the subject of the proposal;

(3)   if the collateral is consumer goods, the collateral is not in the possession of the debtor when the debtor consents to the acceptance; and

(4)   subsection (e) does not require the secured party to dispose of the collateral or the debtor waives the requirement pursuant to Section 9-624.

(b)   [Purported acceptance ineffective.] A purported or apparent acceptance of collateral under this section is ineffective unless:

(1)   the secured party consents to the acceptance in an authenticated record or sends a proposal to the debtor; and

(2)   the conditions of subsection (a) are met.

(c)   [Debtor's consent.] For purposes of this section:

(1)   a debtor consents to an acceptance of collateral in partial satisfaction of the obligation it secures only if the debtor agrees to the terms of the acceptance in a record authenticated after default; and

(2)   a debtor consents to an acceptance of collateral in full satisfaction of the obligation it secures only if the debtor agrees to the terms of the acceptance in a record authenticated after default or the secured party:

(A)   sends to the debtor after default a proposal that is unconditional or subject only to a condition that collateral not in the possession of the secured party be preserved or maintained;

(B)   in the proposal, proposes to accept collateral in full satisfaction of the obligation it secures; and

(C)   does not receive a notification of objection authenticated by the debtor within 20 days after the proposal is sent.

(d) [Effectiveness of notification.] To be effective under subsection (a)(2), a notification of objection must be received by the secured party:

(1)   in the case of a person to which the proposal was sent pursuant to Section 9-621, within 20 days after notification was sent to that person; and

(2)   in other cases:

(A)   within 20 days after the last notification was sent pursuant to Section 9-621; or

(B)   if a notification was not sent, before the debtor consents to the acceptance under subsection (c).

(e) [Mandatory disposition of consumer goods.] A secured party that has taken possession of collateral shall dispose of the collateral pursuant to Section 9-610 within the time specified in subsection (f) if:

(1)   60 percent of the cash price has been paid in the case of a purchase-money security interest in consumer goods; or

(2)   60 percent of the principal amount of the obligation secured has been paid in the case of a non-purchase-money security interest in consumer goods.

(f) [Compliance with mandatory disposition requirement.] To comply with subsection (e), the secured party shall dispose of the collateral:

(1)   within 90 days after taking possession; or

(2)   within any longer period to which the debtor and all secondary obligors have agreed in an agreement to that effect entered into and authenticated after default.

(g) [No partial satisfaction in consumer transaction.] In a consumer transaction, a secured party may not accept collateral in partial satisfaction of the obligation it secures.

ANALYSIS

The authorization of partial retention in satisfaction in business transactions resolves an open point under old Article 9. Old §§ 9-506 and 9-505(2) did not expressly authorize retention in partial satisfaction. So the issue was whether such a result could be achieved through post-default modification of the debtor's redemption right. *See Secured Transactions* § 8.05[4]. Retention in partial satisfaction will allow the creditor to become the owner of the collateral without making a disposition under new § 9-610 and to still have a debt claim for the portion of the obligation not satisfied.

Official Comment

1. **Source.** Former Section 9-505.

2. **Overview.** This section and the two sections following deal with strict foreclosure, a procedure by which the secured party acquires the debtor's interest in the collateral without the need for a sale or other disposition under Section 9-610. Although these provisions derive from former Section 9-505, they have been entirely reorganized and substantially rewritten. The more straightforward approach taken in this Article eliminates the fiction that the secured party always will present a "proposal" for the retention of collateral and the debtor will have a fixed period to respond. By eliminating the need (but preserving the possibility) for proceeding in that fashion, this section eliminates much of the awkwardness of former Section 9-505. It reflects the belief that strict foreclosures should be encouraged and often will produce better results than a disposition for all concerned.

Subsection (a) sets forth the conditions necessary to an effective acceptance (formerly, retention) of collateral in full or partial satisfaction of the secured obligation. Section 9-621 requires in addition that a secured party who wishes to proceed under this section notify certain other persons who have or claim to have an interest in the collateral. Unlike the failure to meet the conditions in subsection (a), under Section 9-622(b) the failure to comply with the notification requirement of Section 9-621 does not render the acceptance of collateral ineffective. Rather, the acceptance can take effect notwithstanding the secured party's noncompliance. A person to whom the required notice was not sent has the right to recover damages under Section 9-625(b). Section 9-622(a) sets forth the effect of an acceptance of collateral.

3. **Conditions to Effective Acceptance.** Subsection (a) contains the conditions necessary to the effectiveness of an acceptance of collateral. Subsection (a)(1) requires the debtor's consent. Under subsections (c)(1) and (c)(2), the debtor may consent by agreeing to the acceptance in writing after default. Subsection (c)(2) contains an alternative method by which to satisfy the debtor's-consent condition in subsection (a)(1). It follows the proposal-and-objection model found in former Section 9-505: The debtor consents if the secured party sends a proposal to the debtor and does not receive an objection within 20 days. Under subsection (c)(1), however, that silence is

not deemed to be consent with respect to acceptances in partial satisfaction. Thus, a secured party who wishes to conduct a "partial strict foreclosure" must obtain the debtor's agreement in a record authenticated after default. In all other respects, the conditions necessary to an effective partial strict foreclosure are the same as those governing acceptance of collateral in full satisfaction. (But see subsection (g), prohibiting partial strict foreclosure of a security interest in consumer transactions.)

The time when a debtor consents to a strict foreclosure is significant in several circumstances under this section and the following one. See Sections 9-620(a)(1), (d)(2), 9-621(a)(1), (a)(2), (a)(3). For purposes of determining the time of consent, a debtor's conditional consent constitutes consent.

Subsection (a)(2) contains the second condition to the effectiveness of an acceptance under this section-the absence of a timely objection from a person holding a junior interest in the collateral or from a secondary obligor. Any junior party-secured party or lienholder-is entitled to lodge an objection to a proposal, even if that person was not entitled to notification under Section 9-621. Subsection (d), discussed below, indicates when an objection is timely.

Subsections (a)(3) and (a)(4) contain special rules for transactions in which consumers are involved. See Comment 12.

4. **Proposals.** Section 9-102 defines the term "proposal." It is necessary to send a "proposal" to the debtor only if the debtor does not agree to an acceptance in an authenticated record as described in subsection (c)(1) or (c)(2). Section 9-621(a) determines whether it is necessary to send a proposal to third parties. A proposal need not take any particular form as long as it sets forth the terms under which the secured party is willing to accept collateral in satisfaction. A proposal to accept collateral should specify the amount (or a means of calculating the amount, such as by including a per diem accrual figure) of the secured obligations to be satisfied, state the conditions (if any) under which the proposal may be revoked, and describe any other applicable conditions. Note, however, that a conditional proposal generally requires the debtor's agreement in order to take effect. See subsection (c).

5. **Secured Party's Agreement; No "Constructive" Strict Foreclosure.** The conditions of subsection (a) relate to actual or implied consent by the debtor and any secondary obligor or holder of a junior security interest or lien. To ensure that the debtor cannot unilaterally cause an acceptance of collateral, subsection (b) provides that compliance with these conditions is necessary but not sufficient to cause an acceptance of collateral. Rather, under subsection (b), acceptance does not occur unless, in addition, the secured party consents to the acceptance in an authenticated record or sends to the debtor a proposal. For this reason, a mere delay in collection or disposition of collateral does not constitute a "constructive" strict foreclosure. Instead, delay is a factor relating to whether the secured party acted in a commercially reasonable manner for purposes of Section 9-607 or 9-610. A debtor's

voluntary surrender of collateral to a secured party and the secured party's acceptance of possession of the collateral does not, of itself, necessarily raise an implication that the secured party intends or is proposing to accept the collateral in satisfaction of the secured obligation under this section.

6. **When Acceptance Occurs.** This section does not impose any formalities or identify any steps that a secured party must take in order to accept collateral once the conditions of subsections (a) and (b) have been met. Absent facts or circumstances indicating a contrary intention, the fact that the conditions have been met provides a sufficient indication that the secured party has accepted the collateral on the terms to which the secured party has consented or proposed and the debtor has consented or failed to object. Following a proposal, acceptance of the collateral normally is automatic upon the secured party's becoming bound and the time for objection passing. As a matter of good business practice, an enforcing secured party may wish to memorialize its acceptance following a proposal, such as by notifying the debtor that the strict foreclosure is effective or by placing a written record to that effect in its files. The secured party's agreement to accept collateral is self-executing and cannot be breached. The secured party is bound by its agreement to accept collateral and by any proposal to which the debtor consents.

7. **No Possession Requirement.** This section eliminates the requirement in former Section 9-505 that the secured party be "in possession" of collateral. It clarifies that intangible collateral, which cannot be possessed, may be subject to a strict foreclosure under this section. However, under subsection (a)(3), if the collateral is consumer goods, acceptance does not occur unless the debtor is not in possession.

8. **When Objection Timely.** Subsection (d) explains when an objection is timely and thus prevents an acceptance of collateral from taking effect. An objection by a person to which notification was sent under Section 9-621 is effective if it is received by the secured party within 20 days from the date the notification was sent to that person. Other objecting parties (i.e., third parties who are not entitled to notification) may object at any time within 20 days after the last notification is sent under Section 9-621. If no such notification is sent, third parties must object before the debtor agrees to the acceptance in writing or is deemed to have consented by silence. The former may occur any time after default, and the latter requires a 20-day waiting period. See subsection (c).

9. **Applicability of Other Law.** This section does not purport to regulate all aspects of the transaction by which a secured party may become the owner of collateral previously owned by the debtor. For example, a secured party's acceptance of a motor vehicle in satisfaction of secured obligations may require compliance with the applicable motor vehicle certificate-of-title law. State legislatures should conform those laws so that they mesh well with this section and Section 9-610, and courts should construe those laws and this section harmoniously. A secured party's acceptance of collateral in the

possession of the debtor also may implicate statutes dealing with a seller's retention of possession of goods sold.

10. **Accounts, Chattel Paper, Payment Intangibles, and Promissory Notes.** If the collateral is accounts, chattel paper, payment intangibles, or promissory notes, then a secured party's acceptance of the collateral in satisfaction of secured obligations would constitute a sale to the secured party. That sale normally would give rise to a new security interest (the ownership interest) under Sections 1-201(37) and 9-109. In the case of accounts and chattel paper, the new security interest would remain perfected by a filing that was effective to perfect the secured party's original security interest. In the case of payment intangibles or promissory notes, the security interest would be perfected when it attaches. See Section 9-309. However, the procedures for acceptance of collateral under this section satisfy all necessary formalities and a new security agreement authenticated by the debtor would not be necessary.

11. **Role of Good Faith.** Section 1-203 imposes an obligation of good faith on a secured party's enforcement under this Article. This obligation may not be disclaimed by agreement. See Section 1-102. Thus, a proposal and acceptance made under this section in bad faith would not be effective. For example, a secured party's proposal to accept marketable securities worth $1,000 in full satisfaction of indebtedness in the amount of $100, made in the hopes that the debtor might inadvertently fail to object, would be made in bad faith. On the other hand, in the normal case proposals and acceptances should be not second-guessed on the basis of the "value" of the collateral involved. Disputes about valuation or even a clear excess of collateral value over the amount of obligations satisfied do not necessarily demonstrate the absence of good faith.

12. **Special Rules in Consumer Cases.** Subsection (e) imposes an obligation on the secured party to dispose of consumer goods under certain circumstances. Subsection (f) explains when a disposition that is required under subsection (e) is timely. An effective acceptance of collateral cannot occur if subsection (e) requires a disposition unless the debtor waives this requirement pursuant to Section 9-624(b). Moreover, a secured party who takes possession of collateral and unreasonably delays disposition violates subsection (e), if applicable, and may also violate Section 9-610 or other provisions of this Part. Subsection (e) eliminates as superfluous the express statutory reference to "conversion" found in former Section 9-505. Remedies available under other law, including conversion, remain available under this Article in appropriate cases. See Sections 1-103, 1-106.

Subsection (g) prohibits the secured party in consumer transactions from accepting collateral in partial satisfaction of the obligation it secures. If a secured party attempts an acceptance in partial satisfaction in a consumer transaction, the attempted acceptance is void.

§ 9-621. NOTIFICATION OF PROPOSAL TO ACCEPT COLLATERAL.

(a) [Persons to which proposal to be sent.] A secured party that desires to accept collateral in full or partial satisfaction of the obligation it secures shall send its proposal to:

(1) any person from which the secured party has received, before the debtor consented to the acceptance, an authenticated notification of a claim of an interest in the collateral;

(2) any other secured party or lienholder that, 10 days before the debtor consented to the acceptance, held a security interest in or other lien on the collateral perfected by the filing of a financing statement that:

(A) identified the collateral;

(B) was indexed under the debtor's name as of that date; and

(C) was filed in the office or offices in which to file a financing statement against the debtor covering the collateral as of that date; and

(3) any other secured party that, 10 days before the debtor consented to the acceptance, held a security interest in the collateral perfected by compliance with a statute, regulation, or treaty described in Section 9-311(a).

(b) [Proposal to be sent to secondary obligor in partial satisfaction.] A secured party that desires to accept collateral in partial satisfaction of the obligation it secures shall send its proposal to any secondary obligor in addition to the persons described in subsection (a).

Official Comment

1. **Source.** Former Section 9-505.

2. **Notification Requirement.** Subsection (a) specifies three classes of competing claimants to whom the secured party must send notification of its proposal: (i) those who notify the secured party that they claim an interest in the collateral, (ii) holders of certain security interests and liens who have filed against the debtor, and (iii) holders of certain security interests who have perfected by compliance with a statute (including a certificate-of-title statute), regulation, or treaty described in Section 9-311(a). With regard to (ii), see Section 9-611, Comment 4. Subsection (b) also requires notification to any secondary obligor if the proposal is for acceptance in partial satisfaction.

Unlike Section 9-611, this section contains no "safe harbor," which excuses an enforcing secured party from notifying certain secured parties and other lienholders. This is because, unlike Section 9-610, which requires that a disposition of collateral be commercially reasonable, Section 9-620 permits the debtor and secured party to set the amount of credit the debtor will receive for the collateral subject only to the requirement of good faith. An effective acceptance discharges subordinate security interests and other subordinate liens. See Section 9-622. If collateral is subject to several liens securing debts much larger than the value of the collateral, the debtor may be disinclined to refrain from consenting to an acceptance by the holder of the senior security interest, even though, had the debtor objected and the senior disposed of the collateral under Section 9-610, the collateral may have yielded more than enough to satisfy the senior security interest (but not enough to satisfy all the liens). Accordingly, this section imposes upon the enforcing secured party the risk of the filing office's errors and delay. The holder of a security interest who is entitled to notification under this section but does not receive it has the right to recover under Section 9-625(b) any loss resulting from the enforcing secured party's noncompliance with this section.

§ 9-622. EFFECT OF ACCEPTANCE OF COLLATERAL.

(a)   [Effect of acceptance.] A secured party's acceptance of collateral in full or partial satisfaction of the obligation it secures:

(1)   discharges the obligation to the extent consented to by the debtor;

(2)   transfers to the secured party all of a debtor's rights in the collateral;

(3)   discharges the security interest or agricultural lien that is the subject of the debtor's consent and any subordinate security interest or other subordinate lien; and

(4)   terminates any other subordinate interest.

(b)   [Discharge of subordinate interest notwithstanding noncompliance.] A subordinate interest is discharged or terminated under subsection (a), even if the secured party fails to comply with this article.

Official Comment

1. **Source.** New.

2. **Effect of Acceptance.** Subsection (a) specifies the effect of an acceptance of collateral in full or partial satisfaction of the secured obligation. The acceptance to which it refers is an effective acceptance. If a purported acceptance is ineffective under Section 9-620, e.g., because the secured party receives a timely objection from a person entitled to notification, then neither

this subsection nor subsection (b) applies. Paragraph (1) expresses the fundamental consequence of accepting collateral in full or partial satisfaction of the secured obligation-the obligation is discharged to the extent consented to by the debtor. Unless otherwise agreed, the obligor remains liable for any deficiency. Paragraphs (2) through (4) indicate the effects of an acceptance on various property rights and interests. Paragraph (2) follows Section 9-617(a) in providing that the secured party acquires "all of a debtor's rights in the collateral." Under paragraph (3), the effect of strict foreclosure on holders of junior security interests and other liens is the same regardless of whether the collateral is accepted in full or partial satisfaction of the secured obligation: all junior encumbrances are discharged. Paragraph (4) provides for the termination of other subordinate interests.

Subsection (b) makes clear that subordinate interests are discharged under subsection (a) regardless of whether the secured party complies with this Article. Thus, subordinate interests are discharged regardless of whether a proposal was required to be sent or, if required, was sent. However, a secured party's failure to send a proposal or otherwise to comply with this Article may subject the secured party to liability under Section 9-625.

§ 9-623. RIGHT TO REDEEM COLLATERAL.

(a) [Persons that may redeem.] A debtor, any secondary obligor, or any other secured party or lienholder may redeem collateral.

(b) [Requirements for redemption.] To redeem collateral, a person shall tender:

(1)   fulfillment of all obligations secured by the collateral; and

(2)   the reasonable expenses and attorney's fees described in Section 9-615(a)(1).

(c) [When redemption may occur.] A redemption may occur at any time before a secured party:

(1)   has collected collateral under Section 9-607;

(2)   has disposed of collateral or entered into a contract for its disposition under Section 9-610; or

(3)   has accepted collateral in full or partial satisfaction of the obligation it secures under Section 9-622.

Official Comment

1. **Source.** Former Section 9-506.

2. **Redemption Right.** Under this section, as under former Section 9-506, the debtor or another secured party may redeem collateral as long as the

secured party has not collected (Section 9-607), disposed of or contracted for the disposition of (Section 9-610), or accepted (Section 9-620) the collateral. Although this section generally follows former Section 9-506, it extends the right of redemption to holders of nonconsensual liens. To redeem the collateral a person must tender fulfillment of all obligations secured, plus certain expenses. If the entire balance of a secured obligation has been accelerated, it would be necessary to tender the entire balance. A tender of fulfillment obviously means more than a new promise to perform an existing promise. It requires payment in full of all monetary obligations then due and performance in full of all other obligations then matured. If unmatured secured obligations remain, the security interest continues to secure them (i.e., as if there had been no default).

3. **Redemption of Remaining Collateral Following Partial Enforcement.** Under Section 9-610 a secured party may make successive dispositions of portions of its collateral. These dispositions would not affect the debtor's, another secured party's, or a lienholder's right to redeem the remaining collateral.

4. **Effect of "Repledging."** Section 9-207 generally permits a secured party having possession or control of collateral to create a security interest in the collateral. As explained in the Comments to that section, the debtor's right (as opposed to its practical ability) to redeem collateral is not affected by, and does not affect, the priority of a security interest created by the debtor's secured party.

§ 9-624. WAIVER.

(a) [Waiver of disposition notification.] A debtor or secondary obligor may waive the right to notification of disposition of collateral under Section 9-611 only by an agreement to that effect entered into and authenticated after default.

(b) [Waiver of mandatory disposition.] A debtor may waive the right to require disposition of collateral under Section 9-620(e) only by an agreement to that effect entered into and authenticated after default.

(c) [Waiver of redemption right.] Except in a consumer-goods transaction, a debtor or secondary obligor may waive the right to redeem collateral under Section 9-623 only by an agreement to that effect entered into and authenticated after default.

ANALYSIS

A drafting assumption is that secured creditors, lien creditors and others who are not debtors or obligors, but who are entitled to notification under new § 9-611(c), will also be able to waive the notification because they are not in the first instance protected by the anti-waiver policy of § 9-602. One could argue that these parties are protected by § 1-102 barring disclaimer of U.C.C. duties of good faith, diligence, reasonableness and care. But it would hardly make sense to deny waivers to these parties which the debtor and secondary obligor can give.

Subsection (b) of this provision did not appear in the August 1998 version of Revised Article 9 issued after NCCUSL's approval. It did not surface as part of the text until the version of November 16, 1998. The ground rules seem to allow much to be done as editorial clean-up after formal approval by the membership of the sponsoring agencies.

Official Comment

1. **Source.** Former Sections 9-504(3), 9-505, 9-506.

2. **Waiver.** This section is a limited exception to Section 9-602, which generally prohibits waiver by debtors and obligors. It makes no provision for waiver of the rule prohibiting a secured party from buying at its own private disposition. Transactions of this kind are equivalent to "strict foreclosures" and are governed by Sections 9-620, 9-621, and 9-622.

[SUBPART 2. NONCOMPLIANCE WITH ARTICLE]

§ 9-625. REMEDIES FOR SECURED PARTY'S FAILURE TO COMPLY WITH ARTICLE.

(a)　[Judicial orders concerning noncompliance.] If it is established that a secured party is not proceeding in accordance with this article, a court may order or restrain collection, enforcement, or disposition of collateral on appropriate terms and conditions.

(b)　[Damages for noncompliance.] Subject to subsections (c), (d), and (f), a person is liable for damages in the amount of any loss caused by a failure to comply with this article. Loss caused by a failure to comply with a request under Section 9-210 may include loss resulting from the debtor's inability to obtain, or increased costs of, alternative financing.

ANALYSIS

Old § 9-507(1) recognizes a cause of action only for violation of default duties in Part 5 of Article 9. New § 9-625(h) gives the debtor an action for failure to comply with any Article 9 provision.

(c) [Persons entitled to recover damages; statutory damages in consumer-goods transaction.] Except as otherwise provided in Section 9-628:

(1) a person that, at the time of the failure, was a debtor, was an obligor, or held a security interest in or other lien on the collateral may recover damages under subsection (b) for its loss; and

ANALYSIS

Although the section purports to give an action to an "obligor," Official Comment 3 specifies that a pure primary obligor who is not a debtor secured party or lien holder may recover damages only for non-compliance with new § 9-616 --the duty to explain the calculation of the deficiency. The theory is that a pure obligor cannot be damaged by the secured party's actions with respect to the collateral.

(2) if the collateral is consumer goods, a person that was a debtor or a secondary obligor at the time a secured party failed to comply with this part may recover for that failure in any event an amount not less than the credit service charge plus 10 percent of the principal amount of the obligation or the time-price differential plus 10 percent of the cash price.

(d) [Recovery when deficiency eliminated or reduced.] A debtor whose deficiency is eliminated under Section 9-626 may recover damages for the loss of any surplus. However, a debtor or secondary obligor whose deficiency is eliminated or reduced under Section 9-626 may not otherwise recover under subsection (b) for noncompliance with the provisions of this part relating to collection, enforcement, disposition, or acceptance.

(e) [Statutory damages: noncompliance with specified provisions.] In addition to any damages recoverable under subsection (b), the debtor, consumer obligor, or person named as a debtor in a filed record, as applicable, may recover $500 in each case from a person that:

(1)   fails to comply with Section 9-208;

(2)   fails to comply with Section 9-209;

(3)   files a record that the person is not entitled to file under Section 9-509(a);

(4)   fails to cause the secured party of record to file or send a termination statement as required by Section 9-513(a) or (c);

(5)   fails to comply with Section 9-616(b)(1) and whose failure is part of a pattern, or consistent with a practice, of noncompliance; or

(6)   fails to comply with Section 9-616(b)(2).

(f) [Statutory damages: noncompliance with Section 9-210.] A debtor or consumer obligor may recover damages under subsection (b) and, in addition, $500 in each case from a person that, without reasonable cause, fails to comply with a request under Section 9-210. A recipient of a request under Section 9-210 which never claimed an interest in the collateral or obligations that are the subject of a request under that section has a reasonable excuse for failure to comply with the request within the meaning of this subsection.

(g) [Limitation of security interest: noncompliance with Section 9-210.] If a secured party fails to comply with a request regarding a list of collateral or a statement of account under Section 9-210, the secured party may claim a security interest only as shown in the statement included in the request as against a person that is reasonably misled by the failure.

Official Comment

1. **Source.** Former Section 9-507.

2. **Remedies for Noncompliance; Scope.** Subsections (a) and (b) provide the basic remedies afforded to those aggrieved by a secured party's failure to comply with this Article. Like all provisions that create liability, they are subject to Section 9-628, which should be read in conjunction with Section 9-605. The principal limitations under this Part on a secured party's right to enforce its security interest against collateral are the requirements that it

proceed in good faith (Section 1-203), in a commercially reasonable manner (Sections 9-607 and 9-610), and, in most cases, with reasonable notification (Sections 9-611 through 9-614). Following former Section 9-507, under subsection (a) an aggrieved person may seek injunctive relief, and under subsection (b) the person may recover damages for losses caused by noncompliance. Unlike former Section 9-507, however, subsections (a) and (b) are not limited to noncompliance with provisions of this Part of Article 9. Rather, they apply to noncompliance with any provision of this Article. The change makes this section applicable to noncompliance with Sections 9-207 (duties of secured party in possession of collateral), 9-208 (duties of secured party having control over deposit account), 9-209 (duties of secured party if account debtor has been notified of an assignment), 9-210 (duty to comply with request for accounting, etc.), 9-509(a) (duty to refrain from filing unauthorized financing statement), and 9-513(a) or (c) (duty to provide termination statement). Subsection (a) also modifies the first sentence of former Section 9-507(1) by adding the references to "collection" and "enforcement." Subsection (c)(2), which gives a minimum damage recovery in consumer-goods transactions, applies only to noncompliance with the provisions of this Part.

3. **Damages for Noncompliance with This Article.** Subsection (b) sets forth the basic remedy for failure to comply with the requirements of this Article: a damage recovery in the amount of loss caused by the noncompliance. Subsection (c) identifies who may recover under subsection (b). It affords a remedy to any aggrieved person who is a debtor or obligor. However, a principal obligor who is not a debtor may recover damages only for noncompliance with Section 9-616, inasmuch as none of the other rights and duties in this Article run in favor of such a principal obligor. Such a principal obligor could not suffer any loss or damage on account of noncompliance with rights or duties of which it is not a beneficiary. Subsection (c) also affords a remedy to an aggrieved person who holds a competing security interest or other lien, regardless of whether the aggrieved person is entitled to notification under Part 6. The remedy is available even to holders of senior security interests and other liens. The exercise of this remedy is subject to the normal rules of pleading and proof. A person who has delegated the duties of a secured party but who remains obligated to perform them is liable under this subsection. The last sentence of subsection (d) eliminates the possibility of double recovery or other over-compensation arising out of a reduction or elimination of a deficiency under Section 9-626, based on noncompliance with the provisions of this Part relating to collection, enforcement, disposition, or acceptance. Assuming no double recovery, a debtor whose deficiency is eliminated under Section 9-626 may pursue a claim for a surplus. Because Section 9-626 does not apply to consumer transactions, the statute is silent as to whether a double recovery or other over-compensation is possible in a consumer transaction.

Damages for violation of the requirements of this Article, including Section 9-609, are those reasonably calculated to put an eligible claimant in the position that it would have occupied had no violation occurred. See Section 1-106. Subsection (b) supports the recovery of actual damages for committing a breach of the peace in violation of Section 9-609, and principles of tort law supplement this subsection. See Section 1-103. However, to the extent that damages in tort compensate the debtor for the same loss dealt with by this Article, the debtor should be entitled to only one recovery.

4. **Minimum Damages in Consumer-Goods Transactions.** Subsection (c)(2) provides a minimum, statutory, damage recovery for a debtor and secondary obligor in a consumer-goods transaction. It is patterned on former Section 9-507(1) and is designed to ensure that every noncompliance with the requirements of Part 6 in a consumer-goods transaction results in liability, regardless of any injury that may have resulted. Subsection (c)(2) leaves the treatment of statutory damages as it was under former Article 9. A secured party is not liable for statutory damages under this subsection more than once with respect to any one secured obligation. See Section 9-628(e). Nor is a secured party liable under this subsection for failure to comply with Section 9-616. See Section 9-628(d).

Following former Section 9-507(1), this Article does not include a definition or explanation of the terms "credit service charge," "principal amount," "time-price differential," or "cash price," as used in subsection (c)(2). It leaves their construction and application to the court, taking into account the subsection's purpose of providing a minimum recovery in consumer-goods transactions.

5. **Supplemental Damages.** Subsections (e) and (f) provide damages that supplement the recovery, if any, under subsection (b). Subsection (e) imposes an additional $500 liability upon a person who fails to comply with the provisions specified in that subsection, and subsection (f) imposes like damages on a person who, without reasonable excuse, fails to comply with a request for an accounting or a request regarding a list of collateral or statement of account under Section 9-210. However, under subsection (f), a person has a reasonable excuse for the failure if the person never claimed an interest in the collateral or obligations that were the subject of the request.

6. **Estoppel.** Subsection (g) limits the extent to which a secured party who fails to comply with a request regarding a list of collateral or statement of account may claim a security interest.

§ 9-626. ACTION IN WHICH DEFICIENCY OR SURPLUS IS IN ISSUE.

(a) [Applicable rules if amount of deficiency or surplus in issue.] In an action arising from a transaction, other than a consumer transaction, in which the amount of a deficiency or surplus is in issue, the following rules apply:

(1)   A secured party need not prove compliance with the provisions of this part relating to collection, enforcement, disposition, or acceptance unless the debtor or a secondary obligor places the secured party's compliance in issue.

(2)   If the secured party's compliance is placed in issue, the secured party has the burden of establishing that the collection, enforcement, disposition, or acceptance was conducted in accordance with this part.

(3)   Except as otherwise provided in Section 9-628, if a secured party fails to prove that the collection, enforcement, disposition, or acceptance was conducted in accordance with the provisions of this part relating to collection, enforcement, disposition, or acceptance, the liability of a debtor or a secondary obligor for a deficiency is limited to an amount by which the sum of the secured obligation, expenses, and attorney's fees exceeds the greater of:

(A)   the proceeds of the collection, enforcement, disposition, or acceptance; or

(B)   the amount of proceeds that would have been realized had the noncomplying secured party proceeded in accordance with the provisions of this part relating to collection, enforcement, disposition, or acceptance.

(4)   For purposes of paragraph (3)(B), the amount of proceeds that would have been realized is equal to the sum of the secured obligation, expenses, and attorney's fees unless the secured party proves that the amount is less than that sum.

(5)   If a deficiency or surplus is calculated under Section 9-615(f), the debtor or obligor has the burden of establishing that the amount of proceeds of the disposition is significantly below the range of prices that a complying disposition to a person other than the secured party, a person related to the secured party, or a secondary obligor would have brought.

(b)   [Non-consumer transactions; no inference.] The limitation of the rules in subsection (a) to transactions other than consumer transactions is intended to leave to the court the determination of the proper rules in consumer transactions. The court may not infer from that limitation the nature of the proper rule in consumer transactions and may continue to apply established approaches.

ANALYSIS

The adoption of the rebuttable presumption rule for business transactions may well make the courts (and juries?) more willing to find a violation of disposition duties by a secured creditor. A creditor does not face a penalty forfeiture of its deficiency for every violation of the disposition rules. In jurisdictions which adhere to the absolute bar rule for consumer transactions, it will not be surprising to see discrepancies as to disposition duties arise in consumer and business transactions, even in situations where the text of Article 9 does not draw distinctions between these different terms of financing.

Official Comment

1. **Source.** New.

2. **Scope.** The basic damage remedy under Section 9-625(b) is subject to the special rules in this section for transactions other than consumer transactions. This section addresses situations in which the amount of a deficiency or surplus is in issue, i.e., situations in which the secured party has collected, enforced, disposed of, or accepted the collateral. It contains special rules applicable to a determination of the amount of a deficiency or surplus. Because this section affects a person's liability for a deficiency, it is subject to Section 9-628, which should be read in conjunction with Section 9-605. The rules in this section apply only to noncompliance in connection with the "collection, enforcement, disposition, or acceptance" under Part 6. For other types of noncompliance with Part 6, the general liability rule of Section 9-625(b)-recovery of actual damages-applies. Consider, for example, a repossession that does not comply with Section 9-609 for want of a default. The debtor's remedy is under Section 9-625(b). In a proper case, the secured party also may be liable for conversion under non-UCC law. If the secured party thereafter disposed of the collateral, however, it would violate Section 9-610 at that time, and this section would apply.

3. **Rebuttable Presumption Rule.** Subsection (a) establishes the rebuttable presumption rule for transactions other than consumer transactions. Under paragraph (1), the secured party need not prove compliance with the relevant provisions of this Part as part of its prima facie case. If, however, the debtor or a secondary obligor raises the issue (in accordance with the forum's rules of pleading and practice), then the secured party bears the burden of proving that the collection, enforcement, disposition, or acceptance complied. In the event the secured party is unable to meet this burden, then paragraph (3)

explains how to calculate the deficiency. Under this rebuttable presumption rule, the debtor or obligor is to be credited with the greater of the actual proceeds of the disposition or the proceeds that would have been realized had the secured party complied with the relevant provisions. If a deficiency remains, then the secured party is entitled to recover it. The references to "the secured obligation, expenses, and attorney's fees" in paragraphs (3) and (4) embrace the application rules in Sections 9-608(a) and 9-615(a).

Unless the secured party proves that compliance with the relevant provisions would have yielded a smaller amount, under paragraph (4) the amount that a complying collection, enforcement, or disposition would have yielded is deemed to be equal to the amount of the secured obligation, together with expenses and attorney's fees. Thus, the secured party may not recover any deficiency unless it meets this burden.

4. **Consumer Transactions.** Although subsection (a) adopts a version of the rebuttable presumption rule for transactions other than consumer transactions, with certain exceptions Part 6 does not specify the effect of a secured party's noncompliance in consumer transactions. (The exceptions are the provisions for the recovery of damages in Section 9-625.) Subsection (b) provides that the limitation of subsection (a) to transactions other than consumer transactions is intended to leave to the court the determination of the proper rules in consumer transactions. It also instructs the court not to draw any inference from the limitation as to the proper rules for consumer transactions and leaves the court free to continue to apply established approaches to those transactions.

Courts construing former Section 9-507 disagreed about the consequences of a secured party's failure to comply with the requirements of former Part 5. Three general approaches emerged. Some courts have held that a noncomplying secured party may not recover a deficiency (the "absolute bar" rule). A few courts held that the debtor can offset against a claim to a deficiency all damages recoverable under former Section 9-507 resulting from the secured party's noncompliance (the "offset" rule). A plurality of courts considering the issue held that the noncomplying secured party is barred from recovering a deficiency unless it overcomes a rebuttable presumption that compliance with former Part 5 would have yielded an amount sufficient to satisfy the secured debt. In addition to the nonuniformity resulting from court decisions, some States enacted special rules governing the availability of deficiencies.

5. **Burden of Proof When Section 9-615(f) Applies.** In a non-consumer transaction, subsection (a)(5) imposes upon a debtor or obligor the burden of proving that the proceeds of a disposition are so low that, under Section 9-615(f), the actual proceeds should not serve as the basis upon which a deficiency or surplus is calculated. Were the burden placed on the secured party, then debtors might be encouraged to challenge the price received in every disposition to the secured party, a person related to the secured party, or a secondary obligor.

6. **Delay in Applying This Section.** There is an inevitable delay between the time a secured party engages in a noncomplying collection, enforcement, disposition, or acceptance and the time of a subsequent judicial determination that the secured party did not comply with Part 6. During the interim, the secured party, believing that the secured obligation is larger than it ultimately is determined to be, may continue to enforce its security interest in collateral. If some or all of the secured indebtedness ultimately is discharged under this section, a reasonable application of this section would impose liability on the secured party for the amount of any excess, unwarranted recoveries but would not make the enforcement efforts wrongful.

§ 9-627. DETERMINATION OF WHETHER CONDUCT WAS COMMERCIALLY REASONABLE.

(a) [Greater amount obtainable under other circumstances; no preclusion of commercial reasonableness.] The fact that a greater amount could have been obtained by a collection, enforcement, disposition, or acceptance at a different time or in a different method from that selected by the secured party is not of itself sufficient to preclude the secured party from establishing that the collection, enforcement, disposition, or acceptance was made in a commercially reasonable manner.

(b) [Dispositions that are commercially reasonable.] A disposition of collateral is made in a commercially reasonable manner if the disposition is made:

(1)   in the usual manner on any recognized market;

(2)   at the price current in any recognized market at the time of the disposition; or

(3)   otherwise in conformity with reasonable commercial practices among dealers in the type of property that was the subject of the disposition.

(c) [Approval by court or on behalf of creditors.] A collection, enforcement, disposition, or acceptance is commercially reasonable if it has been approved:

(1)   in a judicial proceeding;

(2)   by a bona fide creditors' committee;

(3)   by a representative of creditors; or

(4)   by an assignee for the benefit of creditors.

(d) [Approval under subsection (c) not necessary; absence of approval has no effect.] Approval under subsection (c) need not be obtained, and lack of approval does not mean that the collection, enforcement, disposition, or acceptance is not commercially reasonable.

Official Comment

1. **Source.** Former Section 9-507(2).

2. **Relationship of Price to Commercial Reasonableness.** Some observers have found the notion contained in subsection (a) (derived from former Section 9-507(2)) (the fact that a better price could have been obtained does not establish lack of commercial reasonableness) to be inconsistent with that found in Section 9-610(b) (derived from former Section 9-504(3) (every aspect of the disposition, including its terms, must be commercially reasonable). There is no such inconsistency. While not itself sufficient to establish a violation of this Part, a low price suggests that a court should scrutinize carefully all aspects of a disposition to ensure that each aspect was commercially reasonable.

The law long has grappled with the problem of dispositions of personal and real property which comply with applicable procedural requirements (e.g., advertising, notification to interested persons, etc.) but which yield a price that seems low. This Article addresses that issue in Section 9-615(f). That section applies only when the transferee is the secured party, a person related to the secured party, or a secondary obligor. It contains a special rule for calculating a deficiency or surplus in a complying disposition that yields a price that is "significantly below the range of proceeds that a complying disposition to a person other than the secured party, a person related to the secured party, or a secondary obligor would have brought."

3. **Determination of Commercial Reasonableness; Advance Approval.** It is important to make clear the conduct and procedures that are commercially reasonable and to provide a secured party with the means of obtaining, by court order or negotiation with a creditors' committee or a representative of creditors, advance approval of a proposed method of enforcement as commercially reasonable. This section contains rules that assist in that determination and provides for advance approval in appropriate situations. However, none of the specific methods of disposition specified in subsection (b) is required or exclusive.

4. **"Recognized Market."** As in Sections 9-610(c) and 9-611(d), the concept of a "recognized market" in subsections (b)(1) and (2) is quite limited; it applies only to markets in which there are standardized price quotations for property that is essentially fungible, such as stock exchanges.

§ 9-628. NONLIABILITY AND LIMITATION ON LIABILITY OF SECURED PARTY; LIABILITY OF SECONDARY OBLIGOR.

(a) [Limitation of liability of secured party for noncompliance with article.] Unless a secured party knows that a person is a debtor or obligor, knows the identity of the person, and knows how to communicate with the person:

(1) the secured party is not liable to the person, or to a secured party or lienholder that has filed a financing statement against the person, for failure to comply with this article; and

(2) the secured party's failure to comply with this article does not affect the liability of the person for a deficiency.

(b) [Limitation of liability based on status as secured party.] A secured party is not liable because of its status as secured party:

(1) to a person that is a debtor or obligor, unless the secured party knows:

(A) that the person is a debtor or obligor;

(B) the identity of the person; and

(C) how to communicate with the person; or

(2) to a secured party or lienholder that has filed a financing statement against a person, unless the secured party knows:

(A) that the person is a debtor; and

(B) the identity of the person.

ANALYSIS

See the text analysis to new § 9-605.

(c) [Limitation of liability if reasonable belief that transaction not a consumer-goods transaction or consumer transaction.] A secured party is not liable to any person, and a person's liability for a deficiency is not affected, because of any act or omission arising out of the secured party's reasonable belief that a transaction is not a consumer-goods transaction or a consumer transaction or that goods are not consumer goods, if the secured party's belief is based on its reasonable reliance on:

(1)　a debtor's representation concerning the purpose for which collateral was to be used, acquired, or held; or

(2)　an obligor's representation concerning the purpose for which a secured obligation was incurred.

ANALYSIS

Subsection (c)(1) comes close to saying that a contractual stipulation that the goods are not consumer goods will control insofar as the debtor/creditor relationship is concerned. Of course, the stipulation is not controlling if the creditor knows that it is false. For the case law on this issue under old Article 9, see *Secured Transactions* § 20.01[2].

(d)　[Limitation of liability for statutory damages.] A secured party is not liable to any person under Section 9-625(c)(2) for its failure to comply with Section 9-616.

(e)　[Limitation of multiple liability for statutory damages.] A secured party is not liable under Section 9-625(c)(2) more than once with respect to any one secured obligation.

Official Comment

1. **Source.** New.

2. **Exculpatory Provisions.** Subsections (a), (b), and (c) contain exculpatory provisions that should be read in conjunction with Section 9-605. Without this group of provisions, a secured party could incur liability to unknown persons and under circumstances that would not allow the secured party to protect itself. The broadened definition of the term "debtor" underscores the need for these provisions.

If a secured party reasonably, but mistakenly, believes that a consumer transaction or consumer-goods transaction is a non-consumer transaction or non-consumer-goods transaction, and if the secured party's belief is based on its reasonable reliance on a representation of the type specified in subsection (c)(1) or (c)(2), then this Article should be applied as if the facts reasonably believed and reasonably relied upon were true. For example, if a secured party reasonably believed that a transaction was a non-consumer transaction and its belief was based on reasonable reliance on the debtor's misrepresentation that the collateral secured an obligation incurred for business purposes, the rebuttable presumption rule would apply under 9-626(b). Of course, if the secured party's belief is not reasonable or, even if reasonable, is not based on reasonable reliance on the debtor's misrepresentation, this limitation on liability is inapplicable.

3. **Inapplicability of Statutory Damages to Section 9-616.** Subsection (d) excludes noncompliance with Section 9-616 entirely from the scope of statutory damage liability under Section 9-625(c)(2).

4. **Single Liability for Statutory Minimum Damages.** Subsection (e) ensures that a secured party will incur statutory damages only once in connection with any one secured obligation.

PART 7 TRANSITION

§ 9-701. EFFECTIVE DATE. This [Act] takes effect on July 1, 2001.

ANALYSIS

At the last minute, NCCUSL decided to move the delayed effective date back from January 1 to July 1, 2001. This allows one more legislative year to sell the Revised Article 9 to the state legislature that may be skeptical of some of its provisions. In addition, it means that Revised Article 9 may not be referred to as the "Y2K+1 bug."

Official Comment

A uniform law as complex as Article 9 necessarily gives rise to difficult problems and uncertainties during the transition to the new law. As is customary for uniform laws, this Article is based on the general assumption that all States will have enacted substantially identical versions. While always important, uniformity is essential to the success of this Article. If former Article 9 is in effect in some jurisdictions, and this Article is in effect in others, horrendous complications may arise. For example, the proper place in which to file to perfect a security interest (and thus the status of a particular security interest as perfected or unperfected) would depend on whether the matter was litigated in a State in which former Article 9 was in effect or a State in which this Article was in effect. Accordingly, this section contemplates that States will adopt a uniform effective date for this Article. Any one State's failure to adopt the uniform effective date will greatly increase the cost and uncertainty surrounding the transition.

Other problems arise from transactions and relationships that were entered into under former Article 9 or under non-UCC law and which remain outstanding on the effective date of this Article. The difficulties arise primarily because this Article expands the scope of former Article 9 to cover additional types of collateral and transactions and because it provides new methods of perfection for some types of collateral, different priority rules, and different choice-of-law rules governing perfection and priority. This Section and the other sections in this Part address primarily this second set of problems.

§ 9-702. SAVINGS CLAUSE.

(a)   [Pre-effective-date transactions or liens.] Except as otherwise provided in this part, this [Act] applies to a transaction or lien within its scope, even if the transaction or lien was entered into or created before this [Act] takes effect.

(b)   [Continuing validity.] Except as otherwise provided in subsection (c) and Sections 9-703 through 9-708:

(1)   transactions and liens that were not governed by [former Article 9], were validly entered into or created before this [Act] takes effect, and would be subject to this [Act] if they had been entered into or created after this [Act] takes effect, and the rights, duties, and interests flowing from those transactions and liens remain valid after this [Act] takes effect; and

(2)   the transactions and liens may be terminated, completed, consummated, and enforced as required or permitted by this [Act] or by the law that otherwise would apply if this [Act] had not taken effect.

(c)   [Pre-effective-date proceedings.] This [Act] does not affect an action, case, or proceeding commenced before this [Act] takes effect.

Official Comment

1. **Pre-Effective-Date Transactions.** Subsection (a) contains the general rule that this Article applies to transactions, security interests, and other liens within its scope (see Section 9-109), even if the transaction or lien was entered into or created before the effective date. Thus, secured transactions entered into under former Article 9 must be terminated, completed, consummated, and enforced under this Article. Subsection (b) is an exception to the general rule. It applies to valid, pre-effective-date transactions and liens that were not governed by former Article 9 but would be governed by this Article if they had been entered into or created after this Article takes effect. Under subsection (b), these valid transactions, such as the creation of agricultural liens and security interests in commercial tort claims, retain their validity under this Article and may be terminated, completed, consummated, and enforced under this Article. However, these transactions also may be terminated, completed, consummated, and enforced by the law that otherwise would apply had this Article not taken effect.

2. **Judicial Proceedings Commenced Before Effective Date.** As is usual in transition provisions, subsection (c) provides that this Article does not affect litigation pending on the effective date.

§ 9-703. SECURITY INTEREST PERFECTED BEFORE EFFECTIVE DATE.

(a) [Continuing priority over lien creditor: perfection requirements satisfied.] A security interest that is enforceable immediately before this [Act] takes effect and would have priority over the rights of a person that becomes a lien creditor at that time is a perfected security interest under this [Act] if, when this [Act] takes effect, the applicable requirements for enforceability and perfection under this [Act] are satisfied without further action.

(b) [Continuing priority over lien creditor: perfection requirements not satisfied.] Except as otherwise provided in Section 9-705, if, immediately before this [Act] takes effect, a security interest is enforceable and would have priority over the rights of a person that becomes a lien creditor at that time, but the applicable requirements for enforceability or perfection under this [Act] are not satisfied when this [Act] takes effect, the security interest:

(1) is a perfected security interest for one year after this [Act] takes effect;

(2) remains enforceable thereafter only if the security interest becomes enforceable under Section 9-203 before the year expires; and

(3) remains perfected thereafter only if the applicable requirements for perfection under this [Act] are satisfied before the year expires.

ANALYSIS

The distinctive feature of the transition scheme is the duty to refile or perfect within one year of the effectiveness of Revised Article 9 if the method of perfection used under old Article 9 is not effective to perfect the interest under the new Article 9.

Example A: First Bank perfects a security interest in Debtor Co.'s bank account by common law pledge or assignment prior to the effective date of Revised Article 9. However, First Bank does not establish control over the bank account under § 9-104. Revised Article 9 becomes effective on July 1, 2001. The perfection of First Bank's interest lapses if First Bank fails to obtain control by July 1, 2002.

Example B: Farmer Equipment Dealer perfects a security interest in farmer's tractor by a local filing before Article 9 becomes effective. Assuming Revised Article 9 becomes effective on July 1, 2001, Farm Equipment Dealer must file in the designated state office specified by new § 9-501(2) by July 1, 2002 to prevent the lapse of its interest. There is to be no non-real estate-related local filing under Revised Article 9.

Example C: Small Loan Company perfects a security interest in the VCR of Borrower by local filing. This type of filing, a non-purchase-money filing by a small loan company against consumer goods not protected by the FTC's Credit Practices Rule, may be the most common form of a U.C.C. filing. *See Secured Transactions* § 20.04[1]. Revised Article 9 becomes effective on July 1, 2001. Small Loan Company must file centrally by July 1, 2002 to prevent the lapse of its interest.

Example D: Valley Finance perfects an interest in the inventory of Debtor Corp., a Delaware corporation, by filing in Florida where the inventory is located. Revised Article 9 becomes effective on July 1, 2001. Valley Finance must file in Delaware by July 1, 2002 to prevent the lapse of its interest.

Examples 2 through 4 illustrate why Revised Article 9 will be regarded as a pest by some financers, assuming that it is adopted as proposed and with the recommended transition provisions. If not "Y2K+2.5," some other pejorative will emerge. Will a state legislature in a jurisdiction which now has local filing as to equipment used in farming operations and consumer goods adopt this transition provision over the opposition of farm equipment dealers and small loan companies?

Official Comment

1. **Perfected Security Interests Under Former Article 9 and This Article.** This section deals with security interests that are perfected (i.e., that are enforceable and have priority over the rights of a lien creditor) under former Article 9 or other applicable law immediately before this Article takes effect. Subsection (a) provides, not surprisingly, that if the security interest would be a perfected security interest under this Article (i.e., if the transaction satisfies this Article's requirements for enforceability (attachment) and perfection), no further action need be taken for the security interest to be a perfected security interest.

2. **Security Interests Enforceable and Perfected Under Former Article 9 but Unenforceable or Unperfected Under This Article.** Subsection (b)

deals with security interests that are enforceable and perfected under former Article 9 or other applicable law immediately before this Article takes effect but do not satisfy the requirements for enforceability (attachment) or perfection under this Article. Except as otherwise provided in Section 9-705, these security interests are perfected security interests for one year after the effective date. If the security interest satisfies the requirements for attachment and perfection within that period, the security interest remains perfected thereafter. If the security interest satisfies only the requirements for attachment within that period, the security interest becomes unperfected at the end of the one-year period.

Example 1: A pre-effective-date security agreement in a consumer transaction covers "all securities accounts." The security interest is properly perfected. The collateral description was adequate under former Article 9 (see former Section 9-115(3)) but is insufficient under this Article (see Section 9-108(e)(2)). Unless the debtor authenticates a new security agreement describing the collateral other than by "type" (or Section 9-203(b)(3) otherwise is satisfied) within the one-year period following the effective date, the security interest becomes unenforceable at the end of that period.

Other examples under former Article 9 or other applicable law that may be effective as attachment or enforceability steps but may be ineffective under this Article include an oral agreement to sell a payment intangible or possession by virtue of a notification to a bailee under former Section 9-305. Neither the oral agreement nor the notification would satisfy the revised Section 9-203 requirements for attachment.

Example 2: A pre-effective-date possessory security interest in instruments is perfected by a bailee's receipt of notification under former 9-305. The bailee has not, however, acknowledged that it holds for the secured party's benefit under revised Section 9-313. Unless the bailee authenticates a record acknowledging that it holds for the secured party (or another appropriate perfection step is taken) within the one-year period following the effective date, the security interest becomes unperfected at the end of that period.

3. **Interpretation of Pre-Effective-Date Security Agreements.** Section 9-102 defines "security agreement" as "an agreement that creates or provides for a security interest." Under Section 1-201(3), an "agreement" is a "bargain of the parties in fact." If parties to a pre-effective-date security agreement describe the collateral by using a term defined in former Article 9 in one way and defined in this Article in another way, in most cases it should be presumed that the bargain of the parties contemplated the meaning of the term under former Article 9.

Example 3: A pre-effective-date security agreement covers "all accounts" of a debtor. As defined under former Article 9, an "account" did not include a right to payment for lottery winnings. These rights to payment are "accounts" under this Article, however. The agreement of the parties presumptively created a security interest in "accounts" as defined in former

Article 9. A different result might be appropriate, for example, if the security agreement explicitly contemplated future changes in the Article 9 definitions of types of collateral-e.g., " 'Accounts' means 'accounts' as defined in the UCC Article 9 of [State X], *as that definition may be amended from time to time.*" Whether a different approach is appropriate in any given case depends on the bargain of the parties, as determined by applying ordinary principles of contract construction.

§ 9-704. SECURITY INTEREST UNPERFECTED BEFORE EFFECTIVE DATE.

A security interest that is enforceable immediately before this [Act] takes effect but which would be subordinate to the rights of a person that becomes a lien creditor at that time:

(1) remains an enforceable security interest for one year after this [Act] takes effect;

(2) remains enforceable thereafter if the security interest becomes enforceable under Section 9-203 when this [Act] takes effect or within one year thereafter; and

(3) becomes perfected:

(A) without further action, when this [Act] takes effect if the applicable requirements for perfection under this [Act] are satisfied before or at that time; or

(B) when the applicable requirements for perfection are satisfied if the requirements are satisfied after that time.

Official Comment

This section deals with security interests that are enforceable but unperfected (i.e., subordinate to the rights of a person who becomes a lien creditor) under former Article 9 or other applicable law immediately before this Article takes effect. These security interests remain enforceable for one year after the effective date, and thereafter if the appropriate steps for attachment under this Article are taken before the one-year period expires. (This section's treatment of enforceability is the same as that of Section 9-703.) The security interest becomes a perfected security interest on the effective date if, at that time, the security interest satisfies the requirements for perfection under this Article. If the security interest does not satisfy the requirements for perfection until sometime thereafter, it becomes a perfected security interest at that later time.

Example: A security interest has attached under former Article 9 but is unperfected because the filed financing statement covers "all of debtor's personal property" and controlling case law in the applicable jurisdiction has determined that this identification of collateral in a financing statement is insufficient. Upon the effective date of this Article, the financing statement becomes sufficient under Section 9-504(2). On that date the security interest becomes perfected. (This assumes, of course, that the financing statement is filed in the proper filing office under this Article.)

§ 9-705. EFFECTIVENESS OF ACTION TAKEN BEFORE EFFECTIVE DATE.

(a) [Pre-effective-date action; one-year perfection period unless reperfected.] If action, other than the filing of a financing statement, is taken before this [Act] takes effect and the action would have resulted in priority of a security interest over the rights of a person that becomes a lien creditor had the security interest become enforceable before this [Act] takes effect, the action is effective to perfect a security interest that attaches under this [Act] within one year after this [Act] takes effect. An attached security interest becomes unperfected one year after this [Act] takes effect unless the security interest becomes a perfected security interest under this [Act] before the expiration of that period.

(b) [Pre-effective-date filing.] The filing of a financing statement before this [Act] takes effect is effective to perfect a security interest to the extent the filing would satisfy the applicable requirements for perfection under this [Act].

(c) [Pre-effective-date filing in jurisdiction formerly governing perfection.] This [Act] does not render ineffective an effective financing statement that, before this [Act] takes effect, is filed and satisfies the applicable requirements for perfection under the law of the jurisdiction governing perfection as provided in [former Section 9-103]. However, except as otherwise provided in subsections (d) and (e) and Section 9-706, the financing statement ceases to be effective at the earlier of:

(1) the time the financing statement would have ceased to be effective under the law of the jurisdiction in which it is filed; or

(2) June 30, 2006.

(d) [Continuation statement.] The filing of a continuation statement after this [Act] takes effect does not continue the effectiveness of the financing statement filed before this [Act] takes effect. However, upon the timely filing of a continuation statement after this [Act] takes effect and in accordance with the law of the jurisdiction governing perfection as provided in Part 3, the effectiveness of a financing statement filed in the same office in that jurisdiction before this [Act] takes effect continues for the period provided by the law of that jurisdiction.

(e) [Application of subsection (c)(2) to transmitting utility financing statement.] Subsection (c)(2) applies to a financing statement that, before this [Act] takes effect, is filed against a transmitting utility and satisfies the applicable requirements for perfection under the law of the jurisdiction governing perfection as provided in [former Section 9-103] only to the extent that Part 3 provides that the law of a jurisdiction other than jurisdiction in which the financing statement is filed governs perfection of a security interest in collateral covered by the financing statement.

(f) [Application of Part 5.] A financing statement that includes a financing statement filed before this [Act] takes effect and a continuation statement filed after this [Act] takes effect is effective only to the extent that it satisfies the requirements of Part 5 for an initial financing statement.

Official Comment

1. **General.** This section addresses primarily the situation in which the perfection step is taken under former Article 9 or other applicable law before the effective date of this Article, but the security interest does not attach until after that date.

2. **Perfection Other Than by Filing.** Subsection (a) applies when the perfection step is a step other than the filing of a financing statement. If the step that would be a valid perfection step under former Article 9 or other law is taken before this Article takes effect, and if a security interest attaches within one year after this Article takes effect, then the security interest becomes a perfected security interest upon attachment. However, the security interest becomes unperfected one year after the effective date unless the requirements for attachment and perfection under this Article are satisfied within that period.

3. **Perfection by Filing: Ineffective Filings Made Effective.** Subsection (b) deals with financing statements that were filed under former Article 9 and which would not have perfected a security interest under the former Article (because, e.g., they did not accurately describe the collateral or were filed in the wrong place), but which would perfect a security interest under this Article. Under subsection (b), such a financing statement is effective to perfect a security interest to the extent it complies with this Article. Subsection (b) applies regardless of the reason for the filing. For example, a secured party need not wait until the effective date to respond to the change this Article makes with respect to the jurisdiction whose law governs perfection of certain security interests. Rather, a secured party may wish to prepare for this change by filing a financing statement before the effective

date in the jurisdiction whose law governs perfection under this Article. When this Article takes effect, the filing becomes effective to perfect a security interest (assuming the filing satisfies the perfection requirements of this Article). Note, however, that Section 9-706 determines whether a financing statement filed before the effective date operates to continue the effectiveness of a financing statement filed in another office before the effective date.

4. **Perfection by Filing: Change in Applicable Law.** Subsection (c) provides that a financing statement filed in the proper jurisdiction under former Section 9-103 remains effective for all purposes, despite the fact that Part 3 of this Article would require filing of a financing statement in a different jurisdiction. This means that, during the early years of this Article's effectiveness, it may be necessary to search the files not only in the jurisdiction whose law governs perfection under this Article but also (if different) in the jurisdiction(s) whose law governed perfection under former Article 9. To limit this burden, subsection (c) provides that a financing statement filed in the jurisdiction determined by former Section 9-103 becomes ineffective at the earlier of the time it would become ineffective under the law of that jurisdiction or June 30, 2006. The June 30, 2006, limitation addresses some nonuniform versions of former Article 9 that extended the effectiveness of a financing statement beyond five years. Note that a financing statement filed before the effective date may remain effective beyond June 30, 2006, if subsection (d) (concerning continuation statements) or (e) (concerning transmitting utilities) or Section 9-706 (concerning initial financing statements that operate to continue pre-effective-date financing statements) so provides.

Subsection (c) is an exception to Section 9-703(b). Under the general rule in Section 9-703(b), a security interest that is enforceable and perfected on the effective date of this Article is a perfected security interest for one year after this Article takes effect, even if the security interest is not enforceable under this Article and the applicable requirements for perfection under this Article have not been met. However, in some cases subsection (c) may shorten the one-year period of perfection; in others, if the security interest is enforceable under Section 9-203, it may extend the period of perfection. A financing statement that remains effective under subsection (c) may be amended (but generally may not be continued) after this Article takes effect by filing an amendment in the office where the financing statement was filed.

Example 1: On July 3, 1996, D, a State X corporation, creates a security interest in certain manufacturing equipment located in State Y. On July 6, 1996, SP perfects a security interest in the equipment under former Article 9 by filing in the office of the State Y Secretary of State. See former Section 9-103(1)(b). This Article takes effect in States X and Y on July 1, 2001. Under Section 9-705(c), the financing statement remains effective for the first five days of July, 2001, after which it lapses. See former Section 9-403. Had SP continued the effectiveness of the financing statement by filing a continuation statement in State Y under former Article 9 before July 1, 2001, the financing statement would have remained effective to perfect the security interest through June 30, 2006. See subsection (c)(2). Alternatively, SP could have filed an initial financing statement in State X under subsection (b) or Section 9-706 before the State Y financing statement lapsed. Had SP done so, the security interest would have remained perfected without interruption until the State X financing statement lapsed.

5. **Continuing Effectiveness of Filed Financing Statement.** A financing statement filed before the effective date of this Article may be continued only by filing in the State and office designated by this Article. This result is accomplished in the following manner: Subsection (d) indicates that, as a general matter, a continuation statement filed after the effective date of this Article does not continue the effectiveness of a financing statement filed under the law designated by former Section 9-103. Instead, an initial financing statement must be filed under Section 9-706. The second sentence of subsection (d) contains an exception to the general rule. It provides that a continuation statement is effective to continue the effectiveness of a financing statement filed before this Article takes effect if this Article prescribes not only the same jurisdiction but also the same filing office.

Example 2: On November 8, 2000, D, a State X corporation, creates a security interest in certain manufacturing equipment located in State Y. On November 15, 2000, SP perfects a security interest in the equipment under former Article 9 by filing in office of the State Y Secretary of State. See former Section 9-103(1)(b). This Article takes effect in States X and Y on July 1, 2001. Under Section 9-705(c), the financing statement ceases to be effective in November, 2005, when it lapses. See Section 9-515. Under this Article, the law of D's location (State X, see Section 9-307) governs perfection. See Section 9-301. Thus, the filing of a continuation statement in State Y after the effective date would not continue the effectiveness of the financing statement. See subsection (d). However, the effectiveness of the financing statement could be continued under Section 9-706.

Example 3: The facts are as in Example 2, except that D is a State Y corporation. Assume State Y adopted former Section 9-401(1) (second alternative). State Y law governs perfection under Part 3 of this Article. (See Sections 9-301, 9-307.) Under the second sentence of subsection (d), the timely filing of a continuation statement in accordance with the law of State Y continues the effectiveness of the financing statement.

Example 4: The facts are as in Example 3, except that the collateral is equipment used in farming operations and, in accordance with former Section 9-401(1) (second alternative) as enacted in State Y, the financing statement was filed in State Y, in the office of the Shelby County Recorder of Deeds. Under this Article, a continuation statement must be filed in the office of the State Y Secretary of State. See Section 9-501(a)(2). Under the second sentence of subsection (d), the timely filing of a continuation statement in accordance with the law of State Y operates to continue a pre-effective-date financing statement only if the continuation statement is filed in the same office as the financing statement. Accordingly, the continuation statement is not effective in this case, but the financing statement may be continued under Section 9-706.

Example 5: The facts are as in Example 3, except that State Y enacted former Section 9-401(1) (third alternative). As required by former Section 9-401(1), SP filed financing statements in both the office of the State Y Secretary of State and the office of the Shelby County Recorder of Deeds. Under this Article, a continuation statement must be filed in the office of the State Y Secretary of State. See Section 9-501(a)(2). The timely filing of a continuation statement in that office after this Article takes effect would be effective to continue the effectiveness of the financing statement (and thus continue the perfection of the security interest), even if the financing statement filed with the County Recorder lapses.

6. **Continuation Statements.** In some cases, this Article reclassifies collateral covered by a financing statement filed under former Article 9. For example, collateral consisting of the right to payment for real property sold would be a "general intangible" under the former Article but an "account" under this Article. To continue perfection under those circumstances, a continuation statement must comply with the normal requirements for a continuation statement. See Section 9-515. In addition, the pre-effective-date financing statement and continuation statement, taken together, must satisfy the requirements of this Article concerning the sufficiency of the debtor's name, secured party's name, and indication of collateral. See subsection (f).

Example 6: A pre-effective-date financing statement covers "all general intangibles" of a debtor. As defined under former Article 9, a "general intangible," would include rights to payment for lottery winnings. These rights to payment are "accounts" under this Article, however. A post-effective-date continuation statement will not continue the effectiveness of the pre-effective-date financing statement with respect to lottery winnings unless it amends the indication of collateral covered to include lottery winnings (e.g., by adding "accounts," "rights to payment for lottery winnings," or the like). If the continuation statement does not amend the indication of collateral, the continuation statement will be effective to continue the effectiveness of the financing statement only with respect to "general intangibles" as defined in this Article.

Example 7: The facts are as in Example 6, except that the pre-effective-date financing statement covers "all accounts and general intangibles." Even though rights to payment for lottery winnings are "general intangibles" under former Article 9 and "accounts" under this Article, a post-effective-date continuation statement would continue the effectiveness of the pre-effective-date financing statement with respect to lottery winnings. There would be no need to amend the indication of collateral covered, inasmuch as the indication ("accounts") satisfies the requirements of this Article.

§ 9-706. WHEN INITIAL FINANCING STATEMENT SUFFICES TO CONTINUE EFFECTIVENESS OF FINANCING STATEMENT.

(a) [Initial financing statement in lieu of continuation statement.] The filing of an initial financing statement in the office specified in Section 9-501 continues the effectiveness of a financing statement filed before this [Act] takes effect if:

(1)   the filing of an initial financing statement in that office would be effective to perfect a security interest under this [Act];

(2)   the pre-effective-date financing statement was filed in an office in another State or another office in this State; and

(3)   the initial financing statement satisfies subsection (c).

(b) [Period of continued effectiveness.] The filing of an initial financing statement under subsection (a) continues the effectiveness of the pre-effective-date financing statement:

(1)   if the initial financing statement is filed before this [Act] takes effect, for the period provided in [former Section 9-403] with respect to a financing statement; and

(2)   if the initial financing statement is filed after this [Act] takes effect, for the period provided in Section 9-515 with respect to an initial financing statement.

(c) [Requirements for initial financing statement under subsection (a).] To be effective for purposes of subsection (a), an initial financing statement must:

(1)   satisfy the requirements of Part 5 for an initial financing statement;

(2)   identify the pre-effective-date financing statement by indicating the office in which the financing statement was filed and providing the dates of filing and file numbers, if any, of the financing statement and of the most recent continuation statement filed with respect to the financing statement; and

(3)   indicate that the pre-effective-date financing statement remains effective.

Official Comment

1. **Continuation of Financing Statements Not Filed in Proper Filing Office Under This Article.** This section deals with continuing the effectiveness of financing statements that are filed in the proper State and office under

former Article 9, but which would be filed in the wrong State or in the wrong office of the proper State under this Article. Section 9-705(d) provides that, under these circumstances, filing a continuation statement after the effective date of this Article in the office designated by former Article 9 would not be effective. This section provides the means by which the effectiveness of such a financing statement can be continued if this Article governs perfection under the applicable choice-of-law rule: filing an initial financing statement in the office specified by Section 9-501.

Although it has the effect of continuing the effectiveness of a pre-effective-date financing statement, an initial financing statement described in this section is not a continuation statement. Rather, it is governed by the rules applicable to initial financing statements. (However, the debtor need not authorize the filing. See Section 9-707.) Unlike a continuation statement, the initial financing statement described in this section may be filed any time during the effectiveness of the pre-effective-date financing statement-even before this Article is enacted-and not only within the six months immediately prior to lapse. In contrast to a continuation statement, which extends the lapse date of a filed financing statement for five years, the initial financing statement has its own lapse date, which bears no relation to the lapse date of the pre-effective-date financing statement whose effectiveness the initial financing statement continues. See subsection (b).

As subsection (a) makes clear, the filing of an initial financing statement under this section *continues* the effectiveness of a pre-effective-date financing statement. If the effectiveness of a pre-effective-date financing statement lapses before the initial financing statement is filed, the effectiveness of the pre-effective-date financing statement cannot be continued. Rather, unless the security interest is perfected otherwise, there will be a period during which the security interest is unperfected before becoming perfected again by the filing of the initial financing statement under this section.

If an initial financing statement is filed under this section before the effective date of this Article, it takes effect when this Article takes effect (assuming that it is ineffective under former Article 9). Note, however, that former Article 9 determines whether the filing office is obligated to accept such an initial financing statement. For the reason given in the preceding paragraph, an initial financing statement filed before the effective date of this Article does not continue the effectiveness of a pre-effective-date financing statement unless the latter remains effective on the effective date of this Article. Thus, for example, if the effectiveness of the pre-effective-date financing statement lapses before this Article takes effect, the initial financing statement would not continue its effectiveness.

2. **Requirements of Initial Financing Statement Filed in Lieu of Continuation Statement.** Subsection (c) sets forth the requirements for the initial financing statement under subsection (a). These requirements are needed to inform searchers that the initial financing statement operates to

continue a financing statement filed elsewhere and to enable searchers to locate and discover the attributes of the other financing statement. A single initial financing statement may continue the effectiveness of more than one financing statement filed before this Article's effective date. See Section 1-102(5)(a) (words in the singular include the plural). If under this Article the collateral is of a type different from its type under former Article 9-as would be the case, e.g., with a right to payment of lottery winnings (a "general intangible" under former Article 9 and an "account" under this Article), then subsection (c) requires that the initial financing statement indicate the type under this Article.

§ 9-707. PERSONS ENTITLED TO FILE INITIAL FINANCING STATEMENT OR CONTINUATION STATEMENT.

A person may file an initial financing statement or a continuation statement under this part if:

(1)   the secured party of record authorizes the filing; and

(2)   the filing is necessary under this part:

(A)   to continue the effectiveness of a financing statement filed before this [Act] takes effect; or

(B)   to perfect or continue the perfection of a security interest.

Official Comment

This section permits a secured party to file an initial financing statement or continuation statement necessary under this Part to continue the effectiveness of a financing statement filed before this Article takes effect or to perfect or otherwise continue the perfection of a security interest. Because a filing described in this section typically operates to continue the effectiveness of a financing statement whose filing the debtor already has authorized, this section does not require authorization from the debtor.

§ 9-708. PRIORITY.

(a)   [Law governing priority.] This [Act] determines the priority of conflicting claims to collateral. However, if the relative priorities of the claims were established before this [Act] takes effect, [former Article 9] determines priority.

(b)   [Priority if security interest becomes enforceable under Section 9-203.] For purposes of Section 9-322(a), the priority of a security interest that becomes enforceable under Section 9-203 of this [Act] dates from the time this [Act] takes effect if the security interest is perfected under this [Act] by the filing of a financing statement before this [Act] takes effect which would not have been effective to perfect the security interest under [former Article 9]. This subsection does not apply to conflicting security interests each of which is perfected by the filing of such a financing statement.

Official Comment

1. **Law Governing Priority.** Ordinarily, this Article determines the priority of conflicting claims to collateral. However, when the relative priorities of the claims were established before this Article takes effect, former Article 9 governs.

Example 1: In 1999, SP-1 obtains a security interest in a right to payment for goods sold ("account"). SP-1 fails to file a financing statement. This Article takes effect on July 1, 2001. Thereafter, on August 1, 2001, D creates a security interest in the same account in favor of SP-2, who files a financing statement. This Article determines the relative priorities of the claims. SP-2's security interest has priority under Section 9-322(a)(1).

Example 2: In 1999, SP-1 obtains a security interest in a right to payment for goods sold ("account"). SP-1 fails to file a financing statement. In 2000, D creates a security interest in the same account in favor of SP-2, who likewise fails to file a financing statement. This Article takes effect on July 1, 2001. Because the relative priorities of the security interests were established before the effective date of this Article, former Article 9 governs priority, and SP-1's security interest has priority under former Section 9-312(5)(b).

Example 3: The facts are as in Example 2, except that, on August 1, 2001, SP-2 files a proper financing statement under this Article. Until August 1, 2001, the relative priorities of the security interests were established before the effective date of this Article, as in Example 2. However, by taking the affirmative step of filing a financing statement, SP-2 established anew the relative priority of the conflicting claims after the effective date. Thus, this Article determines priority. SP-2's security interest has priority under Section 9-322(a)(1).

As Example 3 illustrates, relative priorities that are "established" before the effective date do not necessarily remain unchanged following the effective date. Of course, unlike priority contests among unperfected security interests, some priorities are established permanently, e.g., the rights of a buyer of property who took free of a security interest under former Article 9.

One consequence of the rule in subsection (a) is that the mere taking effect of this Article does not of itself adversely affect the priority of conflicting claims to collateral.

Example 4: In 1999, SP-1 obtains a security interest in a right to payment for lottery winnings (a "general intangible" as defined in former Article 9 but an "account" as defined in this Article). SP-1's security interest is unperfected because its filed financing statement covers only "accounts." In

2000, D creates a security interest in the same right to payment in favor of SP-2, who files a financing statement covering "accounts and general intangibles." Before this Article takes effect on July 1, 2001, SP-2's perfected security interest has priority over SP-1's unperfected security interest under former 9-312(5). Because the relative priorities of the security interests were established before the effective date of this Article, former Article 9 continues to govern priority after this Article takes effect. Thus, SP-2's priority is not adversely affected by this Article's having taken effect.

Note that were this Article to govern priority, SP-2 would become subordinated to SP-1 under Section 9-322(a)(1), even though nothing changes other than this Article's having taken effect. Under Section 9-704, SP-1's security interest would become perfected; the financing statement covering "accounts" adequately covers the lottery winnings and complies with the other perfection requirements of this Article, e.g., it is filed in the proper office.

Example 5: In 1999, SP-1 obtains a security interest in a right to payment for lottery winnings-a "general intangible" (as defined under former Article 9). SP-1's security interest is unperfected because its filed financing statement covers only "accounts." In 2000, D creates a security interest in the same right to payment in favor of SP-2, who makes the same mistake and also files a financing statement covering only "accounts." Before this Article takes effect on July 1, 2001, SP-1's unperfected security interest has priority over SP-2's unperfected security interest, because SP-1's security interest was the first to attach. See former Section 9-312(5)(b). Because the relative priorities of the security interests were established before the effective date of this Article, former Article 9 continues to govern priority after this Article takes effect. Although Section 9-704 makes both security interests perfected for purposes of this Article, both are unperfected under former Article 9, which determines their relative priorities.

2. **Financing Statements Ineffective Under Former Article 9 but Effective Under This Article.** If this Article determines priority, subsection (b) may apply. It deals with the case in which a filing that occurs before the effective date of this Article would be ineffective to perfect a security interest under former Article 9 but effective under this Article. For purposes of Section 9-322(a), the priority of a security interest that attaches after this Article takes effect and is perfected in this manner dates from the time this Article takes effect.

Example 6: In 1999, SP-1 obtains a security interest in D's existing and after-acquired instruments and files a financing statement covering "instruments." In 2000, D grants a security interest in its existing and after-acquired accounts in favor of SP-2, who files a financing statement covering "accounts." After this Article takes effect on July 1, 2001, one of D's account debtors gives D a negotiable note to evidence its obligation to pay an overdue account. Under the first-to-file-or-perfect rule in Section 9-322(a), SP-1 would have priority in the instrument, which constitutes SP-2's proceeds. SP-1's filing in 1999 was earlier than SP-2's in 2000. However, subsection (b) provides that, for purposes of Section 9-322(a), SP-1's priority dates from the time this Article takes effect (July 1, 2001). Under Section 9-322(b), SP-2's priority with respect to the proceeds (instrument) dates from its filing as to the original collateral (accounts). Accordingly, SP-2's security interest would be senior.

Subsection (b) does not apply to conflicting security interests each of which is perfected by a pre-effective-date filing that was not effective under former Article 9 but is effective under this Article.

Example 7: In 1999, SP-1 obtains a security interest in D's existing and after-acquired instruments and files a financing statement covering "instruments." In 2000, D grants a security interest in its existing and after-acquired instruments in favor of SP-2, who files a financing statement covering "instruments." After this Article takes effect on July 1, 2001, one of D's account debtors gives D a negotiable note to evidence its obligation to pay an overdue account. Under the first-to-file-or-perfect rule in Section 9-322(a), SP-1 would have priority in the instrument. Both filings are effective under this Article, see Section 9-705(b), and SP-1's filing in 1999 was earlier than SP-2's in 2000. Subsection (b) does not change this result.

APPENDIX I   CONFORMING AMENDMENTS TO OTHER ARTICLES

§ 1-105. TERRITORIAL APPLICATION OF THE ACT; PARTIES' POWER TO CHOOSE APPLICABLE LAW.

*   *   *

(2) Where one of the following provisions of this Act specifies the applicable law, that provision governs and a contrary agreement is effective only to the extent permitted by the law (including the conflict of laws rules) so specified:

Rights of creditors against sold goods.	Section 2-402.
Applicability of the Article on Leases.	Sections 2A-105 and 2A-106.
Applicability of the Article on Bank Deposits and Collections.	Section 4-102.
Governing law in the Article on Funds Transfers.	Section 4A-507.
Letters of Credit.	Section 5-116.
Bulk sales subject to the Article on Bulk Sales.	Section 6-103.
[If a State adopts the repealer of Article 6, then this item should be deleted.]	
Applicability of the Article on Investment Securities.	Section 8-110.
~~Perfection provisions of the Article on Secured Transactions.~~	~~Section 9-103.~~
<u>Law governing perfection, the effect of perfection or nonperfection, and the priority of security interests and agricultural liens.</u>	<u>Sections 9-301 through 9-307.</u>

ANALYSIS

Under § 1-105, the parties can choose the controlling law so long as the jurisdiction selected bears a reasonable relation to the transaction. In contrast, the choice of law rules in new § 9-307 are mandatory. The relationship between 1-105 and the mandating Article 9 rules is complex. Under Revised Article 9, the mandatory rules govern issues by perfection, the effect or perfection or non-perfection and the priority issues dealt with in Part 3 of the Revised Article. The private agreement can select the law to govern other issues involved in the rights and duties of the debtor and creditor, including attachment and default issues. The controlling choice of law as issues raised by Part 4 of Revised Article 9 is left to other law. *See Secured Transactions*, Chapter 5.

Official Comment

* * *

6. ~~Section 9-103~~ Sections 9-301 through 9-307 should be consulted as to the rules for perfection of security interests and agricultural liens ~~and the effects~~, the effect of perfection and nonperfection, and priority.

§ 1-201. GENERAL DEFINITIONS. Subject to additional definitions contained in the subsequent Articles of this Act which are applicable to specific Articles or Parts thereof, and unless the context otherwise requires, in this Act:

* * *

(9) "Buyer in ordinary course of business" means a person ~~who~~ that buys goods in good faith, ~~and~~ without knowledge that the sale ~~to him is in violation of~~ violates the ~~ownership~~ rights ~~or security interest~~ of ~~a third party~~ another person in the goods, and ~~buys~~ in the ordinary course from a person, other than a pawnbroker, in the business of selling goods of that kind ~~but does not include a pawnbroker. All persons who sell minerals or the like (including oil and gas) at wellhead or minehead shall be deemed to be persons~~ A person buys goods in the ordinary course if the sale to the person comports with the usual or customary practices in the kind of business in which the seller is engaged or with the seller's own usual or customary practices. A person that sells oil, gas, or other minerals at the wellhead or minehead is a person in the business of selling goods of that kind. ~~"Buying"~~ A buyer in ordinary course of business may ~~be~~ buy for cash, ~~or~~ by exchange of other property, or on secured or unsecured credit, and ~~includes receiving~~ may acquire goods or documents of title under a pre-existing contract for sale ~~but does not include a transfer in bulk or as security for or in total or partial satisfaction of a money debt.~~ Only a buyer that takes possession of the goods or has a right to recover the goods from the seller under Article 2 may be a buyer in ordinary course of business. A person that acquires goods in a transfer in bulk or as security for or in total or partial satisfaction of a money debt is not a buyer in ordinary course of business.

*   *   *

ANALYSIS

Case law under old Article 9 allow buyers to qualify as buyers in ordinary course even though they have not taken possession. These buyers take free of the security interests created by their seller even though the buyers' interests are secret. *See Secured Transactions* §§ 7.05[2][a]; 7A.20[4]. Revised Article 9 will require the buyer to have possession or a right to recover the goods. However, the proposed amendment for § 2-502 will give the consumer buyer that has paid all or part of the price a right to recover goods which have been identified to the contract. Moreover, a buyer unable to cover has a right to repleve identified good under § 2-716. Thus it will still be possible for a prepaying consumer buyer or a buyer unable to cover to qualify as a buyer in ordinary course even though the buyer has not taken possession of the goods. *See Secured Transactions* § 1A.09[2].

(32) "Purchase" includes taking by sale, discount, negotiation, mortgage, pledge, lien, <u>security interest,</u> issue or re-issue, gift, or any other voluntary transaction creating an interest in property.

*   *   *

(37) "Security interest" means an interest in personal property or fixtures which secures payment or performance of an obliga-tion. ~~The retention or reservation of title by a seller of goods notwithstanding shipment or delivery to the buyer (Section 2-401) is limited in effect to a reservation of a "security interest".~~ The term also includes any interest of a <u>consignor and a</u> buyer of accounts<u>,</u> ~~or~~ chattel paper, ~~which~~ <u>a payment intangible, or a promissory note in a transaction that</u> is subject to Article 9. The special property interest of a buyer of goods on identification of those goods to a contract for sale under Section 2-401 is not a "security interest", but a buyer may also acquire a "security interest" by complying with Article 9. ~~Unless a consignment is intended as security, reservation of title thereunder is not a "security interest", but a consignment in any event is subject to the provisions on consignment sales (Section 2-326).~~ <u>Except as otherwise provided in Section 2-505, the right of a seller or lessor of goods under Article 2 or 2A to retain or acquire possession</u>

of the goods is not a "security interest", but a seller or lessor may also acquire a "security interest" by complying with Article 9. The retention or reservation of title by a seller of goods notwithstanding shipment or delivery to the buyer (Section 2-401) is limited in effect to a reservation of a "security interest".

* * *

Official Comment

* * *

9. "Buyer in Ordinary Course of Business." From Section 1, Uniform Trust Receipts Act. The definition has been expanded to make clear the type of person protected. Its major significance lies in Section 2-403 and in the Article on Secured Transactions (Article 9).

~~The reference to minerals and the like makes clear that a buyer in ordinary course buying minerals under the circumstances described takes free of a prior mortgage created by the sellers. See Comment to Section 9-103.~~

~~A pawnbroker cannot be a buyer in ordinary course of business because the person from whom he buys goods (or acquires ownership after foreclosing an initial pledge) is typically an ordinary user and not a person engaged in selling goods of that kind.~~

The first sentence of paragraph (9) makes clear that a buyer from a pawnbroker cannot be a buyer in ordinary course of business. The second sentence tracks Section 6-102(1)(m). It explains what it means to buy "in the ordinary course." The penultimate sentence prevents a buyer that does not have the right to possession as against the seller from being a buyer in ordinary course of business. Concerning when a buyer obtains possessory rights, see Sections 2-502 and 2-716. However, the penultimate sentence is not intended to affect a buyer's status as a buyer in ordinary course of business in cases (such as a "drop shipment") involving delivery by the seller to a person buying from the buyer or a donee from the buyer. The requirement relates to whether *as against the seller* the buyer or one taking through the buyer has possessory rights.

* * *

32. "Purchase." Section 58, Uniform Warehouse Receipts Act; Section 76, Uniform Sales Act; Section 53, Uniform Bills of Lading Act; Section 22, Uniform Stock Transfer Act; Section 1, Uniform Trust Receipts Act. Rephrased. With the addition of taking "by . . . security interest," the revised definition makes explicit what formerly was implicit.

*   *   *

37. "Security Interest." See Section 1, Uniform Trust Receipts Act. ~~The present definition is elaborated, in view especially of the complete coverage of the subject in Article 9. Notice that in view of the Article the term includes the interest of certain outright buyers of certain kinds of property. Section 1-201(37) is being amended at the same time that the Article on Leases (Article 2A) is being promulgated as an amendment to this Act.~~ The definition of "security interest" was revised in connection with the promulgation of Article 2A and also to take account of the expanded scope of Article 9 as revised in the 1998 Official Text. It includes the interest of a consignor and the interest of a buyer of accounts, chattel paper, payment intangibles, or promissory notes. See Section 9-109. It also makes clear that, with certain exceptions, *in rem* rights of sellers and lessors under Articles 2 and 2A are not "security interests." Among the rights that are not security interests are the right to withhold delivery under Section 2-702(1), 2-703(a), or 2A-525, the right to stop delivery under Section 2-705 or 2A-526, and the right to reclaim under Section 2-507(2) or 2-702(2).

*   *   *

§ 2-103. DEFINITIONS AND INDEX OF DEFINITIONS.

*   *   *

(3) The following definitions in other Articles apply to this Article:

"Check".	Section 3-104.
"Consignee".	Section 7-102.
"Consignor".	Section 7-102.
"Consumer goods".	Section ~~9-109~~ 9-102.
"Dishonor".	Section ~~3-507~~ 3-502.
"Draft".	Section 3-104.

*   *   *

§ 2-210. DELEGATION OF PERFORMANCE; ASSIGNMENT OF RIGHTS.

*   *   *

(2) ~~Unless~~ Except as otherwise provided in Section 9-406, unless otherwise agreed, all rights of either seller or buyer can be assigned except where the assignment would materially change the duty of the other party, or increase materially the

burden or risk imposed on him by his contract, or impair materially his chance of obtaining return performance. A right to damages for breach of the whole contract or a right arising out of the assignor's due performance of his entire obligation can be assigned despite agreement otherwise.

(3) The creation, attachment, perfection, or enforcement of a security interest in the seller's interest under a contract is not a transfer that materially changes the duty of or increases materially the burden or risk imposed on the buyer or impairs materially the buyer's chance of obtaining return performance within the purview of subsection (2) unless, and then only to the extent that, enforcement actually results in a delegation of material performance of the seller. Even in that event, the creation, attachment, perfection, and enforcement of the security interest remain effective, but (i) the seller is liable to the buyer for damages caused by the delegation to the extent that the damages could not reasonably be prevented by the buyer, and (ii) a court having jurisdiction may grant other appropriate relief, including cancellation of the contract for sale or an injunction against enforcement of the security interest or consummation of the enforcement.

* * *

Legislative Note: Succeeding subsections must be renumbered.

Official Comment

3. Under subsection (2) rights which are no longer executory such as a right to damages for breach or a right to payment of an "account" as defined in the Article on Secured Transactions (Article 9) may be assigned although the agreement prohibits assignment. In such cases no question of delegation of any performance is involved. The assignment of a "contract right" as defined in the Article on Secured Transactions (Article 9) is not covered by this subsection. Subsection (2) is subject to Section 9-406, which makes rights to payment for goods sold ("accounts"), whether or not earned, freely alienable notwithstanding a contrary agreement or rule of law.

*   *   *

§ 2-312. WARRANTY OF TITLE AND AGAINST INFRINGEMENT; BUYER'S OBLIGATION AGAINST INFRINGEMENT.

*   *   *

Official Comment

*   *   *

5. Subsection (2) recognizes that sales by sheriffs, executors, certain foreclosing lienors and persons similarly situated ~~are~~ may be so out of the ordinary commercial course that their peculiar character is immediately apparent to the buyer and therefore no personal obligation is imposed upon the seller who is purporting to sell only an unknown or limited right. This subsection does not touch upon and leaves open all questions of restitution arising in such cases, when a unique article so sold is reclaimed by a third party as the rightful owner.

Foreclosure sales under Article 9 are another matter. Section 9-610 provides that a disposition of collateral under that section includes warranties such as those imposed by this section on a voluntary disposition of property of the kind involved. Consequently, unless properly excluded under subsection (2) or under the special provisions for exclusion in Section 9-610, a disposition under Section 9-610 of collateral consisting of goods includes the warranties imposed by subsection (1) and, if applicable, subsection (3).

*   *   *

§ 2-326. SALE ON APPROVAL AND SALE OR RETURN; ~~CONSIGNMENT SALES AND~~ RIGHTS OF CREDITORS.

(1) Unless otherwise agreed, if delivered goods may be returned by the buyer even though they conform to the contract, the transaction is

(a) a "sale on approval" if the goods are delivered primarily for use, and

(b) a "sale or return" if the goods are delivered primarily for resale.

(2) ~~Except as provided in subsection (3), goods~~ Goods held on approval are not subject to the claims of the buyer's creditors until acceptance; goods held on sale or return are subject to such claims while in the buyer's possession.

~~(3) Where goods are delivered to a person for sale and such person maintains a place of business at which he deals in goods of the kind involved, under a name other than the name of the person making delivery, then with respect to claims of creditors of the person conducting the business the goods are deemed to be on sale or return. The provisions of this subsection are applicable even though an agreement purports to reserve title to the person making delivery until payment or resale or uses such words as "on consignment" or "on memorandum". However, this subsection is not applicable if the person making delivery~~

~~(a) complies with an applicable law providing for a consignor's interest or the like to be evidenced by a sign, or~~

~~(b) establishes that the person conducting the business is generally known by his creditors to be substantially engaged in selling the goods of others, or~~

~~(c) complies with the filing provisions of the Article on Secured Transactions (Article 9).~~

~~(4)~~ (3) Any "or return" term of a contract for sale is to be treated as a separate contract for sale within the statute of frauds section of this Article (Section 2-201) and as contradicting the sale aspect of the contract within the provisions of this Article on parol or extrinsic evidence (Section 2-202).

Official Comment

1. ~~A~~ Both a "sale on approval" ~~or~~ and a "sale or return" ~~is distinct~~ should be distinguished from other types of transactions with which they frequently have ~~frequently~~ been confused. ~~The type of "sale on approval," "on trial" or "on satisfaction" dealt~~ A "sale on approval," sometimes also called a sale "on trial" or "on satisfaction," deals with a contract under which the seller undertakes a ~~particular business~~ risk in order to satisfy ~~his~~ its prospective buyer with the appearance or performance of the goods ~~in question~~ that are sold. The goods are delivered to the proposed purchaser but they remain the property of the seller until the buyer accepts them. The price has already been agreed. The buyer's willingness to receive and test the goods is the consideration for the seller's engagement to deliver and sell. ~~The type of "sale or return" involved herein~~ A "sale or return," on the other hand, typically is a sale to a merchant whose unwillingness to buy is overcome only by the seller's engagement to take back the goods (or any commercial unit of goods) in lieu of payment if they fail to be resold. A sale or return is a present sale of goods which may be undone at the buyer's option. Accordingly, subsection (2) provides that goods delivered on approval are not subject to the prospective buyer's creditors until acceptance, and goods delivered in a sale or return are subject to the buyer's creditors while in the buyer's possession.

These two transactions are so strongly delineated in practice and in general understanding that every presumption runs against a delivery to a consumer being a "sale or return" and against a delivery to a merchant for resale being a "sale on approval."

2. The right to return goods for failure to conform to the contract of sale does not make the transaction a "sale on approval" or "sale or return" and has nothing to do with this section ~~and the following section~~ or Section 2-327. ~~The present~~ This section is not concerned with remedies for breach of contract. It deals instead with a power given by the contract to turn back the goods even though they are wholly as warranted. This section nevertheless presupposes that a contract for sale is contemplated by the parties, although that contract may be of the particular character ~~here described~~ that this section addresses (i.e., a sale on approval or a sale or return).

~~Where the~~ If a buyer's obligation as a buyer is conditioned not on its personal approval but on the article's passing a described objective test, the risk of loss by casualty pending the test is properly the seller's and proper return is at its expense. On the point of "satisfaction" as meaning "reasonable satisfaction" ~~where~~ when an industrial machine is involved, this Article takes no position.

~~2. Pursuant to the general policies of this Act which require good faith not only between the parties to the sales contract, but as against interested third parties, subsection (3) resolves all reasonable doubts as to the nature of the transaction in favor of the general creditors of the buyer. As against such creditors words such as "on consignment" or "on memorandum", with or without words of reservation of title in the seller, are disregarded when the buyer has a place of business at which he deals in goods of the kind involved. A necessary exception is made where the buyer is known to be engaged primarily in selling the goods of others or is selling under a relevant sign law, or the seller complies with the filing provisions of Article 9 as if his interest were a security interest. However, there is no intent in this Section to narrow the protection afforded to third parties in any jurisdiction which has a selling Factors Act. The purpose of the exception is merely to limit the effect of the present subsection itself, in the absence of any such Factors Act, to cases in which creditors of the buyer may reasonably be deemed to have been misled by the secret reservation.~~

3. Subsection ~~(4)~~ (3) resolves a conflict in the ~~pre-existing~~ pre-UCC case law by ~~recognition~~ recognizing that an "or return" provision is so definitely at odds with any ordinary contract for sale of goods that ~~where written agreements are~~ if a written agreement is involved ~~it~~ the "or return" term must be contained in a written memorandum. The "or return" aspect of a sales contract must be treated as a separate contract under the Statute of Frauds section and as contradicting the sale insofar as questions of parol or extrinsic evidence are concerned.

4. Certain true consignment transactions were dealt with in former Sections 2-326(3) and 9-114. These provisions have been deleted and have been replaced by new provisions in Article 9. See, e.g., Sections 9-109(a)(4); 9-103(b); 9-319.

§ 2-502. BUYER'S RIGHT TO GOODS ON SELLER'S REPUDIATION, FAILURE TO DELIVER, OR INSOLVENCY.

(1) Subject to subsections (2) and (3) and even though the goods have not been shipped a buyer who has paid a part or all of the price of goods in which he has a special property under the provisions of the immediately preceding section may on making and keeping good a tender of any unpaid portion of their price recover them from the seller if:

(a) in the case of goods bought for personal, family, or household purposes, the seller repudiates or fails to deliver as required by the contract; or

(b) in all cases, the seller becomes insolvent within ten days after receipt of the first installment on their price.

(2) The buyer's right to recover the goods under subsection (1)(a) vests upon acquisition of a special property, even if the seller had not then repudiated or failed to deliver.

ANALYSIS

The consumer buyer's rights to recover the goods under § 2-502(1)(a) or under § 2-716 are declared to vest on the acquisition of the buyer's special property interest, *i.e.*, when the goods are identified to contract of sale. *See* § 2-501. In theory, a security interest granted by the seller after identification of the goods to the sales contract can only attach to the seller's interest in the goods at that point. Thus, a consumer buyer is to take free of post-identification security interests created by the seller when the buyer could recover the goods from the seller under §§ 2-502 or 2-716, even though the buyer does not qualify as a buyer in ordinary course. These provisions were part of the last minute debtor/creditor compromise. It seems likely, however, that a floating lien security interest held by a creditor of the seller will attach to the goods before or simultaneously with this identification to a particular sales contract. In which case, the buyer must be a buyer in ordinary course or the creditor must authorize the sale for the buyer to take free of the floating lien. *See Secured Transactions* § 1A.09[2].

One bankruptcy court has held that Section 2-502 of the present U.C.C., giving a prepaying buyer a right to goods on the seller's insolvency, is preempted by Section 365 of the Bankruptcy Code. Diesel Performance Inc. v. G. Paoletti (*In re* G. Paoletti, Inc.), 205 B.R. 251, 34 U.C.C. Rep. Serv. 2d 987 (Bankr. N.D. Cal. 1997). Similar challenges may be made to the expanded protections for pre-paying buyers contained in new §§ 2-502(1)(a) and 2-716.

(3) If the identification creating his special property has been made by the buyer he acquires the right to recover the goods only if they conform to the contract for sale.

Official Comment

1. This section gives an additional right to the buyer as a result of identification of the goods to the contract in the manner provided in Section 2-501. The buyer is given a right to <u>recover</u> the goods ~~on the seller's insolvency occurring~~, <u>conditioned upon making and keeping good a tender of any unpaid portion of the price, in two limited circumstances. First, the buyer may recover goods bought for personal, family, or household purposes if the seller repudiates the contract or fails to deliver the goods. Second, in any case, the buyer may recover the goods if the seller becomes insolvent within 10 days after he the seller receives the first installment on their price. The buyer's right to recover the goods under this section is an exception to the usual rule, under which the disappointed buyer must resort to an action to recover damages.</u>

2. The question of whether the buyer also acquires a security interest in identified goods and has rights to the goods when insolvency takes place after the ten-day period provided in this section depends upon compliance with the provisions of the Article on Secured Transactions (Article 9).

3. <u>Under subsection (2), the buyer's right to recover consumer goods under subsection (1)(a) vests upon acquisition of a special property, which occurs upon identification of the goods to the contract. See Section 2-501. Inasmuch as a secured party normally acquires no greater rights in its collateral that its debtor had or had power to convey, see Section 2-403(1) (first sentence), a buyer who acquires a right to recover under this section will take free of a security interest created by the seller if it attaches to the goods after the goods have been identified to the contract. The buyer will take free, even if the buyer does not buy in ordinary course and even if the security interest is perfected. Of course, to the extent that the buyer pays the price after the security interest attaches, the payments will constitute proceeds of the security interest.</u>

~~3.~~ <u>4.</u> Subsection ~~(2)~~ <u>(3)</u> is included to preclude the possibility of unjust enrichment<u>,</u> which ~~exists~~ <u>would exist</u> if the buyer were permitted to recover goods even though they were greatly superior in quality or quantity to that called for by the contract for sale.

§ 2-716. BUYER'S RIGHT TO SPECIFIC PERFORMANCE OR REPLEVIN.

(1) Specific performance may be decreed where the goods are unique or in other proper circumstances.

(2) The decree for specific performance may include such terms and conditions as to payment of the price, damages, or other relief as the court may deem just.

(3) The buyer has a right of replevin for goods identified to the contract if after reasonable effort he is unable to effect cover for such goods or the circumstances reasonably indicate that such effort will be unavailing or if the goods have been shipped under reservation and satisfaction of the security interest in them has been made or tendered. In the case of goods bought for personal, family, or household purposes, the buyer's right of replevin vests upon acquisition of a special property, even if the seller had not then repudiated or failed to deliver.

Official Comment

* * *

3. The legal remedy of replevin is given to the buyer in cases in which cover is reasonably unavailable and goods have been identified to the contract. This is in addition to the buyer's right to recover identified goods on the seller's insolvency (Section 2-502) under Section 2-502. For consumer goods, the buyer's right to replevin vests upon the buyer's acquisition of a special property, which occurs upon identification of the goods to the contract. See Section 2-501. Inasmuch as a secured party normally acquires no greater rights in its collateral that its debtor had or had power to convey, see Section 2-403(1) (first sentence), a buyer who acquires a right of replevin under subsection (3) will take free of a security interest created by the seller if it attaches to the goods after the goods have been identified to the contract. The buyer will take free, even if the buyer does not buy in ordinary course and even if the security interest is perfected. Of course, to the extent that the buyer pays the price after the security interest attaches, the payments will constitute proceeds of the security interest.

*   *   *

§ 2A-103. DEFINITIONS AND INDEX OF DEFINITIONS.

*   *   *

(3) The following definitions in other Articles apply to this Article:

"Account".	Section ~~9-106~~ 9-102(a)(2).
"Between merchants".	Section 2-104(3).
"Buyer".	Section 2-103(1)(a).
"Chattel paper".	Section ~~9-105(1)(b)~~ 9-102(a)(11).
"Consumer goods".	Section ~~9-109(1)~~ 9-102(a)(23).
"Document".	Section ~~9-105(1)(f)~~ 9-102(a)(30).
"Entrusting".	Section 2-403(3).
~~"General intangibles".~~	~~Section 9-106.~~
"General intangible".	Section 9-102(a)(42).
"Good faith".	Section 2-103(1)(b).
"Instrument".	Section ~~9-105(1)(i)~~ 9-102(a)(47).
"Merchant".	Section 2-104(1).
"Mortgage".	Section ~~9-105(1)(j)~~ 9-102(a)(55).
"Pursuant to commitment".	Section ~~9-105(1)(k)~~ 9-102(a)(68).
"Receipt".	Section 2-103(1)(c).
"Sale".	Section 2-106(1).
"Sale on approval".	Section 2-326.
"Sale or return".	Section 2-326.
"Seller".	Section 2-103(1)(d).

*   *   *

§ 2A-303. ALIENABILITY OF PARTY'S INTEREST UNDER LEASE CONTRACT OR OF LESSOR'S RESIDUAL INTEREST IN GOODS; DELEGATION OF PERFORMANCE; TRANSFER OF RIGHTS.

(1) As used in this section, "creation of a security interest" includes the sale of a lease contract that is subject to Article 9, Secured Transactions, by reason of Section ~~9-102(1)(b)~~ 9-109(a)(3).

(2) Except as provided in ~~subsections~~ subsection (3) and ~~(4)~~ Section 9-407, a provision in a lease agreement which (i) prohibits the voluntary or involuntary transfer, including a transfer by sale, sublease, creation or enforcement of a security interest, or attachment, levy, or other judicial process, of an interest of a party under the lease contract or of the lessor's residual interest in the goods, or (ii) makes such a transfer an event of default, gives rise

to the rights and remedies provided in subsection ~~(5)~~ (4), but a transfer that is prohibited or is an event of default under the lease agreement is otherwise effective.

~~(3) A provision in a lease agreement which (i) prohibits the creation or enforcement of a security interest in an interest of a party under the lease contract or in the lessor's residual interest in the goods, or (ii) makes such a transfer an event of default, is not enforceable unless, and then only to the extent that, there is an actual transfer by the lessee of the lessee's right of possession or use of the goods in violation of the provision or an actual delegation of a material performance of either party to the lease contract in violation of the provision. Neither the granting nor the enforcement of a security interest in (i) the lessor's interest under the lease contract or (ii) the lessor's residual interest in the goods is a transfer that materially impairs the prospect of obtaining return performance by, materially changes the duty of, or materially increases the burden or risk imposed on, the lessee within the purview of subsection (5) unless, and then only to the extent that, there is an actual delegation of a material performance of the lessor.~~

~~(4)~~ (3) A provision in a lease agreement which (i) prohibits a transfer of a right to damages for default with respect to the whole lease contract or of a right to payment arising out of the transferor's due performance of the transferor's entire obligation, or (ii) makes such a transfer an event of default, is not enforceable, and such a transfer is not a transfer that materially impairs the prospect of obtaining return performance by, materially changes the duty of, or materially increases the burden or risk imposed on, the other party to the lease contract within the purview of subsection ~~(5)~~ (4).

~~(5)~~ (4) Subject to ~~subsections~~ subsection (3) and ~~(4)~~ Section 9-407:

(a) if a transfer is made which is made an event of default under a lease agreement, the party to the lease contract not making the transfer, unless that party waives the default or otherwise agrees, has the rights and remedies described in Section 2A-501(2);

(b) if paragraph (a) is not applicable and if a transfer is made that (i) is prohibited under a lease agreement or (ii) materially impairs the prospect of obtaining return performance by, materially changes the duty of, or materially increases the burden or risk imposed on, the other party to the lease contract, unless the party not making the transfer agrees at any time to the transfer in the lease contract or otherwise, then, except as limited by contract, (i) the transferor is liable to the party not making the transfer for damages caused by the transfer to the extent that the damages could not reasonably be prevented by the party not making the transfer and (ii) a court having jurisdiction may grant other appropriate relief, including cancellation of the lease contract or an injunction against the transfer.

~~(6)~~ (5) A transfer of "the lease" or of "all my rights under the lease", or a transfer in similar general terms, is a transfer of rights and, unless the language or the circumstances, as in a transfer for security, indicate the contrary, the transfer is a delegation of duties by the transferor to the transferee. Acceptance by the transferee constitutes a promise by the transferee to perform those duties. The promise is enforceable by either the transferor or the other party to the lease contract.

~~(7)~~ (6) Unless otherwise agreed by the lessor and the lessee, a delegation of performance does not relieve the transferor as against the other party of any duty to perform or of any liability for default.

~~(8)~~ (7) In a consumer lease, to prohibit the transfer of an interest of a party under the lease contract or to make a transfer an event of default, the language must be specific, by a writing, and conspicuous.

Official Comment

1. Subsection (2) states a rule, consistent with Section ~~9-311~~ 9-401(b), that voluntary and involuntary transfers of an interest of a party under the lease contract or of the lessor's residual interest, including by way of the creation or enforcement of a security interest, are effective, notwithstanding a provision in the lease agreement prohibiting the transfer or making the transfer an event of default. Although the transfers are effective, the provision in the lease agreement is nevertheless enforceable, but only as provided in subsection ~~(5)~~ (4). Under subsection ~~(5)~~ (4) the prejudiced party is limited to the remedies on "default under the lease contract" in this Article and, except as limited by this Article, as provided in the lease agreement, if the transfer has been made an event of default. Section 2A-501(2). Usually, there will be a specific provision to this effect or a general provision making a breach of a covenant an event of default. In those cases where the transfer is prohibited, but not made an event of default, the prejudiced party may recover damages; or, if the damage remedy would be ineffective adequately to protect that party, the court can order cancellation of the lease contract or enjoin the transfer. This rule that such provisions generally are enforceable is subject to ~~subsections (3) and (4)~~ subsection (3) and Section 9-407, which make such provisions unenforceable in certain instances.

2. ~~The first such instance is described in subsection (3). A~~ Under Section 9-407, a provision in a lease agreement which prohibits the creation or enforcement of a security interest, including sales of lease contracts subject to

Article 9 (~~Sections 9-102(1)(b) and 9-104(f)~~ Section 9-109(a)(3)), or makes it an event of default is generally not enforceable, reflecting the policy of Section 9-406 and former Section 9-318(4). ~~However, inasmuch as the creation of a security interest includes the sale of a lease contract, if there are then unperformed duties on the part of the lessor/seller, there could be a delegation of duties in the sale, and, if such a delegation actually takes place and is of a material performance, a provision in a lease agreement prohibiting it or making it an event of default would be enforceable, giving rise to the rights and remedies stated in subsection (5). The statute does not define "material." The parties may set standards to determine its meaning. The term is intended to exclude delegations of matters such as accounting to a professional accountant and the performance of, as opposed to the responsibility for, maintenance duties to a person in the maintenance service industry.~~

~~3. For similar reasons, the lessor is entitled to protect its residual interest in the goods by prohibiting anyone but the lessee from possessing or using them. Accordingly, under subsection (3) if there is an actual transfer by the lessee of its right of possession or use of the goods in violation of a provision in the lease agreement, such a provision likewise is enforceable, giving rise to the rights and remedies stated in subsection (5). A transfer of the lessee's right of possession or use of the goods resulting from the enforcement of a security interest granted by the lessee in its leasehold interest is a "transfer by the lessee" under this subsection.~~

~~4. Finally, subsection (3) protects against a claim that the creation or enforcement of a security interest in the lessor's interest under the lease contract or in the residual interest is a transfer that materially impairs the prospect of obtaining return performance by, materially changes the duty of, or materially increases the burden or risk imposed on the lessee so as to give rise to the rights and remedies stated in subsection (5), unless the transfer involves an actual delegation of a material performance of the lessor.~~

~~5. While it is not likely that a transfer by the lessor of its right to payment under the lease contract would impair at a future time the ability of the lessee to obtain the performance due the lessee under the lease contract from the lessor, if under the circumstances reasonable grounds for insecurity as to receiving that performance arise, the lessee may employ the provision of this Article for demanding adequate assurance of due performance and has the remedy provided in that circumstance. Section 2A-401.~~

~~6. Sections 9-206 and 9-318(1) through (3) also are relevant. Section 9-206 sanctions an agreement by a lessee not to assert certain types of claims or defenses against the lessor's assignee. Section 9-318(1) through (3) deal with, among other things, the other party's rights against the assignee where Section 9-206(1) does not apply. Since the definition of contract under Section 1-201(11) includes a lease agreement, the definition of account debtor under Section 9-105(1)(a) includes a lessee of goods. As a result, Section 9-206~~

~~applies to lease agreements, and there is no need to restate those sections in this Article. The reference to "defenses or claims arising out of a sale" in Section 9-318(1) should be interpreted broadly to include defenses or claims arising out of a lease inasmuch as that section codifies the common law rule with respect to contracts, including lease contracts.~~

~~7.~~ 3. Subsection ~~(4)~~ (3) is based upon Section 2-210(2) and Section ~~9-318(4)~~ 9-406. It makes unenforceable a prohibition against transfers of certain rights to payment or a provision making the transfer an event of default. It also provides that such transfers do not materially impair the prospect of obtaining return performance by, materially change the duty of, or materially increase the burden or risk imposed on, the other party to the lease contract so as to give rise to the rights and remedies stated in subsection ~~(5)~~ (4). Accordingly, a transfer of a right to payment cannot be prohibited or made an event of default, or be one that materially impairs performance, changes duties or increases risk, if the right is already due or will become due without further performance being required by the party to receive payment. Thus, a lessor can transfer the right to future payments under the lease contract, including by way of a grant of a security interest, and the transfer will not give rise to the rights and remedies stated in subsection ~~(5)~~ (4) if the lessor has no remaining performance under the lease contract. The mere fact that the lessor is obligated to allow the lessee to remain in possession and to use the goods as long as the lessee is not in default does not mean that there is " remaining performance" on the part of the lessor. Likewise, the fact that the lessor has potential liability under a "non-operating" lease contract for breaches of warranty does not mean that there is " remaining performance". In contrast, the lessor would have " remaining performance" under a lease contract requiring the lessor to regularly maintain and service the goods or to provide "upgrades" of the equipment on a periodic basis in order to avoid obsolescence. The basic distinction is between a mere potential duty to respond which is not " remaining performance," and an affirmative duty to render stipulated performance. Although the distinction may be difficult to draw in some cases, it is instructive to focus on the difference between "operating" and "non-operating" leases as generally understood in the marketplace. Even if there is " remaining performance" under a lease contract, a transfer for security of a right to payment that is made an event of default or that is in violation of a prohibition against transfer does not give rise to the rights and remedies under subsection ~~(5)~~ (4) if it does not constitute an actual delegation of a material performance under ~~subsection (3)~~ Section 9-407.

~~8.~~ 4. The application of either the rule of ~~subsection (3)~~ Section 9-407 or the rule of subsection ~~(4)~~ (3) to the grant by the lessor of a security interest in the lessor's right to future payment under the lease contract may produce the same result. Both ~~subsections~~ provisions generally protect security transfers by the lessor in particular because the creation by the lessor of a security interest or the enforcement of that interest generally will not prejudice the lessee's rights if it does not result in a delegation of the lessor's duties. To the contrary, the receipt of loan proceeds or relief from the enforcement of an antecedent debt normally should enhance the lessor's ability to perform its duties under the lease contract. Nevertheless, there are circumstances where relief might be justified. For example, if ownership of the goods is transferred pursuant to enforcement of a security interest to a party whose ownership would prevent the lessee from continuing to possess the goods, relief might be warranted. See 49 U.S.C. § 1401(a) and (b) which places limitations on the operation of aircraft in the United States based on the citizenship or corporate qualification of the registrant.

9. 5. Relief on the ground of material prejudice when the lease agreement does not prohibit the transfer or make it an event of default should be afforded only in extreme circumstances, considering the fact that the party asserting material prejudice did not insist upon a provision in the lease agreement that would protect against such a transfer.

10. 6. Subsection (5) (4) implements the rule of subsection (2). Subsection (2) provides that, even though a transfer is effective, a provision in the lease agreement prohibiting it or making it an event of default may be enforceable as provided in subsection (5) (4). See Brummond v. First National Bank of Clovis, 656 P.2d 884, 35 U.C.C.Rep.Serv. (Callaghan) 1311 (N.Mex.1983), stating the analogous rule for Section 9-311. If the transfer prohibited by the lease agreement is made an event of default, then, under subsection 5(a) (4)(a), unless the default is waived or there is an agreement otherwise, the aggrieved party has the rights and remedies referred to in Section 2A-501(2), viz. those in this Article and, except as limited in the Article, those provided in the lease agreement. In the unlikely circumstance that the lease agreement prohibits the transfer without making a violation of the prohibition an event of default or, even if there is no prohibition against the transfer, and the transfer is one that materially impairs performance, changes duties, or increases risk (for example, a sublease or assignment to a party using the goods improperly or for an illegal purpose), then subsection 5(b) (4)(b) is applicable. In that circumstance, unless the party aggrieved by the transfer has otherwise agreed in the lease contract, such as by assenting to a particular transfer or to transfers in general, or agrees in some other manner, the aggrieved party has the right to recover damages from the transferor and a court may, in appropriate circumstances, grant other relief, such as cancellation of the lease contract or an injunction against the transfer.

11. 7. If a transfer gives rise to the rights and remedies provided in subsection (5) (4), the transferee as an alternative may propose, and the other party may accept, adequate cure or compensation for past defaults and adequate assurance of future due performance under the lease contract. Subsection (5) (4) does not preclude any other relief that may be available to a party to the lease contract aggrieved by a transfer subject to an enforceable prohibition, such as an action for interference with contractual relations.

~~12.~~ 8. Subsection ~~(8)~~ (7) requires that a provision in a consumer lease prohibiting a transfer, or making it an event of default, must be specific, written and conspicuous. See Section 1-201(10). This assists in protecting a consumer lessee against surprise assertions of default.

~~13.~~ 9. Subsection ~~(6)~~ (5) is taken almost verbatim from the provisions of Section ~~2-210(4)~~ 2-210(5). The subsection states a rule of construction that distinguishes a commercial assignment, which substitutes the assignee for the assignor as to rights and duties, and an assignment for security or financing assignment, which substitutes the assignee for the assignor only as to rights. Note that the assignment for security or financing assignment is a subset of all security interests. Security interest is defined to include "any interest of a buyer of . . . chattel paper". Section 1-201(37). Chattel paper is defined to include a lease. Section ~~9-105(1)(b)~~ 9-102. Thus, a buyer of leases is the holder of a security interest in the leases. That conclusion should not influence this issue, as the policy is quite different. Whether a buyer of leases is the holder of a commercial assignment, or an assignment for security or financing assignment should be determined by the language of the assignment or the circumstances of the assignment.

§ 2A-307. PRIORITY OF LIENS ARISING BY ATTACHMENT OR LEVY ON, SECURITY INTERESTS IN, AND OTHER CLAIMS TO GOODS.

(1) Except as otherwise provided in Section 2A-306, a creditor of a lessee takes subject to the lease contract.

(2) Except as otherwise provided in ~~subsections~~ subsection (3) ~~and (4)~~ and in Sections 2A-306 and 2A-308, a creditor of a lessor takes subject to the lease contract unless~~:~~

~~(a)~~ the creditor holds a lien that attached to the goods before the lease contract became enforceable~~;~~

~~(b) the creditor holds a security interest in the goods and the lessee did not give value and receive delivery of the goods without knowledge of the security interest; or~~

~~(c) the creditor holds a security interest in the goods which was perfected (Section 9-303) before the lease contract became enforceable.~~

~~(3) A lessee in the ordinary course of business takes the leasehold interest free of a security interest in the goods created by the lessor even though the security interest is perfected (Section 9-303) and the lessee knows of its existence.~~

~~(4) A lessee other than a lessee in the ordinary course of business takes the leasehold interest free of a security interest to the extent that it secures future advances made after the secured party acquires knowledge of the lease or more than 45~~

~~days after the lease contract becomes enforceable, whichever first occurs, unless the future advances are made pursuant to a commitment entered into without knowledge of the lease and before the expiration of the 45-day period.~~

(3) Except as otherwise provided in Sections 9-317, 9-321, and 9-323, a lessee takes a leasehold interest subject to a security interest held by a creditor of the lessor.

Official Comment

*   *   *

3. To take priority over the lease contract, and the interests derived therefrom, the creditor must come within ~~one of three exceptions~~ the exception stated ~~within the rule. First,~~ in subsection (2)~~(a)~~ or within one of the provisions of Article 9 mentioned in subsection (3). Subsection (2) provides that where the creditor holds a lien (Section 2A-103(1)(r)) that attached before the lease contract became enforceable (Section 2A-301), the creditor does not take subject to the lease. ~~Second, subsection (2)(b) provides that when the creditor holds a security interest (Section 1-201(37)), whether or not perfected, the creditor has priority over a lessee who did not give value (Section 1-201(44)) and receive delivery of the goods without knowledge (Section 1-201(25)) of the security interest. As to other lessees, under subsection (2)(c) a secured creditor holding a perfected security interest before the time the lease contract became enforceable (Section 2A-301) does not take subject to the lease. With respect to this provision, the lessee in these circumstances is treated like a buyer so that perfection of a purchase money security interest does not relate back (Section 9-301).~~ Subsection (3) provides that a lessee takes its leasehold interest subject to a security interest except as otherwise provided in Sections 9-317, 9-321, or 9-323.

4. The rules of this section operate in favor of whichever party to the lease contract may enforce it, even if one party perhaps may not, e.g., under Section 2A-201(1)(b).

~~5. The rules stated in subsections (2)(b) and (c), and the rule in subsection (3), are is best understood by reviewing a hypothetical. Assume that a merchant engaged in the business of selling and leasing musical instruments obtained possession of a truck load of musical instruments on deferred payment terms from a supplier of musical instruments on January 6. To secure payment of such credit the merchant granted the supplier a security interest in the instruments; the security interest was perfected by filing on January 15. The merchant, as lessor, entered into a lease to an individual of one of the musical instruments supplied by the supplier; the lease became enforceable on January 10. Under subsection (2)(b) the lessee will prevail (assuming the lessee qualifies thereunder) unless subsection (c) provides otherwise. Under the rule stated in subsection (2)(c) a priority dispute between the~~

~~supplier, as the lessor's secured creditor, and the lessee would be determined
by ascertaining on January 10 (the day the lease became enforceable) the
validity and perfected status of the security interest in the musical instrument
and the enforceability of the lease contract by the lessee. Nothing more
appearing, under the rule stated in subsection (2)(c), the supplier's security
interest in the musical instrument would not have priority over the lease
contract. Moreover, subsection (2) states that its rules are subject to the rules
of subsections (3) and (4). Under this hypothetical the lessee should qualify
as a "lessee in the ordinary course of business". Section 2A-103(1)(o).
Subsection (3) also makes clear that the lessee in the ordinary course of
business will win even if he or she knows of the existence of the supplier's
security interest.~~

~~6. Subsections (3) and (4), which are modeled on the provisions of Section
9-307(1) and (3), respectively, state two exceptions to the priority rule stated
in subsection (2) with respect to a creditor who holds a security interest. The
lessee in the ordinary course of business will be treated in the same fashion
as the buyer in the ordinary course of business, given a priority dispute with
a secured creditor over goods subject to a lease contract.~~

§ 2A-309. LESSOR'S AND LESSEE'S RIGHTS WHEN GOODS BECOME FIXTURES.

(1) In this section:

* * *

(b) a "fixture filing" is the filing, in the office where a <u>record of
a</u> mortgage on the real estate would be filed or recorded, of a
financing statement covering goods that are or are to become
fixtures and conforming to the requirements of Section ~~9-402(5)~~
<u>9-502(a) and (b)</u>;

* * *

§ 4-210. SECURITY INTEREST OF COLLECTING BANK IN ITEMS, ACCOMPANYING DOCUMENTS AND PROCEEDS.

* * *

(c) Receipt by a collecting bank of a final settlement for an item
is a realization on its security interest in the item, accompanying
documents, and proceeds. So long as the bank does not receive
final settlement for the item or give up possession of the item or
accompanying documents for purposes other than collection, the
security interest continues to that extent and is subject to Article
9, but:

(1) no security agreement is necessary to make the security interest enforceable (Section ~~9-203(1)(a)~~ 9-203(b)(3)(A));

(2) no filing is required to perfect the security interest; and

(3) the security interest has priority over conflicting perfected security interests in the item, accompanying documents, or proceeds.

§ 5-118. SECURITY INTEREST OF ISSUER OR NOMINATED PERSON.

(a) An issuer or nominated person has a security interest in a document presented under a letter of credit to the extent that the issuer or nominated person honors or gives value for the presentation.

(b) So long as and to the extent that an issuer or nominated person has not been reimbursed or has not otherwise recovered the value given with respect to a security interest in a document under subsection (a), the security interest continues and is subject to Article 9, but:

(1) a security agreement is not necessary to make the security interest enforceable under Section 9-203(b)(3);

(2) if the document is presented in a medium other than a written or other tangible medium, the security interest is perfected; and

(3) if the document is presented in a written or other tangible medium and is not a certificated security, chattel paper, a document of title, an instrument, or a letter of credit, the security interest is perfected and has priority over a conflicting security interest in the document so long as the debtor does not have possession of the document.

Official Comment

1. This section gives the issuer of a letter of credit or a nominated person thereunder an automatic perfected security interest in a "document" (as that term is defined in Section 5-102(a)(6)). The security interest arises only if the document is presented to the issuer or nominated person under the letter of credit and only to the extent of the value that is given. This security interest is analogous to that awarded to a collecting bank under Section 4-210. Subsection (b) contains special rules governing the security interest arising under this section. In all other respects, a security interest arising under this section is subject to Article 9. See Section 9-109. Thus, for example, a security interest arising under this section may give rise to a security interest in proceeds under Section 9-315.

2. Subsection (b)(1) makes a security agreement unnecessary to the creation of a security interest under this section. Under subsection (b)(2), a security interest arising under this section is perfected if the document is presented in a medium other than a written or tangible medium. Documents that are written and that are not an otherwise-defined type of collateral under Article 9 (e.g., an invoice or inspection certificate) may be goods, in which an issuer or nominated person could perfect its security interest by possession. Because the definition of document in Section 5-102(a)(6) includes records (e.g., electronic records) that may not be goods, subsection (b)(2) provides for automatic perfection (i.e., without filing or possession).

Under subsection (b)(3), if the document (i) is in a written or tangible medium, (ii) is not a certificated security, chattel paper, a document of title, an instrument, or a letter of credit, and (iii) is not in the debtor's possession, the security interest is perfected and has priority over a conflicting security interest. If the document is a type of tangible collateral that subsection (b)(3) excludes from its perfection and priority rules, the issuer or nominated person must comply with the normal method of perfection (e.g., possession of an instrument) and is subject to the applicable Article 9 priority rules. Documents to which subsection (b)(3) applies may be important to an issuer or nominated person. For example, a confirmer who pays the beneficiary must be assured that its rights to all documents are not impaired. It will find it necessary to present all of the required documents to the issuer in order to be reimbursed. Moreover, when a nominated person sends documents to an issuer in connection with the nominated person's reimbursement, that activity is not a collection, enforcement, or disposition of collateral under Article 9.

One purpose of this section is to protect an issuer or nominated person from claims of a beneficiary's creditors. It is a fallback provision inasmuch as issuers and nominated persons frequently may obtain and perfect security interests under the usual Article 9 rules, and, in many cases, the documents will be owned by the issuer, nominated person, or applicant.

UCC Article 6, Alternative A:

Legislative Note: To take account of differences between former Article 9 and revised Article 9, a State that repeals Article 6 after revised Article 9 takes effect must make the following changes to Alternative A. First, inasmuch as revised Article 9 contains no counterpart of former Section 9-111, the reference to that section in Section 1 of the repealer should be deleted, and Section 4 of the repeal bill should allude to former Section 9-111. Second, the last entry in Section 1-105(2) should be amended as shown above in this Appendix.

UCC Article 6, Alternative B:

§ 6-102. DEFINITIONS AND INDEX OF DEFINITIONS.

(1) In this Article, unless the context otherwise requires:

(a) "Assets" means the inventory that is the subject of a bulk sale and any tangible and intangible personal property used or held for use primarily in, or arising from, the seller's business and sold in connection with that inventory, but the term does not include:

(i) fixtures (Section 9-313(1)(a) 9-102(a)(41)) other than readily removable factory and office machines;

(ii) the lessee's interest in a lease of real property; or

(iii) property to the extent it is generally exempt from creditor process under nonbankruptcy law.

* * *

(2) The following definitions in other Articles apply to this Article:

(a) "Buyer."   Section 2-103(1)(a).
(b) "Equipment."   Section 9-109(2) 9-102(a)(33).
(c) "Inventory."   Section 9-109(4) 9-102(a)(48).
(d) "Sale."   Section 2-106(1).
(e) "Seller."   Section 2-103(1)(d).

* * *

§ 6-103. APPLICABILITY OF ARTICLE.

* * *

(3) This Article does not apply to:

(a) a transfer made to secure payment or performance of an obligation;

(b) a transfer of collateral to a secured party pursuant to Section 9-503 9-609;

(c) a sale disposition of collateral pursuant to Section 9-504 9-610;

(d) retention of collateral pursuant to Section 9-505 9-620;

* * *

§ 7-503. DOCUMENT OF TITLE TO GOODS DEFEATED IN CERTAIN CASES.

(1) A document of title confers no right in goods against a person who before issuance of the document had a legal interest or a perfected security interest in them and who neither

(a) delivered or entrusted them or any document of title covering them to the bailor or his nominee with actual or apparent authority to ship, store or sell or with power to obtain delivery under this Article (Section 7-403) or with power of disposition under this Act (Sections 2-403 and ~~9-307~~ 9-320) or other statute or rule of law; nor

(b) acquiesced in the procurement by the bailor or his nominee of any document of title.

* * *

§ 8-102. DEFINITIONS.

* * *

Official Comment

* * *

7. "Entitlement holder." This term designates those who hold financial assets through intermediaries in the indirect holding system. Because many of the rules of Part 5 impose duties on securities intermediaries in favor of entitlement holders, the definition of entitlement holder is, in most cases, limited to the person specifically designated as such on the records of the intermediary. The last sentence of the definition covers the relatively unusual cases where a person may acquire a security entitlement under Section 8-501 even though the person may not be specifically designated as an entitlement holder on the records of the securities intermediary.

A person may have an interest in a security entitlement, and may even have the right to give entitlement orders to the securities intermediary with respect to it, even though the person is not the entitlement holder. For example, a person who holds securities through a securities account in its own name may have given discretionary trading authority to another person, such as an investment adviser. Similarly, the control provisions in Section 8-106 and the related provisions in Article 9 are designed to facilitate transactions in which a person who holds securities through a securities account uses them as collateral in an arrangement where the securities intermediary has agreed that if the secured party so directs the intermediary will dispose of the positions. In such arrangements, the debtor remains the entitlement holder but has agreed that the secured party can initiate entitlement orders. <u>Moreover, an entitlement holder may be acting for another person as a nominee, agent, trustee, or in another capacity. Unless the entitlement holder is itself acting as a securities intermediary for the other person, in which case the other person would be an entitlement holder with respect to the securities entitlement, the relationship between an entitlement holder and another person for whose benefit the entitlement holder holds a securities entitlement is governed by other law.</u>

8. "Entitlement order." This term is defined as a notification communicated to a securities intermediary directing transfer or redemption of the financial asset to which an entitlement holder has a security entitlement. The term is used in the rules for the indirect holding system in a fashion analogous to the use of the terms "indorsement" and "instruction" in the rules for the direct holding system. If a person directly holds a certificated security in registered form and wishes to transfer it, the means of transfer is an indorsement. If a person directly holds an uncertificated security and wishes to transfer it, the means of transfer is an instruction. If a person holds a security entitlement, the means of disposition is an entitlement order. <u>An entitlement order includes a direction under Section 8-508 to the securities intermediary to transfer a financial asset to the account of the entitlement holder at another financial intermediary or to cause the financial asset to be transferred to the entitlement holder in the direct holding system (e.g., the delivery of a securities certificate registered in the name of the former entitlement holder).</u> As noted in Comment 7, an entitlement order need not be initiated by the entitlement holder in order to be effective, so long as the entitlement holder has authorized the other party to initiate entitlement orders. See Section 8-107(b).

* * *

§ 8-103. RULES FOR DETERMINING WHETHER CERTAIN OBLIGATIONS AND INTERESTS ARE SECURITIES OR FINANCIAL ASSETS.

* * *

(f) A commodity contract, as defined in Section ~~9-115~~ 9-102(a)(15), is not a security or a financial asset.

§ 8-106. CONTROL.

(a) A purchaser has "control" of a certificated security in bearer form if the certificated security is delivered to the purchaser.

(b) A purchaser has "control" of a certificated security in registered form if the certificated security is delivered to the purchaser, and:

(1) the certificate is indorsed to the purchaser or in blank by an effective indorsement; or

(2) the certificate is registered in the name of the purchaser, upon original issue or registration of transfer by the issuer.

(c) A purchaser has "control" of an uncertificated security if:

(1) the uncertificated security is delivered to the purchaser; or

(2) the issuer has agreed that it will comply with instructions originated by the purchaser without further consent by the registered owner.

(d) A purchaser has "control" of a security entitlement if:

(1) the purchaser becomes the entitlement holder; or

(2) the securities intermediary has agreed that it will comply with entitlement orders originated by the purchaser without further consent by the entitlement holder; or

(3) another person has control of the security entitlement on behalf of the purchaser or, having previously acquired control of the security entitlement, acknowledges that it has control on behalf of the purchaser.

ANALYSIS

This additional way of obtaining control over securities entitlements is designed to allow a creditor to obtain control through an agent or bailee. Note, however, that a broker could acknowledge that it holds control on behalf of a bank or other financer with respect to entitlements held with it.

(e) If an interest in a security entitlement is granted by the entitlement holder to the entitlement holder's own securities intermediary, the securities intermediary has control.

(f) A purchaser who has satisfied the requirements of subsection (c)(2) or (d)(2) has control, even if the registered owner in the case of subsection (c)(2) or the entitlement holder in the case of subsection (d)(2) retains the right to make substitutions for the uncertificated security or security entitlement, to originate instructions or entitlement orders to the issuer or securities intermediary, or otherwise to deal with the uncertificated security or security entitlement.

(g) An issuer or a securities intermediary may not enter into an agreement of the kind described in subsection (c)(2) or (d)(2) without the consent of the registered owner or entitlement holder, but an issuer or a securities intermediary is not required to enter into such an agreement even though the registered owner or entitlement holder so directs. An issuer or securities intermediary that has entered into such an agreement is not required to confirm the existence of the agreement to another party unless requested to do so by the registered owner or entitlement holder.

Official Comment

1. The concept of "control" plays a key role in various provisions dealing with the rights of purchasers, including secured parties. See Sections 8-303 (protected purchasers); 8-503(e) (purchasers from securities intermediaries); 8-510 (purchasers of security entitlements from entitlement holders); 9-115(4) 9-314 (perfection of security interests); 9-115(5) 9-328 (priorities among conflicting security interests).

Obtaining "control" means that the purchaser has taken whatever steps are necessary, given the manner in which the securities are held, to place itself in a position where it can have the securities sold, without further action by the owner.

* * *

4. Subsection (d) specifies the means by which a purchaser can obtain control over of a security entitlement. Two Three mechanisms are possible, analogous to those provided in subsection (c) for uncertificated securities. Under subsection (d)(1), a purchaser has control if it is the entitlement holder. This subsection would apply whether the purchaser holds through the same intermediary that the debtor used, or has the securities position transferred to its own intermediary. Subsection (d)(2) provides that a purchaser has control if the securities intermediary has agreed to act on entitlement orders originated by the purchaser if no further consent by the entitlement holder is required. Under subsection (d)(2), control may be achieved even though the transferor original entitlement holder remains listed as the entitlement holder. Finally, a purchaser may obtain control under subsection (d)(3) if another person has control and the person acknowledges that it has control on the purchaser's behalf. Control under subsection (d)(3) parallels the delivery of certificated securities and uncertificated securities under Section 8-301. Of course, the acknowledging person cannot be the debtor.

This section specifies only the minimum requirements that such an arrangement must meet to confer "control"; the details of the arrangement can be specified by agreement. The arrangement might cover all of the positions in a particular account or subaccount, or only specified positions.

There is no requirement that the control party's right to give entitlement orders be exclusive. The arrangement might provide that only the control party can give entitlement orders, or that either the entitlement holder or the control party can give entitlement orders. See subsection (f).

The following examples illustrate the ~~rules~~ application of subsection (d):

Example 1. Debtor grants Alpha Bank a security interest in a security entitlement that includes 1000 shares of XYZ Co. stock that Debtor holds through an account with Able & Co. Alpha also has an account with Able. Debtor instructs Able to transfer the shares to Alpha, and Able does so by crediting the shares to Alpha's account. Alpha ~~Bank~~ has control of the 1000 shares under subsection (d)(1). Although Debtor may have become the beneficial owner of the new securities entitlement, as between Debtor and Alpha, Able has agreed to act on Alpha's entitlement orders because, as between Able and Alpha, ~~because~~ Alpha ~~Bank is~~ has become the entitlement holder. See Section 8-506.

Example 2. Debtor grants Alpha Bank a security interest in a security entitlement that includes 1000 shares of XYZ Co. stock that Debtor holds through an account with Able & Co. Alpha ~~Bank~~ does not have an account with Able. Alpha ~~Bank~~ uses Beta as its securities custodian. Debtor instructs Able to transfer the shares to Beta, for the account of Alpha ~~Bank~~, and Able does so. Alpha ~~Bank~~ has control of the 1000 shares under subsection (d)(1). As in Example 1, although Debtor may have become the beneficial owner of the new securities entitlement, as between Debtor and Alpha, Beta has agreed to act on Alpha's entitlement orders because, as between Beta and Alpha, ~~because~~ Alpha ~~is~~ has become the entitlement holder.

Example 3. Debtor grants Alpha Bank a security interest in a security entitlement that includes 1000 shares of XYZ Co. stock that Debtor holds through an account with Able & Co. Debtor, Able, and Alpha ~~Bank~~ enter into an agreement under which Debtor will continue to receive dividends and distributions, and will continue to have the right to direct dispositions, but Alpha ~~Bank~~ also has the right to direct dispositions. Alpha ~~Bank~~ has control of the 1000 shares under subsection (d)(2).

Example 4. Able & Co., a securities dealer, grants Alpha Bank a security interest in a security entitlement that includes 1000 shares of XYZ Co. stock that Able holds through an account with Clearing Corporation. Able causes Clearing Corporation to transfer the shares into ~~Alpha Bank's~~ Alpha's account at Clearing Corporation. As in Example 1, Alpha ~~Bank~~ has control of the 1000 shares under subsection (d)(1).

Example 5. Able & Co., a securities dealer, grants Alpha Bank a security interest in a security entitlement that includes 1000 shares of XYZ Co. stock that Able holds through an account with Clearing Corporation. Alpha ~~Bank~~ does not have an account with Clearing Corporation. It holds its securities through Beta Bank, which does have an account with Clearing Corporation.

Able causes Clearing Corporation to transfer the shares into ~~Beta Bank's~~ Beta's account at Clearing Corporation. Beta ~~Bank~~ credits the position to Alpha's account with Beta ~~Bank.~~ As in Example 2, Alpha ~~Bank~~ has control of the 1000 shares under subsection (d)(1).

Example 6. Able & Co. a securities dealer, grants Alpha Bank a security interest in a security entitlement that includes 1000 shares of XYZ Co. stock that Able holds through an account with Clearing Corporation. Able causes Clearing Corporation to transfer the shares into a pledge account, pursuant to an agreement under which Able will continue to receive dividends, distributions, and the like, but Alpha ~~Bank~~ has the right to direct dispositions. As in Example 3, Alpha ~~Bank~~ has control of the 1000 shares under subsection (d)(2).

Example 7. Able & Co. a securities dealer, grants Alpha Bank a security interest in a security entitlement that includes 1000 shares of XYZ Co. stock that Able holds through an account with Clearing Corporation. Able, Alpha, and Clearing Corporation enter into an agreement under which Clearing Corporation will act on instructions from Alpha with respect to the XYZ Co. stock carried in Able's account, but Able will continue to receive dividends, distributions, and the like, and will also have the right to direct dispositions. As in Example 3, Alpha ~~Bank~~ has control of the 1000 shares under subsection (d)(2).

Example 8. Able & Co. a securities dealer, holds a wide range of securities through its account at Clearing Corporation. Able enters into an arrangement with Alpha Bank pursuant to which Alpha provides financing to Able secured by securities identified as the collateral on lists provided by Able to Alpha on a daily or other periodic basis. Able, Alpha, and Clearing Corporation enter into an agreement under which Clearing Corporation agrees that if at any time Alpha directs Clearing Corporation to do so, Clearing Corporation will transfer any securities from Able's account at Alpha's instructions. Because Clearing Corporation has agreed to act on Alpha's instructions with respect to any securities carried in Able's account, at the moment that Alpha's security interest attaches to securities listed by Able, Alpha obtains control of those securities under subsection (d)(2). There is no requirement that Clearing Corporation be informed of which securities Able has pledged to Alpha.

Example 9. Debtor grants Alpha Bank a security interest in a security entitlement that includes 1000 shares of XYZ Co. stock that Debtor holds through an account with Able & Co. Beta Bank agrees with Alpha to act as Alpha's collateral agent with respect to the security entitlement. Debtor, Able, and Beta enter into an agreement under which Debtor will continue to receive dividends and distributions, and will continue to have the right to direct dispositions, but Beta also has the right to direct dispositions. Because Able has agreed that it will comply with entitlement orders originated by Beta without further consent by Debtor, Beta has control of the security entitlement (see Example 3). Because Beta has control on behalf of Alpha, Alpha also has control under subsection (d)(3). It is not necessary for Able to enter into an agreement directly with Alpha or for Able to be aware of Beta's agency relationship with Alpha.

*   *   *

7. The term "control" is used in a particular defined sense. The requirements for obtaining control are set out in this section. The concept is not to be interpreted by reference to similar concepts in other bodies of law. In particular, the requirements for "possession" derived from the common law of pledge are not to be used as a basis for interpreting subsection (c)(2) or (d)(2). Those provisions are designed to supplant the concepts of "constructive possession" and the like. A principal purpose of the "control" concept is to eliminate the uncertainty and confusion that results from attempting to apply common law possession concepts to modern securities holding practices.

The key to the control concept is that the purchaser has the ~~present~~ ability to have the securities sold or transferred without further action by the transferor. There is no requirement that the powers held by the purchaser be exclusive. For example, in a secured lending arrangement, if the secured party wishes, it can allow the debtor to retain the right to make substitutions, ~~or~~ to direct the disposition of the uncertificated security or security entitlement, or otherwise to give instructions or entitlement orders. (As explained in Section 8-102, Comment 8, an entitlement order includes a direction under Section 8-508 to the securities intermediary to transfer a financial asset to the account of the entitlement holder at another financial intermediary or to cause the financial asset to be transferred to the entitlement holder in the direct holding system (e.g., by delivery of a securities certificate registered in the name of the former entitlement holder).) Subsection (f) is included to make clear the general point stated in ~~subsection~~ subsections (c) and (d) that the test of control is whether the purchaser has obtained the requisite power, not whether the debtor has retained other powers. There is no implication that retention by the debtor of powers other than those mentioned in subsection (f) is inconsistent with the purchaser having control. Nor is there a requirement that the purchaser's powers be unconditional, provided that further consent of the entitlement holder is not a condition.

Example 10. Debtor grants to Alpha Bank and to Beta Bank a security interest in a security entitlement that includes 1000 shares of XYZ Co. stock that Debtor holds through an account with Able & Co. By agreement among the parties, Alpha's security interest is senior and Beta's is junior. Able agrees to act on the entitlement orders of either Alpha or Beta. Alpha and Beta each has control under subsection (d)(2). Moreover, Beta has control notwithstanding a term of Able's agreement to the effect that Able's obligation to act on Beta's entitlement orders is conditioned on the Alpha's consent. The crucial distinction is that Able's agreement to act on Beta's entitlement orders is not conditioned on Debtor's further consent.

Example 11. Debtor grants to Alpha Bank a security interest in a security entitlement that includes 1000 shares of XYZ Co. stock that Debtor holds thought an account with Able & Co. Able agrees to act on the entitlement orders of Alpha, but Alpha's right to give entitlement orders to the securities intermediary is conditioned on the Debtor's default. Alternatively, Alpha's right to give entitlement orders is conditioned upon Alpha's statement to Able that Debtor is in default. Because Able's agreement to act on Beta's entitlement orders is not conditioned on Debtor's further consent, Alpha has control of the securities entitlement under either alternative.

In many situations, it will be better practice for both the securities intermediary and the purchaser to insist that any conditions relating in any way to the entitlement holder be effective only as between the purchaser and the entitlement holder. That practice would avoid the risk that the securities intermediary could be caught between conflicting assertions of the entitlement holder and the purchaser as to whether the conditions in fact have been met. Nonetheless, the existence of unfulfilled conditions effective against the intermediary would not preclude the purchaser from having control.

§ 8-110. APPLICABILITY; CHOICE OF LAW.

* * *

(e) The following rules determine a "securities intermediary's jurisdiction" for purposes of this section:

(1) If an agreement between the securities intermediary and its entitlement holder ~~specifies that it is governed by the law of a particular jurisdiction~~ governing the securities account expressly provides that a particular jurisdiction is the securities intermediary's jurisdiction for purposes of this part, this article, or this [Act], that jurisdiction is the securities intermediary's jurisdiction.

(2) If paragraph (1) does not apply and an agreement between the securities intermediary and its entitlement holder governing the securities account expressly provides that the agreement is governed by the law of a particular jurisdiction, that jurisdiction is the securities intermediary's jurisdiction.

~~(2)~~ (3) If neither paragraph (1) nor paragraph (2) applies and an agreement between the securities intermediary and its entitlement holder ~~does not specify the governing law as provided in paragraph (1), but~~ governing the securities account expressly ~~specifies~~ provides that the securities account is maintained at an office in a particular jurisdiction, that jurisdiction is the securities intermediary's jurisdiction.

~~(3)~~ (4) If ~~an agreement between the securities intermediary and its entitlement holder does not specify a jurisdiction as provided in paragraph (1) or (2),~~ none of the preceding paragraphs applies, the securities intermediary's jurisdiction is the jurisdiction in which ~~is located~~ the office identified in an account statement as the office serving the entitlement holder's account is located.

~~(4)~~ (5) If ~~an agreement between the securities intermediary and its entitlement holder does not specify a jurisdiction as provided in paragraph (1) or (2) and an account statement does not identify an office serving the entitlement holder's account as provided in paragraph (3),~~ none of the preceding paragraphs applies, the securities intermediary's jurisdiction is the jurisdiction in which ~~is located~~ the chief executive office of the securities intermediary is located.

(f) A securities intermediary's jurisdiction is not determined by the physical location of certificates representing financial assets, or by the jurisdiction in which is organized the issuer of the financial asset with respect to which an entitlement holder has a security entitlement, or by the location of facilities for data processing or other record keeping concerning the account.

Official Comment

*   *   *

3. Subsection (b) provides that the law of the securities intermediary's jurisdiction governs the issues concerning the indirect holding system that are dealt with in Article 8. Paragraphs (1) and (2) cover the matters dealt with in the Article 8 rules defining the concept of security entitlement and specifying the duties of securities intermediaries. Paragraph (3) provides that the law of the security intermediary's jurisdiction determines whether the intermediary owes any duties to an adverse claimant. Paragraph (4) provides that the law of the security intermediary's jurisdiction determines whether adverse claims can be asserted against entitlement holders and others.

Subsection (e) determines what is a "securities intermediary's jurisdiction." The policy of subsection (b) is to ensure that a securities intermediary and all of its entitlement holders can look to a single, readily-identifiable body of law to determine their rights and duties. Accordingly, subsection (e) sets out a sequential series of tests to facilitate identification of that body of law. Paragraph (1) of subsection (e) permits specification of the ~~governing law~~ securities intermediary's jurisdiction by agreement. In the absence of such a specification, the law chosen by the parties to govern the securities account determines the securities intermediary's jurisdiction. See paragraph (2). Because the policy of this section is to enable parties to determine, in advance and with certainty, what law will apply to transactions governed by this Article, the validation of the parties' selection of governing law by agreement is not conditioned upon a determination that the jurisdiction whose law is chosen bear a "reasonable relation" to the transaction. See Section 4A-507; compare Section 1-105(1). That is also true with respect to the similar provisions in subsection (d) of this section and in Section ~~9-103(6)~~ 9-305. The remaining paragraphs in subsection (e) contain additional default rules for determining the securities intermediary's jurisdiction.

* * *

5. The following examples illustrate how a court in a jurisdiction which has enacted this section would determine the governing law:

Example 1. John Doe, a resident of Kansas, maintains a securities account with Able & Co. Able is incorporated in Delaware. Its chief executive offices are located in Illinois. The office where Doe transacts business with Able is located in Missouri. The agreement between Doe and Able specifies that ~~it is governed by~~ Illinois ~~law~~ is the securities intermediary's (Able's) jurisdiction. Through the account, Doe holds securities of a Colorado corporation, which Able holds through Clearing Corporation. The rules of Clearing Corporation provide that the rights and duties of Clearing Corporation and its participants are governed by New York law. Subsection (a) specifies that a controversy concerning the rights and duties as between the issuer and Clearing Corporation is governed by Colorado law. Subsections (b) and (e) specify that a controversy concerning the rights and duties as between the Clearing Corporation and Able is governed by New York law, and that a controversy concerning the rights and duties as between Able and Doe is governed by Illinois law.

* * *

7. The choice of law provisions concerning security interests in securities and security entitlements are set out in Section ~~9-103(6)~~ 9-305.

§ 8-301. DELIVERY.

(a) Delivery of a certificated security to a purchaser occurs when:

(1) the purchaser acquires possession of the security certificate;

(2) another person, other than a securities intermediary, either acquires possession of the security certificate on behalf of the purchaser or, having previously acquired possession of the certificate, acknowledges that it holds for the purchaser; or

(3) a securities intermediary acting on behalf of the purchaser acquires possession of the security certificate, only if the

certificate is in registered form and ~~has been~~ is (i) registered in the name of the purchaser, (ii) payable to the order of the purchaser, or (iii) specially indorsed to the purchaser by an effective indorsement and has not been indorsed to the securities intermediary or in blank.

* * *

Official Comment

* * *

2. Subsection (a) defines delivery with respect to certificated securities. Paragraph (1) deals with simple cases where purchasers themselves acquire physical possession of certificates. Paragraphs (2) and (3) of subsection (a) specify the circumstances in which delivery to a purchaser can occur although the certificate is in the possession of a person other than the purchaser. Paragraph (2) contains the general rule that a purchaser can take delivery through another person, so long as the other person is actually acting on behalf of the purchaser or acknowledges that it is holding on behalf of the purchaser. Paragraph (2) does not apply to acquisition of possession by a securities intermediary, because a person who holds securities through a securities account acquires a security entitlement, rather than having a direct interest. See Section 8-501. Subsection (a)(3) specifies the limited circumstances in which delivery of security certificates to a securities intermediary is treated as a delivery to the customer. Note that delivery is a method of perfecting a security interest in a certificated security. See Section 9-313(a), (e).

* * *

§ 8-302. RIGHTS OF PURCHASER.

(a) Except as otherwise provided in subsections (b) and (c), a purchaser ~~upon delivery~~ of a certificated or uncertificated security ~~to a purchaser, the purchaser~~ acquires all rights in the security that the transferor had or had power to transfer.

(b) A purchaser of a limited interest acquires rights only to the extent of the interest purchased.

(c) A purchaser of a certificated security who as a previous holder had notice of an adverse claim does not improve its position by taking from a protected purchaser.

Official Comment

1. Subsection (a) provides that ~~if a~~ purchaser of a certificated or uncertificated security ~~is delivered (Section 8-301) to a purchaser in a transfer, the~~

~~purchaser~~ acquires all rights that the transferor had or had power to transfer. This statement of the familiar "shelter" principle is qualified by the exceptions that a purchaser of a limited interest acquires only that interest, subsection (b), and that a person who does not qualify as a protected purchaser cannot improve its position by taking from a subsequent protected purchaser, subsection (c).

2. Although this section provides that a purchaser acquires a property interest in a certificated or uncertificated security ~~upon "delivery,"~~ it does not state that a person can acquire an interest in a security only by ~~delivery~~ <u>purchase</u>. Article 8 <u>also</u> is not a comprehensive codification of all of the law governing the creation or transfer of interests in securities <u>by purchase</u>. For example, the grant of a security interest is a transfer of a property interest, but the formal steps necessary to effectuate such a transfer are governed by Article 9 not by Article 8. Under the Article 9 rules, a security interest in a certificated or uncertificated security can be created by execution of a security agreement under Section 9-203 and can be perfected by filing. A transfer of an Article 9 security interest can be implemented by an Article 8 delivery, but need not be.

Similarly, Article 8 does not determine whether a property interest in certificated or uncertificated security is acquired under other law, such as the law of gifts, trusts, or equitable remedies. Nor does Article 8 deal with transfers by operation of law. For example, transfers from decedent to administrator, from ward to guardian, and from bankrupt to trustee in bankruptcy are governed by other law as to both the time they occur and the substance of the transfer. The Article 8 rules do, however, determine whether the issuer is obligated to recognize the rights that a third party, such as a transferee, may acquire under other law. See Sections 8-207, 8-401, and 8-404.

§ 8-502. ASSERTION OF ADVERSE CLAIM AGAINST ENTITLEMENT HOLDER.

* * *

Official Comment

* * *

3. The following examples illustrate the operation of Section 8-502.

* * *

Example 4. Debtor holds XYZ Co. shares in a securities account with Able & Co. As collateral for a loan from Bank, Debtor grants Bank a security interest in the security entitlement to the XYZ Co. shares. Bank perfects by a method which leaves Debtor with the ability to dispose of the shares. See Section ~~9-115~~ 9-312. In violation of the security agreement, Debtor sells the XYZ Co. shares and absconds with the proceeds. Assume -implausibly -that Bank is able to trace the XYZ Co. shares and show that the "same shares" ended up in Buyer's securities account with Baker & Co. Section 8-502 precludes any action by Bank against Buyer, whether framed in constructive trust or other theory, provided that Buyer acquired the security entitlement for value and without notice of adverse claims.

* * *

Example 6. Debtor grants Alpha Co. a security interest in a security entitlement that includes 1000 shares of XYZ Co. stock that Debtor holds through an account with Able & Co. Alpha also has an account with Able. Debtor instructs Able to transfer the shares to Alpha, and Able does so by crediting the shares to Alpha's account. Alpha has control of the 1000 shares under Section 8-106(d). (The facts to this point are identical to those in Section 8-106, Comment 4, Example 1, except that Alpha Co. was Alpha Bank.) Alpha next grants Beta Co. a security interest in the 1000 shares included in Alpha's security entitlement. See Section 9-207(c)(3). Alpha instructs Able to transfer the shares to Gamma Co., Beta's custodian. Able does so, and Gamma credits the 1000 shares to Beta's account. Beta now has control under Section 8-106(d). By virtue of Debtor's explicit permission or by virtue of the permission inherent in Debtor's creation of a security interest in favor of Alpha and Alpha's resulting power to grant a security interest under Section 9-207, Debtor has no adverse claim to assert against Beta, assuming implausibly that Debtor could "trace" an interest to the Gamma account. Moreover, even. if Debtor did hold an adverse claim, if Beta did not have notice of Debtor's claim, Section 8-502 will preclude any action by Debtor against Beta, whether framed in constructive trust or other theory.

* * *

§ 8-510. RIGHTS OF PURCHASER OF SECURITY ENTITLEMENT FROM ENTITLEMENT HOLDER.

(a) ~~An~~ In a case not covered by the priority rules in Article 9 or the rules stated in subsection (c), an action based on an adverse claim to a financial asset or security entitlement, whether framed in conversion, replevin, constructive trust, equitable lien, or other theory, may not be asserted against a person who purchases a security entitlement, or an interest therein, from an entitlement holder if the purchaser gives value, does not have notice of the adverse claim, and obtains control.

(b) If an adverse claim could not have been asserted against an entitlement holder under Section 8-502, the adverse claim cannot be asserted against a person who purchases a security entitlement, or an interest therein, from the entitlement holder.

(c) In a case not covered by the priority rules in Article 9, a purchaser for value of a security entitlement, or an interest therein, who obtains control has priority over a purchaser of a security entitlement, or an interest therein, who does not obtain control. ~~Purchasers~~ Except as otherwise provided in subsection (d), purchasers who have control rank ~~equally, except that a~~ according to priority in time of:

(1) the purchaser's becoming the person for whom the securities account, in which the security entitlement is carried, is maintained, if the purchaser obtained control under Section 8-106(d)(1);

(2) the securities intermediary's agreement to comply with the purchaser's entitlement orders with respect to security entitlements carried or to be carried in the securities account in which the security entitlement is carried, if the purchaser obtained control under Section 8-106(d)(2); or

(3) if the purchaser obtained control through another person under Section 8-106(d)(3), the time on which priority would be based under this subsection if the other person were the secured party.

(d) A securities intermediary as purchaser has priority over a conflicting purchaser who has control unless otherwise agreed by the securities intermediary.

Official Comment

* * *

4. Subsection (c) specifies a priority rule for cases where an entitlement holder transfers conflicting interests in the same security entitlement to different purchasers. It follows the same principle as the Article 9 priority rule for investment property, that is, control trumps non-control. Indeed, the most significant category of conflicting "purchasers" may be secured parties. Priority questions for security interests, however, are governed by the rules in Article 9. Subsection (c) applies only to cases not covered by the Article 9 rules. It is intended primarily for disputes over conflicting claims arising out of repurchase agreement transactions that are not covered by the other rules set out in Articles 8 and 9.

The following example illustrates subsection (c):

Example 4. Dealer holds securities through an account at Alpha Bank. Alpha Bank in turns holds through a clearing corporation account. Dealer transfers securities to RP1 in a "hold in custody" repo transaction. Dealer then transfers the same securities to RP2 in another repo transaction. The repo to RP2 is implemented by transferring the securities from Dealer's regular account at Alpha Bank to a special account maintained by Alpha Bank for Dealer and RP2. The agreement among Dealer, RP2, and Alpha Bank provides that Dealer can make substitutions for the securities but RP2 can direct Alpha Bank to sell any securities held in the special account. Dealer becomes insolvent. RP1 claims a prior interest in the securities transferred to RP2.

In this example Dealer remained the entitlement holder but agreed that RP2 could initiate entitlement orders to Dealer's security intermediary, Alpha Bank. If RP2 had become the entitlement holder, the adverse claim rule of Section 8-502 would apply. Even if RP2 does not become the entitlement holder, the arrangement among Dealer, Alpha Bank, and RP2 does suffice to give RP2 control. Thus, under Section 8-510(c), RP2 has priority over RP1, because RP2 is a purchaser who obtained control, and RP1 is a purchaser who did not obtain control. The same result could be reached under Section 8-510(a) which provides that RP1's earlier in time interest cannot be asserted as an adverse claim against RP2. The same result would follow under the Article 9 priority rules if the interests of RP1 and RP2 are characterized as "security interests," see Section 9-115(5)(a) 9-328(1). The main point of the rules of Section 8-510(c) is to ensure that there will be clear rules to cover the conflicting claims of RP1 and RP2 without characterizing their interests as Article 9 security interests.

The priority rules in Article 9 for conflicting security interests also include a default temporal priority rule of pro rata treatment for cases where multiple secured parties have obtained control but omitted to specify their respective rights by agreement. See Section 9-115(5)(b) 9-328(2) and Comment 6 5 to Section 9-115 9-328. Because the purchaser priority rule in Section 8-510(c) is intended to track the Article 9 priority rules, it too has a pro rata temporal priority rule for cases where multiple non-secured party purchasers have obtained control but omitted to specify their respective rights by agreement. The rule is patterned on Section 9-328(2).

5. If a securities intermediary itself is a purchaser, subsection (d) provides that it has priority over the interest of another purchaser who has control. Article 9 contains a similar rule. See Section 9-328(3).

APPENDIX II MODEL PROVISIONS FOR PRODUCTION-MONEY PRIORITY

Legislative Note: States that enact these model provisions should add the following definitions to Section 9-102(a) following the definition of "proceeds" and preceding the definition of "promissory note", renumbering paragraphs in 9-102(a) accordingly:

( ) "Production-money crops" means crops that secure a production-money obligation incurred with respect to the production of those crops.

( ) "Production-money obligation" means an obligation of an obligor incurred for new value given to enable the debtor to produce crops if the value is in fact used for the production of the crops.

( ) "Production of crops" includes tilling and otherwise preparing land for growing, planting, cultivating, fertilizing, irrigating, harvesting, and gathering crops, and protecting them from damage or disease.

MODEL § [9-103A]. "PRODUCTION-MONEY CROPS"; "PRODUCTION-MONEY OBLIGATION"; PRODUCTION-MONEY SECURITY INTEREST; BURDEN OF ESTABLISHING.

(a) A security interest in crops is a production-money security interest to the extent that the crops are production-money crops.

(b) If the extent to which a security interest is a production-money security interest depends on the application of a payment to a particular obligation, the payment must be applied:

(1) in accordance with any reasonable method of application to which the parties agree;

(2) in the absence of the parties' agreement to a reasonable method, in accordance with any intention of the obligor manifested at or before the time of payment; or

(3) in the absence of an agreement to a reasonable method and a timely manifestation of the obligor's intention, in the following order:

(A) to obligations that are not secured; and

(B) if more than one obligation is secured, to obligations secured by production-money security interests in the order in which those obligations were incurred.

(c) A production-money security interest does not lose its status as such, even if:

(1) the production-money crops also secure an obligation that is not a production-money obligation;

(2) collateral that is not production-money crops also secures the production-money obligation; or

(3) the production-money obligation has been renewed, refinanced, or restructured.

(d) A secured party claiming a production-money security interest has the burden of establishing the extent to which the security interest is a production-money security interest.

Legislative Note: This section is optional. States that enact this section should place it between Sections 9-103 and 9-104 and number it accordingly, e.g., as Section 9-103A or 9-103.1.

Official Comment

1. **Source.** New.

2. **Production-Money Priority; "Production-Money Security Interest."** This section is patterned closely on Section 9-103, which defines "purchase-money security interest." Subsection (b) makes clear that a security interest can obtain production-money status only to the extent that it secures value that actually can be traced to the direct production of crops. To the extent that a security interest secures indirect costs of production, such as general living expenses, the security interest is not entitled to production-money treatment.

MODEL § [9-324A]. PRIORITY OF PRODUCTION-MONEY SECURITY INTERESTS AND AGRICULTURAL LIENS.

(a) Except as otherwise provided in subsections (c), (d), and (e), if the requirements of subsection (b) are satisfied, a perfected production-money security interest in production-money crops has priority over a conflicting security interest in the same crops and, except as otherwise provided in Section 9-327, also has priority in their identifiable proceeds.

(b) A production-money security interest has priority under subsection (a) if:

(1) the production-money security interest is perfected by filing when the production-money secured party first gives new value to enable the debtor to produce the crops;

(2) the production-money secured party sends an authenticated notification to the holder of the conflicting security interest not less than 10 or more than 30 days before the production-money secured party first gives new value to enable the debtor to

produce the crops if the holder had filed a financing statement covering the crops before the date of the filing made by the production-money secured party; and

(3) the notification states that the production-money secured party has or expects to acquire a production-money security interest in the debtor's crops and provides a description of the crops.

(c) Except as otherwise provided in subsection (d) or (e), if more than one security interest qualifies for priority in the same collateral under subsection (a), the security interests rank according to priority in time of filing under Section 9-322(a).

(d) To the extent that a person holding a perfected security interest in production-money crops that are the subject of a production-money security interest gives new value to enable the debtor to produce the production-money crops and the value is in fact used for the production of the production-money crops, the security interests rank according to priority in time of filing under Section 9-322(a).

(e) To the extent that a person holds both an agricultural lien and a production-money security interest in the same collateral securing the same obligations, the rules of priority applicable to agricultural liens govern priority.]

Legislative Note: This section is optional. States that enact this section should place it between Sections 9-324 and 9-325 and number it accordingly, e.g., as Section 9-324A or 9-324.1.

Official Comment

1. **Source.** New; replaces former Section 9-312(2).

2. **Priority of Production-Money Security Interests and Conflicting Security Interests.** This section replaces the limited priority in crops afforded by former Section 9-312(2). That priority generally was been thought to be of little value for its intended beneficiaries. This section attempts to balance the interests of the production-money secured party with those of a secured party who has previously filed a financing statement covering the crops that are to be produced. For example, to qualify for priority under this section, the production-money secured party must notify the earlier-filed secured party prior to extending the production-money credit. The notification affords the earlier secured party the opportunity to prevent subordination by extending the credit itself. Subsection (d) makes this explicit. If the holder of a security interest in production-money crops which conflicts with a production-money security interest gives new value for the production of the crops, the security interests rank according to priority in time of filing under Section 9-322(a).

3. **Multiple Production-Money Security Interests.** In the case of multiple production-money security interests that qualify for priority under subsection (a), the first to file has priority. See subsection (c). Note that only a security interest perfected by filing is entitled to production-money priority. See subsection (b)(1). Consequently, subsection (c) does not adopt the first-to-file-or-perfect formulation.

4. **Holder of Agricultural Lien and Production-Money Security Interest.** Subsection (e) deals with a creditor who holds both an agricultural lien and an Article 9 production-money security interest in the same collateral. In these cases, the priority rules applicable to agricultural liens govern. The creditor can avoid this result by waiving its agricultural lien.

INDEX

[References are to sections of the Official 1998 version of Article 9, and to author's analysis, identified by the notation "*-Analysis*"]

B

C

E

N

O

PROMISSORY NOTES